International ~~Legal Argument in the~~ Perman~~ent Court of~~ International Justice

The Rise of the International Judiciary

The International Court of Justice at The Hague is the principal judicial organ of the United Nations, and the successor of the Permanent Court of International Justice (1923–46), which was the first real permanent court of justice at the international level. This book analyses the ground-breaking contribution of the Permanent Court to international law, in terms of both judicial technique and the development of legal principle.

The book draws on hitherto unpublished archival material left by judges and other persons involved in the work of the Permanent Court, giving fascinating insights into many of its most important decisions and the individuals who made them (Huber, Anzilotti, Moore, Hammerskjöld and others). At the same time, it examines international legal argument in the Permanent Court, basing its approach on a developed model of international legal argument that stresses the intimate relationships between international and national lawyers and between international and national law.

OLE SPIERMANN is Lecturer in International Law at the University of Copenhagen. He specialises in international law and international dispute settlement. He is a member of the Executive Council of the International Law Association as well as the ILA Committees on International Commercial Arbitration and Foreign Investment. Dr Spiermann is an associate with Jonas Bruun Law Firm, Copenhagen.

CAMBRIDGE STUDIES IN INTERNATIONAL AND COMPARATIVE LAW

Established in 1946, this series produces high quality scholarship in the fields of public and private international law and comparative law. Although these are distinct legal sub-disciplines, developments since 1946 confirm their interrelation.

Comparative law is increasingly used as a tool in the making of law at national, regional and international levels. Private international law is now often affected by international conventions, and the issues faced by classical conflicts rules are frequently dealt with by substantive harmonisation of law under international auspices. Mixed international arbitrations, especially those involving state economic activity, raise mixed questions of public and private international law, while in many fields (such as the protection of human rights and democratic standards, investment guarantees and international criminal law) international and national systems interact. National constitutional arrangements relating to 'foreign affairs', and to the implementation of international norms, are a focus of attention.

The Board welcomes works of a theoretical or interdisciplinary character, and those focusing on the new approaches to international or comparative law or conflicts of law. Studies of particular institutions or problems are equally welcome, as are translations of the best work published in other languages.

A list of books in the series can be found at the end of this volume.

International Legal Argument in the Permanent Court of International Justice

The Rise of the International Judiciary

Ole Spiermann
University of Copenhagen

CAMBRIDGE
UNIVERSITY PRESS

CAMBRIDGE UNIVERSITY PRESS
Cambridge, New York, Melbourne, Madrid, Cape Town, Singapore,
São Paulo, Delhi, Dubai, Tokyo, Mexico City

Cambridge University Press
The Edinburgh Building, Cambridge CB2 8RU, UK

Published in the United States of America by Cambridge University Press, New York

www.cambridge.org
Information on this title: www.cambridge.org/9780521172844

First published 2005
First paperback edition 2010

A catalogue record for this publication is available from the British Library

Library of Congress Cataloguing in Publication data
Spiermann, Ole.
International legal argument in the Permanent Court of International Justice : the rise
of the international judiciary / by Ole Spiermann.
    p.   cm. – (Cambridge studies in international and comparative law (Cambridge,
England : 1996))
Includes bibliographical references and index.
ISBN 0 521 83685 9 (HB)
1. Permanent Court of International Justice.   2. International courts – History – 20th
century. I. Title. II. Series.
KZ6260.S65   2004
341.5′52 – dc22   2003069728

ISBN 978-0-521-83685-2 Hardback
ISBN 978-0-521-17284-4 Paperback

The future will be ours.

B. C. J. Loder, 1920

I should like to compare our decisions to ships which are intended to be launched on the high seas of international criticism.

Max Huber, 1927

The drawback of an experiment, carried on on this scale, is that it must succeed.

Åke Hammarskjöld, 1935

The Permanent Court of International Justice was the most important link.

J. Gustavo Guerrero, 1946

Contents

Foreword

From the point of view of international courts and tribunals we live in paradoxical times. There is more activity than ever in the professional memory of the present generation of international lawyers. Some at least of the cases – not only before the International Court but also (and perhaps even more so) before the WTO Dispute Settlement Body, the various human rights and international criminal courts and the *ad hoc* tribunals and commissions – are of considerable importance. The cumulation of cases is developing the jurisprudence of specific areas of international law in a rapid way. And yet there is a pervasive sense that the whole 'system' is insecure, uncertain in its constitutional underpinnings, erratic in the political support for it and largely unrelated to key issues facing the world at this time.

This being so, a study of the foundations of international decision-making by the first permanent international court is of renewed interest. The Permanent Court of International Justice was not seen by its members or by governments as a prelude or an overture to something else; it was the beginning of a distinctive and permanent institution. It faced its own problems of the elaboration of international judicial technique and the development of the law amidst political uncertainty and a wavering mandate. Dr Spiermann clearly identifies the focus of the work as 'the use of international legal argument outside the *Buchrecht*, that is, in practice'. Its significance for us is enhanced given the close continuity between the Permanent Court and the International Court, not just in terms of formal rules (the Statute of the new Court being a virtual copy of the old) but also in terms of the practice – the 'received stock of concepts' and techniques which were not received from elsewhere but had to be invented, the ways of handling advisory and contentious cases that developed as a result. These emerged from the *practice* of the

Permanent Court. How they did so, and the tensions and disagreements faced by the participants in the process, form the core of this splendid book.

These days, our expectations of doctoral theses have been lowered to fit the one size that funding bodies will allow. They are in many cases rather apprentice works than master pieces even in the original sense of that term. But Dr Spiermann's work transcends the limits of the genre, and will be of permanent value. His careful account, based on substantial archival research and on new sources of insight, permits an evaluation of the Permanent Court which is both balanced and positive. At the same time, practice is related to theory: the work makes a contribution to thinking about the underpinnings of international legal reasoning and its relation to the law we are all first taught, national law from one or another country and the accompanying national legal traditions. For beyond the historical account of the Permanent Court there is also a subtle theory about the 'sources' of international law, which has sprung, as Dr Spiermann argues, from '[t]he national lawyer's need for international law'. The dynamic between international and national here is thoughtfully analysed, even if we may end where we began with a conviction that the traditions of legal thought and process intersect and cannot be captured by dualistic categories.

Dr Spiermann is to be warmly congratulated. Hereafter the history of the Permanent Court will not be able to be written except by reference to this work.

James Crawford
Lauterpacht Research Centre for International Law
University of Cambridge
28 February 2004

Acknowledgments

This book is an extended and thoroughly revised version of a thesis submitted to the University of Cambridge in 1999 for the degree of Doctor of Philosophy. It represents the outcome of years of contemplation that began way back in 1993 in Copenhagen. The bulk of the work was carried out during my years in Cambridge, beginning in 1995 when I was enrolled in the LLM programme in international law. I stayed on for another three years as a doctorate student in that unique atmosphere of international legal research that I had come to identify with, first of all, Professor James Crawford and Professor Philip Allott.

Professor Crawford was the supervisor of my LLM thesis, 'Mrs Butterfingers' Essay on Sovereignty'. He continued as my supervisor for the first two years of my PhD research, and he also kindly helped me in the last intense weeks before submission of the thesis, and again before submission of this manuscript. His broadmindedness, efficiency and general interest in legal research provided an exceptional atmosphere in which to explore new ideas. In my last year of research, when Professor Crawford was on sabbatical, Professor Vaughan Lowe took over the supervision of my research. Professor Lowe introduced me to the welcome, though onerous, concept of archival research, which soon took me around Europe and to the United States. I have consistently been aware of what a privilege it has been to have such excellent scholars to guide me. I give them my warmest thanks.

I also thank my examiners, Professor Philip Allott and Professor John G. Merrills, for valuable criticism. The viva took place in the same rooms in Trinity College, Cambridge in which I had originally discussed the prospects of a doctorate with Professor Allott. I also wish to thank Professor Martti Koskenniemi, who read the revised manuscript of this book and provided me with much appreciated comments.

Professor Koskenniemi's *From Apology to Utopia* has served as a source of inspiration since the very beginning of my research in international law. Thanks also to my parents and sister and to Mrs Ciara Damgaard, Mr Knut Hammarskjöld, Ms Joanna Harrington, Dr Ulrich Huber, Mr Thomas Holst Laursen, Mr Amnon Lev, Mr Per Magid and Miss Anna Stamhus Nielsen, and to Ms Finola O'Sullivan, Dr Alison Powell, Mr Martin Gleeson and all at the Press who have brilliantly carried out the publication of this book.

It is with happiness that I reminisce on my visits to the Archives du Ministère des Affaires Etrangères at the Quai d'Orsay, the Bundesarchiv in Koblenz, the Harvard Law School Library in the 'other' Cambridge, the Kungliga biblioteket in Stockholm, the Library of Congress in Washington DC, the Nationaalarchief in The Hague, the National Archives and Records Administration in Maryland, the Peace Palace Library in The Hague, the Public Record Office in London, the Rigsarkivet in Copenhagen, the Universitäts- und Landesbibliothek Münster and the Zentralbibliothek in Zurich. Thanks also to the staffs at the League of Nations Archives in Geneva, the Squire Law Library in Cambridge, the Yale University Library in New Haven, the Memorial Hall of the M. Adachi Foundation in Kyoto and the Minnesota Historical Society in St Paul.

The Danish Research Academy generously funded my PhD research. I am pleased also to record my thanks to the British Council, which contributed towards the costs of my LLM year, and to the Anglo-Danish Society, the University of Copenhagen, Jesus College, Cambridge and the Axel H's Rejselegat. I also thank the Augustinus Fonden, the Axel H's Rejselegat, the Davids Samling, the Margot og Thorvald Dreyers Fond, the Finneske Legat, the Gangstedfonden and the Knud Højgaards Fond for providing generous funding towards the costs of archival research and other expenses incurred while revising the manuscript at the University of Copenhagen.

The present work is dedicated to Karina, who I thank last and most.

Copenhagen
1 October 2003

Table of cases

Table of treaties

Abbreviations

Adatci papers	Memorial Hall of the M. Adachi Foundation, Kyoto, Japan; references to [document no. in accordance with the list in *Dr M. Adachi: Conscience of the World* (Tokyo, 1969), pp. 18–28]
AJIL	*American Journal of International Law*
AJIL Supp.	*Supplement to the American Journal of International Law*
American Society Proceedings	American Society of International Law, *Proceedings of the Annual Meeting*
Annuaire	*Annuaire de l'Institut de Droit International*
Ann. français	*Annuaire Français de Droit International*
Annual Digest	Annual Digest and Reports of Public International Law Cases
AYIL	*Australian Yearbook of International Law*
Borchard papers	*Edwin M. Borchard papers*, Yale University Library, Manuscripts and Archives, New Haven, Connecticut, United States; references to [box no.].[folder no.]
BYIL	*British Yearbook of International Law*
CMLR	*Common Market Law Review*
DSR	World Trade Organization, *Dispute Settlement Reports*
ECHR Reports	European Court of Human Rights, *Reports of Judgments and Decisions*

ECHR Series A   *Publications of the European Court of Human Rights: Judgments and Decisions*
ECR   European Court of Justice, *European Court Reports*
EJIL   *European Journal of International Law*
van Eysinga papers   *Papieren van Prof. Jhr. W. J. M. van Eysinga*, Nationaalarchief, The Hague, The Netherlands; references to [folder no.]
FO   British Government Papers (*General Correspondence of Foreign Office*), Public Record Office, London, England; references to [series no.]/[original file no.]
Grotius Transactions   *Transactions of the Grotius Society*
GYIL   *German Yearbook of International Law*
Hammarskjöld papers   *Hammarskjöldska Arkivet: Åke Hammarskjöld, 1893–1937*, Kungliga biblioteket, Stockholm, Sweden; references to [box no.]
HILJ   *Harvard International Law Journal*
HLR   *Harvard Law Review*
Huber papers   *Nachlass von Max Huber*, Zentralbibliothek Zürich, Zurich, Switzerland; references to [box no.].[folder no.]
Hudson papers   *Manley O. Hudson Papers*, Harvard Law School Library, Cambridge, Massachusetts, United States; references to [box no.].[folder no.]
Hughes papers   *Charles Evans Hughes papers*, Manuscript Division, Library of Congress, Washington DC, United States; references to [reel no.]
ICJ Reports   International Court of Justice, *Reports of Judgments, Advisory Opinions and Orders*
ICLQ   *International and Comparative Law Quarterly*

ICSID Reports	Reports of Cases Decided under the Convention on the Settlement of Investment Disputes between States and Nationals of Other States
IJIL	*Indian Journal of International Law*
ILM	*International Legal Materials*
ILR	*International Law Reports*
Jessup papers	*Philip C. Jessup papers*, Manuscript Division, Library of Congress, Washington DC, United States; references to [box no.]
Kellogg papers	*Frank Billings Kellogg Papers*, Minnesota Historical Society, St Paul, Minnesota, United States; references to [reel no.]
League of Nations Archives	League of Nations Papers, United Nations Library at Geneva, Geneva, Switzerland; references to [original file no.]
LJIL	*Leiden Journal of International Law*
LPICT	*Law and Practice of International Courts and Tribunals*
LQR	*Law Quarterly Review*
Moore papers	*John Bassett Moore papers*, Manuscript Division, Library of Congress, Washington DC, United States; references to [box no.]
NARA	United States Government Papers (*Department of State*), National Archives and Records Administration, Washington DC, United States; references to [series no.]/[original file no.]
NJIL	*Nordic Journal of International Law*
NYUJILP	*New York University Journal of International Law and Politics*
Official Journal	League of Nations, Official Journal
ÖZöRV	*Österreichische Zeitschrift für öffentliches Recht und Völkerrecht*
Procès-Verbal of Council	League of Nations, *Procès-Verbal of the Session of the Council*

Quai d'Orsay	French Government Papers, Archives du Ministère des Affaires étrangères, Paris, France; references to [box no. in Serié SdN/Secrétariat générale]
RDILC	*Revue de Droit International et de Legislation Comparée*
Records of Assembly: Committees	League of Nations, *The Records of the Assembly: Meetings of the Committees*
Records of Assembly: Plenary	League of Nations, *The Records of the Assembly: Plenary Meetings*
Recueil des Cours	*Recueil des Cours de l'Académie de Droit International*
RGDIP	*Revue Générale de Droit International Public*
RIAA	*Reports of International Arbitral Awards*
Rigsarkivet	Danish Government Papers (*Udenrigsministeriet*), Rigsarkivet, Copenhagen, Denmark; references to [box no.]
Rivista	*Rivista di Diritto Internazionale*
Root papers	*Elihu Root papers*, Manuscript Division, Library of Congress, Washington DC, United States; references to [box no.]
Schücking papers (Koblenz)	*Nachlaß Schücking*, Bundesarchiv, Koblenz, Germany; references to [reel no.]
Schücking papers (Münster)	*Nachlaß Schücking*, Universitäts- und Landesbibliothek Münster, Münster, Germany; references to [box no.].[folder no.]
Series A	*Publications of the Permanent Court of International Justice: Collection of Judgments, 1923–1930*
Series A/B	*Publications of the Permanent Court of International Justice: Collection of Judgments and Advisory Opinions, 1931–1940*
Series B	*Publications of the Permanent Court of International Justice: Collection of Advisory Opinions, 1922–1930*

Series C	*Publications of the Permanent Court of International Justice: Acts and Documents Relating to Judgments and Advisory Opinions*
Series D	*Publications of the Permanent Court of International Justice: Acts and Documents Concerning the Organization of the Court*
Series D No. 2 (1922)	*Publications of the Permanent Court of International Justice: Preparation of the Rules of Court, 1922*
Series D No. 2, Add.1 (1926)	*Publications of the Permanent Court of International Justice: Revision of the Rules of Court, 1926*
Series D No. 2, Add.2 (1931)	*Publications of the Permanent Court of International Justice: Modification of the Rules, 1931*
Series D No. 2, Add.3 (1936)	*Publications of the Permanent Court of International Justice: Elaboration of the Rules of Court of March 11th, 1936*
Series E	*Publications of the Permanent Court of International Justice: Annual Reports*
UNCIO	*Documents of the United Nations Conference on International Organization* (22 vols., London and New York, 1945–55)
US	United States Supreme Court Reports
Wehberg papers	*Nachlaß Wehberg*, NL 199, Bundesarchiv, Koblenz, Germany; references to [box no.]
YICJ	*Yearbook of the International Court of Justice*
YILC	*Yearbook of the International Law Commission*
YJIL	*Yale Journal of International Law*
YLJ	*Yale Law Journal*
ZaöRV	*Zeitschrift für ausländisches öffentliches Recht und Völkerrecht*

PART 1

The Permanent Court of International Justice

1   A project of international justice

From arbitration to adjudication

As the predecessor of the present International Court of Justice, the Permanent Court of International Justice was a historic 'melting-pot' of ideals about international justice and, according to some, international community as well as notions of international law. It was the culmination so far of a persistent movement towards, in prosaic terms, more effective settlement of international disputes. The twentieth century had opened with a call for international justice, a growing hope of sustaining peace through international adjudication and law.[1] Although cold water was inevitably poured on the belief in international adjudication being a real, trustworthy alternative to warfare,[2] the century witnessed several successful projects of international justice, with more now underway. This was partly due to the legacy of the Permanent Court where international law was brought down to earth, as it were, and given a practical edge. In this context, the world, at last, experienced the rise of the international judiciary.

The Permanent Court of International Justice was preceded by the Permanent Court of Arbitration established under the 1899 and 1907 Conventions for the Pacific Settlement of International Disputes, which have been described as 'in a sense a codification of the law of pacific settlement up to that time'.[3] In Articles 15 (1899) and 37 (1907), 'international

---

[1] On earlier responses to this call, see W. Evans Darby, *International Tribunals: A Collection of the Various Schemes Which Have Been Propounded and of Instances Since 1815* (London, 1900); and Hans Wehberg, *The Problem of an International Court of Justice* (Oxford, 1918), pp. 128–71.

[2] See H. Triepel, *Die Zukunft des Völkerrechts* (Leipzig, 1916), pp. 13–16.

[3] Manley O. Hudson, *The Permanent Court of International Justice, 1920–1942* (2nd edn, New York, 1943), p. 4.

3

arbitration' was defined as having 'for its object the settlement of disputes between States by judges of their own choice on the basis of respect for law'.[4] The name of the Permament Court of Arbitration was a misnomer, as has often been noted.[5] In retrospect, its historical importance was to serve as a point of departure for more ambitious projects of international justice that aimed at adjudication, as opposed to arbitration. According to Hersch Lauterpacht, 'there was a tendency to deny the judicial character of arbitration, as it then existed, in order to strengthen the argument for the establishment of a true international court able to develop International Law by the continuity of its pronouncements and the permanency of its personnel'.[6]

The distinction between arbitration and adjudication related to national law: adjudication implemented ideals of a court of justice taken from national legal systems, whereas, from the perspective of those systems, arbitration was exceptional, consensual and *ad hoc*. The plans for a Court of Arbitral Justice and an International Prize Court were put before the Second Peace Conference at The Hague in an attempt to meet the standards of adjudication. The plans miscarried, however, due to

---

[4] Cf. *Article 3, Paragraph 2, of the Treaty of Lausanne (Frontier between Turkey and Iraq)*, Series B No. 12 (1925) at 26; and *Interpretation of the Greco-Turkish Agreement of December 1st, 1926 (Final Protocol, Article IV)*, Series B No. 16 (1928) at 22–3. See also *Dubai–Sharjah Border Arbitration*, 91 ILR 543 (1981) at 574–5; and *Case concerning Maritime Delimitation and Territorial Questions between Qatar and Bahrain* (Merits), ICJ Reports [2001] 40 at para. 113.

[5] Criticism of the name was raised at the First Peace Conference: see James Brown Scott (ed.), *The Proceedings of the Hague Peace Conferences: The Conference of 1899* (London, 1920), pp. 755–6, 775–7 and 652; cf. *ibid.*, pp. 709–17 and 597–8. And criticism of the institution was commonplace at the Second Peace Conference: see James Brown Scott (ed.), *The Proceedings of the Hague Peace Conferences: The Conference of 1907* (London, 1920–1), vol. 1, pp. 344 and 347 and also vol. 2, pp. 234, 319, 327 and 596: 'Instead of a permanent court, the Convention of 1899 gave but the phantom of a court, an impalpable specter, or to be more precise yet, it gave us a recorder with a list' (Asser); 'In a word, the Permanent Court is not permanent because it is not composed of permanent judges; it is not accessible because it has to be constituted for each case; it is not a court because it is not composed of judges' (Brown Scott); 'What then, is this court whose members do not even know one another? The Court of 1899 is but an idea which occasionally assumes shape and then again disappears' (Martens); 'The present Permanent Court has not gone far in the direction of establishing and developing international law. Each case is isolated, lacking both continuity and connection with the other' (Choate). See also Advisory Committee of Jurists, *Procès-Verbaux of the Proceedings of the Committee (16 June–24 July 1920, with Annexes)* (The Hague, 1920), pp. 694–5 and 698.

[6] L. Oppenheim, *International Law* (5th edn by H. Lauterpacht, London, 1935–7), vol. 2, p. 23, note 1. John Bassett Moore took issue with this view in 1917: see Charles Cheney Hyde, *International Law Chiefly as Interpreted and Applied in the United States* (2nd edn, Boston, 1947), vol. 2, p. 1580, note 3.

disagreement over the method of electing the members of the courts,[7] and also because of an open-ended list of sources of law to be applied.[8] Instead, in 1908 five states established the Central American Court of Justice for ten years. It was soon accused for not abiding by the highest standards of adjudication.[9]

In 1920, a crucial step towards adjudication was launched in Article 14 of the Covenant of the League of Nations, according to which:

> The Council shall formulate and submit to the Members of the League for adoption plans for the establishment of a Permanent Court of International Justice. The Court shall be competent to hear and determine any dispute of an international character which the parties thereto submit to it. The Court may also give an advisory opinion upon any dispute or question referred to it by the Council or by the Assembly.

Article 14 thus envisaged a judicial body entrusted with two kinds of jurisdiction: contentious jurisdiction over 'any dispute of an international character which the parties . . . submit to it' and advisory jurisdiction over 'any dispute or question referred to it by the Council or by the Assembly'. Still, it was later referred to as 'a curious fact that the question of the exact legal character of the new Court of International Justice was never settled in an authoritative way by those who framed the Covenant'.[10] The notion of an international court, although not formally an organ of the League, had been included in an early suggestion for a Covenant of a League of Nations submitted by Colonel House to President Wilson. According to House, an international court was 'a necessary part of the machinery' and 'might well prove the strongest part of it'.[11] Room was made for an international court in some of the drafts submitted by governments. On the initiative of Lord Robert Cecil, a provision on plans for the establishment of a Permanent Court of International Justice found its way into the 'Hurst-Miller draft', which Wilson laid before the Commission on the League of Nations at its first meeting at the Paris Peace Conference on 3 February 1919.[12] He did

---

[7] *Proceedings of the Conference of 1907*, vol. 2, pp. 619–24 and vol. 1, p. 168.

[8] *Ibid.*, vol. 1, pp. 190–1.

[9] Cf. Jean Eyma, *La Cour de justice Centre Américaine* (Paris, 1928), pp. 171–6; Hudson, *Permanent Court*, pp. 45–70; Jean Allain, *A Century of International Adjudication* (The Hague, 2000), pp. 88–91; and Ian Brownlie, *Principles of Public International Law* (6th edn, Oxford, 2003), p. 677, note 43.

[10] League of Nations, *The Permanent Court of International Justice* (Geneva, 1921), p. 6.

[11] See David Hunter Miller, *The Drafting of the Covenant* (New York, 1928), vol. 1, p. 13 and also vol. 2, p. 8.

[12] See *ibid.*, vol. 1, pp. 61–4, 67 and 69 and also vol. 2, pp. 234, 265–6, 321–2 and 348–9.

so with the words '[a] living thing is born';[13] the same words fitted the Permanent Court. Advisory jurisdiction was not a part of the draft until a proposal to this effect was agreed upon at a meeting between President Wilson and Lord Cecil on 18 March 1919.[14] There was some effort not to allow this jurisdiction to be confused with so-called 'obligatory' or 'compulsory' jurisdiction.[15]

It was within the framework of Article 14 that the Statute of the Permanent Court was drawn up, initially under the guidance of a specific notion of adjudication that had been put well in the appendix to a memorandum of the Secretariat of the League of Nations. Referring to 'the Courts of Justice of the different countries', the Secretariat explained that 'arbitration is distinguished from judicial procedure in the strict sense of the word by three features: the nomination of the arbitrators by the parties concerned, the selection by these parties of the principles on which the tribunal should base its findings, and finally its character of voluntary jurisdiction'.[16] In his report on the organisation

---

[13] F. P. Walters, *A History of the League of Nations* (Oxford, 1952), p. 1.

[14] Miller, *Drafting of the Covenant*, vol. 1, pp. 290, 297, 391 and 405–6 and also vol. 2, pp. 585, 662, 670 and 688. Cf. the French proposal, *ibid.*, vol. 2, pp. 348–9 and 353.

[15] *Ibid.*, vol. 1, pp. 290, 379–80, 393, 413 and 416.

[16] Advisory Committee of Jurists, *Documents Presented to the Committee Relating to Existing Plans for the Establishment of a Permanent Court of International Justice* (The Hague, 1920), p. 113; and also James Brown Scott, *The Project of a Permanent Court of International Justice and Resolutions of the Advisory Committee of Jurists* (Washington DC, 1920), pp. 12, 28, 46, 49, 68–9, 93–5, 99–100 and 137; B. C. J. Loder, 'The Permanent Court of International Justice and Compulsory Jurisdiction' (1921–2) 2 *BYIL* 6; Olaf Hoijer, *La Solution pacifique des litiges internationaux avant et depuis la Société des Nations* (Paris, 1925), pp. 480–2 and 496–7; Démètre Negulesco, 'La Jurisprudence de la Cour permanente de Justice internationale' (1926) 33 *RGDIP* 194 at 195 and 207; Åke Hammarskjöld in (1927) 33-I *Annuaire*, pp. 819 and 821; and Jean Garnier-Coignet, 'Procédure judiciaire et procédure arbitrale: etude de droit international positif' (1930) 6 *Revue de Droit International* 123 at 146. Cf. Antonio Sanchez de Bustamante y Sirvén, *The World Court* (New York, 1925), pp. 151–4; Max Huber in (1927) 33-I *Annuaire*, p. 762, note 1; John Bassett Moore, 'General Introduction' and 'Notes on the Historical and Legal Phases of the Adjudication of International Disputes' in John Bassett Moore (ed.), *International Adjudications Ancient and Modern: History and Documents, Modern Series* (New York, 1929), pp. xv and xxxviii; Oppenheim/Lauterpacht, *International Law*, vol. 2, pp. 22–3, 45 and 88–9; and Manley O. Hudson, *International Tribunals: Past and Future* (Washington DC, 1944), p. 100. In 1924, three Protocols entered into force which in Articles 12, 13 and 15 of the Covenant substituted 'arbitration or judicial settlement' for 'arbitration': cf. Paul De Vineuil, 'The Permanent Court of International Justice and the Geneva "Peace Protocol"' (1925) 17 *Rivista* 144 at 148–50; Åke Hammarskjöld, 'The Permanent Court of International Justice and its Place in International Relations' (1930) 9 *International Affairs* 467 at 472; and Åke Hammarskjöld, 'International Justice' in League of Nations, *Ten Years of World Co-operation* (London, 1930), p. 125 at p. 139.

of a Permanent Court of International Justice submitted to the Council of the League of Nations at its second session in February 1920, Léon Bourgeois wrote: 'In addition to national Courts of Law, whose duty it is to administer the laws of each State within its territorial limits, there is room for an international tribunal entrusted with the important task of administering international law and enforcing among the nations the *cuique suum* which is the law which governs human intercourse'.[17]

In early 1920, the Council of the League of Nations appointed the ten members of the Advisory Committee of Jurists to formulate the first draft.[18] The Advisory Committee was assisted by the Under-Secretary-General of the League of Nations, Dionisio Anzilotti, and a young member of the Secretariat, Åke Hammarskjöld (who had drafted the appendix just quoted).[19] On 24 July 1920, the Advisory Committee adopted a draft-scheme which was in accordance with the specific notion of adjudication set out in the Secretariat's memorandum. Of course, the draft-scheme itself was to become a binding code of procedure, also regulating, in what became Article 38, the law to be applied. In addition, the draft-scheme contained provisions on the election of judges and compulsory jurisdiction, according to which a state should be capable of bringing a case against another state without the latter having to consent to the specific proceedings.

Thus, the Advisory Committee had succeeded in settling the issue of electing the judges.[20] There was to be a general election every ninth year. The candidates would be nominated by the members of the Permanent Court of Arbitration divided into 'national' groups, while the judges were elected jointly by the Council and the Assembly of the League. On Elihu Root's initiative, and inspired by the bicameral legislative process in the United States,[21] the draft-scheme struck a balance between recognising the privileged status of the Great Powers, which then dominated the Council, and observing a principle of sovereign equality that was the institutional philosophy of the Assembly. After much debate, the Advisory Committee also adopted provisions on judges *ad hoc*.[22] A party to a

---

[17] *Procès-verbal of Council* 1920–5, p. 5.
[18] On the work of the Advisory Committee, see Ole Spiermann, '"Who Attempts Too Much Does Nothing Well": The 1920 Advisory Committee of Jurists and the Statute of the Permanent Court of International Justice' (2002) 73 *BYIL* 187.
[19] Van Hamel's note, 14 April 1920, League of Nations Archives 21-3833-859.
[20] Advisory Committee, *Procès-verbaux*, pp. 101–66.
[21] *Ibid.*, pp. 108–9.
[22] *Ibid.*, pp. 528–39, 575–7 and 720–2; and see Spiermann, 'Advisory Committee', pp. 230–5.

dispute before the Permanent Court which did not have a judge of its nationality on the bench would be allowed to choose a person to sit as a judge *ad hoc*. The Dutch member, B. C. J. Loder, had been opposed on principle because, in his view, the institution of judges *ad hoc* 'involved the idea of arbitration instead of justice'; he was criticised, however, by the President of the Advisory Committee, Baron Descamps, for having 'confused national and international legal organisations; a complete analogy between these two organisations could not be established'.[23]

The members of the Advisory Committee disagreed as to whether every good national judge would make a good international judge.[24] There would not seem to have been an exact notion of the international judge; rather, they were to be moulded from national lawyers, and to distinguish themselves from the latter, as the Permanent Court began its work. In the report of the Advisory Committee, it was stated that 'there will be, besides Jurisconsults, great judges, who may have only encountered questions of International Law indirectly or rarely during their careers', the focus being on 'those judges most capable of rising above the level of national justice to international affairs'.[25] According to Bourgeois, 'the Court will contain representatives of the different judicial systems into which the world is divided and . . . the judgments of the Court will therefore be the result of the co-operation of entirely different thought and systems'.[26]

While national lawyers may have agreed, broadly speaking, on which disputes and questions were suitable for submission to an international court, and by implication also on the scope of international law, their expectations as to which solutions and answers were correct and their understanding of the content of international law would almost unavoidably have been coloured by national tendencies and traditions. It had been taken for granted when preparing the draft-scheme that 'it would be one of the Court's important tasks to contribute, through its jurisprudence, to the development of international law'.[27] President

---

[23] Advisory Committee, *Procès-verbaux*, pp. 531 and 532–3, respectively.

[24] Doubts were expressed by several members: see *ibid.*, pp. 448 (Ricci-Busatti), 449 (Descamps), 553 (Lapradelle) and 611 and 645 (Altamira), which should be contrasted with the views of Phillimore and Root, *ibid.*, pp. 191 and 448, respectively; see also Scott, *Project of a Permanent Court*, pp. 26 and 51.

[25] Advisory Committee, *Procès-verbaux*, pp. 695 and 707.

[26] *Procès-verbal* of Council 1920–10, p. 175.

[27] Advisory Committee, *Procès-verbaux*, pp. 534 and 695; and Scott, *Project of a Permanent Court*, pp. 68–9, 128 and 137; Jean Morellet, *L'organisation de la Cour permanente de Justice internationale* (Paris, 1921), pp. 28–9 and 135; Elihu Root, 'The Permanent Court of

Loder subsequently referred to 'the fact that it was the duty of the Court to build up international jurisprudence',[28] while in a pamphlet published by the League of Nations it was noted that '[i]t is for the Court itself to make out what is international law, and it is in this domain that the jurisprudence of the Court will have its greatest importance as a means of codifying the law of nations'.[29] In the words of one enthusiastic commentator: 'La jurisprudence de la nouvelle Cour permanente, composée de magistrats indépendants et compétents, pourra aussi exercer une influence très utile et féconde sur l'évolution du droit international. L'idée est ancienne, mais sa réalisation est nouvelle.'[30]

The subject of compulsory jurisdiction had caused the Advisory Committee the most trouble.[31] It was generally agreed that the jurisdiction of the Permanent Court should be limited to disputes between states.[32] The outstanding question was whether, by becoming a party to the Court Protocol to which the Statute was appended, a state accepted the Permanent Court's jurisdiction in its future disputes, or at least in some types of dispute, so that unlike arbitration a dispute could subsequently be brought before the Permanent Court unilaterally by one state without the consent of the other party or parties. The view prevailed in the Advisory Committee that it had to start not with Article 14 of the Covenant but at the point where the work of the Second Peace Conference had come to a standstill.[33] Article 34 of the draft-scheme entrusted

International Justice' (1923) 17 *American Society Proceedings* 1 at 6; D. G. Nyholm, 'La Cour permanente de Justice internationale' in P. Munch (ed.), *Les Origines et l'oeuvre de la Société des Nations* (Copenhagen, 1924), vol. 2, p. 241 at pp. 254–5; and A. de Lapradelle, *Influence de la Société des Nations sur le développement du droit des gens* (Paris, 1932–3), 1re leçon, p. 21. In the same token, it should be stressed that the Advisory Committee had submitted a proposal on Conferences for the Advancement of International Law: see Advisory Committee, *Procès-verbaux*, pp. 497, 519–20 and 747–8; and Spiermann, 'Advisory Committee', pp. 227–8 and 252–3.

[28] Series D No. 2 (1922) at 89 and see also Advisory Committee, *Procès-verbaux*, p. 294.

[29] League of Nations, *Permanent Court*, pp. 10 and 17 (which publication was in substance a reproduction of a paper prepared by Åke Hammarskjöld: see *ibid.*, p. 3, note 1). It was stated explicitly that the rejection of the proposal on Conferences for the Advancement of International Law 'largely increases the importance of the rôle of the Court in creating International Law by its jurisprudence': *ibid.*, p. 17. See also Bourgeois in *Procès-verbal of Council 1920-8*, p. 165.

[30] Hoijer, *Solution pacifique*, p. 515.

[31] Advisory Committee, *Procès-verbaux*, pp. 224–93, 541–4, 582–3 and 651–2 and see Hammarskjöld to Van Hamel, 15 July 1920, Hammarskjöld papers 480.

[32] Advisory Committee, *Procès-verbaux*, pp. 204–17.

[33] *Ibid.*, pp. 15–19 (Descamps) and also, in particular, *ibid.*, pp. 43 and 696–7 and Advisory Committee, *Documents*, pp. 7–23 and 113–19. See also Spiermann, 'Advisory Committee', pp. 197–8 and 201.

the Permanent Court with 'jurisdiction (and this without any special convention giving it jurisdiction) to hear and determine cases of a legal nature'. Such compulsory jurisdiction had not, however, been approved by all members of the Advisory Committee. The notion failed the test of realities in the mind of the Japanese member, Minéitcirô Adatci,[34] and shortly afterwards it was turned down in the Council as being contrary to Article 14 of the Covenant.[35] As Professor Manley O. Hudson put it, compulsory jurisdiction 'was the outstanding feature of the draft-scheme to occupy the attention of the Council and the Assembly'.[36] The Council's amendment, a step away from adjudication and back towards arbitration, was publicly regretted by leading members of the Advisory Committee, namely B. C. J. Loder and Lord Phillimore.[37] Similar criticism was raised in the Third Committee of the First Assembly, to which the Council referred the draft Statute. But compulsory jurisdiction made no re-entry into the Statute, which was appended to the Protocol of Signature Relating to the Statute of the Permanent Court of International Justice provided for by Article 14 of the Covenant of the League of Nations signed on 16 December 1920. While the final Article 34 of the Statute provided that '[o]nly States or Members of the League of Nations can be parties in cases before the Court', according to Article 36:

The jurisdiction of the Court comprises all cases which the parties refer to it and all matters specially provided for in Treaties and Conventions in force.

The Members of the League of Nations and the States mentioned in the Annex to the Covenant may, either when signing or ratifying the Protocol to which the present Statute is adjoined, or at a later moment, declare that they recognize as compulsory *ipso facto* and without special agreement, in relation to any other Member or State accepting the same obligation, the jurisdiction of the Court in all or any of the classes of legal disputes concerning:

    (a)   the interpretation of a treaty;
    (b)   any question of international law;
    (c)   the existence of any fact which, if established, would constitute a breach of an international obligation;
    (d)   the nature or extent of the reparation to be made for the breach of an international obligation.

---

[34] *Ibid.*, pp. 541–3.
[35] See Annex 118 in *Procès-verbal of Council* 1920-10, p. 161 and also *ibid.*, p. 21.
[36] Hudson, *Permanent Court*, p. 191; and see also League of Nations, *Permanent Court*, p. 10.
[37] See Loder, 'Permanent Court', pp. 20–6; and Lord Phillimore, 'The Third Committee: The Permanent Court of International Justice' in Lord Robert Cecil and Lord Phillimore (eds.), *The First Assembly* (London, 1921), p. 147 at pp. 167 and 170; and also Phillimore in *Hansard*, HL, vol. 69, col. 107, 16 November 1927.

The declaration referred to above may be made unconditionally or on condition of reciprocity on the part of several or certain Members or States, or for a certain time.

In the event of a dispute as to whether the Court has jurisdiction, the matter shall be settled by the decision of the Court.

Consequently, states could give their consent to the Permanent Court's contentious jurisdiction in two different forms. As laid down in the first paragraph, a so-called 'Special Agreement' could be concluded with particular reference to submitting an existing dispute to the Permanent Court, or the dispute could fall within a generally defined category of disputes contained in a compromissory clause which had been agreed to beforehand, often as part of a larger treaty regime. The broadest compromissory clause was the so-called 'Optional Clause' contained in the second paragraph.[38] It was a compromise reached in the First Assembly following a Brazilian delegate's fierce criticism of the decision depriving the Permanent Court of its compulsory jurisdiction.[39] The Optional Clause was not made an integral part of the Statute and so did not provide for compulsory jurisdiction proper.

The Statute contained no provisions on the Permanent Court's advisory jurisdiction expressly provided for in Article 14 of the Covenant. A provision drafted by the Advisory Committee developing the distinction

---

[38] Technically speaking, the Optional Clause was Part B of the Court Protocol of 16 December 1920, in essence a reproduction of Article 36(2) of the Statute: 'The undersigned, being duly authorized thereto, further declare, on behalf of their Government, that, from this date, they accept as compulsory, *ipso facto* and without special convention, the jurisdiction of the Court in conformity with Article 36, paragraph 2, of the Statute of the Court under the following conditions: . . .'. As there is no strict requirement as to form, it would seem permissible to use the expression 'Optional Clause' when referring to Article 36(2). Cf. Hudson, *Permanent Court*, pp. 451–2; and Shabtai Rosenne, *The Law and Practice of the International Court, 1920–1996* (The Hague, 1997), p. 728, but see already *Case concerning the Legal Status of the South-Eastern Territory of Greenland*, Series A/B No. 48 (1932) at 270 and *The Electricity Company of Sofia and Bulgaria* (Preliminary Objection), Series A/B No. 77 (1939) at 80.

[39] See *Records of Assembly: Committees* 1920, pp. 406–8 and 617. The proposal to insert provisions concerning compulsory jurisdiction in 'a special agreement' or a separate 'convention' or 'proposal' had already been advanced in a report submitted by the Italian Government to the Council, see *ibid.*, p. 498, and by Ricci-Busatti, who had not looked in vain for support: *ibid.*, pp. 380–1. The proposal was possibly inspired by the Swiss Government's amendment submitted in 1907 to the Second Peace Conference: see *Records of Assembly: Plenary* 1920, pp. 440 (Hagerup) and 490 (Motta) and also *Proceedings of the Conference of 1907*, vol. 2, pp. 66–7, 468–9, 473, 492 and 881–2; Max Huber, *Denkwürdigkeiten, 1907–1924* (Zürich, 1974), pp. 42–4 and 173–4; and Max Huber, 'Schiedsrichterliche und richterliche Streiterledigung: Ein Überblick' (1961/66) 56 *Die Friedens-Warte* 105 at 110 and 114.

between 'disputes' and 'questions' had been suppressed in the Assembly.[40] According to the draft provision adopted by the Advisory Committee, '[w]hen it shall give an opinion upon a question which forms the subject of an existing dispute, it shall do so under the same conditions as if the case had been actually submitted to it for decision'.[41] One reason for suppressing it had been the argument of a French representative, Henri Fromageot, that the Covenant 'contained a provision in accordance with which the Court could not refuse to give advisory opinions' and that '[i]t was therefore unnecessary to include a rule to the same effect in the constitution of the Court'.[42]

On 14 September 1929, the Protocol Concerning the Revision of the Statute of the Permanent Court of International Justice containing a few minor amendments to the Statute was signed; it took effect in 1936. In particular, the posts of deputy-judges, who filled vacancies, were abolished and a series of provisions on the Permanent Court's advisory jurisdiction were copied from the Rules of Court and from the Permanent Court's 'case law'. Although it became an organ of the United Nations in 1945, the drafting of the Statute of the International Court of Justice, appended to the Charter of the United Nations, was really another minor revision;[43] thus, in 1971, Judge Aréchaga referred to the Statute as 'an international instrument which has successfully withstood half a century of application'.[44] One of the amendments adopted in 1945 was the abolition of the general election, while key provisions like Articles 34 and 36 were left essentially untouched. The relationship between the International Court and the Permanent Court thus became one of predecessor and successor.[45]

At the inauguration ceremony in 1946, President Guerrero, who had also been the last President of the Permanent Court, said that '[i]n the

---

[40] *Records of Assembly: Committees* 1920, p. 401.

[41] Advisory Committee, *Procès-verbaux*, pp. 567 and 732 and also Lapradelle in *ibid.*, p. 585 and Scott, *Project of a Permanent Court*, p. 112.

[42] *Records of Assembly: Committees* 1920, p. 401.

[43] See the report of the First Committee of the Commission on Judicial Organizations, 13 UNCIO, p. 384.

[44] Eduardo Jiménez de Aréchaga, 'Judges Ad Hoc in Advisory Proceedings' (1971) 31 *ZaöRV* 697 at 698.

[45] See *Case concerning the Aerial Incident of July 27th, 1955* (Preliminary Objections), ICJ Reports [1959] 127 at 158–9; and *Military and Paramilitary Activities in and against Nicaragua* (Jurisdiction and Admissibility), ICJ Reports [1984] 392 at para. 32; and also Mohamed Shahabuddeen, *Precedent in the World Court* (Cambridge, 1996), pp. 22–3.
Cf. Mohamed Samed M. Amr, *The Role of the International Court of Justice as the Principal Judicial Organ of the United Nations* (The Hague, 2003), pp. 20–2.

long chain of institutions created to secure the pacific settlement of international disputes, the Permanent Court of International Justice was the most important link'.[46] In Professor Philip C. Jessup's words, 'the International Court of Justice is in a very real sense the continuation of the Permanent Court of International Justice'.[47] The former has been described as 'le *Doppelgänger* ou le reflet de miroir' of the latter.[48] Explicit references to decisions of the Permanent Court found wider use in the decisions of its successor than in its own. As Judge Higgins put it, 'the ICJ is the legal successor to the PCIJ, and the jurisprudence of the latter remains pertinent and compelling to this day'.[49] Likewise, Judge Bedjaoui has observed that the International Court of Justice 'is scarcely more than a mere replica or continuation of the Permanent Court of International Justice'.[50] He added that '[e]ven today, the present Court makes unstinting use of the jurisprudence of the PCIJ, not only because of its quality but also because, conceptually, there has been no substantial evolution of the judicial function from one Court to the other'. The omission in Article 1 of the new Statute of any reference to the Permanent Court of Arbitration was a belated reflection of the very different nature of the Permanent Court, and thus also of the International Court.

At the time of its establishment, the Permanent Court was the most sophisticated judicial body internationally, 'the first standing court of potentially global competence';[51] so was the International Court in 1946. The Permanent Court saw the rise of an international judiciary and partly due to its legacy rival projects in the form of permanent, specialised courts, many of them regional, have emerged. Some regional courts are closer than the International Court to adjudication and the associated ideals of a national court of justice. Thus, treaties under the European Union entrust the European Court of Justice with a broad compulsory jurisdiction. While the International Court is only open to

---

[46] YICJ 1946–47, p. 37; see also Huber, 'Schiedsrichterliche und richterliche Streiterledigung', pp. 108 and 113.

[47] Philip C. Jessup, *A Modern Law of Nations: An Introduction* (Hamden, 1947), p. 147; and also Percy Spender, 'The Office of the President of the International Court of Justice' (1965) 1 *AYIL* 9 at 9.

[48] Georges Abi-Saab, 'De l'evolution de la Cour internationale: reflexions sur quelques tendances recentes' (1992) 96 *RGDIP* 273 at 275.

[49] Rosalyn Higgins, 'The ICJ, the ECJ, and Integrity of International Law' (2003) 52 *ICLQ* 1 at 3.

[50] Mohamed Bedjaoui, *The New World Order and the Security Council* (Dordrecht, 1994), p. 75.

[51] Philippe Sands and Pierre Klein, *Bowett's Law of International Institutions* (5th edn, London, 2001), p. 352.

states, the European Court of Justice and other international courts such as the European Court of Human Rights also have jurisdiction to entertain disputes between an individual and a state. So did numerous bodies established under the peace treaties that brought an end to the First World War. Such bodies can be highly effective, but they are normally specialised, their jurisdiction being centred on the interpretation of one or a few treaties. The International Court has remained the most authoritative international court of general jurisdiction, occupying the position as the principal judicial organ of the world as well as the United Nations. It has remained 'la suprême magistrature internationale'.[52] To quote a leading commentator: 'While there is no formal hierarchy of international courts and tribunals, the pre-eminence of the Permanent Court and the present International Court is today generally accepted. Any other international adjudicatory body which ignored relevant dicta and decisions of the International Court would jeopardize its credibility'.[53]

The significance of the Permanent Court

At the opening meeting of the Advisory Committee of Jurists, Bourgeois had been explicit as to 'what a large place in our eyes the Court of Justice must take in the international organisation of the world'.[54] Internationalists at the time saw the Permanent Court as 'le facteur de centralisation qui . . . s'est manifesté de plus en plus dans la communauté internationale';[55] its personnel were styled 'officials of the community of States';[56] and its decisions were said to 'become part and parcel of the legal sense of the community'.[57] In short, it was 'one of the most important organs of the international community'.[58] Such views have long been abandoned, the Permanent Court now being associated by many with a distant and less sophisticated past. In Professor Philip Allott's view, the Permanent Court was one among 'many previous attempts

---

[52] Huber in (1954) 45-II *Annuaire*, p. 62.
[53] Rosenne, *Law and Practice*, pp. 1609 and 1612; and see James Crawford, *International Law as an Open System: Selected Essays* (London, 2002), pp. 36–7.
[54] Advisory Committee, *Procès-verbaux*, p. 11.
[55] Max Sørensen, *Les Sources du droit international: étude sur la jurisprudence de la Cour permanente de Justice internationale* (Copenhagen, 1946), pp. 154 and 253.
[56] Series E No. 16 (1939–45), p. 11.
[57] H. Lauterpacht, 'The So-Called Anglo-American and Continental Schools of Thought in International Law' (1931) 12 *BYIL* 31 at 53.
[58] Oppenheim/Lauterpacht, *International Law*, vol. 2, p. 50, note 1.

at international pseudo-constitutionalism'.[59] But, to use the words of another commentator, 'somewhat ironically . . . [state sovereignty] was upheld and celebrated by institutions [such as the Permanent Court] that had been created in the hope that they somehow would curtail sovereignty'.[60] In 1972, at the commemoration of the fiftieth anniversary of the Permanent Court, it was characterised by Sir Muhammad Zafrulla Khan, then President of the International Court, as 'a stage in the progress towards on organized international community based on peace and justice different from those which had preceded it not merely in degree but also in kind'.[61] Today, many international lawyers may assume that in the interval vast changes occurred and that a study of the decisions of the Permanent Court, dating back to the period between 1922 and 1940, can be little more than a contribution to a neglected field of international legal history. On this view, the Permanent Court is the estranged companion of a past considered overcome.

For example, according to Shabtai Rosenne:

[l]ooking back, the cases which were referred to the Permanent Court were not major in the sense that the judicial pronouncement would have a forward reach beyond merely deciding the disputes before that Court. They may have been important in their day, both politically and legally. With the one major exception of the cases which the Court decided in the year 1951 . . . virtually the same assessment could fairly be made of the work of the present Court up to 1966.[62]

In the following sentence, Rosenne notes that '[m]any international lawyers consider that the major contribution of the Permanent Court to the development of international law was concentrated on the law of treaties – a core topic of international law, it is true, but not the only one'. Consequently, within its main field, that of treaty interpretation,[63]

---

[59] Philip Allott, *The Health of Nations: Society and Law Beyond the State* (Cambridge, 2002), p. 250.

[60] Antony Anghie, 'Colonialism and the Birth of International Institutions: Sovereignty, Economy, and the Mandate System of the League of Nations' (2002) 34 *NYUJILP* 513 at 544.

[61] YICJ 1971-2, p. 132.

[62] Shabtai Rosenne, 'Presentation' in Connie Peck and Roy S. Lee (eds.), *Increasing the Effectiveness of the International Court of Justice* (The Hague, 1997), p. 466 at p. 468. See also Rosenne, *Law and Practice*, pp. 3–4, 8, 19–21, 28–30, 33–8, 93–5, 101, 167, 181–2, 393–8 and 1061; however, this work contains plenty of references to decisions of the Permanent Court and also numerous statements that are more favourable to it, e.g., ibid., pp. 175, 285, 667, 776–7, 832–3, 1072–3, 1379–80, 1609–10, 1623–7 and 1679. Cf. Shabtai Rosenne, *The World Court* (5th edn, Dordrecht, 1995), pp. 15–20, 245–6 and 258.

[63] Cf. Maurice Houlard, *La Nature juridique des traités internationaux et son application aux théories de la nullité, de la caducité et de la révision des traités* (Bourdeaux, 1936), p. 63;

the Permanent Court might have made a contribution, seemingly reducing the significance of Rosenne's just-quoted conclusion to those fields in which the Permanent Court did not operate and so made no contribution to international law, past or present.

It takes a careful analysis of the entire case law of the Permanent Court to decide in which fields it did operate, and where its decisions may have had a direct or indirect impact. According to Rosenne, the International Court, 'standing on the building blocks laid by its predecessor, has by now extracted almost all that it possibly can from the Statute as it was conceived originally'.[64] This is a special case of treaty interpretation. Referring to five branches of procedural law, i.e. intervention by third states, contentious jurisdiction, provisional measures of protection, default of appearance and advisory jurisdiction, Rosenne argues that 'for each of these topics, treated in a few lines of generality in the Statute and which hardly occurred in the Permanent Court, the present Court has now created a substantial body of law'.[65] Of course, there have been several important developments in the scope and content of international law since the heyday of the Permanent Court, many of which could not have been predicted in the inter-war period.[66] Also, the interpretation of the Statute of the International Court has evolved and new initiatives have been taken, some of which are truly progressive (while others are quite restrictive).[67] This is inevitable and fully in agreement with general principles of treaty interpretation. Nevertheless, a perusal of the decisions of the International Court will demonstrate that also within such fields as its jurisdiction, whether contentious or advisory, or provisional measures, there are not only some building blocks laid by the Permanent Court but also several explicit references to its decisions. In 1972, halfway between the end of the Permanent Court's activity and the present, President Khan told his audience that 'the Permanent Court built up a corpus of procedural law appropriate to a permanent

---

Hudson, *Permanent Court*, p. 631; Sørensen, *Sources du droit international*, p. 57; and Eduardo Jiménez de Aréchaga, 'The Work and the Jurisprudence of the International Court of Justice 1947–1986' (1987) 58 *BYIL* 1 at 31. Of course, interpretation of contemporary treaties – whether law-making or not, see Marcelle Jokl, *De l'interprétation des traités normatifs d'après la doctrine et la jurisprudence internationales* (Paris, 1935), p. 179 – remains an essential part of the International Court's workload; see also Rosenne, *Law and Practice*, p. 172.

[64] Rosenne, 'Presentation', p. 472.   [65] *Ibid.*, p. 473.

[66] See Shahabuddeen, *Precedent*, pp. 116–17.

[67] Cf. Stephen M. Schwebel, 'Reflections on the Role of the International Court of Justice' (1986) 61 *Washington Law Review* 1061 at 1069.

international tribunal which has proved of great value and assistance to the present Court'.[68]

In Rosenne's own words, as his standard work on the International Court 'progressed from its initial edition in 1957 through those of 1965 and 1985 to date, the impression has grown stronger that, whatever the present Court's superficial resemblances to and descent from the Permanent Court, it cannot today be regarded as being the same institution under a new name, or as meeting the same needs'.[69] This resembles an experience common among internationalists as new institutions and contexts emerge and steal the attention. Rosenne refers to 1951 as marking 'the end of an international court as an instrument for applying Eurocentered inherited international law and the start of its conversion into the organ of truly universal international law applied in an international community for which the Charter is the controlling instrument'.[70] But it would seem a sheer coincidence if among all the decisions rendered between 1922 and 1966 only three decisions delivered in 1951 still have a bearing on international law, let alone the structures of international legal argument. Many probably regard also the year 1951 as obsolete; Rosenne himself has written that the International Court has 'rendered important services in the evolution of international law through the United Nations and in the peaceful settlement of international disputes, more in the last decade than in the first forty years of its existence since 1946, and more than in the whole existence, from 1922, of its predecessor, the Permanent Court of International Justice'.[71]

A wealth of similar statements can be found in the writings of Professor Edward McWhinney. In his view, '[t]he ethnic-cultural and value base'

---

[68] YICJ 1971–2, p. 133. It has been suggested that in the beginning of the 1970s the first phase in the interpretation of the procedural law of the International Court and its predecessor dating back to 1922 came to an end and was replaced by a second phase, these being termed, respectively, 'l'affirmation de l'autonomie formelle de la Cour vis-à-vis des Parties' and 'vers une arbitralisation de la Cour', see Abi-Saab, 'De l'evolution de la Cour internationale', pp. 281–93.

[69] Rosenne, Law and Practice, p. 8. Cf., e.g., Rosenne, The World Court, pp. 169–74; and Shabtai Rosenne, 'The Composition of the Court' in Leo Gross (ed.) The Future of the International Court of Justice (Dobbs Ferry, 1976), p. 377 at pp. 382–5, 388, 390 and 427–8; this view found no expression earlier when the docket of the International Court did not compare well to the activity of its predecessor, see, e.g., Shabtai Rosenne, 'On the Non-Use of the Advisory Competence of the International Court of Justice' (1963) 39 BYIL 1 at 34–6.

[70] Rosenne, 'Presentation', p. 470; and Rosenne, Law and Practice, pp. 21, 28 and 38.

[71] Rosenne, The World Court, p. xvi.

of the Permanent Court 'is simply too narrow . . . in a new, pluralistic World Community for too much automatic legal respect or legal deference to be accorded, today, to such jurisprudence from yesterday'.[72] This may not be a particularly surprising statement given that McWhinney casts the International Court in the light of comparative law.[73] Yet it cannot stand close scrutiny. According to McWhinney, 'from the work of the "old" Court of the between-the-two-World-Wars era, only *Eastern Carelia*, and *Austro-German Customs Union* ("the *Customs Regime* case"), seem particularly relevant to the contemporary International Court'.[74] This is an extraordinary choice: the *Eastern Carelia* opinion has been distinguished several times by the principal judicial organ of the United Nations, while the *Customs Regime* opinion was one of the most poorly reasoned and hotly disputed decisions in the history of the Permanent Court. Numerous other decisions keep being referred to by the International Court and other international courts. They also continue to occupy writers contributing to the most diversified fields of international law.

The year 1966 was in many respects a turning-point in the history of the International Court, yet it seems open to doubt whether it was also such a sharp dividing line in the case law of the International Court and its predecessor as has been ventured by Rosenne and McWhinney.[75] The trends which McWhinney identifies in decisions after 1966 – that is, in particular, 'a highly functional, problem-solving approach that emphasises the spirit of the law and the main trends in its historical unfolding' – were present in the Permanent Court in the 1920s, but

---

[72] Edward McWhinney, *Supreme Courts and Judicial Law-Making: Constitutional Tribunals and Constitutional Review* (Dordrecht, 1986), p. 298.

[73] See, e.g., Edward McWhinney, 'The Legislative Rôle of the World Court in an Era of Transition' in Rudolf Bernhard *et al.* (eds.), *Völkerrecht als Rechtsordnung – Internationale Gerichtsbarkeit – Menschenrechte: Festschrift für Hermann Mosler* (Berlin, 1983), p. 567 at p. 567; and Edward McWhinney, *Judicial Settlement of International Disputes: Jurisdiction, Justiciability and Judicial Law-Making on the Contemporary International Court* (Dordrecht, 1991), pp. 25 and 133.

[74] McWhinney, *Judicial Settlement*, p. xviii.

[75] Cf. *ibid.*, pp. xvii, 20, 23 and 156; but see Edward McWhinney, '"Internationalizing" the International Court: The Quest for Ethno-Cultural and Legal-Systematic Representativeness' in Emmanuel G. Bello and Bola A. Ajibola (eds.), *Essays in Honour of Judge Taslim Olawale Elias* (Dordrecht, 1992), p. 277 at pp. 279–82 and 288; Edward McWhinney, 'The Role and Mission of the International Court in an Era of Historical Transition' in Nandasiri Jasentuliyana (ed.), *Perspectives on International Law: Essays in Honour of Judge Manfred Lachs* (The Hague, 1995), p. 217 at pp. 218, 220 and 224; and Edward McWhinney, 'The International Court and Judicial Law-Making: Nuclear Tests Re-visited' in Jerzy Makarczyk (ed.), *Theory of International Law at the Threshold of the 21st Century: Essays in Honour of Krzysztof Skubiszewski* (The Hague, 1996), p. 509 at pp. 511–16.

somewhat lacking in the 1930s.[76] The importance of the second judgment delivered in 1966 in the *South West Africa* case is by now one of the classical questions of international dispute settlement and I have no desire whatsoever to embark upon it here. Suffice it to say that there are obvious similarities between the *Customs Regime* opinion delivered in 1931 and the *South West Africa* case and that history appears to be repeating itself,[77] it being no coincidence, for example, that the two great revisions of the Rules of Court took place in, respectively, the 1930s and the 1970s.

It might be just as convincing to take the opposite view to that of Rosenne and McWhinney. Writing in 1976, Professor J. H. W. Verzijl concluded:

Personally, I am of the opinion that the attitude of sovereign judicial independence taken by the Permanent Court vis-à-vis the litigant parties and the disputes submitted to it was superior to that adopted by the present International Court, an appraisal which necessarily also applies to the intrinsic value of its judgments and advisory opinions. Especially the clearly marked propensity of the present Court to abstain from pronouncing unambiguous decisions upon various legal questions of extreme importance diminishes to a great extent the value of its case law.[78]

There are good substantive reasons for focusing on the work of the Permanent Court, independently of its historical significance. It is, for various reasons, the best-documented international court of the twentieth century. This provides an important ground for dusting off these decisions of the past, also in relation to international legal argument in practice, yet it has not been the decisive factor. Although its work lies long back, what remains so particularly attractive about the Permanent Court and its decisions is that they were pioneers. This was 'a golden era in international adjudication',[79] in which, according to Professor Vaughan Lowe, '[i]nternational law . . . arguably reached the stage of practical completeness'.[80] The Permanent Court became 'an institution in the real

---

[76] Cf. *ibid.*, pp. 156 and also 25 and 46.
[77] Cf. Judge Jessup's dissenting opinion appended to *South West Africa* (Second Phase), ICJ Reports [1966] 6 at 416.
[78] J. H. W. Verzijl, *International Law in a Historical Perspective* (Leiden, 1976), vol. 8, p. 606.
[79] Edward McWhinney, *The World Court and the Contemporary International Law-Making Process* (Alphen aan den Rijn, 1979), p. 164; and see also Sørensen, *Sources du droit international*, pp. 27 and 56.
[80] A. V. Lowe, 'The Politics of Law-Making: Are the Method and Character of Norm Creation Changing?' in Michael Byers (ed.), *The Role of Law in International Politics* (Oxford, 2000), p. 207 at p. 211.

sense of the term', and this was the context in which the international judiciary took form.[81] In 1972, when the International Court celebrated the fiftieth anniversary of the Permanent Court, it did so under the title 'Commemoration of the Fiftieth Anniversary of the Institution of the International Judicial System'. On this occasion, in his speech already referred to twice, President Khan said that 'it is not merely the ideals and objectives in view in 1922 which have survived and grown, but also the methods which were adopted for the achievement of those objectives'.[82]

Simply because the Permanent Court was first, it formulated some often-quoted statements regarding international adjudication, which, as remarked by Sir Robert Jennings, make for the draftsman an easy initial run.[83] For example, in the *Mavrommatis* case, the Permanent Court defined a dispute as 'a disagreement on a point of law or fact, a conflict of legal views or of interests between two persons';[84] in the *Eastern Carelia* opinion, it held that '[t]he Court, being a Court of Justice, cannot, even in giving advisory opinions, depart from the essential rules guiding their activity as a Court';[85] in the *Free Zones* case, it stated that 'the judicial settlement of international disputes, with a view to which the Court has been established, is simply an alternative to the direct and friendly settlement of such disputes between the Parties';[86] and, in the *Electricity Company* case, it pronounced that 'the parties to a case must abstain from any measure capable of exercising a prejudicial effect in regard to the execution of the decision to be given and, in general, not allow any step of any kind to be taken which might aggravate or extend the dispute'.[87]

The Permanent Court put international law into practice, and it did so within a novel context.[88] No permanent international court preceded the Permanent Court, while a number of international courts have taken over and carried on other projects of international justice. The Permanent Court formulated principles to solve what many would regard as a phenomenon of recent origin, namely competition between jurisdictions

---

[81] Cf. President Winiarski in YICJ 1961–2, p. 2.   [82] YICJ 1971–2, p. 127.

[83] R. Y. Jennings, 'The Judiciary, International and National, and the Development of International Law' (1996) 45 *ICLQ* 1 at 10.

[84] *Case of the Mavrommatis Palestine Concessions* (Jurisdiction), Series A No. 2 (1924) at 11.

[85] *Status of Eastern Carelia*, Series B No. 5 (1923) at 29.

[86] *Case of the Free Zones of Upper Savoy and the District of Gex* (First Phase), Series A No. 22 (1929) at 13.

[87] *The Electricity Company of Sofia and Bulgaria* (Interim Measures of Protection), Series A/B No. 79 (1939) at 199.

[88] See also L. Oppenheim, *The League of Nations and its Problems* (Oxford, 1919), pp. 62–3.

of different international courts and tribunals.[89] Being the first truly permanent court of international significance, the members of the Permanent Court faced a series of new issues, or perhaps old issues cast in a novel, more urgent light, which generated considerable thoroughness as to the use of international legal argument. In erecting this new edifice, the judges had to care about the disputes to come as well as the past and the actual dispute before them. There is no doubt that the eleven men who met in the Peace Palace in 1922 saw themselves as being in an unprecedented situation. Whereas subsequent international courts have been able to draw on an ever-expanding repository of judicial precedent, the Permanent Court was often left without any such guidance (and thus also without any such means of rationalising or embellishing its decisions). Indeed, parts of the International Court's work cannot be properly appreciated without thorough knowledge of the Permanent Court, while the opposite does not apply. According to Jennings:

The International Court of Justice, at its fiftieth anniversary, will have existed just about twice as long as its predecessor, the Permanent Court of International Justice. It was the accepted success of that Court that ensured the constitution of its successor. Yet it seems fair to say that the record of the present Court compares quite well with that of its distinguished predecessor. Many PCIJ decisions are still frequently relied upon – *Mavrommatis Concessions, Factory at Chorzów*, the *Legal Status of Eastern Greenland*, and the *Lotus* cases come immediately to mind – but, with the exception perhaps of the *Eastern Greenland* decision, these cases tend to be consulted for somewhat technical lawyers' law. They can hardly be said to have had the sort of major impact upon the general system of international law and relations that one finds, for example, in the present Court's Advisory Opinion in the *Reparation for Injuries Suffered in the Service of the United Nations* case; or to have given a new and lasting direction to the law of the sea in general, as in the *Anglo-Norwegian Fisheries* case, and the *Continental Shelf* cases.[90]

---

[89] Thus, forum selection principles were suggested in *Case of the Mavrommatis Palestine Concessions* (Jurisdiction), Series A No. 2 (1924) at 31–2, *Case concerning the Factory at Chorzów* (Claim for Indemnity) (Jurisdiction), Series A No. 9 (1927) at 30 and *Rights of Minorities in Upper Silesia (Minority Schools)*, Series A No. 15 (1928) at 23, while the question of *lis pendens* was touched upon in *Case concerning Certain German Interests in Polish Upper Silesia* (Jurisdiction), Series A No. 6 (1925) at 19–20 and *Case concerning the Factory at Chorzów* (Claim for Indemnity) (Jurisdiction), Series A No. 9 (1927) at 31–2. See also Yuval Shany, *The Competing Jurisdictions of International Courts and Tribunals* (Oxford, 2003), pp. 230–4 and 239–41.

[90] R. Y. Jennings, 'The International Court of Justice after Fifty Years' (1995) 89 *AJIL* 493 at 493; and see also R. Y. Jennings, 'The Role of the International Court of Justice' (1997) 58 *BYIL* 1 at 5. Cf. W. Michael Reisman, 'Lassa Oppenheim's Nine Lives' (1994) 19 *YJIL* 255 at 257, 273 and 274.

It may well be true that the greatest importance of the Permanent Court is that it was an 'accepted success';[91] it had created 'a heritage worth preserving and nurturing'.[92] However, this success was in part a consequence of its decisions and use of international legal argument, notable examples being decisions enlightening the functioning and jurisdiction of an international court. The *Reparation for Injuries Suffered in the Service of the United Nations* opinion was fundamental to the understanding of the then embryonic United Nations, so were decisions of the Permanent Court in respect of a different and now obsolete organisation, that is, the League of Nations (and also the International Labour Organization, which is still in existence); indeed, in its opinion the International Court referred to decisions of its predecessor.[93] It has been said that 'the PCIJ, perhaps out of necessity, hesitantly laid the foundations for some of the more vital doctrines of the discipline, and in particular invented the curiously paired doctrines of attributed powers and implied powers: the heart, many would think with some justification, of the law of international organizations'.[94]

It requires close scrutiny of the case law to determine the importance of the decisions of the Permanent Court, and also all the decisions of the present International Court not mentioned by Jennings, to international law, whether past or present. The need for such scrutiny only becomes less urgent if the question is approached from an 'optimist' point of view that has dogged internationalists throughout history, considering an ever closer approximation to national systems as the evolutionary logic of any international system:

Since the notion that a court that could adjudicate upon sovereign rights was a novelty, the Permanent Court of International Justice, when it was formed after World War I, functioned within this milieu of nineteenth century concepts of sovereignty. Its approach to questions of international law naturally registered the same individualistic attitude to state sovereignty.

[91] See Hudson, *International Tribunals*, pp. 238–9; Edvard Hambro, 'The International Court of Justice' (1949) 3 *Yearbook of World Affairs* 188 at 190 and 203–4; Shabtai Rosenne, *The World Court: What It Is and How It Works* (Leiden, 1962), pp. 24–7; and Stephen M. Schwebel, 'The Docket and Decisionmaking Process of the International Court of Justice' (1989) 13 *Suffolk Transnational Law Journal* 543 at 544–5.

[92] Schwebel, 'Reflections on the Role', p. 1063.

[93] See *Reparation for Injuries Suffered in the Service of the United Nations*, ICJ Reports [1949] 174 at 182–3 and 184. As regards the League of Nations, see President Anzilotti in Committee of Jurists on the Statute of the Permanent Court of International Justice, *Minutes of the Session Held at Geneva, March 11th–19th, 1929* (League of Nations Document C.166.M.66.1929.V, 1929), p. 59; cf. Hudson, *Permanent Court*, pp. 400–2.

[94] Jan Klabbers, 'The Life and Times of the Law of International Organizations' (2001) 70 *NJIL* 287 at 290; cf. Jan Klabbers, *An Introduction to International Institutional Law* (Cambridge, 2002), pp. 61–3 and 67.

The post-World War II world is different. As the hitherto impenetrable dykes of State sovereignty spring ever-increasing leaks, there flow through them, into domestic systems, universal concepts and controls in such matters as health, communications and the environment. Various regional interests and global concerns prevent all efforts at merely domestic management of a nation's affairs. Further, the individualistic concepts of State sovereignty are yielding also to collectivist concepts, as international law adapts itself to the needs of a collectivist world.[95]

It takes an 'optimist' interpretation of the evolution of international law to conclude that international legal argument as used in the Permanent Court is no longer relevant. In my view, as I shall revert to in Chapters 2 and 3, the structures of international legal argument in the International Court are the same as those in the Permanent Court, which is a fine context in which to study these structures more closely.

From *Buchrecht* to practice

Whereas the fathers of the Permanent Court had to remove major political and conceptual obstacles in order to achieve its establishment, the Permanent Court's work and decisions encountered new impediments, some political, while others, though more technical, were associated with international legal theory at the time. No doubt, what Professor Martti Koskenniemi has said about Georg Jellinek in his brilliant *tour de force* through the history of *Buchrecht* in the period 1870 to 1960 applies to many of Jellinek's contemporaries and also his successors, namely that 'though he had concluded a marriage of convenience with law his real love remained with philosophy'.[96] When in 1911 Professor Lassa Oppenheim coined the term '*Buchrecht*', he thought of 'a system erected by greater or smaller authorities on the foundations of state practice and in its details often uncertain and contested'.[97] Oppenheim regarded it as 'a well-known fact that not only the legal systems which prevail in the several States differ, but also that there are differences concerning

[95] Christopher Gregory Weeramantry, 'Expanding the Potential of the World Court' in Nandasiri Jasentuliyana (ed.), *Perspectives on International Law: Essays in Honour of Judge Manfred Lachs* (The Hague, 1995), p. 309 at pp. 341–2. A possible source of inspiration might have been Judge Alvarez' dissenting opinion in *Fisheries*, ICJ Reports [1951] 116 at 146.

[96] Martti Koskenniemi, *The Gentle Civilizer of Nations: The Rise and Fall of International Law, 1870–1960* (Cambridge, 2001), p. 199.

[97] L. Oppenheim, *Die Zukunft des Völkerrecht* (Leipzig, 1911), p. 11; '*Buchrecht*' was translated into 'book-law' in the English edition: L. Oppenheim, *The Future of International Law* (Oxford, 1921), p. 5. See also S. Séfériadès, 'Aperçus sur la coutume juridique internationale et notamment sur son fondement' (1936) 43 *RGDIP* 129 at 130.

the fundamental conceptions of justice, law, procedure, and evidence'.[98] This was Oppenheim's argument for each state having a judge on the international bench. At the same time, it was a plausible source of the uncertainty and contests, which in Oppenheim's view characterised the content of the *Buchrecht* at the time the Permanent Court took up its work.

Had Oppenheim been writing a century later, it may perhaps be doubted whether he would have taken this term into use. According to Lord McNair, speaking in 1962, 'the feature of the past half-century has been the gradual transformation of international law from a book-law occasionally supplemented by treaties into a case-law constantly supplemented by treaties'.[99] In a weighty contribution written in the same period, it was noted that '[t]he permanence of the [Permanent] Court, and the acceptance of its jurisdiction in some degree by most of the states of the world, meant that its decisions had a far greater persuasive force than those of any previous international tribunal; case law became a more important contributing factor to the development of international law'.[100] Likewise, in his classic series of lectures published in 1934, *The Development of International Law by the Permanent Court of International Justice*, Hersch Lauterpacht dealt with 'the creation, development and clarification of an imposing body of rules of international law of varying degrees of crystallisation'.[101] There is some truth to these statements. But, even when decisions and treaties are available, they are not necessarily a panacea for uncertainty and contests over the content of international law. The selection of which passages to quote, and the reading given to them, might be influenced by, *inter alia*, a lawyer's

---

[98] Oppenheim, *League of Nations*, pp. 64–5 and 67.

[99] Arnold D. McNair, *The Expansion of International Law* (Jerusalem, 1962), p. 54; and see previously Arnold D. McNair, *The Development of International Justice* (New York, 1954), p. 16; and Arnold D. McNair, 'La Termination et la dissolution des traités' (1928) 22 *Recueil des Cours* 463 at 463 and 474. See also R. Y. Jennings, 'An International Lawyer Takes Stock' (1990) 39 *ICLQ* 513 at 519; and Shahabuddeen, *Precedent*, p. 15.

[100] J. L. Simpson and Hazel Fox, *International Arbitration: Law and Practice* (London, 1959), p. 19.

[101] H. Lauterpacht, *The Development of International Law by the Permanent Court of International Justice* (London, 1934), p. 8; and see also Moore, 'General Introduction', pp. vii and ix; Hudson, *International Tribunals*, p. 110; McNair, *Development of International Justice*, p. 16; George Schwarzenberger, *International Law as Applied by International Courts and Tribunals* (3rd edn, London, 1957), vol. 1, p. xix; R. Y. Jennings, 'The Progress of International Law' (1958) 34 *BYIL* 334 at 338–9; C. H. M. Waldock, 'General Course on Public International Law' (1962) 106 *Recueil des Cours* 1 at 13; and Shahabuddeen, *Precedent*, p. 15.

positions under the *Buchrecht*. In his narrative of 'the rise and fall of international law' between 1870 and 1960, Koskenniemi essentially neglects international adjudication.

Many analyses of the precedential value of decisions of the International Court and its predecessor have followed the list of sources of legal rules contained in Article 38 of the Statute of the International Court:

The Court, whose function is to decide in accordance with international law such disputes as are submitted to it, shall apply:

> (a) international conventions, whether general or particular, establishing rules expressly recognized by the contesting States;
> (b) international custom, as evidence of a general practice accepted as law;
> (c) the general principles of law recognized by civilized nations;
> (d) subject to the provisions of Article 59, judicial decisions and the teachings of the most highly qualified publicists of the various nations, as subsidiary means for the determination of rules of law.[102]

The rather artificial discussions caused by the wording of the last provision, according to which the International Court 'shall apply . . . subject to the provisions of Article 59, judicial decisions . . . as subsidiary means for the determination of the rules of law',[103] bears witness to the fact that more than anything else Article 38 is itself a product of the *Buchrecht*. Max Sørensen's doctoral thesis from 1946, *Les sources du droit international: Etude sur la jurisprudence de la Cour Permanente de Justice Internationale*, showed that, when one categorises *dicta* of the Permanent Court along the lines of Article 38 and sources theory in general, one is not using the theory to describe the decisions but the decisions to describe the theory.

The overall conception of an international court developing rules that are collectable in a 'case law' suggests a not altogether realistic view on how a decision is normally reached by a collegiate body and how the reasons for that decision are assembled. Part of this view is the assumption

---

[102] As for Article 38(1), the main difference from the Statute of the Permanent Court is the words 'whose function is to decide in accordance with international law such disputes as are submitted to it': see 13 UNCIO, pp. 164, 284–5 and 392.

[103] According to Article 59, '[t]he decision of the Court has no binding force except between the parties and in respect of that particular case'. As pronounced by the Permanent Court in 1926, '[t]he object of this article is simply to prevent legal principles accepted by the Court in a particular case from being binding upon other States or in other disputes': *Case concerning Certain German Interests in Polish Upper Silesia* (Merits), Series A No. 7 (1926) at 19; and see *Procès-verbal of Council* 1920-10, p. 173 and *Records of Assembly: Committees* 1920, p. 512.

that the international court will follow whichever pronouncement may be contained in a previous decision.[104] It was supported by Lauterpacht in the following way:

> The Court follows its own decisions for the same reasons for which all courts – whether bound by the doctrine of precedent or not – do it, namely, because such decisions are a depository of legal experience to which it is convenient to adhere; because they embody what the Court thinks is the law; because respect for decisions given in the past makes for continuity and stability, which are of the essence of orderly administration of justice; and because judges do not like, if they can help it, to admit that they were previously in the wrong.[105]

It will usually be inadequate, however, in analysing the decisions of a collegiate judicial body to treat the body as a disembodied institutional voice and to use the singular when referring to the group of judges. As for the Permanent Court, Lauterpacht would seem to have neglected the unprecedented situation in which the judges found themselves. They had markedly different backgrounds, not limited to the divisions between judges from civil law systems and judges from common law systems.[106] There were judges with a previous career in international law and judges whose past experiences belonged to national law, diplomacy or politics; judges who believed in the idea of a *société des nations* and judges who remained sceptical; judges who were favourably disposed towards the Great Powers and judges who laid emphasis on the rule of law (or of international law).

In general, decisions of international courts are drafted by shifting groups of judges representing shifting majorities. The *motifs* only reach their final form after several judges have arrived at a compromise between their individual views, which may well have been divergent and potentially irreconcilable, even though leading to the same result. Often there are ellipses and gaps in the *motifs*, or different passages may tend to contradict each other because they are the contributions of different minds. Even though the *motifs* are usually silent, the overruling of holdings in previous decisions can hardly be avoided, unless members of an international court agree on more issues than lawyers in general. Thus, there are bound to be discussions about, for example, the limits to the court's jurisdiction and the methods of treaty interpretation and also

---

[104] Cf. Hudson, *Permanent Court*, p. 628; and see also Hudson in YILC 1949, p. 104, referring to 'an advisory opinion of the Permanent Court of International Justice, the authority of which could not be challenged'; cf. *ibid.*, pp. 256 and 288.

[105] Lauterpacht, *Development by the Permanent Court*, p. 8; cf. *ibid.*, p. 88.

[106] Cf. Lauterpacht, 'Schools of Thought', p. 31.

perhaps the importance of sovereignty and the nature of international law, and some of these discussions may not lead to a single resolution.

All this is trite learning, yet it is essential. By way of illustration one may point to the exposition by J. P. Fockema Andreae in *An Important Chapter from the History of Legal Interpretation: The Jurisdiction of the First Permanent Court of International Justice (1922–1940)*. In the first part of this book, Andreae presented what he called on 'outline', a 'picture' and a 'fragment' of principles of treaty interpretation in the Permanent Court.[107] He attempted to piece together several quotes, or fragments, from the published decisions into a general, intelligible model of treaty interpretation. Although the writer clearly wanted to be successful in his attempt, and also to congratulate the Permanent Court,[108] he did not quite succeed in hiding his disappointment caused by the impossibility to have all or just most quotes to fit the same general model. This led Andreae to write:

When observing the instability of the structure of judgments and advisory opinions of the Court . . . and even more so when watching the strong differences of opinion in the very bosom of the Court brought up for discussion there, one naturally wonders what are the chief causes of this state of things. Many people have racked their brains about it and the last word has certainly not been spoken on this subject yet. There is little chance of that happening very soon either, because the problem is extremely complicated and shows many a subtle fact, but it is worth deep contemplation because it would be of the greatest importance to the legal security of States and citizens, as well as to the development of legal science and jurisdiction if one could add more (in regard to its principles) to the knowledge of judicial judgment.[109]

Unlike many of his contemporaries, Andreae was explicit as to the complexity of collective decision-making.[110] Perhaps the reason why this fact is seldom taken seriously when analysing the decisions of a collegiate body is not only the lack of time and documentation but also a certain disinterest as to what were the views represented on the bench. Sir Robert Jennings has underlined '[t]he tendency all too often, of both writers and courts, . . . to cite isolated passages from judgments, almost as if they were passages from Holy Writ, with little or no attempt to qualify

---

[107] See J. P. Fockema Andreae, *An Important Chapter from the History of Legal Interpretation: The Jurisdiction of the First Permanent Court of International Justice, 1922–1940* (Leiden, 1948), pp. 14–69.

[108] *Ibid.*, pp. 7–8 and 140–2.   [109] *Ibid.*, pp. 116 and also 107, 133 and 136.

[110] *Ibid.*, p. 139. See also, in the context of Article 52 of the ICSID Convention, *Compania de Aguas del Aconquija, SA & Vivendi Universal (Compagnie Générale des Eaux) v. Argentina* (Annulment), 6 ICSID Reports 340 (2002) at para. 65.

their meaning in relation to the submissions and arguments of the parties, or to the facts of the particular case, or to the context of the judgment in which the passage occurs'.[111] According to Jennings, '[b]y such use of citations of selected passages from decisions, almost any proposition can be given the appearance of being vested with judicial authority'. In 1935, the registrar of the Permanent Court, Åke Hammarskjöld, observed that:

> the *dicta* of the Court are almost always carefully limited to particular situations arising in concrete cases; and if one takes these *dicta* as a basis in estimating the Court's contribution to positive international law, there is always the risk of generalisations which may only correspond remotely to the Court's past and present views, to say nothing of the opinions it may adopt in the future. Many of the admirable works which have already been devoted to the Court's jurisprudence (in the continental sense of the word) have not succeeded in avoiding this danger.[112]

Certainly, ellipses and contradictions in the *motifs* add to the role of the reader, who will have to interpret and even to quote selectively. Indeed, the present understanding of some of the Permanent Court's key decisions says more about the preconceived ideas, or hidden agendas, of readers and of international legal theory than about the attitudes of the judges themselves.

One kind of agenda was to boost the popularity of the Permanent Court. For example, while Professor Hudson, not only author of the seminal *The Permanent Court of International Justice, 1920–1942: A Treatise* and the leading American commentator but also, in Manfred Lachs' words, 'the chronicler of the World Court',[113] happily expressed the hope that the Permanent Court would give 'new foundation and fresh vigor to international law',[114] his not-so-secret aspiration was the adherence of the United States to the Court Protocol and, in the long run, the League of Nations (neither of which was ever achieved).[115] In his overview of treaty interpretation in the Permanent Court, Hudson ventured that 'the

---

[111] R. Y. Jennings, 'Role of the International Court' (1997) 58 *BYIL* 1 at 41–2; and also R. Y. Jennings, 'The Judicial Function and the Rule of Law' in *International Law at the Time of its Codification: Essays in Honour of Roberto Ago* (Milan, 1987), vol. 3, p. 139 at pp. 142–3.

[112] Åke Hammarskjöld, 'The Permanent Court of International Justice and the Development of International Law' (1935) 14 *International Affairs* 797 at 797.

[113] Manfred Lachs, *The Teacher in International Law: Teachings and Teaching* (The Hague, 1982), p. 100.

[114] Manley O. Hudson, 'The Fifth Year of the Permanent Court of International Justice' (1927) 21 *AJIL* 26 at 35.

[115] See Michael Dunne, *The United States and the World Court, 1920–1935* (London, 1988), pp. 4–5, 66, 72, 87 and 157–8. On Hudson's assistance to the League of Nations in the

Court has appreciated the necessity of its maintaining a consistent attitude in dealing with the texts which have come before it, and the result has been both a clarification of the legal situations to which the texts have related and a significant contribution to the approach to be made in international law to the interpretation and application of conventional arrangements'.[116] To achieve his overall goal required considerable 'propaganda', a point on which Hudson was clear.

Similarly, after the British Government had ratified the Optional Clause in 1929, conferring jurisdiction on the Permanent Court, W. E. Beckett, who was then the Second Legal Adviser at the Foreign Office, urged his colleagues to defend and indeed popularise the Permanent Court and its decisions.[117]

However, as already indicated, the most common kind of hidden agenda was and is the *Buchrecht*. It may induce theorists to adopt the notion of an international court having a duty to 'develop' and 'clarify' international law in accordance with some blueprint, as opposed to 'make' international law on a different basis. In Lauterpacht's view:

the habit of being influenced, consciously or unconsciously, by conclusions previously formed *in pari materia* is an inevitable mental process to which judges like others are subject, and experience has shown that Article 59 and the reference to it in Article 38 have not hindered the Court in its task of consolidating and enlarging the *corpus juris gentium*. In fact, while the political conditions of the world have not permitted the Court to apply the rule of law to important political controversies directly threatening peace, it has been amply fulfilling the other part of its task which was expected of it at the time of its establishment. It has become an effective agency for developing and clarifying International Law.[118]

---

summer periods, see also Terry L. Deibel, *Le Secrétariat de la Société des Nations et l'internationalisme américain, 1919–1924* (Geneva, 1972), pp. 16 and also 113–32.

[116] Hudson, *Permanent Court*, p. 631.

[117] Beckett's comments, 1 December 1931, FO 371 C8740/673/3; and see W. E. Beckett, 'Decisions of the Permanent Court of International Justice on Points of Law and Procedure of General Application' (1930) 11 *BYIL* 1; W. E. Beckett, 'Les Questions d'intérêt général au point de vue juridique dans la jurisprudence de la Cour permanente de Justice internationale' (1932) 39 *Recueil des Cours* 135; and W. E. Beckett, 'Les Questions d'intérêt général au point de vue juridique dans la jurisprudence de la Cour permanente de Justice internationale (juillet 1932–juillet 1934)' (1934) 50 *Recueil des Cours* 193. On Beckett's impact, see G. G. Fitzmaurice, *The Law and Procedure of the International Court of Justice* (Cambridge, 1986), pp. xxix and 2, note 1.

[118] Oppenheim/Lauterpacht, *International Law*, vol. 2, pp. 65–6; cf. L. Oppenheim, *International Law* (4th edn by Arnold D. McNair, London, 1926–8), vol. 2, pp. 56–7. See conversely Walther Schücking, 'Le Développement du Pacte de la Société des Nations' (1927) 20 *Recueil des Cours* 353 at 420 and 427.

The decisions of the Permanent Court are regularly associated with 'positivism', as with much from the past, the prime reason being its judgment in *The Lotus*.[119] In the *Nuclear Weapons* opinion, President Bedjaoui appended a declaration in which as regards *The Lotus* he submitted that '[t]he resolutely positivist, voluntarist approach of international law still current at the beginning of the century – and which the Permanent Court did not fail to endorse . . . – has been replaced by an objective conception of international law, a law more readily seeking to reflect a collective juridical conscience and respond to the social necessities of States organized as a community'.[120] No doubt, this is an 'optimist' version of present day international law, which has had its equivalents in the past and will have more so in the future. In 2002, Judges Higgins, Kooijmans and Buergenthal referred to *The Lotus* as 'the high water mark of laissez-faire in international relations'.[121] They identified a 'vertical notion of the authority of action . . . significantly different from the horizontal system of international law envisaged in the "*Lotus*" case'. However, this was due to new treaty rules regarding so-called 'universal' jurisdiction, as distinct from a transformation of the basis of international law. What is of importance here is to underline that *The Lotus* was precisely the one decision in respect of which persons surrounding

---

[119] E.g., Louis Cavaré, 'L'arrêt du "Lotus" et le positivisme juridique' (1930) 10 *Travaux juridiques et économiques de l'Université de Rennes* 144 at 148; Arthur Steiner, 'Fundamental Conceptions of International Law in the Jurisprudence of the Permanent Court of International Justice' (1936) 30 *AJIL* 414 at 416; Ijaz Hussain, *Dissenting and Separate Opinions at the World Court* (Dordrecht, 1984), pp. 53, 64 and 77; Georges Abi-Saab, 'The International Court as a World Court' in Vaughan Lowe and Malgosia Fitzmaurice (eds.), *Fifty Years of the International Court of Justice: Essays in Honour of Sir Robert Jennings* (Cambridge, 1996), p. 3 at p. 4; Bruno Simma and Andreas L. Paulus, 'The Responsibility of Individuals for Human Rights Abuses in Internal Conflicts: A Positivist View' (1999) 93 *AJIL* 302 at 304; and Outi Korhonen, *International Law Situated: An Analysis of the Lawyer's Stance Towards Culture, History and Community* (The Hague, 2000), p. 207. Likewise, two otherwise well-balanced studies: David Kennedy, 'A New World Order: Yesterday, Today, and Tomorrow' (1994) 4 *Transnational Law & Contemporary Problems* 329 at 364 and David Kennedy, 'International Law and the Nineteenth Century: History of an Illusion' (1996) 65 *NJIL* 385 at 402–3; cf. David Kennedy, 'My Talk at the ASIL: What is New Thinking in International Law?' (2000) 94 *American Society Proceedings* 104 at 116. See also, more generally, Hans Morgenthau, 'Positivism, Functionalism, and International Law' (1940) 34 *AJIL* 260 at 264. Cf. Pellet, YILC 1998-I, p. 28.

[120] *Legality of the Threat or Use of Nuclear Weapons*, ICJ Reports [1996] 226 at 290–1. Cf. the dissenting opinions of Judges Shahabuddeen and Weeramantry, *ibid.*, pp. 393 and 396 and 495–6, respectively.

[121] See Judges Higgins, Kooijmans and Buergenthal's joint separate opinion at para. 51 in *Case concerning the Arrest Warrant of 11 April 2000*, ICJ Reports [2002] 3.

the Permanent Court were most explicit in complaining about theorists, and others, having misconstrued the *motifs*.[122]

As for a more detailed illustration of the role of the reader, it is worthwhile to dwell on Lauterpacht's above-mentioned lectures from 1934. They have not only been perhaps the most influential interpretation of the decisions of the Permanent Court and, through a later edition, its successor. They will also guide us towards the use of international legal argument outside the *Buchrecht*, that is, in practice, with which this book is concerned. The skeleton of Lauterpacht's argument was fairly simple. Of the two main threads that he saw running through the decisions, 'judicial caution' and 'judicial legislation', the former was subordinated to the latter,[123] which in turn was translated into the principle that international law should be effective.[124] The reason why Article 38(1)(c) of the Statute was not referred to in the Permanent Court's decisions was that the principle of effectiveness absorbed the general principles.[125] Lauterpacht concluded that 'the work of the Court can to a large extent be conceived in terms of a restrictive interpretation of claims of State sovereignty'.[126] At this point, the scholar's independent voice had become apparent, as had his theoretical agenda, which was to refute various sovereignty-based arguments and dogmas.[127] What Lauterpacht had originally described as the Permanent Court's genuine contribution to international law, '[j]udicial legislation, conceived as a process of changing the existing law',[128] was in the end treated as a necessity, 'a matter of judicial duty'.[129] By then Lauterpacht had rationalised the Permanent Court's decisions, formerly described as 'revolutionary', 'drastic' and 'striking', along the lines of his own agenda, making them seem statements of the obvious. He made a detour round the Permanent Court's decisions in *The Lotus* and the

---

[122] See Michel de la Grotte, 'Les Affaires traitées par la Cour permanente de Justice internationale pendant la periode 1926–1928' (1929) 10 *RDILC* 387 at 387; and Huber in (1931) 36-I *Annuaire*, p. 79.

[123] Lauterpacht, *Development by the Permanent Court*, pp. 43–4.

[124] *Ibid.*, pp. 69–70, 50 and 84.   [125] *Ibid.*, p. 82.

[126] *Ibid.*, pp. 89 and 104; cf., for an early hint, *ibid.*, p. 33. See also H. Lauterpacht, *The Function of Law in the International Community* (Oxford, 1933), pp. 208–9.

[127] See H. Lauterpacht, *Private Law Sources and Analogies of International Law* (London, 1927), pp. 43 *et seq.*; H. Lauterpacht, *Function of Law*, pp. 3–4; and Oppenheim/Lauterpacht, *International Law*, vol. 1, pp. 117–18. Cf. Shabtai Rosenne, 'Sir Hersch Lauterpacht's Concept of the Task of the International Judge' (1961) 55 *AJIL* 825 at 828–31; and Korhonen, *International Law Situated*, pp. 194 and 259.

[128] Lauterpacht, *Development by the Permanent Court*, pp. 45 and also 68.

[129] *Ibid.*, pp. 105 and 107; see also *ibid.*, p. 50.

Customs Regime case in order to give his lectures the desired degree of coherence.[130]

The second edition, which appeared in 1958, also covering the first nine years of the International Court, was based on the old text, yet it was more than an update. Lauterpacht had become much more critical about 'judicial legislation',[131] which no longer trumped 'judicial caution'.[132] Also, the principle of effectiveness was a mere shadow of itself, being subordinated to the static intentions of the parties,[133] while room was made for sovereignty.[134] In consequence, new chapters on 'the limits of the principle of effectiveness' and 'the recognition of claims of sovereignty' had been added.[135] Lauterpacht no longer saw a hierarchy between 'judicial caution' and 'judicial legislation', or between 'effectiveness' and 'sovereignty'.[136] Indeed, he was clear on 'the disadvantages of any attempt to study the work of the Court with the view to extracting from it rigid rules'.[137] There were only some different 'trends and principles', which made up the International Court's 'indirect but significant contribution towards the development of the law of nations'.[138] This watered-down conclusion was a disappointment, given the title and given the strict, rule-oriented definition of developing international law.[139] Yet it ought not to be regretted.

The fact that in 1954 Lauterpacht had succeeded McNair as a judge of the International Court might have contributed towards the abandonment of the original, theoretical agenda and thus of arguably the most influential theory of the development of international law by judicial fiat. Lauterpacht had certainly adopted a more welcoming attitude towards the International Court overruling old 'precedents'.[140] More importantly, Lauterpacht underlined that in practice international legal argument was far more sophisticated than the *Buchrecht* hinted at and a new reason why Article 38(1)(c) had not been needed.[141] Lauterpacht

---

[130] *Ibid.*, pp. 21–3 and 103–4.
[131] H. Lauterpacht, *The Development of International Law by the International Court* (London, 1958), pp. 156–7, 179, 221–3, 266, 283 and 399.
[132] *Ibid.*, pp. 83–4, 152 and 227.   [133] *Ibid.*, pp. 229 and 243.
[134] Cf. *ibid.*, pp. 229, 293 and 331.   [135] *Ibid.*, pp. 282–93 and 334–400.
[136] See *ibid.*, pp. 230, 341 and 396–7.   [137] *Ibid.*, p. 293.   [138] *Ibid.*, p. 400.
[139] See *ibid.*, p. 18; and also Koskenniemi, *Gentle Civilizer of Nations*, pp. 403–5. The reason why Koskenniemi's conclusion is not quite as bleak might be that he does not compare the second edition to the first: cf. *ibid.*, pp. 412 and 536–9.
[140] *Ibid.*, pp. 14–15, 18–20, 29, 62, 66–7 and 398; *The Lotus* had remained a prime target (*ibid.*, pp. 20 and 28), while the criticism of the *Customs Regime* opinion had disappeared (*ibid.*, pp. 47–8).
[141] *Ibid.*, pp. 165–6 and also 396; cf. *ibid.*, p. 282.

seemed to share the experience expressed by his predecessor, Lord McNair, in the following way:

> Whereas I may have thought, as a teacher or as the author of a book or an article, that I had adequately examined some particular rule of law, I have constantly found that, when I have been confronted with the same rule of law in the course of writing a professional opinion or of contributing to a judgment, I have been struck by the different appearance that the rule of law may assume when it is being examined for the purpose of its application in practice to a set of ascertained facts.[142]

When a lawyer undertakes the application of international law to a specific case, international law seems to change, or in other words, much of what has been taken for granted in theory falls apart. The work of the Permanent Court and subsequent international courts has not merely contributed 'case law' as a new source of international law in addition to treaty and custom. Rather, it has changed the way in which international law is approached. There is more to international legal argument in practice than what is conventionally accounted for in the *Buchrecht*, including Article 38 of the Statute of the International Court.

Chapters 2 and 3 in this book attempt to encapsulate, wholly or in part, what is that 'more' for readers not only pursuing their own agendas. These chapters are concerned with the ways in which lawyers use international law to solve disputes and questions in practice, for example within the framework of an international court. It is not about the content of international law at any given time, let alone an attempt *de lege ferenda* to call into question solutions known to practising lawyers. The focus is on the circumstances and the structures within which substantive international law unfolds. As such Chapters 2 and 3 set out to develop a descriptive model of international legal argument, which can be used in analysing the decisions of the Permanent Court in Chapters 5 to 7. Because of the unprecedented activity of the Permanent Court, it is justified to go into some detail not only in describing this model but also the basis of international law upon which it rests.

---

[142] McNair, *Development of International Justice*, pp. 16–17; the passage is quoted by R. Y. Jennings, 'Gerald Gray Fitzmaurice' (1985) 55 *BYIL* 1 at 49. See also Sørensen, *Sources du droit international*, p. 144.

PART 2

International legal argument

2   The basis of international law

Conceptions of the state

Back in 1899, only a few of the positions now occupied by international lawyers had been provided for. Yet 1899 was a significant year. Governments met at the First Peace Conference at The Hague to set an example of codifying international law in treaties. They reached agreement on the establishment of the first international court of a permanent character, at least nominally – the Permanent Court of Arbitration. The nineteenth century had witnessed a remarkable growth in the number of treaties, and their subject matters, many of which were also governed by national law. In the same period constitutional democracy had spread widely. While it remained a government prerogative to represent the state internationally, for example when consenting to be bound by a treaty, parliamentary bodies had become centres of national law-making processes.

In 1899, Professor Heinrich Triepel in *Völkerrecht und Landesrecht* addressed the topical issue of the relationship between international and national law. It is one of the few nineteenth-century books on international law that was quoted, or at least cited, throughout the twentieth century. Triepel has been seen as the main exponent of the dualist theory, according to which national and international law are separate legal systems. One consequence of this view is that acts contrary to international law may be valid under national law, and *vice versa*. The systems were described by Triepel as circles that perhaps touched but never overlapped.[1] Triepel grounded his dualist theory on differences between the two systems as regards their subjects and the relationships they

---

[1] H. Triepel, *Völkerrecht und Landesrecht* (Leipzig, 1899), p. 111; and see *ibid.*, pp. 256–64.

governed, as well as the sources of their rules.[2] There was nothing new about reserving individuals and their relationships to national law: this was one of several points on which Triepel's theory was in line with the work of his predecessors.[3]

Völkerrecht und Landesrecht provides an instructive contrast to the analysis in this chapter of the basis of international law. Without challenging Triepel's fundamental idea of dualism, national and international law may be seen not only as two separate circles, whether overlapping or not. From another point of view, which is equally valid, they are separate parts of the same bigger circle of law. Triepel himself referred to national and international law as both being '*Rechtstheile*',[4] or parts of law, and while the differences in sources ensured separation, and thus dualism, the differences he envisaged in subjects and relationships suggested coordination. *Völkerrecht und Landesrecht* demands attention because of Triepel's struggle with well-known conceptions of the state and the contexts in which such conceptions present themselves. This struggle took place at an unanalysed level of *Völkerrecht und Landesrecht* and contributed to some of the more obscure elements of Triepel's theory. Triepel's successors may focus on the parallel use of the conceptions of the state and regard them as tools, rather than obscure presuppositions, in analysing international legal argument. It is not that the conceptions are unfamiliar. It is that the emphasis has been on their definition in the abstract, rather than on the practical application given to them in different contexts. Bringing out this level in Triepel's pioneering work lays bare the basis of international law and gives new insight into the structures of international legal argument. Thus, in *Völkerrecht und Landesrecht* there were:

---

[2] *Ibid.*, pp. 9 and 253–4. According to Triepel, it was, logically speaking, not a condition for the systems being separate that they had different subjects, nor that they governed different kinds of relationships between the subjects; however, they had to regulate different parts of these relationships: see *ibid.*, pp. 11, 19–20 and 22. By implication, there could be no true conflict between international and national law: *ibid.*, pp. 23, 26 and 254; cf., as regards '*die Reception*' of one system into the other, *ibid.*, pp. 169–73 and 211–36. See also L. Oppenheim, *International Law* (London, 1905–6), vol. 1, pp. 25–6 and, as a reminiscence of his earlier work, Dionisio Anzilotti, *Cours de droit internaional* (Paris, 1929), p. 63. Cf. G.-A. Walz, 'Les Rapports du droit international et du droit interne' (1937) 61 *Recueil des Cours* 379 at 407–8, 424 and 426–7.

[3] Cf. Triepel, *Völkerrecht und Landesrecht*, pp. 21, 121–2 and 329.

[4] See *ibid.*, pp. 2–3, 8 and 111.

The state as a national sovereign

National law, which according to Triepel governed the relations between individuals and between individuals and the state, was seen as the creation of the state. The state could make law, and change it, at will. 'Jeder Staat', Triepel wrote, 'nun regelt durch seine Rechtsordnung "Beziehungen" aller der Subjekte, die er sich unterworfen denkt, d. h. für die nach seiner Meinung seine Autorität bestimmend ist.'[5]

While Triepel embraced the conception of the state as a sovereign in the context of national law, he ruled out the possibility of using this conception in the context of international law, which governed the relations between states.[6] Triepel emphatically opposed the theory of *Selbstverpflictung*, according to which the binding force of international law rested on, and only endured for so long as it was in accordance with, the will of the single state.[7] 'Einen Rechtssatz, der nicht als Macht über den Subjekten steht, an die er sich wendet, kann ich', Triepel wrote, 'mir nicht denken, und einen Rechtssatz, der solche Macht ist, kann nicht eines dieser Subjekte durch einen Machtspruch gegen sich selbst hervorbringen.'[8] Instead, law made unilaterally was but 'äusseres Staatsrecht',[9] external public law that the state could make, but also change at will.

Accordingly, one finds in *Völkerrecht und Landesrecht* the conception of the state as a national sovereign (i.e., the conception of the state as a sovereign used in the context of national law), but no conception of the

[5] *Ibid.*, pp. 12 and also 9 and 257 (in the French translation, published in 1920: 'Chaque Etat règle par son système juridique les relations entre les sujets qu'il considère comme lui étant soumis, c'est-à-dire sur lesquels, à son avis, son autorité s'exerce de façon souveraine.').

[6] *Ibid.*, pp. 18 and also 22 and 32.

[7] *Ibid.*, pp. 18–19, 77 and 131–4. For the theory of *Selbstverpflictung*, see Karl Magnus Bergbohm, *Staatsverträge und Gesetze als Quellen des Völkerrechts* (Dorpat, 1877), pp. 19 and 39; and Georg Jellinek, *Die rechtliche Natur der Staatenverträge: Ein Beitrag zur juristischen Construction des Völkerrechts* (Vienna, 1880), pp. 7 and, in particular, 23 and 34–45. Of course, as is also the case with Triepel, it is possible to give a more sophisticated interpretation of the theory than the caricature prevailing among international lawyers in general; as regards Jellinek, see Martti Koskenniemi, *The Gentle Civilizer of Nations: The Rise and Fall of International Law, 1870–1960* (Cambridge, 2001), pp. 198–206; and also Martti Koskenniemi, *From Apology to Utopia: The Structure of International Legal Argument* (Helsinki, 1989), pp. 102–5.

[8] Triepel, *Völkerrecht und Landesrecht*, pp. 78–9 and also 268 ('Je ne peux pas me représenter une règle de droit, qui n'est pas un pouvoir au-dessus des sujets auxquels elle s'applique, et, si elle est un pouvoir au-dessus des sujets, l'un d'eux ne peut pas, par une décision souveraine, la créer contre lui-même.').

[9] *Ibid.*, p. 79.

state as an international sovereign (i.e., the conception of the state as a sovereign used in the context of international law).

The state as an international law subject

In the context of international law, Triepel preferred the conception of the state as a law subject.[10] If this was at variance with the concept of sovereignty, 'dann würde es die höchste Zeit sein, an eine noch gründlichere Revision dieses berüchtigten Begriffs zu geben, als er sie schon in neuerer Zeit von berufenen Händen erfahren hat'.[11] According to Triepel, bindingness was a condition that lawyers had to presuppose, and which they could not justify in terms of law.[12] By expressly adopting the conception of the state as an international law subject, Triepel was of the view that he had made clear the difference between his theory and the theory of *Selbstverpflictung*. Once made, a rule of international law was unaffected by change in the state's will; it was, in Triepel's words, an 'autonomer Rechtssatz', an autonomous legal rule.[13]

In support of the rival theory of monism, according to which national and international law are integral parts of one legal system, writers questioned the conception of the state as an international law subject. Thus, one argument for the unity of national and international law was that individuals were the real subjects of both.[14] However, there was not much 'reality' to this or other conceptual challenges of monism; for the consequence of national law being in conflict with international law was simply that of state responsibility, which was the same consequence envisaged by the dualist theory.[15]

---

[10] *Ibid.*, pp. 78–9 and also H. Triepel, *Die Zukunft des Völkerrechts* (Leipzig, 1916), pp. 4–5.

[11] Triepel, *Völkerrecht und Landesrecht*, p. 76, note 2 ('il serait grand temps de procéder à une révision de ce concept fameux d'une manière encore plus approfondie que ne l'ont fait à l'époque moderne des esprits célèbres.').

[12] *Ibid.*, pp. 81–2; cf. *ibid.*, pp. 103–10.   [13] *Ibid.*, pp. 60, 71 and 75; cf. *ibid.*, p. 82.

[14] See Alfred Verdross, *Die Einheit des rechtlichen Weltbildes auf Grundlage der Völkerrechtsverfassung* (Tübingen, 1923), p. 47; Hans Kelsen, *Das Problem der Souveränität und die Theorie des Völkerrechts* (2nd edn, Tübingen, 1928), pp. 128 and 130–4; and also, e.g., Joseph L. Kunz, 'La Primauté du droit des gens' (1925) 6 *RDILC* 556 at 586–7; Maurice Bourquin, 'Régles générales du droit international de la paix' (1931) 35 *Recueil des Cours* 5 at 139–41; and B. Mirkine-Guetzévitch, 'Droit international et droit constitutionnel' (1931) 38 *Recueil des Cours* 311 at 321–2. For a different version, see Léon Duguit, *Traité de droit constitutionnel* (3rd edn, Paris, 1927), vol. 1, pp. 184–99; and Georges Scelle, *Précis de droit de gens* (Paris, 1932), vol. 1, p. 31. See also H. Lauterpacht, 'Règles générales du droit de la paix' (1937) 62 *Recueil des Cours* 99 at 126, 130 and 211; cf. *ibid.*, pp. 216–27.

[15] Hans Kelsen, 'Les Rapports de système entre le droit interne et le droit international public' (1926) 14 *Recueil des Cours* 231 at 314–17.

The state as an international co-sovereign

Having severed the link between changes in the state's will and in international law, Triepel still had to explain the origins of international law in the first place, and how it changed. Triepel has not been the only international lawyer with a theoretical bent to make quite a demand on his or her creativity in devising a generally applicable law-making process. Holding that there was no legislator above the states,[16] Triepel saw the making of international law as a matter for states acting jointly.[17] His solution was to have the states collectively as the international sovereign, it being understood that this international sovereign was nothing but an aggregate of the several states.[18] This conception of the state as an international co-sovereign made Triepel adopt the distinction known in German legal theory between a contract (*Vertrag*) and legislation seen as a law-making agreement (*Vereinbarung*).[19] A *Vertrag* was an exchange in relation to which the two states did not have a common will but independent wills, each wanting something different from the other party.[20] It was seen as 'die Vereinigung mehrerer Personen',[21] which gave rise to personal rights and obligations ('subjektive Rechte oder Pflichten'), but not law.[22] The *Vereinbarung* was distinguished from the *Vertrag* by its subject matter: the *Vereinbarung* was an agreement between two or more states laying down common rules of general application.[23] Only here did Triepel see a common will, an international sovereign, and thus international law,[24] or 'objektives Recht'.[25]

Many of Triepel's critics have failed to see the practical difference from the theory of *Selbstverpflictung*.[26] Triepel stressed that a state could not

[16] Triepel, *Völkerrecht und Landesrecht*, p. 96.   [17] *Ibid.*, pp. 32 and also 66–7.
[18] See *ibid.*, pp. 45, 51–2, 67, 70, 79, 92 and 258. Cf. the references to notions of an international community, *ibid.*, pp. 27–8, 76, 102, 268 and 383.
[19] Cf. *ibid.*, pp. 49–50 and 64–7; and see, in particular, Karl Binding, *Die Gründung des norddeutschen Bundes: Ein Beitrag zur Lehre von der Staatenschöpfung* (Leipzig, 1889), pp. 69–70. Cf. Erich Kaufmann, *Das Wesen des Völkerrechts und die clausula rebus sic stantibus* (Tübingen, 1911), pp. 161–70.
[20] Triepel, *Völkerrecht und Landesrecht*, pp. 32–45.
[21] *Ibid.*, p. 44 ('l'accord de plusieurs personnes').
[22] *Ibid.*, pp. 47–8, 61 and 71. If breached, the *Vertrag* terminated: *ibid.*, p. 89.
[23] *Ibid.*, pp. 49–74.   [24] *Ibid.*, p. 63.
[25] See also Triepel's definition of a legal rule, or rather law-making, the essence of which was 'eines dem Einzelwillen überlegenen Willens', that is, a will superior to the individual wills: *ibid.*, pp. 28–9, 31, 45–6, 57, 61–2 and 70.
[26] E.g., Hugo Krabbe, *Die moderne Staats-idee* (The Hague, 1919), p. 293; Wiktor Sukiennicki, *La Souveraineté des états en droit international moderne* (Paris, 1927), p. 221; Bourquin, 'Régles générales', pp. 49–50; Rudolf Laun, *Der Wandel der Ideen Staat und Volk als*

change a *Vereinbarung* single-handedly as if it were the international sovereign;[27] moreover, he linked the *Vereinbarung* to the conception of the state as an international law subject.[28] Nevertheless, Triepel appeared to regard the states collectively as having the power to change as well as make international law, just as one would have expected to be the case with a theory of *Selbstverpflictung*.[29] Indeed, it would seem to have been the notion of the international sovereign not only making, but also changing international law that prompted Triepel to reject the conception of the state as an international sovereign in the first place.

Triepel could have avoided much criticism had he not upheld the notion of international law being changed at sovereign or co-sovereign will. If the changing of international law was governed by international law, a state could have been a subject under old international law and at the same time take part in the making of new international law; for it still depended on international law whether the law so made trumped and thus changed the old law. This would have had no implications for Triepel's overall theory of dualism,[30] while arguably making it more consistent with the conception of the state as an international law subject. What is more, Triepel would not have had to shun the conception of the state as an international sovereign, which after all might have been accurate. In particular, it was for each state to decide on its own whether to participate in a *Vereinbarung*.[31] Expressing consent, or will, remained a sovereign rather than a co-sovereign act. A certain unease might have persisted because of doubt as to the hierarchical relationship between the conception of the state as an international sovereign, or sovereignty, and the conception of the state as an international law subject, or bindingness. Although his conception of the state as an international co-sovereign was criticised for sliding into a predominant conception of the state as an international sovereign, Triepel would seem

---

äussering des Weltgewissens (Barcelona, 1933), pp. 20–1; Paul Guggenheim, *Lehrbuch des Völkerrechts: Unter Berücksichtigung der internationalen und schweizerischen Praxis* (Basel, 1948), vol. 1, p. 20; and J. L. Brierly, 'The Basis of Obligation in International Law' in Hersch Lauterpacht and Humphrey Waldock (eds.), *The Basis of Obligation in International Law and Other Papers by the Late James Leslie Brierly* (Oxford, 1958), p. 1 at pp. 15–16. See also Ulrich M. Gassner, *Heinrich Triepel: Leben und Werk* (Berlin, 1999), pp. 459–70.

[27] Triepel, *Völkerrecht und Landesrecht*, p. 88.

[28] *Ibid.*, pp. 78–9; see also *ibid.*, pp. 47–9 concerning Bergbohm, *Staatsverträge und Gesetze*, p. 81, according to whom the state should be conceived as an international sovereign, as opposed to an international law subject.

[29] Triepel, *Völkerrecht und Landesrecht*, pp. 88–90.   [30] Cf. *ibid.*, pp. 62 and 258.

[31] As for Triepel's version of a theory of the persistent objector, see *ibid.*, pp. 75 and 83–6.

to have no doubt that the conception of the state as an international law subject was the superior or preferred conception.

The dualist distinction between a national and an international context provides the background against which conceptions of the state are seen; thus there are the conception of the state as a 'national' sovereign, the conception of the state as an 'international' sovereign, or co-sovereign, and the conception of the state as an 'international' law subject. Here the terms 'national' and 'international' signify the legal system in relation to which the conceptions are being defined: the national sovereign is the master of national law; the international sovereign is the master of international law.

As in *Völkerrecht und Landesrecht*, international legal theory is usually built on the two conceptions that are defined in relation to international law, i.e., the conception of the state as an 'international' sovereign and the conception of the state as an 'international' law subject. Thus, the making of international law has been associated with the conception of the state as an international sovereign, inducing theorists to consider both the changing of international law and its binding force, whether or not it is changed. The hierarchy between the conceptions of the state as an international sovereign and as an international law subject, or simply between sovereignty and bindingness, has given rise to a burning issue in international legal theory, referred to by Professor Hans Kelsen as '[d]as Problem der Souveränität'.[32] In most contexts of national law, discussions of 'positivism' versus 'natural law' died out early in the twentieth century, or at least were relegated to the realm of 'pure' theory. To a certain degree, however, the dichotomy remained current in the context of international law writings, even for those who were not avowed theorists. Here 'positivism' meant that group of theories founded on state will and emphasising sovereignty; 'natural law' was that group of theories expressly or implicitly rejecting positivism and emphasising sources of law apart from the will of the state.

The inter-war period was particularly rich in dichotomies related to a general, ontological hierarchy between sovereignty and bindingness, examples being monism with state primacy versus monism with international law primacy, or the constitutive theory of recognition of new

---

[32] Kelsen, *Problem der Souveränität*, p. 103; and also, e.g., Sukiennicki, *Souveraineté des états*, p. 55; Brierly, 'Basis of Obligation', p. 43; David Kennedy, 'Theses about International Law Discourse' (1980) 23 *GYIL* 353 at 361; and H. L. A. Hart, *The Concept of Law* (2nd edn, Oxford, 1994), p. 220.

states versus the notion that their creation was governed by international law,[33] and so on. More recently, Professor David Kennedy has
forced the entirety of international legal argument into a corresponding dichotomy between 'hard' and 'soft' arguments;[34] he has been joined
by Professor Martti Koskenniemi, who distinguishes between 'ascending'
and 'descending' arguments.[35] The ambition of other theories, perhaps
less abstract, has been to go 'beyond' sovereignty, thereby securing the
conception of the state as an international law subject as the hierarchically privileged conception. Such ambitions are a traditional virtue
of internationalists, but the virtue is now so venerable it forces us to
enquire why this continuous effort has not got anywhere.[36]

The different ways in which the dichotomy between sovereignty and
bindingness continues to express itself in the works of theorists involve
precisely the kind of insistence that gives international legal theory
a bad name among practising international lawyers. As suggested by
Völkerrecht und Landesrecht, it is rather trivial, to a practitioner at least,
that international law is binding; and to look for the explanation in
international law, and so to assume the system to be self-referential, is
certainly a misconception. Nevertheless, in theory it has been difficult to
progress, mainly because theorists have only been concerned with 'international' conceptions of the state, i.e., as an international sovereign and

---

[33] As to the latter view, see N. Politis, 'Le Problème des limitations de la souveraineté et
la théorie de l'abus des droits dans les rapports internationaux' (1925) 6 *Recueil des
Cours* 5 at 21; Alfred Verdross, 'La Fondement du droit international' (1927) 16 *Recueil
des Cours* 251 at 311–19; Viktor Bruns, 'Völkerrecht als Rechtsordnung I' (1929) 1 *ZaöRV*
1 at 35; Hans Kelsen, 'Théorie générale du droit international public' (1932) 42 *Recueil
des Cours* 121 at 261; Scelle, *Précis de droit de gens*, pp. 77–8; and Lauterpacht, *Function of
Law*, p. 96; and also Hermann Mosler, 'Völkerrecht als Rechtsordnung' (1976) 36 *ZaöRV*
6 at 40–1; Ulrich Fastenrath, *Lücken im Völkerrecht* (Berlin, 1991), p. 248; Louis Henkin,
International Law: Politics and Values (Dordrecht, 1995), p. 10; and Philip Allott, 'The
Concept of International Law' (1999) 10 *EJIL* 23 at 37. Cf. Max Huber's analysis in (1931)
36-I *Annuaire*, pp. 84–5; and James Crawford, *The Creation of States in International Law*
(Oxford, 1979), p. 422.

[34] David Kennedy, *International Legal Structures* (Baden-Baden, 1987), p. 29 and previously
Kennedy, 'Theses', pp. 361–2; for an updated version, set in a predominantly American
context, see David Kennedy, 'When Renewal Repeats: Thinking Against the Box' (2000)
32 *NYUJILP* 335 at 340–97, 401 and 456.

[35] Koskenniemi, *Apology to Utopia*, pp. 40–1.

[36] When theorists go the whole hog and strike the pejorative word 'sovereignty' off the
vocabulary of international law, they add to the importance of the word, or rather to
the meanings of the word; nobody would care about striking off an irrelevant word;
cf. Henkin, *International Law*, p. 8 ('[s]overeignty is a bad word') and also, e.g., Fernando
R. Téson, 'The Kantian Theory of International Law' (1992) 92 *Columbia Law Review* 53 at
54 and 92; Neil MacCormick, 'Beyond the Sovereign State' (1994) 56 *Modern Law Review*
1; and Thomas M. Franck, *Fairness in International Law and Institutions* (Oxford, 1995),
p. 4.

as an international law subject. Koskenniemi has provided numerous examples indicating that to ground international law on the conception of the state as an international sovereign cannot be accepted.[37] The following passage illustrates an argument repeated throughout Koskenniemi's *From Apology to Utopia*:

Just like individuality can exist only in relation to community – and becomes, in that sense, dependent on how it is viewed from a non-individual perspective – a State's sphere of liberty, likewise, seemed capable of being determined only by taking a position beyond liberty. The paradox is that assuming the existence of such a position undermines the original justification of thinking about statehood in terms of an initial, pre-social liberty.

The ambiguity about the modern doctrine of sovereignty follows from this paradox. On the one hand, we seem incapable of conceptualizing the State or whatever liberties it has without reflecting on the character of the social relations which surround it. The sphere of liberty of a member of society must, by definition, be delimited by the spheres of liberty of the other members of that society. But the delimitation of freedoms in this way requires that we do not have to rely on the self-definition of the members of their liberties. In other words, a State's sphere of liberty must be capable of determination from a perspective which is external to it. On the other hand, we cannot derive the State completely from its social relations and its liberty from an external (and overriding) normative perspective without losing the State's individuality as a nation and the justification for its claims to independence and self-determination.[38]

Koskenniemi infers that the 'modern doctrine' of state sovereignty, and international legal argument in general, is indeterminate. However, the better view is that international law does not rest on the 'external' conception of the state as an international sovereign.[39]

Against this background, this chapter tracks the basis of international law back to the conception of the state as a national sovereign, that is, the 'internal' conception of the state as a sovereign defined in relation to national law. True, it is the conception of the state as a *national* sovereign because it relates to national law; it defines the sources and subjects of national law as well as the relationships governed by national law. But then in order to come round to, and conceive of, international law, one has to be a national lawyer – that is, a lawyer concerned with one or

---

[37] Thus, the argument that the international lawyer cannot 'know better' than the international sovereign what international law has been consented to: see Koskenniemi, *Apology to Utopia*, pp. 218–19, 243, 263, 278–9, 286–7, 297, 304, 310–11, 319–20, 326, 338, 340–1, 357, 377–8 and 381.

[38] *Ibid.*, p. 193. See also, e.g., as regards sources theory, *ibid.*, pp. 267–91, treaty interpretation, *ibid.*, pp. 291–302, and custom, *ibid.*, pp. 343–89.

[39] Cf. *ibid.*, pp. 223–35.

other national legal system – or at least to be familiar with national lawyers' ways of reasoning. International law is the response to a need, felt by national lawyers, for law that separates and complements the several national legal systems. It is because of its bearing on the conception of the state as a national sovereign that international law, though 'international', is 'law' (and as such binding) and the reason why it is offered as part of university courses in national law. The *Buchrecht* contains uncountable pointers towards this basis of international law. But, as Koskenniemi's critique serves to illustrate, the consequences have not been fully appreciated.[40]

The national lawyer's need for international law may be given various interpretations, some of which are sociological or otherwise meta-legal, but basically this need is conceptual, and legal, in nature. International law mirrors the conception of the state as a national sovereign, embedded in national law, and covers issues for which national law is found insufficient. Being based on the conception of the state as a national sovereign, national law is unsuited to govern issues conceived by national lawyers, for whatever reason, as being related to more than one state. They could only be resolved by a national legal system of a state insisting that the other states involved are subjected to it. But that would be tantamount to a refusal to recognise these issues as being issues *between* states, or at least between sovereign and independent states. Instead, such issues between states are referred to international law. National lawyers have a sense of internationalism and share a fairly specific notion as to which issues involve the interests of more than one national sovereign.[41] An external perspective on the sovereign legislator or the national legal system is not needed. It is possible from within the system to imagine and reject, or at least be critical of, the notion of another national sovereign being a national law subject. The 'external' view on this national sovereign is generated by, and is dependent on, the 'internal' system mastered by another national sovereign. The cardinal dichotomy, national versus international, does not translate as internal versus external but as one national sovereign versus more national sovereigns, or single versus plural. The underlying rationale

---

[40] See *ibid.*, pp. 52–263 and, as a further example, Oppenheim, *International Law*, pp. 11–12, 17, 45, 54, 58, 102, 148–9, 159–61, 170–7 and 193, holding *ibid.*, p. 54, that '[t]he necessity for a Law of Nations did not arise until a multitude of States absolutely independent of one another had successfully established themselves'; and also L. Oppenheim, *The League of Nations and its Problems* (London, 1919), pp. 77–8. Cf. James Crawford, *International Law as an Open System: Selected Essays* (London, 2002), pp. 101–3.

[41] Cf. Koskenniemi, *Apology to Utopia*, pp. 29, 217, 222–3 and 263.

being one of coexistence between several national sovereigns, the term 'the international law of coexistence' will be employed in this book. Professor Roberto Ago once said that '[t]hese rules were born under the impetus of specific needs of organization and development of stable relations among sovereign political entities, which, although deeply differentiated, were at the same time bound to live together in the same geopolitical milieu, to entertain multiform relations whether their interests coincided or conflicted'.[42]

To quote Professor Richard Falk, '[i]nternational law, in contrast to domestic law, is much like a Victorian lady and must depend upon an excess of self-restraint to achieve virtue'.[43] That the rationale behind international law is to complement national law explains the duality of coordination and separation, which characterises the relationship between national and international law. The two legal systems are coordinated in the sense that international law governs issues for which national law is unsuited. From this point of view, it is as if national and international law were two parts of one big circle of law. It is because the normal point of view is that of a specific national legal system, as opposed to international law, that the term 'dualism' has much wider currency than the term 'pluralism'.[44] However, at the same time, national and international law are separate circles; it only makes sense to refer issues to international law if international law is in turn treated as a legal system independent of national law, thus, to use the terminology favoured by, for example, Triepel, having a source different from national law. The international law of coexistence is 'static', as opposed to 'dynamic', in the sense that its scope is not determined through an international law-making process. In contrast, its scope is

---

[42] Roberto Ago, 'Pluralism and the Origins of the International Community' (1977) 3 *Italian Yearbook of International Law* 3 at 29; and similarly, e.g., Paul Vinogradoff, 'Historical Types of International Law' (1923) 1 *Bibliotheca Visseriana* 1 at 7; Hermann Mosler, *The International Society as a Legal Community* (Alphen aan den Rijn, 1980), pp. 1–6; Prosper Weil, 'Towards Relative Normativity in International Law?' (1983) 77 *AJIL* 413 at 418–20; C. F. Amerasinghe, 'The Historical Development of International Law: Universal Aspects' (2001) 39 *Archiv des Völkerrechts* 367 at 367; David J. Bederman, *International Law in Antiquity* (Cambridge, 2001), pp. 2, 18, 47, 74–6, 88–91, 135–6, 207–8, 274–5 and 278–9; and Randall Lesaffer, 'The Grotian Tradition Revisited: Change and Continuity in the History of International Law' (2002) 73 *BYIL* 103 at 136. See, conversely, Antony Anghie, 'Finding the Peripheries: Sovereignty and Colonialism in Nineteenth Century International Law' (1999) 40 *HILJ* 1 at 25, 34–49 and 67.

[43] Richard A. Falk, *The Role of Domestic Courts in the International Legal Order* (Syracuse, 1964), p. 53.

[44] Cf. Hans Kelsen, *Principles of International Law* (2nd edn by Robert W. Tucker, New York, 1966), p. 553.

determined by the insufficiency of national law and so by reference to the conception of the state as a national sovereign. What is left to be determined, or developed, in one way or another is its content. The questions that the international law of coexistence entertains have been defined by national law, or the insufficiency of national law, while the answers to those questions are to be developed by international law as a legal system in its own right.

Triepel saw contracts between sovereigns as giving rise only to obligations, but not law.[45] However, having regard to the small number of states and the importance of treaty-making, one may wonder whether this was an adequate use of the term 'law'. Most lawyers define and treat treaties as a source of law with the result that there is another branch of international law besides the international law of coexistence. The obligations arising under contracts between sovereigns, whether unilateral, bilateral or multilateral, are allocated to international law and there treated as 'law', making it convenient to refer to the state undertaking obligations as an international, as opposed to a national, sovereign; and to the state subsequently bound as an international law subject. This may be referred to as 'the international law of cooperation'. It is due to the international law of cooperation that an international law-making process exists, which is 'dynamic' in character, the outcome of which can be whatever is preferred by politicians.

The terms 'international law of coexistence' and 'international law of cooperation' have been used before, and in more or less the same meanings as indicated above, notably in Professor Wolfgang Friedmann's *The Changing Structure of International Law*. A main theme of the book was the distinction between 'the traditional international law, essentially concerned with the interstate rules of mutual respect for state sovereignty and abstention from interference in such sovereignty, and the newer, positive international law of co-operation'.[46] Although the

---

[45] Likewise, G. G. Fitzmaurice, 'Some Problems Regarding the Formal Sources of International Law' in *Symbolae Verzijl* (La Haye, 1958), p. 153 at pp. 154 and 157–60; D. P. O'Connell, *International Law* (2nd edn, London, 1970), vol. 1, p. 21; Bin Cheng, 'Some Remarks on the Constituent Element(s) of General (or So-Called Customary) International Law' in Antony Anghie and Garry Sturgess (eds.), *Legal Visions of the 21st Century: Essays in Honour of Judge Christopher Weeramantry* (The Hague, 1998), p. 377 at p. 379; and Ian Brownlie, *Principles of Public International Law* (6th edn, Oxford, 2003), p. 4. See also *Delimitation of the Maritime Boundary in the Gulf of Maine Area*, ICJ Reports [1984] 246 at para. 83; and H. W. A. Thirlway, 'The Law and Procedure of the International Court of Justice, 1960–1989: Part Two' (1990) 61 *BYIL* 1 at 21–2.

[46] Wolfgang Friedmann, *The Changing Structure of International Law* (London, 1964), p. 251. As for Friedmann's definition of the international law of coexistence, see *ibid.*,

international law of coexistence was seen as essential,[47] according to Friedmann international law had fundamentally changed due to a move from coexistence to cooperation.[48] Friedmann presented the international law of coexistence and the international law of cooperation as two branches of international law;[49] yet, and possibly because he was concerned only with a broad outline of international law, he also justified the international law of cooperation in terms of coexistence. Thus, 'it may be predicted that either international society will more and more develop these positive and formative aspects of international law, or that mankind will destroy itself, whether through war, or through ruinous and destructive competition and exploitation of the resources of the earth short of war'.[50]

This book does not assimilate issues belonging to the international law of cooperation and the international law of coexistence in terms of substance, nor adhere to the notion of international legal argument as having a single structure, whether changing or not. True, the basis of the international law of cooperation is the same as that of the international of coexistence, namely the conception of the state as a national sovereign. It is because contracts between sovereigns are not suited to be governed by the national legal system of one national sovereign that they are allocated to international law; the conceptions of the state as an international sovereign and as an international law subject follow from this allocation. But a key difference between the two branches of international law is the reason why issues are, or become, international in the first place. Issues coming within the international law of

pp. 15–16, 37, 61–2, 89 and 297–8. The international law of cooperation was introduced *ibid.*, pp. 37 and 61–3; see also Wolfgang Friedmann, 'Some Impacts of Social Organization on International Law' (1956) 50 *AJIL* 475 at 507; and Wolfgang Friedmann, *Law in a Changing Society* (London, 1959), p. 460.

[47] Friedmann, *Changing Structure*, pp. 214, 298 and 370.

[48] *Ibid.*, pp. 62 and 64. Cf. Georges Abi-Saab, 'Cours générale de droit international public' (1987) 207 *Recueil des Cours* 9 at 324–7; Georges Abi-Saab, 'Whither the International Community?' (1998) 9 *EJIL* 248 at 254–65; Albert Bleckmann, *Allgemeine Staats- und Völkerrechtslehre: Vom Kompetenz- zum Kooperationsvölkerrecht* (Cologne, 1995), pp. 696–9, 963–9 and *passim*; and Sienho Yee, 'Towards an International Law of Co-progressiveness' in Sienho Yee and Wang Tieya (eds.), *International Law in the Post-Cold War World: Essays in Memory of Li Haopei* (London, 2001), p. 18 at pp. 19, 23, 27, 30–1 and 37.

[49] Friedmann, *Changing Structure*, pp. 14–15, 37, 58 and *passim*.

[50] *Ibid.*, pp. 94 and also 364. In this respect, Friedmann was aided by general principles of law, see *ibid.*, pp. 188–9, 192 and 371; cf. as to the importance of treaties, *ibid.*, pp. 37, 68, 122 and 124. See also Friedmann, 'Impacts of Social Organization', p. 475. Cf. George Schwarzenberger, *The Frontiers of International Law* (London, 1962), pp. 29–34.

coexistence are international in kind, their subject matter being international. In contrast, the international law of cooperation is comprised of contracts that are international in form, the parties being states, but not necessarily in kind: they may well regulate issues which national lawyers would not have identified as concerning the interests of more states had a contract not been entered into. It is precisely because only the form of these contracts relates to the conception of the state as a national sovereign that in dealing with their substance, whether scope or content, other, 'international' conceptions of the state are felicitous.

The idea that in law, as elsewhere, the international flows from the national can be illustrated by returning to Jeremy Bentham's *An Introduction to the Principles of Morals and Legislation*, first published in 1789. When defining the limits of criminal jurisdiction, Bentham remarked, as if in passing, that the law of nations, as the *jus gentium* was then termed, was actually a law between nations, or states. It was on this occasion that Bentham coined the word 'international', following a French writer, Henri-François d'Aguesseau, who had already substituted the term 'droit entre les gens' for 'droit des gens'.[51] According to Bentham, transactions between the sovereign of a state and 'a private member' of another state might be regulated by national law, just like 'any transactions which may take place between individuals who are subjects of different states'. 'There remain', Bentham added, 'the mutual transactions between sovereigns, as such, for the subject of that branch of jurisprudence which may be properly and exclusively termed international.'

How to regulate those transactions was, or so Bentham claimed, 'a question that must rest till the nature of the thing called a law shall have been more particularly unfolded'. Likewise, according to his draft essay on war, '[w]hen a state has sustained what it looks upon as an injury, in respect of property, from another state – there being no common superior ready chosen for them – it must either submit to the injury, or get the other state to join in the appointment of a common judge, or go to war'.[52] These being the options, most lawyers have contributed to unfolding an international law that could complement the national legal systems and advise the judge, whether 'common' or not, thereby

---

[51] Jeremy Bentham, *An Introduction to the Principles of Morals and Legislation* (2nd edn, London, 1823), p. 326.

[52] Jeremy Bentham, 'Principles of International Law' in John Bowring (ed.), *The Works of Jeremy Bentham* (Edinburgh, 1843), vol. 2, p. 535 at p. 544 (manuscripts from 1786–9). As for the four essays brought together, somewhat controversially, in John Bowring's collection of the works of Jeremy Bentham, see, e.g., Gunhild Hoogensen, 'Bentham's International Manuscripts Versus the Published "Works"' (2001) 4 *Journal of Bentham Studies* 1.

providing a legal remedy to the insufficiency of national law. Actually, Bentham himself recommended a codification – 'new international laws to be made upon all points which remain unascertained; that is to say, upon the greater number of points in which the interests of two states are capable of collision'.[53]

Two hundred years later the choice between such terms as 'international law' and 'law of nations' is not likely to excite. English-speaking lawyers still employ the term 'international law', and their francophone colleagues use the term 'droit international', while German-speaking lawyers adhere to 'Völkerrecht', their equivalent to 'law of nations'. Yet Triepel's countrymen do not take international law to be confined to the classical issues under the international law of coexistence, for which 'the interests of two states are capable of collision' despite the lack of codification and treaties. International law has been broadening due to contracts between sovereigns being treated as treaties under the international law of cooperation and having whatever scope and content preferred by politicians. Treaties have introduced subjects of international law other than states and generally have brought many issues within the reach of international law, issues not traditionally seen as international (and therefore considered by many national lawyers as more suitable for national law).[54] But they are not at the heart of internationalism.

It is common for institutions operating under human rights instruments, for example, to make observations such as the following, concerning the European Convention on Human Rights: 'Unlike international treaties of the classic kind, the Convention comprises more than mere reciprocal engagements between contracting States. It creates, over and above a network of mutual, bilateral undertakings, objective obligations which, in the words of the Preamble, benefit from a 'collective enforcement'.[55] Because individuals may invoke responsibility and bring claims of their own before the European Court, the term 'supranational' has been taken up.[56] In the context of the European Community, the European Court of Justice once said that 'the Community

---

[53] Bentham, 'Principles of International Law', p. 540. Cf. Jeremy Bentham, *A Comment on the Commentaries and, A Fragment on Government* (London, 1977), pp. 36–7 and 370–2 (manuscript from 1774–6).

[54] Cf. Friedmann, *Changing Structure*, pp. 216, 218, 221, 242–3 and 368.

[55] *Ireland v. United Kingdom*, ECHR Series A No. 25 (1978) at para. 239. Similarly, e.g., from the Inter-American Court of Human Rights, *Restrictions to the Death Penalty*, Advisory Opinion OC-3/83, 70 ILR 449 (1983) at para. 50 and, from the United Nations Human Rights Committee, General Comment No. 24, 107 ILR 65 (1994) at 69–70.

[56] See Appl. 46827/99 and 46951/99, *Mamatkulov and Abdurasulovic v. Turkey* (6 February 2003) at para. 106. Cf. *Matthews v. United Kingdom*, ECHR Reports 1999-I at para. 44.

constitutes a new legal order of international law for the benefit of which the states have limited their sovereign rights, albeit within limited fields, and the subjects of which comprise not only Member States but also their nationals'.[57] The following year, the European Court of Justice added that '[b]y contrast with ordinary international treaties, the EEC Treaty has created its own legal system which, on the entry into force of the Treaty, became an integral part of the legal systems of the Member States and which their courts are bound to apply'.[58] Reflections such as these occasionally lead international courts to adopt the language of constitutionalism in preference to Bentham's internationalism.[59] Perhaps this is also just a matter of form. But even if not, the above-quoted claims to depart from internationalism, or at least from 'classic' and 'ordinary' internationalism, suggest that international law is widely assumed only to govern relations between states and to do so on a basis of strict reciprocity. This is very much a Benthamite conception.

In this light, one ought to appreciate the virtue of the neologism invented by Bentham, namely that it gives expression to a definition by species and genus. International law is law (the genus) between, or *inter*, states (the species). Recalling the devastating troubles of legal theory for centuries in defining the concept of law,[60] it is obvious that this smooth standard definition of international law as being law between states ends a defining task of a different kind. The definition refers back to a definition of national law as law within, or *intra*, the state, which no doubt precedes the definition of international law. Indeed, the concept of law can hardly be distinguished from the concept of national law,[61] whereas at some point it was commonplace to ask whether international

---

[57] Case 26/62, *Van Gend en Loos* v. *Nederlandse administratie der Belastingen* [1963] ECR 1 at 12.

[58] Case 6/64, *Costa* v. *ENEL* [1964] ECR 585 at 593. Cf. Opinion 1/91, *Draft Agreement Relating to the Creation of the European Economic Area* [1991] ECR I-6079 at para. 21; and Case E-1/94, *Ravintoloitsijain Liiton Kustannus Oy Restamark* [1994–5] EFTA Court Report 15 at para. 77.

[59] E.g., *Loizidou* v. *Turkey* (Preliminary Objections), ECHR Series A No. 310 (1995) at para. 75; and Case 294/83, *Les Verts* v. *Parliament* [1986] ECR 1339 at para. 23. Cf. Case E-2/97, *Mag Instrument Inc.* v. *California Trading Company* [1997] EFTA Court Report 127 at para. 25; and Case E-9/97, *Sveinbjörnsdóttir* v. *Iceland*, [1998] EFTA Court Report 95 at para. 59.

[60] According to Professor Philip Allott, '[a] mystery to many people who are not lawyers, the law is a puzzle to itself': Philip Allott, *The Health of Nations: Society and Law Beyond the State* (Cambridge, 2002), p. 37.

[61] E.g., Jeremy Bentham, *A Fragment on Government; or a Comment on the Commentaries* (2nd edn, London, 1823), p. 2; John Westlake, *A Treatise on Private International Law* (7th edn by Norman Bentwich, London, 1925), pp. 3–4; Lauterpacht, *Function of Law*, p. 406; Hans Kelsen, *General Theory of Law and State* (Cambridge, MA, 1945), pp. 181–207; Alf Ross, *On Law and Justice* (London, 1958), p. 59; Joseph Raz, *The Authority of Law: Essays on Law and*

law is really law (and for many, to think that it is not). International law is, at least in the eyes of national lawyers, the continuous 'vanishing point of Jurisprudence',[62] yet it is a 'point of Jurisprudence'. In 1929, Lauterpacht was able to conclude that 'there is, quite apart from judgments of prize courts, hardly a branch of international law which has not received judicial treatment at the hands of municipal tribunals'.[63]

In short, the term 'international law' invites one to see international law against a background coloured by national law. In Triepel's view, the sources, subjects and relationships with which national law was concerned were different from those of international law. This was not a curious coincidence, but an expression, perhaps crude, of the systems and their scope, as distinct from their validity, being coordinated. The conception of the state as a national sovereign is projected on to international legal argument because international law is a creation by the national legal mind. A way of over-stating the point was the defunct custom, mostly restricted to German lawyers, of referring to international law as 'auswärtiges Staatsrecht' or 'äusseres Staatenrecht'.[64] Taking a broader view, Triepel found the virtue of the German tradition in an allegedly more profound understanding of international law. In his view, '[e]s hat dem deutschen Völkerrechte nur zum Vorteile gereicht, daß alle namhaften Völkerrechtslehrer von anderen juristischen Disziplinen

---

Morality (Oxford, 1979), pp. 98–9; H. L. A. Hart 'Definition and Theory in Jurisprudence' in H. L. A. Hart, *Essays in Jurisprudence and Philosophy* (Oxford, 1983), p. 21 at p. 32; Ronald Dworkin, *Law's Empire* (London, 1986), pp. 102–3, 93 and 190; and Roger Cotterrell, *The Sociology of Law: An Introduction* (2nd edn, London, 1992), pp. 38–43. Cf. Gidon Gottlieb, 'The Nature of International Law: Towards a Second Concept of Law' in Cyril E. Black and Richard A. Falk (eds.), *The Future of the International Legal Order* (Princeton, 1972), vol. 4, p. 331; and Ian Brownlie, 'The Reality and Efficacy of International Law' (1981) 52 *BYIL* 1 at 6 and 8.

[62] Thomas Erskine Holland, *The Elements of Jurisprudence* (13th edn, Oxford, 1924), p. 392; and also H. Lauterpacht, 'The Problem of the Revision of the Law of War' (1952) 29 *BYIL* 360 at 382.

[63] H. Lauterpacht, 'Decisions of Municipial Courts as a Source of International Law' (1929) 10 *BYIL* 65 at 67; and see also R. Y. Jennings, 'The Judiciary, International and National, and the Development of International Law' (1996) 45 *ICLQ* 1 at 2–3.

[64] See, respectively, Johann Jakob Moser, *Deutsches auswärtiges Staatsrecht* (Leipzig, 1772) and Georg Friedrich von Martens, *Précis du droit des gens moderne de l'Europe* (2nd edn by Charles Vergé, Paris, 1864), pp. 40–1 and 46. The latter expression was taken to its extreme and seen as a synonym with all international law in G. W. F. Hegel, *Grundlinien der Philosophie des Rechts* (Cambridge, 1991), pp. 281 and 366–71 (originally published 1821). Cf. Johann Caspar Bluntschli, *Das moderne Völkerrecht der civilisirten Staaten als Rechtsbuch dargestellt* (3rd edn, Nördlingen, 1878), p. 59; and August Wilhelm Heffter, *Das europäische Völkerrecht der Gegenwart auf den bisherigen Grundlagen* (8th edn by F. Heinr. Geffcken, Berlin, 1888), p. 1.

hergekommen sind und diese auch noch neben dem Völkerrechte gepflegt haben'.[65] It seems likely that Triepel had in mind the classical issues that for centuries have been taught to students of international law; those are issues where 'the interests of two states are capable of collision' due to their subject matter, or kind, as opposed to their form.

At the beginning of the twenty-first century, this international law of coexistence is still the international law that lawyers first encounter. The international law of coexistence is what is normally offered as part of university courses in national law, what provides the key topics of general textbooks on international law, and what is instinctively thought of by lawyers, if they are asked about international law at a later point in their careers. In short, the international law of coexistence is part of lawyers' law. As observed by Professor Clive Parry, '[i]t . . . remains essentially true that one can have a very fair idea of international law without having read a single treaty; and that one cannot gain any very coherent idea of the essence of international law by reading treaties alone'.[66] In the international law of coexistence, one finds the central principles of how to separate and complement the powers of the several sovereign states; principles which were known to Jeremy Bentham and Heinrich Triepel as well as their predecessors. In the twentieth century, a few topics were added, most of which were recognisable to national legal reasoning. For example, the members of the newly established International Criminal Court will certainly be overburdened with literature, if not prosecutions. Similarly, the trinity of *jus cogens* rules, *erga omnes* obligations (and rights) and international crimes has generated an extraordinary bulk of literature.[67] However, its practical impact has been insignificant. Besides, it is not exactly that this trinity is unprecedented in international legal theory, the history of which is inseparable from the natural law tradition.

---

[65] H. Triepel, 'Ferdinand von Martitz: Ein Bild seines Lebens und seines Wirkens' (1922) 30 *Niemeyers Zeitschrift für Internationales Recht* 155 at 162; cf. Triepel, *Völkerrecht und Landesrecht*, pp. 79 and 112–14 (translation: 'It has only enriched German international law that all renowned teachers in international law have come from other legal disciplines, which they have continued to pursue along with international law.').

[66] Clive Parry, *The Sources and Evidences of International Law* (Manchester, 1965), pp. 34–5.

[67] As for the basic texts, see Article 53 of the Vienna Convention on the Law of Treaties; *Barcelona Traction, Light and Power Company, Limited* (Merits), ICJ Reports [1970] 3 at para. 33; and Article 19 of the International Law Commission's Draft Articles on State Responsibility as adopted on first reading, YILC 1977-II.2, pp. 95–122.

The textbook standard is more or less to neglect the international law of cooperation,[68] which indeed cannot be fully accounted for in terms of the conception of the state as a national sovereign and to a large extent is international only in form. Lawyers who engage in the study of some specific treaty system, often because of the institutions or judicial bodies taking part in it, may soon find themselves devising their own discipline in isolation from 'general' international law. European Community law is a prime example, but there are many other possible examples, such as human rights law, international environmental law and world trade law.[69] It is true that writers of general textbooks are at great pains to stress, like Triepel, that the key characteristic of international legal rules is not their international subject matter but their international genesis, whether in the form of explicit contracts between states, their common usage or some other element. Textbooks on international law normally open with a self-contained theory of sources. But then sources theory does not stand alone. It is, almost without exception, accompanied by an examination of the nature of international law and a discussion of its relationship with national law. What is more, hardly any lawyer is introduced to international law by way of general books on international law. Many are introduced by way of books on national law. *An Introduction to Principles of Morals and Legislation* was meant to serve as an introduction to a penal code; it was only because of such questions as to the limits of criminal jurisdiction that Bentham dealt with inter-national law. Today books on constitutional law, procedural law or jurisprudence, or perhaps books on incorporated treaty regimes more or less treated as national law, like European Union law or human rights law, will already have introduced students to the international law of coexistence by the time they come to international law (if this subject is taken at all).

As regards the classical topics of international law passed on through generations, the judgment of the Chamber of the International Court in the *Delimitation of the Maritime Boundary in the Gulf of Maine Area* case contains a noteworthy passage. Provoked by the inherent vagueness of the concept of equity used in maritime delimitation following the *North Sea Continental Shelf* cases, the Chamber stated:

---

[68] Cf. Friedmann, *Changing Structure*, p. 66.

[69] Cf. Donald M. McRae, 'The Contribution of International Trade Law to the Development of International Law' (1996) 260 *Recueil des Cours* 99 at 147–51; and Donald M. McRae, 'The WTO in International Law: Tradition Continued or New Frontier?' (2000) 3 *Journal of International Economic Law* 27 at 29.

A body of detailed rules is not to be looked for in customary international law which in fact comprises a limited set of norms for ensuring the co-existence and vital co-operation of the members of the international community, together with a set of customary rules whose presence in the opinio juris of States can be tested by induction based on the analysis of a sufficiently extensive and convincing practice, and not by deduction from preconceived ideas.[70]

The following year, possibly in response to this passage, the full Court held that '[i]t is of course axiomatic that the material of customary international law is to be looked for primarily in the actual practice and opinio juris of States, even though multilateral conventions may have an important role to play in recording and defining rules deriving from custom, or indeed in developing them'.[71] The conception of *opinio juris* cherished by so many of Triepel's successors would seem nicely to fit his conception of the co-sovereign act in the form of a *Vereinbarung*: 'Nur ein zu einer Willenseinheit durch Willenseinigung zusammengeflossener Gemeinwille mehrerer oder vieler Staaten kann die Quelle von Völkerrecht sein.'[72]

The classical core of international law, referred to in 1984 by the Chamber as 'norms for ensuring the co-existence and vital co-operation of the members of the international community' and here just termed the international law of coexistence, has been justified in various ways (just as the notion of an 'international community' has had several meanings). What since the beginning of the twentieth century has been justified by reference to consent and *opinio juris* had been associated previously, before law evolved into a discipline independent of, in particular, theology and philosophy, with natural law ideas of virtue, justice, reason,

---

[70] *Delimitation of the Maritime Boundary in the Gulf of Maine Area*, ICJ Reports [1984] 246 at para. 111 and also para. 81.

[71] *Continental Shelf (Libya v. Malta)*, ICJ Reports [1985] 13 at para. 27, subsequently quoted in *Military and Paramilitary Activities in and against Nicaragua* (Merits), ICJ Reports [1986] 14 at para. 183 and *Legality of the Threat or Use of Nuclear Weapons*, ICJ Reports [1996] 226 at para. 64.

[72] Triepel, *Völkerrecht und Landesrecht*, pp. 32 and 50, and also, as regards customary international law as *Vereinbarung*, *ibid.*, pp. 84 and 94–103 ('Seule peut être source du droit international une volonté commune (*Gemeinwille*) de plusieurs ou de nombreux Etats, constituant une unité de volonté (*Willenseinheit*) au moyen d'une union des volontés (*Willenseinigung*).'). See also Bin Cheng, 'Opinio Juris: A Key Concept in International Law that is Much Misunderstood' in Sienho Yee and Wang Tieya (eds.), *International Law in the Post-Cold War World: Essays in Memory of Li Haopei* (London, 2001), p. 56 at pp. 66–7, according to whom '[i]t is the concordance of the generality of *opiniones individuales juris generalis* of the subjects of international law which forms the *opinio generalis juris generalis*'.

conscience juridique, etc.[73] But whatever its justification, or camouflage, and whatever its name, the scope of the international law of coexistence has remained basically the same; it has shown a high degree of stability over the centuries.

The rationale behind the international law of coexistence, the actual source from which it flows, will not be found unless one visits the universe of national legal reasoning. It makes sense to distinguish between a national and an international context, and it is impossible to conceive of the one without the other, yet the former remains the *raison d'être* of the latter, just as the conception of the state as a national sovereign forms the essence of sovereignty. While the scope of international law can be expressed in terms of national lawyers' need for a complementary and residual legal system, any attempt at determining the scope of national law by reference to some need shared by international lawyers would be unsuccessful. A legal system termed 'inter-national' and concerned with 'points in which the interests of two states are capable of collision' is a residual system, one that conceptually presupposes national law, not a system from which national law can be derived or otherwise determined. Those opposed are concerned not with the law, nor its conceptual deep structure, but with meta-legal justifications of law already given.

Before developing a model of international legal argument along these lines, the following section provides three introductory examples involving the conception of the state as a national sovereign. As for all three examples, the absent articulation of this conception has made possible a series of inadequacies over which international legal theory has drawn a Latin veil. Thus, lawyers refer to '*non liquet*', '*opinio juris*' and '*pacta sunt servanda*', and hope that the lack of clarity of these notions will be concealed by their familiar foreign expression.

The national sovereign in international legal argument

Non liquet *and Article 38 of the Statute*

A famous provision of the Statute of the Permanent Court, which in 1945 was incorporated into the Statute of the International Court, gave

---

[73] See François Geny, *Méthode d'interprétation et sources en droit privé positif* (2nd edn, Paris, 1919), p. 360, note 4; Maurice Bourquin, 'Régles générales du droit international de la paix' (1931) 35 *Recueil des Cours* 5 at 62; and Paul Guggenheim, 'L'origine de la notion de l'"opinio juris sive necessitatis" comme deuxième élément de la coutume dans l'histoire du droit des gens' in *Hommage d'une génération de juristes au Président Basdevant* (Paris, 1960), p. 258. As for the *conscience juridique*, cf. Triepel, *Völkerrecht und Landesrecht*, pp. 30–1.

guidance as to how the Permanent Court should decide the disputes to which it had been referred. Despite its archaic form, Article 38(1), which was devised by the Advisory Committee, has remained the principal text used by international lawyers in describing the sources, or origins, of international law. While some of the members of the Advisory Committee stressed that the Permanent Court should develop international law, none were willing without express consent of the parties to vest it with the powers of a sovereign legislator.

Two of the sources, treaty and custom, were not in dispute, but the proposal of Descamps to include 'the rules of international law as recognised by the legal conscience of civilised nations [la conscience juridique des peuples civilisés]' met strong opposition from, especially, Root and Phillimore.[74] In the end, a compromise was worked out and Article 38 now provides for 'the general principles of law recognized by civilized nations'.[75] Before reaching this compromise, the question of a non liquet had been aired by Francis Hagerup.[76] The original supporters of the President's proposal developed the argument that, without a third source, the Permanent Court would in some cases have no option but to declare that international law was not clear (non liquet), thereby ending the proceedings without giving an answer to the specific issues raised.[77] Perhaps this argument convinced some members of the Advisory Committee; but Phillimore founded his approval of the third source on principles of common law,[78] while Root accepted the compromise only because the formula reproduced pronouncements of the United States Supreme Court.[79]

Two members of the Advisory Committee, Arturo Ricci-Busatti and Albert de Lapradelle, stressed that adding yet another source did not necessarily exclude the possibility of a non liquet.[80] This was true, of course.[81] In theory, the exclusion of a non liquet, which Hersch

---

[74] See Advisory Committee of Jurists, Procès-Verbaux of the Proceedings of the Committee (16 June–24 July 1920, with Annexes) (The Hague, 1920), pp. 306 and 293 (Descamps), 286–7, 293–4 and 308–10 (Root) and 295 (Phillimore).

[75] Ibid., pp. 344 and 331.   [76] Ibid., pp. 296 and 307.

[77] Ibid., pp. 294 (Loder) and 295–6 (Lapradelle).   [78] Ibid., pp. 316 and 335.

[79] See James Brown Scott, The Project of a Permanent Court of International Justice and Resolutions of the Advisory Committee of Jurists (Washington DC, 1920), pp. 107–11, referring to, inter alia, Thirty Hogheads of Sugar v. Boyle, 13 US (9 Cranch) 191 (1815) at 198 and The Paquete Habana, 175 US 677 (1900) at 700; see also Hilton v. Guyot, 159 US 113 (1895) at 228.

[80] Advisory Committee, Procès-verbaux, pp. 336 and 338.

[81] Cf. Articles 18 and 28 of the 1928 General Act for the Pacific Settlement of International Disputes; and also Article 12 of the Draft on Arbitral Procedure, YILC

Lauterpacht regarded as a general principle in itself,[82] would seem to have the potential to turn sources theory into a mere cipher. In order to avoid a *non liquet*, lawyers may take the view that they need international law, regardless of the possible emptiness of the 'sources' of international law. Ricci-Busatti pointed to a possible solution to this problem. In his view, '[t]hat which is not forbidden is allowed'.[83] So if in a specific case the Permanent Court concluded that no international law was applicable, it would have to infer that the state in question had been allowed to do what it did. In cases where there was no international law, Ricci-Busatti was willing to substitute the conception of the state as a national sovereign for the conception of the state as an international law subject. Indeed, given there was no international law applicable, it made no sense to refer to a conception of the state defined by reference to international law.

This solution to the problem of a *non liquet* was so simple that it ought to have prevented a prolonged discussion. But the spectre of a *non liquet* has haunted lawyers envisaging issues which, in their view, unquestionably come within international law;[84] the principle '[t]hat which is not forbidden is allowed' is conditional upon there being no international law applicable, but as regards these issues, being international in kind, legal analysis points in the opposite direction. Whatever the so-called sources of international law, there has been an unmistakable

---

1952-II, pp. 63–4 and YILC 1952-I, pp. 217–18; and Article 42(2) of the ICSID Convention. See, however, H. Lauterpacht, 'The British Reservations to the Optional Clause' (1930) 10 *Economica* 137 at 167.

[82] Lauterpacht, *Function of Law*, p. 67. No doubt, the concept of a *non liquet* comes from national law; cf. A. G. Koroma, 'International Justice in Relation to the International Court of Justice' in Kalliopi Koufa (ed.), *International Justice* (Thessaloniki, 1997), p. 421 at p. 455, according to whom 'a declaration of *non liquet* . . . could be tantamount to a denial of justice'; and also Mohammed Bedjaoui, 'Expediency in the Decisions of the International Court of Justice' (2000) 71 *BYIL* 1 at 11.

[83] Advisory Committee, *Procès-verbaux*, pp. 314–15. Phillimore and Hagerup appeared to accept this view, while it was questioned by De Lapradelle, *ibid.*, pp. 316, 317 and 320, respectively. Cf. Triepel, *Völkerrecht und Landesrecht*, p. 382.

[84] See H. Lauterpacht, 'Some Observations on the Prohibition of "Non Liquet" and the Completeness of the Law' in *Symbolae Verzijl* (1958), p. 196 at p. 211; Julius Stone, '*Non Liquet* and the Function of Law in the International Community' (1959) 35 *BYIL* 124 at 132 and 159; G. G. Fitzmaurice, 'The Problem of Non-Liquet: Prolegomena to a Restatement' in *Mélanges offerts à Charles Rousseau: La communauté internationale* (Paris, 1974), p. 89 at pp. 105–10; and Daniel Bodansky, '*Non Liquet* and the Incompleteness of International Law' in Laurence Boisson de Chazournes and Philippe Sands (eds.), *International Law, the International Court of Justice and Nuclear Weapons* (Cambridge, 1999), p. 153 at pp. 163–5; cf., however, *ibid.*, pp. 156–7. See also *New Jersey v. Delaware*, 291 US 361 (1933) at 383–4.

need for international law, as national law is by definition inadequate or unsuited. Ricci-Busatti, on his part, did not find that the principle '[t]hat which is not forbidden is allowed' was pertinent to all cases as to which no 'positive rule of international law' applied. On the contrary, 'there are other principles of the same character (that which forbids the abuse of right or that of *res judicata*, etc.), and certain general rules of equity and justice which come into play in each case'.[85]

This is further illustrated by the position adopted by Descamps. In respect of the phrase 'any question of international law' as used in Article 13(2) of the Covenant of the League of Nations, defining which disputes were 'generally suitable for submission to arbitration', Descamps said that it had been 'suggested by the fact that there are two kinds of international law: the law founded on special conventions, and general international law'.[86] His view appeared to be that 'general international law' was more than positive rules, whether based on treaty or custom. When Descamps defended his original draft provision on the sources of international law against Root's criticism, he said that:

it is absolutely impossible and supremely odious to say to the judge that, although in a given case a perfectly just solution is possible: 'You must take a course amounting to a refusal of justice' merely because no definite convention or custom appeared. What, therefore, is the difference between my distinguished opponent and myself? He leaves the judge in a state of compulsory blindness forced to rely on subjective opinions only; I allow him to consider the cases that come before him with both eyes open.[87]

In other words, cases were foreseen that came within Article 13(2) of the Covenant but for which there were no 'positive rules', that is, 'no definite convention or custom' with which to solve them. In Descamps' words, 'if the competence of the Court were confined within the limits of positive recognised rules, too often it would have to non-suit the parties'.[88] Even Root would seem to have come round. At a later point, he said about re-election of judges and the continuity of the Permanent Court's case law: 'This continuity was still more important in international law than in the case of a national jurisdiction, since, in the latter case, positive law could always be applied, whereas an international judge must often be guided by his own conceptions of law.'[89]

[85] Advisory Committee, *Procès-verbaux*, p. 315.   [86] *Ibid.*, p. 264.
[87] *Ibid.*, pp. 323 and also 318. Descamps also relied on the Martens clause: see *ibid.*, pp. 323–4 and 310 and also 511. See also his reference to equity, *ibid.*, p. 48.
[88] *Ibid.*, p. 320.   [89] *Ibid.*, p. 471.

The discussion in the Advisory Committee revealed a need for international law that went beyond the positive rules then identified with treaty and custom. By implication, the scope of international law could not be said to have been defined by positive rules, or at least not solely by such rules. The members of the Advisory Committee did not need sources to know the scope of international law. It was because they knew there was more to international law than what was covered by 'positive rules' that they looked for additional sources, not the other way around. Theirs was not so much a discussion about treaties as about how to respond to a need for international law when treaties are lacking. Custom was found insufficient, hence the third source, termed 'the general principles of law recognised by civilised nations', was called for. This phrase had been coined, or at least used, by the United States Supreme Court, and the principles in question were supposedly to be found by national lawyers by some process of collective introspection. This points to the rationale behind international law as precisely being to complement national law where seen by national lawyers as insufficient. In such cases, it may be supposed that national lawyers belonging to different national legal systems can be brought to seek the same international basis for their decision-making, even though no legal rules have yet crystallised. In 1920, national lawyers were in need of more answers from international law than there were positive rules to provide. And so the Permanent Court had to make law; it had to fill the scope of the international law of coexistence.

In fact, no such specific dispute as the Advisory Committee had in view would seem to have been met with a *non liquet*. Instead, the phrase has been broadened to include the much less significant phenomenon of inconclusive statements on general questions of international law.[90] But specific cases involving the interests of a plurality of national sovereigns have been given a solution in international law, often specific to the facts of the actual case, which in turn may be seen and justified as a result of general principles or 'customary' law. It is simply a corollary of the basis of this international law of coexistence to say that where there is no

---

[90] For such statements, see *Jurisdiction of the European Commission of the Danube between Galatz and Braila*, Series B No. 14 (1927) at 68; *Interpretation of the Statute of the Memel Territory* (Merits), Series A/B No. 49 (1932) at 321; *Reparation for Injuries Suffered in the Service of the United Nations*, ICJ Reports [1949] 174 at 185–6; and *Legality of the Threat or Use of Nuclear Weapons*, ICJ Reports [1996] 226 at para. 2 (E) of the advice. The phrase has been used in yet other contexts, e.g., in relation to the *Haya de la Torre Case*, ICJ Reports [1951] 71 at 81: see J. H. W. Verzijl, *The Jurisprudence of the World Court* (Leiden, 1965), vol. 1, p. 15.

international law – that is, where there is no need for international law –
national law applies and thus that which is not forbidden is allowed.

Custom and opinio juris

While normally regarded as the two main sources of international law,
treaty and custom are characterised by sets of questions so different
that one may well wonder why they are mentioned so often in the same
breath. In practice, as for treaties, the acts of states, as international
sovereigns, whereby obligations are undertaken, and in respect of which
the states are to be conceived as international law subjects, are normally
well established. What needs elaboration is the scope and content. When
it comes to custom, it would seem to be the other way round. As to
questions of theory, whereas in respect of treaties it is asked why they
are binding, in respect of custom it is asked how they got their scope
and, in particular, their content. To put it crudely, the conception of
the state as an international law subject creates problems in relation to
treaties, while the conception of the state as an international sovereign
is taken for granted. In relation to custom, the latter conception is the
problem, since what is looked for is not an equivalent to the principle
pacta sunt servanda, but a law-making process.

  Custom is normally seen as a concept consisting of two elements:
the presence of a consistent and general practice among states (*usus*),
and a consideration on the part of those states that their practice is in
accordance with international law (*opinio juris*). Since the beginning of
the twentieth century the second element, *opinio juris*, has been what
pointed to a law-making process. Just as treaty-making, it was centred
on consent and thus reflected the conception of the state as an international sovereign. But when combined with the other element of the
bipartite concept, that is, practice, a paradox seems to arise:

> Cette théorie selon laquelle les actes constituant la coutume doivent être
> exécutés dans l'intention d'accomplir une obligation juridique ou d'exercer un
> droit (dans le sens technique du mot), c.-à-d. d'exécuter une règle de droit déjà
> en vigueur . . . a pour conséquence que le droit coutumier ne peut prendre
> naissance que par une erreur des sujets constituant la coutume.[91]

In an attempt to circumvent this paradox, one writer has thrown it into
relief by referring to '*l'opinio juris* comme le sentiment d'être lié par

---

[91] Hans Kelsen, 'Théorie du droit international coutumier' (1939) 1 *Revue internationale de
la théorie du droit* 253 at 263.

une norme à laquelle on consent'.[92] The subject is simultaneously the sovereign law-maker, an assertion that, as Triepel pointed out, may not be so far from the theory of *Selbstverpflictung*.

Various suggestions have been put forward on how to separate, in time, the state as an international sovereign from the state as an international law subject.[93] Some writers, including Triepel, have arguably achieved this by adopting a fully-fledged analogy between custom and treaty, thus defining the former as the implicit variant of the latter.[94] This step solves the problem, at least as regards the conception of the state as an international sovereign. Most lawyers, however, have been reluctant to press the treaty analogy so far, even though they have applied a similar distinction between two phases, one in which the custom was made and another, the present, in which it is applied. *Opinio juris* has been construed as the interpretation or evaluation by states in the latter phase of what happened in the former phase, namely that a binding custom was made.[95]

In the *North Sea Continental Shelf* cases, the International Court held that '[n]ot only must the acts concerned amount to a settled practice, but they must also be such, or be carried out in such a way, as to be evidence of a belief that this practice is rendered obligatory by the existence of a rule of law requiring it'.[96] The International Court also noted that '[t]here are many international acts, e.g. in the field of ceremonial and protocol, which are performed almost invariably, but which are motivated only by considerations of courtesy, convenience or tradition, and not by any sense of legal duty'.[97] The suggestion seemed to be that the bipartite

---

[92] Birgitte Stern, 'La Coutume au coeur du droit international' in *Mélanges offerts à Paul Reuter* (1981), p. 479 at p. 488; cf. Maarten Bos, *A Methodology of International Law* (Amsterdam, 1984), p. 65.

[93] Cf. Roberto Ago, 'Droit positif et droit international' (1957) 3 *Ann. français* 14 at 57–9.

[94] See Triepel, *Völkerrecht und Landesrecht*, pp. 95–6; and also Oppenheim, *International Law*, p. 22; André Weiss, *Manuel de droit international privé* (9th edn, Paris, 1925), p. xxix; Anzilotti, *Cours*, pp. 67–8 and 73–7; Arrigo Cavaglieri, *Corso di diritto internazionale* (3rd edn, Napoli, 1934), p. 56; Karl Strupp, 'Les Règles générales du droit de la paix' (1934) 47 *Recueil des Cours* 263 at 301–4; and S. Séfériadès, 'Aperçus sur la coutume juridique internationale et notamment sur son fondement' (1936) 43 *RGDIP* 129 at 131–5, 145 and 176.

[95] E.g., Max Sørensen, *Les Sources du droit international: Etude sur la jurisprudence de la Cour permanente de Justice internationale* (Copenhagen, 1946), p. 106; Charles de Visscher, 'Coutume et traité en droit international public' (1955) 59 *RGDIP* 353 at 356; Eric Suy, *Les Actes juridiques unilatéraux en droit international public* (Paris, 1962), p. 228; Alfred Verdross, 'Entstehungsweisen und Geltungsgrund des universellen völkerrechtlichen Gewohnheitsrechts' (1969) 29 *ZaöRV* 635 at 640; and G. J. H. van Hoof, *Rethinking the Sources of International Law* (Deventer, 1983), p. 95.

[96] *North Sea Continental Shelf*, ICJ Reports [1969] 3 at para. 77.   [97] *Ibid.*

conception of custom does not describe how custom is made. It is a definition by species and genus, the purpose of which is to distinguish existing customs, however made, from existing 'courtesy, convenience or tradition'. This leaves very little for international lawyers to say in this context about a law-making process and the state as an international sovereign. International lawyers know custom when they see it, as it were, but they do not know where it comes from.

Significantly, as pointed to by Professor Max Sørensen as regards the decisions of the Permanent Court, *opinio juris* has been referred to principally where rejecting an alleged custom:

Chose remarquable, d'ailleurs, ni la Cour, ni les juges dissidents ne se sont jamais intéressés à l'élément psychologique pour affirmer l'existence d'une coutume. La pratique générale et constante leur a suffi pour conclure qu'une règle coutumière avait été créée et pouvait servir de base de leurs décisions. On a recouru à l'élément psychologique seulement dans le sens négatif que son absence a empêché l'affirmation d'une règle coutumière.[98]

In Sørensen's view, 'la faculté de libre appréciation à l'égard des éléments qui constituent traditionnellement la coutume internationale' was 'la clef de voûte du problème de la coutume en droit international'.[99] Kelsen originally presented *opinio juris* as a cover-up for extra-legal considerations such as justice or equity.[100] But he later adopted a more moderate view.[101] Kelsen's original conclusion seemed misplaced if one takes into account the fact that a key argument of his in favour of monism was that, with respect to its scope . . .

[t]he analysis of international law has shown that most of its norms are incomplete norms which receive their completion from the norms of national law. Thus, the international legal order is significant only as part of a universal legal order which comprises also all the national legal orders. The analysis has further led to the conclusion that the international legal order determines the territorial, personal, and temporal coexistence of a multitude of States. We have finally seen that the international legal order restricts the material sphere of validity of their own matters that could otherwise have been arbitrarily regulated by the State.[102]

---

[98] Sørensen, *Sources du droit international*, p. 110.   [99] *Ibid.*, p. 111.

[100] Kelsen, 'Droit international coutumier', pp. 265–6.

[101] Although he maintained the position that it was a fiction to assume that customary law was only binding upon a state that had given its consent, see Hans Kelsen, *Principles of International Law* (New York, 1952), pp. 313 and 316. In the second edition of this work, the editor, Professor Robert W. Tucker, advocated a somewhat different view similar to that to be articulated in the *North Sea Continental Shelf* cases: see Kelsen, *Principles of International Law*, pp. 450–1 and vii.

[102] Kelsen, *General Theory*, p. 363.

It is an important insight, which Triepel shared,[103] that basic principles of international law normally categorised as custom, including those concerning jurisdiction, presuppose and thus accommodate the conception of the state as a national sovereign. Lawyers certainly have more to say about this branch of international law. What needs to be taken into account, however, is not the conception of the state as an international sovereign, but the conception of the state as a national sovereign.[104] The international law normally categorised as custom, or general principles, is the product of national lawyers being in need of law different from national law to settle, to quote Bentham once again, cases in which, despite the lack of codification or treaties, 'the interests of two states are capable of collision'. Accordingly, the law-making process in respect of the international law of coexistence is confined to its content; the scope has been determined in advance. If one puts *opinio juris* in this light, limiting its bearing to the content, as opposed to the scope, of the international law of coexistence, Kelsen's apparent paradox vanishes (although, of course, the question remains whether *opinio juris* is an adequate way in which to describe how the content is to be determined).

There are many ways in which to express the general condition of the international law of coexistence that its scope has been determined in advance. Ian Brownlie employs the distinction between formal sources (the law-making process, the scope of international law) and material sources (evidences as to the outcome of the law-making process, the content of international law). According to Brownlie, who does not see a treaty as a source of law, but like Triepel as a source of obligation, '[i]n

---

[103] Triepel, *Völkerrecht und Landesrecht*, pp. 270–1; cf. *ibid.*, pp. 255, 387 and 439.

[104] See also Lazare Kopelmanas, 'Custom as a Means of the Creation of International Law' (1937) 18 *BYIL* 127 at 130 and 132–5; Paul Guggenheim, 'Les Deux éléments de la coutume en droit international' in *La technique et les principes du droit public: Etudes en l'honneur de Georges Scelle* (Paris, 1950), vol. 1, p. 275 at pp. 280–1; Philip Allott, 'Language, Method and the Nature of International Law' (1971) 45 *BYIL* 79 at 103–4; Anthony A. D'Amato, *The Concept of Custom in International Law* (Ithaca, 1971), pp. 29–31 and 79–80; Peter Haggenmacher, 'La Doctrine des deux éléments du droit coutumier dans la pratique de la Cour internationale' (1986) 90 *RGDIP* 5 at 11–12; Christian Tomuschat, 'Obligations Arising for States without or against Their Will' (1993) 241 *Recueil des Cours* 195 at 237 and 291–300; V. D. Degan, *Sources of International Law* (The Hague, 1997), pp. 88, 172, 179–80 and 217; Michael Byers, *Custom, Power and the Power of Rules* (Cambridge, 1999), p. 148; and Anthea Elizabeth Roberts, 'Traditional and Modern Approaches to Customary International Law: A Reconciliation' (2001) 95 *AJIL* 757 at 764. In respect of a narrowly defined category of axiomatic principles, see Sørensen, *Sources du droit international*, p. 117 and Charles de Visscher, *Théories et réalites en droit international public* (4th edn, Paris, 1970), p. 412 and also Anzilotti, *Cours*, p. 68.

a sense "formal sources" do not exist in international law. As a substitute, and perhaps an equivalent, there is the principle that the general consent of states creates rules of general application.'[105] That is to say, international law is already here, so there is no need for a law-making process. Indeed, at a later point Brownlie adds that 'the whole of the law could be expressed in terms of the coexistence of sovereignties'.[106] The scope of the international law of coexistence having been determined already, the questions to answer being known, the international lawyer's task is to produce the answers and so provide the content of international law for which one may imagine a variety of (material) sources.

One should not read Article 38(1) in isolation from the provisions in the Statute defining its addressee, that is, the international judge. These provisions, which also go back to the draft-scheme adopted by the Advisory Committee, would not seem to be aiming narrowly at the international lawyer. In its report, the Advisory Committee stated that it had had in mind lawyers who possessed 'the openmindedness necessary in international law suits' and were 'capable of rising above the level of national justice to international affairs'.[107] As mentioned in Chapter 1, the members of the Advisory Committee disagreed as to whether every good national judge would make a good international judge. One could imagine a similar debate in respect of any kind of specialised tribunal within a national legal system. According to Article 2, '[t]he Court shall be composed of independent judges, elected regardless of their nationality from among persons of high moral character, who possess the qualifications required in their respective countries for appointment to the highest judicial offices, or are jurisconsults of recognized competence in international law'. So the judges would be either eminent national lawyers, suitable for election to the highest judicial offices in national legal systems, or international lawyers 'of recognized competence'.

In selecting the candidates for election, the so-called national group which makes the nomination under Article 4 of the Statute is 'recommended to consult its highest court of justice, its legal faculties and schools of law, and its national academies and national sections of international academies devoted to the study of law'. Once again prominent national lawyers, whether members of courts, faculties or academies, are given a role, this time as advisors in selecting the candidates for election. As regards the electors, Article 9 provides:

---

[105] See Brownlie, *Principles*, p. 3.   [106] *Ibid.*, p. 287.
[107] Advisory Committee, *Procès-verbaux*, pp. 698 and 707.

At every election, the electors shall bear in mind not only that the persons to be elected should individually possess the qualifications required, but also that in the body as a whole the representation of the main forms of civilization and of the principal legal systems of the world should be assured.

In the Advisory Committee, the phrase 'the representation of the main forms of civilization and of the principal legal systems of the world' had been devised to guarantee each of the Great Powers a judge.[108] Yet it is noteworthy that one way to express this idea was by referring to 'the principal national legal systems'. In its report, the Advisory Committee stated that there had been no intention of referring to 'the various systems of International Law'. While national lawyers may have agreed, broadly speaking, on the scope of international law, their conception of the content of international law would almost unavoidably have been coloured by national tendencies and traditions suggesting parochial views of international law. Thus, Root later said about the work in the Advisory Committee: 'We passed hours and hours and days in that committee in discussing subjects where the only difference was not in our discussion or in what we were saying, but in a different set of ideas in the backs of our heads.'[109] In a passage that emphasised the formidable task facing the judges to be elected, the report of the Advisory Committee stated:

Doubtless, on certain matters, for instance in Naval Prize Law, two systems of European jurisprudence exist, or at any rate did exist before the War; perhaps, on some points, differences still exist between the respective methods used by Europeans, Americans or Asiatics, in dealing with questions of International Law; but no matter what the main national tendencies in International Law may be, the meaning of the expression adopted by the Committee is not and cannot be to maintain existing distinctions between various conceptions of International Law, for such an intention would be opposed to the guiding principle upon which the establishment of a single Court of Justice for all nations is based: that is to say, the principle of the unity and universality of International Law.[110]

---

[108] See Descamps' proposal to this effect, *ibid.*, pp. 28, 49, 111, 132–3, 356 and 362. Cf. Advisory Committee of Jurists, *Documents Presented to the Committee Relating to Existing Plans for the Establishment of a Permanent Court of International Justice* (The Hague, 1920), p. 37; and Scott, *Project of a Permanent Court*, pp. 20 and 63.

[109] Elihu Root, *Men and Policies: Addresses* (Cambridge, 1925), p. 400.

[110] Advisory Committee, *Procès-verbaux*, pp. 709–10 and also *ibid.*, pp. 200 (Lapradelle), 308 (Root), 369–70 (Altamira) and 384 (Adatci). Cf. A. de Lapradelle, *Influence de la Société des Nations sur le développement du droit des gens* (Paris, 1932–3), 9e leçon, p. 13; and Scott, *Project of a Permanent Court*, pp. 63–4. See also Pierre-Marie Dupuy, 'The Danger of Fragmentation or Unification of the International Legal System and the International Court of Justice' (1999) 31 *NYUJILP* 791 at 791–2.

By referring to 'the principal legal systems of the world' in Article 9, what the Advisory Committee had in mind was the 'distinct systems of legal education' and so to 'ensure that, no matter what points of national law may be involved in an international suit, all shall be equally comprehended'.[111] It was added that it was not enough to recommend representation of 'the great legal systems of the world'. It was 'an essential condition' that also the main forms of civilisation were represented 'if the Permanent Court of International Justice is to be a real World Court for the Society of all Nations'.[112] That being said, there would seem to have been no shared understanding in the Advisory Committee as to the exact meaning of 'the main forms of civilization and the principal legal systems of the world'.

To sum up, there had been no clear distinction, at least not at the time when originally the Statute was framed, between international and national lawyers. It was not a view prevailing in the Advisory Committee that in 1920 international judges were available for a new Permanent Court. International judges were rather an ideal, which it was hoped could be achieved by moulding national judges and other national lawyers. Thus, individual members of the Advisory Committee referred to national judges who 'internationalise[d] themselves – as M. Adatci liked to express it, to "deify" themselves' – or who were 'not denationalised but super-nationalised'.[113] At the same time, the need for making international law international was envisaged.

Conclusions on non liquet and opinio juris

There are two main conclusions to be drawn from the first two examples as to the use of conceptions of the state. First, an essential element of such conceptions is the context in relation to which they are defined. Secondly, the basis of international law rests on the conception of the state as a sovereign defined in relation to national law, as opposed to international law, that is, the state as a national sovereign. International

---

[111] See also Scott, *Project of a Permanent Court*, pp. 53, 62–3, 65 and 89. On the other hand, Adatci and Fernandes later said that there had been no intention to secure a strict distribution of judges according to geography: see *Records of Assembly: Committees* 1920, p. 304. Cf. ICSID, *History of the ICSID Convention: Documents Concerning the Origin and the Formulation of the Convention* (Washington DC, 1968), vol. 2, pp. 728, 768 and 809.

[112] Advisory Committee, *Procès-verbaux*, p. 710; cf. Sandra L. Bunn-Livingstone, *Juricultural Pluralism vis-à-vis Treaty Law: State Practice and Attitudes* (The Hague, 2002), p. 46.

[113] See Advisory Committee, *Procès-verbaux*, pp. 187 (Adatci) and 534 (Lapradelle), respectively.

law is in existence long before the conception of the state as an international sovereign is put to work and before possible concerns about *Selbstverpflictung* – or about the conception of the state as an international law subject and bindingness – present themselves.

The problem of a *non liquet* reflects a demand for international law that does not flow from the so-called sources of international law. This demand, or need, originates from national lawyers and gives rise to international law. Without it there would be no international law. If the conception of the state as a national sovereign is neglected, the basis of the international law of coexistence becomes so blurred as to defy definition; the inability to explain the basis of international law has constituted an unending contest of wit and word, 'a mysterious phenomenon',[114] as indicated by the emptiness of '*opinio juris*'. Once the national lawyer has come to the conclusion that the interests of more than one national sovereign are involved, the national law of one can only be applied if neglecting that the others are also sovereign. Instead, international issues are referred to international law and, as a consequence, international law is born. This international law of coexistence is fundamental and basic; it is part of lawyers' law and constitutes the necessary minimum of international law. It is taken for granted in the same way as national law is taken for granted. Its scope is coordinated with national law, whereas in terms of validity and also content it has to be separated from national law in order to achieve the purpose of complementing it.

Although the conception of the state as a national sovereign has a fundamental role in international law, this is different from its role in national law. The need for a residual and complementary legal system is due not so much to the notion of a national sovereign exercising supreme power within a national legal system as to the situation in which another national sovereign is made subject to this power. Although this 'external' view on the national sovereign depends on the 'internal' national legal system of another national sovereign, it is and remains an external view. In the context of national law, the national sovereign embodies a power, a competence, while in respect of international law the national sovereign is rather an object or a datum, a given condition,[115] the presence of which prompts the need for a residual and complementary legal system. Accordingly, in addition to being 'basic', the international law of coexistence may be seen as 'static'. Its

---

[114] Degan, *Sources*, p. 142.   [115] Crawford, *Open System*, p. 26.

scope is not the result of a law-making process but is derived from facts, namely the existence of a plurality of states. Its content is a different matter (but neither is this a product of the state acting as a national sovereign).

None of this implies that the various legal systems cannot be separated, or that dualism, or pluralism, has been excluded as a theory.[116] Indeed, theories of monism never occupied centre stage. There was, for example, no justification for Kelsen to infer from some substantive principles of one legal system that all legal systems were integrated also in terms of validity.[117] Although Triepel and his followers also advanced arguments based on substantive law, substance is not a synonym for validity. In principle, as a matter of national law, the national sovereign is not prevented from regulating single-handedly, in the national legal system, issues related to a plurality of states. But national lawyers are unlikely to feel comfortable about such regulation if not in accordance with the content of the international law of coexistence.

In addition to the international law of coexistence, there is the international law of cooperation. As Bentham stressed, there are contracts that are national and contracts that are international, the latter being contracts between sovereigns. This is just another example of coordination between the national and the international context. Yet the example is special because contracts are international due to their form, but not necessarily due to their subject matter. It is for states to decide what to give the form of a contract. And so, since national law is unsuited to govern these contracts between sovereigns, they account for an international law-making process and give rise to international law that is 'dynamic', as opposed to 'static'. This international law of cooperation is separated from national law not only as regards its validity and content, but also as regards its scope. Before turning to the model of international legal argument, a further example involving the use, or non-use, of the conception of the state as a national sovereign must be mentioned. This example concerns the international law of cooperation and a third Latin veil, namely *pacta sunt servanda*. It is mainly in respect of the international law of cooperation that lawyers use the two conceptions of the state defined in relation to international law, that is, the state as an international sovereign and the state as an international law

---

[116] Cf. *Elettronica Sicula SpA*, ICJ Reports [1989] 15 at paras. 73 and 124.
[117] Cf. Kelsen, *Problem der Souveränität*, pp. 122–3; and Lauterpacht, *Function of Law*, p. 411.

subject. Although these conceptions, and international law in general, would not have been conceivable had it not been for the conception of the state as a national sovereign, the latter must nevertheless leave room for the two conceptions defined in relation to international law. Again, as regards the conception of the state as a national sovereign, it should here be seen as a fact, as opposed to a power or competence.

Treaty and pacta sunt servanda

A treaty is by definition binding in international law. It is, according to a narrow definition, 'an agreement concluded between States in written form and governed by international law, whether embodied in a single instrument or in two or more related instruments and whatever its designation'.[118] A treaty is a binding agreement. Therefore, it may seem a little puzzling that there is said to be a 'fundamental principle of the law of treaties',[119] according to which a treaty is binding; for if not binding, there would be no treaty in the first place.[120] Perhaps what it really means is not that treaties are binding, a tautology, but that, for example, certain texts are treated by international law as treaties, meaning that their content is binding.[121]

But even if the principle *pacta sunt servanda* serves international lawyers as a synonym for the concept of treaty (*pactum*), this is not its sole meaning. Another meaning was conveyed by inserting the expression 'in force' in Article 26 of the Vienna Convention. Under the heading '*pacta sunt servanda*', Article 26 provides that '[e]very treaty in force is

[118] Article 2(1)(a) of the 1969 Vienna Convention on the Law of Treaties; see also Article 2(1)(a) of the 1986 Vienna Convention on the Law of Treaties between States and International Organizations or between International Organizations; and YILC 1982-II.2, p. 18.

[119] YILC 1966-II, p. 211.

[120] E.g., Angelo Piero Sereni, *The Italian Conception of International Law* (New York, 1943), p. 249; H. W. A. Thirlway, *International Customary Law and Codification* (Leiden, 1972), pp. 38–9; Roberto Lavalle, 'About the Alleged Customary Law Nature of the Rule Pacta Sunt Servanda' (1983) 33 ÖZöRV 9 at 11; and Jan Klabbers, *The Concept of Treaty in International Law* (The Hague, 1996), p. 40. Cf. Fitzmaurice, YILC 1959-II, p. 53; *Exchange of Greek and Turkish Populations*, Series B No. 10 (1925) at 20; and Clive Parry, 'The Law of Treaties' in Max Sørensen (ed.), *Manual of Public International Law* (London, 1968), p. 175 at p. 207.

[121] E.g., Hans Kelsen, 'Contribution à la théorie du traité international' (1936) 10 *Revue Internationale de la Théorie du Droit* 253 at 255; Joseph L. Kunz, 'The Meaning and the Range of the Norm *Pacta Sunt Servanda*' (1945) 39 *AJIL* 180 at 181; Brierly, 'Basis of Obligation', p. 10; and Thirlway, *International Customary Law*, pp. 27 and 38.

binding upon the parties to it and must be performed by them in good faith'. Behind the reference to 'in force' lies an interpretation of 'binding' (*servanda*), which signifies the period, the length of which is determined by combining the rules on the entry into force with those on the termination of a treaty. When so interpreted, it may be said, and is indeed commonly said, that the principle *pacta sunt servanda* stands in opposition to the various grounds for terminating a treaty, including the *rebus sic stantibus* rule. Here the principle *pacta sunt servanda* is a synonym for the rules governing the entry into force of a treaty; alternatively, it may be seen as reflecting the rules governing the termination of treaties and the changing of international law.[122]

The expression 'in force' is not the only significant element of Article 26. There is also the notion of good faith, which in the Vienna Convention has a bearing on principles of treaty interpretation. Relying on the interpretation given by the Permanent Court to some discrimination bans, among other examples, the International Law Commission's commentary on Article 26 inferred that 'the obligation must not be evaded by a merely literal application of the clauses'.[123] It was also said to be 'clearly implicit' that 'a party must abstain from acts calculated to frustrate the object and purpose of the treaty'. The commentary on Article 20 of the Harvard Draft Convention on the Law of Treaties, similarly linking the principle *pacta sunt servanda* and the notion of good faith, explained the rationale behind the latter notion by quoting Cornelius van Bynkershoek: 'Respect for treaty obligations, he concluded, was more necessary in international law than respect for contracts in private law, because there was no superior power competent to compel the parties to a treaty to observe its stipulations.'[124] According to Bin

---

[122] See Waldock, in United Nations Conference on the Law of Treaties, *Official Records* (New York, 1969–71), vol. 1, p. 158. The expression 'in force' gave rise to much debate, *ibid.*, pp. 150–8 and 427–8 and also vol. 2 (1970), pp. 44–9, possibly because the International Law Commission had not reached agreement on including it, see YILC 1964-I, pp. 23–32 and YILC 1966-I.2, pp.32–7; the expression was adopted in *Gabčíkovo-Nagymaros Project*, ICJ Reports [1997] 7 at para. 114.

[123] YILC 1966-II, pp. 211 and 221; and Waldock, YILC 1964-II, p. 8. The example goes back to Arnold D. McNair, *The Law of Treaties: British Practice and Opinions* (2nd edn, Oxford, 1961), pp. 540–1; see also George Schwarzenberger, *International Law and Order* (London, 1971), p. 118; and *Gabčíkovo-Nagymaros Project*, ICJ Reports [1997] 7 at para. 142.

[124] Cornelius van Bynkershoek, *Quaestionum Juris Publici Libri Duo* (Oxford, 1930), p. 191 (originally published 1737), as quoted in (1935) 29 *AJIL Supp.*, p. 982. See also Emmerich de Vattel, *Le Droit des gens ou principes de la loi naturelle* (Washington DC, 1916), pp. 161–2, 188, 191–2, 200 and 201 (originally published 1758).

Cheng, referring to the Harvard Draft Convention, '[p]acta sunt servanda, now an indisputable rule of international law, is but an expression of the principle of good faith which above all signifies the keeping of faith, the pledged faith of nations as well as that of individuals'.[125]

Unlike the term 'in force', the notion of good faith does not link the principle *pacta sunt servanda* to already existing rules but, on the contrary, to doubts about rules and about the conception of the state as an international law subject in general. International law is 'no superior power'. What is unveiled here is a third meaning attributed to the principle *pacta sunt servanda* – not a synonym for the concept of treaty, nor for rules governing the entry into force or termination of a treaty. Its primary function is to underline the conception of the state as an international law subject in the eyes of lawyers feeling uneasy about this conception. As such feelings are strongest when deciding whether obligations should be executed, the principle *pacta sunt servanda* has been reinforced in the context of treaty interpretation by an appeal to the notion of good faith. This explains why, according to the European Court of Justice, 'the *pacta sunt servanda* principle . . . constitutes a fundamental principle of any legal order and, in particular, the international legal order'.[126] Repeated invocations of the principle *pacta sunt servanda* and the notion of good faith bear witness to the conception of the state as an international law subject actually losing ground: systems secure in their normative character do not need to repeat themselves. In the *Nuclear Tests* cases, the International Court saw the notion of good faith as the basis of the binding character of some unilateral declarations as well as of the principle *pacta sunt servanda*. On that occasion the International Court laid down the principle that a 'restrictive interpretation is called for' when deciding to what extent a unilateral declaration is binding.[127]

[125] Bin Cheng, *General Principles of Law as Applied by International Courts and Tribunals* (London, 1953), p. 113.

[126] Case C-162/96, *Racke v. Hauptzollamt Mainz* [1998] ECR I-3698 at para. 49.

[127] *Nuclear Tests (Australia v. France)*, ICJ Reports [1974] 253 at paras. 44 and 46 and (*New Zealand v. France*), ICJ Reports [1974] 457 at paras. 47 and 49; cf. H. W. A. Thirlway, 'The Law and Procedure of the International Court of Justice, 1960–1989: Part One' (1989) 60 BYIL 1 at 16–17. The *dictum* was quoted in *Military and Paramilitary Activities in and against Nicaragua* (Jurisdiction and Admissibility), ICJ Reports [1984] 392 at para. 60, and it was confirmed in *Military and Paramilitary Activities in and against Nicaragua* (Merits), ICJ Reports [1986] 14 at para. 261 and *Frontier Dispute (Burkina Faso v. Mali)*, ICJ Reports [1986] 554 at para. 40. Cf. as to a certain unease regarding a unilateral statement, *Case of the SS Wimbledon*, Series A No. 1 (1923) at 29 and 41.

In the Vienna Convention, Article 26 is accompanied by a provision, Article 27, according to which '[a] party may not invoke the provisions of its internal law as justification for its failure to perform a treaty'. The aim of Article 27 is to isolate the conception of the state as a national sovereign from international law, as well as to subordinate the conception of the state as an international sovereign to the conception of the state as an international law subject.[128] But then it is precisely in regard to treaty provisions that seek to regulate the sovereign in the context of its national law, that is, the national sovereign, that the notion of good faith springs to mind.[129] It allows, according to Shabtai Rosenne, 'a fair degree of freedom of action in interpreting and applying the terms of the treaty-obligation in a concrete case'.[130] Likewise, according to Sir Gerald Fitzmaurice, 'the correct interpretation of a treaty having been ascertained, it then becomes the duty of the parties to carry it out reasonably, equitably and in good faith'.[131] In preparing the Convention on the Settlement of Investment Disputes between States and Nationals of Other States, Aron Broches, who as General Counsel of the International Bank for Reconstruction and Development was the principal architect of the ICSID Convention, at one point stated that 'it was necessary to leave some freedom to the Contracting States to interpret in good faith the principal concept laid down in the Convention'.[132]

On this view, it is one thing to say that a treaty has been concluded and entered into force and quite another thing to conclude that the conception of the state as a sovereign is irrelevant. Indeed, the conception of the state as a national sovereign may influence treaty interpretation so that it permits the national sovereign 'a fair degree of freedom', even

---

[128] Cf. *Affaire de l'île de Timor*, 11 RIAA 490 (1914) at 496–7 and the 'subjective' interpretation based on the intention of the international sovereigns, *ibid.*, pp. 499–503.

[129] See *North Atlantic Coast Fisheries Case*, 11 RIAA 167 (1910) at 187 and *Case concerning Rights of Nationals of the United States of America in Morocco*, ICJ Reports [1952] 176 at 212.

[130] Shabtai Rosenne, *Developments in the Law of Treaties, 1945–1986* (Cambridge, 1989), p. 176; and also Shabtai Rosenne, 'Interpretation of Treaties in the Restatement and the International Law Commission's Draft Articles: A Comparison' (1966) 5 *Columbia Journal of Transnational Law* 205 at 223; see also Mustafa Kamil Yasseen, 'L'interprétation des traités d'après la Convention de Vienne sur le droit des traités' (1976) 151 *Recueil des Cours* 1 at 21; and Wolfram Karl, *Vertrag und spätere Praxis im Völkerrecht* (Berlin, 1983), p. 185.

[131] YILC 1959-II, p. 54.

[132] ICSID, *History*, vol. 2, p. 903; and see also *ibid.*, pp. 211, 758 and 1021.

if resulting in a restrictive interpretation of the treaty in question. In extreme cases, the conception of the state as a sovereign leads lawyers operating in an international context towards the theory of *Selbstverpflictung* with the result that the conception of the state as an international sovereign opposes and challenges the conception of the state as an international law subject and, thereby, the binding force of treaty law. When introducing what became Article 26, Sir Humphrey Waldock, the special rapporteur, thought that 'it may be desirable to underline a little that the obligation to observe treaties is one of good faith and not *stricti juris*'.[133] And according to Professor Elisabeth Zoller, '[u]n Etat peut parfaitement remplir ses obligations découlant d'un traité, mais violer le principe de bonne foi'.[134]

Lawyers who start from a position of doubt as to whether the state is really an international law subject easily find themselves caught in an infinite regress; for why is the principle *pacta sunt servanda* binding? Then one is looking for what Hans Kelsen termed a '*Stufenbau*', that is, a hierarchy of rules, and in particular for the summit. H. L. A. Hart, a legal theorist, has referred to the principle *pacta sunt servanda* in the context of 'the minimum content of Natural Law'.[135] Kelsen at one point, and also Italian scholars like Dionisio Anzilotti, held that the principle *pacta sunt servanda* is the supreme rule that cannot be justified by other rules, i.e., the *Grundnorm* of international law.[136] That hollow term may appear to be the only difference between this view and Triepel's conclusion that a principle securing the binding force of already binding treaties is not needed.[137] But then one should not disregard the doubts about the conception of the state as an international law subject. Triepel did not share those doubts, but they make most lawyers identify the need for

---

[133] YILC 1964-II, p. 7; and see George Schwarzenberger, 'The Fundamental Principles of International Law' (1955) 87 *Recueil des Cours* 195 at 300; cf. YILC 1964-I, pp. 23–32.

[134] Elisabeth Zoller, *La Bonne foi en droit international public* (Paris, 1977), p. 81; contrast, however, McNair, *The Law of Treaties*, pp. 465 and 540 *et seq.*; and also Robert Kolb, *La Bonne foi en droit international public* (Geneva, 2000), p. 275.

[135] Hart, *Concept of Law*, p. 193; and also Henkin, *International Law*, p. 28. Cf. Verdross, *Einheit des rechtlichen Weltbildes*, pp. 7–8; G. G. Fitzmaurice, 'The Law and Procedure of the International Court of Justice 1954–9: General Principles and Sources of International Law' (1959) 36 *BYIL* 183 at 195; and McNair, *The Law of Treaties*, p. 493.

[136] Kelsen, 'Rapports de système', p. 265; Kelsen, *Problem der Souveränität*, p. 137; and Anzilotti, *Cours*, p. 44; cf., however, Kelsen, *General Theory*, p. 369.

[137] Triepel, *Völkerrecht und Landesrecht*, pp. 81–2; cf. *ibid.*, pp. 103–10. See also Ch. Rousseau, *Principes généraux du droit international public* (Paris, 1944), p. 363.

international law justifying international law; thus, lawyers normally take the view that the principle *pacta sunt servanda* belongs to so-called customary international law.

For present purposes, it suffices to conclude that apparently conceptions of the state as a sovereign are not alien to international lawyers operating in the context of the international law of cooperation already made, either as the conception of the state as a national sovereign, or as a change in the hierarchy between the conception of the state as an international sovereign and the conception of the state as an international law subject (to the effect that changing international law becomes a question of sovereign will rather than international law). On the other hand, while the different meanings given to *pacta sunt servanda* suggest that the conception of the state as a national sovereign may have a say in respect of the international law of cooperation, this is clearly not uncontroversial: only one of the three meanings attributed to *pacta sunt servanda* exemplifies such a role. Basically, contracts between sovereigns are allocated to international law due to the insufficiency of national law, it being assumed that they are binding and so should not be distrusted by lawyers. As stressed in the *Border and Transborder Armed Actions* case, a principle of good faith 'is not in itself a source of obligation where none would otherwise exist';[138] nor should it or conceptions of the state as a sovereign weaken obligations that do exist.[139] In a preliminary award rendered under the auspices of the Court of Arbitration of the International Chamber of Commerce, the sole arbitrator found, correctly, that '[a] sovereign state must be sovereign enough to make a binding promise both under international law and municipal law'.[140]

---

[138] *Border and Transborder Armed Actions* (Jurisdiction and Admissibility), ICJ Reports [1988] 69 at para. 105; and also *Land and Maritime Boundary between Cameroon and Nigeria* (Preliminary Objections), ICJ Reports [1998] 275 at para. 39.

[139] Cf. Article 300 of the United Nations Convention on the Law of the Sea and *Land and Maritime Boundary between Cameroon and Nigeria* (Preliminary Objections), ICJ Reports [1998] 275 at para. 38, in which the International Court linked a principle of good faith to the doctrine of abuse of rights used by the Permanent Court in certain cases: see *Case concerning Certain German Interests in Polish Upper Silesia* (Merits), Series A No. 7 (1926) at 30; *Case of the Free Zones of Upper Savoy and the District of Gex* (Second Phase), Series A No. 24 (1930) at 12; and *Case of Free Zones of Upper Savoy and the District of Gex* (Third Phase), Series A/B No. 46 (1932) at 167. While in the *Upper Silesia* case the presumption against states abusing rights was used in respect of a treaty not yet in force, in the *Free Zones* case it paved the way for a restrictive interpretation of existing treaty obligations.

[140] ICC Case No. 2321, as reproduced in Sigvard Jarvin and Yves Derains (eds.), *Collection of ICC Arbitral Awards 1974–1985* (Paris, 1990), p. 8 at p. 10.

A definition of state

Although there would be no conception of the state as an international sovereign, nor a conception of the state as an international law subject, if not for the conception of the state as a national sovereign, it is crucial to keep separate the two former conceptions defined in relation to international law from the latter conception. When combined, the three conceptions of the state used here, and which are all considered necessary, exclude a unitary structure for international legal argument. Instead, international legal argument has two structures. Given the basis of international law, as complementary and residual, it could not be any different, nor can the structures be changed by lawyers.

This can be illustrated by Article 1 of the 1933 Montevideo Convention on Rights and Duties of States. According to this provision, '[t]he State as a person of international law should possess the following qualifications: (a) a permanent population; (b) a defined territory; (c) government; and (d) capacity to enter into relations with the other States'. The core is the classical conception of the state as the government of a population, i.e., the state as a national sovereign. But to this conception has been added territory, by implication acknowledging that the national sovereign is part of a world containing several national sovereigns. This generates the need for an international law of coexistence that separates the several national sovereigns; it is commonly presented in the form of custom, or general principles. Also added, at least in the Montevideo Convention, has been the capacity to enter into relations with other states and thus to be an international actor in a broad, factual sense, one aspect being the state as an international sovereign. It has a legal impact in particular when taking part in the making of treaties, here referred to as the international law of cooperation.

According to the model developed and explained in Chapter 3, any exercise in international legal argument will lead the lawyer to the conception of the state as a national sovereign, the international law of coexistence or the international law of cooperation. First, the conception of the state as a national sovereign and the international law of coexistence, currently termed 'customary' or 'general' international law, are dealt with. Afterwards, attention is turned towards the international law of cooperation, that is, treaty law, which reflects the conception of the state as an international sovereign. The two structures in which the international law of coexistence and the international law of cooperation take part are termed, respectively, the 'basic' and the 'dynamic' structure of international legal argument. The basic structure advances from the conception of the state as a national sovereign to the international law of coexistence; the dynamic structure advances from the international law of cooperation to the conception of the state as a national sovereign. The relationship between the structures is the subject of the following section. Finally, the basic assumption that international legal argument originates with conceptions of the state, as opposed to some notion of an international community or the like, is explained.

3   The double structure of international legal argument

The basic structure

The national principle of self-containedness

Most lawyers work and think on the basis of a national legal system: they are 'national' lawyers. As such most rarely pay regard to international law. The standard approach is to see the national legal system as being self-contained, capable of solving on its own disputes and other issues as they present themselves. Where dealing with an issue belonging to the vast domain within which national lawyers regard national law as being self-contained, a national lawyer will be at least sceptical, if not dismissive, of an argument as to the relevance of international law. This starting-point may be termed 'the national principle of self-containedness'. For example, the state is seen as perfectly capable on its own, that is, in its national law, to regulate the relationship between individuals, and between individuals and the state; thus individuals are not normally a concern for the international law of coexistence.[1] In respect of a treaty-based regime part of which clearly has direct effect on individuals, the European Court of Justice indeed takes the view that

---

[1] For an especially clear statement, many would say 'overstatement', see *South West Africa* (Second Phase), ICJ Reports [1966] 6 at paras. 49–50; cf. *Legal Consequences for States of the Continued Presence of South Africa in Namibia (South West Africa) notwithstanding Security Council Resolution 276 (1970)*, ICJ Reports [1971] 16 at para. 131; and *United States Diplomatic and Consular Staff in Tehran*, ICJ Reports [1980] 3 at para. 91. In respect of companies, see *Anglo-Iranian Oil Co. Case* (Jurisdiction), ICJ Reports [1952] 93 at 112; and *Barcelona Traction, Light and Power Company, Limited* (Merits), ICJ Reports [1970] 3 at para. 38. Cf., e.g., Arbitrator Dupuy in *Texaco Overseas Petroleum Company and California Asiatic Oil Company v. Libya*, 53 ILR 420 (1977) at paras. 32–5 and 40–51; *AGIP v. Congo*, 1 ICSID Reports 306 (1979) at 324; and *Sandline International Inc. v. Papua New Guinea*, 117 ILR 554 (1998) at 560.

in a very fundamental sense it 'constitutes a new legal order of international law'.[2]

In the *Military and Paramilitary Activities in and against Nicaragua* case, the International Court referred to 'matters in which each State is permitted, by the principle of State sovereignty, to decide freely'. By way of illustration, the International Court pointed to 'the choice of a political, economic, social and cultural system, and the formulation of foreign policy'.[3] These are broadly defined categories for which a national lawyer will not see the need for anything but national law, at least not as a starting-point. Previously, in the *Nationality Decrees* opinion, the Permanent Court had pointed to 'certain matters which, though they may very closely concern the interests of more than one State, are not, in principle, regulated by international law'.[4] As a consequence, 'each State is sole judge', meaning that even when two states reached irreconcilable results, for example, if one proscribed what the other prescribed, or imposed the same duty on a subject where it could only be fulfilled in relation to one, the conflict would not be regarded as so serious as to make the lawyer look behind the national principle of self-containedness.

This principle is basically a projection of a deep-rooted value of national law, namely the conception of the state as a national sovereign. The translation of the definition of sovereignty in the original French version of Jean Bodin's *Les Six livres de la république* is 'the absolute and perpetual power of a commonwealth', while the same definition in the Latin version published a year later translates as 'supreme and absolute power over citizens and subjects'.[5] The former formulation is echoed in the passages from the *Nationality Decrees* opinion and the *Military and Paramilitary Activities in and against Nicaragua* case quoted above; the latter formulation reflects the European Court of Justice's presumption against the involvement of the individual in international law.

From self-containedness to the international law of coexistence

Not each and every issue falls within the sweeping formulas by which Jean Bodin defined sovereignty. Bodin, writing within the tradition of

---

[2] Case 26/62, *Van Gend en Loos* v. *Nederlandse administratie der belastingen* [1963] ECR 1 at 12.
[3] *Military and Paramilitary Activities in and against Nicaragua* (Merits), ICJ Reports [1986] 14 at para. 205; see previously *Western Sahara*, ICJ Reports [1975] 12 at para. 94; and *United States Diplomatic and Consular Staff in Tehran* (Provisional Measures), ICJ Reports [1979] 7 at para. 25.
[4] *Nationality Decrees in Tunis and Morocco*, Series B No. 4 (1923) at 23–4.
[5] See Jean Bodin, *On Sovereignty* (Cambridge, 1992), p. 1 (originally published 1576).

natural law, was clear on this. '[I]f we say', he wrote, 'that to have absolute power is not to be subject to any law at all, no prince of this world will be sovereign, since every earthly prince is subject to the laws of God and of nature and to various human laws that are common to all peoples.'[6] According to Bodin, 'absolute power' meant that 'persons who are sovereign must not be subject in any way to the commands of someone else and must be able to give the law to subjects'.[7] The one premise which has made national law the doorway to international law is not peculiar to the tradition of natural law. Every national lawyer, including the most rigid positivist, will subscribe to 'the legal maxim that one equal cannot command another'.[8]

In Triepel's words, 'das Landesrecht unfähig ist, Verhältnisse von Staat zu Staat, die als Beziehungen der Koordination gedacht werden müssen, von sich aus zu regeln'.[9] As for certain categories of issues, national lawyers concerned with one national legal system have recognised the involvement of other national sovereigns, particularly where a serious clash between the interests of several national sovereigns has been identified. As a corollary, they have felt a need for a complementary legal system that unlike national legal systems is not subject to a single sovereign; this system is the international law of coexistence. To quote Triepel again, 'im Bereiche des staatlichen Rechts ungemein zahlreiche Stellen giebt, an denen sich Niemand, der zum vollen Verständnisse des Landesrechts an sich gelangen will, der Nothwendigkeit verschliessen kann, die Brücke zum Völkerrecht hinüberzuschlagen'.[10]

One example of issues regulated by the international law of coexistence is another state's coercion with regard to the choices referred to by the International Court in the *Military and Paramilitary Activities in and against Nicaragua* case. Such coercion gives rise to a clash between states, the prevention of which is the rationale behind the traditional principle of non-intervention.[11] Another example is the principle of

---

[6] *Ibid.*, p. 10.   [7] *Ibid.*, p. 11.   [8] *Ibid.*, p. 20.

[9] H. Triepel, *Völkerrecht und Landesrecht* (Leipzig, 1899), p. 22 ('le droit interne est incapable de régler de lui-même les rapports d'Etat à Etat qui doivent être considérés comme rapports de coordination'). See also Max Huber, 'Die Fortbildung des Völkerrechts auf dem Gebiete des Prozess- und Landkriegsrechts durch die II. internationale Friedenskonferenz im Haag 1907' (1908) 2 *Jahrbuch des öffentlichen Rechts der Gegenwart* 470 at 501.

[10] Triepel, *Völkerrecht und Landesrecht*, p. 3 ('il y a des endroits extraordinairement nombreux dans le droit étatique, où quiconque veut arriver à une pleine intelligence du droit interne doit se soumettre à la nécessité de passer le pont qui conduit au droit international').

[11] *Military and Paramilitary Activities in and against Nicaragua* (Merits), ICJ Reports [1986] 14 at para. 205; and also *Corfu Channel Case* (Merits), ICJ Reports [1949] 4 at 35.

diplomatic protection: while individual rights have been far from the centre of the international law of coexistence, a state's treatment of an alien may nevertheless give rise to a legal dispute between that state and another state under the international law of coexistence. According to Emmerich de Vattel:

> Whoever ill-treats a citizen indirectly injures the State, which must protect that citizen. The sovereign of the injured citizen must avenge the deed and, if possible, force the aggressor to give full satisfaction or punish him, since otherwise the citizen will not obtain the chief end of civil society, which is protection.[12]

The so-called fathers of international law, writers like Francisco de Vitoria, Alberico Gentili and Hugo Grotius, concerned themselves with international law (*jus gentium*) because they wrote on issues that were seen as international, as opposed to national. Vitoria lectured on the meeting between the Spanish and the Indians, which took place far to the west of the Azores; Gentili was originally asked for his opinion on the immunity of the Spanish ambassador to England, a Catholic involved in plans to overthrow the English Queen; and Grotius got involved in international law through a case before a prize court concerning questions of prize and booty and also Portugal's alleged jurisdiction over the Indian Ocean. All three writers assumed that these issues could not be dealt with simply by applying one sovereign's national law to the case before them.[13] In their subsequent writings, they all made contributions to the law of war, the archetype of an inter-state dispute which is not left to the national law of one of the sovereign states.[14] For, to quote Montesquieu, '[o]ffensive force is regulated by the right of nations, which is the political law of the nations considered in their relation with each other'.[15]

---

[12] Emmerich de Vattel, *Le Droit des gens ou principes de la loi naturelle* (Washington DC, 1916), p. 136 (originally published 1758).

[13] See Francisco de Vitoria, *De Indis Relectio Prior* (Washington DC, 1917), pp. 131–4 (originally published 1532); Alberico Gentili, *De Legationibus Libri Tres* (New York, 1924), pp. 97, 108 and 111 (originally published 1585); and Hugo Grotius, *De Iure Praedae Commentarius* (London, 1950), pp. 26–9, 51–2, 135, 231–2, 238–40, 245–6 and 258–9 (manuscript from 1604).

[14] See Alberico Gentili, *De Iure Belli Libri Tres* (Oxford, 1933), pp. 3–11 (originally published 1612); and Hugo Grotius, *De Jure Belli ac Pacis Libri Tres* (Oxford, 1925), prolegomena, para. 26 (originally published 1625).

[15] Charles de Montesquieu, *The Spirit of the Laws* (Cambridge, 1989), p. 138 (originally published 1748). See also Sir Robert Jennings' tribute to Sir Humphrey Waldock in R. Y. Jennings, *Collected Writings of Sir Robert Jennings* (The Hague, 1998), p. 1395 at p. 1397.

As a term for this lawyers' international law, '*jus gentium*' was to be replaced by 'the law of nations', which in turn was overtaken by Bentham's 'international law'. It was treated as a legal system in its own right; for only by being independent of all national legal systems would it be a location to which national lawyers could refer disputes and other issues between sovereigns. And as they did so, national lawyers promoted a project of international law that aimed at coexistence, containing various principles necessary to smooth out potential disputes between the several national sovereigns and their national legal systems. This international law of coexistence is the minimum of international law, unrelated to treaty obligations and applying to all states, new as well as old.

Separating state powers

The prime response to the need for an international law of coexistence has been the definition, in Kelsen's phraseology, of 'spheres of validity',[16] separating those powers of the several national sovereigns that may otherwise give rise to serious disputes. This has been done by giving each state jurisdiction, *prima facie* exclusive, over its own land territory.[17] In respect of the exercise of power (enforcement), the Permanent Court called the territorial separation 'the first and foremost restriction imposed by international law upon a State'.[18] For the same reason, and as Vitoria exemplified, questions of title to territory, and also of delimitation, form essential parts of the international law of coexistence.[19] To a large extent 'sovereignty' and 'territory' are interchangeable, thus the term 'territorial sovereignty'. For example, the essence of a so-called 'state succession' is a transfer of title to territory.[20]

---

[16] Hans Kelsen, *General Theory of Law and State* (Cambridge, MA, 1945), pp. 208–9.

[17] E.g., *Corfu Channel Case* (Merits), ICJ Reports [1949] 4 at 35.

[18] *The Case of the SS Lotus*, Series A No. 10 (1927) at 18; see also Arbitrator Huber in *Island of Palmas Case*, 2 RIAA 829 (1928) at 838–9.

[19] On the need for a solution to title and delimitation cases, see e.g., *Legal Status of Eastern Greenland*, Series A/B No. 53 (1933) at 46; and *The Minquiers and Ecrehos Case*, ICJ Reports [1953] 47 at 67; see also the related principle of stability articulated in *Case concerning the Temple of Preah Vihear* (Merits), ICJ Reports [1962] 6 at 34; *Aegean Sea Continental Shelf*, ICJ Reports [1978] 3 at para. 85; and *Territorial Dispute (Libya v. Chad)*, ICJ Reports [1994] 6 at paras. 72–3.

[20] See common Article 2 of the 1978 Vienna Convention on Succession of States in Respect of Treaties and the 1983 Vienna Convention on Succession of States in Respect of State Property; and also *Frontier Dispute (Burkina Faso v. Mali)*, ICJ Reports [1986] 554 at para. 30 and *Land, Island and Maritime Frontier Dispute (El Salvador v. Honduras)*, ICJ Reports [1992] 351 at para. 399.

With respect to a few select issues it is not the territorial state that enjoys exclusive jurisdiction. The representatives of a state are normally exempted from the jurisdiction of other states even when present in their territories.[21] Gentili is by no means the only lawyer introduced to international law through a case concerning diplomatic immunity.

The law of the sea which binds a state even though no treaty obligations have been undertaken centres on defining and separating state powers. According to the *Fisheries Jurisdiction* case, 'the rules of international maritime law have been the product of mutual accommodation, reasonableness and cooperation'.[22] The need for principles of maritime delimitation is not in doubt.[23] The separation of state powers is also the focus of air law and the law regarding outer space. It was in respect of the latter field that Bin Cheng coined the term 'instant custom',[24] that is, a 'custom' that is clearly not a custom proper. It has been applied to new areas of human activity where lawyers have faced an immediate need for international law, the continental shelf being a further example in addition to outer space.[25]

Once separated, one state may not intervene with the way in which another state exercises its powers; in particular, in the absence of a supervening principle, physical intervention, including warfare, is excluded.[26] On the other hand, the acts of one state are not binding on another

---

[21] Cf. *Colombian–Peruvian Asylum Case*, ICJ Reports [1950] 266 at 274; *United States Diplomatic and Consular Staff in Tehran* (Provisional Measures), ICJ Reports [1979] 7 at paras. 38–40; *United States Diplomatic and Consular Staff in Tehran*, ICJ Reports [1980] 3 at para. 92; *Case concerning the Arrest Warrant of 11 April 2000*, ICJ Reports [2002] 3 at paras. 53–4; and *Case concerning Avena and other Mexican Nationals*, ICJ Reports [2004] (not yet reported) at para. 47 (31 March 2004).

[22] *Fisheries Jurisdiction (United Kingdom v. Iceland)*, ICJ Reports [1974] 3 at para. 53.

[23] E.g., *Fisheries*, ICJ Reports [1951] 116 at 132; and *North Sea Continental Shelf*, ICJ Reports [1969] 3 at para. 83. See also the decision of the Central American Court of Justice in *Gulf of Fonseca (El Salvador v. Nicaragua)*, (1917) 11 *AJIL* 674 at 711–12.

[24] Bin Cheng, 'United Nations Resolutions on Outer Space: "Instant" International Customary Law?' (1965) 5 *IJIL* 23; and also R. Y. Jennings, 'What is International Law and How Do We Tell It When We See It' (1981) 37 *Schweizerisches Jahrbuch für internationales Recht* 59 at 67–71; Bin Cheng, 'Some Remarks on the Constituent Element(s) of General (or So-Called Customary) International Law' in Antony Anghie and Garry Sturgess (eds.), *Legal Visions of the 21st Century: Essays in Honour of Judge Christopher Weeramantry* (The Hague, 1998), p. 377 at pp. 381 and 389; and Bin Cheng, 'Opinio Juris: A Key Concept in International Law That Is Much Misunderstood' in Sienho Yee and Wang Tieya (eds.), *International Law in the Post-Cold War World: Essays in Memory of Li Haopei* (London, 2001), p. 56 at p. 65.

[25] Cf. James Crawford and Thomas Viles, 'International Law on a Given Day' in Konrad Ginther *et al.* (eds.), *Festschrift für Karl Zemanek* (Berlin, 1994), p. 45.

[26] *Military and Paramilitary Activities in and against Nicaragua* (Merits), ICJ Reports [1986] 14 at paras. 188 and 202.

state. They are under no obligation to recognise the actions of a national sovereign unless international law provides otherwise (while there is no access to counter-measures so long as no violation of international law has occurred).

Supervening state powers: common, substantive standards

While being the prime response to the need for the international law of coexistence, territorial separation of state powers cannot answer all questions that are referred from national law to international law. Certain questions require that the international law of coexistence provides a common, substantive standard for inter-state behaviour; it has to determine how a state should employ its jurisdiction, as opposed to merely choosing which state should enjoy exclusive jurisdiction.[27]

In addition to defining exactly which issues are international, and to what extent, the need for common, substantive standards is what has fuelled academic debates throughout the centuries and given rise to some of the most celebrated instances of judicial law-making internationally. While the insufficiency of national law determines the scope of the international law of coexistence, it does not determine its content. On the contrary, the answers to be given to the questions referred from national law are for international law to decide. Analogies from this or that part of a specific national legal system are inadequate. In many cases, international lawyers have abstained from wrapping up their answers in the language of general rules, or principles. Rather, these have been specific answers to specific questions. Still, there are some examples of highly developed substantive standards with a long tradition under the international law of coexistence.

For example, a state's interest in its nationals has to a certain extent been recognised so as to confer a right of diplomatic protection on the former in respect of the latter; according to the Permanent Court, 'it is the bond of nationality between the State and the individual which alone confers upon the State the right of diplomatic protection'.[28]

---

[27] Cf. Wolfgang Friedmann, *The Changing Structure of International Law* (London, 1964), pp. 60, 89–90 and 298.

[28] *The Panevezys–Saldutiskis Railway Case*, Series A/B No. 76 (1939) at 16; and see also, e.g., *Case of the Mavrommatis Palestine Concessions* (Jurisdiction), Series A No. 2 (1924) at 12; *Nottebohm Case* (Second Phase), ICJ Reports [1955] 4 at 24; and *Barcelona Traction, Light and Power Company, Limited* (Merits), ICJ Reports [1970] 3 at paras. 36–7 and 85–7. A 'genuine link' between the state and the national may be required in order not to generate more conflict with other states, see *Nottebohm Case* (Second Phase), ICJ Reports [1955] 4 at 21; the same rationale underlies *Barcelona Traction, Light and Power Company, Limited* (Merits), ICJ Reports [1970] 3 at paras. 78, 94 and 96.

Diplomatic protection has been described as 'a very sensitive area of international relations'.[29] It derogates from the national principle of self-containedness where a national of another state suffers from serious maltreatment. In a case where the territorial state has denied an alien, for example, his or her life or property, or a fair trial, lawyers have recognised a conflict between the interests of the two states for which the international law of coexistence must provide a solution. A similar rationale motivates the principles of humanitarian law.[30] It has been extended to internal armed conflicts precisely because, according to the International Criminal Tribunal for the Former Yugoslavia, 'the large-scale nature of civil strife, coupled with the increasing interdependence of States in the world community, has made it more and more difficult for third States to remain aloof'.[31] In the age of the United Nations the human rights movement may have changed some 'names'. Certain rights previously reserved for 'aliens' are now arguably conferred on individuals irrespective of nationality, and perhaps it can be argued that individuals themselves are able to lay down claims for compensation in case of violation.[32] Be that as it may, the substantive scope of this part of the international law of coexistence has not been significantly enlarged.[33] The human rights movement has largely been confined to treaty law, and to institutions specific to each treaty.

Protection of aliens and principles of humanitarian law, and also the equivalent human rights, are some of the examples of the international

---

[29] *Barcelona Traction, Light and Power Company, Limited* (Merits), ICJ Reports [1970] 3 at para. 37.

[30] *Legality of the Threat or Use of Nuclear Weapons*, ICJ Reports [1996] 226 at paras. 75–82; cf. *Corfu Channel Case* (Merits), ICJ Reports [1949] 4 at 22.

[31] *Prosecutor v. Tadic* (Jurisdiction), 105 ILR 453 (1995) at para. 97. See also Liesbeth Zegveld, *Accountability of Armed Opposition Groups in International Law* (Cambridge, 2002), p. 16.

[32] Thus, from the Inter-American Court of Human Rights, *Rodríguez Case* (Compensation), 95 ILR 306 (1989) at para. 25; and *Aloeboetoe et al. v. Suriname* (Compensation), 116 ILR 260 (1993) at para. 43; cf. *Prosecutor v. Tadic* (Jurisdiction), 105 ILR 453 (1995) at para. 42; and *Distomo Massacre Case*, (2003) 42 ILM 1030 (2003) at 1037. See also Mohamed Bennouna, 'Preliminary Report on Diplomatic Protection' (United Nations Document A/CN.4/484, 1998), para. 52; and John Dugard, 'First Report on Diplomatic Protection' (United Nations Document A/CN.4/506, 2000), paras. 46 and 175–84.

[33] Cf. *Barcelona Traction, Light and Power Company, Limited* (Merits), ICJ Reports [1970] 3 at paras. 34 and 89–91; and also YILC 1977-II.2, p. 46. The list of so-called 'customary' rights produced by the United Nations Human Rights Committee in General Comment No. 24 corresponds to a large extent with traditional standards of treating aliens, see 107 ILR 65 (1994) at 70; see also American Law Institute, *Restatement (Third) of the Foreign Relations Law of the United States, as Adopted and Promulgated May 14, 1986* (St Paul, MN, 1987), vol. 2, pp. 161–75; and International Law Association, *Report on the 66th Conference* (1994), pp. 29 and 544–9.

law of coexistence not merely choosing which state should enjoy exclusive jurisdiction but determining how a state has to employ its jurisdiction. Other substantive standards indicating a need for the international law of coexistence include the principle of good neighbourliness.[34] In the *Island of Palmas* case, Sole Arbitrator Huber exhibited many of these tendencies, stating that territorial sovereignty implied 'the obligation to protect within the territory the rights of other States, in particular their right to integrity and inviolability in peace and in war, together with the rights which each State may claim for its national in foreign territory'.[35]

There are more examples. In addition to the various needs for solving serious clashes of state interests, translating into rights and obligations, there are the 'secondary' principles on the responsibility incurred by states that do not abide by their 'primary' obligations. No doubt the need for the international law of coexistence is only satisfied where the 'primary' obligations are supplemented by 'secondary' principles laying down the consequences of the 'primary' obligations being breached.[36] On the other hand, the need for the international law of coexistence has not developed so far as to include 'tertiary' principles on the judicial settlement of disputes. Appeals in this context to the international law of coexistence normally link international dispute settlement to some issue that is clearly international in kind, such as inter-state wars. The old saying that international dispute settlement can end wars has

---

[34] As regards the latter, see *Island of Palmas Case*, 2 RIAA 829 (1928) at 839; *Trail Smelter Case*, 3 RIAA 1938 (1941) at 1965; and *Corfu Channel Case* (Merits), ICJ Reports [1949] 4 at 22; see also, with respect to the environment, *Legality of the Threat or Use of Nuclear Weapons*, ICJ Reports [1996] 226 at para. 29; and *Gabčíkovo-Nagymaros Project*, ICJ Reports [1997] 7 at paras. 53, 112 and 140.

[35] *Island of Palmas Case*, 2 RIAA 829 (1928) at 839; in respect of diplomatic protection, see Arbitrator Huber in *Affaire des biens britanniques au Maroc espagnol*, 2 RIAA 615 (1924) at 636 and 649.

[36] *Case concerning the Factory at Chorzów* (Claim for Indemnity) (Jurisdiction), Series A No. 9 (1927) at 21; and *Case concerning the Factory at Chorzów* (Claim for Indemnity) (Merits), Series A No. 17 (1928) at 29 and 47; see also *Affaire des biens britanniques au Maroc espagnol*, 2 RIAA 615 (1924) at 632; and, of course, the Draft Articles on Responsibility of States for Internationally Wrongful Acts as finally adopted by the International Law Commission in 2001. On the distinction between primary and secondary rules, see Roberto Ago, YILC 1969-II, p. 127 and also YILC 1963-II, pp. 227–8 and YILC 1970-II, p. 306; see also James Crawford, 'First Report on State Responsibility' (United Nations Document A/CN.4/490, 1998), paras. 13–16; 'Report of the International Law Commission to the General Assembly' (United Nations Document A/56/10, 2001), pp. 59–62, paras. 1–4; and James Crawford, *The International Law Commission's Articles on State Responsibility: Introduction, Text and Commentaries* (Cambridge, 2002), pp. 14–16.

not been taken to the point of arguing that the international law of coexistence regulates international dispute settlement in the same way as it regulates warfare. The international law of coexistence establishes no courts, nor does it confer extra jurisdiction on the existing international courts established under treaties.[37] It imposes a duty to negotiate 'in good faith' at most.[38]

The inherent vagueness of the international law of coexistence

Although most issues come within the national principle of self-containedness, national lawyers tend to refer some issues to the international law of coexistence. In those instances, coexistence between states is conditional on international law providing a solution, or so national lawyers reason. Charles de Montesquieu, the great prophet of national legal ideals, summarised the residual need for international law in the following way: 'All nations have a right of nations; and even the Iroquois, who eat their prisoners, have one. They send and receive embassies; they know rights of war and peace: the trouble is that their right of nations is not founded on true principles.'[39] Triepel pointed to 'Seerecht, Gesandtschafts- und Konsularrecht, Militärrecht, das sogenannte internationale Privat- und Strafrecht' and also to 'Souveränetät, Staatenverbindung, Staatsgebiet, Staatsservituten, Staatsangehörigkeit, Bedeutung, Abschluss, Wirksamkeit, Inhalt der Staatsverträge'.[40] H. L. A. Hart noted that 'we expect international law, but not morality, to tell us such things as the number of days a belligerent vessel may stay for refuelling or repairs in a neutral port; the width of territorial waters; the methods to be used in their measurement. All these things are necessary and desirable provisions for legal rules to make.'[41]

---

[37] See famously *Status of Eastern Carelia*, Series B No. 5 (1923) at 27; and also *Interpretation of Peace Treaties*, ICJ Reports [1950] 65 at 71; *Case of the Monetary Gold Removed from Rome in 1943*, ICJ Reports [1954] 19 at 32; *Continental Shelf (Libya v. Malta)* (Intervention), ICJ Reports [1984] 3 at paras. 14 and 35; and *Legality of Use of Force (Yugoslavia v. United States)*, ICJ Reports [1999] 916 at para. 19; see also *Case of the Free Zones of Upper Savoy and the District of Gex* (First Phase), Series A No. 22 (1929) at 13; *North Sea Continental Shelf*, ICJ Reports [1969] 3 at para. 87; and *Military and Paramilitary Activities in and against Nicaragua* (Merits), ICJ Reports [1986] 14 at paras. 290–1.

[38] Cf. *North Sea Continental Shelf*, ICJ Reports [1969] 3 at para. 85.

[39] Montesquieu, *Spirit of the Laws*, p. 8.

[40] Triepel, *Völkerrecht und Landesrecht*, pp. 2 and 5 ('[d]roit maritime, droit d'ambassade et de consular, droit militaire, ce qu'on appelle le droit privé international et le droit pénal international'; 'souveraineté, unions d'Etats, territoire d'Etat, servitudes internationales, nationalité, importance, conclusion, effets, contenu des traités internationaux').

[41] H. L. A. Hart, *The Concept of Law* (2nd edn, Oxford, 1994), pp. 229–30.

Hart's focus on 'legal rules' should not, however, be taken at face value.[42] The international law of coexistence contains few rules which attach well-defined consequences to well-defined antecedents, whether facts or conditions. While the definition of issues as international may often be clear-cut, more or less, it is a completely different matter for international law to provide a solution to the issues so referred from national law. Vagueness often seems unavoidable in cases where the need for the international law of coexistence cannot be met by relying on the territorial separation of states. This is the case where the issue is one of title to such territory; instead, the International Court has relied on 'the rule of equity' in maritime delimitation.[43] The territorial separation of states is also immaterial in cases where a need is felt not for separating state powers but for supervening them. It will often be possible to take some analogy from national law, an example being the classical principles regarding aliens. However, such an analogy is not always adopted. Moreover, from the perspective of a variety of national legal systems, analogies cannot be expected to produce anything close to an exact rule.

Nevertheless, in relation to an actual dispute between states a *non liquet* would be something of a surprise. One technique is for an international court to sidestep the international law of coexistence and its inherent vagueness, instead relying on the previous behaviour of particular states in some construction of acquiescence or implied consent. International lawyers may also seek comfort in the fact that the international law of coexistence is a law of exception, a law for the gaps. Basically, it is triggered by the need for specific solutions in specific instances of what are seen as serious clashes between national sovereigns. Thus, another technique is for international lawyers to confront issues of coexistence only when they materialise in specific cases, not worrying so much about general rules. The inherent vagueness of the international law of coexistence has not prevented lawyers from coming up with specific solutions in specific cases. The International Court has indeed drawn maritime boundaries despite the fact that at a general level it has not gone far in giving meaning to the term 'equity'. An often-quoted passage from the award rendered in the *Eastern Extension, Australasia & China Telegraph Co.* case comes to mind:

---

[42] Cf. *ibid.*, pp. 259–63.
[43] *North Sea Continental Shelf*, ICJ Reports [1969] 3 at para. 88; but see *ibid.*, para. 85.

International law, as well as domestic law, may not contain, and generally does not contain, express rules decisive of particular cases; but the function of jurisprudence is to resolve the conflict of opposing rights and interests by applying, in default of any specific provision of law, the corollaries of general principles, and so to find – exactly as in the mathematical sciences – the solution of the problem. This is the method of jurisprudence; it is the method by which the law has been gradually evolved in every country resulting in the definition and settlement of legal relations as well between States as between private individuals.[44]

Owing to its inherent vagueness, it may be difficult not to engage in an act of some law-making when applying the international law of coexistence; indeed, leaving aside attempts at codification, if there is a law-making process involved as regards the content of the international law of coexistence – as opposed to its scope, which is relatively well defined – it is controlled by lawyers assumed to apply the law, as distinct from politicians assumed to make it. According to Sir Robert Jennings, 'international legal scholars have an influence probably unparalleled since the jurisconsults of classical Roman law'.[45] As a result, the content of the international law of coexistence may be less static than its scope.

There are many factors that may influence what kind of response lawyers give when confronted with the need for the international law of coexistence. Some are of an ideological or cultural character,[46] concerning 'the spirit of the laws',[47] while others reflect values of a wider application associated with coexistence. The dominant factors are probably connected with legal tradition. State practice is yet another factor, but a subsidiary element at that, partly because any analysis of such

---

[44] See *Eastern Extension, Australasia & China Telegraph Co., Limited* v. *United States*, 6 RIAA 112 (1923) at 114–15; the President of the Tribunal, Henri Fromageot, was the spiritual father of Article 38(2) of the Statute of the International Court, providing that Article 38(1) 'shall not prejudice the power of the Court to decide a case *ex aequo et bono*, if the parties agree thereto', see *Records of Assembly: Committees* 1920, pp. 385–6 and 403 and also Series D No. 2, Add.3 (1936), p. 314.

[45] R. Y. Jennings, 'International Lawyers and the Progressive Development of International Law' in Jerzy Makarczyk (ed.), *Theory of International Law at the Threshold of the 21st Century: Essays in Honour of Krzysztof Skubiszewski* (The Hague, 1996), p. 413 at p. 413. See also Mohammed Bedjaoui, 'L'opportunité dans les décisions de la Cour internationale de Justice' in Laurence Boisson de Chazournes and Vera Gowlland-Debbas (eds.), *The International Legal System in Quest of Equity and Universality: Liber Amicorum Georges Abi-Saab* (The Hague, 2001), p. 563 at pp. 573–88.

[46] Cf. Friedmann, *Changing Structure*, pp. 297, 325, 331 and 379.

[47] See Philip Allott, *The Health of Nations: Society and Law Beyond the State* (Cambridge, 2002), pp. 246–7.

practice is fraught with practical difficulties.[48] It is neither practice, nor *opinio juris*, but a need felt by national lawyers for another kind of law other than national law that leads to the employment of so-called custom, or even of general principles, and in general drives this basic structure of international legal argument.

Some of the specific solutions given to specific cases, when taken together, may form a rule in relation to which it might be natural to conceive of the state as an international law subject. On very rare occasions, such rules may contradict each other where an incident involves more than one issue international in kind, an example being the *Legality of the Threat or Use of Nuclear Weapons* opinion concerning humanitarian law and 'the fundamental right of every State to survival'.[49] Apart from that, the formulation of rules will only be possible in the core of the international law of coexistence, like the exercise of power, as opposed to, for example, jurisdiction to legislate or adjudicate. Most of the specific solutions bred by the international law of coexistence can hardly be generalised. Indeed, it was the lack of rules combined with the need for an international law of coexistence that caused the discussion on *non liquet* in the Advisory Committee and brought in the formula of general principles.

Of course, members of formal or informal codification bodies such as the International Law Commission and the Institut de Droit International occasionally undertake the task of improving the law, or are asked to suggest what would be a progressive development of it. The same can be said about members of international courts, who may indeed find bold generalisations a convenient way to boost their argument. But precisely because such generalisations serve a specific decision in a specific case, there is no guarantee that they will be applied to subsequent cases. What can be expressed in general terms is often nothing but a need for

---

[48] Cf. *Military and Paramilitary Activities in and against Nicaragua* (Merits), ICJ Reports [1986] 14 at paras. 184 and 186.

[49] *Legality of the Threat or Use of Nuclear Weapons*, ICJ Reports [1996] 226 at para. 96. At first, the International Court stated that the use of nuclear weapons 'in fact seems scarcely reconcilable' with humanitarian law, *ibid.*, para. 95, while in para. 2(E) of the advice it stated that 'the threat or use of nuclear weapons would generally be contrary to the rules of international law applicable in armed conflict, and in particular the principles and rules of humanitarian law'. Significantly, the field as for which the International Court could not 'conclude definitively whether the threat or use of nuclear weapons would be lawful or unlawful' was relatively well defined, namely 'in an extreme circumstance of self-defence, in which the very survival of a State would be at stake'; this was the field where humanitarian law possibly yielded to another rule of the international law of coexistence.

international law without an articulation of any such law; this is basically the case, for example, with the balancing tests of state interests in the field of jurisdiction to legislate.[50]

The fact that national lawyers feel a need for international law does not make general rules readily available. Whereas this need determines the questions that confront international lawyers, and so determines the scope of the international law of coexistence, it does not help in finding the answers and determining its content. The result is an exceptional branch of law, where rules are rare. Yet it is law, or at least international law, for at the centre one finds an unmistakable need for law in specific cases.

The dynamic structure

The law of treaties

One aspect of the international law of coexistence neglected up to this point is the law of treaties. These are principles that govern, *inter alia*, the entry into force and the termination of treaties as well as their interpretation and application. Jean Bodin mentioned the principle *pacta sunt servanda* and assumed that contracts between sovereigns were regulated not by some national legal system but by *jus gentium*.[51] Both Gentili and Grotius made contributions to the law of treaties, so did later writers like Christian Wolff and Emmerich de Vattel.

It is generally assumed that contracts between private persons, and between a state and a private person, can be governed by a single system of national law.[52] The need for (private) international law is thought to go no further than, at most, a need for choosing between different national legal systems (although there have been attempts, also in recent times, to establish a '*lex mercatoria*' guided by a definition

---

[50] See International Law Association, *Report on the 67th Conference* (1996), pp. 520–32; and, e.g., A. V. Lowe, 'Public International Law and the Conflict of Laws: The European Response to the United States Export Administration Regulations' (1984) 33 *ICLQ* 515; *Timberlane Lumber Company et al.* v. *Bank of America et al.*, 66 ILR 270 (1976) at 280–6; and *Mannington Mills* v. *Congoleum Corp.*, 595 F 2d 1287 (1979) at 1296–8; cf. *Hartford Fire Insurance Co. and Others* v. *California and Others*, 100 ILR 566 (1993) at 585–8 and 596–602.

[51] Jean Bodin, *The Six Books of a Commonweale* (Cambridge, MA, 1962), pp. 72–3 and 112 (originally published 1576); see also Bodin, *On Sovereignty*, p. 45.

[52] See *Case concerning the Payment of Various Serbian Loans Issued in France*, Series A No. 20 (1929) at 41; cf. Grotius, *Jure Belli ac Pacis*, p. 390; and Vattel, *Le Droit des gens*, p. 160 (but see *ibid.*, p. 186).

of internationalism based on transborder elements, as distinct from involvement of the interests of a plurality of states).[53] But, as Bentham noted, '[t]here remain then the mutual transactions between sovereigns as such, for the subject of that branch of jurisprudence which may be properly and exclusively termed international'.[54]

History records no period about which it is known that contracts were not concluded between sovereigns. In the short history of international law, the Peace of Westphalia from 1648 holds a position equal to Grotius' *De Jure Belli ac Pacis Libri Tres*. Statesmen have continued to conclude contracts, the number and scope of which began to increase exponentially in the nineteenth century. It has hardly been suggested that these contracts come within national law. In the absence of an explicit provision to this effect, national lawyers would be surprised to hear if a contract between two or more sovereigns were made subject to the national law of one. Such contracts are international and presumably governed by (public) international law.[55]

Accordingly, the international law of coexistence accommodates a law of treaties capable of solving the specific questions that arise within the context of treaties. As with other issues, the need for supervening state powers does not in itself breed general rules or principles, as distinct from specific solutions, but the law of treaties is particularly rich in analogies taken from national legal systems.[56] As regards principles of treaty interpretation, Professor Dionisio Anzilotti, about whom it has

---

[53] Thus, it has become a minority view to find the basis of private international law in comity of nations or equivalent notions reflecting a need for coexistence between states: cf. Joseph Story, *Commentaries on the Conflict of Laws* (8th edn by Melville M. Bigelow, Boston, 1883), pp. 35–6, who relied on the following principle framed by Ulricus Huber in the seventeenth century: '[T]he rulers of every empire from comity admit that the laws of every people in force within its own limits ought to have the same force everywhere, so far as they do not prejudice the powers of rights of other governments, or of their citizens.' *Ibid.*, p. 29. For an English translation of Huber's brief monograph, *De Conflictu Legum in Diversis Imperiis*: see Ernest G. Lorenzen, *Selected Articles on the Conflict of Laws* (New Haven, 1947), pp. 162–80. Story, in turn, coined the term 'private international law': see Story, *Commentaries on Conflict of Laws*, pp. 9–10.

[54] Jeremy Bentham, *An Introduction to the Principles of Morals and Legislation* (2nd edn, London, 1823), p. 327. These include contracts between a state and an international organisation composed of states; cf. *Reparation for Injuries Suffered in the Service of the United Nations*, ICJ Reports [1949] 174 at 179–80.

[55] Cf., as regards treaty interpretation, *Maffezini v. Spain* (Jurisdiction), 5 ICSID Reports 396 (2000) at para. 29.

[56] Equally rich in analogies are the 'secondary' rules on state responsibility: cf. Crawford, *State Responsibility*, p. 21.

been said, correctly, that 'no judge has been so generous with the draft-ing of interpretation rules',[57] wrote that:

En l'absence de normes obligatoires d'interprétation, les divergences très impor-tantes qui subsistent entre quelques critères admis, à cet égard, dans les divers ordres juridiques, ne peuvent qu'avoir des répercussions sur l'interprétation du droit international, en rendant singulièrement plus difficile d'arriver à des con-clusions concordantes . . . Cette diversité de méthodes et de tendances qui est, sans aucun doute, un des principaux obstacles à l'interprétation uniforme des normes internationales, fera, de plus en plus, sentir sa fâcheuse influence à mesure que se développera l'activité des organes judiciaires internationaux dans lesquels toutes les tendances doivent être représentées et dans lequels il est besoin de faciliter à tout prix la possibilité d'arriver à un même résultat.[58]

On a general level the concept of treaty is rather vague. Whether a treaty has been concluded is 'a question of fact',[59] which depends on interpreta-tion.[60] Treaty obligations do not have to be contained in a text, nor is the conclusion of a treaty necessarily an explicit act. A pattern of behaviour, or just a single act or omission, can be sufficient, thus the doctrine of acquiescence. Implied treaties are sometimes couched in the language of custom, although they are still treated as treaties. One example is so-called 'local custom',[61] another is what according to one commenta-tor is termed 'modern custom . . . derived by a deductive process that begins with general statements of rules rather than particular instances of practice'.[62] As regards issues coming within the scope of the interna-tional law of coexistence, international courts may be keen to conceive and refer to implied treaties in order to compensate for the inherent vagueness of the international law of coexistence (and as an alternative to judicial law-making with a wider bearing).

---

[57] J. P. Fockema Andreae, *An Important Chapter from the History of Legal Interpretation: The Jurisdiction of the First Permanent Court of International Justice, 1922–1940* (Leiden, 1948), p. 129.

[58] Dionisio Anzilotti, *Cours de droit internaional* (Paris, 1929), pp. 113–14.

[59] Cf. *Status of Eastern Carelia*, Series B No. 5 (1923) at 26 and 28.

[60] *Aegean Sea Continental Shelf*, ICJ Reports [1978] 3 at para. 96; and *Maritime Delimitation and Territorial Questions between Qatar and Bahrain* (Jurisdiction and Admissibility), ICJ Reports [1994] 112 at paras. 22–5.

[61] Cf. *Colombian–Peruvian Asylum Case*, ICJ Reports [1950] 266 at 276–8; and *Case concerning Right of Passage over Indian Territory* (Merits), ICJ Reports [1960] 6 at 39; and also *Jurisdiction of the European Commission of the Danube between Galatz and Braila*, Series B No. 14 (1927) at 17; and *Free City of Danzig and International Labour Organization*, Series B No. 18 (1930) at 12–13.

[62] Anthea Elizabeth Roberts, 'Traditional and Modern Approaches to Customary International Law: A Reconciliation' (2001) 95 *AJIL* 757 at 758; and see *ibid.*, pp. 764–5, 768–70 and 776–9.

Extending international law: the international law of cooperation and conceptions of the state

The result of contracts between states being allocated to international law, and the treatment of them as 'law', as opposed to mere 'obligations', is that international law is extended and that international legal argument knows another structure in addition to the basic structure. This is so, although prominent writers belonging to the natural law tradition like Grotius and Vattel fitted treaty law into the basic structure, which is based on the conception of the state as a national sovereign. In their view, treaty law should supplement the inherently vague international law of coexistence, normally on a basis of reciprocity, and so be confined to those issues for which national lawyers identified a need for international law.[63] In the twentieth century, if not before, treaties would seem to have outgrown that conception.[64] Many, if not most, treaties might have come into existence to regulate issues considered by negotiators and politicians as being international, interesting a plurality of states, although below the threshold of the international law of coexistence.

A consequence of the international law of cooperation belonging to a different structure of international legal argument is the use of other conceptions of the state than the state as a national sovereign. Thus, treaty-making has invited international lawyers to conceive of the state, not as a national sovereign but, in some instances, as an international sovereign. Because the making of the international law of cooperation takes place independently of the national context, and so the conception of the state as a national sovereign, whether seen as a competence or a fact, it seems adequate to conceive of the state that agrees to treaty engagements as an international sovereign. Here, the starting-point of international law is not the question: is there such a serious clash between national sovereigns that international law must be deemed to

---

[63] Cf. Grotius, *Jure Belli ac Pacis*, pp. 394–7, 413–14 and 418–19; and Vattel, *Le Droit des gens*, pp. 165–9, 171, 207 and 213–14. See also Gentili, *Iure Belli*, p. 425; and Christian Wolff, *Jus Gentium Methodo Scientifica Pertractatum* (Oxford, 1934), p. 191 (originally published 1749).

[64] Although there are examples to the contrary: see Alf Ross, *A Text-book of International Law* (London, 1947), pp. 57, 77–8, 184, 223, 227–30, 237, 239 and 271–2; George Schwarzenberger, *The Frontiers of International Law* (London, 1962), pp. 30–1; and Friedmann, *Changing Structure*, p. 94. A restatement of this view is the overall message, it would seem, of Evangelos Raftopoulos, *The Inadequacy of the Contractual Analogy in the Law of Treaties* (Athens, 1990). Cf. Ole Spiermann, 'A National Lawyer Takes Stock: Professor Ross' Textbook and Other Forays into International Law' (2003) 14 *EJIL* 675 at 687–9.

exist for the purpose of regulating it? The question is rather: have international sovereigns made international law, i.e., have they concluded a treaty?

An affirmative answer to the former question leads one to the international law of coexistence, while an affirmative answer to the latter question to the international law of cooperation. In both cases it would seem appropriate now to conceive of the state as an international law subject rather than as a national or an international sovereign. When, in 2002, Judges Higgins, Kooijmans and Buergenthal identified a 'vertical notion of the authority of action . . . significantly different from the horizontal system of international law envisaged in the "*Lotus*" case',[65] they relied on newer treaties regarding so-called 'universal' jurisdiction and so on the conception of the state as an international law subject, as opposed to the conception of the state as a national sovereign. The conception of the state as an international law subject has much appeal in respect of the international law of cooperation, which also mainly consists of rules. In contrast, most specific cases coming within the international law of coexistence are solved not by subsuming facts under a rule in respect of which the state can be seen as an international law subject, but by considering the need for international law to prevent, or regulate, a specific clash between states conceived of as national sovereigns. Besides, in respect of issues international in kind, which come within the international law of coexistence, the conception of the state as a national sovereign points towards international law, making the adoption of a conception of the state as an international law subject less urgent.

It is also necessary to consider the consequences of giving negative answers to the above-mentioned questions, as if to say that no international law is involved. As to the question: is there such a serious clash between national sovereigns that international law must be deemed to exist for the purpose of regulating it?, a negative answer lets the matter rest with the national principle of self-containedness; then each national sovereign is a 'sole judge'. Similarly, there is the implication of a negative answer to the question: have international sovereigns made international law? Here, where international law is lacking, it makes no sense to conceive of the state in terms of international law, that is, as an international law subject or as an international sovereign. For these cases,

---

[65] See Judges Higgins, Kooijmans and Buergenthal's joint separate opinion, para. 51, in *Case concerning the Arrest Warrant of 11 April 2000*, ICJ Reports [2002] 3.

only the conception of the state as a national sovereign remains, and thus each state is deemed to be free; 'all that can be required of a State is that it should not overstep the limits which international law places upon its jurisdiction; within these limits, its title to exercise jurisdiction rests in its sovereignty'.[66]

The overall difference between the two structures of international legal argument has to do with three conceptions of the state. The basic structure centres on the conception of the state which is familiar to national law, namely the state as a national sovereign. This conception came to the fore in the writings of, among others, Jean Bodin and Charles de Montesquieu. The basic structure of argument has national law as its starting-point and recognises only a residual need for international law. In contrast, the dynamic structure has been underpinned by the conception of the state as an international sovereign and the conception of the state as an international law subject, the latter being hierarchically superior to the former. It evolves out from international law and only recognises state freedom, including national law-making, as a residual solution if no international law has been made.

Although a distinction between the making and the application of international law may be relevant as regards the international law of cooperation, interpreting the rules that it contains may be complicated, notably if the interpreter does not abide by the conception of the state as an international law subject. It is difficult not to see the abandonment, even if only temporarily, of the conception of the state as an international law subject as a challenge to the binding force of international law, yet there are many, also somewhat less dramatic forms, in which the attractiveness of other conceptions of the state may express themselves. Contracts between sovereigns are allocated to international law, as opposed to national law, and their treated not only as 'obligations', but as 'law'; the interpreter's choice of conception of the state depends on his or her notion of law in the specific context, as well as on whether it is truly accepted that the contract equates to 'law', as opposed to mere 'obligations'.

That the interpreter may have a choice, albeit not a free choice, is indicated by the variety of general principles of treaty interpretation, the first principle being that where there is a treaty there is also an

---

[66] *The Case of the SS Lotus*, Series A No. 10 (1927) at 19; and see also *Military and Paramilitary Activities in and against Nicaragua* (Merits), ICJ Reports [1986] 14 at para. 269; and *Legality of the Threat or Use of Nuclear Weapons*, ICJ Reports [1996] 226 at para. 52.

interpretation, that is, an answer to each and every specific question as to the meaning (and application) of the treaty.[67] Also, in this context, a *non liquet* looks a remote possibility.

Schools of treaty interpretation

The International Law Commission had been working on codifying the law of treaties virtually since its establishment in 1949; when finally adopting its draft in 1966 it was referred to as 'the opus magnum of the International Law Commission'.[68] Treaty interpretation was the last topic approached by the Commission, as the first three special rapporteurs on the law of treaties had not dealt with it. It was no secret, however, that two of the special rapporteurs, Sir Hersch Lauterpacht and Sir Gerald Fitzmaurice, held strong and differing views on the subject. Lauterpacht interpreted the decisions of the Permanent Court and its successor, the International Court, in accordance with a 'subjective' school of treaty interpretation, which was 'subjective' in the sense that it gave priority to the intention of the parties.[69] In contrast, Fitzmaurice systematised the decisions of the International Court so that they were informed by an 'objective' school of treaty interpretation centring on the text of the treaty.[70] The differences between the two schools were emphasised within the work of the Institut de Droit International

---

[67] See Articles 16 (1899) and 38 (1907) of the Hague Conventions for the Pacific Settlement of International Disputes; Article 13(2) of the Covenant of the League of Nations; and Article 36(2) of the Statute of the International Court. From the early practice of the latter, see *Admission of a State to the United Nations (Charter, Art. 4)*, ICJ Reports [1947–8] 57 at 61. See also Charles de Visscher, *Problèmes d'interprétation judiciaire en droit international public* (Paris, 1963), pp. 22–5.

[68] Manfred Lachs, 'The Law of Treaties: Some General Reflections on the Report of the International Law Commission' in Pierre Lalive and Jacques Freymond (eds.), *Recueil d'études de droit international en hommage à Paul Guggenheim* (Geneva, 1968), p. 391 at p. 391.

[69] E.g., H. Lauterpacht, *The Development of International Law by the Permanent Court of International Justice* (London, 1934), p. 69; H. Lauterpacht, 'Restictive Interpretation and the Principle of Effectiveness in the Interpretation of Treaties' (1949) 26 *BYIL* 48 at 62, 69 and 75–6; and H. Lauterpacht, *The Development of International Law by the International Court* (London, 1958), pp. 27 and 227; cf., however, (1950) 43-I *Annuaire*, pp. 370–3, 380 and 383–6.

[70] See G. G. Fitzmaurice, 'The Law and Procedure of the International Court of Justice: Treaty Interpretation and Certain Other Treaty Points' (1951) 28 *BYIL* 1 at 9–10; and G. G. Fitzmaurice, 'The Law and Procedure of the International Court of Justice, 1951–54: Treaty Interpretation and Other Treaty Points' (1957) 34 *BYIL* 203 at 211–12. Cf. H. W. A. Thirlway, 'The Law and Procedure of the International Court of Justice, 1960–1989: Part Three' (1991) 62 *BYIL* 1 at 18–19.

on treaty interpretation. Lauterpacht had been the Institut's first rapporteur on the matter, but following his election to the International Court it had been with Fitzmaurice as the new rapporteur that in 1956 the Institut adopted its resolution favouring objective, textual interpretation.[71]

Sir Humphrey Waldock, the International Law Commission's fourth and final special rapporteur on the law of treaties, was naturally influenced by the preceding discussions. Waldock tried to evade the battleground by playing down the importance of the decisions of the International Court and its predecessor in this their main field. In his third report to the Commission, which introduced the topic of treaty interpretation, the special rapporteur wrote:

The jurisprudence of international tribunals furnishes examples of all the different approaches to interpretation – textual, subjective and teleological. But it also shows that, if the textual method of interpretation predominates, none of these approaches is exclusively the correct one, and that their use in any particular case is to some extent a matter of choice and appreciation. This does not necessarily mean that there is no obligatory rule in regard to methods of interpretation; but it does mean that there is a certain discretionary element also on this point.[72]

Consequently, Waldock recommended the Commission in its draft to omit 'principles whose appropriateness in any given case depends so much on the particular context and on a subjective appreciation of varying circumstances'.

It did not follow from a principle depending on 'the particular context' that 'a subjective appreciation of varying circumstances' was involved in applying the principle. Yet this conclusion was approved by the Commission.[73] The general rule of interpretation contained in Article 31 of the 1969 Vienna Convention on the Law of Treaties does not take a decisive stand on the dispute between the objective and the subjective schools of interpretation.[74] However, there is more to be said about treaty interpretation, especially if one abandons the notion that principles of treaty

---

[71] See (1956) 46 *Annuaire*, pp. 364–5. It was heavily relied upon in *Asian Agricultural Products Limited v. Sri Lanka*, 4 ICSID Reports 246 (1990) at 263–6; cf. *ibid.*, p. 270.

[72] YILC 1964-II, p. 54.   [73] YILC 1966-II, p. 218.

[74] Article 31(1) reads: 'A treaty shall be interpreted in good faith in accordance with the ordinary meaning to be given to the terms of the treaty in their context and in the light of its object and purpose.' This objective approach is balanced by Article 31(4), according to which '[a] special meaning shall be given to a term if it is established that the parties so intended'. Cf. McDougal, in United Nations Conference on the Law of Treaties, *Official Records* (New York, 1969–71), vol. 1, p. 168.

interpretation must be applicable to all instances of interpretation.[75] During the discussions in the International Law Commission, there was a tendency to view treaty interpretation as, in Shabtai Rosenne's words, 'an academic intellectual exercise performed in the abstract'.[76] And the objective and subjective schools are indeed divided by questions of the highest academic order, but with some practical importance, namely the notion of a treaty and, by implication, the conception of the state.[77]

The notion of a treaty is defined in relation to a conception of the state, either as a binding agreement between states or as an instrument, normally a text, binding upon states. Here the term 'states' carries two different connotations. As for the former definition, a treaty is an agreement between international sovereigns. This definition, which resembles that of a contract in national law, or a *Vertrag* in *Völkerrecht und Landesrecht*, fuels a subjective approach to treaty interpretation, that is, an approach focusing on the intentions of the international law-makers and possibly the preparatory work, or subsequent practice. In contrast, the latter definition reflects the conception of the state as an international law subject and corresponds to Triepel's *Vereinbarung*. In this case, the analogy being an act of legislation, the interpreter will be prompted to emancipate the treaty from its fathers, thus giving it a more objective interpretation based on its text or its object and purpose (teleological interpretation).

The report submitted by Lauterpacht to the Institut in 1950, and the ensuing debate, illustrates the importance of conceptions of the state to treaty interpretation. Lauterpacht gave no explicit reason as to why he saw the unveiling of the common intentions of the parties as the crux of treaty interpretation, yet his general preference for the conception of the state as an international sovereign was indicated by his reasoned rejections of other principles of treaty interpretation. For example, teleological interpretation was approached somewhat reluctantly for the interpreter 'ne faudrait pas remplir ces fonctions quasi-législatives de manière si délibérée ou si énergique qu'on soit fondé à reprocher au tribunal de substituer sa propre intention à celle des

---

[75] Cf. Lauterpacht, 'Restrictive Interpretation', pp. 51–2; J. H. W. Verzijl, *The Jurisprudence of the World Court* (Leiden, 1965), vol. 1, pp. 504–5; Antonio Cassese, *International Law* (Oxford, 2001), p. 133; and Ian Brownlie, *Principles of Public International Law* (6th edn, Oxford, 2003), pp. 398 and 602. As for Verzijl, cf. *Pinson v. Mexico*, 5 RIAA 329 (1928) at 422.

[76] YILC 1964-I, p. 289.

[77] Cf. Julius Stone, 'Fictional Elements in Treaty Interpretation: A Study in the International Judicial Process' (1953–4) 1 *Sydney Law Review* 344 at 364.

Parties',[78] that is, the states, not the interpreters, were the international sovereigns. A general, sovereignty-based principle of restrictive interpretation was rejected because international sovereigns presumably did not want to restrict international law: 'les traités ont pour objet réel de déroger à des principes généraux reconnus et de limiter la liberté d'action des Etats par l'énoncé d'obligations spécifiques.'[79] And textual interpretation, if standing alone, was said to give 'une impression troublante d'inachève' and indeed to be equal to 'adopter la méthode de la "Begriffsjurisprudenz"'.[80]

Objective interpretation is often justified by the presumption that the text reflects the intentions of the parties. But while Lauterpacht could support this presumption,[81] lawyers favouring objective interpretation do not normally treat it as merely a starting-point. Indeed, textual interpretation, if producing a 'clear' result, is often said to be the end of interpretation, even though other indications as to the intentions of the parties can easily disturb clarity; the same goes for teleological interpretation. Whereas a conclusion based solely on the text, or the object and purpose, seems premature to the subjective school, it is embraced by the objective school because, in the mind of the interpreter, the conception of the state as an international law subject has been substituted for the conception of the state as an international sovereign. It is true that lawyers are seldom explicit on this point, yet a shift towards focusing on the conception of the state as an international law subject underlay the views of, for example, Sir Eric Beckett, one of the main opponents of Lauterpacht's report. According to Beckett, 'the treaty, when once signed, assumes, if I may so put it, a sort of life of its own'.[82] Similarly, Lord McNair appeared to conceive of states as international law subjects, as opposed to international sovereigns, when writing that:

[i]l me paraît que plus on permet le recours aux travaux préparatoires, plus on introduit un élément d'incertitude et plus on relâche les liens obligeant les parties. Plus on encourage les avocats à fouiller dans une masse de travaux préparatoires, plus on affaiblit les termes du traité.[83]

Max Huber made statements similar to those of Beckett and McNair and, in a passage that was later quoted in the International Law Commission's commentary on its general rule of interpretation, he added

---

[78] (1950) 43-I *Annuaire*, p. 421.   [79] *Ibid.*, p. 407.   [80] *Ibid.*, pp. 395 and 397.
[81] *Ibid.*, p. 387.   [82] *Ibid.*, p. 444.
[83] *Ibid.*, p. 450. A similar rationale lay behind Vattel's famous first principle of interpretation, according to which '[i]t is not permissible to interpret what has no need of interpretation': Vattel, *Le Droit des gens*, pp. 199 and 213; cf. *ibid.*, p. 191.

that '[l]e texte signé est, sauf de rares exceptions, la seule et la plus récente expression de la volonté commune des parties'.[84] Thereby, Huber assumed that the states were no longer international sovereigns but, it may be inferred, international law subjects. In 1968, referring to this argument, Jiménez de Aréchaga noted: 'If respect for the wording of a treaty that had been signed and ratified was not something sacred, if the parties were to be allowed freely to invoke their supposed real will, an essential advantage of written and conventional law would be lost.'[85]

Let it be added that, to use Rosenne's words again, whatever the 'academic exercise performed in the abstract', choices between principles of interpretation are hardly general ones between 'schools'.[86] The choice depends on the specific issue and the circumstances of the case. The idea is not that the interpreter's choice of conception of the state is necessarily the sole factor determining the preferred method of interpretation. But this conception has an impact. In a specific case, if one conceives of the state as an international law subject, the issue stays with the international law of cooperation and an objective interpretation is more compelling. On the other hand, by adopting the conception of the state as an international sovereign, the interpreter is concerned with the act of international law-making that drew, and draws, the line between the international law of cooperation and the residual principle of state freedom. This may reflect a certain doubt as to the making of the international law of cooperation and involve, in the words of Sir Humphrey Waldock, 'very real dangers . . . for the integrity of the meaning of the treaty';[87] but it may also just be a witness to a Benthamite conception of the international law of cooperation as being law, or perhaps relational rights and obligations, between states, as opposed to law above states.

A somewhat parallel case is the interpretation of declarations submitted under the Optional Clause contained in Article 36(2) of the Statute of the International Court of Justice. If such declarations contain reservations, questions of interpretation arise which are not treated as ordinary questions of treaty interpretation. This is because construing reservations has to do with the law-making act of the international sovereign, as distinct from a treaty text, the content of which is binding on the participating states conceived of as international law subjects. There is

---

[84] (1952) 44-I *Annuaire*, p. 199, as quoted in YILC 1966-II, p. 220, note 128.
[85] *Law of Treaties Conference*, vol. 1, p. 170.
[86] Cf. Lauterpacht in (1950) 43-I *Annuaire*, pp. 424–32; and Beckett, *ibid.*, p. 442.
[87] *Law of Treaties Conference*, vol. 1, p. 184.

a difference between interpreting Article 36(2) of the Statute and interpreting the declarations submitted under this provision. In the words of
the International Court, 'the provisions of . . . [the Vienna] Convention
[on the Law of Treaties] may only apply analogously to the extent compatible with the *sui generis* character of the unilateral acceptance of the
Court's jurisdiction'.[88] As regards the declarations submitted under the
Optional Clause, the International Court has referred to 'the principle of
interpretation whereby a reservation to a declaration of acceptance of
the compulsory jurisdiction of the Court is to be interpreted in a natural
and reasonable way, with appropriate regard for the intentions of the
reserving State and the purpose of the reservation'.[89]

That being said, it is a little odd to refer to unilateral acceptances
as having a '*sui generis* character', taking into account the present conception of treaty reservations following *Reservations to the Convention on
the Prevention and Punishment of the Crime of Genocide*.[90] According to one
authority, although concerned with a different matter, 'taking refuge
in the concept of *sui generis* is always a solution of last resort and an
admission of helplessness'.[91] All treaty engagements are undertaken by
unilateral acts and it is difficult to see the ground on which to distinguish the interpretation of treaty reservations in general from the
interpretation of reservations contained in declarations submitted under
the Optional Clause (cf. Article 2(1)(d) of the Vienna Convention on the
Law of Treaties) or unilateral declarations generally.[92] The view that,
in respect of the Optional Clause, reservations 'do not by their terms

---

[88] *Fisheries Jurisdiction (Spain v. Canada)*, ICJ Reports [1998] 432 at para. 46. As for the
special character of the Optional Clause: see *Military and Paramilitary Activities in and
against Nicaragua* (Jurisdiction and Admissibility), ICJ Reports [1984] 392 at paras.
59–60, relying on *Nuclear Tests (Australia v. France)*, ICJ Reports [1974] 253 at paras. 43
and 46 and *(New Zealand v. France)*, ICJ Reports [1974] 457 at paras. 46 and 49; and also,
e.g., C. H. M. Waldock, 'Decline of the Optional Clause' (1955–6) 32 *BYIL* 244 at 254;
and Shabtai Rosenne, *The Law and Practice of the International Court, 1920–1996* (The
Hague, 1997), pp. 769–70 and 822–31. Cf. Malgosia Fitzmaurice, 'The Optional Clause
System and the Law of Treaties: Issues of Interpretation in Recent Jurisprudence of the
International Court of Justice' (1999) 20 *AYIL* 127.

[89] *Ibid.*, para. 54; and see also *Anglo-Iranian Oil Co. Case* (Jurisdiction), ICJ Reports [1952] 93
at 104–5; *Case of Certain Norwegian Loans*, ICJ Reports [1957] 9 at 27; *Aegean Sea
Continental Shelf*, ICJ Reports [1978] 3 at paras. 63–81; and *Aerial Incident of 10 August
1999*, ICJ Reports [2000] 12 at paras. 42–4.

[90] ICJ Reports [1951] 15.

[91] Alain Pellet, 'Fourth Report on Reservations to Treaties' (United Nations Document
A/CN.4/499, 1999), para. 50.

[92] See also Hersch Lauterpacht, YILC 1953-II, pp. 102–3, referring to *Question of Jaworzina
(Polish–Czechoslovakian Frontier)*, Series B No. 8 (1923) at 30.

derogate from a wider acceptance already given' but rather 'operate to define the parameters of the State's acceptance' applies to reservations to multilateral treaties in general.[93] And, indeed, the International Law Commission has broadened the interpretative approach of the International Court in respect of declarations under the Optional Clause and applied it to treaty reservations.[94] The difference between interpreting reservations and treaties is, it should be added, mainly due to the subjective school not being dominant in treaty interpretation.

Decisions adopted by organs of international organisations pursuant to a constituting treaty may also be considered in this context. A significant example is resolutions adopted by the Security Council under Chapter VII of the United Nations Charter, which may be binding under Article 25. In deciding whether a particular resolution was binding, the International Court adopted a 'subjective' approach:

> The language of a resolution of the Security Council should be carefully analysed before a conclusion can be made as to its binding effect. In view of the nature of the powers under Article 25, the question whether they have been in fact exercised is to be determined in each case, having regard to the terms of the resolution to be interpreted, the discussions leading to it, the Charter provisions invoked and, in general, all circumstances that might assist in determining the legal consequences of the resolution of the Security Council.[95]

This suggests that in the context of the Security Council, at least when deciding on the binding nature of a resolution, states are seen as international sovereigns negotiating political solutions rather than international law subjects bound by the solutions thus adopted.[96] The latter

---

[93] Cf. *Fisheries Jurisdiction (Spain v. Canada)*, ICJ Reports [1998] 432 at para. 44; and also *Case concerning Right of Passage over Indian Territory* (Merits), ICJ Reports [1960] 6 at 34; and *Southern Pacific Properties (Middle East) Limited v. Egypt* (Jurisdiction No. 2), 3 ICSID Reports 131 (1988) at 142 and 158.

[94] See Commentary on Guideline 1.3.1, paras. 5–12, as adopted on first reading: YILC 1999-II.2, para. 470. Cf. Alain Pellet, 'Third Report on Reservations to Treaties' (United Nations Document A/CN.4.491/Add.4, 1998), paras. 386–414; and Alain Pellet, 'Fifth Report on Reservations to Treaties' (United Nations Document A.CN.4/508/Add.1, 2000), paras. 179–96. See also Victor Rodríguez Cedeno, 'Fourth Report on Unilateral Acts of States' (United Nations Document A/CN.4/519, 2001), paras. 126–53; and Victor Rodríguez Cedeno, 'Fifth Report on Unilateral Acts of States' (United Nations Document A/CN.4/525/Add.1, 2002), paras. 123–35.

[95] *Legal Consequences for States of the Continued Presence of South Africa in Namibia (South West Africa) notwithstanding Security Council Resolution 276 (1970)*, ICJ Reports [1971] 15 at para. 114.

[96] See C. F. Amerasinghe, 'Interpretation of Texts in Open International Organizations' (1994) 65 *BYIL* 175 at 264; and Michael C. Wood, 'The Interpretation of Security Council Resolutions' (1998) 2 *Max Planck Yearbook of United Nations Law* 73 at 93–5.

conception of the state would suggest a more objective approach than adopted by the International Court.[97]

The openness of the international law of cooperation

Contracts are binding, whether the parties are individuals or states. But, unlike contracts between individuals, contracts between states are allocated to international law. National law is unsuited because the contracts are binding and international in form, the parties being states. As a framework for this international law of cooperation, a need has arisen for the international law of coexistence to provide its own law of contracts, that is, the law of treaties, of which treaty interpretation forms an integral part.

Treaty interpretation, 'the life of the dead letter',[98] has produced a worse impression on international lawyers than necessary. In what has been said to be an 'understatement',[99] the International Law Commission heralded '[t]he interpretation of documents' as 'to some extent an art, not an exact science'.[100] But, whereas the achievements of lawyers seldom excite talent scouts from the art world, to greet treaty interpretation, and law in general, as a science is perhaps to anticipate one or two scientific revolutions, and accompanying paradigm shifts, that have yet to come. Although it may make little sense to say very much about the subject without reference to a specific treaty, the cacophony of general principles is not just a result of so much depending on politicians, or the law-making process. In particular, the overarching dispute between an objective and a subjective school is mainly due to disagreement as to how specific treaties are conceived and the accompanying conceptions of the state, either as an international law subject or as an international sovereign. More examples, which relate to the hierarchy between the two structures of international legal argument, are provided in the following sections.

---

[97] Cf. Jochen Abr. Frowein, 'Unilateral Interpretation of Security Council Resolutions: A Threat to Collective Security?' in Christiane Philipp (ed.), *Liber Amicorum Günther Jaenicke: Zum 85. Geburtstag* (Berlin, 1998), p. 97 at p. 99. It should be added that authorisations of the use of force may be interpreted strictly as a consequence of the conception of the state as a national sovereign and the international law of coexistence, as opposed to the national principle of self-containedness; cf. *ibid.*, p. 112. Similarly, Frowein and Krisch in Bruno Simma (ed.), *The Charter of the United Nations: A Commentary* (2nd edn, Oxford, 2002), pp. 713 and 759.

[98] Robert Phillimore, *Commentaries upon International Law* (3rd edn, London, 1882), vol. 2, p. 95.

[99] Anthony Aust, *Modern Treaty Law and Practice* (Cambridge, 2000), p. 184.

[100] YILC 1966-II, p. 218.

It is possible to avoid some of the general confusion prompted by the totality of equally valid principles of treaty interpretation by solidifying them. While the conception of the state as an international sovereign, and thus subjective interpretation, may be relevant in respect of reservations to multilateral treaties, when interpreting the content of multilateral treaties, as accepted by states, the favoured conception would seem to be the state as an international law subject, the result being an objective treaty interpretation. Basically, this is simply a reflection of the conception of the state as an international law subject being hierarchically superior over the conception of the state as an international sovereign (or, in other words, the changing of international law being governed by international law).

The double structure

Recapitulation

The mainstay of the model of international argument used in this book is three different conceptions of the state, namely the conceptions of the state as a national sovereign, as an international sovereign and as an international law subject. On this basis, lawyers deal with and discuss international law within two structures. The main question is not one of choosing between the intentions of the different conceptions of the state, but one of extensions and the categorisation of issues within the structures.

One of the two structures, the basic structure, advances from the national principle of self-containedness (and the conception of the state as a national sovereign) to the international law of coexistence (still mainly the conception of the state as a national sovereign); the line dividing the two categories reflects national lawyers' needs for a common legal system that supplements the several national legal systems in respect of issues involving conflicting state interests (thus also based on the conception of the state as a national sovereign). The other, dynamic structure advances from the international law of cooperation (and, at least as a starting-point, the conception of the state as an international law subject) to the residual principle of sovereignty (the conception of the state as a national sovereign), the dividing line being generated by treaty making (reflecting the conception of the state as an international sovereign).

Dividing lines are drawn between the national principle of self-containedness and the international law of coexistence and between the international law of cooperation and the residual principle of state freedom. Within each structure the issue in question is either placed within international law, whether the international law of coexistence or the international law of cooperation, or, if there is no international law, with the state conceived of as a national sovereign, free to make national law, whether expressed in terms of self-containedness or residual freedom. What makes each of the two structures normative is that, in practice as well as in principle, lawyers do not have a free hand in categorising issues. It is not left with the individual lawyer to decide whether there is such a clash between the interests of national sovereigns that it triggers the international law of coexistence. Nor can it be said to be a matter of the individual lawyer's will whether a treaty has been concluded, explicitly or implicitly.

The two structures of international legal argument are in a sense the opposite of each other: the basic structure advances from the national to the international, the dynamic structure from the international to the national. Each and every issue may be categorised within both structures, often with different results. Accordingly, even if accepting that each structure taken on its own is normative, the question remains whether choosing between the structures is governed by international law. An answer in the negative and this model of international legal argument would reproduce the indeterminacy arguments advanced by, among others, Professors Kennedy and Koskenniemi.[101] They are part of a 'critical' legal studies movement associated with a particular national legal system.[102] The opposite structures with which they are concerned have mainly to do with the justification of international law and so not relevant to international legal argument as such;[103] this is because they

---

[101] Cf. David Kennedy, *International Legal Structures* (Baden-Baden, 1987), pp. 29–54 and *passim*; and Marti Koskenniemi, *From Apology to Utopia: The Structure of International Legal Argument* (Helsinki, 1989), pp. 42–50.

[102] See Roberto Mangabeira Unger, *The Critical Legal Studies Movement* (Cambridge, MA, 1983).

[103] Concerning unilateral declarations, *rebus sic stantibus* and custom, see Kennedy, *International Legal Structures*, pp. 54–99 and 104–5: '[i]t is about the sources of normative authority in a system of autonomous sovereigns'; '[s]ources discourse is the doctrinal counterpart to the obsession of theory with questions of the legitimacy, strength, and authority of international law'. Likewise in respect of jurisdiction, diplomatic protection and state responsibility, *ibid.*, pp. 151–88; and in respect of the law of the sea, the use of force and humanitarian law, *ibid.*, pp. 201–86. See also Koskenniemi, *Apology to Utopia*, pp. 25, 44 and 50: 'I shall argue . . . that law is incapable of providing convincing justifications to the solution of normative problems'; cf., however, *ibid.*, pp. 201 and 205.

ground international legal argument, and its indeterminacy, on the conception of the state as an international sovereign, as distinct from the conception of the state as a national sovereign. The model developed in this book is ultimately based on the latter conception and reflects the opposite view that international law is essential where choosing between the basic and the dynamic structures of international legal argument. Thus, there are not merely two structures of international legal argument, but a double structure in which the two structures are hierarchically ordered. The questions where in each structure to categorise a specific issue, and which structure to treat as the hierarchically privileged, form a pertinent and sometimes difficult task confronting, for example, the members of an international court. Categorising specific issues within the double structure may be uncertain; obviously, categorisations may also change over time. Nevertheless, it takes a distortion of international law, alienating it from national as well as international lawyers, to conclude that lawyers may choose between the two structures at will as if moving in vicious circles.

Taking the two structures together as a double structure of international legal argument, discussions of a general hierarchy between sovereignty and bindingness are misconceived. From the international lawyer's point of view, sovereignty does not carry a fixed, general meaning, nor are sovereignty and international law mutually exclusive. Sovereignty is neither *passé*, nor all-embracing. In respect of issues coming within the national principle of self-containedness, it can be said that sovereignty restricts, if not excludes, international law (sovereignty *contra legem*), while the international law of coexistence may furnish examples of international law determining sovereignty (sovereignty *infra legem*). In yet other cases, those that fall under the international law of cooperation, international law can indeed be said to have gone beyond sovereignty, thus the conception of the state as an international law subject, which implies that sovereignty is not, *prima facie*, relevant in treaty interpretation. In respect of issues that do not fall under the international law of cooperation, while belonging to the same dynamic structure of international legal argument, there is a residual principle of state freedom that makes sovereignty supplement international law (sovereignty *praeter legem*). In addition, sovereignty determines international law in the sense that states are free to conclude treaties.

The variety of meanings given to sovereignty emphasises the importance of the hierarchical relationship between the two structures of which the double structure consists. As already pointed to, an issue may

be categorised within both structures with different results. Such difference, of course, does not materialise if the issue belongs to the national
principle of self-containedness under the basic structure and the residual principle of freedom under the dynamic structure; for both principles point back to the conception of the state as a national sovereign.
Moreover, if categorised with the international law of coexistence under
the basic structure, there is hardly any doubt that the residual principle of state freedom under the dynamic structure yields; or rather, the
residual principle leads back to the conception of the state as a national
sovereign, which in turn points to the international law of coexistence.
Problems as to the hierarchical relationship between the two structures
of international legal argument are limited to issues that under the
dynamic structure are categorised with the international law of cooperation, and so in practice these problems find their most urgent form
in treaty interpretation. The international law of cooperation is a fixed
part of the double structure, yet in a specific case an interpreter may not
conceive of the state as an international law subject and it will affect
his or her interpretation. In addition to the dispute within the dynamic
structure between objective and subjective schools of treaty interpretation, and the underlying conceptions of the state as an international law
subject and an international sovereign, other principles of treaty interpretation appeal to interpreters, depending on how much room they
give to the basic structure of international legal argument based on the
conception of the state as a national sovereign and the categorisation of
the subject matter, or issue, thereunder. This will be illustrated in the
following.

The national principle of self-containedness in treaty interpretation

The principle of restrictive interpretation, according to which the interpretation which is less onerous to the obligated state should be preferred, causing less interference with its freedom, does not follow from
the conception of the state as an international law subject, nor the conception of the state as an international sovereign: it has to do with the
conception of the state as a national sovereign. When a treaty regulates
an issue otherwise within the national principle of self-containedness,
an interpreter conceiving the state as a national sovereign will be drawn
towards a restrictive interpretation, possibly while invoking principles
of good faith and *pacta sunt servanda*. An example is European Community law, where one of the main concepts is that of a Community, or
even a Union, having partly replaced the national sovereigns so that it

enjoys the benefits of hitherto national prerogatives. By way of contrast, Community lawyers portray treaty interpretation under international law as according a pivotal status to restrictive interpretation, thereby operating in a peculiar 'school' of thought that certainly says more about Community law than treaty interpretation in general.[104]

Two other examples may be mentioned. In the early case law of the European Court of Human Rights, it defined its own task as one of reviewing the decision of the national authorities rather than itself subsuming the facts of the case under the provisions in the Convention.[105] This approach was a witness to state authorities being seen as the more appropriate master of individuals. Consequently, for example, in the judgment delivered in *Handyside* v. *United Kingdom*, the doctrine of the margin of appreciation served to lessen the burdens imposed on the national sovereign. Despite the fact that this approach was subsequently brought into disrepute in the first *Sunday Times* case, it has been regularly, though erratically, used by the Court.[106] In 1998, when the

---

[104] Cf. Otto Riese, 'Über den Rechtsschutz innerhalb der Europäischen Gemeinschaften' (1966) 1 *Europarecht* 24 at 27; A. M. Donner, 'The Constitutional Powers of the Court of Justice of the European Communities' (1974) 11 *CMLR* 127 at 135; Hans Kutscher, 'Methods of Interpretation as Seen by a Judge at the Court of Justice' in *Judicial and Academic Conference 27–28 September 1976* (Luxembourg, 1976), p. 1 at p. 31; G. Federico Mancini, 'The Making of a Constitution for Europe' (1989) 26 *CMLR* 595 at 596; and J. H. H. Weiler, 'The Transformation of Europe' (1991) 100 *YLJ* 2403 at 2416; and also F. Matscher, 'Methods of Interpretation of the Convention' in R. St J. Macdonald *et al.* (eds.), *The European System for the Protection of Human Rights* (1993), p. 63 at p. 66. See also Ole Spiermann, 'The Other Side of the Story: An Unpopular Essay on the Making of the European Community Legal Order' (1999) 10 *EJIL* 763 at 788.

[105] A striking illustration of this approach, which is still dominant, is *Wemhoff* v. *Germany*, ECHR Series A No. 7 (1968) at para. 12; see also, e.g., *Case relating to Certain Aspects of the Laws on the Use of Languages in Education in Belgium* (Merits), ECHR Series A No. 6 (1968) at 24–5; *Handyside* v. *United Kingdom*, ECHR Series A No. 24 (1976) at paras. 58 and 50; and *Sunday Times* v. *United Kingdom (No. 1)*, ECHR Series A No. 30 (1979) at para. 59.

[106] See *Handyside* v. *United Kingdom*, ECHR Series A No. 24 (1976) at para. 48; and *Sunday Times* v. *United Kingdom (No. 1)*, ECHR Series A No. 30 (1979) at para. 59; see also C. H. M. Waldock, 'The Effectiveness of the System Set up by the European Convention on Human Rights' (1980) 1 *Human Rights Law Journal* 1 at 8; G. G. Fitzmaurice, 'Some Reflections on the European Convention on Human Rights – and on Human Rights' in Rudolf Bernhardt *et al.* (eds.), *Festschrift für Hermann Mosler* (Berlin, 1983) p. 203 at pp. 218–19; Matscher, 'Methods of Interpretation', p. 77; and R. St J. Macdonald, 'The Margin of Appreceation' in R. St J. Macdonald *et al.* (eds.), *The European System for the Protection of Human Rights* (Dordrecht, 1993), p. 83 at pp. 83–4 and 122–4. On the 'doctrine', see Elias Kastanas, *Unité et diversité: notions autonomes et marge d'appréciation des états dans la jurisprudence de la Cour européenne des droits de l'homme* (Brussels, 1996); Howard Charles Yourow, *The Margin of Appreciation Doctrine in the Dynamics of the European Human Rights Jurisprudence* (The Hague, 1996); and

Appellate Body of the World Trade Organization touched briefly upon the principle of restrictive interpretation, it relied on the judgments of the International Court in the *Nuclear Tests* cases.[107] There, however, restrictive interpretation was invoked in the special context of unilateral statements. Rather than the content of the obligations undertaken, the International Court's restrictive interpretation concerned the preliminary question as to whether any obligations had been undertaken at all and thus the sovereign act of the international sovereign.[108]

A restrictive interpretation is not the only possible result of the national principle of self-containedness. It may also prompt an 'analogous' interpretation under which international law is brought to resemble a particular national legal system. As has been said in the context of comparative law, '[m]ost fundamental, of course, is the fact that legal terms receive their meaning and coloration from the legal culture in which the person using them normally operates'.[109] Although seldom a technique used deliberately by interpreters, its attraction lies in the fact that international law does not change national law so long as it is not substantively different from national law; this brings comfort to national lawyers, in particular those who regard the content of a particular national legal system as natural, perhaps even not open to debate. It serves the same purpose as restrictive interpretation in that national law does not have to be changed.

Forming treaty provisions in the images of national law, or values or ideals taken from national law, may be not only permissible but also indispensable. Thus, objective treaty interpretation may pay regard to substantive national law in various ways, notably where treaty

---

Y. Arai-Takahashi, *The Margin of Appreciation Doctrine and the Principle of Proportionality in the Jurisprudence of the ECHR* (Oxford, 2002). Cf. in general Marc-André Eissen, 'La Cour européenne des droits de l'homme' (1986) 102 *Revue du droit public et de la science politique en France et à l'étranger* 1539 at 1580–7.

[107] *European Communities: Measures Concerning Meat and Meat Products (Hormones)*, [1998] DSR 135 at para. 165. This report was referred to in *SGS Société Générale de Surveillance SA* v. *Pakistan (Jurisdiction)*, (2003) 18 *ICSID Review-Foreign Investment Law Journal* 307 (2003), para. 171, note 178.

[108] Cf. *Nuclear Tests (Australia v. France)*, ICJ Reports [1974] 253 at para. 44 and *(New Zealand v. France)*, ICJ Reports [1974] 457 at para. 47. But see Victor Rodríguez Cedeno, 'Fourth Report on Unilateral Acts of States' (United Nations Document A/CN.4/519, 2001), paras. 126–48 and 153.

[109] Peter Herzog, 'The Need for a Comparative Perspective' in Thomas E. Carbonneau (ed.), *Resolving Transnational Disputes Through International Arbitration* (Charlottesville, 1984), p. 75 at p. 76. See also, e.g., Arthur Nussbaum, 'Rise and Fall of the Law-of-Nations Doctrine in the Conflict of Laws' (1942) 42 *Columbia Law Review* 189 at 200.

regulation resembles structural or institutional aspects of national law. The pedestrian example is a so-called 'domestic' analogy taken from a plurality of national legal systems in order to plug a gap in a treaty. Such analogies will normally coincide with an effective or teleological interpretation of the treaty. For example, it will be in accordance with the object and purpose of a treaty establishing an international institution to fill a gap in the treaty by adopting an analogy from national law if and when this aspect of the treaty-based institution can be said to be modelled on national institutions. Some examples of domestic analogies were given by Phillimore when in 1920 the Advisory Committee of Jurists dealt with general principles in the context of the Permanent Court, namely 'certain principles of procedure . . . and the principle of res judicata, etc.'.[110] Such examples of domestic analogies are characterised by the treaty itself referring to national law, often implicitly due to its purpose. Thus, it is the international law of cooperation, which points back to national law. However, the use of national institutions and structures as models, and the assimilation of treaty-based institutions and structures into 'precedents' set by national legal systems, is sometimes taken further than what is suggested by the treaty itself and so by what is herein referred to as 'domestic analogies'. This is so where these institutions or structures are used not to plug gaps in accordance with the purpose of a treaty establishing an international institution or structure, but to define that very purpose. This will be referred to as 'analogical interpretation'. The essence of analogical interpretation is changing the content and purpose of the treaty in order to imitate internationally the conception of the state as national lawyers know it, that is, the national sovereign. A lawyer engaged in an analogical interpretation, as opposed to using domestic analogies, is a lawyer amending rather than interpreting or applying the treaty. Admittedly, it can be difficult in practice to distinguish between interpretation that stems from a treaty purpose and interpretation that reflects a purpose imposed on the treaty, yet these are opposite techniques. Comparable, and equally regrettable, are the less frequent attempts at filling in the content of

---

[110] Advisory Committee of Jurists, *Procès-Verbaux of the Proceedings of the Committee (16 June–24 July 1920, with Annexes)* (The Hague, 1920), p. 335. See also H. Lauterpacht, *Private Law Sources and Analogies of International Law* (London, 1927), pp. 203–11; Bin Cheng, *General Principles of Law as Applied by International Courts and Tribunals* (London, 1953), pp. 257–386; and *Application for Review of Judgement No. 158 of the United Nations Administrative Tribunal*, ICJ Reports [1973] 166 at para. 36; and also *LaGrand Case*, ICJ Reports [2001] 466 at para. 102.

the international law of coexistence by taking analogies from a specific system of national law.

The international law of coexistence in treaty interpretation

A different approach to interpretation may be adopted by an interpreter if the treaty regulates an issue so as to possibly overturn the result produced under the international law of coexistence, as distinct from the national principle of self-containedness. Writers belonging to the natural law tradition may well have regarded such a treaty as null and void. In a specific case, an interpreter may look through the treaty, as it were, focusing on the conception of the state as a national sovereign, or the conception of the state as an international law subject, as the case may be. In most cases this should be sufficient to secure a result in accordance with the international law of coexistence, thus in practice following the natural law tradition (and possibly pre-empt an embryonic tradition of *jus cogens*).

For example, in an address commemorating the fortieth anniversary of the Permanent Court in 1962, Judge Winiarski, then President of the International Court, said:

In a period such as the present, the function of the Court is sometimes a particularly arduous one, but it must not be forgotten that alongside rules in evolution that are part of customary or treaty law, which in the main are rules of particular application, there are almost immutable rules and principles which are necessary because they meet the deep-seated needs of the international community and of which von Liszt said in his positivist construct that they constitute 'den festen Grundstock des ungeschriebenen Völkerrechts, seinen ältesten, wichtigsten, heiligsten Bestand'.[111]

A significant example is the *Legal Consequences for States of the Continued Presence of South Africa in Namibia (South West Africa) notwithstanding Security Council Resolution 276 (1970)* opinion in which the International Court interpreted a mandate entered into in 1920 with the League of Nations acting under Article 22 of its Covenant. Referring to the text of the Covenant, the International Court held that, 'viewing the institutions of 1919, the Court must take into consideration the changes which have occurred in the supervening half-century, and its interpretation cannot remain unaffected by the subsequent development of law, through the

---

[111] YICJ 1961–2, pp. 2–3; and see Franz von Liszt, *Das Völkerrecht* (12th edn by Max Fleischmann, Berlin, 1925), p. 116.

Charter of the United Nations and by way of customary law'.[112] The International Court added that 'an international instrument has to be interpreted and applied within the framework of the entire legal system prevailing at the time of interpretation'.

If in need of ornamentation, one way to formulate the approach is to identify the international law of coexistence with 'rational' state behaviour, presuming that coexistence will be preserved. Still, it ought to be taken into account that many aspects of the international law of coexistence are inherently vague and that here treaty law is often most welcome, almost whatever its content.

Problems of international legal argument

The double structure of international legal argument has different forms depending on the hierarchical position of the basic structure in respect of issues coming within the international law of cooperation. Supposedly, a national lawyer will be tempted to find more room for the basic structure than an international lawyer. Or to put it differently, what distinguishes an international lawyer from a national lawyer in respect of treaty interpretation is his or her ability to disregard the national principle of self-containedness and to be critical about, though open to, the use of analogies taken from national law and the international law of coexistence.

There have been many instances of interpreting treaties in accordance with the international law of coexistence, whereas, with the possible exception of two decisions in the *Free Zones* case,[113] there would seem to be no clear examples of the International Court or its predecessor interpreting treaties restrictively due to the national principle of self-containedness. More than eighty years of case law leaves no space for a principle of restrictive interpretation. Contracts between sovereigns are allocated to international law precisely to avoid the conception of the state as a national sovereign, and accordingly such contracts are underpinned by the view that they should be given full effect in law. The adequate conceptions of the state are the conceptions of the state as an international sovereign and as an international law subject, the

---

[112] *Legal Consequences for States of the Continued Presence of South Africa in Namibia (South West Africa) notwithstanding Security Council Resolution 276 (1970)*, ICJ Reports [1971] 16 at para. 53; and see Lachs, 'Law of Treaties', p. 401.

[113] *Case of the Free Zones of Upper Savoy and the District of Gex* (Second Phase), Series A No. 24 (1930) at 12; and *Case of Free Zones of Upper Savoy and the District of Gex* (Third Phase), Series A/B No. 46 (1932) at 167.

latter being hierarchically superior. This view was expressed by a tribunal under the International Centre for Settlement of Investment Disputes in *Amco* v. *Indonesia*, relying on the conception of the state as an international sovereign:

> In the first place, like any other conventions, a convention to arbitrate is not to be construed restrictively, nor, as a matter of fact, broadly or liberally. It is to be construed in a way which leads to find out and to respect the common will of the parties: such a method of interpretation is but the application of the fundamental principle *pacta sunt servanda*, a principle common, indeed, to all systems of internal law and to international law.
>
> Moreover – and this is again a general principle of law – any convention, including conventions to arbitrate, should be construed in good faith, that is to say by taking into account the consequences of their commitments the parties may be considered as having reasonably and legitimately envisaged.[114]

As regards the content of the international law of cooperation as well as the international law of coexistence, it is essential that the international lawyer is not prejudiced by a peculiar national legal system, for example by automatically taking analogies from that particular system.

In sum, there are three essential aspects of international legal argument which will be of particular interest to an analysis of the decisions of the Permanent Court undertaken in the light of the double structure, namely (1) the role in international legal argument of the national lawyer and of the conception of the state as a national sovereign; (2) the role of the international lawyer, as distinct from any national lawyer, notably in treaty interpretation but also in determining the content of the international law of coexistence; and (3) the variety in international legal argument, reflecting what has here been described as the categorisation of issues within the double structure of international legal argument, and the hierarchical relationship between the two structures.

The international community

Although not an integral part of the double structure of international legal argument, an evolutionary approach has at all material times had a certain currency in international legal theory, the *Buchrecht*. It has been well put by Professor David Kennedy:

---

[114] *Amco Asia Corporation and Others* v. *Indonesia* (Jurisdiction), 1 ICSID Reports 389 (1983) at para. 14; cf. *Ceskoslovenska Obchodni Banka AS* v. *Slovakia* (Jurisdiction), 5 ICSID Reports 335 (1999) at para. 34.

For more than a century, international lawyers have imagined each new moment as the overcoming of sovereignty, formalism, autonomy, politics, and the coming into being of law, pragmatism and international community. More than a hundred years ago, they were already proclaiming the arrival of institutions, pragmatism, community, globalization. At the same time, that which has been thought finally overcome continually returns, not only as an evil foe but as a newly attractive reform.[115]

Notions of an international community as an overarching set of values or ideals have been espoused by internationalists over the centuries,[116] yet they do not fit into the model of international argument set forth in this chapter. They are seen here as parts of a troubling inheritance of national lawyers. It is one thing to argue, as has been done in Chapter 2, that international law cannot be fully appreciated without paying regard to the national lawyer, and quite another thing to conclude that international lawyers should always adopt the national lawyer's point of view. The view taken here is that notions of an international community are simply another result of overstating the role of national lawyers in international law. This is not to reject *ubi societas, ibi jus* in the context of international law. But the relevant communities are the national or state communities, not an international community, which is perhaps rather an international 'uncommunity' or 'unsociety'.[117] Conversely, most notions of an international community are difficult to reconcile with a model of international legal argument that is ultimately based on the conception of the state as a national sovereign.[118]

---

[115] David Kennedy, 'My Talk at the ASIL: What is New Thinking in International Law?' (2000) 96 *American Society Proceedings* 104 at 106.

[116] It has arguably been part of a professional commitment: see David Kennedy, 'A New World Order: Yesterday, Today, and Tomorrow' (1994) 4 *Transnational Law & Contemporary Problems* 329 at 335–8; Martti Koskenniemi, 'Between Commitment and Cynicism: Outline for a Theory of International Law as Practice' in *Collection of Essays by Legal Advisers of States, Legal Advisers of International Organizations and Practitioners in the Field of International Law* (New York, 1999), p. 495 at pp. 497–9; and David Kennedy, 'When Renewal Repeats: Thinking Against the Box' (2000) 32 *NYUJILP* 335 at 424 and 469–70. It is certainly an understatement to say that '[d]ie internationale Gemeinschaft ist in der Gegenwart zu einem Modebegriff geworden': Christian Tomuschat, 'Die internationale Gemeinschaft' (1995) 33 *Archiv des Völkerrechts* 1 at 1.

[117] See Philip Allott, *Eunomia: New Order for a New World* (Oxford, 1990), pp. 243–50. Allott, it should be added, believes that this unsociety might be changed and, indeed, is changing: see *ibid.*, pp. 3–4 and *passim* and also Allott, *Health of Nations*, pp. 59, 152–7, 310–15 and 419–21.

[118] See René-Jean Dupuy, *La Communauté internationale entre le mythe et l'histoire* (Paris, 1986), p. 40; and also Alfred Zimmern, *The League of Nations and the rule of law, 1918–1935* (London, 1936), p. 98: 'The rules of international law, as they existed

It does not take much effort to find out that the national lawyer has been essential to current understandings of international law. In addition to generating the need for an international law applicable to issues international in kind, or in form, the national lawyer has also had a say in evaluating and conceiving the resulting international law, normally under the assumption that international law ought to be self-contained to the same degree as national legal systems. Generally speaking, the view that international law is a travesty of law or of the ideals of national law, and that it is bound to remain a primitive legal system, is well known. It is opposed to the belief in a dramatic evolution of international law, yet they are both corollaries, an 'optimist' and a 'pessimist', of the same phenomenon of lawyers giving national law too much space in their understanding of international law, and possibly also in their international legal argument.

There are two sides of the 'optimist' view dealt with here. On the one hand, the international law of the past tends to be disparaged. It is often identified with the international law of coexistence, as if coexistence will not continue to be a problem and as if cooperation will be a novelty. On the other hand, the international law of the future is associated with the highest of aspirations. Professor Friedmann, for one, argued that 'the international legal order will no doubt either have to be equipped with a more clearly established hierarchy of norms, and more powerful sanctions, or decline and perish. The present is the era of either dawn or twilight.'[119] Each period of the twentieth century has known its modish writers who tried to look behind state sovereignty, searching for a better, more 'legal' code of international law than Bentham's internationalism. On this view, rather than being profoundly and richly influenced by its history, international law is subject to a rapid evolution that makes the past look uninteresting. It is assumed that international law, or rather some 'international law of co-progressiveness',[120] will take on many of the characteristics of national law. The upshot of 'the international community' is certain aspects of international relations that remind the internationalist of a 'community', that is, a

---

previous to 1914, were, with a few exceptions, not the outcome of the experience of the working of a world-society. They were simply the result of the contacts between a number of self-regarding political units – stars whose course, as they moved majestically through a neutral firmament, crossed one another from time to time.'

[119] Friedmann, *Changing Structure*, p. 88.

[120] Sienho Yee, 'Towards an International Law of Co-progressiveness' in Sienho Yee and Wang Tieya (eds.), *International Law in the Post-Cold War World: Essays in Memory of Li Haopei* (London, 2001), p. 18 at pp. 19, 28 and 37–9.

model state, a national sovereign. Leaving aside the making of federal constitutions, and also constitutions of unitary states by way of treaties, there is no 'super-State'.[121] Yet the notion of the 'world state' goes hand in hand with the conception of the state as a national sovereign. There is hardly any possible root for the notion of an international community other than one's conception of a national community, and perhaps various sub-communities, those being the legally relevant communities known. The notion of an international community is a reflection of the conception of the (world) state as a national sovereign; in the words of Andreas Paulus, it 'transfers the notion of community to the international sphere: Just as domestic societies have developed into collectivities sharing common values and projects, in the age of globalization, the international sphere seems to be developing slowly into a realm of shared purposes and values.'[122]

Of course, there are many ways in which to justify the results produced under the international law of coexistence, one possibility being to see it as a legal manifestation of some international community. However, as with other kinds of justification, it has not to do with the law; it does not make it, nor does it improve or undermine it or otherwise change it. In particular, there are no clear examples of the notion of an international community being taken seriously to the point of influencing the scope or content of the international law of coexistence. Nor has it changed the hierarchical relationship between the basic and dynamic structures of international legal argument. Accordingly, it must find its possible impact, if any, within the dynamic structure and the international law of cooperation. Certainly, the notion of an international community makes certain treaty regimes more appealing than others and also provides a blueprint for analysing such regimes; for example, some of the more portentous approaches towards treaties reflecting national constitutional traditions, such as human rights conventions, and also other instances of lawyers substituting constitutionalism for internationalism,

---

[121] Cf. *Reparation for Injuries Suffered in the Service of the United Nations*, ICJ Reports [1949] 174 at 179; and *Interpretation of the Agreement of 25 March 1951 between the WHO and Egypt*, ICJ Reports [1980] 73 at para. 37.

[122] Andreas Paulus, 'The Influence of the United States on the Concept of the "International Community"' in Michael Byers and Georg Nolte (eds.), *United States Hegemony and the Foundations of International Law* (Cambridge, 2003), p. 57 at p. 86. See generally Andreas L. Paulus, *Die internationale Gemeinschaft im Völkerrecht: Eine Untersuchung zur Entwicklung des Völkerrechts im Zeitalter der Globalisierung* (Munich, 2001), pp. 9–223.

notably in Europe. Simma and Paulus have argued that 'what the [United Nations] Charter undoubtedly did achieve was the translation of the concept of the "international community" from an abstract notion to something approaching institutional reality'.[123]

In treaty interpretation, one might imagine the conception of the state as a national sovereign being used as a guiding principle, as opposed to a jealous prerogative, in what would be a new form of analogical interpretation.[124] Compared to the national principle of self-containedness, it would not necessarily impose the content of a specific national legal system on the treaty, but rather the ideals belonging to such a system and possibly shared with other systems. While interpretations based on the national principle of self-containedness are normally cursed, at least when not wrapped in the language of good faith, this other form of analogical interpretation might be praised, the reason being its communitarian ring.[125] When determining its own jurisdiction, an international court is likely to face the question whether it has an implied jurisdiction due to its nature as a court of justice, or whether its jurisdiction must always and entirely rest on specific state consent. Whether this is an analogical interpretation proper can only be ascertained when taking into account the underlying treaty and its purposes, including a possible purpose of final resolution of disputes. In the context of the Permanent Court, a first attempt to distinguish analogical interpretation from domestic analogies was made when omitting the provision in the draft-scheme prepared by the Advisory Committee on compulsory

---

[123] Bruno Simma and Andreas L. Paulus, 'The "International Community": Facing the Challenge of Globalization' (1998) 9 *EJIL* 266 at 274.

[124] As regards analogies from principles of interpretation in national legal systems, see Sandra L. Bunn-Livingstone, *Juricultural Pluralism vis-à-vis Treaty Law: State Practice and Attitudes* (The Hague, 2002), pp. 99–126 and 307–8.

[125] Cf. Rudolf Bernhardt, 'Thoughts on the Interpretation of Human-Rights Treaties' in Franz Matscher and Herbert Petzold (eds.), *Studies in Honour of Gérard J. Wiarda* (1988), p. 65 at pp. 66–7; Ganshof van der Meersch in *ibid.*, p. 201 at p. 219; Paul Mahoney, 'Judicial Activism and Judicial Self-Restraint in the European Court of Human Rights: Two Sides of the Same Coin' (1990) 11 *Human Rights Law Journal* 57 at 86; François Ost, 'The Original Canons of Interpretation of the European Court of Human Rights' in Mireille Delmas-Marty (ed.), *The European Convention for the Protection of Human Rigths: International Protection Versus National Restrictions* (Dordrecht, 1992), p. 283 at pp. 295 and 305; Matscher, 'Methods of Interpretation', pp. 68–70 and 74; and J. G. Merrills, *The Development of International Law by the European Court of Human Rights* (2nd edn, Manchester, 1993), pp. 85, 200 and 238–53; and also Donner, 'Constitutional Powers', p. 135; Anna Bredimas, *Methods of Interpretation and Community Law* (Amsterdam, 1978), pp. 136–7 and 179–80; and Mancini, 'Making of a Constitution', p. 612.

jurisdiction.[126] Whatever the form of an analogical interpretation, such interpretations are all instances of interpreters overstating their identities as national lawyers. It makes no difference whether they are idealists, as are most 'optimists', or cynics, as are many 'pessimists'.

No doubt, the international law of cooperation changes over time. But then an analysis of the double structure of international legal argument is not a description of rules, existing or past. It has to do with the way in which rules, at any period, are interpreted and applied. And there is no reason to assume that these aspects of international legal argument change any more than the international law of coexistence. Theory might evolve, but that is not necessarily of importance to the use of international legal argument in practice. The international law of cooperation will continue to proliferate, but there is little indication that the processes of interpretation and exegesis have been or are being transformed. To quote Professor James Crawford, '[o]ur system is one which international lawyers of four generations ago would have had no particular difficulties in recognising or working with, once they had got over its bulk'.[127] To the extent that politicians are influenced by notions of an international community, those notions may naturally influence treaty-making. This influence can easily be accommodated within the double structure of international legal argument as just another part of the international law of cooperation, the interpretation of which is preferably 'objective'. The notion of an international community may also inspire judges and others to produce grand statements where they have no implications, yet the notion evaporates as soon as the international lawyer moves on to applying international legal argument to specific cases. Thus, in her study of judges from the Third World, Michele Sicart-Bozec concludes that 'force est de constater que, malgré les "revolutions structurelles" annoncées dans tous les domaines, le droit international

---

[126] According to the report of the Advisory Committee, '[n]ot only is it obvious that the constituent Statute of the Court can confer upon it the degree of competence, which the States drawing up the Statute, wish to give it, but also, in the opinion of the majority of the Committee, the grant of such powers, though perhaps not strictly in accordance with the letter of the Covenant, follows its spirit so exactly that it would seem a great pity, now that the Court is being definitely organised, not to complete the progress made by this last provision', Advisory Committee, *Procès-verbaux*, pp. 727–8. See also Ole Spiermann, '"Who Attempts Too Much Does Nothing Well": The 1920 Advisory Committee of Jurists and the Statute of the Permanent Court of International Justice' (2002) 73 *BYIL* 187 at 197–8, 200, 210–11, 241 and 254–5.

[127] James Crawford, *International Law as an Open System: Selected Essays* (London, 2002), pp. 17 and also 37–8.

n'a pas été bouleversé à la Cour Internationale de Justice'.[128] According to Kennedy, '[i]t is not surprising that as international lawyers have worked to build a legal system outside the state, they have pursued issues that parallel the traditional forms of domestic law: legislation, administration and adjudication'.[129] Whether surprising or not, it is essential not to lose the curb on the would-be national lawyer lurking within most of us claiming to be international lawyers.

In sum, the evolutionary, or even revolutionary, approach to international law is not caused by international law. It is a consequence of the national lawyer being given too much space, and it is 'flatly wrong'.[130] The differences between the past and the future are the differences between international law that is different from national law and international law that is akin to national law, which Professor Dupuy has referred to as 'droit institutionnel'.[131] What particularly interests the 'optimists' about the present is to find the omens of this future among the reminiscences of the past. Novel institutions may be spellbinding 'optimists' for a while, but the spell is almost inevitably broken since the 'optimist' ethos is not embedded in international law. Although once praised in the name of progress, international institutions may soon find that a high price can be charged for having been associated with 'optimism'; down the road to the cerebral rarity shop they may even find themselves potential objects of ridicule because, after all, they are not close enough to the ideals of national law.

While 'the international community' is often referred to in individual opinions appended to decisions of the International Court, carrying a variety of meanings as the omnibus term it is, it has seldom found expression in the *motifs*. Recently, President Guillaume has pointed to the term in a separate opinion as being 'ill-defined'.[132] On the other hand, there are some well-known *dicta*.[133] In 1949, the International Court referred to 'fifty States, representing the vast majority of the members of

---

[128] Michelle Sicart-Bozec, *Les Juges du tiers monde à la Cour internationale de Justice* (Paris, 1986), pp. 185 and also 299–306.

[129] Kennedy, 'My Talk at the ASIL', p. 108; and also Kennedy, 'Renewal Repeats', p. 349.

[130] Thomas M. Franck, *The Power of Legitimacy among Nations* (New York, 1990), p. 196.

[131] Dupuy, *Communauté internationale*, pp. 40 and 48–57.

[132] See President Guillaume's separate opinion, para. 15, appended to *Case concerning the Arrest Warrant of 11 April 2000*, ICJ Reports [2002] 3. See also Gilbert Guillaume, *La Cour internationale de Justice à l'aube du XXIème siècle* (Paris, 2003), pp. 189–97.

[133] See also Manfred Lachs, 'Quelques réflexions sur la communauté internationale' in *Le Droit international au service de la paix, de la justice et du developpement: Mélanges Michel Virally* (Paris, 1991), p. 349 at pp. 355–6.

the international community';[134] in 1969, the International Court took account of 'the case of general or customary law rules and obligations which, by their very nature, must have equal force for all members of the international community';[135] in 1970, there was the famous, although rather narrow, *dictum* concerning 'the obligations of a State towards the international community as a whole',[136] that is, it would seem, the aggregate of all states; in 1971, the International Court referred to as 'the injured entity . . . a people which must look to the international community for assistance in its progress towards the goals for which the sacred trust was instituted';[137] and in 1980, the International Court considered it 'to be its duty to draw the attention of the entire international community, of which Iran itself has been a member since time immemorial, to the irreparable harm that may be caused by events of the kind now before the Court'.[138]

No decision rivals the *Legality of the Threat or Use of Nuclear Weapons* opinion with its eight references to the term 'the international community', which confirm that the term is used mainly for ornamentation. Most of these references had to do with the international law of cooperation and were shorthand for the international sovereigns taken together.[139] Treaties were taken to express 'an increasing concern in the international community',[140] while resolutions, though not binding in themselves but which pointed towards possible future law-making, gave voice to 'the desire of a very large section of the international community'.[141] In the absence of treaties, the International Court referred to 'the international community' being 'profoundly divided' and stressed the conflicting views of 'an appreciable section of the international community'.[142] Also, the *motifs* identified '182 States' with 'the vast majority of the international community',[143] and they referred to 'a growing

---

[134] *Reparation for Injuries Suffered in the Service of the United Nations*, ICJ Reports [1949] 174 at 185.

[135] *North Sea Continental Shelf*, ICJ Reports [1969] 3 at para. 63.

[136] *Barcelona Traction, Light and Power Company, Limited* (Merits), ICJ Reports [1970] 3 at para. 33.

[137] *Legal Consequences for States of the Continued Presence of South Africa in Namibia (South West Africa) notwithstanding Security Council Resolution 276 (1970)*, ICJ Reports [1971] 16 at para. 127.

[138] *United States Diplomatic and Consular Staff in Tehran*, ICJ Reports [1980] 3 at para. 92.

[139] Cf. Christian Tomuschat, 'Obligations Arising for States without or against Their Will' (1993) 241 *Recueil des Cours* 195 at 222 and 227; but see *ibid.*, pp. 231–2.

[140] *Legality of the Threat or Use of Nuclear Weapons*, ICJ Reports [1996] 226 at para. 62.

[141] *Ibid.*, para. 73 and also paras. 100 and 103.

[142] *Ibid.*, paras. 67 and 96, respectively.   [143] *Ibid.*, para. 100.

awareness of the need to liberate the community of States and the international public from the dangers resulting from the existence of nuclear weapons'.[144]

This leaves one reference, which was used so as to ornament results produced under the international law of coexistence, the content of which had been clarified and strengthened by parallel treaty-making:

The extensive codification of humanitarian law and the extent of the accession to the resultant treaties, as well as the fact that the denunciation clauses that existed in the codification instruments have never been used, have provided the international community with a corpus of treaty rules the great majority of which had already become customary and which reflected the most universally recognized humanitarian principles.[145]

In a declaration appended to the advisory opinion, President Bedjaoui underlined 'the emergence of the concept of "international community" and its sometimes successful attempts at subjectivization'.[146] The *motifs* only bore out the first part of that statement, nor would 'subjectivization' seem to have been achieved in any other case dealt with by the International Court or its predecessor. Indeed, as President Bedjaoui in the same breath referred to 'the social necessities of States organized as a community', the statement about 'successful attempts at subjectivization' lost much of its potential effect.

In international legal argument as administered in practice, the role left to the notion of an international community is of an ornamental character, whether in justifying the results produced by the international law of coexistence or in wrapping up certain select parts of the international law of cooperation.[147] Thus there is, in Koskenniemi's words, 'this gap between our presumptuous rhetoric and our timid self-image'.[148] Such ornamentation is harmless, yet can be worrisome. For it is a testimony to national lawyers being given a role too large, and while the 'optimist' version and various notions of an international community attract most sympathy, by far the largest potential for the national lawyer is with the national principle of self-containedness. There are

---

[144] *Ibid.*, para. 63.   [145] *Ibid.*, para. 82.   [146] *Ibid.*, p. 270.

[147] Cf. William D. Jackson in Kenneth W. Thompson (ed.), *Community, Diversity, and a New World Order* (1994), p. 3 at pp. 4 and 6–7; and Don Greig, ' "International Community", "Interdependence" and All That . . . Rhetorical Correctness?' in Gerard Kreijen *et al.* (eds.), *State Sovereignty, and International Governance* (Oxford, 2002), p. 521 at p. 531.

[148] Cf. Martti Koskenniemi, 'International Law in a Post-Realist Era' (1995) 16 *AYIL* 1 at 2 and see also *ibid.*, p. 7.

examples of grand 'optimist' rhetoric being followed by interpretations that are either restrictive or analogous. Communitarian phraseology may serve to remove critical questions as to whether the interpretation so ornamented reflects the conception of the state as a national sovereign.

Perhaps the most prominent example is the concepts of *jus cogens* and *erga omnes*. Although narrow in scope, and with little practical bearing, they fit the 'optimist' notion of an international community, a cornucopia of analogical interpretations approximating it to a world state.[149] But these concepts might just as well be seen as expressions of an opposite, 'pessimist' bent which questions the hierarchical relationship between the conceptions of the state as an international law subject and as an international sovereign, and which may even give priority to the conception of the state as a national sovereign. The introduction of the concept of *jus cogens* in the Vienna Convention on the Law of Treaties, or peremptory rules, proceeded on the assumption that third state interests, leaving aside community interests, were rarely acknowledged in international law. Had it not been for a rather extreme version of what Bruno Simma has referred to as 'bilateralism',[150] two states would often be prevented from derogating *inter partes* from general international law due to the presence of third state interests of a superior kind (cf. Article 41(1)(b) of the Vienna Convention), and the concept of *jus cogens* would hardly have been seen as progressive. Arguably, the concept of *jus cogens* in its present meaning was only introduced because international lawyers enthralled by a notion of an international community had difficulties in giving the conception of the state as an international law subject preference over the conception of the state as an international sovereign through the recognition of third state interests. That such difficulties may not have been surmounted, is suggested by the field of application of *jus cogens* being supremely unclear and also by the reluctance displayed by the International Court in defining which obligations and rights are *erga omnes*.[151] The celebrated *dictum* in the

---

[149] Cf. Tomuschat, 'Internationale Gemeinschaft', pp. 1–3; and Paulus, *Internationale Gemeinschaft*, p. 423.

[150] See Bruno Simma, 'From Bilaterlism to Community Interest in International Law' (1994) 250 *Recueil des Cours* 217 at 230–3.

[151] Cf. *Barcelona Traction, Light and Power Company, Limited* (Merits), ICJ Reports [1970] 3 at paras. 33–4 and 91; *East Timor*, ICJ Reports [1995] 90 at para. 29; and *Application of the Convention on the Prevention and Punishment of the Crime of Genocide* (Preliminary Objections), ICJ Reports [1996] 595 at para. 31.

Barcelona Traction, Light and Power Company case concerning obligations *erga omnes* owed to 'the international community as a whole', and in respect of which all states can be held to have a legal interest in their protection, is somewhat restricted in scope compared to the approach taken by, for example, the International Court in the first phase of the *South West Africa* case.[152] There have been attempts at expanding the concept of *jus cogens* to yet other fields, such as state responsibility, diplomatic protection, treaty reservations and state immunity, and accordingly to apply further, possibly more significant legal consequences to it.[153] While some of these attempts are without a basis in international law, it must be considered in respect of others whether the legal consequences in question apply to rules other than *jus cognes* rules, or lawyers will end up with a concept of *jus cogens* that pleases the 'optimist' notion of an international community, but which for purposes of international law might be a far too narrow and fairly eccentric exception to widespread 'bilateralism'.

The epitome of an international lawyer's approach to the content of international law is not further analogies taken from national law, unless invited by the international law of cooperation, or the international law of coexistence. Indeed, an international lawyer's approach would be exactly the opposite: to give the international law of

---

[152] Cf. *Barcelona Traction, Light and Power Company, Limited* (Merits), ICJ Reports [1970] 3 at para. 33–4; and *South West Africa Cases* (Preliminary Objections), ICJ Reports [1962] 319 at 343; see also Anzilotti, *Cours*, pp. 517–18.

[153] Cf. Article 41 of the International Law Commission's Draft Articles on Responsibility of States for Internationally Wrongful Acts; but see James Crawford, 'First Report on State Responsibility' (United Nations Document A/CN.4/490/Add.3, 1998), paras. 87, 98 and 101; and James Crawford, 'Third Report on State Responsibility' (United Nations Document A/CN.4/507/Add.4, 2000), paras. 373–5 and 410–11; John Dugard, 'First Report on Diplomatic Protection' (United Nations Document A/CN.4/506, 2000), para. 89; Alain Pellet, 'Third Report on Reservations to Treaties' (United Nations Document A/CN.4/491, 1998), para. 25; and 'Report of the Working Group on Jurisdictional Immunities of States and Their Property' (United Nations Document A/CN.4/L.576, 1999), Appendix; and, e.g., *Al-Adsani* v. *United Kingdom*, ECHR Reports 2001-XI at paras. 61 and 66. The latter judgment was based on a supremely wide, and incorrect, concept of *jus cogens* as being not merely peremptory but hierarchically superior, which can be found in decisions of the International Criminal Tribunal for the Former Yugoslavia: see *Prosecutor* v. *Furundzija*, 38 ILM 317 (1998) at para. 153 and also, e.g., Yasseen in *Law of Treaties Conference*, vol. 1, pp. 295–6 and vol. 2, p. 103 and Paulus, *Internationale Gemeinschaft*, p. 362. See conversely, as for the use of the concept of *jus cogens* in respect of circumstances precluding wrongfulness: Article 26 of the Draft Articles on Responsibility of States for Internationally Wrongful Acts; and Ole Spiermann, 'Humanitarian Intervention as a Necessity and the Threat or Use of *Jus Cogens*' (2002) 71 *NJIL* 523.

cooperation as well as the international law of coexistence a sphere in which they are treated as independent and to avoid, in particular, being inspired by the national principle of self-containedness as well as sub-jecting the conception of the state as an international law subject to the conception of the state as an international sovereign. For international law is to be treated as a legal system in its own right.

PART 3

International legal argument in the Permanent Court of International Justice

4   Revisiting the Permanent Court

Approach and material

In studying international legal argument as unfolding in the decisions of an international court, the question is what to do if one's analysis of the decisions is not to be only superficially about that court. The shifting divisions between the judges, the emergence and decline of what Lauterpacht termed 'trends and principles',[1] the varying influence of specific judges over time and the numerous implicit overrulings of former decisions are all interrelated aspects that warrant a chronological analysis of the decisions of the same international court. Of course, no description takes the form of a one-way process of cognition, yet that ought not to prevent lawyers from analysing the decisions of international courts. A model of international legal argument concerned with the practical use of international law in specific cases, as distinct from the *Buchrecht*, is essential. Account must be taken of the written and oral pleadings of the parties appearing before the international court, yet the focus is on the decisions of, and therefore international legal argument within, the Permanent Court.

On one occasion, having regard to the increasing interest among scholars in commenting on the decisions of the Permanent Court, President Huber suggested to his colleagues that 'the work in preparing our decisions must be such that if our critics – whether learned men or politicians – could be admitted to the private sittings of the Court, they would remain with the impression that the evolution of our judgments is really worthy of the Court'.[2] A straight line can be drawn from this suggestion

---

[1] H. Lauterpacht, *The Development of International Law by the International Court* (London, 1958), p. 400.
[2] Präsidentreden, 15 June 1926, Huber papers 25.2.

to the paragraph at the end of the *Legality of the Threat or Use of Nuclear Weapons* opinion in which the International Court took the unusual step of advising the readers of the opinion 'that its reply to the question put to it by the General Assembly rests on the totality of the legal grounds set forth by the Court above . . . each of which is to be read in the light of the others'. 'Some of these grounds are', it was added, 'not such as to form the object of formal conclusions in the final paragraph of the Opinion; they nevertheless retain, in the view of the Court, all their importance.'[3] Referring to this paragraph, Judge Ferrari Bravo has said that:

[i]l faut donc, et c'est ma conclusion finale, ne pas s'arrêter aux conclusions, mais lire tout l'arrêt (ou l'avis consultatif), parce qu'il y a des choses qui ne se retrouvent pas dans le dispositif pour la simple raison qu'on n'a pas pu former une majorité, ni dans un sens ni dans l'autre. Ces choses toutefois existent et donneront un jour des fruits.[4]

The official publications of the Permanent Court are complete and well organised.[5] In addition to its decisions and all material relating to the proceedings, the Permanent Court published all minutes of the meetings concerning the making, amendment and revision of the internal Rules of Court; and it brought out an annual report containing a digest of decisions taken in its application of the Statute and Rules, which indeed is 'indispensable to a study of the work of the Court'.[6]

Although the deliberations are confidential, and remain so, as time goes by it becomes possible to gain some insight into the deliberations and thereby to improve one's understanding of the decisions. Material that can supplement the official publications enters the public domain. This is worthy of scrutiny not only in order to disclose what happened on the bench, but also in order to understand the different personalities that made up the collegiate body. As will become clear in Chapters 5 to 7, various analyses relating to the decisions and the deliberations soon emanated from persons with the most intimate knowledge of the work

---

[3] *Legality of the Threat or Use of Nuclear Weapons*, ICJ Reports [1996] 226 at para. 104. See also *Polish Postal Service in Danzig*, Series B No. 11 (1925) at 30, referring to *The Pious Funds Case*, 9 RIAA 11 (1902) at 12.

[4] Luigi Ferrari Bravo, 'La Cour internationale de justice aujourd'hui' in Kalliopi Kaufa (ed.), *International Law of the Turn of the Century* (Thessaloniki, 1998), p. 17 at p. 67.

[5] Cf. Manley O. Hudson, *The Permanent Court of International Justice, 1920–1942* (2nd edn, New York, 1943), pp. 307–8.

[6] L. Oppenheim, *International Law* (5th edn by H. Lauterpacht, London, 1935–7), vol. 2, p. 70, note 2.

of the Permanent Court. There is also the academic work and other published writings, including memoirs, left by members of the inner circle, their biographies and obituaries.

A further, essential source is the several collections of primary material. Published series of diplomatic documents tend to neglect the Permanent Court,[7] although valuable files are kept in the archives of governments and international institutions.[8] Generally, the papers left by former judges and others with a thorough knowledge of the Permanent Court are the most interesting. Chapters 5 to 7 are based on such material,[9] which has produced some useful insights into the world of the Permanent Court, including the deliberation room, although it is neither complete, nor necessarily representative. What is certain, however, is that primary material made accessible to the general public is much richer when it comes to the Permanent Court as compared to the more recent international courts.

There have been attempts to rationalise the decisions of the Permanent Court in terms of the burning political issues at the time, or of sociological reflections more generally. The inter-war period witnessed a remarkable outpouring of so-called 'realist' jurisprudential theory, yet in respect of the Permanent Court those attempts have not been entirely successful, nor does the archival material suggest that majorities of the Permanent Court were driven by considerations other than those which

---

[7] Thus, *Akten zur Deutschen auswärtigen Politik, 1918–1945* (Göttingen, 1950–); *Documents diplomatiques belges, 1920–1940* (Brussels, 1964–6); *Documents diplomatiques français, 1920–32* (Paris, 1997–) and *1932–1939* (Paris, 1963–84); *Documents on British Foreign Policy, 1919–1939* (London, 1947–86); *I documenti diplomatici Italiani, 1918–1939* (Rome, 1953–); and *La prassi Italiana di diritto internazionale, 1919–1925* (Rome, 1995). More informative for the present purposes are *Documenten betreffende de buitenlandse politiek van Nederland, 1919–1945* ('s-Gravenhage, 1976–) and, in particular, *Documents diplomatiques suisses, 1848–1945* (Bern, 1979–92).

[8] Cf. José Sette Camara, 'Behind the World Bench' in Manuel Rama-Montaldo (ed.), *El derecho internacional en un mundo en transformación* (Montevideo, 1994), p. 1069 at p. 1075.

[9] Namely the papers left by Edwin Borchard, W. J. M. van Eysinga, Åke Hammarskjöld, Max Huber, Manley O. Hudson, Philip C. Jessup, Frank B. Kellogg, John Bassett Moore, Elihu Root, Walther Schücking and Hans Wehberg and the archives of the British Foreign Office, the French Ministry of Foreign Affairs and the Danish Ministry of Foreign Affairs as well as National Archives and Records Administration in the United States. I have also been in contact with the Memorial Hall of the M. Adachi Foundation, which keeps the papers of Minéitcirô Adatci, and visited the Istituto di Diritto Internazionale 'D. Anzilotti' in Pisa, Italy. The League of Nations Archives have been consulted, but unfortunately without any significant result. The archives of the Permanent Court itself are not accessible to the public; see also Registry of the International Court of Justice, *The International Court of Justice* (4th edn, The Hague, 1996), p. 67.

can be accommodated within international legal argument. In the political history of the League of Nations, the Permanent Court is but a footnote, partly because it did not deal with the main political issues of the day. The key political discussions were not directly relevant to its decision-making, with the possible exception of the *Customs Regime* opinion delivered in 1931. It would seem acceptable as a starting-point to assume that judges in the Permanent Court were not animated by national or personal biases of a non-legal kind, although there can be no doubt that international legal argument occasionally left them with certain discretion. Also in this respect the writings left by the members of the Permanent Court, both official and private, have been preferred to more or less arbitrary forays into a *Zeitgeist* defined in political or sociological terms.

Structure of the remaining chapters

Chapters 5 to 7 are devoted to the pioneering decisions rendered by the Permanent Court between 1922 and 1940. They will demonstrate the practical significance of international law as a residual and complementary legal system and the structures of international legal argument erected thereon. When taken as a whole the decisions of the Permanent Court illustrate the double structure of international legal argument detailed in Chapter 3, including what have been presented as key aspects of international legal argument. In order to describe these and other aspects of international legal argument in the Permanent Court, Chapters 5 to 7 apply the terminology developed in Chapters 2 and 3. It is true that this terminology is not to be found in the text of the decisions, nor were the judges necessarily conscious of the double structure of international legal argument. Rather the terminology is used as a way of analysing the decisions, in the hope that both the terminology and the underlying model may shed light on the use of legal argument by the first permanent court of international law at a formative period of the development of international legal argument.

The decisions of the Permanent Court can be grouped into three periods. The first period started with the first general election of judges in 1921 and the inauguration of the Permanent Court in 1922 and ran until the end of 1924. This was the foundational period during which Judges Anzilotti and Huber became rather influential in the work of the Permanent Court. Judge Huber's election as President of the Permanent Court in late 1924 marked the beginning of the second period, a period which saw a series of remarkable examples of the double structure of international legal argument, including the judgment in *The Lotus*. This period moulded an international lawyer's approach to international law, not confined to national legal reasoning and the conception of the state as a national sovereign. It is difficult to identify precisely when the second period came to an end and the third began. The two overlapped during Judge Anzilotti's presidency between 1928 and 1930, but the second period had clearly come to an end in 1931 when the composition of the bench changed in accordance with the results of the second general election of judges. Between 1931 and 1940 the Permanent Court changed its use of the double structure of international legal argument. The hierarchy between the two structures that compose the double structure was changed and more space was found for the conception of the state as a national sovereign at the expense of the two other conceptions of the state. Thus, the overarching theme of the third period was a national lawyer's approach to international law.

Within each of the three periods a handful of decisions have been singled out for detailed analysis. They will often be the cases in which members of the bench differed in their categorisation within the structures of international legal argument or as regards the hierarchical relationship between the structures. Other decisions selected relate to such controversial decisions in significant ways. Aspects of most of the other decisions will be dealt with as well, as will the work of commentators on the Permanent Court. The overall approach is chronological, but the chronology will be interrupted where necessary to preserve the continuity of analysis.

5   The foundational period, 1922–1924

The Permanent Court as composed after the first general election

The judges

As the Court Protocol had entered into force at the time of the opening of the Second Assembly in September 1921, the first general election of judges took place on 14 September 1921.[1] The judges were to be elected under Article 2 of the Statute 'amongst persons of high moral character, who possess the qualifications required in their respective countries for appointment to the highest judicial offices, or are jurisconsults of recognized competence in international law'. According to Article 9, 'the whole body . . . should represent the main forms of civilization and the principal legal systems of the world'. In the Assembly, just before the election, Minéitcirô Adatci had said that this 'extremely important article . . . emphasises the universal character of the institution, for as the various States accept the clause enjoining mutual obligation, the Court of International Justice will become a complete world organisation'.[2] The successful candidates were rather diverse in terms of their experience and had a range of ages.[3]

A number of judges had made significant contributions to international legal theory. Max Huber (forty-seven years old in 1921) was a Swiss professor in international law from Zurich, who had spent the war as legal adviser to the Swiss Federal Council. Huber's doctoral thesis from 1898 on state succession had been much referred to, and in 1910 he had

---

[1] See *Records of Assembly: Plenary* 1921, pp. 235–58, 272–3, 279, 281–2, 290–1 and 293–4.
[2] *Ibid.*, p. 241; and also Advisory Committee of Jurists, *Procès-Verbaux of the Proceedings of the Committee (16 June–24 July 1920, with Annexes)* (The Hague, 1920), p. 384.
[3] See Series E No. 1 (1922–5), pp. 14–27.

published a mature piece on the foundation, past and possible future of international law: *Beiträge zur Kenntnis der soziologischen Grundlagen des Völkerrechts und der Staatengesellschaft*. This was an attempt to provide an alternative to positivist approaches to international law.[4] According to Huber, international law was only at its beginning, something that had induced him to advocate theory that, *de lege ferenda*, approached international relations from a broader, 'sociological' perspective.[5] Pending further development, international law had to reflect closely the reality of international relations, notably the territorial setting necessary for a minimum of coexistence.[6] Huber traced the few departures from this 'realism' back to the natural law tradition, which had made a series of proposals, some of which, he said, had subsequently been accepted in state practice.[7] Huber's piece was republished in 1928 under the more ambitious title *Die soziologischen Grundlagen des Völkerrechts*.

Among the other judges a major figure was the Italian professor Dionisio Anzilotti (fifty-two years old), whose name was prominently associated with doctrines of positivism and dualism. But Anzilotti's work and interests obviously covered a much wider field. One of his first publications was a pioneering work from 1892 on the sociology of law: *La filosofia del diritto e la sociologia*.[8] In 1929, the first volume of Anzilotti's

---

[4] Max Huber, *Die Soziologischen Grundlagen des Völkerrechts* (Berlin, 1928), p. 6; and see also Oliver Diggelmann, *Anfänge der Völkerrechtssoziologie: die Völkerrechtskonzeptionen von Max Huber und Georges Schelle im Vergleich* (Zurich, 2000), pp. 24–8, 67 and 107–8. Huber considered this to be his most significant scientific contribution: see Max Huber, *Denkwürdigkeiten, 1907–1924* (Zurich, 1974), p. 51. One may speculate whether it takes anything less than a complete neglect of what was to come after the First World War – combined with an exaggeration of the role of international law in international politics that Huber certainly did not subscribe to – to claim that '[t]he fact that it [that is, Huber's book] reached its optimistic conclusion only four years before the war suggests that something was wrong in its argument': Martti Koskenniemi, *The Gentle Civilizer of Nations: The Rise and Fall of International Law, 1870–1960* (Cambridge, 2001), p. 228.

[5] Huber, *Soziologischen Grundlagen des Völkerrechts*, pp. 4–6 and 98; see also Max Huber, *Die Staatensuccession: Völkerrechtliche und Staatsrechtliche Praxis in XIX. Jahrhundert* (Leipzig, 1898), pp. 4 and 26–40.

[6] Huber, *Soziologischen Grundlagen des Völkerrechts*, pp. 9–10 and 45–9. As to possible ends, see also Max Huber, 'Die Fortbildung des Völkerrechts auf dem Gebiete des Prozess- und Landkriegsrechts durch die II. internationale Friedenskonferenz im Haag 1907' (1908) 2 *Jahrbuch des öffentlichen Rechts der Gegenwart* 470 at 473; Max Huber, 'Die geschichtlichen Grundlagen des heutigen Völkerrechts' (1922–3) 16 *Wissen und Leben* 261 at 278–81; and Max Huber, 'On the Place of the Law of Nations in the History of Mankind' in *Symbolae Verzijl* (The Hague, 1958), p. 190 at pp. 193–5.

[7] Huber, *Soziologischen Grundlagen des Völkerrechts*, pp. 11, 34–5, 42 and 55–6.

[8] Reprinted in Società italiana per l'organizzazione internazionale, *Opere di Dionisio Anzilotti* (Padua, 1963), vol. 4, pp. 495–671. It has indeed been suggested that Anzilotti

authoritative textbook on public international law was translated into French, *Cours de droit international*. Anzilotti had advised the Italian government on numerous occasions before 1920, the year in which he was appointed as Under-Secretary-General of the League of Nations.[9]

Another well-known professor was John Bassett Moore (sixty-one years old), the American editor of two quasi-official publications, *History and Digest of International Arbitrations* from 1898 and *A Digest of International Law* from 1906. While clearly not an admirer of theory, Moore was an expert on the history of American diplomacy. He had assisted the Department of State on various occasions and, according to Elihu Root, he had 'an accurate mind, great learning in International Law, and practical experience in International affairs'.[10] It has been said that he 'became synonymous at the beginning of the twentieth century with the American approach to international law'.[11] In Moore's own words, he was at The Hague not because he shared 'Wilson's visionary supposition that the war had made everything over and created a new world and particularly a new European world, but solely because I think that the peaceful processes of judicial tribunals are preferable to contentions by arms, and that it is desirable that the judicial habit should be cultivated and strengthened'.[12] In his view, 'the prime qualification' of an international judge was not to 'be an "internationalist"' but someone with real experience of international affairs.[13] Moore had been elected even though the United States was not a party to the Court Protocol (and

coined the phrase 'sociology of law': see C. J. M. Schuyt, *Rechtssociologie: een terreinverkenning* (Rotterdam, 1971), p. 15, referred to in Jan Klabbers, 'The Sociological Jurisprudence of Max Huber: An Introduction' (1992) 43 ÖZöRV 197 at 200.

[9] Of the eleven Under-Secretaries-General and Directors serving in the early Secretariat, five had been professors: see Egon F. Ranshofen-Wertheimer, *The International Secretariat: A Great Experiment in International Administration* (Washington DC, 1945), pp. 404–5.

[10] Root to Phillimore, 13 September 1921, Root papers 139.

[11] W. Michael Reisman, 'Lassa Oppenheim's Nine Lives' (1994) 19 *YJIL* 255 at 256.

[12] Moore to [Mrs] Moore, 1 February 1922, Moore papers 49. It may be added that Moore did not see himself as first and foremost a professor (or, at least, he did not want other people to see him as such). In his opinion, it was 'most important that a judge should know life and have had experience with men and affairs. The greatest failure I have known as international judge was a man merely of books and theoretic formulas, who had no experience of life and affairs': Moore to Phillips, 29 December 1921, Moore papers 176.

[13] Moore to Finlay, 26 March 1923, Moore papers 177. What Judge Moore meant by this was perhaps not obvious. In a letter to a Brazilian diplomat, he explained his position: 'Alvarez is what they call an "internationalist". That is not the sort of man who makes a good judge. For a judge we need an all-round, capable man of affairs, who would make a successful lawyer or business man – a man of sober, sound judgment, without crotchets or fads, such as our "internationalists" usually have,' Moore to Da Gama, 27 March 1923, Moore papers 177. In another letter, Judge Moore wrote that 'a clear and

even though the United States group in the Permanent Court of Arbitration had nominated no candidates for the election).

André Weiss (sixty-three years old), the French judge, was a professor in private international law and for a long time also a *jurisconsulte adjoint* to the French Ministry of Foreign Affairs. He was the author of a well-known text, *Manuel de droit international privé*, the ninth edition of which appeared in 1925. Treating private international law as a branch of law at international, as opposed to national, level, Weiss, in the introduction, discussed what is herein referred to as the international law of coexistence, the sources of which were said to be national law, state consent and doctrine.[14]

Antonio Sanchez de Bustamante (fifty-six years old) from Cuba was a professor in both public and private international law, between which he saw an intimate relationship. De Bustamante also ran a lucrative law firm in Havana. In 1924, he published an introduction to 'the World Court', which in 1925 appeared in an English translation. In the 1930s, a French translation of a bulky treatise, *Droit international public*, appeared.

In addition to the five professors in international law, the bench included three judges who had had long careers as members of national courts, including one from the Privy Council, Lord Finlay (seventy-nine years old). In an earlier period of his professional life, Finlay had been a professor in international law, and he had taken part 'in most if not all the larger international arbitrations in which Great Britain has been involved in the last twenty years'.[15] B. C. J. Loder (seventy-two years old)

---

firm grasp of legal principles' are qualifications that, though 'very important', 'are often lacking in persons who figure as "internationalists"': Moore to Balogh, 11 October 1924, Borchard papers 6.89. In 1946, Alvarez was elected to the International Court of Justice, where he became an active dissenter pursuing a 'new international law', the 'optimist' flavour of which was more attractive to theorists than his colleagues on the bench; cf. *Admission of a State to the United Nations (Charter, Art. 4)*, ICJ Reports [1947–8] 57 at 67–72; *Corfu Channel Case* (Merits), ICJ Reports [1949] 4 at 39–48; *Competence of the Assembly regarding Admission to the United Nations*, ICJ Reports [1950] 4 at 12–21; *International Status of South-West Africa*, ICJ Reports [1950] 128 at 174–85; *Colombian–Peruvian Asylum Case*, ICJ Reports [1950] 266 at 290–302; *Reservations to the Convention on the Prevention and Punishment of the Crime of Genocide*, ICJ Reports [1951] 15 at 49–55; *Fisheries*, ICJ Reports [1951] 116 at 145–53; *Anglo-Iranian Oil Co. Case* (Jurisdiction), ICJ Reports [1952] 93 at 124–35; *The Minquiers and Ecrehos Case*, ICJ Reports [1953] 47 at 73; and *Effect of Awards of Compensation made by the United Nations Administrative Tribunal*, ICJ Reports [1954] 47 at 67–75.

[14] See André Weiss, *Manuel de droit international privé* (9th edn, Paris, 1925), pp. ix–x and xxiii–xxxiii and also in (1922) 29 *Annuaire*, pp. 163–4; cf. André Weiss, *Traité théorique et pratique de droit international privé* (2nd edn, Paris, 1912), vol. 3, pp. 5–7, 15–16, 49–52, 62–3 and 66 and Weiss, *Manuel de droit international privé*, pp. 357, 374–5, 381 and 383.

[15] Hurst's memorandum, 30 April 1920, FO 372 T5215/1202/329.

had been a judge of the Dutch Supreme Court. He had previously represented his country at international conferences and had been active in the drafting of the Statute. He had been appointed a member of the Advisory Committee on the initiative of Dr J. A. van Hamel, the head of the Legal Section of the Secretariat of the League of Nations and a fellow countryman, according to whom Loder 'has worked a good deal on the question of international jurisdiction, and whose name as well as personality are very much appreciated by several of the eminent jurists who are going to be Members of the Committee'.[16] Another member from a small neutral state was D. G. Nyholm (sixty-three years old), a Danish judge who had served some twenty years with the mixed courts at Cairo. His main publication was a partly idealistic plan for *le tribunal mondial* published in 1918 and in the light of which he saw the Permanent Court.[17] Neither Nyholm nor Loder were renowned as experts on international law but they extolled the traditional virtue of international justice as an alternative to warfare.

Like Loder, the Spanish judge, Rafael Altamira (fifty-five years old), had been a member of the Advisory Committee of Jurists. He was an historian who dealt with legal subjects only occasionally. According to James Brown Scott, 'Mr Altamira repeatedly expressed the view in the proceedings of the Committee, that the success of the court would depend upon the quality of its judges, and that moral qualities had more importance than scientific ability'.[18] Japan was represented by Yorozu Oda

[16] Van Hamel's memorandum, 2 October 1919, League of Nations Archives 21-1345-88; and see Ole Spiermann, '"Who Attempts Too Much Does Nothing Well": The 1920 Advisory Committee of Jurists and the Statute of the Permanent Court of International Justice' (2002) 73 *BYIL* 187 at 190, note 13. Van Hamel had told some of the members of the Advisory Committee that the Permanent Court ought not to be detached from 'the League of Nations machinery': see van Hamel's memorandum, 21 June 1920, League of Nations Archives 21-4992-4959. Perhaps this was the reason why subsequently Loder dubbed the Permanent Court 'one of the principal organs of the League' (which, however, 'exercises its powers in full and sovereign independence'): see Series D No. 2 (1922) at 326. Cf. Manley O. Hudson, *The Permanent Court of International Justice, 1920–1942* (2nd edn, New York, 1943), pp. 111–12.

[17] Cf. D. G. Nyholm, 'La Cour permanente de Justice internationale' in P. Munch (ed.), *Les Origines et l'oeuvre de la Société des Nations* (Copenhagen, 1924), vol. 2, p. 241 at pp. 241–8 and 260–3. Nyholm had not been alone in submitting such plans: see generally Lord Phillimore, 'Schemes for Maintaining General Peace' in *Peace Handbooks Issued by the Historical Section of the Foreign Office* (London, 1920), vol. 25, no. 160 at pp. 23–65; and Chr. L. Lange, 'Préparation de la Société des Nations pendant la guerre' in P. Munch (ed.), *Les Origines et l'oeuvre de la Société des Nations* (Copenhagen, 1923), vol. 1, p. 1 at pp. 8–43.

[18] James Brown Scott, *The Project of a Permanent Court of International Justice and Resolutions of the Advisory Committee of Jurists* (Washington DC, 1920), p. 51; and see Advisory

(fifty-three years old), a professor in administrative law and an expert in ancient Chinese law. Another judge, Ruy Barbosa (seventy-two years old), a Brazilian statesman, never came to The Hague due to illness. In 1923, he was replaced by Epitacio da Silva Pessôa (fifty-six years old),[19] a lawyer and former President of Brazil as well as former member of the Federal Supreme Court, who – according to a previous tribute by Moore – was 'a consummate product of his country's intellectual and spiritual life'.[20]

The Statute provided for four deputy-judges for the purposes of filling vacancies. At the first general election, two former national judges were elected: F. V. N. Beichmann (sixty-two years old) from Norway and Michailo Yovanovitch (sixty-six years old) from Yugoslavia. In addition were elected a widely experienced Romanian lawyer, Demètre Negulesco (forty-six years old), and from China, Wang Chung-hui (forty years old), 'the country's foremost jurist',[21] who had been educated partly in the United States. In 1920, under the debates in the Third Committee of the First Assembly on the Statute of the Permanent Court, Negulesco had proposed that the judges should be irremovable and appointed for life. 'It should not be forgotten', he had said, 'that the judges of the Permanent Court would have the supremely important task of creating the new international law which was necessary.'[22]

Except for Altamira, Loder, Negulesco and Wang, and also Pessôa, the names of the successful candidates were known from the list maintained by the bureau of the Permanent Court of Arbitration. It generally paid off for the candidates to be known in advance not only by their own governments but also by representatives of the other states present at Geneva at the time of the general election. In 1919, Anzilotti, de Bustamante, Pessôa and Weiss had represented their respective governments at the Paris Peace Conference; Beichmann, Huber and Loder, although from neutral states, had been entrusted with missions to the Conference.

Committee, *Procès-verbaux*, pp. 369–70 and 447; cf. *ibid.*, pp. 611, 645 and 698. In 1927, at the time of electing a new President of the Permanent Court, Weiss was reported as having said that 'seule la candidature Altamira pourrait être opposée à celle du juge italien, mais M. Altamira n'a pas l'autorité juridique de son collègue', Note, 29 November 1927, Quai d'Orsay 2400B.

[19] See *Records of Assembly: Plenary* 1923, pp. 23–4.

[20] John Bassett Moore, *The Collected Papers of John Bassett Moore* (New York, 1944), vol. 5, p. 59; and see also Moore to Root, 2 July 1923, Moore papers 177.

[21] Robert Thomas Pollard, *China's Foreign Relations, 1917–1931* (New York, 1933), pp. 94 and 281.

[22] *Records of Assembly: Committees* 1920, p. 282.

Huber, Loder and Negulesco had been delegates to the Assembly, while Anzilotti had been in charge of the League's efforts in turning Article 14 of the Covenant into a living thing. Each state represented on the Council fought for a judge and succeeded, with the exception of Belgium, in securing a judge or (in the case of China) a deputy-judge.

The legal adviser to the British Foreign Office, Sir Cecil Hurst, found the result of the first general election disappointing.[23] His main criticism was that 'there are far too many professors and legal advisers and too few judges'. But in the period immediately prior to the establishment of the Permanent Court, there were few who by profession were international arbitrators, let alone international judges. It was said at the time that 'there are two quite distinct opinions in this matter, the first that lack of this experience will be a serious drawback, the second that it will really have very little importance in the kind of work that the judges will be called upon to undertake'.[24] For his part, like Phillimore and some other members of the Advisory Committee, Hurst valued judicial experience in the fields of national law above academic or diplomatic expertise in international law. He ended his internal memorandum on the election in the following way:

The Court only contains three men who have had judicial experience. It is made up of three judges, three legal advisers and five professors. I think I can safely prophesy that it will be completely dominated by Lord Finlay and Loder, assisted by a vast fund of information which Moore will provide, and troubled with a certain amount of narrow obstructiveness from Anzilotti and Huber. I doubt if the rest will count.[25]

At the time of their election, Anzilotti, Beichmann, de Bustamante, Moore and Weiss were members of the Institut de Droit International, and Huber and Loder were *associés*.[26] Nine years later, Altamira, Negulesco and Oda had also been invited to join the Institut.[27]

The preliminary session

The preliminary session of the Permanent Court in early 1922 was attended by all ordinary judges except the South American judges. The

---

[23] See Hurst's memorandum, 15 September 1921, FO 371 W10008/22/98.

[24] Sweetser to Root, 17 September 1921, Moore papers 176.

[25] Cf. Alexander P. Fachiri, *The Permanent Court of International Justice: Its Constitution, Procedure and Work* (2nd edn, London, 1932), p. 16. Judge Nyholm agreed in the criticism that there were too few magistrates; indeed, he regarded himself as the only one; cf. Nyholm, 'Cour permanente', p. 250; and Nyholm to Minister, 6 June 1928, Rigsarkivet H-12-14.

[26] See (1921) 28 *Annuaire*, pp. xvii–xxv.   [27] See (1931) 37-II *Annuaire*, pp. xii–xxiv.

Permanent Court was to elect a president, frame its rules of procedure and settle various other matters. The election of a president was a sensitive issue. The choice would seem to have been between Judge Finlay, the most senior judge,[28] and Judge Loder, who was a national of the neutral state in which the Peace Palace was situated.[29] The election of a president was seen by some as politically important. A United States diplomat submitted the following observations:

Already, I understand that much interest centers in the selection of the President of the Court. There appear to be two candidates under consideration – namely, Lord Finlay, of England, and Mr B. C. J. Loder, of the Netherlands. Mr Loder claims, I believe, to have the support of France and Spain, and in addition gossip is to the effect that the States represented on the Court which were neutral during the war will also cast their votes in his favor. Lord Finlay is supposed to have the support of Italy. The attitude of the United States, Cuba and Brazil is unknown, but their votes are important if Lord Finlay is to have any chance of becoming the President of the Court.

Mr Loder is, I believe, well known to the Department. He was the Dutch representative on the Commission of Jurists convoqued by the Council of the League of Nations for the establishment of a project of statute for a Permanent Court of International Justice, and is one of the foremost authorities on international law in the Netherlands. He has, however, a somewhat excitable and nervous temperament, and I gather that his selection as President, while perhaps personally agreeable to M. van Karnebeek, would not be viewed especially favorably by other members of the Foreign Office nor by the Dutch personnel of the Court of Arbitration, nor in certain other Dutch circles. I hear the remark from Dutchmen of prominence that the selection of Lord Finlay would undoubtedly add to the prestige of the Court and would therefore be in the interests of the Court itself. It is said that the French are most active in the support of Mr Loder and believe that the appointment of a British Judge as President would convey the impression to the world at large that the Court was under the influence of British jurisprudence. There is also the argument that Lord Finlay is rather too old to assume the responsibilities connected with the office of President.[30]

At the first meeting, Judge Finlay proposed Judge Loder as chairman, and Judge Loder was subsequently elected president, although, as noted

---

[28] See Carlin's note, 13 December 1921, *Documents diplomatiques suisses, 1848–1945* (Bern, 1979–92), vol. 8, p. 382; and also [William] Finlay to Hurst, 6 February 1922, FO 371 W1219/505/98; Green to Moore, 8 December 1921, Moore papers 176; and Moore to Johnson, 9 February 1932, Moore papers 177.

[29] As regards the election of the President of the Advisory Committee, see Spiermann, 'Advisory Committee', pp. 193–5. Back then, Loder had stressed that the question of electing a president 'was really not one of age but a material question of the greatest importance': see Hammarskjöld's memorandum, 15 June 1920, Hammarskjöld papers 500.

[30] Phillips to Secretary of State, 18 January 1922, NARA 500 C114/169.

by Max Huber, the vote was not unanimous.[31] It was reported that 'Lord Finlay's action has created a most favorable impression in Dutch circles, and is one more evidence of the cleverness with which the British are co-operating with their Dutch neighbors across the Channel'.[32] On the proposal of Judge Anzilotti, the election of the vice-president of the Permanent Court was postponed, but eventually Judge Weiss was elected by a majority.[33]

In comparison, the judges' election of Åke Hammarskjöld as registrar of the Permanent Court was less controversial. In 1920, he had been appointed to a position in the Legal Section of the Secretariat of the League, having the launch of the Permanent Court under Anzilotti's supervision as his main occupation. They had assisted the Advisory Committee of Jurists and followed the matter closely on its way through the political processes of the League. Hammarskjöld had prepared the preliminary session of the Permanent Court at which he appeared as its acting secretary and it was, in Anzilotti's words, 'impossible de trouver un autre candidat qui a une intelligence aussi élevée et a un dévouement aussi complet réunisse une connaissance de l'organisation de la Cour comparable à celle qu'en a M. Hammarskjöld'.[34] When the time had come for the draft-scheme adopted by the Advisory Committee to be submitted to the Council of the League, Anzilotti had told Sir Eric Drummond, the Secretary-General of the League, that Hammarskjöld 'is quite well acquainted with every question discussed by the Committee and I regard his presence at San Sebastian [as] almost as necessary as mine'.[35] According to James Brown Scott, who had accompanied Root to the session of the Advisory Committee, 'Mr Hammarskjöld inherits a great name, and he seems destined to increase its lustre if health and years are added to ability and tact, poise and judgment'.[36] In February 1922, Åke Hammarskjöld was twenty-eight years old.

---

[31] See Series D No. 2 (1922) at 1 and 5; and also Max Huber, *Denkwürdigkeiten, 1907–1924* (Zurich, 1974), p. 270. Nine votes were cast in favour of Judge Loder, with Judge Weiss obtaining two votes. Elihu Root, who had met Loder at the session of the Advisory Committee, was reported as having said that 'the Court did exactly the right thing in making him President': see Moore to Loder, 14 March 1922, Moore papers 177.

[32] Phillips to Secretary of State, 6 February 1922, NARA 500 C114/170.

[33] See Series D No. 2 (1922) at 4–5 and 26. Judge Weiss obtained seven votes, Judge Anzilotti three votes and Judge Huber and Deputy-Judge Beichmann one vote each.

[34] Anzilotti to Moore, 4 November 1921, Moore papers 176.

[35] Anzilotti to Drummond, 17 July 1920, League of Nations Archives 21-5729-4959.

[36] Scott, *Project of a Permanent Court*, p. 9. See also Spiermann, 'Advisory Committee', pp. 190–1; and Dorothy V. Jones, *Toward a Just World: The Critical Years in the Search for International Justice* (Chicago, 2002), pp. 24–8.

The Rules of Court were adopted at the preliminary session.[37] Chapter 1 covered the constitution and work of the Permanent Court, while Chapter 2 dealt with the Permanent Court's contentious procedure in Articles 32–70 and its advisory procedure in Articles 71–74. The specific authorisation in Article 23 of the Statute to replace 15 June as the opening date of the Permanent Court's ordinary session was not employed; the same provision authorised the president to summon an extraordinary session 'whenever necessary'.

As to the form of the decisions, Articles 62 and 71 of the Rules did not require that a judgment or an advisory opinion contain the result of the vote on the *dispositif*, or advice, nor were dissenters under a duty publicly to declare their dissent, much less to append a dissenting opinion. However, although it was officially unknown how many judges dissented from the Permanent Court's decisions, and the identity of such judges, the foundational period between 1922 and 1924 appeared to have seen no examples of judges voting against the *dispositif* or advice without making their vote public.[38]

The Permanent Court's advisory jurisdiction was not referred to in the Statute and it kept being suppressed in the Rules. At the preliminary session, the judges had had before them a report by Judge Moore which was highly critical of the advisory jurisdiction,[39] and for the time being Articles 71–74 of the Rules left most questions unanswered.[40] Eventually answers had to be given as the Permanent Court responded to the several requests made by the Council of the League for opinions pursuant to Article 14 of the Covenant. Indeed, these kept the Permanent Court alive during the first years of its existence.[41]

Hammering out the Rules of Court had not been an altogether easy task for the newly elected judges to complete. Judge Moore later recalled that '[t]here were many cloudy and stormy days in February and March 1922'.[42] At the time, although originally quite optimistic,[43] Judge Moore had reported as follows:

---

[37] See Rules of Court adopted on 24 March 1922, Series D No. 1 (1926) at 66–82.

[38] See Series D No. 2, Add.1 (1926) at 209.

[39] Series D No. 2 (1922) at 383–98; and also John Bassett Moore, 'The Organization of the Permanent Court of International Justice' (1922) 22 *Columbia Law Review* 497 at 507–8.

[40] Series D No. 2 (1922) at 398 and 98–9, 159–61 and 219–21.

[41] In 1927, Hudson wrote that the advisory jurisdiction 'has proved so useful that people now think it indispensable. That is my own opinion also.' See Hudson to Borchard, 25 November 1927, Hudson papers 76.7.

[42] Moore to Nyholm, 20 May 1928, Moore papers 176.

[43] Moore to [Mrs] Moore, 11 February 1922, Moore papers 49.

Ld Finlay, in our talk, said it had seemed to be supposed that we were to be 'supermen', but that it seemed to be turning out that we were very inferior men, since we spent our time in discussing and disagreeing over trivial questions of detail which ought not to be dealt with at all. I replied that, at the present rate, we might go on until November next . . . There is, I may say, a marked tendency on the part of the Latins to act together, and to this group I would assign Max Huber, although he is from German Switzerland. Of course, they might say that the rest exhibit a similar tendency; but I think that the votes of the rest of us usually coincide with our reasons, and that we do not divide in our reasoning and then vote in union. I think that what I have called the 'Latin' group rather expected my general support, and this expectation may have been strengthened by my voting with them on the first question that came before us. Subsequently, however, I have often disappointed them.[44]

Among the members of this 'Latin group', Judge Moore drew attention to Judge Anzilotti, 'a man of great independence of mind, . . . [who] perhaps is often led to vote in a certain way lest he may seem to be swayed by the opinions of others and particularly of those of Mr Loder, the President of the Court'. He added that Judge Anzilotti 'may have an excessive tendency to differ, especially with those by whom he would wish not to be unduly influenced'. Like Judge Moore, Judge Huber complained about certain judges, in particular President Loder and Judge Nyholm, automatically subjecting the Permanent Court to procedural principles taken from civil law. However, Judge Huber added that 'Anzilotti und ich, meistens von Moore unterstützt, vertraten den Standpunkt, daß der Internationale Gerichtshof die richterliche Unabhängigkeit und die Stabilität seiner Zusammensetzung mit der nationalen Justiz gemein habe, nicht aber sein Verfahren, in dem die Parteien souveräne Staaten sind, und daß er mit dem Massenbetrieb staatlicher Gerichte sich nicht vergleichen lasse'.[45]

In another letter written on 13 February 1922, on which day the judges had discussed various questions relating to technical assessors in cases concerning communications and transit,[46] Judge Moore added to his picture:

---

[44] Moore to [Mrs] Moore, 13 February 1922, Moore papers 49.
[45] Huber, *Denkwürdigkeiten*, p. 272 (translation: 'Anzilotti and I, normally supported by Moore, held the view that the Permanent Court shared with the national judiciary the judicial independence and the permanency of its bench, but not its procedure, the parties being sovereign states, and that the Permanent Court could not be compared with the mass-industry that are national courts.').
[46] See Series D No. 2 (1922) at 34–8.

I really feel much concern about the future of our work. Saturday's discussion was bad enough, but today's was really disheartening. You ought to see the record of the discussions. I always speak briefly, and try to confine my remarks to the fundamental point. I refrain as much as possible from speaking at all. Ld Finlay follows the same course, and so does Mr Loder. But the flood of talk goes on, and inundates us! Mr Yovanovitch, the Serbian, I may remark, makes no speeches at all, as he can command only his native tongue and German. He sits with an interpreter behind him, and has all he can do to catch enough to vote on. The Japanese, Mr Oda, speaks French which only one of the French–English interpreters, who sits by him, can understand, but I do him only justice when I say that, when he says anything, it is very brief and to the point. Mr Weiss, the French judge, speaks rather frequently, but the principal orators are Huber and Anzilotti. Today, most of the talking was done by Huber. He is impulsive and discursive, and raises all sorts of points, and until he comes to vote it is hard to know where he stands or how he intends to range himself.

. . .

It is an incalculable misfortune that we have on the Court any one who was connected with previous discussions and particularly with the formulation of the Statute. Anzilotti, Huber, Altamira and Loder were all so connected. In consequence they cannot free themselves from the prepossessions and the disturbing influences of prior debates. Whenever a topic is taken up, their minds revert to the questions that were threshed over, but not settled, and they proceed – particularly Huber and Anzilotti – to debate as if no statute had been passed, losing sight of the fact that we must look for our powers to our charter and not to previous proposals. This is the situation in which we actually find ourselves.[47]

Outlook for the Permanent Court

Writing about the Hague Peace Conferences and the Permanent Court of Arbitration in the tradition of the *Buchrecht*, Professor Walther Schücking had submitted that '[d]er stolze Friedenspalast, der dort von tausend fleißigen Händen aufgeführt ist, ist nur das Symbol einer neuen Zeit'.[48] The early 1920s was the time for similarly 'optimist' statements about the future of international adjudication, yet on the bench balanced and unsentimental views prevailed. Certainly, those who would become the leading members of the Permanent Court in the following years did not cherish 'that "pathetic fallacy" . . . that war was about disputes, and could be controlled by providing a court for the pacific settlement

---

[47] Moore to [Mrs] Moore, 13 February 1922, Moore papers 49.
[48] Walther Schücking, *Der Staatenverband der Haager Konferenzen* (Munich, 1912), p. ix (in the English translation: '[t]he stately Peace Palace, which has been built there by a thousand industrious hands, is merely the symbol of a new age'). See also Weiss, *Manuel de droit international privé*, pp. xv–xvi.

of disputes, as if that were a straight alternative, and as if wars must always have a lawyer's idea of a dispute at the core'.[49] At an early point, Judge Anzilotti had asked:

What are we warranted to expect of this new Organisation of International Justice? There are two categories of persons: those who envisage the Court as the opening up of a new epoch in international relations, and those who cannot mention the Court without a mocking smile on their lips or in their hearts. Both categories are mistaken, and the first rather more than the latter.[50]

At the inaugural meeting of the Permanent Court on 15 February 1922, President Loder had made the same point.[51] In Judge Anzilotti's view, '[t]his and no other is the *raison d'être* and the function of the Court: to facilitate and develop the solution according to law, not of the great international conflicts, but of the ordinary disputes which to-day are less adequately dealt with by diplomacy, an organisation little suited for the purpose'. As for those who expected 'more of new devices than is reasonable or practical', Judge Moore took the view that '[t]his is because human beings do not sufficiently take into account their limitations. No human institution can survive without public confidence and support. I trust that the new international tribunal may turn out to have this assurance of usefulness and permanency.'[52]

In a publication issued by the League of Nations, but which was substantially a reproduction of a paper prepared by Åke Hammarskjöld, the following was said about the Permanent Court:

The importance of the new Court for the development of international law and for the maintenance of peace rests, above all, upon its personal and material competence. The importance of the Court is great and should not be underrated. However, it would be dangerous to attribute to the Court an importance that could not belong to it. Upon exaggerated hopes or confidence would follow – as was the case with regard to the Permanent Court of Arbitration – the blackest scepticism. This scepticism would constitute a very great danger to the young institution and would jeopardise the blessings that the world is entitled to expect from its creation and activities.

. . .

---

[49] R. Y. Jennings, 'The "World Court" is Necessarily a Regional Court' in Daniel Bardonnet (ed.), *The Peaceful Settlement of International Disputes in Europe: Future Prospects* (Dordrecht, 1991), p. 305 at p. 306.

[50] See Dionisio Anzilotti, 'The Permanent Court of International Justice' (being a translation by Hammarskjöld of the manuscript of a speech given in 1923), Hammarskjöld papers 478.

[51] See Series D No. 2 (1922) at 329.

[52] Moore to Balch, 24 September 1921, Moore papers 217.

To create little by little, by practical and successive solutions, a conscience of justice within the community of nations, and to make that community love the conception of justice, to compel nations to feel and appreciate the invaluable blessings of law, that is what those who are equally far from sharing the thoughtless enthusiasm of some, and the unwarrantable scepticism of others, may confidently expect from this new institution.[53]

Just after his election, Max Huber had written to Professor Manley O. Hudson: 'The Court is, I think, rather well composed, but, I fear, that it is too numerous. Very much will depend on its first decisions. I hope and I trust that they will be absolutely impartial, this is important above all.'[54] To Judge Moore, he had written that:

I always was of [the] opinion that public opinion, including the lawyers, have a tendency to overrate the importance and effectiveness of an international judiciary for international peace, but it is nevertheless very gratifying that this opinion exists and it is our duty to give credit to it and to deepen and strengthen the esteem in which international arbitration is held in the world. The moral responsibility of the Court in deciding the first cases and in giving their argumentation is immense. The world is disgusted with politics of interest and influence and longs for an institution of real impartiality. We must not only be impartial but even try to avoid the appearance of partiality.[55]

The Permanent Court and advisory opinions

The International Labour Organization opinions

In 1922, at its first session, the Permanent Court delivered three advisory opinions concerning the Constitution of the International Labour Organization. The judges had disagreed on how to approach the Constitution. A United States diplomat formerly at The Hague was informed that 'the Court has worked with less friction than it did last winter, but the burden of work on two or three of us was really heavy'.[56] Also, again according to Judge Moore, '[t]he burden of Court work came to rest very heavily on some of the members, of whom I was one . . . We

---

[53] League of Nations, *The Permanent Court of International Justice* (Geneva, 1921), p. 20; as for Hammarskjöld's role, see *ibid.*, p. 3, note 1. Cf. Wilhelm G. Grewe, *The Epochs of International Law* (3rd edn, Berlin, 2000), p. 618.

[54] Huber to Hudson, 10 November 1921, Hudson papers 9.8.

[55] Huber to Moore, 21 October 1921, Moore papers 176; and see Huber, *Denkwürdigkeiten*, p. 305. Cf. Advisory Committee, *Procès-verbaux*, p. 721, in which the presence of judges *ad hoc* was justified by referring to the principle that '[j]ustice . . . must not only be just, but appear so'.

[56] Moore to Phillips, 15 August 1922, Moore papers 49 and NARA 500 C114/360.

rendered in all three opinions, after numerous public hearings and many private deliberations.[57] In President Loder's view, 'we lost a considerable amount of time in scarcely useful discussions'.[58]

As for the first opinion concerning the nomination of a delegate to the International Labour Conference, a suggestion made by Judge Finlay had been adopted to the effect that the *motifs* should be made as short as possible, quashing an earlier draft.[59] The reasoning, as finally adopted, was confined to the specific provision in question.[60] It conveyed a common-sense flavour and avoided references to principles of treaty interpretation. In contrast, in the second opinion, that is, the *Competence of the International Labour Organization* opinion on whether the competence of the International Labour Organization extended to agriculture, different views and principles were intermingled as the *motifs* touched on and gave support to almost every general principle of treaty interpretation.[61] Since the Permanent Court drew a veil over the disagreements – with the result that none of their views were adequately treated in the *motifs* – an analysis of the first two opinions would not be of much value. Indeed, when preparing the second *Competence of the International Labour Organization* opinion in 1926, the judges disagreed as to the interpretation of 'les précédents' from 1922, Judges de Bustamante, Loder, Nyholm, Oda and Pessôa forming a minority.[62] The third opinion was, on the other hand, uncontroversial, the *motifs* brief and unexciting.[63]

---

[57] Moore to Borchard, 15 August 1922, Moore papers 48.

[58] Loder to Moore, 29 December 1922, Moore papers 177.

[59] See Finlay to Moore, 15 July 1922, Moore papers 177; Finlay to Hammarskjöld, 16 July 1922 and Hammarskjöld to Finlay, 16 July 1922, both Hammarskjöld papers 480.

[60] *Nomination of the Workers' Delegate to the International Labour Conference*, Series B No. 1 (1922) at 17–27.

[61] *International Labour Organization and the Conditions of Agricultural Labour*, Series B No. 2 (1922) at 21–41. See also Hammarskjöld to [Hjalmar] Hammarskjöld, 13 August 1922, Hammarskjöld papers 29. Judge Weiss and Deputy-Judge Negulesco declared a dissent from the advice that the International Labour Organization was competent in the field of agriculture and the latter filed 'an "opinion" for private circulation': see Moore to Huber, 15 August 1922, Moore papers 177. The second opinion was quoted twice by the International Law Commission in its commentary on the general rule of treaty interpretation: see YILC 1966-II, pp. 221–2. The second and third opinions would seem to have been prepared by Judge Moore, Distr. 3046, van Eysinga papers 145, possibly in collaboration with Judges Anzilotti and Finlay: see Moore to Finlay, 7 August 1922, Moore papers 176.

[62] See Eleventh session, *Procès-Verbal* 16 (8 July 1926), reproduced in Epitácio Pessôa, *Côrte permanente de justiça international (1923–1930)* (Rio de Janeiro, 1960), p. 109.

[63] *International Labour Organization and the Methods of Agricultural Production*, Series B No. 3 (1922) at 53–9.

The two subsequent opinions were more informative. These were the *Nationality Decrees* opinion rendered at the second session early in 1923 and the *Eastern Carelia* opinion, which was delivered later the same year at the third session. Using the terminology of the model developed in Chapter 3, both opinions raised the question how to fit the institutions established under the Covenant into the double structure of international legal argument. Unlike the first session in 1922, Judge Huber was present at the later sessions, and his account of the sessions in 1923 and 1924 was later published as part of his memoirs, *Denkwürdigkeiten, 1907–1924*.

The Nationality Decrees *opinion*

Towards the end of 1922, the Permanent Court was requested to advise upon the competence of the Council of the League of Nations in respect of a dispute between France and the United Kingdom. The resulting opinion was an early demonstration of the basic structure of international legal argument not being dominating in all kinds of cases; in particular, it could not prevent the articulation of an international lawyer's approach to treaty interpretation.

In the French protectorates of Tunis and Morocco, decrees had been promulgated designating certain individuals born within the territories as Tunisian and Moroccan subjects respectively. Another set of decrees had made them French subjects. Some of the affected persons (who were affected in the sense that they were conscripted into the French army) were British subjects, and the British Government brought the matter before the Council. Under Article 15(1) of the Covenant, the Council was competent to make recommendations upon 'any dispute likely to lead to a rupture, which is not submitted to arbitration'. In response the French Government invoked the exception contained in Article 15(8):

If the dispute between the parties is claimed by one of them, and is found by the Council, to arise out of a matter which by international law is solely within the domestic jurisdiction of that party, the Council shall so report, and shall make no recommendation as to its settlement.[64]

The Council requested the Permanent Court to advise whether paragraph 8 was applicable to the actual dispute.

---

[64] In French, Article 15(8) provided: 'Si l'une des parties prétend et si le Conseil reconnaît que le différend porte sur une question que le droit international laisse à la compétence exclusive de cette partie, le Conseil le constatera dans un rapport, mais sans recommander aucune solution.'

Paragraph 8 was part of an institutional arrangement, the interpretation of which would be influenced by how an interpreter in this context conceived the state. The English version of paragraph 8 provided that 'by international law' some matters came within 'the domestic jurisdiction', thus the provision, exceptionally, appeared to contain a reference, as it were, to the categorisation of the institutional arrangement within the structures of international legal argument and possibly also their hierarchical relationship. The question of how to understand and treat that reference, not necessarily corresponding with the interpreter's own sense of the hierarchy between the basic and the dynamic structures, was further complicated by differences between the two authoritative versions of the Covenant. This led to a hesitant introduction to the Permanent Court's analysis:

> Special attention must be called to the word '*exclusive*' in the French text, to which the word '*solely*' (within the domestic jurisdiction) corresponds in the English text. The question to be considered is not whether one of the parties to the dispute is or is not competent in law to take or to refrain from taking a particular action, but whether the jurisdiction claimed belongs *solely* to that party.
>
> From one point of view, it might well be said that the jurisdiction of a State is *exclusive* within the limits fixed by international law – using this expression in its wider sense, that is to say, embracing both customary law and general as well as particular treaty law. But a careful scrutiny of paragraph 8 of Article 15 shows that it is not in this sense that exclusive jurisdiction is referred to in that paragraph.
>
> The words 'solely within the domestic jurisdiction' seem rather to contemplate certain matters which, though they may very closely concern the interests of more than one State, are not, in principle, regulated by international law. As regards such matters, each State is sole judge [*seul maître de ses décisions*].[65]

As for the English version of Article 15(8), the term 'solely' led the Permanent Court to suggest that 'more than one State' could be interested in the matter. These interests were not defined by reference to international law; they were the interests of national sovereigns. In the structure of international legal argument based on the conception of the state as a national sovereign, where matters 'are not . . . regulated', i.e., where there is no clash between state interests so serious that it triggers the international law of coexistence, the matter rests with the national principle of self-containedness. Likewise, in the beginning of its report on

---

[65] *Nationality Decrees in Tunis and Morocco*, Series B No. 4 (1923) at 23–4; cf. *ibid.*, pp. 21–2 as to the wording of the request for the advisory opinion.

the Aaland Islands, which like the *Nationality Decrees* opinion was mainly a product of Max Huber's drafting, a Commission of International Jurists had seen paragraph 8 as 'an attribute of the sovereignty of every State'.[66]

Accordingly, the English version of Article 15(8) referred to the basic structure of international legal argument, which contains the national principle of self-containedness. In this structure, while the 'matter' had been categorised with the national principle of self-containedness, it was quite another question how to categorise another state's interference with that matter. As suggested by the word 'solely', this question could well come within the international law of coexistence. Huber explained the distinction as follows:

Le Pacte est basé, comme le droit international commun, sur les Etats comme unités territoriales indépendantes. L'article XV, al. 8, constitue une application du principe proclamé par l'article X. Le Membre de la S. D. N. ne doit subir aucune intervention de la part de la S. D. N. dans ses affairs intérieures, quel que soit l'intérêt que d'autres Etats pourraient y avoir.[67]

The *Nationality Decrees* opinion explored the rationale behind Article 15(8) in terms of a principle of non-intervention under the international law of coexistence, which on this occasion was given a rather broad scope. According to the *motifs*, 'at a given point' the League's interest in being able to make recommendations gave 'way to the equally essential interest of the individual State to maintain intact its independence in matters which international law recognises to be solely within its jurisdiction'.[68] 'Without this reservation', the Permanent Court explained, 'the internal affairs of a country might, directly they appeared to affect the interests of another country, be brought before the Council and form the subject of recommendations by the League of Nations.' In Huber's view:

---

[66] *Aaland Islands Case*, Official Journal 1920 Special Supplement No. 3 (1920) at 5. On Huber's part in the drafting, see Huber, *Denkwürdigkeiten*, pp. 164–5 and 276.

[67] (1931) 36-I *Annuaire*, pp. 78 and see also 79 and 82–6. According to Article 10 of the Covenant, '[t]he Members of the League undertake to respect and preserve as against external aggression the territorial integrity and existing political independence of all Members of the League'.

[68] Series B No. 4 (1923) at 25. The report by the Commission of International Jurists contained similar considerations expressed in Huber's phraseology: 'Any other solution would amount to an infringement of sovereign rights of a State and would involve the risk of creating difficulties and a lack of stability which would not only be contrary to the very idea embodied in the term "State", but would also endanger the interests of the international community': *Aaland Islands Case*, Official Journal 1920, Special Supplement No. 3 (1920) at 5. Likewise, Arbitrator Huber in *Affaire des biens britanniques au Maroc espagnol*, 2 RIAA 615 (1924) at 642; see also (1931) 36-I *Annuaire*, p. 83. Cf. Elihu Root in (1920) 14 *American Society Proceedings*, p. 33.

L'idée de compétences exclusives concrètes (compétences qui, très probable-
ment, ont préoccupé les auteurs de l'article XV, al. 8, du Pacte) a pour but
d'éviter que des compétences considérées en général comme exclusives puis-
sent éventuellement fléchir devant des considérations tirées de l'idée de la
communauté internationale (p. ex. collision entre le droit de commerce et autres
droits dits fondamentaux des Etats avec la souveraineté territoriale, limitation
de l'action pénale au territoire de l'Etat du délit commis, etc.).[69]

With a view to the dispute in question, the *motifs* stated that 'in the
present state of international law, questions of nationality are, in the
opinion of the Court, in principle within this reserved domain'. Weiss
inferred that '[l]es règles concernant la nationalité sont du domaine de
la législation interne de chaque Etat'.[70] That questions of nationality 'in
principle' came within 'this reserved domain' meant that the matters
themselves were not regulated by the international law of coexistence
and that another state's interference with them came within the international law of coexistence, being an illegal intervention.[71]

However, this was not the end of the *motifs*. According to the same
paragraph of the *motifs*, '[t]he question whether a certain matter is or
is not solely within the jurisdiction of a State is an essentially relative
question; it depends upon the development of international relations'.[72]
So in addition to the matter 'in principle' coming within the national
principle of self-containedness, and other states' interferences with the
matter under the international law of coexistence, the *motifs* laid down
a further condition for applying paragraph 8. It was 'limited by rules
of international law' so that if a state had undertaken treaty obligations, paragraph 8, the *motifs* stated, 'then ceases to apply as regards
those States which are entitled to invoke such rules', the dispute taking on 'an international character'.[73] It was because of this possibility of treaty-making that the scope of paragraph 8 was 'an essentially

---

[69] (1931) 36-I *Annuaire*, p. 85.
[70] See Weiss, *Manuel de droit international privé*, p. 3; and likewise Negulesco in Shabtai
Rosenne (ed.), *Conference for the Codification of International Law* (New York, 1975), vol. 3,
p. 910; cf. Series C No. 2 at 45 and 94–5. See also YILC 1997-II.2, p. 18.
[71] Cf. Rundstein in Shabtai Rosenne (ed.), *Committee of Experts for the Progressive Codification
of International Law* (New York, 1972), vol. 2, pp. 35–6; the British Government in
Codification Conference, vol. 1, p. 17; Ian Brownlie, 'The Relations of Nationality in Public
International Law' (1963) 39 *BYIL* 284 at 286–8 and 297–8; and P. Weis, *Nationality and
Statelessness in International Law* (2nd edn, Alphen aan den Rijn, 1979), p. 88.
[72] Series B No. 4 (1923) at 24.   [73] *Ibid.*

relative question'.[74] This shift to the other, dynamic structure of international legal argument did not follow from the reference contained in Article 15(8). True, in the opening passage the Permanent Court had associated the French version of Article 15(8), which referred to 'une question que le droit international laisse à la compétence exclusive de cette partie', with the residuum of international law 'in its wider sense'. But according to the same opening passage, 'careful scrutiny' had made the Permanent Court select the basic structure of international legal argument, representing a continuum from the national principle of self-containedness to the international law of coexistence, in preference to the dynamic structure and the residual principle of state freedom; this 'scrutiny' might well have included the drafting history of paragraph 8.[75] But then there was more to the interpretation of Article 15(8) than linking the reference contained in the provision to the basic structure. According to Huber:

[74] See Huber in (1931) 36-I *Annuaire*, pp. 86 and 83. It has been said that the *dictum* is one among 'several seminal contributions to the contemporary international law of human rights': Stephen M. Schwebel, 'The Roles of the Security Council and the International Court of Justice in the Application of International Humanitarian Law' (1995) 27 *NYUJILP* 731 at 748; and that 'this dictum may be retrospectively called the ground of modern human rights law, even its declaration of independence': Nathaniel Berman, 'Imperial Rivalry and the Genealogy of Human Rights: *The Nationality Decrees Case*' (2000) 94 *American Society Proceedings* 51 at 51; cf. Nathaniel Berman, 'The *Nationality Decrees Case*, or, Of Intimacy and Consent' (2000) 13 *LJIL* 265 at 290–1. According to Judge Ammoun, 'the same Court nevertheless continued faithful to a certain positivism which culminated in the Judgment in 1927 in the *Lotus* case and constantly influenced its subsequent Judgments': see Judge Ammoun's separate opinion in *Barcelona Traction, Light and Power Company, Limited* (Merits), ICJ Reports [1970] 3 at 313. These and most other commentators have focused on this leg of the interpretation, which Gaetano Arangio-Ruiz has termed the 'international law criterion'. His own 'reinterpretation' of the series of cases on domestic jurisdiction starting with the *Nationality Decrees* opinion is an attempt to isolate the other leg, that is, the national principle of self-containedness: see Gaetano Arangio-Ruiz, 'The Plea of Domestic Jurisdiction before the International Court of Justice: Substance or Procedure?' in Vaughan Lowe and Malgosia Fitzmaurice (eds.), *Fifty Years of the International Court of Justice: Essays in Honour of Sir Robert Jennings* (Cambridge, 1996), p. 440 at pp. 457–8; similarly, Martti Koskenniemi, *From Apology to Utopia: The Structure of International Legal Argument* (Helsinki, 1989), pp. 215 and 219–20.

[75] David Hunter Miller, *The Drafting of the Covenant* (New York, 1928), vol. 1, p. 322 and vol. 2, pp. 350, 566 and 700. See the pleadings of the French Government, Series C No. 2 (Supp.) at 19–23 and Series C No. 2 at 57 and 71–89; cf. *ibid.*, p. 215 and, on behalf of the British Government, *ibid.*, pp. 24 and 26. Instead of an 'international law criterion', a political criterion had been suggested previously in the report on the merits in the *Aaland Islands* case submitted by the Commission of Rapporteurs on 16 April 1921: see Document du Conseil B7, 21/68/106, p. 22.

[l]a thèse selon laquelle l'alinéa 8 de l'article XV mettrait à l'écart la S. D. N. chaque fois que le conflit porterait sur une question intérieure semble trouver un appui dans les idées des auteurs du Pacte, mais elle est nettement contraire à son esprit et n'est aucunement exigée par le texte.[76]

Paragraph 8 was only a facet of the institutional arrangement in Article 15, and the Permanent Court resisted making its interpretation dependent on the reference in paragraph 8 to the basic structure of international legal argument. This was because the Permanent Court's own categorisation of the institutional arrangement did not lead it to the basic structure; and because it took the dynamic structure to be hierarchically superior. Despite the reference contained in paragraph 8, the Permanent Court, guided by 'son esprit', saw Article 15 as a whole in the light of the other, dynamic structure advancing from the international law of cooperation to the residual principle of freedom. The *motifs* did at no point doubt the hierarchical superiority of the dynamic structure over the basic structure. Accordingly, the Permanent Court dubbed the definition of the Council's powers in paragraph 1 'the fundamental principle', while paragraph 8 was 'an exception to the principles affirmed in the preceding paragraphs and does not therefore lend itself to an extensive interpretation'.[77] The Permanent Court did not interpret Article 15(1) and the Council's powers restrictively, even though the national principle of self-containedness was suggested, nor in accordance with a sweeping principle of non-intervention under the international law of coexistence. Those powers were rather given an effective interpretation in accordance with the conception of the state as an international law subject. To the extent that 'l'idée de la communauté internationale' had found expression in the international law of cooperation, the Permanent Court was willing to derogate from the drafting history of paragraph 8. Huber was clear on this:

Jusqu'à la création de la S. D. N. et jusqu'au Pacte de Paris les Etats possédaient une compétence exclusive sur la manière dont ils voulaient liquider ou ne pas liquider leurs différends avec d'autres Etats. Cette compétence qui comprenait le droit à la guerre et partant à la négation des droits et même de l'existence d'autres Etats est une conception au fond incompatible avec celle de la communauté internationale et remontant à une période antérieure à celle-ci.

---

[76] (1931) 36-I *Annuaire*, pp. 81 and also 83, according to which Article 15(8) 'a été inséré dans le Pacte pour des raisons politiques déterminées, et non pas pour des considérations tirées du système du Pacte ou du droit international en général'.

[77] Series B No. 4 (1923) at 24 and 25.

Cette limitation de la compétence exclusive est l'événement le plus important dans l'évolution des compétences de l'Etat dans le domaine international.[78]

That the Permanent Court categorised the institutional arrangement differently, and gave preference to the dynamic structure over the basic structure, despite the reference contained in paragraph 8, became abundantly clear when applying paragraph 8 to the facts of the case. According to the Permanent Court, paragraph 8 was inapplicable where 'the legal grounds (titres) relied on are such as to justify the provisional conclusion that they are of juridical importance for the dispute submitted to the Council'.[79] A higher threshold, for example an 'opinion upon the merits of the legal grounds (titres)', would, the Permanent Court said, 'hardly be in conformity with the system established by the Covenant for the pacific settlement of international disputes'. On behalf of the French Government, Professor Lapradelle had made such an exceedingly long speech on the merits of the dispute that it had become rather difficult to hold that the disputed matters could be pronounced on without regard to various treaties.[80] This conclusion was also helped by the Permanent Court's conception of the nature of protectorates, which, in accordance with the views held by Anzilotti, were not a fixed category under international law but to be decided in each case on the basis of 'the special conditions under which they were created'.[81] As a result, paragraph 8 did not apply to the dispute in question.[82]

The Permanent Court's reference to 'the system established by the Covenant for the pacific settlement of international disputes' suggested

---

[78] (1931) 36-I Annuaire, p. 86.   [79] Series B No. 4 (1923) at 26.

[80] As for the relevant part of Professor Lapradelle's speech, see Series C No. 2 at 155–91, which caused Sir Douglas Hogg's brilliant reply on behalf of the British Government, ibid., pp. 200–3, 206–11 and 245; cf. the French Government, ibid., pp. 215–17 and 240. In 1928, Hammarskjöld was reported as having said to a Danish diplomat that only in one case had the oral proceedings influenced the Permanent Court's decision, namely in the case of Hogg due to his 'overlegne Beherskelse af Fakta og Ret og sine common sense betragtninger', that is, his superior command of the factual and legal questions involved as well as his common sense considerations: see despatch to Cohn, 10 May 1928, Rigsarkivet H-12-16. For an attempt to read the Nationality Decrees opinion in the light of the merits of the dispute, possibly assuming that the Permanent Court's interpretation was limited to a choice between the contentions brought forward by the parties, see Berman, 'Nationality Decrees Case', pp. 290–5.

[81] Series B No. 4 (1923) at 27; and likewise Dionisio Anzilotti, Cours de droit internaional (Paris, 1929), pp. 232–3 and 236–7; cf. Huber, Die Staatensuccession, pp. 170–1; and Arbitrator Huber in Affaire des biens britanniques au Maroc espagnol, 2 RIAA 615 (1924) at 648–9. See also Waldock, YILC 1972-II, p. 4; and James Crawford, The Creation of States in International Law (Oxford, 1979), pp. 142, 186–7 and 207.

[82] Series B No. 4 (1923) at 27–31.

a teleological interpretation of Article 15, reflecting the conception of the state as an international law subject. That categorisation of the institutional arrangement within the dynamic structure overshadowed the reference contained in paragraph 8 to the basic structure of international legal argument, and thus the conception of the state as a national sovereign. Indeed, it did so to such a degree that, in Lauterpacht's words, 'in the future no State will invoke with any hope of success the domestic jurisdiction clause'.[83] A crucial lesson of the *Nationality Decrees* opinion was that the Permanent Court was not likely to turn the hierarchy between the dynamic and basic structures of international legal argument upside-down and look through the conception of the state as an international law subject simply because of the wording of the provision in question, or its preparatory work.

The *Nationality Decrees* opinion also made a contribution towards fitting the powers of the institutions established by, or at least mentioned in, the Covenant into what is here referred to as the double structure. This was so, despite the absence of explicit reasoning. For example, the only reason in the *motifs* for a provisional conclusion as to the 'juridical importance' of treaty rules being preferred in the first place was the sweeping reference to 'the system'. This required a considerable amount of creativity on the reader's part. Lauterpacht took the view that the 'provisional' conclusion had to be an opinion on the merits. For if the 'provisional' conclusion proved wrong, Lauterpacht wrote, 'that would mean that the matter is within the domestic jurisdiction of the defendant State, and that the relevancy, as provisionally assumed, did not in fact exist'.[84] Lauterpacht's argument neglected, among other things, that Article 15(8) was to be applied by the Council, not a court of justice.[85] According to the Permanent Court, the Council should make 'such recommendations as are deemed just and proper in the circumstances with a view to the maintenance of peace'.[86] The test laid down by the Permanent Court had nothing to do with abstract debates as to which

---

[83] H. Lauterpacht, *The Development of International Law by the Permanent Court of International Justice* (London, 1934), p. 85; and see also Judge Lauterpacht's dissenting opinion appended to *Interhandel Case*, ICJ Reports [1959] 6 at 121–2; cf. the judgment, *ibid.*, pp. 24–5. A preliminary objection based on a notion of domestic jurisdiction was actually upheld in *Case of Certain Norwegian Loans*, ICJ Reports [1957] 9 at 24–5; cf. Judge Lauterpacht's separate opinion, *ibid.*, pp. 51–2. See also *Aegean Sea Continental Shelf*, ICJ Reports [1978] 3 at paras. 59 and 78.

[84] H. Lauterpacht, *The Function of Law in the International Community* (Oxford, 1933), pp. 362–3. Cf. C. H. M. Waldock, 'The Plea of Domestic Jurisdiction before International Legal Tribunals' (1954) 31 *BYIL* 96 at 111–14.

[85] Cf. *ibid.*, p. 176, note 2.   [86] Series B No. 4 (1923) at 25.

disputes were justiciable. It was about the system of dispute settlement under the Covenant, a treaty, and despite the absence of explicit reasoning, the Permanent Court was clearly unwilling to treat the Council as a judicial body.

According to one Paul de Vineuil, a commentator who explicitly undertook to discern the rationale behind the loose test, 'malgré le risque évident de mal interpréter les intentions de la Cour', there were two main reasons: first, if the Council were to apply a stricter test it would have to go further into the dispute, thereby making paragraph 8 'une arme qui se retourne contre celui qui s'en sert'; secondly, since paragraph 8 referred to what 'by international law' was solely a matter of domestic jurisdiction, a stricter test would have been a legal test approximating compulsory jurisdiction, which, according to this commentator, was why such a test would be contrary to 'the system established by the Covenant for the pacific settlement of international disputes'.[87] In other words, dispute settlement had been categorised within the dynamic structure of international legal argument so that in the absence of specific treaty obligations the residual principle of freedom applied.

'Paul de Vineuil' was a pseudonym of Åke Hammarskjöld, the Registrar of the Permanent Court. Not only had he first-hand knowledge of the deliberations, according to Max Huber, 'Paul de Vineuil's' analysis was based on a first draft of the *motifs* prepared by three judges. As to why the Permanent Court had preferred virtual gaps in the *motifs*, Huber explained:

Das Gutachten wurde von mir entworfen, und trotz starker – von mir, Anzilotti und Beichmann bedauerter – Streichungen ist es fast ganz das Produkt meiner Redaktion, auch in der endgültigen Fassung. Bei der Beratung zeigte es sich, wie wenig die Richter mit der inneren Struktur des Völkerbundpaktes wirklich vertraut waren; daher ihr Bestreben, die Erwägungen, die für die Kenner des Paktes ausschlaggebend, ihnen aber fremd waren, auszuschalten. So konnten Anzilotti, Beichmann und ich nur durch Drohung mit einem Sondergutachten erzielen, daß die für uns wichtigsten Gedanken wenigstens in einer bis fast zur Unverständlichkeit komprimierten Form im Gutachten Platz fanden. Hammarskjöld hat nachher unsere Gedanken in einer Abhandlung in der 'Revue de Droit international de Vinewil' [*sic.*] klar dargelegt.[88]

[87] See Paul de Vineuil, 'Les Leçons du quantrième avis consultatif de la Cour permanente de Justice internationale' (1923) 4 *RDILC* 291 at 299; and also Hammarskjöld in (1932) 37 *Annuaire*, p. 417. Cf. Walther Schücking and Hans Wehberg, *Die Satzung des Völkerbundes* (2nd edn, Berlin, 1924), pp. 591–2.

[88] Huber, *Denkwürdigkeiten*, p. 276 (translation: 'The opinion was drafted by me and the final product was almost entirely due to my drafting, despite widespread deletions, which I, Anzilotti and Beichmann regretted. The deliberations demonstrated that the

According to Judge Moore, '[t]he question before us was not complicated, but a week was consumed in hearing the arguments of counsel, and this was followed by a somewhat prolonged discussion, rather minute in its details, as to what the opinion should or should not contain'.[89] Huber's account of the deliberations may be compared to a letter written by Judge Moore to Judge Finlay about 'the revised draft opinion':

I am sorry to be compelled to think that the revision is much more open to exception than was the original draft. While I do not find that anything to which objection was made has been omitted, I encounter numerous passages, wholly or partly new, which are altogether unacceptable.

After all that was said at our last conference upon the importance of confining our opinion to the question before the Court, and the general approval with which this seemed to meet, I am astonished to find that the revised draft actually puts the Court . . . in the place of the Council, and then proceeds through a number of pages . . . to elaborate and lay down rules by which the Council must be governed. Not only is this in itself improper, but the rules laid down are, in my opinion, quite inadmissible, and would virtually deprive the Council of the power to find that a matter is within the exclusive competence of one of the parties. This is all the more strange, since the general design of what is said seems to have been to limit the Council's powers of interposition. But, in any event, all that is said on this subject is purely gratuitous. It is not within the terms of reference.

As bootless discussions are undesirable, and as some of our colleagues apparently cannot be brought to accept the distinction, which I conceive to be fundamental, between holding that the particular matter now before the Court is not one of exclusive national competence, and laying down a general rule for the government of the Council in all conceivable cases, I think my best course, in the interest of all concerned, will be to file a brief concurring opinion, referring to Art. 59 of the Statute as applying by analogy to Advisory Opinions, and containing substantially the short statement I read the other day.[90]

It is remarkable that Hammarskjöld made an attempt to add to the *motifs* a rationale that had been rejected, or at least suppressed, by members

judges had only a limited understanding of the inner structure of the Covenant; hence their endeavour to eliminate the considerations which were decisive for the experts on the Covenant, but with which they were unfamiliar. Only by threatening to append a separate opinion did Anzilotti, Beichmann and I arrange for the thoughts that we regarded as being most important to be included, though in a form so compressed that it became almost unintelligible. Subsequently Hammarskjöld has explained our thoughts in an article by Vineuil in the Revue de Droit International.').

[89] Moore to de Bustamante, 15 March 1923, Moore papers 49.

[90] Moore to Finlay, 29 January 1923, Moore papers 177; and see also Moore to Finlay, 4 February 1923, Moore papers 177. Cf. *Certain Expenses of the United Nations (Article 17, Paragraph 2, of the Charter)*, ICJ Reports [1962] 151 at 167–8.

of the Permanent Court. Part of the immediate background of 'Paul de Vineuil's' article was an early, perfidious case-note in the *American Journal of International Law*, which had aroused much ill-feeling with Judges Anzilotti and Huber.[91] 'Paul de Vineuil's' article had actually been authorised by President Loder.[92]

More articles followed and in an attempt to persuade Hudson to follow 'Vineuil's' lead in his annual review articles on the Permanent Court's work, Hammarskjöld explained that 'the Vineuil articles as a rule are written with the precise intention of indicating the angle from which the various decisions should be envisaged'.[93] The articles were written to shed light on decisions of the Permanent Court which 'have been very widely misunderstood'. 'Paul de Vineuil' did not merely point out the various misunderstandings: he provided his readers with a correct understanding of the decisions. In plugging the gaps in the *motifs*, 'Paul de Vineuil' selected a view from among the possibly conflicting views that had cancelled out each other in the course of the deliberations. It will become clear that on most occasions the views of 'Paul de Vineuil' perfectly matched those of Judge Huber, with whom Hammarskjöld was on exceptionally good terms.[94] According to Huber, Hammarskjöld made considerable contributions during the deliberations.[95]

In the *Nationality Decrees* opinion, a mere 'provisional conclusion' as to the Council's powers had been accepted, according to 'Paul de Vineuil', partly because compulsory jurisdiction of a judicial kind was alien to the Covenant and thus fell outside (this part of) the international law of cooperation. Even if this way of drawing the line between the international law of cooperation and the residual principle of freedom had been backed by a majority, it would undoubtedly have been controversial. It was arguably at variance with the draft-scheme adopted by the Advisory Committee of Jurists – and certainly with strong views held by President

---

[91] See Anzilotti to Hammarskjöld, 15 May 1923, Hammarskjöld papers 478 and Hammarskjöld to Hudson, 24 March 1923, Hudson papers 8.31 regarding Charles Noble Gregory, 'An Important Decision by the Permanent Court of International Justice' (1923) 17 *AJIL* 298 at 306; see also Moore to Gray, August 1923 (not sent), Moore papers 177; and Manley O. Hudson, 'The Second Year of the Permanent Court of International Justice' (1924) 18 *AJIL* 1 at 6 and 30, note 114.

[92] Hammarskjöld to de Visscher, 13 February 1923, Hammarskjöld papers 488.

[93] Hammarskjöld to Hudson, 21 August 1924 and 29 February 1924, both Hudson papers 8.32.

[94] See Peter Vogelsanger, *Max Huber: Recht, Politik, Humanität aus Glauben* (Frauenfeld, 1967), p. 140; and also Huber, *Denkwürdigkeiten*, pp. 185, 186 and 271.

[95] Max Huber, 'In Memoriam Åke Hammarskjöld (1893–1937)' in Åke Hammarskjöld, *Juridiction internationale* (Leiden, 1938), p. 7 at pp. 19–20.

Loder, according to whom the Permanent Court had been vested with compulsory jurisdiction in consequence of Article 14 of the Covenant.[96] In the following request for an advisory opinion, in the *Eastern Carelia* case, it became harder to veil this disagreement since the new case fell to be decided by the judges' conception of the Permanent Court and its functions under the Covenant and the Statute.

The Eastern Carelia *opinion*

The request for an advisory opinion in the *Eastern Carelia* case arose out of a dispute between Finland and Russia. The Finnish Government contended that – in a declaration mentioned only in a *procès-verbal* of the meeting at which the two states had signed the Dorpat Treaty, recognising Finland's independence – Russia had undertaken certain obligations towards Finland as regards the status and treatment of the inhabitants of Eastern Carelia.

At the time Russia was not a member of the League and, therefore, had not 'once and for all', as the Permanent Court said, consented to the Covenant and the system of dispute settlement set up by Articles 12–16.[97] Having characterised independence as 'a fundamental principle of international law [*la base même du droit international*]', the Permanent Court added: 'It is well established in international law that no State can, without its consent, be compelled to submit its disputes with other States either to mediation or to arbitration, or to any other kind of pacific settlement.' In other words, dispute settlement did not come within the international law of coexistence, but in the absence of consent the residual principle of freedom applied. According to Article 17 of the Covenant, the Permanent Court went on, the actual dispute between

---

[96] For Loder's – unconvincing – interpretation of the Covenant, see Advisory Committee, *Procès-verbaux*, pp. 249–51; *Records of Assembly: Plenary* 1920, pp. 445–6; and B. C. J. Loder, 'The Permanent Court of International Justice and Compulsory Jurisdiction' (1921–2) 2 *BYIL* 6; see also Hammarskjöld to Van Hamel, 23 June 1920, Hammarskjöld papers 480; and Spiermann, 'Advisory Committee', p. 210. Indeed, President Loder had taken the view that 'the preliminary question and the question "au fond" are so narrowly connected that an answer to the first can only be based on a conviction about the second', Loder to Moore, 29 December 1922, Moore papers 177.

[97] *Status of Eastern Carelia*, Series B No. 5 (1923) at 27. In 1922, the Permanent Court had decided, by eight votes to three, not to include Russia in the list of states entitled to appear before the Permanent Court, even though the recognition that Russia lacked at the time had to do with its government rather than its status as a state; cf. Series E No. 1 (1922–5) at 260–1; and also the various excerpts from *procès-verbaux* kept as van Eysinga papers 134. On the initiative of the Secretariat of the League, Russia was added to the list in 1925: see *ibid.*, p. 261.

Finland and Russia could only be entertained if Russia 'apart from any existing obligations' gave its consent, which it had not done. As the dispute could not be submitted 'for solution according to the methods provided for in the Covenant',[98] any 'intervention' by the Council would be *ultra vires*, and it was concluded that '[t]he Court therefore finds it impossible to give its opinion'.[99] This line of reasoning was straightforward, applying the conception of the state as an international sovereign to Russia. So long as Russia had not undertaken any treaty obligations, a residual principle of state freedom applied. It may be added that this part of the *motifs* closely reflected a note prepared by Judge Anzilotti.[100]

Perhaps it could have been asked why the Permanent Court had to scrutinise the Council's powers *ex officio* and made the giving of an opinion conditional upon the Council not having acted *ultra vires*. Max Huber, referring to Judge Anzilotti and himself, gave a short answer to this question: 'Wir erkannten – und Anzilottis Scharfblick war dies vor mir klar geworden – daß die Erstattung des geforderten Gutachtens einer Umgehung des Völkerbundpaktes gleichkäme und daß das Gericht daher dem Auftrag des Rates gar nicht nachkommen dürfe.'[101] There seemed to be no doubt about this analogy from Article 36(4) of the Statute, which applied the principle of *compétence-de-la-compétence* to the Permanent Court's contentious jurisdiction.[102]

---

[98] Series B No. 5 (1923) at 28.   [99] *Ibid.*

[100] See 'Memorandum by Mr Moore', Distr. 361, undated, p. 12, Moore papers 180.

[101] Huber, *Denkwürdigkeiten*, p. 277 (translation: 'We realised – and Anzilotti's keen mind had made him realise this before I did – that allowing the requested opinion would be equal to circumventing the Covenant and that therefore the Court ought not to comply with the Council's request at all.').

[102] See the Registrar's report, Series D No. 2, Add.3 (1936) at 837; and also *Rio Grande Irrigation and Land Company, Limited v. United States*, 6 RIAA 131 (1923) at 135–6. Cf., in respect of procedural aspects, *Questions relating to Settlers of German Origin in Poland*, Series B No. 6 (1923) at 22. The following year, in his dissenting opinion appended to the Permanent Court's judgment in the *Mavrommatis* case, Judge Moore stated that '[t]here are certain elementary conceptions common to all systems of jurisprudence, and one of these is the principle that a court of justice is never justified in hearing and adjudging the merits of a cause of which it has not jurisdiction': see Series A No. 2 (1924) at 57–8, which can be compared to *Rights of Minorities in Upper Silesia (Minority Schools)*, Series A No. 15 (1928) at 23. One may also recall the judgment of the United States Supreme Court in *Marbury v. Madison*, 5 US (1 Cranch) 137 (1803); according to Judge Moore, Chief Justice Marshall had had 'a power, penetration and simplicity of thought never surpassed if ever equalled on the bench, judicially to establish the system of constitutional law which has so vitally contributed not only to the unity and power of the United States but to the development of legal and political action throughout the world': Moore to Stone, 26 August 1924, Moore papers 52.

At the time the Permanent Court met to begin its deliberations, Judges Anzilotti, Finlay, Huber and Moore and Deputy-Judge Wang were prepared to lodge a dissenting opinion should a majority decide to give the advisory opinion requested by the Council.[103] In the end, these judges became the backbone of the narrow majority decision. Judge Moore later wrote that:

I have not hesitated to say, in talking with my friends, that, if the decision in the Eastern Carelia case had been contrary to what, by 7 to 4, it actually was, I would have resigned from the Court at the end of the session, for the simple reason that it would have been a waste of time to continue on a professorly 'world' tribunal, which had by its want of independence destroyed all possibility of ever being more than a mere subordinate and subservient agency of the Council of the League. I have never told you the inner history of the Eastern Carelia case. It brought us close to the precipice.[104]

Judges Altamira, de Bustamante, Nyholm and Weiss dissented without appending any opinions. Later Judge de Bustamante explained that, in his view, the Permanent Court should not review the Council's competence *ex officio*,[105] while Judge Nyholm perhaps put into practice his view that ideally the consent of the respondent was not needed before '*le tribunal mondial*'.[106] Judge Altamira soon declared that in his view the Permanent Court's advisory jurisdiction should be treated as fundamentally different from its 'judicial function properly so-called',[107] the Permanent Court's role being to give secret advice to the League organs.

The members of the majority would also seem to have disagreed on the reasons for their result. Indeed, Judge Moore submitted a memorandum in which he made the following proposal:

The notification [to the Russian Government] was given by the Court in conformity with the terms of the Resolution of the Council, which requested the Court

---

[103] Huber, *Denkwürdigkeiten*, pp. 277–8.

[104] Moore to Chamberlain, 9 July 1925, Moore papers 54.

[105] Antonio Sanchez de Bustamante y Sirvén, 'La función consultiva del Tribunal Permanente de Justicia Internacional' (1924) 73 *Revista general de legislación y jurisprudencia* 519 at 520–1; and Antonio Sanchez de Bustamante y Sirvén, *The World Court* (New York, 1925), p. 278.

[106] D. G. Nyholm, *Le Tribunal mondial* (Cairo, 1918), pp. 12–15 and 29; and see Nyholm, 'Cour permanente', p. 260.

[107] See Rafael Altamira y Crevea, 'El Tribunal Permanente de Justicia Internacional' (1925–6) 6 *Anales de la Universidad de Valencia* 155 at 163; and Rafael Altamira y Crevea, *La Sociedad de las Naciones y el Tribunal Permanente de Justicia Internacional* (Madrid, 1931), pp. 234–42 and 257; and also Series D No. 2, Add.1 (1926) at 193, 293–4, 286–7 and 264; Series E No. 4 (1927–8) at 77–8; and Series D No. 2, Add.3 (1936) at 925.

to give an advisory opinion on the question presented to it, 'taking into consideration the information which the various countries concerned may equally present to the Court'. If, as was thus expressly admitted, the Court, in order to give its opinion, needed 'information' from the parties, we are not justified in interpreting the Resolution of the Council as meaning that that information should be obtained from only one of the parties and its friends.

The refusal of the Russian Government placed it beyond the power of the Court to obtain information from both sides, and thus rendered the Court unable to deal with the question without an assumption of power which finds no countenance either in the terms of the Covenant or in the Resolution of the Council.

While I fully concur in what Lord Finlay has said on the subject of obligatory or compulsory jurisdiction, yet, in view of what the President and other members of the Court have stated, and particularly of what M. Anzilotti has observed upon the possible obligations of Members of the League as between themselves, I am not disposed to press that subject to the point of dividing the Court on the present question. On the contrary, with a view to unite the Court, I prefer to take the course which I have just sketched; a course which appears to be plainly marked out in Resolution, and which, while it recognizes and respects the independence of nations, involves no compromise of the independence and judicial character of the Court and no reflection or criticism on the action of the Council.

In pursuing this course we may, apart from some passages on obligatory jurisdiction, still use as the basis of our discussion the draft prepared by Lord Finlay, with the omission of certain passages which perhaps might be interpreted as prejudging the question between Finland and Russia, and the insertion of such passages as are necessary to incorporate the solution above suggested.[108]

Although the Permanent Court had already reached the conclusion that due to the Council's lack of competence it could not give an opinion, the *motifs* continued and, in accordance with Judge Moore's proposal, 'other cogent reasons [*d'autres raisons péremptoires*]' for the same conclusion were added.[109] In its final form, this second line of reasoning, which turned on the Permanent Court's own competence, gave the *Eastern Carelia* opinion its controversial flavour and made it an interesting example of international legal argument.

At first, and in accordance with Judge Moore's proposal,[110] it was noted that the main question underlying the dispute between Finland and Russia, namely whether the declaration mentioned in the *procès-verbal* was of a legal character, was 'really one of fact'.[111] Contentious proceedings

---

[108] 'Memorandum by Mr Moore', Distr. 361, undated, Moore papers 180, pp. 15–16.
[109] Series B No. 5 (1923) at 28.
[110] 'Memorandum by Mr Moore', Distr. 361, undated, Moore papers 180, pp. 5 and 9.
[111] Series B No. 5 (1923) at 28 and also 26.

between the parties involved were generally regarded as being better suited to resolve facts; for although there was no 'absolute rule that the request for an advisory opinion may not involve some enquiry as to facts', it was 'certainly expedient that the facts upon which the opinion of the Court is desired should not be in controversy, and it should not be left to the Court itself to ascertain what they are'.[112] Then an intriguing paragraph followed:

> The Court is aware of the fact that it is not requested to decide a dispute, but to give an advisory opinion. This circumstance, however, does not essentially modify the above considerations. The question put to the Court is not one of abstract law, but concerns directly the main point of the controversy between Finland and Russia, and can only be decided by an investigation into the facts underlying the case. Answering the question would be substantially equivalent to deciding the dispute between the parties. The Court, being a Court of Justice, cannot, even in giving advisory opinions, depart from the essential rules guiding their activity as a Court [son activité de tribunal].[113]

The exact bearing of this paragraph was not entirely clear. In general terms it suggested that, for whatever reason (other than the Council's incompetence), the Permanent Court was not competent to give the advisory opinion requested, or at least that it should use a discretionary power under Article 14 of the Covenant to decline it.

On the face of it, the contrast to the *Nationality Decrees* opinion could not have been sharper. In its previous decision the Permanent Court had undone, as it were, an express exception to the Council's powers under Article 15 of the Covenant, whereas in the *Eastern Carelia* opinion the Permanent Court added, or at least strengthened, an exception to the Permanent Court's powers under Article 14.[114] Part of the reason for this contrast was suggested by what was the most apparent aspect of the above-quoted paragraph. Whatever the implications of the holding that '[t]he Court, being a Court of Justice, cannot . . . depart from the essential rules guiding their activity as a Court',[115] the three dots in this quotation

---

[112] Ibid., p. 28; cf. *Jurisdiction of the European Commission of the Danube between Galatz and Braila*, Series B No. 14 (1927) at 46.

[113] Series B No. 5 (1923) at 28–9.

[114] Cf. the deliberate suppression of a distinction based on Article 14 of the Covenant between requests for advisory opinions upon a specific 'dispute' and upon a general 'question' in the late phase of the drafting of the Statute: *Records of Assembly: Committees* 1920, pp. 386–8. Taking the reports on the *Aaland Islands* case as an example, Max Huber had said that '[h]ad they affected the actual conflict, the . . . procedure might have proved dangerous': *ibid.*, p. 387.

[115] Series B No. 5 (1923) at 29.

substitute for an insertion, namely 'even in giving advisory opinions', which is reasonably intelligible. Implying that it was not for 'a Court of Justice' to give advisory opinions in the first place, the insertion recalled the essence of the report submitted by Judge Moore at the preliminary session. In a virtual crusade against the advisory jurisdiction provided for in Article 14 of the Covenant, Judge Moore had elaborated on the notion that '[a] Court of Justice, whether national or international, is essentially a judicial body'.[116] According to Judge Moore, the advisory jurisdiction was 'not an appropriate function of a Court of Justice': the opinions, not being obligatory, were 'at variance with the fundamental design of the Permanent Court of International Justice' and 'would tend not only to obscure but also to change the character of the Court' so that in the end its advisory jurisdiction 'would inevitably bring the Court into disrepute'.[117] The notion of a court of justice to which Judge Moore repeatedly compared the Permanent Court was just his notion of a national court.[118] Moore regarded the reference to the Permanent Court 'being a Court of Justice' as 'the most vital utterance in the whole opinion, because it was the source and the foundation of the position the Court took'.[119] According to Moore, in the *Eastern Carelia* opinion the majority had agreed that '[t]he giving of advisory opinions by the Court at the request of the Council is in no wise compulsory upon the Court' and they had applied 'the right of the courts to determine for themselves whether they would or would not answer a particular question'.[120]

The *Eastern Carelia* opinion was an early example of analogical interpretation having a possible role in defining the Permanent Court's jurisdiction. Frankly, the only bit of international law that was not 'advisory' before the Council, a political organ, was the Covenant. The Council was not obliged to restrict its recommendation for the settlement of a dispute under Article 15 of the Covenant to one based on international

---

[116] Series D No. 2 (1922) at 383; and also Series D No. 2, Add.1 (1926) at 294–6; and Judge Anzilotti's dissenting opinion in *Consistency of Certain Danzig Legislative Decrees with the Constitution of the Free City*, Series A/B No. 65 (1935) at 60.

[117] See Series D No. 2 (1922) at 397–8; Judge Moore also referred to Huber's concerns, *ibid.*, p. 394.

[118] See John Bassett Moore, 'Fifty Years of International Law' (1936–7) 50 *HLR* 395 at 416; as to the rejection of the United States Supreme Court to give an advisory opinion in 1793, see also Manley O. Hudson, 'Advisory Opinions of National and International Courts' (1923–4) 37 *HLR* 970 at 976; and Charles Evans Hughes, *The Supreme Court of the United States: Its Foundation, Methods and Achievements: An Interpretation* (New York, 1928), pp. 30–1.

[119] Moore to Walsh, 19 January 1926, Moore papers 172.

[120] Moore to Miller, 13 October 1926, Moore papers 172.

law; even if the opinions of the Permanent Court had been termed obligatory, in the context of the Council's political bargaining they would still
have been only advisory. And so the *motifs* of the *Eastern Carelia* opinion
indicated that in 1922 Judge Moore had taken a position as extreme as
Judge Altamira's. 'The Court cannot regret', the *motifs* ended, 'that the
question has been put, as all must now realize that the Council has
spared no pains in exploring every avenue which might possibly lead to
some solution with a view to settling a dispute between two nations.'[121]
When originally submitting his report, Judge Moore had written that '[i]t
seems to have received general assent, but it will be discussed, and some
may not come out where they think they stand now'.[122] Indeed, it seems
to have been Judge Moore himself who came up with that appeasing
ending of the *motifs*.[123]

Many years later Moore confessed that 'I have always felt peculiar satisfaction with the part I bore in the Eastern Carelia case, in which the
Court by a majority vote refused to permit itself to be used in that way',
that is, 'for political purposes'.[124] In a previous letter, Moore had told
that Huber 'gave his efforts and influence to make this view effective,
and thus helped to save the court from being made in that instance a
partisan political catspaw'.[125] However, the possible objections of some
members of the majority to Judge Moore's arguably analogical interpretation could be a reason why the above-quoted paragraph was so obscure.
In particular, the initial reference to 'the above considerations' not being
modified by the case coming within the Permanent Court's advisory, as
opposed to contentious, jurisdiction seemed almost deliberately open-
ended. Did it only refer to the considerations about enquiries into facts,
or did it also refer to the considerations about Russia's not having given
its consent, thus making this an impediment not only to the Council
but also, and independently, to the Permanent Court undertaking the
dispute?

On a narrow reading, the less wide scope of the advisory jurisdiction
as compared to the contentions jurisdiction, and therefore the need
for specific consent, could be limited to cases in which the facts were

---

[121] Series B No. 5 (1923) at 29; and see Anzilotti's lecture, undated, Hammarskjöld papers
478; and Huber to Hudson, 24 August 1925, Hudson papers 130.1.
[122] Moore to [Mrs] Moore, 11 February 1922, Moore papers 49.
[123] See 'Memorandum by Mr Moore', Distr. 361, undated, Moore papers 180, p. 17.
[124] Moore to Stone, 8 March 1932, Moore papers 172.
[125] Moore to de Wolf, 23 December 1930, Moore papers 172 and NARA 500 C114/Advisory
opinions/90.

in dispute. Actually, the paragraph contained a reference to the question of 'an investigation into the facts', while the following paragraph added, using a phrase suggested by Judge Moore, that 'the investigation which, as the terms of the Council's Resolution had foreshadowed, would require the consent and co-operation of both parties'.[126] When writing his memorandum, Judge Moore had suggested as a compromise a course comparable to the narrow reading.[127] However, at that time the part of the *motifs* containing the second line of reasoning had not been drafted. There can hardly be any doubt that Judge Moore's own views warranted a broader reading so that, even if the Council was competent to undertake a specific dispute, the Permanent Court could not give an advisory opinion that in reality would decide a dispute between states if the states involved had not consented to the Permanent Court exercising such jurisdiction.[128] Judge Anzilotti and perhaps Judge Finlay, who played a significant role in drafting the opinion, adhered to this reading,[129] so did 'Paul de Vineuil',[130] though possibly for other reasons than Judge Moore.

[126] Series B No. 5 (1923) at 29.

[127] See 'Memorandum by Mr Moore', Distr. 361, undated, Moore papers 180, pp. 13–15.

[128] See John Bassett Moore, *International Law and Some Current Illusions and Other Essays* (New York, 1924), pp. 126–33; John Bassett Moore, 'The Permanent Court of International Justice' (1924) 197 *International Conciliation* 91 at 106; Moore, 'Fifty Years', pp. 416–17; and Moore, *Collected Papers*, vol. 7, p. 29.

[129] As regards Judge Finlay's view, see Finlay to Hammarskjöld, 24 June 1923, Hammarskjöld papers 480; and Finlay to Hurst, 24 February 1926, FO 371 W1559/30/98. As for Judge Finlay's role in the drafting of the opinion, see Moore to Finlay, 4 July 1923 and Finlay to Moore, 16 July 1923, both Moore papers 177. Judge Anzilotti advocated the broader reading: see *Customs Regime between Germany and Austria (Protocol of March 19th, 1931)*, Series A/B No. 41 (1931) at 68–9; and *Consistency of Certain Danzig Legislative Decrees with the Constitution of the Free City*, Series A/B No. 65 (1935) at 60–1; while the narrow reading was sufficient in *Free City of Danzig and International Labour Organization*, Series B No. 18 (1930) at 20; cf. Dionisio Anzilotti, 'Der Ständige Internationale Gerichtshof (Cour permanente de Justice Internationale)' in Julius Magnus (ed.), *Die Höchsten Gerichte der Welt* (Leipzig, 1929), p. 623 at p. 625; and see also Charles de Visscher, 'Dionisio Anzilotti' (1951) 6 *La Comunità Internazionale* 247 at 251; and José María Ruda, 'The Opinions of Judge Dionisio Anzilotti at the Permanent Court of International Justice' (1992) 3 *EJIL* 100 at 122. Some months before the *Eastern Carelia* opinion, Judge Anzilotti had publicly 'insisted upon the complete independence of the Court from the Council and the Assembly of the League of Nations and upon its being a World-Court rather than a Court of the League': see Anzilotti to Hammarskjöld, 16 March 1923, Hammarskjöld papers 478.

[130] Paul de Vineuil, 'Les Rèsultats de la troisième session de la Cour permanente de Justice internationale' (1923) 4 *RDILC* 573 at 585; for the background, see Hammarskjöld to Hudson, 21 August 1924, Hudson papers 8.32. Hammarskjöld upheld this interpretation when subsequently speaking with an American diplomat about revision of the Statute: see Norweb to Secretary of State, 13 February 1929,

On this broader reading, the *Eastern Carelia* opinion and the *Nationality Decrees* opinion shared the assumption that the Covenant vested neither the Council nor the Permanent Court with compulsory jurisdiction of a judicial kind; thus the residual principle of freedom applied in respect of both. In fact, 'Paul de Vineuil' indicated that the *Eastern Carelia* opinion should be seen as a consequence of the *Nationality Decrees* opinion.[131] Although the Council had recommended France and the United Kingdom to go to the Permanent Court, the formal request for an advisory opinion appeared only after the Permanent Court had pressed for it.[132] The two governments merely wanted an advisory opinion, but they treated the case as a contentious proceeding instituted by a special agreement.[133] That had encouraged the Permanent Court to assimilate its advisory and contentious jurisdictions further. Max Huber, for one, took the view that when the Council was willing to employ its right to request an advisory opinion in this way when members of the League were concerned, it had to give similar treatment to 'dem unbeliebten und schwachen Rußland': anything else would be a 'politisch-parteiischen Handhabung des Völkerbundpaktes'.[134] The point had been clearly stated in the draft prepared by Judge Finlay.[135]

No doubt Judges Anzilotti, Finlay, Huber and Moore had exercised considerable influence when drafting the *motifs*, yet the majority also comprised President Loder and two other judges. There were indications that one or more judges took a very different stand on the Permanent Court's competence. This was not so much about whether a broad or a narrow reading of the above-quoted passage was the correct one. It was more

---

NARA 500 C114/748. A narrower reading was suggested in Paul de Vineuil, 'The Permanent Court of International Justice and the Geneva "Peace Protocol"' (1925) 17 *Rivista* 144 at 155–6; but see Åke Hammarskjöld, 'International Justice' in League of Nations, *Ten Years of World Co-operation* (London, 1930), p. 125 at p. 143.

[131] De Vineuil, 'Troisième session', p. 585; and see Hammarskjöld to Hudson, 24 July 1923, Hammarskjöld papers 481.

[132] See Series C No. 2 at 248–60; and Hammarskjöld to Hurst, 7 November 1922, FO 372 T13056/224/317.

[133] See also the French Government, Series C No. 2 at 52–4; and, as a reminder, the report by Judges Anzilotti, Loder and Moore, Series E No. 4 (1927–8) at 76; and Åke Hammarskjöld, 'La Cour permanente de Justice internationale à la neuvième session de l'Assemblée de la Société des Nations' (1928) 9 *RDILC* 665 at 720–1. Cf. *Nationality Decrees in Tunis and Morocco*, Series B No. 4 (1923) at 26, in which the Permanent Court referred to 'the request submitted to the Court by the Council' and 'the competence conferred upon the Court by the Council's resolution'.

[134] Huber, *Denkwürdigkeiten*, p. 277 (translation 'the unpopular and weak Russia'; 'a politically biased application of the Covenant').

[135] See 'Memorandum by Mr Moore', Distr. 361, undated, Moore papers 180, pp. 10–11.

about whether the second line of reasoning had any value at all. On an analogical interpretation contrary to that of Judge Moore, abandoning the second line of reasoning would be one step towards vesting the Permanent Court with a compulsory jurisdiction. Compared to the first line of reasoning regarding the Council's incompetence, the second was couched in less clear terms. Indeed, and although there were attractive ways to escape this apparent contradiction of the second line of reasoning,[136] at the very beginning of the Permanent Court's substantive reasoning it had been deemed 'unnecessary' to decide 'whether questions for an advisory opinion, if they relate to matters which form the subject of a pending dispute between nations, should be put to the Court without the consent of the parties'.[137] When introducing the second line of reasoning it was presented as merely a matter of expediency,[138] although at the end of the *motifs* it was put on the same footing as the first line of reasoning.[139] Later Moore warned that 'the Court indicated that its conclusion might have been different if Russia had been a Member of the League'.[140]

Having received the Permanent Court's advisory opinion, the Council of the League opposed the second line of reasoning in such express terms that Judge Moore considered it a 'scarcely veiled admonition levelled at the Court',[141] 'a most improper and indefensible act'.[142] It was because of the Council's blunt reaction that, in 'Paul de Vineuil's' view, 'il peut être opportun de tâcher de formuler d'une manière très précise ce principe' on which the decision relied.[143] It prompted Judge Moore to take an active role in stiffening the American conditions for adherence to the Court Protocol, constructing the infamous fifth reservation according

---

[136] E.g., Arnold D. McNair, 'The Council's Request for an Advisory Opinion' (1926) 7 *BYIL* 1 at 7; and Hudson, *Permanent Court*, p. 489; cf. A. Nicolayévitch Mandelstam, 'La Conciliation internationale d'après le pacte et la jurisprudence du Conseil de la Société des Nations' (1926) 14 *Recueil des Cours* 333 at 399, note 1.

[137] Series B No. 5 (1923) at 27.   [138] *Ibid.*, p. 28.   [139] See *ibid.*, p. 29.

[140] Moore, 'Suggestions for Consideration, as to Clauses to Follow the First Two Paragraphs (the Recitals) of the Draft of Resolution', undated, Moore papers 172.

[141] Moore to Huber, 18 September 1926, Huber papers 24.1 and Moore papers 172; cf. Official Journal 1923, pp. 1336–7.

[142] Moore to Fletcher, 21 June 1926, Moore papers 172. On the other hand, Judge Moore took the view that the Council's action 'explains some things that I had not before understood': Moore to Borchard, 30 September 1924, Borchard papers 6.89.

[143] De Vineuil, 'Troisième session', p. 585; see also Hammarskjöld to Sweetser, 23 August 1926, Hammarskjöld papers 485; and Åke Hammarskjöld, 'Le Règlement revisé de la Cour permanente de Justice internationale' (1927) 8 *RDILC* 322 at 354, note 24. Cf. Schücking and Wehberg, *Satzung des Völkerbundes*, p. 643.

to which the Permanent Court could not, 'without the consent of the United States, entertain any request for an advisory opinion touching any dispute or question in which the United States has or claims an interest'.[144] The point was that 'the matter should be so settled not only that the Court cannot revert itself, but also that the Council cannot ask it to do so'.[145] Indeed, Moore later explained that 'any weakening of paragraph 5 constitutes a wrong to the court and a menace to its independence'.[146] Professor Hudson did not fully share Judge Moore's view as to the importance of the reservations and made it widely known that Judge Moore had had a hand in framing them.[147] In a letter to Professor Jessup, Hudson wrote that:

---

[144] See Moore to Huber, 18 September 1926, Huber papers 24.1 and Moore papers 172 and 177; and also Philip C. Jessup, *Elihu Root* (New York, 1938), vol. 2, p. 432; Denna Frank Fleming, *The United States and the World Court, 1920–1966* (2nd edn, New York, 1968), pp. 60–4; and Michael Dunne, *The United States and the World Court, 1920–1935* (London, 1988), pp. 139–47. See also Moore to Bayard, 16 December 1925, Moore to Bosten, 15 August 1932 and 26 August 1932, and Moore to Rood, 6 October 1933, all Moore papers 172. Cf. Moore to Borchard, 10 December 1925, Borchard papers 6.90; Moore to Pepper, 21 December 1925, Moore to Walsh, 19 January 1926, Pepper to Moore, 28 January 1926, Moore to Stone, 28 January 1926, Moore to Pepper, 1 February 1926, Pepper to Wickersham, 22 July 1929 and Moore to Pepper, 5 August 1929 and 12 August 1929, all Moore papers 172. When originally proposing that the United States should adhere, Judge Moore had not suggested any conditions as regards the Permanent Court's advisory jurisdiction: see Moore to Hughes, 27 September 1922, Moore papers 176 and NARA 500 C114/269; and also Moore to Hughes, 4 April 1923 and Moore to Gray, August 1923 (not sent), both Moore papers 177. Unsurprisingly, the fifth reservation was met with scepticism: see 'Minutes of the Conference of State Signatories of the Protocol of Signature of the Statute of the Permanent Court of International Justice, Held at Geneva from September 1st to 23rd, 1926' (League of Nations Document V.Legal.1926.V.26, 1926), pp. 77–8; and Drummond to Hudson, 25 February and 30 March 1926, both Hudson papers 75.2. However, an American diplomat could report from The Hague that the members of the Permanent Court considered that 'the reservations laid down by the United States Government are not only unobjectionable but will really add to the character and influence of the Court itself': Tobin to Secretary of State, 28 April 1926, NARA 500 C114/508.

[145] Moore to Chamberlain, 9 July 1925, Moore papers 54; and likewise Root to Phillimore, 27 July 1926, Root papers 141; and Elihu Root, 'The Objections to the Permanent Court of International Justice Because It Gives Advisory Opinions', 25 May 1925, Root papers 195 and NARA 500 C114/Advisory opinions/31.

[146] Moore to de Wolf, 23 December 1930, Moore papers 172 and NARA 500 C114/Advisory opinions/90.

[147] Thus, a crucial letter of 21 December 1925 from Judge Moore to Senator Pepper, Moore papers 172, was widely circulated on the initiative of Hudson: see Hudson to Hammerskjöld, 5 March 1926, Hudson papers 130.1; Hudson to Drummond, 12 March 1926, Hudson papers 75.2; and Drummond to Hurst, 26 March 1926, FO 371 W2723/30/98.

I think you treat a little too seriously the argument that the Council would have attempted to undo something which the Court did. I knew all about the situation at the time and made several drafts of a resolution for the Council. There was only a desire to guard against the possible future effect of one passage in the Court's opinion relating to the power of the Council to request advisory opinions. Of course the big bugs who sat on the Council did not understand the question as did their legal advisers, but it really deserves no serious treatment.[148]

No wonder commentators have never agreed on the better interpretation of the *Eastern Carelia* opinion. The International Court itself has given the *Eastern Carelia* opinion different interpretations. In the *Interpretation of Peace Treaties* opinion, while adopting the broader reading of the second line of reasoning, the International Court distinguished the *Eastern Carelia* opinion on the ground that the International Court is itself an organ of the United Nations and so holds a position unlike that of its predecessor (which had not been an organ of the League).[149] On the other hand, in the *Western Sahara* opinion the International Court held that 'lack of competence of the League to deal with a dispute involving non-member States which refused its intervention was a decisive reason for the Court's declining to give an answer'.[150] The International Court seemed willing also to adopt the second line of reasoning, but it preferred the narrow reading.[151] It would only abide by a broader reading in certain circumstances; according to the *motifs*, '[a]n instance of this would be when the circumstances disclose that to give a reply would have the effect of circumventing the principle that a State is not obliged to allow its disputes to be submitted to judicial settlement without its consent'.[152] However, and in accordance with how the *Eastern Carelia* opinion had been distinguished in previous decisions, this did not apply where the object of the request for an advisory opinion is

---

[148] Hudson to Jessup, 22 December 1925, Hudson papers 75.3; see also Hudson, *Permanent Court*, p. 500.

[149] See *Interpretation of Peace Treaties*, ICJ Reports [1950] 65 at 71; and also *Reservations to the Convention on the Prevention and Punishment of the Crime of Genocide*, ICJ Reports [1951] 15 at 19; *Certain Expenses of the United Nations (Article 17, Paragraph 2, of the Charter)*, ICJ Reports [1962] 151 at 155; *Legal Consequences for States of the Continued Presence of South Africa in Namibia (South West Africa) notwithstanding Security Council Resolution 276 (1970)*, ICJ Reports [1971] 12 at para. 32; *Western Sahara*, ICJ Reports [1975] 12 at para. 41; and also, e.g., *Legality of the Threat or Use of Nuclear Weapons*, ICJ Reports [1996] 226 at paras. 14–15. See also Geza de Magyary, *La Juridiction de la Cour permanente de Justice internationale* (Paris, 1931), pp. 90–5.

[150] *Western Sahara*, ICJ Reports [1975] 12 at para. 30.

[151] *Ibid.*, paras. 45–7.   [152] *Ibid.*, para. 33.

'to obtain from the Court an opinion which the General Assembly deems of assistance to it for the proper exercise of its functions'.[153]

In sum, the implications of the holding in the *Eastern Carelia* opinion that '[t]he Court, being a Court of Justice, cannot, even in giving advisory opinions, depart from the essential rules guiding their activity as a Court' have been curtailed. It mainly, though obscurely, is seen as a warning that the International Court can only undertake 'legal' disputes and, more significantly, is guided by an international rule of law reflecting domestic analogies.[154] Judge Shahabuddeen has commented on this notion of an international rule of law:

The history of the creation of the Permanent Court makes it clear that the concept of a court of justice to which the Court was intended to conform was that of a court of justice as generally understood in municipal law. That being so, warnings about the danger of transposing municipal law ideas to the international plane would not seem apt in this context. The fact that the Court was to function on the international plane was not regarded as importing any substantial modifications of the essential elements of that conception in its application to the Court.[155]

As regards the *Eastern Carelia* opinion itself, in more recent doctrinal writings there has been a tendency towards complete neglect of the second line of reasoning. In accordance with the interpretation given by the International Court, commentators hold that general consent derived from Article 14 of the Covenant would always have been a sufficient

---

[153] *Ibid.*, para. 39.

[154] See *Certain Expenses of the United Nations (Article 17, Paragraph 2, of the Charter)*, ICJ Reports [1962] 151 at 155; and also *Case concerning the Northern Cameroons* (Preliminary Objections), ICJ Reports [1963] 15 at 30; and *Legality of the Threat or Use of Nuclear Weapons*, ICJ Reports [1996] 226 at para. 13. Cf. *Judgments of the Administrative Tribunal of the International Labour Organisation upon Complaints made against the United Nations Educational, Scientific and Cultural Organization*, ICJ Reports [1956] 77 at 84–5.

[155] Judge Shahabuddeen's dissenting opinion in *Land, Island and Maritime Frontier Dispute (El Salvador v. Honduras)* (Intervention), ICJ Reports [1990] 3 at 33; referring to *Case of the Free Zones of Upper Savoy and the District of Gex* (Second Phase), Series A No. 24 (1930) at 15; and also *Constitution of the Maritime Safety Committee of the Inter-Governmental Maritime Consultative Organization*, ICJ Reports [1960] 150 at 153; *Case concerning the Northern Cameroons* (Preliminary Objections), ICJ Reports [1963] 15 at 29; *Application for Review of Judgement No. 158 of the United Nations Administrative Tribunal*, ICJ Reports [1973] 166 at para. 24; *Application for Review of Judgement No. 273 of the United Nations Administrative Tribunal*, ICJ Reports [1982] 325 at para. 22; and *Applicability of the Obligation to Arbitrate under Section 21 of the United Nations Headquarters Agreement of 26 June 1947*, ICJ Reports [1988] 12 at para. 40. See also *LaGrand Case*, ICJ Reports [2001] 466 at para. 102; and Shabtai Rosenne, *The Law and Practice of the International Court, 1920–1996* (The Hague, 1997), pp. 86, 172–3 and 1014–20.

ground for jurisdiction.[156] Still, many, if not most, agree with 'Paul de Vineuil': as regards cases where the request for an advisory opinion concerned a dispute, as opposed to a question, the Permanent Court would have required specific consent from the parties involved, thereby turning this part of the Permanent Court's advisory jurisdiction into a contentious jurisdiction. The best view, however, would seem to be that the *motifs* were inconclusive as to where to draw the line between the international law of cooperation and the residual principle of freedom. In Judge Huber's draft of the *Nationality Decrees* opinion, a similar point regarding the Permanent Court's lack of compulsory jurisdiction had been deleted by other judges.[157] In the *Eastern Carelia* opinion, had the Council not acted *ultra vires*, a majority of the Permanent Court would probably have given the advisory opinion requested, although Judges Anzilotti, Huber and Moore would have lodged dissenting opinions, jointly or separately.

It may be justified at this point to quote from a letter written in 1932 to Professor Brierly, in which Moore recalled the views represented on the bench some ten years before. Having referred to the opposition of Judge Finlay and himself against the proposal advanced by Judge Anzilotti at the preliminary session for secret advisory opinions to the League,[158] Judge Moore wrote:

In the attitude to which I have referred I always thought that Anzilotti was influenced by his previous connection with the Secretariat at Geneva, which led him originally to incline to the view that the advisory function was designed to enable the court to help the Council in its perplexities, even to the extent of conferring with it in secret and giving it secret counsel. Nor was Anzilotti at the outset by any means alone in that view. The ideas of many were very hazy

---

[156] See Kenneth James Keith, *The Extent of the Advisory Jurisdiction of the International Court of Justice* (Leiden, 1971), pp. 89–97, who relied on, among others, Georges Abi-Saab, *Les Exceptions préliminaires dans la procédure de la Cour internationale* (Paris, 1967), pp. 78–9; and the very differently aimed analysis of Gabriele Salvioli, 'La Jurisprudence de la Cour permanente de Justice internationale' (1926) 12 *Recueil des Cours* 3 at 90–2; see also *ibid.*, p. 53. Keith has been followed by, e.g., Michla Pomerance, *The Advisory Function of the International Court* (Baltimore, 1973), pp. 287–9; C. H. M. Waldock, *Aspects of the Advisory Jurisdiction of the International Court of Justice* (Geneva, 1976), p. 3; and Mohamed Shahabuddeen, *Precedent in the World Court* (Cambridge, 1996), pp. 112–13.

[157] Cf. Åke Hammarskjöld, 'Sidelights on the Permanent Court of International Justice' (1927) 25 *Michigan Law Review* 327 at 339; and Åke Hammarskjöld, 'Quelques aspects de la fonction consultative de la Cour permanente de Justice internationale' in *Festgabe für Max Huber zum sechzigsten Gerburtstag 28. Dezember 1934* (Zurich, 1934), p. 146 at pp. 148–9.

[158] See Series D No. 2 (1922) at 160.

on the subject. The statute did not mention advisory opinions, and I think a majority of the members of the court came to The Hague under the impression that, in consequence of this omission, we were not empowered to deal with the subject. It was soon learned, however, that the Council would soon approach us with requests for opinions, and the tendency to comply was greatly strengthened by the lack of any prospect of litigation. Perceiving the drift, I saw the importance of assimilating advisory activities to judicial proceedings, so as to preserve the court's judicial character, and my first effort in that direction was the preparation of the memorandum to which I have referred. Lord Finlay, with his experience on the Judicial Committee of the Privy Council, of course did not have to be convinced. Huber, after reading the memorandum, accepted its conclusions. Loder ranged himself with us. We carried the day. But the size of our majority was somewhat deceptive. The attempt of the Council to censure the court for its refusal in the Eastern Carelia case had an effect. Other incidents had an unsettling influence. Altamira presented a formal proposal for conference and secrecy. I immediately made a formal protest. These things are published in the Annual Reports edited by the Registrar of the court. Altamira's proposal actually remained pending, without a vote, until the United States Senate, by its Reservations, expressly required open judicial procedure in advisory matters. Altamira then withdrew his proposal.[159]

The Permanent Court's assimilation of its advisory jurisdiction to its contentious jurisdiction, and what Professor de Visscher has referred to as '[l]'éternel problème de la conciliation de la fonction consultative avec le caractère essentiellement judiciaire de la Cour',[160] may be seen as another example of the influence of national legal reasoning. It was probably easier for the members of the Permanent Court to find a common ground as regards advisory jurisdiction if assimilated to contentious jurisdiction. For while contentious jurisdiction is well known in national legal systems, there would appear to be no agreement as to the wisdom of vesting a court of justice with advisory jurisdiction.[161]

Conclusions

The *Nationality Decrees* opinion was a clear rejection on the Permanent Court's part of conceiving the state as a national sovereign in that

---

[159] Moore to Brierly, 15 February 1932, Moore papers 178.

[160] Charles de Visscher, *Aspects récents du droit procédural de la Cour internationale de justice* (Paris, 1966), p. 198.

[161] See also Moore to Borchard, 7 November 1927, Borchard papers 6.92, in which Judge Moore pointed to the fact that, while 'the procedure adopted by the Court in the matter of advisory opinions yields a result analogous to a judgment', states may find it easier to submit the dispute to the Permanent Court under its advisory jurisdiction, as opposed to its contentious jurisdiction, an example being the *Nationality Decrees* opinion.

specific case. Even though Article 15(8) of the Covenant contained, on the Permanent Court's own reading, a reference to the structure of international legal argument that contains the national principle of self-containedness, and also the international law of coexistence, the *motifs* were marked by the conception of the state as an international law subject. On the other hand, in the *Eastern Carelia* opinion, Article 14 of the Covenant had been given a somewhat narrow interpretation. But that was not due to the national principle of self-containedness. The Permanent Court's contentious and advisory jurisdictions being assimilated, it was the result of the Covenant not vesting it with compulsory jurisdiction.

In addition, the Permanent Court's first advisory opinions hinted at the influence of judges thinking as national lawyers. It had resulted in analogical interpretation rather than restrictive interpretation: in relation to the Permanent Court's advisory jurisdiction, such an analogical interpretation had a restrictive flavour in Judge Moore's version, while supposedly an extensive version had been advocated by President Loder, among others.

The remaining part of this chapter focuses on the first two judgments of the Permanent Court in contentious proceedings. The judgment in *The Wimbledon*, also delivered at the Permanent Court's third session, considered in detail the basic structure of international legal argument based on the conception of the state as a national sovereign. A year later, in its judgment in the *Mavrommatis* case, the Permanent Court again had to consider its jurisdiction and the possibilities of analogical interpretation. The Permanent Court also delivered four more advisory opinions. As they resembled *The Wimbledon* structurally, they will be mentioned in this connection.

The Wimbledon and territorial sovereignty

The case of a clear text

The Wimbledon was the first decision to which dissenting opinions were appended. They unveiled a general disagreement on the bench as to the categorisation of the subject matter of the dispute within the double structure of international legal argument. The joint dissenting opinion of Judges Anzilotti and Huber concerned, as it said, 'a point which affects the interpretation of international conventions in general'.[162] So did the

---

[162] *Case of the SS Wimbledon*, Series A No. 1 (1923) at 35.

dissenting opinion of Judge *ad hoc* Schücking. Compared to previous decisions *The Wimbledon* provides a more explicit and thorough illustration of the hierarchy between the basic and the dynamic structures of international legal argument that make up the double structure.

The case arose out of an incident taking place in March 1921 at the western approach of the Kiel Canal. German authorities had refused the *SS Wimbledon*, flying the British flag, access to the Kiel Canal on its way to Danzig because it carried weapons intended for a belligerent (Poland technically being in a state of war with Russia). The four Principal Allied and Associated Powers, France, Italy, Japan and the United Kingdom, instituted proceedings before the Permanent Court under Article 386(1) of the Versailles Treaty.[163] They contended that Germany, despite being a neutral in the Russo-Polish war, had been under a treaty obligation to give free access to the *SS Wimbledon*. This contention was based on Article 380 of the Versailles Treaty, providing that '[t]he Kiel Canal and its approaches shall be maintained free and open to the vessels of commerce and of war of all nations at peace with Germany on terms of entire equality'.

In the *motifs* of the Permanent Court's judgment, which had been prepared by a drafting committee chaired by Judge Weiss and were supported by a majority of nine,[164] the substantive argument began as follows:

The Court considers that the terms of article 380 are categorical and give rise to no doubt. It follows that the canal has ceased to be an internal and national navigable waterway, the use of which by the vessels of states other than the riparian state is left entirely to the discretion of that state, and that it has become an international waterway intended to provide under treaty guarantee easier access to the Baltic for the benefit of all nations of the world.[165]

This opening hinted at the basic tension that divided the judges in *The Wimbledon*. On the one hand, there was the case of objective treaty

---

[163] According to this provision, '[i]n the event of violation of any of the conditions of Articles 380 to 386, or of disputes as to the interpretation of these articles, any interested Power can appeal to the jurisdiction instituted for the purpose by the League of Nations'. The Permanent Court pronounced that '[i]t will suffice to observe for the purposes of this case that each of the four Applicant Powers has a clear interest in the execution of the provisions relating to the Kiel Canal, since they all possess fleets and merchant vessels flying their respective flags': *ibid.*, p. 20. The Polish Government intervened under Article 63 of the Statute: see *ibid.*, p. 13.

[164] An early 'Projet d'Arrêt' can be found in Schücking papers (Münster) XII.4.

[165] Series A No. 1 (1923) at 22.

interpretation and a 'clear' text. Before the Permanent Court, the Principal Allied and Associated Powers had relied on Vattel's first principle of treaty interpretation, according to which 'it is not permissible to interpret what has no need of interpretation'.[166] The dissenters agreed that if a literal interpretation was given to Article 380 the German authorities had been under an obligation to give access to the *SS Wimbledon*.[167] However, as the above-quoted passage from the *motifs* indicated, the 'clear' text derogated from the national principle of self-containedness under which the use of 'an internal and national navigable waterway' was 'left entirely to the discretion of' Germany, the national sovereign. *The Wimbledon* brought out a tension between the conception of the state as an international law subject and the conception of the state as a national sovereign. The resulting use of international legal argument reached its most complicated level in the *motifs*, partly because the majority there responded to views expressed in the dissenting opinions. For this reason, the dissenting opinions will be dealt with first.

The dissenting opinions

In the dissenting opinions the conception of the state as a national sovereign partly substituted for the conception of the state as an international law subject under a 'clear' treaty text. As a result, the dynamic structure of international legal argument partly gave way to the basic structure. Judge *ad hoc* Schücking relied on the notion of an international servitude and the 'teaching of writers', according to whom 'all treaties concerning servitudes must be interpreted restrictively in the sense that the servitude, being an exceptional right resting upon the territory of a foreign State, should limit as little as possible the sovereignty of that State'.[168] This was an example of the national principle of self-containedness influencing treaty interpretation.

Although also seeing the conception of the state as a national sovereign behind the 'clear' text, Judges Anzilotti and Huber took a different approach, holding that:

for the purpose of the interpretation of contracts which take the form of international conventions, account must be taken of the complexity of interstate

---

[166] Emmerich de Vattel, *Le Droit des gens ou principes de la loi naturelle* (Washington DC, 1916), p. 199 (originally published 1758), as quoted in Series C No. 3 (Add.) at 68.

[167] See Series A No. 1 (1923) at 39 (Judges Anzilotti and Huber) and 44 (Judge *ad hoc* Schücking).

[168] *Ibid.*, p. 43.

relations and of the fact that the contracting parties are independent political entities. Though it is true that when the wording of a treaty is clear its literal meaning must be accepted as it stands, without limitation or extension, it is equally true that the words have no value except in so far as they express an idea; but it must not be presumed that the intention was to express an idea which leads to contradictory or impossible consequences or which, in the circumstances, must be regarded as going beyond the intention of the parties. The purely grammatical interpretation of every contract, and more especially of international treaties, must stop at this point.[169]

The joint dissenting opinion added that '[t]he right of a State to adopt the course which it considers best suited to the exigencies of its security and to the maintenance of its integrity, is so essential that, in case of doubt, treaty stipulations cannot be interpreted as limiting it, even though these stipulations do not conflict with such an interpretation'.[170] The 'right [liberté]' referred to was not the national principle of self-containedness, but part of 'the rights and duties of neutrality'.[171]

Principles of neutrality form part of the international law of coexistence. In Huber's view, they were a crucial part of the setting of territorially separated states.[172] The fathers of international law acknowledged various conflicts of interests between belligerents and non-belligerents for which common solutions were needed. The traditional position may be summarised in a formula balancing the interests of the various national sovereigns. So long as a non-belligerent does not seriously interfere with the activities or interests of a belligerent, for example by tolerating another belligerent's transport of military material across its territory, the neutral is entitled to have its territory and activities respected by the belligerents.

It was in accordance with Huber's 'sociological' approach to international law that, in the overriding interest of peace, the text of a treaty was presumed to yield to the core principles of the international law of coexistence that made up, as it were, the subsistence level of states. The Wimbledon was very much a test for Huber's approach and so, of course, he was unhappy with the result reached by the majority. According to Max Huber, the judgment proved that:

---

[169] Ibid., p. 36.   [170] Ibid., pp. 37 and also 38 and 40.

[171] See ibid., pp. 35 and 41; see also Judge ad hoc Schücking, ibid., pp. 45–7. The same expression, 'la liberté de l'Etat', had been employed in the Nationality Decrees opinion in the context of a principle of non-intervention under the international law of coexistence: see Nationality Decrees in Tunis and Morocco, Series B No. 4 (1923) at 24.

[172] Huber, Soziologischen Grundlagen des Völkerrechts, p. 48.

mehrere der Richter mit dem Völkerrecht gar nicht vertraut waren, und zwar nicht nur mit Einzelheiten; sondern Struktur und Wesen des Völkerrechts, seine tiefgreifenden Unterschiede gegenüber dem nationalen – bürgerlichen und öffentlichen – Recht kamen ihnen gar nicht genügend zum Bewußtsein . . . Nur ein durch Unkenntnis des Völkerrechts erklärbarer juristischer Formalismus konnte der Mehrheit das Gefühl der Sicherheit bei ihrer am Buchstaben hängenden Vertragsinterpretation geben.[173]

The judgment

As hinted at in the opening of the *motifs*, and unlike Judges Anzilotti and Huber, the majority had not completely rejected as irrelevant the view that the text of Article 380 of the Versailles Treaty derogated from the national principle of self-containedness. Although later Moore found it 'proper to say that the judgment of the Court was based, not on the general principles of international law, but specifically upon Article 380 of the Versailles Treaty',[174] some members of the majority might well have been reluctant to ground the reasoning solely on the conception of the state as an international law subject under a 'clear' treaty provision. According to the *motifs*, it was 'of a very controversial nature, whether in the domain of international law, there really exist servitudes analogous to the servitudes of private law', yet it did not reject the principle of restrictive interpretation articulated in the dissenting opinion of Judge *ad hoc* Schücking. According to the majority:

the fact remains that Germany has to submit to an important limitation of the exercise of the sovereign rights which no one disputes that she possesses over the Kiel Canal. This fact constitutes a sufficient reason for the restrictive interpretation, in case of doubt, of the clause which produces such a limitation. But the Court feels obliged to stop at the point where the so-called restrictive interpretation would be contrary to the plain terms of the article and would destroy what has been clearly granted.[175]

---

[173] Huber, *Denkwürdigkeiten*, p. 280 (translation: 'several of the judges were not familiar with international law, a lack of familiarity not only with some details of international law but with its nature and overall structure. The judges were not sufficiently mindful of its far-reaching differences from national law, both civil and public . . . Due to their ignorance of international law the majority could feel confident about their treaty interpretation only by adopting a legal formalism, which was riveted to the letter of the law.'). See also Fritz Wartenweiler, *Max Huber: Spannungen und Wandlungen in Werden und Wirken* (Zurich, 1953), pp. 159–60.

[174] John Bassett Moore, 'Permanent Court of International Justice at The Hague' 27 December 1943, Moore papers 180, p. 16.

[175] Series A No. 1 (1923) at 24–5.

This was an empty gesture, of course, the Permanent Court having already held that the text was 'clear'.[176] But the conception of the state as a national sovereign appeared again as the Permanent Court faced the main contention of the German Government, namely that if Article 380 of the Versailles Treaty was given the interpretation suggested by the text, it would conflict with Germany's obligations towards Russia, which had not consented to be bound by the Versailles Treaty. According to the German Government, it would be incompatible with the international law of coexistence and Germany's duties as a neutral in a war between Poland and Russia to give passage to a vessel loaded with weapons for Poland.[177]

In its written pleadings the German Government inferred from its neutrality 'un droit tout personnel et imprescriptible qu'un Etat ne saurait s'engager d'avance à ne pas exercer'.[178] An arrangement that detracted in this right 'devraient être considérés comme non obligatoires'.[179] Before the Permanent Court, the German agent tried to tone down the somewhat imprudent ring of this argument. He explained that it was only 'from a moral point of view' that such an arrangement should be regarded as non-binding.[180] The majority, however, seized on the obscurity and, 'in the classical statement of a governing axiom',[181] explained that:

[t]his contention has not convinced the Court; it conflicts with general considerations of the highest order [considérations d'intérêt général de l'ordre le plus élevé]. It is also gainsaid by consistent international practice and is at the same time contrary to the wording of Article 380 which clearly contemplates time of war as well as time of peace. The Court declines to see in the conclusion of any Treaty by which a State undertakes to perform or refrain from performing a particular act an abandonment of its sovereignty. No doubt any convention creating an obligation of this kind places a restriction upon the exercise of the sovereign

---

[176] However, referring to Judge Loder's dissenting opinion in *The Case of the SS Lotus*, Series A No. 10 (1927) at 35, it has been said that 'it is not astonishing' that Judge Loder, who grew up 'in a country where the so-called legal rule "exceptiones sunt strictissimae interpretationis" is handled with a certain predilection and lavishness, appealed to this rule', J. P. Fockema Andreae, *An Important Chapter from the History of Legal Interpretation: The Jurisdiction of the First Permanent Court of International Justice, 1922–1940* (Leiden, 1948), p. 22.

[177] See Series C No. 3 (Add.) at 42–6.

[178] *Ibid.*, p. 49.   [179] *Ibid.*, p. 149.   [180] Series C No. 3-I at 342.

[181] Schwebel, YILC 1980-II.1, p. 188 and also YILC 1980-II.2, p. 126. The 'axiom' had been expressed earlier: see Arbitrator Hines in *Cession of Vessels and Tugs for Navigation on the Danube*, 1 RIAA 97 (1921) at 103; and also Loder in Advisory Committee, *Procès-verbaux*, p. 133; and Spiermann, 'Advisory Committee', p. 204.

rights of the State, in the sense that it requires them to be exercised in a certain way. But the right of entering into international engagements is an attribute of State sovereignty.[182]

This rejection of an argument that would seem to have been advanced by nobody in no way contributed towards the Permanent Court's overcoming the contention of the German Government as to its alleged duties as a neutral towards Russia. Nevertheless, the above-quoted passage indicated a shift in the majority's reasoning. The conception of the state as an international law subject was no longer the main plank of the reasoning. Thus, unlike an earlier opinion, the Permanent Court did not hold that Article 380 'is a part of the Treaty and constitutes an obligation by which the Parties to the Treaty are bound to one another'.[183] Instead, the Permanent Court was willing to contemplate the conception of the state as a national sovereign upon which, it said, 'an obligation of this kind places a restriction'. And, since the Permanent Court had departed from the conception of the state as an international law subject, its counter-argument was grounded on the conception of the state as an international sovereign.[184] Thus, in what may be termed 'the *Wimbledon* statement', the Permanent Court held that 'the right of entering into international engagements is an attribute of State sovereignty'.

This is, of course, a famous *dictum*; it makes a nice quotation. Recently, referring to the theoretical dichotomy between sovereignty and bindingness as 'the sovereignty dilemma', Professor Jan Klabbers has written:

Instead of being plagued by the sovereignty dilemma, the *Wimbledon* court had managed to make a virtue out of a vice; it had squared the circle, and its solution

[182] Series A No. 1 (1923) at 25. In their joint dissenting opinion, Judges Anzilotti and Huber interpreted the submissions of the German Government so that they related to the interpretation of the Versailles Treaty, as opposed to the hierarchical relationship between this treaty and 'a neutral duty': see *ibid.*, p. 35. On the other hand, a similar display of eagerness was *Jurisdiction of the European Commission of the Danube between Galatz and Braila*, Series B No. 14 (1927) at 36.

[183] See *Nomination of the Workers' Delegate to the International Labour Conference*, Series B No. 1 (1922) at 19 as regards Article 389(3) of the Versailles Treaty.

[184] As a matter of international legal argument in general, it cannot be said that '[w]hatever the mastery over its domestic law that the Burundian State derives from its sovereignty, it is obliged, by virtue of this same sovereignty, to respect its international undertakings'; for here 'sovereignty' first implies the conception of the state as a national sovereign, then the conception of the state as an international sovereign, which is different: cf. the award of the ICSID tribunal in *Goetz and others* v. *Burundi*, 6 ICSID Reports 5 (1998) at para. 120; and also, referring to the *Wimbledon* statement, *ibid.*, para. 65. Cf. James Crawford, *International Law as an Open System: Selected Essays* (London, 2002), p. 345.

has been with us since 1923, internalized as probably no other international legal dogma has become internalized in the collective mind of the 'invisible college of international lawyers'.[185]

It is important to stress, however, that the *Wimbledon* statement was pronounced only once the conception of the state as an international law subject had given way to the conception of the state as a national sovereign and the basic structure of international legal argument. Rather than restating the former conception as hierarchically superior, a claim that had, for example, underpinned the *Nationality Decrees* opinion,[186] the Permanent Court relied on the third conception of the state, i.e. as an international sovereign, and so regained control of the dynamic structure of international legal argument. In this light, a rather more critical appraisal of the *Wimbledon* statement would seem to be appropriate.[187]

On the facts of the case, the switching forth and back between the structures of international legal argument underlined the conflict between 'international engagements' undertaken towards some states under the international law of cooperation and obligations owed to other states under the international law of coexistence. Being unwilling to settle for this conflict,[188] the majority took up the conception of the state as a national sovereign and challenged the German Government's interpretation of the international law of coexistence. The Permanent Court described at length 'the precedents' afforded by the Suez Canal and, in particular, the Panama Canal. This was Judge Moore's field.[189] The judgment drew heavily on the view of 'the United States and the nations of the world' regarding the obligations of the former as a neutral sovereign over the Panama Canal.[190] In conclusion, it was held that

---

[185] Jan Klabbers, 'Clinching the Concept of Sovereignty: Wimbledon Redux' (1998) 3 *Austrian Review of International and European Law* 345 at 364.

[186] Cf. *ibid.*, pp. 349–50.

[187] Interestingly, Klabbers does not refer to the Permanent Court's allusion to a principle of restrictive interpretation, cf. *ibid.*, pp. 359–64, but see *ibid.*, pp. 350 and 362 as regards the first *Competence of the International Labour Organization* opinion. Of course, not all theorists have been convinced by the *Wimbledon* statement: see, e.g. Esa Paasivirta, *Participation of States in International Contracts and Arbitral Settlements of Disputes* (Helsinki, 1990), pp. 179–81.

[188] See also Judge *ad hoc* Schücking, Series A No. 1 (1923) at 47.

[189] That Judge Moore took part in the drafting is also suggested by Finlay to Moore, undated, Moore papers 177.

[190] Series A No. 1 (1923) at 27–8.

the two 'precedents' served to 'invalidate in advance' the application of arguments based on neutrality to the Kiel Canal.[191]

The dissenters happily commented on the Suez and Panama Canals, which they saw as being governed by special treaty regimes that were more explicit, and 'clear', on neutrality than the Versailles Treaty. In the same breath, the dissenters held that these regimes provided no precedent as to the international law of coexistence.[192]

According to Max Huber, substantial amendments to the *motifs* were adopted at the final reading of the draft.[193] This was possibly due to the criticisms raised in the dissenting opinions. The joint dissenting opinion of Judges Anzilotti and Huber only dealt with the Suez and Panama 'precedents'. The *motifs*, however, at least in their final form, fused the neutrality argument based on the two 'precedents' with an argument concerning change of territorial status *erga omnes*. This second argument was only entertained by Judge *ad hoc* Schücking, and only in a somewhat haphazard manner.[194] Yet it was a crucial argument. It buttressed the majority's overall reasoning, adding immediately after the neutrality argument that the Suez and Panama Canals were:

merely illustrations of the general opinion according to which when an artificial waterway connecting two open seas has been permanently dedicated to the use of the whole world, such waterway is assimilated to natural straits in the sense that even the passage of a belligerent man-of-war does not compromise the neutrality of the sovereign State under whose jurisdiction the waters in question lie.[195]

The effect of the Permanent Court's view was clear as it ruled that 'the passage of neutral vessels carrying contraband of war is authorised by Article 380, and cannot be imputed to Germany as a failure to fulfil its

---

[191] *Ibid.*, p. 28.

[192] *Ibid.*, pp. 39–40 (Judges Anzilotti and Huber) and 43–4 and 46 (Judge *ad hoc* Schücking).

[193] Huber, *Denkwürdigkeiten*, p. 287. Indeed, a copy of the 'Projet d'Arrêt' of 11 August 1923 only consists of pages 15–24 in the printed version, see Schücking papers (Münster) XII.4. This copy would not seem to be complete, but it suggests that the substantial amendments to the *motifs* concerned pages 24–34.

[194] Series A No. 1 (1923) at 45–6.

[195] *Ibid.*, p. 28; the reference to 'the general opinion', though deliberately open-ended, probably referred to 'the United States and the nations of the world': cf. *ibid.*, pp. 27–8. It is not evident that *The Wimbledon* was an example of 'strong state practice and weak *opinio juris*': cf. Anthea Elizabeth Roberts, 'Traditional and Modern Approaches to Customary International Law: A Reconciliation' (2001) 95 *AJIL* 757 at 773.

duties as a neutral'.[196] Article 380 being part of a regime with the 'objective' character that the entire territorial setting is vested with under the international law of coexistence, the corresponding rights of Russia under the law of neutrality were reduced accordingly, even though Russia was not a party to the Versailles Treaty. In the opening of its substantive reasoning, on holding that the status of the Kiel Canal had been changed from 'an internal and national navigable waterway' to 'an international waterway', the Permanent Court appeared to think of that change as an 'objective' fact, as opposed to the mere product of relational obligations and rights restricted to the parties to the Versailles Treaty.[197]

A number of writers have tried to rationalise the notion of waterways 'permanently dedicated to the use of the whole world'.[198] It has been seen as potentially more far-reaching than such modern phrases as 'obligations *erga omnes*' and 'rules of *jus cogens*'.[199] But it should be kept in its context of 'the passage of a belligerent man-of-war'. It can hardly justify a general theory of international canals, as the Permanent Court appeared to have in mind only the conflict between Article 380 of the Versailles Treaty and principles of neutrality.

Conclusions

In his *Denkwürdigkeiten*, Max Huber revealed that the joint dissenting opinion appended to *The Wimbledon* was in accordance with the content of a secret protocol appended to the Versailles Treaty.[200] Manley O. Hudson, who might have been in possession of confidential minutes communicated to him by Hammarskjöld,[201] suggested that the majority

---

[196] Series A No. 1 (1923) at 29–30.

[197] Cf. the dissenting opinion of Judges Anzilotti and Huber, which referred to 'the interpretation of contracts which take the form of international conventions': *ibid.*, p. 36. However, see also as regards state succession the dissenting opinion of Judge Oda in *Case of the Mavrommatis Palestine Concessions* (Jurisdiction), Series A No. 2 (1924) at 86.

[198] E.g., Richard Baxter, *The Law of International Waterways – With Particular Regard to Interoceanic Canals* (Cambridge, 1964), pp. 182, 308 and 343. Cf. Waldock, YILC 1964-II, pp. 29–30, who was criticised by El-Erian, YILC 1964-I, p. 98.

[199] Cf. Christine Chinkin, *Third Parties in International Law* (Oxford, 1993), p. 86; and Maurizio Ragazzi, *The Concept of International Obligations Erga Omnes* (Oxford, 1997), pp. 26–7.

[200] Huber, *Denkwürdigkeiten*, p. 280; cf. Series A No. 1 (1923) at 40; and see De Vineuil, 'Troisième session', p. 580. The preparatory work of the Versailles Treaty was secret and had not been relied on in argument before the Permanent Court.

[201] Cf. Hammarskjöld to Hudson, 4 July 1922, 14 July 1922 and 24 July 1923, all Hammarskjöld papers 481.

had been motivated by 'certain pragmatic tests in the minds of the judges which were not brought out into the open'.[202] Perhaps a sneaking suspicion as to its partiality is an inevitable part of being an international court, at least at the time. In 1920, being troubled by such suspicions, Loder had pointed to a main reason underlying them, namely the conception of the state as a national sovereign:

In the case of the Supreme Court whose composition we are now discussing, the danger of partiality is particularly great, even because it will be an International Court. It is the States that will be the parties to the suits it is to try, the States which will have to defend before it their own interests and those of their subjects. And the danger is very real that these mighty organisms will seek to abuse their powerful position by influencing the march of justice. The idea that States, accustomed in their consciousness of power to exert their influence, either through might or through the exercise of cunning and diplomacy, should find their actions judged by a court not of their own choosing, before which they will have to appear, shorn of these attributes of power and greatness, that idea is a novel one, the first fruit of the League of Nations.[203]

However that may be, in *The Wimbledon* the majority demonstrated that within the international law of coexistence a prime argument against neutrality and territorial sovereignty was change of territorial status. A complete cession of territory from one state to another state, or a group of states, cannot be challenged by other states, nor can a partial cession. In this way, by focusing on the international law of coexistence instead of the international law of cooperation, the majority avoided the problem of Russia not being a party to the Versailles Treaty (because, in respect of the international law of coexistence, what triggers international law is not consent to, but a need for, such law). The shift from the international law of cooperation to the international law of coexistence was only possible because neutrality and the territorial setting of states came within the latter. For matters that were not covered by the international law of coexistence – an example being the Permanent Court's own jurisdiction – there was no alternative to the international

---

[202] Hudson, 'Second Year', p. 13; see also Ernst Wolgast, *Der Wimbledonprozeß* (Berlin, 1926), p. 159; and George Schwarzenberger, *International Law as Applied by International Courts and Tribunals* (London, 1986), vol. 4, pp. 213–14 and 241–2.

[203] Cf. B. C. J. Loder, *La Cour permanente de Justice internationale: Discours prononcé à la conférence de l'Association de droit international ('International Law Association'), à Portsmouth, le 28 Mai 1920* (unknown, 1920), p. 6; see also Manfred Lachs, 'A Few Thoughts on the Independence of Judges of the International Court of Justice' (1986–7) 25 *Columbia Journal of Transnational Law* 593 at 594.

law of cooperation and the need for consent, as exemplified by the *Eastern Carelia* opinion.

The basic structure of international legal argument: four more advisory opinions

The *Eastern Carelia* opinion had an immediate and formidable effect in the *German Settlers* opinion and the *Acquisition of Nationality* opinion, also delivered in 1923 at the third session of the Permanent Court. In both instances, the Council's questions on the merits were preceded by a request for the Permanent Court's advice as to whether the cases came within the competence of the League, and the first opinion, drafted by Judges Huber and Moore and Deputy-Judge Wang, confirmed the need for assuring the Council's competence before responding to its request for an opinion on the merits.[204] In both opinions, the Permanent Court was so careful in ascertaining the Council's competence that having done so, the questions put by the Council as to the merits had effectively been advised upon as well.[205] Perhaps this was partly an illustration of the question-begging character of many of the arguments advanced by the Polish Government.[206]

Both opinions dealt with the Polish Minorities Treaty, which Article 93 of the Versailles Treaty had made a condition for recognising Poland as an independent state within an enlarged territory. This treaty became the model for other treaties and declarations concerning the protection of minorities in the new states that emerged after the First World War. Together these undertakings made up the scheme for minorities protection. Arguing a restrictive interpretation of the provisions of the Polish Minorities Treaty, the Polish Government recalled the national principle of self-containedness to which a state's treatment of its own nationals and inhabitants was said to belong.[207]

---

[204] *Questions relating to Settlers of German Origin in Poland*, Series B No. 6 (1923) at 19 and 22. On the drafting of the opinion, see Huber to Moore, 22 August [1923], Moore papers 177; Moore to Borchard, 8 September 1931, Moore papers 63 and Borchard papers 7.98; Moore to Hudson, 31 January 1936, Hudson papers 95.10; and Huber, *Denkwürdigkeiten*, p. 281.

[205] See Series B No. 6 (1923) at 23–4; and also *Questions concerning the Acquisition of Polish Nationality*, Series B No. 7 (1923) at 15–16; and Judge Finlay's separate opinion, *ibid.*, pp. 22–3.

[206] Cf. as to the previous reports of Committees of Jurists, Series B No. 6 (1923) at 18 and Series B No. 7 (1923) at 11.

[207] Series C No. 3-I at 459–60, 463, 479, 484, 493 and 770.

It is sufficient here to emphasise two aspects of the opinions. As for the *German Settlers* opinion concerning discrimination in the context of property rights, the Permanent Court sensibly concluded that the Polish Government's declared policy of de-Germanisation amounted to discrimination, if not in law, then in fact.[208] But the Permanent Court did not merely state that the German settlers were treated differently from other Polish nationals. In addition, and in accordance with Max Huber's doctoral thesis, the Permanent Court developed a long, alternative line of reasoning based on general principles of state succession, according to which the settlers' private rights were to be respected by the new territorial sovereign, Poland.[209] This was an early demonstration of the international law of coexistence not resting on consent, at least not in respect of new states (Poland).[210]

In the *Acquisition of Nationality* opinion, which concerned the provision on the acquisition of nationality in Article 4, the Permanent Court again did more than interpret the Polish Minorities Treaty, an exercise that concluded with the observation that the Polish Government's view was 'equivalent, not to interpreting the Treaty, but to reconstructing it'.[211] In addition, the Permanent Court carefully justified Article 4.[212] This supplementary line of reasoning did not have a direct bearing on the

---

[208] Series B No. 6 (1923) at 24–5.

[209] *Ibid.*, pp. 35–6, 38 and 42. And see Huber, *Die Staatensuccession*, pp. 42–3, 57–60, 101, 123, 135, 149–50 and 174; and also Max Sørensen, *Les Sources du droit international: Etude sur la jurisprudence de la Cour permanente de Justice internationale* (Copenhagen, 1946), pp. 182 and 186. Likewise, *Case concerning Certain German Interests in Polish Upper Silesia* (Merits), Series A No. 7 (1926) at 31. For the purpose of securing more freedom in progressively developing the law of state succession, the Permanent Court's pronouncements on acquired rights were given a most restrictive interpretation by Bedjaoui, YILC 1969-II, pp. 74 and 85 and YILC 1969-I, p. 55; and Mohamed Bedjaoui, 'Problèmes récents de succession d'états dans les états nouveaux' (1970) 130 *Recueil des Cours* 455 at 484 and 536, note 12; but see Waldock, YILC 1969-I, pp. 74–5; cf. García Amador, YILC 1957-II, p. 120 and YILC 1959-II, pp. 4 *et seq.*

[210] See C. H. M. Waldock, 'General Course on Public International Law' (1962) 106 *Recueil des Cours* 1 at 52–3; Maurice Mendelson, 'The Subjective Element in Customary International Law' (1995) 66 *BYIL* 177 at 189, note 49; and also *Case of the Mavrommatis Palestine Concessions* (Jurisdiction), Series A No. 2 (1924) at 23–4.

[211] Series B No. 7 (1923) at 20. See also *Affaire relative à l'acquisition de la nationalité polonaise*, 1 RIAA 401 (1924) at 416.

[212] *Ibid.*, pp. 18–20 and also 15–16. Much attention has been given to this justification by Nathaniel Berman, '"But the Alternative is Despair": European Nationalism and the Modernist Renewal of International Law' (1993) 106 *HLR* 1792 at 1834–42; but see Georges Kaeckenbeeck, *The International Experiment of Upper Silesia* (London, 1942), p. 522; and also *Question of Jaworzina (Polish–Czechoslovakian Frontier)*, Series B No. 8 (1923) at 20–1.

international law of coexistence, unlike the principles of state succession in the *German Settlers* opinion. But the justification for derogating from the national principle of self-containedness was akin to pointing to an exceptional need for (international law of) coexistence.[213]

As for the deliberations, Judge Finlay wrote to Mrs Bassett Moore on the day the Permanent Court delivered the *Acquisition of Nationality* opinion that:

[w]e missed your husband very much en chambre de Conseil. I wish we had had more time in which case I think the judgment would have become one harmonious whole! But it will do and I am sure he will read with interest the right conclusions – and the reasons – some right and some wrong. It is just as well to have a little variety – and the endless material for legal debating societies which we have provided![214]

In the *Minorities* opinions, the supplementary lines of reasoning suggested that in this context some of the judges were a little sceptical as to the national principle of self-containedness yielding to the international law of cooperation; they brought in the international law of coexistence, which reflects the same conception of the state as that principle, that is, the conception of the state as a national sovereign. This was the same shift in international legal argument from the dynamic to the basic structure as in *The Wimbledon*. Commentators have tended to associate the *Minorities* opinions and other decisions regarding the minorities scheme with an opposite principle of effective interpretation.[215] One may wonder whether this has been just another consequence of lawyers being unaccustomed to derogate from the national principle of self-containedness, therefore exaggerating the conclusions

---

[213] Cf. *Exchange of Greek and Turkish Populations*, Series B No. 10 (1925) at 19 as regards domicile; and *Case concerning Certain German Interests in Polish Upper Silesia* (Merits), Series A No. 7 (1926) at 70, 74–5 and 79 as regards conceptions of nationality and domicile.

[214] Finlay to [Mrs] Moore, 15 September 1923, Moore papers 177. Judge Finlay had appended individual observations to the *Acquisition of Nationality* opinion, in which he noted that 'I am glad to think that any points on which I differ from the Court are mainly academic and that in the recent case the same result would follow upon either view': Series B No. 7 (1923) at 26.

[215] E.g, Lauterpacht, *Development by the Permanent Court*, pp. 74–5; Nathan Feinberg, 'La Juridiction et la jurisprudence de la Cour permanente de justice internationale en matière de mandats et de minorités' (1937) 59 *Recueil des Cours* 591 at 646–7; Jacob Robinson et al., *Were the Minorities Treaties a Failure?* (New York, 1943), pp. 149–50; and Athanasia Spiliopoulou Åkermark, *Justifications of Minority Protection in International Law* (London, 1997), p. 109.

reached by the Permanent Court in this respect. True, the Permanent Court employed a principle of effective interpretation in construing the Council's competence. Article 12 of the Polish Minorities Treaty linked this competence to the notion of a minority, which in turn was interpreted so that the Council's competence covered questions about the acquisition of nationality by non-inhabitants under Article 4.[216] It was not due to the Permanent Court, however, that the Treaty contained a provision in Article 4 relating neither to Polish nationals nor Polish inhabitants.

The *Jaworzina* opinion delivered at the fourth session in 1923, and the similar *Monastery of Saint-Naoum* opinion delivered at the fifth session in 1924,[217] illustrated another way in which, in addition to the one in *The Wimbledon*, the international law of coexistence may affect the interpretation of treaties regulating territorial questions, the Permanent Court presuming that disputes concerning title to or delimitation of territory had already been resolved.[218] The territorial setting of states could only then serve the international law of coexistence as a means to separate national sovereigns.[219] On this basis the Permanent Court made it clear that treaty provisions concerning territorial questions would be subjected to a strictly objective interpretation, excluding preparatory work.[220] Having accepted that the Principal Allied and Associated Powers had authority to solve the frontier dispute, the Permanent Court held that a subsequent agreement between the two parties involved to the contrary 'was *res inter alios acta* and could not affect the legal situations

---

[216] Series B No. 7 (1923) at 17, referring, it would seem, to Series B No. 6 (1923) at 23 and 25–6.

[217] The *Monastery of Saint-Naoum* opinion was the shorter, perhaps because an effort had been made to ensure a unanimous opinion, in which Judge Moore actually succeeded: see Moore to Deak, 11 February 1941, Moore papers 178.

[218] See *Question of Jaworzina (Polish–Czechoslovakian Frontier)*, Series B No. 8 (1923) at 21, 23, 33–4, 38, 42–3 and 55; and *Question of the Monastery of Saint-Naoum (Albanian Frontier)*, Series B No. 9 (1924) at 15. This approach has been linked to a notion of equity: see Marcelle Jokl, *De l'interprétation des traités normatifs d'après la doctrine et la jurisprudence internationales* (Paris, 1936), p. 94; cf. Andreae, *An Important Chapter*, pp. 102–3. In 1969, the International Court referred to the *Monastery of Saint-Naoum* opinion when holding that there is 'no rule that the land frontiers of a State must be fully delimited and defined, and often in various places and for long periods they are not': see *North Sea Continental Shelf*, ICJ Reports [1969] 3 at para. 46. The International Court would have found more support for that proposition in *Article 3, Paragraph 2, of the Treaty of Lausanne (Frontier between Turkey and Iraq)*, Series B No. 12 (1925) at 21–2.

[219] Cf. Series B No. 8 (1923) at 32.

[220] *Ibid.*, p. 41; see also *ibid.*, pp. 35–7 as regards subsequent practice.

created by the decision' of the organ under the Principal Allied and Associated Powers.[221]

At one point in the *Jaworzina* opinion, the Permanent Court also relied on the frontier in question having for a long time been an international frontier; for, so the not uncontroversial argument went, '[a]lthough Austria and Hungary had common institutions based on analogous laws passed by their legislatures, they were none the less distinct international units'.[222] This argument had been relied on before the Permanent Court,[223] and it corresponded with the views of Judges Anzilotti and Huber,[224] who had drafted the *motifs* together with Judge Weiss.[225] Having found that the frontier dispute had already been given a final and complete solution by a decision taken under the auspices of the Principal Allied and Associated Powers, the Permanent Court was reluctant to forego the possibility there provided for of modifications 'justified by reason of the interests of individuals or of communities'.[226] This may have been as an indirect reference to a principle of self-determination;[227] if so it was a slighting reference, since community interests were to be subordinated to the international authority of the Principal Allied and Associated Powers, who by inference could decide on other grounds than the interests of the communities invodled. On the other hand, the parties having been in direct negotiations about modifications, there was the view that 'direct agreement between the parties regarding the points in dispute' was 'a form of settlement always preferable to the intervention of a third party'.[228] This statement was a rather crude translation

---

[221] *Ibid.*, pp. 55–6. Cf. *Case of the Mavrommatis Palestine Concessions* (Jurisdiction), Series A No. 2 (1924) at 30; and *Rights of Minorities in Upper Silesia (Minority Schools)*, Series A No. 15 (1928) at 33 (the majority) and 51 (Judge Huber).

[222] See *ibid.*, pp. 42–3; and likewise Arbitrator Beichmann in *Affaire des réparations allemandes selon l'article 260 du Traité de Versailles*, 1 RIAA 429 (1924) at 440–1. Cf. Krystyna Marek, *Identity and Continuity of States in Public International Law* (2nd edn, Geneva, 1968), p. 205; and Crawford, *Creation of States*, pp. 290–1 and 404, note 20.

[223] Cf. Series C No. 4 at 330 (Czechoslovak government).

[224] Anzilotti, *Cours*, pp. 154, 158–9, 191 and 195; and Huber, *Soziologischen Grundlagen des Völkerrechts*, p. 23.

[225] Huber, *Denkwürdigkeiten*, p. 281.

[226] As for the Permanent Court's presumption: see Series B No. 8 (1923) at 49 and also 46–8.

[227] Cf. *ibid.*, pp. 39, 40 and 48; and see also *ibid.*, p. 20 regarding 'historical and ethonological factors'.

[228] *Ibid.*, p. 56. In this connection, one may also point to the references to equity in the decision: see *ibid.*, pp. 18, 29, 40 and 51; cf. *ibid.*, p. 21 as to what the Permanent Court was not concerned with. Cf. the submissions of the Polish Government, Series C No. 4 at 12–14 and 87.

of the theoretical position taken by Max Huber, which will be dealt with in the following section.

The *Monastery of Saint-Naoum* opinion would seem to have contributed further to assimilating the Permanent Court's advisory jurisdiction to its contentious jurisdiction. Thus, the Permanent Court held that 'the documents placed before it and the arguments adduced on this point do not suffice to prove that the Conference of Ambassadors was mistaken in holding that the Albanian frontier at Saint Naoum had not been definitely fixed in 1913'.[229] Thereby, the Permanent Court would seem to have modified, if not jettisoned, one of the ways in which 'Paul de Vineuil' suggested that the *Eastern Carelia* opinion could be used:

The point on which an opinion was required was a question of fact; Russia having refused to put in an appearance, the Court was unable to elucidate the facts: if the question had been brought before the Court as a case for judgment a decision might have been given on the Finnish statement only, under the terms of Article 53 of the Statute (judgment by default); but in advisory procedure it is a question of ascertaining the objective truth.[230]

The *Mavrommatis* case and the Permanent Court's contentious jurisdiction

The test for jurisdiction

The *Mavrommatis* case arose out of a dispute between a Greek national, Mr Mavrommatis, and the British Government. Prior to the First World War, when Palestine had been part of the Ottoman Empire, a number of concessions had been granted to Mavrommatis. Some years later, after the collapse of the Ottoman Empire with its defeat in 1918, the British Government, acting as the Mandatory of Palestine under a Mandate negotiated with the League, granted various concessions to a third party partly overlapping those of Mavrommatis (the Rutenberg concessions). In Mavrommatis' view, the British Government thereby violated Protocol XII of the Lausanne Peace Treaty between Turkey and the Allied Powers, including the British Empire and Greece. Eventually the Greek Government intervened and submitted the case to the Permanent Court under Article 26 of the Mandate for Palestine, which provided:

The Mandatory agrees that, if any dispute whatever should arise between the Mandatory and another Member of the League of Nations relating to the

---

[229] Series B No. 9 (1924) at 16.   [230] De Vineuil, 'Geneva "Peace Protocol"', p. 155.

interpretation or the application of the provisions of the Mandate, such dispute, if it cannot be settled by negotiation, shall be submitted to the Permanent Court of International Justice provided for by Article 14 of the Covenant of the League of Nations.

The British Government denied that this compromissory clause was applicable, and thus at its fifth session the Permanent Court had, for the first time in contentious proceedings, to apply Article 36(4) of the Statute, providing that, in 'the event of a dispute as to whether the Court has jurisdiction, the matter shall be settled by the decision of the Court'. A narrow majority of seven judges dismissed the objection, although only in respect of some of Mavrommatis' concessions.

Two conditions were swiftly dealt with in the *motifs*. As for the condition that a dispute existed between the British Government and another member of the League, the Permanent Court relied on 'an elementary principle of international law', namely the principle of diplomatic protection. The Greek Government having taken up the case, '[t]he dispute . . . entered upon a new phase; it entered the domain of international law [*il s'est porté sur le terrain international*], and became a dispute between two States'.[231] The purpose of such diplomatic protection was 'to ensure, in the person of its subjects, respect for the rules of international law'.[232] The principle of diplomatic protection had been anticipated by the Advisory Committee when limiting the Permanent Court's jurisdiction to disputes between states.[233] It made the Permanent Court identify Greece with Mavrommatis and Greece's dispute with his.

The condition that the dispute could not be settled by negotiations was treated rather lightly by the majority. According to the *motifs*, negotiations were required so as to 'clarify' the subject matter of the dispute; on the other hand, the Permanent Court found it 'incompatible with the flexibility which should characterise international relations to require the two Governments to reopen a discussion which has in fact already taken place and on which they rely'.[234] In addition, 'amongst other

---

[231] *Case of the Mavrommatis Palestine Concessions* (Jurisdiction), Series A No. 2 (1924) at 12.

[232] *Ibid.* Cf. the exceptional formalism advanced by Judge de Bustamante, *ibid.*, pp. 81–2; and also de Bustamante, *World Court*, p. 181.

[233] Advisory Committee, *Procès-verbaux*, pp. 204–17 and 723. See also Hammarskjöld to Van Hamel, 25 June 1920, Hammarskjöld papers 480; Scott, *Project of a Permanent Court*, pp. 93–5; and Spiermann, 'Advisory Committee', pp. 208–9.

[234] Series A No. 2 (1924) at 15 and likewise *ibid.*, p. 34; cf. Judge Pessôa, *ibid.*, pp. 88 and 91; but see *Case concerning Certain German Interests in Polish Upper Silesia* (Jurisdiction), Series A No. 6 (1925) at 22; and also Fifth session, *Procès-Verbal* 24 (19 August 1924), reproduced in Pessôa, *Côrte permanente*, p. 106.

considerations', which were not set forth, the Permanent Court held that the states themselves 'are in the best position to judge as to political reasons which may prevent the settlement of a given dispute by diplomatic negotiation'.

What remained to be fulfilled was the third condition, namely that the dispute related 'to the interpretation or the application of the provisions of the Mandate'. This was the major hurdle standing in the way of the Permanent Court's jurisdiction, and it is what makes the *Mavrommatis* case a significant example of international legal argument. As in so many of the decisions on jurisdiction to come, the *Mavrommatis* case divided the Permanent Court. Max Huber has offered this account of the deliberations:

Während in den früheren Sessionen sich immer rasch eine entscheidende Mehrheit für eine bestimmte Lösung fand – mochte auch die Verständigung über die Begründung schwierig sein –, so teilte sich in diesem Fall das Gericht in zwei fast gleich starke Gruppen, die in Erkenntnis der grundsätzlichen Bedeutung des Urteils sich mit einer Schärfe und Leidenschaft gegenübertraten wie sonst nie zuvor. Durch die wenig neutrale Haltung des Präsidenten gegenüber denjenigen, die seine Auffassung nicht teilten, wurde die Stimmung noch wesentlich gereizter. Sie entlud sich denn auch nachher in fünf zum Teil unverhältnismäßig umfangreichen, zum Teil taktlos aggressiven 'Opinions dissententes'.[235]

According to Hammarskjöld, Judge Finlay acted as a judge *ad hoc*, trying to rally his colleagues behind his own government's case.[236] Judge Huber had been inclined to join him and the four other dissenters, partly because of the absence of preceding negotiations,[237] but in the end he went along with the six other members of the bench, including President Loder, who would otherwise have had the casting vote

---

[235] Huber, *Denkwürdigkeiten*, p. 282 (translation 'While at the previous sessions decisive majorities in favour of a specific result had quickly formed, although agreement on the *motifs* had been difficult to achieve, in this case the Court divided into two almost equally strong groups which, recognising the fundamental importance of the judgment, argued against the opinion of the other group with a rigour and a passion never seen before. The hardly neutral attitude of the President towards the group that did not share his view added considerably to the fraught atmosphere. Afterwards this resulted in five 'dissenting opinions', which were, in part, disproportionately long and, in part, tactlessly aggressive.'). By far the longest dissenting opinions were written by Judges Finlay and Moore.

[236] Hammarskjöld to [Hjalmar] Hammarskjöld, 19 August 1924, Hammarskjöld papers 30.

[237] Huber, *Denkwürdigkeiten*, p. 283. It should be noted that the *motifs* referred to 'the very small number and brevity of the subsequent communications exchanged between the two Governments, which communications appear to be irreconcilable with the idea of negotiations properly so-called': Series A No. 2 (1924) at 13.

under Article 55 of the Statute.[238] By the time Judge Huber made up his mind, a draft of the judgment had already been prepared. According to Huber, that draft drew heavily on civil law concepts, an inclination which Anzilotti and Huber saw as a general trait of 'M. Loder et quelques autres anciens juges, qui auraient voulu modeler la Cour sur les tribunaux nationaux'.[239] Together with the Registrar these two judges revised the entire draft, remedying what Huber phrased 'dem Völkerrecht fremde, zivilprozessual gedachte Begründung'.[240] On 26 July 1924, Judge Anzilotti had written the following to Judge Moore, as he had to Judge Finlay:

I am a little afraid that the opinions of a part of the Members of the Court are rather under the influence of the continental system of procedure.

Whatever may be the decision of the Court, it seems to me that it is very important that the judgment of the Court does not appear to have been influenced by one legal system. Of course, our decision must be founded upon international rather than national law; but I think that international law will not help us very much, as the question, as far as I know, never presented itself in international Courts or relations.

I am trying to go through English law, but the task is for me a very long and difficult one and the results which I may reach shall be very poor. Perhaps you will be kind enough to give me some information. I should be very glad indeed if I could get a clear notion of the two following points:

1) Should an American (or English) Court, in a case similar to the case which is now before us, in order either to admit or to reject the preliminary objection to its competency, adopt a definite construction of Article 11 of the Mandate or only a provisional one? In other words: should the construction of Article 11, as adopted in the preliminary judgment, bind the Court when it decides the merits of the case?

---

[238] President Loder indeed used his casting vote at a 'preliminary' vote: see Moore to Finlay, 7 August 1924, Moore papers 52.

[239] Anzilotti to Hammarskjöld, 22 November 1924, Hammarskjöld papers 478. See also, as regards President Loder's point of view, Series D No. 2, Add.1 (1926) at 81–2, 195 and 204–5; and J. H. W. Verzijl, *The Jurisprudence of the World Court* (Leiden, 1965), vol. 1, p. 535. The majority consisted of President Loder, Judges Altamira, Anzilotti, Huber, Nyholm and Weiss and Judge *ad hoc* Caloyanni, all from continental Europe and with some background in civil law; cf. the dissenting opinion of Judge Moore, Series A No. 2 (1924) at 57 *et seq.*, which may be compared to Huber's observations in *Documents diplomatiques suisses*, vol. 8, p. 914 and also *Interpretation of Judgments Nos. 7 and 8 (the Chorzów Factory)*, Series A No. 13 (1927) at 27 (Judge Anzilotti).

[240] See Huber, *Denkwürdigkeiten*, pp. 282–3 (translation: 'a reasoning alien to international law and conceived along the lines of civil procedural law'); see also Wartenweiler, *Max Huber*, p. 147.

2) Is it possible that the Court, who affirmed its competency in a preliminary judgment, recognises that it was not competent in the final judgment?[241]

Judge Moore's reply had been short:

I intend to discuss tomorrow the points you raise in your letter of the 26th, and particularly the President's proposal to dismiss the present plea to the jurisdiction on the strength of a technical rule of procedure which, as I shall show, is not only not recognized in various countries, including the United States, but which is directly contrary to the uniform practice which prevails in international tribunals. Your letter shows that you have fully grasped the importance of this question.

No one can be more desirous than I am always to make the greatest possible progress with our business, but we should not permit ourselves to be hurried into taking decisions the purport of which even those who propose them apparently do not understand.[242]

The final judgment had gone through two different drafting committees, the views of which were markedly different.[243] For example, the *motifs* explicitly refrained from categorising the objection of the British Government as to the Permanent Court's jurisdiction under a specific term, 'whether "competence" and "jurisdiction", *incompétence* and *fin de non-recevoir*'.[244] This could be reminiscent of the constant referrals to civil law concepts in the first draft, or it could be part of Judges Anzilotti and Huber's attempts at remedying that draft. On the other hand, taking into account the just-quoted passage from Judge Moore's letter, it would not seem to have been the first drafting committee that had come up with the principle employed in respect of the condition that the dispute could not be settled by negotiations, and which at a later point in the *motifs* found an even more apt form, namely that '[t]he Court, whose jurisdiction is international, is not bound to attach to matters of form the same degree of importance which they might possess in municipal law'.[245]

A delicate question about origin arises in respect of the often-quoted passage of the *motifs* in which the majority, facing the third condition

---

[241] Anzilotti to Moore, 26 July 1924, Moore papers 51.
[242] Moore to Anzilotti, 27 July 1924, Moore papers 51.
[243] Cf. Edwin M. Borchard, 'The Mavrommatis Concessions Case' (1925) 19 *AJIL* 728 at 728; and Salvioli, 'Jurisprudence', p. 18.
[244] Series A No. 2 (1924) at 10; cf. *Case concerning Certain German Interests in Polish Upper Silesia* (Jurisdiction), Series A No. 6 (1925) at 19.
[245] *Ibid.*, pp. 34 and also 15.

under Article 26 of the Mandate, took note of the absence in the Statute and the Rules of any provisions regarding preliminary objections.[246] It was inferred that the Permanent Court:

therefore is at liberty to adopt the principle which it considers best calculated to ensure the administration of justice, most suited to procedure before an international tribunal and most in conformity with the fundamental principles of international law.

For this reason the Court, bearing in mind the fact that its jurisdiction is limited, that it is invariably based on the consent of the respondent and only exists in so far as this consent has been given, cannot content itself with the provisional conclusion that the dispute falls or not within the terms of the Mandate. The Court, before giving judgment on the merits of the case, will satisfy itself that the suit before it, in the form in which it has been submitted and on the basis of the facts hitherto established, falls to be decided by application of the clauses of the Mandate.[247]

As this test for jurisdiction also seemed to be peculiar to international law, as opposed to civil law, at least partially, it would be fair to surmise that it was due to the second drafting committee; it had taken as its basis the views of Judge Anzilotti,[248] who later called the passage 'a very accurate statement of the principles of international law which govern the Court's jurisdiction'.[249] The implication is that the generally couched test had not necessarily been a leading theme for the judgment taken as a whole, and in particular for what remained of the first draft.

That the general test had been added by the second drafting committee is also suggested by the following paragraph. Here, the Permanent Court distinguished the *Nationality Decrees* opinion, holding that in the *Mavrommatis* case a provisional conclusion as to the applicability of the clause was not sufficient. The Permanent Court stressed that its jurisdiction under Article 26 of the Mandate was 'limited to certain categories of disputes, which are determined according to a legal criterion (the interpretation and application of the terms of the Mandate), and tends therefore to assert the general rule that States may or may not submit

---

[246] As for the Rules of Court, cf. Series D No. 2 (1922) at 201–3 and 213–14 and also 489–90 and 494.

[247] Series A No. 2 (1924) at 16.

[248] See Anzilotti to Huber, 3 August 1924, Huber papers 24.1.

[249] *Case concerning Certain German Interests in Polish Upper Silesia* (Jurisdiction), Series A No. 6 (1925) at 30; see also Series D No. 2, Add.1 (1926) at 83 (Judge Anzilotti) and 88–9 (Judge Huber); as well as Anzilotti, *Cours*, p. 119.

their disputes to the Court at their discretion'.[250] This passage hinted at an essential reason in the *Nationality Decrees* opinion, also drafted by Judges Anzilotti and Huber, for having applied a loose test in respect of the Council's competence under Article 15 of the Covenant, namely that the Council was to remain a political body and was not vested with compulsory jurisdiction of a legal kind.[251]

At this point there seemed to be no doubt that the Permanent Court's jurisdiction was an issue belonging to the international law of cooperation. Thus it rested on treaty-making. The state was bound as an international law subject if consent had been given, but was otherwise free to act as a national sovereign.

Applying the compromissory clause

In its attempt to relate the actual dispute to the interpretation and application of the Mandate, the Greek Government relied on Article 11 of the Mandate, the relevant part of which read:

The Administration of Palestine shall take all necessary measures to safeguard the interests of the community in connection with the development of the

---

[250] Series A No. 2 (1924) at 16–17. See also the judgment of the European Court of Human Rights in *Case relating to Certain Aspects of the Laws on the Use of Languages in Education in Belgium* (Preliminary Objection), ECHR Series A No. 5 (1966) at 16. The European Court expressly preferred the approach adopted in the *Mavrommatis* case to that in the *Nationality Decrees* opinion; it found that the former approach was 'justified by the principle of economy of proceedings, by the logical sequence in which the various questions arise and by the fact that the European Court, like the World Court, has only an attributed jurisdiction derived purely from the consent of States'.

[251] See also Series D No. 2, Add.1 (1926) at 90 (Judge Anzilotti); and Judge Anzilotti's separate opinion in *Customs Regime between Germany and Austria (Protocol of March 19th, 1931)*, Series A/B No. 41 (1931) at 69–70 and also 57, 61–2 and 68; cf., perhaps *de lege ferenda*, Series D No. 2, Add.1 (1926) at 89 and 91 (Judge Huber). In 1924, Arbitrator Huber made an analogy to the interpretation of domestic jurisdiction given in the *Nationality Decrees* opinion: see *Affaire des biens britanniques au Maroc espagnol*, 2 RIAA 615 (1924) at 634–5. In the *Ambatielos* case, the International Court applied a test similar to the *Nationality Decrees* opinion in order not to encroach upon the jurisdiction of a Commission of Arbitration: see *Ambatielos Case* (Merits), ICJ Reports [1953] 10 at 14 and 16–19; contrast the joint dissenting opinion of President McNair and Judges Basdevant, Klaestad and Read, *ibid.*, pp. 28–9 and 31. Similarly, and concerning a less strictly worded compromissory clause, *Judgments of the Administrative Tribunal of the International Labour Organization upon Complaints made against the United Nations Educational, Scientific and Cultural Organization*, ICJ Reports [1956] 77 at 88–9. Cf., however, Judge Shahabuddeen's separate opinion in *Oil Platforms* (Preliminary Objection), ICJ Reports [1996] 803 at 825–32; but see Judge Higgins' separate opinion, *ibid.*, pp. 849–57.

country, and, subject to any international obligations accepted by the Mandatory, shall have full power to provide for public ownership or control of any of the natural resources of the country or of the public works, services and utilities established or to be established therein.

The Permanent Court's interpretation of 'public ownership or control' pointed to the importance of conceptions of the state in treaty interpretation. Holding that this expression was narrower in the English version than the equivalent expression in the French version, 'pleins pouvoirs pour décider quant à la propriété ou au contrôle public', the Permanent Court laid down this principle of interpretation:

The Court is of opinion that, where two versions possessing equal authority exist one of which appears to have a wider bearing than the other, it is bound to adopt the more limited interpretation which can be made to harmonise with both versions and which, as far as it goes, is doubtless in accordance with the common intention of the Parties.[252]

This was an example of the conception of the state as an international sovereign having a restrictive effect on treaty interpretation.[253] It was restrictive in the sense that differences in expressions did not lead the Permanent Court to examine the object and purpose of the treaty; instead, it reduced the meaning of the text to the overlap between the two expressions. This may be compared to the first *Competence of the International Labour Organization* opinion, in which the Permanent Court in a similar case of possible divergence between an English and a French version held that 'the context is the final test'.[254] In the *Mavrommatis* case, the Permanent Court corroborated its different argument partly by allusion to the conception of the state as a national sovereign: 'In the present case this conclusion is indicated with especial force because the question concerns an instrument laying down the obligations of Great Britain in her capacity as Mandatory for Palestine and because the original draft of this instrument was probably made in English.'[255] However, the Permanent Court soon came back to such objective interpretation, and the underpinning conception of the state as an international law subject; this was in order not to 'nullify the expression *contrôle public* in

---

[252] Series A No. 2 (1924) at 19 and also 69–70 (Judge Moore).
[253] Cf. Jean Hardy, 'The Interpretation of Plurilingual Treaties by International Courts and Tribunals' (1961) 37 *BYIL* 72 at 78–80.
[254] *International Labour Organization and the Conditions of Agricultural Labour*, Series B No. 2 (1922) at 35.
[255] Series A No. 2 (1924) at 19.

the French version'.[256] In addition, the Permanent Court could find support for the result of the more objective interpretation in the pleadings of the British Government and so, arguably, the conception of the state as an international sovereign.[257]

The Permanent Court took the view that the Mandatory's granting of the Rutenberg concessions which partly overlapped the concessions held by Mavrommatis was part of an exercise of 'public control'.[258] According to Article 11, this exercise of control had been 'subject to any international obligations accepted by the Mandatory'. The Permanent Court was satisfied that the actual dispute related to the interpretation and application of the Mandate (and that consequently it had jurisdiction under Article 26) if 'the international obligations mentioned in Article 11 affect the merits', or 'affect the Mavrommatis concessions'.[259] It only declined jurisdiction in respect of those concessions that had 'no connection with Article 11 of the Mandate'.[260]

Hammarskjöld found that the Permanent Court's result had been unforeseeable.[261] There are two main reasons why the general consensual test, which had been favoured by the second drafting committee, and the underlying conception of the state as an international sovereign, may seem to have been mere lip-service to a decision already taken in the first drafting committee. First, a provision's 'affecting' a dispute does not seem to imply that the dispute definitively 'falls to be decided by' the provision, as the general consensual test had it.[262] Secondly, the

[256] Ibid., p. 20. Accordingly, the interpretation turned out not to be restrictive: see the dissenting opinion of Judge Moore, ibid., pp. 69–70; and also Yi-ting Chang, The Interpretation of Treaties by Judicial Tribunals (New York, 1933), pp. 146–9; Jokl, Interprétation des traités, pp. 58–69; and Ian Sinclair, The Vienna Convention on the Law of Treaties (2nd edn, Manchester, 1984), pp. 149–50. The above-quoted dictum was rejected by the International Law Commission: see YILC 1966-II, pp. 225–6; and also Waldock, YILC 1964-II, pp. 64–5. Cf. Anzilotti, Cours, pp. 106–7; and Arbitrator Beichmann in Affaire des réparations allemandes selon l'article 260 du Traité de Versailles, 1 RIAA 429 (1924) at 459–67 and 472.

[257] Series A No. 2 (1924) at 21–3; cf. ibid., pp. 49–50 and 52–3 (Judge Finlay).

[258] Ibid., pp. 19–23 and 26. Cf. the dissenting opinion of Judge Moore, ibid., pp. 69–71; and also Moore to Borchard, 11 September 1925, Borchard papers 6.90: 'Perhaps you are right in saying merely that "Some of the minority judges concluded" etc. The papers may not show that they all shared the conclusion. I believe that Pessôa rested on only one point – that there was no "dispute", although, in the course of the oral discussions, he took my view. Possibly Oda did not. Finlay and Bustamante did.' Cf. Borchard, 'The Mavrommatis Concessions Case', p. 731.

[259] Series A No. 2 (1924) at 19, 23 and 26.   [260] Ibid., p. 29.

[261] Hammarskjöld to [Hjalmar] Hammarskjöld, 19 August 1924, Hammarskjöld papers 30.

[262] Cf. Paul De Vineuil, 'Les Decisions de la cinquième Session ordinaire de la Cour permanente de Justice internationale' (1925) 6 RDILC 80 at 108.

reference in Article 11 of the Mandate to 'any international obligations accepted by the Mandatory' appears to have been used to extend the Permanent Court's jurisdiction beyond the Mandate and so the compromissory clause in Article 26.

As for the first point, however, it was not so much about which test to apply as when to apply it. The following passage is illustrative:

> At the present stage of the proceedings the question whether there really has been a breach of these obligations [referred to in Article 11 of the Mandate] can clearly not be gone into; to do so would involve a decision as to the responsibility of the respondent, a thing which the two Governments concerned do not at the moment ask the Court to do. But, in accordance with the principles set out above, the Court is constrained at once to ascertain whether the international obligations mentioned in Article 11 affect the merits of the case and whether any breach of them would involve a breach of the provisions of this article.[263]

The general consensual test had been laid down when thinking of the dispute as defined by the applicant. Because the Permanent Court's jurisdiction rested on consent, also of the respondent, the dispute could only be decided by the Permanent Court if it fell within the compromissory clause. In the just-quoted passage, however, the Permanent Court did not deal with the dispute as defined by the applicant: it dealt with the dispute as seen against the background of, and so as defined by, the compromissory clause.[264] In accordance with this clause, that is, Article 26 of the Mandate, the Permanent Court indicated that it would entertain all questions that fell to be decided by 'the interpretation or application of the provisions of the Mandate'. There was no indication, however, that the Permanent Court would decide the rest of the dispute as defined by the applicant. The only thing the Permanent Court settled in its judgment on the preliminary objection was whether the dispute as defined by the applicant contained some questions that were 'affected' by the Mandate and thus could conceivably be decided on the basis of it. Of course, that made preliminary objections rather weak arguments, but that was simply a reflection of the fact that they concerned the merits of the case and could hardly be separated from them.[265]

---

[263] Series A No. 2 (1924) at 23.

[264] Compare the applicant's definition of the dispute, *ibid.*, p. 17, with the definition of the dispute as later introduced, *ibid.*, p. 19.

[265] See, however, President Loder's intervention, Series C No. 5-I at 27–8; and also the Greek Government, *ibid.*, p. 54. Cf. *Military and Paramilitary Activities in and against Nicaragua* (Jurisdiction and Admissibility), ICJ Reports [1984] 392 at paras. 81 and 83; and *Questions of Interpretation and Application of the 1971 Montreal Convention arising from*

Unlike an objection to the Council's competence based on Article 15(8) of the Covenant, such as that dealt with in the *Nationality Decrees* opinion, an objection to the Permanent Court's jurisdiction did not have to be resolved preliminarily. Often this was an objection not against the proceedings as such, but primarily against the proceedings resulting in a final decision. Even though the Permanent Court had partly dismissed the British Government's preliminary objection, the compromissory clause in Article 26 of the Mandate would determine which questions were answered in the final judgment. Whether the Permanent Court selected the questions to be answered already when deciding on the preliminary objection, instead of in the following judgment on the merits, might more than anything else have been a matter of taste.

It is the second of the above-mentioned points that made the *motifs* seem controversial in relation to the consensual test, as also stressed in the dissenting opinions of Judges Finlay, Moore and Oda.[266] It had to do with using Article 11 of the Mandate and the reference to 'any international obligations accepted by the Mandatory' so as to extend the Permanent Court's jurisdiction beyond the substantive provisions of the Mandate. Looking into the preparatory work, the Permanent Court held that this reference had originally related to a provision in the abortive Sèvres Treaty, which the later Protocol XII of the Lausanne Treaty replaced.[267] It regulated certain concessions granted by the Ottoman Government, in particular the holders' right to claim that their concessions should be either readapted to the new economic circumstances or dissolved with compensation. Under Article 11 of the Mandate, acts of 'public control', including the granting of the Rutenberg concessions, were valid only if done in accordance with Protocol XII.

According to the Greek Government, Protocol XII imposed an obligation on the British Government to recognise the Mavrommatis concessions and, therefore, the Rutenberg concessions were invalid to the extent that they were incompatible with the Mavrommatis concessions. However, Protocol XII contained no compromissory clause. The Permanent Court could only decide on these questions if its jurisdiction under Article 26 of the Mandate covered not only Article 11 of the Mandate but

---

the *Aerial Incident at Lockerbie* (Preliminary Objections) (*Libya* v. *United Kingdom*), ICJ Reports [1998] 9 at paras. 29 and 33 and (*Libya* v. *United States*), ICJ Reports [1998] 115 at paras. 28 and 32; see also Judge Higgins' separate opinion in *Oil Platforms* (Preliminary Objection), ICJ Reports [1996] 803 at 849.

[266] Cf. Series A No. 2 (1924) at 42, 60 and 85, respectively.   [267] Cf. *ibid.*, pp. 24–8.

also Protocol XII. On this point the *motifs* were sparse, possibly due to disagreement between the two drafting committees:

The Court considers that the reservation made in Article 11 regarding international obligations is not a mere statement of fact devoid of immediate legal value [*n'a pas le caractère d'une simple constatation sans valeur juridique directe*], but that, on the contrary, it is intended to afford these obligations within the limits fixed in the article, the same measure of protection as all other provisions of the Mandate.[268]

The preference for Article 11 in this context seemed to confirm the dissenters' view that the phrase 'international obligations accepted by the Mandatory' did not concern the Permanent Court's jurisdiction under Article 26, limited as it was to 'the interpretation or the application of the provisions of the Mandate'. At the root of the Permanent Court's argument was the claim that 'the reservation made in Article 11' was not 'a mere statement of fact devoid of immediate legal value'. The majority had already explained that the reservation had some legal value in the sense that 'the international obligations of the Mandatory are not, *ipso facto*, international obligations of Palestine' and so had to be made applicable to Palestine and its 'wide measure of autonomy' under Article 11.[269] Moreover, as some of the dissenters noted, the reservation precluded the otherwise possible interpretation that Article 11 authorised unrestricted nationalisation.[270] However, in the above-quoted paragraph the majority did not refer to 'legal value' but to 'immediate legal value'. It was only when relied upon before the Permanent Court that obligations got a 'legal value' that was 'immediate'.

This line of reasoning suggested that the limits within which the Permanent Court had jurisdiction were drawn in accordance with a certain notion of a court of justice, rather than reflecting an agreement between states conceived as international sovereigns. It may have seemed unsatisfactory that the Permanent Court could entertain disputes if a violation of 'international obligations accepted by the Mandatory' had been determined, while it had no jurisdiction to make that determination itself. It was perfectly possible, however, that this was what states had agreed

---

[268] *Ibid.*, p. 26.

[269] *Ibid.*, p. 23; and similarly Arbitrator Huber in *Affaire des biens britanniques au Maroc espagnol*, 2 RIAA 615 (1925) at 648. Cf. Anzilotti, *Cours*, p. 131; and see Ago, YILC 1979-II.1, pp. 6–7 and also YILC 1979-II.2, p. 98.

[270] Notably Series A No. 2 (1924) at 47–8 (Judge Finlay). Cf. the reference in the *motifs* to 'the general principle of subrogation', *ibid.*, p. 28; and also Huber, *Die Staatensuccession*, p. 149.

to. Moreover, and possibly more importantly, this argument attributes a specific and questionable purpose to the reference to 'international obligations accepted by the Mandatory'. The reasoning in the *motifs* leading to the opposite conclusion looked like the epitome of analogical interpretation, holding that the better law was the law guarded by a court of justice.[271] This 'institutional' test bred a series of additional problems, which, however, the majority was able to overcome.[272]

Conclusions

The *Mavrommatis* case spelled out a basic tension underlying the understanding of the Permanent Court's jurisdiction. Either a compromissory clause contained in a specific treaty could be dealt with in isolation, the test for jurisdiction being what the states as international sovereigns had agreed to under the specific circumstances; or a compromissory clause could be put in the greater context of the Permanent Court as an institution and given a mainly analogical, and often extensive, interpretation in accordance with notions of what a court of justice ought to be. The underpinning notion was taken from national law and so, in a sense, reflected the conception of the state as a national sovereign.

In the *Mavrommatis* case, Judges Finlay and Moore were strict on the consensual test for jurisdiction, as had also been the case in the *Eastern Carelia* opinion. Indeed, Judge Moore told Professor Borchard that he was 'unable to grasp the majority view in a legal sense'.[273] Borchard having proposed to write an editorial on the *Mavrommatis* case, Judge Moore gave some more information, echoing his complaints about the debates at the preliminary session back in 1922 leading to the adoption of the Rules of Court:

Bustamante privately made the rather significant comment that the decision, as it stood, represented the continent of Europe against the rest of the world. It is a curious fact that the judges who voted for jurisdiction formed a continental bloc, and that all the judges from the rest of the world, civilians as well as Common Law judges, voted contra. Apart from certain personal elements, I think this division was perhaps essentially due to the fact that the plea to the jurisdiction was not grasped by the former group, at least some of whom seemed to think that, if the plea was allowed, the claim could never under any circumstances be

---

[271] Cf. B. C. J. Loder, *La Difference entre l'arbitrage international et la justice internationale* (The Hague, 1923), pp. 21–2.

[272] See Series A No. 2 (1924) at 29–36; cf. YILC 1966-II, p. 212.

[273] Moore to Borchard, 4 September 1924, Borchard papers 6.89.

renewed. I did my best to clear up this misapprehension but my efforts were of no avail so far as the majority were concerned.[274]

On the facts of the specific case, the question of which test to apply not only divided some of the dissenters from the majority; it also divided the majority judges into at least two groups. On the one hand, it may be recalled that in 1920, from the floor of the First Assembly, B. C. J. Loder, who almost certainly took part in the first drafting committee in the *Mavrommatis* case, had told the opponents of compulsory jurisdiction:

You are fighting against time; you will do so in vain . . . Ensure the present for yourselves; the future will be ours . . . We recognise no greatness which is raised above justice, even when it wears the mantle of sovereignty.[275]

On the other hand, the years following the first judgment in the *Mavrommatis* case saw Judge Anzilotti as the main exponent of the consensual test. In a letter to Hammarskjöld written just before the *Nationality Decrees* opinion came up, Judge Anzilotti had explained his position:

Je comprends la *Kompetenz-Kompetenz* de la Cour de cette manière: la Cour a le devoir de s'assurer toujours de sa compétence et de ne prononcer que si elle juge que sa compétence existe; il y a donc toujours, explicite ou implicite, un jugement de la Cour sur sa propre compétence que les parties sont tenues d'accepter et de respecter. Si la Cour s'est trompée, cette obligation des parties n'en subsiste pas moins, en vertu de leur propre volonté.[276]

Two months after the *Mavrommatis* case, in a decision in the *Moroccan Claims*, Arbitrator Huber made room for the view that '[l]e principe de l'indépendance des Etats exclut que leur politique intérieure ou extérieure fasse dans le doute l'object de l'activité d'une juridiction

---

[274] Moore to Borchard, 11 February 1925, Borchard papers 6.90 and Moore papers 53; cf. the dissenting opinion of Judge Moore, Series A No. 2 (1924) at 57 *et seq.*; Moore to Hughes, 12 September 1924 and Moore to Stone, 12 September 1924, both Moore papers 52.

[275] *Records of Assembly: Plenary* 1920, p. 445; and also Loder, 'Permanent Court', p. 26; and B. C. J. Loder, *Speech Delivered by Dr B. C. J. Loder at the Banquet Given by the Anglo-Batavian Society* (The Hague, 1923), pp. 19–22; and N. Politis, 'How the World Court Has Functioned' (1925–6) 4 *Foreign Affairs* 443 at 449. Indeed, in the *Mavrommatis* case, Article 26 was referred to as 'a clause establishing the latter's [that is, the Permanent Court's] compulsory jurisdiction': see Series A No. 2 (1924) at 29; cf. *ibid.*, pp. 41, 43 and 51 (Judge Finlay), 54 and 60 (Judge Moore) and 85 (Judge Oda). Cf. Series D No. 2 (1922) at 330. As for a recent restatement of Loder's original views, see Judge Weeramantry's dissenting opinion in *Fisheries Jurisdiction (Spain v. Canada)*, ICJ Reports [1998] 432 at 512–13.

[276] See Anzilotti to Hammarskjöld, 25 November 1922, Hammarskjöld papers 478.

internationale'.[277] The rationale behind this view, also hinted at in the *Jaworzina* opinion,[278] had been set out by Huber in 1919 when reflecting on the Peace Treaties and the Covenant of the League of Nations. He had distinguished international adjudication from national adjudication in the following terms:

> Das besondere staatliche Interesse dagegen in einem internationalen Konflikt hat für die zwischenstaatliche Rechtsgemeinschaft eine höhere Bedeutung; das Individuelle des Falles verlangt deshalb weitgehende Rücksicht. Lebensinteressen eines Staates können nicht ohne unmittelbare oder latente Gefahr für den Frieden geopfert werden. Das gibt der zwischenstaatlichen Rechtssprechung in vielen Fällen einen hochpolitischen Character, der sich nicht leicht mit einer für alle Staaten bindenden und all Streitigkeiten erfassenden Regelung verträgt.[279]

When, in the *Mavrommatis* case, the Permanent Court had outlined the considerations pertinent to determining the limits of its jurisdiction, it had pointed to those which were 'best calculated to ensure the administration of justice, most suited to procedure before an international tribunal and most in conformity with the fundamental principles of international law'.[280] These three kinds of considerations seem to have reflected, respectively, President Loder's inclination towards analogical interpretation and an institutional test, Judge Huber's concerns about intervention and coexistence being compromised and thus a potentially restrictive test, and Judge Anzilotti's focus on the international law of cooperation and a strictly consensual test. Shabtai Rosenne has described the development as follows:

---

[277] *Affaire des biens britanniques au Maroc espagnol*, 2 RIAA 615 (1924) at 642; and see Huber, *Soziologischen Grundlagen des Völkerrechts*, p. 48. A reminiscence of this view was Hammarskjöld, 'Quelques aspects', p. 158.

[278] *Question of Jaworzina (Polish–Czechoslovakian Frontier)*, Series B No. 8 (1923) at 56.

[279] Max Huber, 'Die konstruktiven Grundlagen des Völkerbundsvertrages' (1922–3) 12 *Zeitschrift für Völkerrecht* 1 at 14 (translation: 'In contrast, the peculiar interest of a state in an international conflict is of greater importance to the international legal community. Therefore, the individuality of cases must be taken into consideration to a greater extent. Vital interests of states cannot be sacrificed without posing an immediate or latent threat to the peace. In many cases, this confers on international adjudication a highly political character, which is not easily reconcilable with the notion of a settlement which is binding on all states and comprising all disputes.'). See also Huber in James Brown Scott (ed.), *The Proceedings of the Hague Peace Conferences: The Conference of 1907* (London, 1920), vol. 2, p. 66; and in (1927) 33-I *Annuaire*, pp. 763–4. Cf. H. Lauterpacht, 'The British Reservations to the Optional Clause' (1930) 10 *Economica* 137 at 158–9.

[280] Series A No. 2 (1924) at 16.

The Permanent Court, after an experimental and tentative start, also made tremendous advances in international judicial procedure. Using as its point of departure the models of procedure in the domestic courts (especially the highest courts), international judicial procedure is today a completely autonomous institution of international law and practice having only superficial resemblances to domestic legal procedure.[281]

Conclusions

Summing up his experiences of the Permanent Court's four sessions in 1923 and 1924 as to the drafting of decisions, Max Huber wrote:

In den Fällen Marokko-Tunis, Ost-Karelien, Deutsche Ansiedler in Polen, Javorzina, Mavrommatis und Neuilly hatte ich wesentlich am Zustandekommen des Entscheides mitgewirkt und die betreffenden Urteile zu einem erheblichen Teil, zwei davon sogar ausschließlich, redigiert. Dabei hatten die Redaktoren stets mindestens vier Fünftel der eigentlich juristischen Begründung zu geben, da die Urteilsberatung meist nur ergab, zu welchem Resultat die Mehrheit gelangt sei, während hinsichtlich der Motive zunächst nur ein Chaos zum Teil widersprechender Standpunkte sichtbar wurde, wobei sich erst noch bei der Redaktion des Urteils zeigte, daß große Teile der Begründung überhaupt erst noch zu finden waren.[282]

This passage ought to be taken as a warning against regarding the votes in favour of a *dispositif* or advice as votes in favour of the *motifs* preceding it. Perhaps not all members of the bench took the same interest in framing thorough *motifs* in order to guard the Permanent Court's reputation,[283] or even to 'develop' international law. The latter notion speaks to the academic lawyer rather than the practitioner, thus perhaps it was

---

[281] Shabtai Rosenne, *The World Court: What It Is and How It Works* (Leiden, 1962), p. 23; and see also Rosenne, *Law and Practice*, pp. 854–5 and 1066–8, referring to *Case of the Mavrommatis Palestine Concessions* (Jurisdiction), Series A No. 2 (1924) at 10 and *Case concerning Certain German Interests in Polish Upper Silesia* (Jurisdiction), Series A No. 6 (1925) at 19.

[282] Huber, *Denkwürdigkeiten*, p. 284 (translation: 'In the cases of *Nationality Decrees, Eastern Carelia, German Settlers, Jaworzina, Mavrommatis* and *Neuilly*, I had an important role in the making of the decisions; in these cases I drafted considerable parts of the decisions, on two occasions even the entire decision. In doing so the editors had to contribute at least four-fifths of the reasoning on the law, since the deliberations for the most part only served to determine the conclusion reached by the majority. With regard to the *motifs*, at first only a chaos of partly contradictory views came to light and it was only during the drafting of the decisions that substantial parts of the reasoning were elaborated.'). Likewise, Walther Schücking, '*Vertrauliche Bemerkungen zur Frage der Revision des Statuts des Weltgerichtshofs*' undated, Schücking papers (Koblenz) 32, pp. 9–10, referring to a conversation with Huber.

[283] Cf. Huber in Series C No. 7-I, p. 18; and Huber, 'Åke Hammarskjöld', p. 19.

not a surprise that Judge Huber and also Judge Anzilotti took part in the drafting on a very regular basis.[284] As the youngest members of the Permanent Court, they also had the first say in the formal deliberations.[285]

As for the Permanent Court's early decisions, '[i]t would', according to one writer, 'be difficult to view the remarkable restraint that the Court displays regarding any substantial analysis of the legal rules advanced for the purpose of reaching judicial conclusions as grounded elsewhere than in policy'.[286] This observation was based on a comparison with international arbitral awards rendered in contemporary cases and so, it would seem, on a neglect of the implications of collegiate decision-making on a bench composed of eleven members. However that may be, prior to this so-called 'remarkable restraint' was the lack of restraint in employing the most general principles in deciding the most specific issues, a somewhat academic tendency.[287] And whatever the use of 'legal rules', the Permanent Court's reasoning was generally quite full.[288]

The overall impression left by the Permanent Court's decisions in the foundational period confirmed Hammarskjöld's evaluation of the discussion of sources in the Advisory Committee of Jurists, namely that '[a]s a purely platonic discussion it was very interesting, but the practical value of it was certainly not great'.[289] The list of sources contained in Article 38 of the Statute was a piece of *Buchrecht*, which hardly contributed anything to the understanding of the Permanent Court's use of international legal argument. Instead, an attempt has been made in this chapter to describe the foundational period of the Permanent Court using the model of international legal argument developed in Chapter 3. To a certain extent, choices between using the basic or the dynamic structure of international legal argument were a result of judges approaching the

---

[284] See Jeffrey B. Golden, 'The World Court: The Qualifications of the Judges' (1978) 14 *Columbia Journal of Law and Social Problems* 1 at 43–4.

[285] Series E No. 2 (1925–6) at 171; and Series D No. 2, Add.1 (1926) at 60.

[286] Richard D. Kearney, 'Sources of Law and the International Court of Justice' in Leo Gross (ed.), *The International Court of Justice: Consideration of Requirements for Enhancing its Rôle in the International Legal Order* (New York, 1976), p. 610 at p. 649.

[287] Cf. Antonio Cassese, *International Law* (Oxford, 2001), p. 157; and also Åke Hammarskjöld, 'The Permanent Court of International Justice and the Development of International Law' (1935) 14 *International Affairs* 797 at 799; and Andreae, *An Important Chapter*, pp. 53 and 129.

[288] Cf. J. H. W. Verzijl, 'Die Rechtsprechung des Ständigen Internationalen Gerichtshofes von 1922 bis Mai 1926' (1924–6) 13 *Zeitschrift für Völkerrecht* 489 at 493.

[289] Hammarskjöld to Van Hamel, 2 July 1920, Hammarskjöld papers 480; cf. *Report of the Informal Inter-Allied Committee on the Future of the Permanent Court of International Justice, 10th February 1944*, Cmd 6531 (London, 1944), p. 19; and also Basdevant's report in 14 UNCIO, p. 843; and H. Lauterpacht, 'The Revision of the Statute of the International Court of Justice' (2002) 1 *LPICT* 55 at 120–1.

cases as national or international lawyers. However, and significantly, such choices were subject to legal argument, as demonstrated by the *Nationality Decrees* opinion and the joint dissenting opinion appended to *The Wimbledon*. This confirms that together the two do not leave international legal argument indeterminate; together they make up a double structure of international legal argument.

Compared to sources theory and other contributions to international legal theory, this double structure would seem to provide a better understanding of *The Wimbledon* and to shed new light on the treatment of the Permanent Court's jurisdiction and its limits. Also, the different weight given to state consent may be explained within the model, that is, the hierarchical relationship between the basic and dynamic structures. On some occasions qualified consent had been required. For example, having noted that the Polish Minorities Treaty derogated from the national principle of self-containedness, the *Minorities* opinions 'qualified' Poland's consent by advancing supplementary lines of reasoning that related to the international law of coexistence. In *The Wimbledon*, the dissenters were reluctant to interpret a treaty provision so as to derogate from the international law of coexistence; in this context 'la liberté de l'Etat' provided for by the international law of coexistence and a principle of non-intervention was seen as particularly strong – much stronger than in its sweeping formulation in the *Nationality Decrees* opinion.[290] The *Jaworzina* and *Monastery of Saint-Naoum* opinions illustrated that the need for the international law of coexistence implied the need for defined territorial borders.

These were examples of judges thinking of the state as a national sovereign as opposed to an international sovereign, thereby playing down the importance of consent. The most striking illustration was the different consequences drawn in the *Eastern Carelia* opinion and the judgment in *The Wimbledon* as regards Russia's not being a party to the Versailles Treaty. In the latter decision, Russia's position as a national sovereign, or even an international law subject, under the international law of coexistence was affected by the Versailles Treaty, as it had changed the territorial status of the Kiel Canal with 'objective' effects under the international law of coexistence, whereas in the former decision Russia was seen as an international sovereign, the consent of which was needed before the Versailles Treaty could be applied. This difference is difficult

---

[290] Cf. *Case of the SS Wimbledon*, Series A No. 1 (1923) at 35; and *Nationality Decrees in Tunis and Morocco*, Series B No. 4 (1923) at 24.

to explain if one does not admit that international law is not only about the conception of the state as an international sovereign, but also to a large extent the conception of the state as a national sovereign.[291]

The variable significance of consent also gave rise to different tests being laid down in the *Nationality Decrees* opinion as to the Council's powers under Article 15 of the Covenant and in the *Eastern Carelia* opinion and the *Mavrommatis* case as to the Permanent Court's jurisdiction. These were occasions on which the judges, with some notable exceptions, did not appear to think as national lawyers, but employed the dynamic structure of international legal argument. They distinguished two different ways of constituting an international institution. The Council and its powers had been constituted under the Covenant while the Permanent Court had been constituted under the Statute as an institution but with no compulsory jurisdiction; its powers had to be based on other sources. Thus, a state could immediately be seen as an international law subject in relation to the Council, while in relation to the Permanent Court it was a national sovereign. It was also an international sovereign, however, and the judgment in the *Mavrommatis* case arguably demonstrated that analogical interpretation of compromissory clauses might nullify the difference between the methods of constituting the institutions.

Also in the *Mavrommatis* case, as the phrase 'any international obligations accepted by the Mandatory' was dealt with at a more abstract level, many judges, including the first drafting committee, made it clear that – unlike Judge Anzilotti in his theoretical writings – they did not ground customary rules on the 'acceptance' of each and every state.[292] Indeed, the Permanent Court's decisions in the foundational period contained many pronouncements on so-called customary law, that is, the international law of coexistence, without making a single reference to '*opinio juris*'.[293] '*Pacta sunt servanda*' and '*non liquet*' were not mentioned either. Whichever the dichotomies known to the *Buchrecht* down the centuries, the key distinction in the foundational period in the Permanent Court was between judges approaching international law as national lawyers and judges who would seem to be more international lawyers.

---

[291] Cf. Sørensen, *Sources du droit international*, p. 98; and Waldock, YILC 1964-II, p. 30.

[292] Series A No. 2 (1924) at 24 and also 28 (the majority), 47 (Judge Finlay) and 68 (Judge Moore); see also *Nationality Decrees in Tunis and Morocco*, Series B No. 4 (1923) at 23; and *The Mavrommatis Jerusalem Concessions* (Merits), Series A No. 5 (1925) at 27.

[293] Cf. *Case of the SS Wimbledon*, Series A No. 1 (1923) at 28 and 36.

6   An international lawyer's approach, 1925–1930

President Huber

At the end of its fifth session, the Permanent Court had to elect a new president. President Loder's rival candidate was Judge Moore, who in a letter to Judge Huber had taken the view that '[e]xisting conditions would not be improved by an embittered but unsuccessful effort to make a change in the presidency, which, as you know, Mr Loder strongly desires to retain; and under no circumstances would I consent to the use of my name for a mere demonstration of dissatisfaction'.[1] What Judge Moore had wanted was 'a substantial majority of my colleagues'. However, repeated voting produced nothing but a series of ties and eventually Judge Moore withdrew his candidacy. A majority of six now favoured the member of the bench who perhaps had exercised the greatest influence on the Permanent Court's work in its foundational period: Judge Huber.[2]

This election was more than a transfer of a title. In 1922, at the Permanent Court's inauguration ceremony, President Loder had said that international law had taken the first step beyond 'the law of force and of selfishness'.[3] This phrase emphasised the vital role which President Loder and other traditionalists attributed to the project of international justice. It also implied that President Loder considered the conception of the state as a national sovereign, and the national sovereign's interests and 'selfishness', that is, the national principle of self-containedness, as the premise from which substantive international law had to develop.[4]

---

[1] Moore to Huber, 27 August 1924, Moore papers 52.
[2] See Max Huber, *Denkwürdigkeiten, 1907–1924* (Zurich, 1974), pp. 298–300.
[3] Series D No. 2 (1922) at 329.
[4] See also Loder in Shabtai Rosenne (ed.), *Committee of Experts for the Progressive Codification of International Law* (New York, 1972), vol. 1, p. 8. Cf. Huber, *Denkwürdigkeiten*, pp. 172, 221 and 269–70.

Upon his election President Huber delivered a speech taking note of 'les limites inhérentes à la justice proprement dite dans le droit international'. But then he added:

Mais cela importe peu: l'essentiel, c'est la croyance en la possibilité et en l'existence d'une institution au-dessus des compétitions plus ou moins brutales ou plus ou moins fines des égoïsmes nationaux, d'une institution qui représente l'impartialité et la justice, principes d'un ordre supérieur. Cette idée de justice internationale est, quoi qu'on en dise, représentée à l'heure actuelle essentielle-ment par notre Cour.[5]

Unlike his predecessor, President Huber did not equate the prosperity of international law with the extinction of the national sovereign's self-ishness. He insisted on international law being 'un ordre supérieur', accentuating the conception of the state as an international law subject. The difference between the two speeches was not simply a reflection of the lapse of a period of three years that lay between their elections. Judge Huber was twenty-five years younger than Judge Loder. In addition there were differences in their professional backgrounds: Judge Loder had had a long career as a national lawyer and was persistent in promoting pro-cedural principles taken from civil law,[6] while Judge Huber had come to the Permanent Court as an international lawyer.

The Registrar made it no secret that there was yet another difference between the two judges, namely that the organisation of the Permanent Court's work would be much improved under President Huber.[7] In 1926, the Permanent Court at last tackled the revision of the Rules of Court, which more and more judges had requested, based on their practical experience of their application.[8] Soon after his election, following the *Exchange of Populations* opinion, President Huber instigated a more influ-ential role for the president in the Permanent Court's work, notably by becoming an *ex officio* member of every drafting committee.[9] President Huber also encouraged the use of written notes from each member of the bench as the starting-point for deliberations, as had been used once under his predecessor, namely in the *Mavrommatis* case.[10] These notes

[5] Series C No. 7-I at 16; cf. Max Huber, *Die Soziologischen Grundlagen des Völkerrechts* (Berlin, 1928), p. 87.
[6] Huber, *Denkwürdigkeiten*, p. 298.
[7] See Hammarskjöld to Huber, 16 September 1924, Huber papers 24.1; and Hammarskjöld to [Hjalmar] Hammarskjöld, 25 January 1925, Hammarskjöld papers 30.
[8] See Revised Rules of Court adopted on 31 July 1926, Series D No. 1 (1926) at 33–65.
[9] See Series E No. 2 (1925–6) at 170–1; and Series D No. 2, Add.1 (1926) at 248–9.
[10] Series E No. 1 (1922–5) at 171.

were preceded only by an exchange of views as to which issues should be discussed. On the basis of the written notes, President Huber would produce a detailed questionnaire, providing a structure for the oral component of the deliberations.[11]

In 1926, at the opening of the eleventh session, President Huber delivered another speech, this time not in public.[12] He suggested that a consultation should take place between the judges before the oral pleadings so that 'nous saurons ce que les plaidoiries devront encore fournir pour nous permettre de juger vraiment en connaissance de cause'. He also urged all judges to engage in the deliberations and the composing of the *motifs*. In his view:

[l]a pire des situations est celle où, des groupements s'étant dessinés, et une majorité s'étant formée, soit lors de la discussion, soit déjà dans les notes individuelles, la discussion se concentre sur la défense des arguments arrivant à un résultat déterminé, et où la minorité se désintéresse en quelque sorte de ce qui doit être la manifestation de la Cour et non pas celle d'une majorité qui s'est formée au sujet d'une affaire déterminée. Les moments où la discussion, sans être épuisée le moins du monde, s'arrête; où le choc des idées opposées n'est qu'un choc mécanique, non pas la base d'une nouvelle évolution, d'une adaptation et d'une compréhension mutuelle, sont pour moi les plus pénibles et je dois le dire que j'ai passé plus d'une fois par des heures où j'ai cru ne plus trouver en moi les forces pour continuer mon travail.

According to the detailed account of the Permanent Court's work in President Huber's *Tagebuch* of 1925–7, this request did not bear much fruit. To Judge Moore, President Huber wrote that 'the evolution of so heterogeneous and numerous a body as the Court is very slow and the individual influence is much limited'.[13]

In the unpublished addendum to his *Denkwürdigkeiten*, covering the years between 1925 and 1959, Huber wrote: 'Wirkliche Völkerrechtskundige waren ausser Moore, Anzilotti, Beichmann, mir und allenfalls dem Cubaner Bustamante nicht da. Deshalb waren wir vier während der ganzen neunjährigen Periode meist das Comité de rédaction, da wir alle der englischen Sprache mächtig waren.'[14] Other

---

[11] Cf. Judge Anzilotti, Series D No. 2, Add.2 (1931) at 241 and 246.
[12] Präsidentreden, 15 June 1926, Huber papers 25.2.
[13] Huber to Moore, 21 January 1926, Moore papers 177.
[14] Max Huber, 'Epilog zu den Denkwürdigkeiten aus meinem Leben niedergeschrieben im Haag 1925–1927' (1959), Huber Papers 17.11, p. 6 (translation: 'Leaving aside Moore, Anzilotti, Beichmann, myself and, at most, Bustamante, there were no real experts in international law. Therefore, during the entire nine-year period the four of us made

judges, including the former President, who was 'strongly opposed to permitting dissenting opinions',[15] began to make secret dissents.[16] In the *Upper Silesia* case, only Judge *ad hoc* Rostworowski openly declared a dissent from the judgment on the merits, but in fact the judges had been evenly split and President Huber only avoided employing his casting vote because Judge Weiss left The Hague before the end of the deliberations.[17] Shortly afterwards, when revising the Rules of Court, Article 62 was amended so that as from 31 July 1926 the final vote would be made public.[18]

During Judge Huber's presidency many of the inchoate tendencies of the foundational period were further pursued. Principles of treaty interpretation were cultivated, with one important context being the Permanent Court's contentious jurisdiction. Governments continued to plead principles of restrictive interpretation that were based on the national principle of self-containedness. In rejecting these and other arguments, the drafting committees eschewed arguments attractive to national lawyers and moulded an international lawyer's approach to international legal argument based on a firm hierarchy between the two structures of international legal argument. In a pure form, this approach may be identified in terms of a distinction between the international law of cooperation and the international law of coexistence with the residual principle of state freedom being applied where no international law could be discerned. During Judges Huber's presidency, the national principle of self-containedness was barely mentioned.

Hammarskjöld continued to play an important role. This was regretted by some: in respect of the Permanent Court's first years of activity, Judge Nyholm had said that Hammarskjöld 'on the basis of his evident professional Greffier capacity rules the whole court';[19] and, despite the

---

up, for the most part, the drafting committee, as we all mastered the English language.'); see also *ibid.*, p. 61; and Max Huber, *Koexistenz und Gemeinschaft: Völkerrechtliche Erinnerungen aus sechs Jahrzehnten* (Zurich, 1956), p. 17.

[15] Moore to Walsh, 19 January 1926, Moore papers 172.

[16] See President Huber, Series D No. 2, Add.1 (1926) at 209 and 215; as for Judge Loder, see *ibid.*, pp. 197 and 212.

[17] See Max Huber, 'Tagebuch, 29. Dez 1924–12. Dez. 1927', Huber papers 25.1, 20 May 1926; and Marcilly's despatch, 26 May 1926, Quai d'Orsay 2406. Cf. *Case concerning Certain German Interests in Polish Upper Silesia* (Merits), Series A No. 7 (1926) at 83.

[18] Series D No. 2, Add.1 (1926) at 200–23; and also Moore to Finlay, 20 July and 27 July 1926, both Moore papers 177; and John Bassett Moore, 'Permanent Court of International Justice: 11th Session (Ordinary), June 15–July 31, 1926', NARA 500 C114/564.

[19] Nyholm to Moore, 6 March 1925, Moore papers 177.

change of president, according to Judge Nyholm, '[t]he whole court is in the hands of the Registrar'.[20] In his speech delivered upon his election as president, President Huber had said that he was 'heureux de savoir que le président de la Cour est très efficacement aidé par le Greffe, dont tous les membres, de haut en bas, nous rendent des services intelligents et dévoués, et qui est dirigé avec un rare talent par Monsieur Hammarskjöld'.[21] Hammarskjöld did not give up his writings on the Permanent Court's decisions, but now they took a less clandestine form. Having been elected an *associé* of the Institut de Droit International, he unveiled the true identity of 'Paul de Vineuil' in a bibliography submitted to the electors.[22] The signature 'Paul de Vineuil' was used once again in commenting on the Permanent Court's decisions in 1929, but in the interval Hammarskjöld adopted a more 'pseudonymous' one: 'Michel de la Grotte'.

Determining the Permanent Court's contentious jurisdiction

The Mavrommatis *case continued*

The Permanent Court's contentious jurisdiction remained a crucial issue during Judge Huber's presidency. Huber himself had expressed doubts as to which disputes were justiciable. There had also been some tension between the notion of jurisdiction based on agreement between international sovereigns and that of jurisdiction based on an ideal of a court of justice under an analogical interpretation. While these different views all had a say in the first judgment in the *Mavrommatis* case, in subsequent decisions the Permanent Court's treatment of jurisdictional questions came closer to its approach to treaty interpretation in general.

The *Mavrommatis* case was decided on the merits at the sixth session in 1925. Although Judge Finlay took part in the majority, not all the divisions of 1924 had been forgotten.[23] As regards 'compétence et préjudice', the draft of the new judgment, which had been produced by a committee that included both President Huber and Judge Anzilotti, won the support of only a narrow majority.[24] The *motifs* as finally adopted stated

[20] Nyholm to Moore, 23 November 1925, Moore papers 177.
[21] Series C No. 7-I at 15.
[22] See (1925) 32 *Annuaire*, p. 567; and Hammarskjöld to de Visscher, 30 September 1925, Hammarskjöld papers 488. Judge Moore received a copy of 'Paul de Vineuil's' latest contribution: see Hammarskjöld to Moore, 27 January 1925, Moore papers 177.
[23] See President Anzilotti's speech in Series E No. 5 (1928-9) at 22.
[24] See Huber, 'Tagebuch', 11 March 1925, 17 March 1925 and 18 March 1925.

that 'even if' the granting of the Rutenberg concessions overlapped the Mavrommatis concessions and contravened Protocol XII to the Lausanne Treaty, Mavrommatis had suffered no loss for which he could claim compensation.[25] A larger majority ruled that Mavrommatis was entitled to have his concessions readapted to the new economic circumstances; a conclusion that was helped not only by the preparatory work to Protocol XII,[26] but which could also be supported by a strict conception of vested rights.[27] Judge Finlay wrote the following to Judge Moore, who was absent:

> The Mavrommatis case has raised Loder in my estimation. He had taken a strong line the other way but turned around completely. I never discussed the case with him – and I am certain that his conviction was that to send the case to experts without a finding by the Court would be fatal to the Court and wrong in law and I honour him for giving effect to this conviction. I think that thanks to his change of attitude the case has ended the right way.[28]

The question of readaptation fell outside the scope – otherwise strictly followed in the *motifs* – of the compromissory clause as it had been construed in 1924.[29] In the course of the proceedings, the parties had agreed to this extension of the Permanent Court's jurisdiction,[30] a *forum prorogatum* that the Permanent Court found room for under Article 36(1) of the Statute.[31] But it was emphasised that the Permanent Court only had jurisdiction to decide on the question of readaptation because of the Special Agreement. The compromissory clause contained in Article 26 of the Mandate did not vest the Permanent Court with jurisdiction to decide the whole dispute as defined by the applicant.

The Upper Silesia *case*

The question of the Permanent Court's contentious jurisdiction re-emerged later the same year in the *Upper Silesia* case, concerning Poland's liquidation of a factory at Chorzów and its alleged expropriation of certain agricultural estates. The German Government referred the case to the Permanent Court under Article 23(1) of the Geneva Convention concerning Upper Silesia, which provided: 'Should differences of opinion

---

[25] *The Mavrommatis Jerusalem Concessions* (Merits), Series A No. 5 (1925) at 45; cf. *ibid.*, pp. 40 and 51.
[26] *Ibid.*, p. 47.   [27] *Ibid.*, p. 49.   [28] Finlay to Moore, 6 April 1925, Moore papers 177.
[29] Series A No. 5 (1925) at 27 and 40–1.   [30] See Series C No. 7-II at 214.
[31] Series A No. 5 (1925) at 27–8, which should be compared to *Case of the Mavrommatis Palestine Concessions* (Jurisdiction), Series A No. 2 (1924) at 30.

respecting the construction and application of Articles 6 to 22 arise between the German and Polish Governments, they shall be submitted to the Permanent Court of International Justice.'

The Polish Government objected to the Permanent Court's jurisdiction. Its main contention was that the disputes as defined by the applicant did not come within the Geneva Convention. According to the Polish Government, the dispute concerned Polish legislation enacted pursuant to provisions in the Versailles Treaty.[32] It was submitted that Germany, and not the two private undertakings in question, had been the real owner of the Chorzów factory, which therefore had been transferred automatically to Poland under Article 256 of the Versailles Treaty.[33] According to the German Government, this and other contentions belonged to the merits,[34] a conclusion with which the Permanent Court agreed, with only Judge *ad hoc* Rostworowski declaring a dissent.[35]

The *motifs* had been drafted by a committee consisting of President Huber and Judges Weiss and Pessôa.[36] On the face of it, they resembled the first judgment in the *Mavrommatis* case and the general test laid down there. As for the submission of the Polish Government that the case was not admissible, the Permanent Court held that 'in estimating the value of the alternative submission to the effect that it should suspend judgment in the suit before it, the Court has not to have regard to "the various codes of procedure and the various legal terminologies" in use in different countries'.[37] As for the test for jurisdiction, the 'essential idea' was, according to Judge Anzilotti, a restatement of the *Mavrommatis* case;[38] yet Judge Anzilotti appended a declaration that advocated a more thorough investigation of the exact limits of the Permanent Court's jurisdiction. The *motifs* held that a dispute as to the scope of a substantive provision contained in Articles 6 to 22 of the Geneva Convention fell within Article 23(1),[39] whereas Judge Anzilotti argued that this was only so if the provision actually applied.[40] Again, this discussion did not concern the limits of the Permanent Court's jurisdiction as such but when to make a decision on those limits. The parties had not yet pleaded the

---

[32] See Series C No. 9–1 at 119–25.

[33] See *ibid.*, pp. 122 and 124, as well as *ibid.*, pp. 42–9 and 92–3.   [34] *Ibid.*, p. 58.

[35] The dissenting opinion was based on the national principle of self-containedness and a principle of restrictive interpretation: see *Case concerning Certain German Interests in Polish Upper Silesia* (Jurisdiction), Series A No. 6 (1925) at 32–3 and 35.

[36] Huber, 'Tagebuch', 13 August 1925.

[37] Series A No. 6 (1925) at 19; cf. *ibid.* as regards 'the doctrine of *litispendance*'.

[38] *Ibid.*, p. 30, referring to *ibid.*, p. 15.   [39] *Ibid.*, pp. 16 and 24–6.   [40] *Ibid.*, p. 30.

merits of the case, something that made the majority anxious about going into the merits.[41]

It is noteworthy that Judge Anzilotti did not comment on the passage in the *motifs*, according to which 'the interpretation of other international agreements is indisputably within the competence of the Court if such interpretation must be regarded as incidental to a decision on a point in regard to which it has jurisdiction'.[42] This principle went back to the *German Settlers* opinion, also partially drafted by Judge Huber,[43] on which the German Government had relied before the Permanent Court.[44] The Permanent Court had then said about the Council's broadly defined competence under the Polish Minorities Treaty, which covered 'any infraction, or any danger of infraction, of any of these obligations', that '[i]n order that the pledged protection may be certain and effective, it is essential that the Council . . . should be competent, incidentally, to consider and interpret the laws or treaties on which the rights claimed to be infringed are dependent'.[45] The *Upper Silesia* case concerned a compromissory clause that was not as broad. Here the principle of incidental jurisdiction was based on the view that the Permanent Court's jurisdiction over differences respecting 'rights, property and interests' regulated by the Geneva Convention was 'not affected by the fact that the validity of these rights is disputed on the basis of texts other than the Geneva Convention'.[46] On the contrary, these other 'texts' came within the Permanent Court's jurisdiction if 'preliminary or incidental'. This was to be decided by an interpretation in respect of which the state was conceived of as an international law subject, the rationale being 'that the application of the Geneva Convention is hardly possible without giving an interpretation of Article 256 of the Treaty of Versailles and the other international stipulations cited by Poland'.[47] In other words, this incidental jurisdiction was necessary for Article 23 of the Geneva Convention to have effect. It was a principle of effectiveness that was dependent on the specific context: unlike the *Mavrommatis* case, or at least the sparse

---

[41] *Ibid.*, p. 15; and Huber, 'Tagebuch', 20 August 1925.

[42] *Ibid.*, p. 18; and see the German Government, Series C No. 9-I at 159–60. Likewise, *Case concerning Certain German Interests in Polish Upper Silesia* (Merits), Series A No. 7 (1926) at 25.

[43] See also Huber, 'Tagebuch', 1 December 1925.

[44] Series C No. 9-1 at 159, 59–60, 68 and 74; cf. the Polish Government, *ibid.*, pp. 94–7.

[45] *Questions relating to Settlers of German Origin in Poland*, Series B No. 6 (1923) at 25.

[46] Series A No. 6 (1925) at 18.

[47] *Ibid.*; and also *Case concerning the Factory at Chorzów* (Claim for Indemnity) (Merits), Series A No. 17 (1928) at 31–2.

reasoning on 'immediate legal value',[48] the *Upper Silesia* case was not a likely example of analogical interpretation.

The judgment on the merits in the *Upper Silesia* case delivered at the tenth session in 1926 was in favour of Germany. It did not, however, give effect to the effective interpretation previously given to the Permanent Court's jurisdiction because, as a third party, Poland was not entitled to rely on the otherwise relevant Armistice Convention and the Protocol of Spa, while Article 256 of the Versailles Treaty was found to be inapplicable.[49] As for the latter, in respect of the factory at Chorzów, the Permanent Court held that on the eve of the entry into force of the Versailles Treaty Germany had really, if obscurely, transferred its rights without abusing them, thereby excluding the factory from the operation of Article 256 of the Versailles Treaty.[50] This doctrine of abuse of rights was linked to a principle of good faith and may indeed have seemed to point back to the national principle of self-containedness.[51] The Permanent Court held that:

Germany undoubtedly retained until the transfer of sovereignty the right to dispose of her property, and only a misuse of this right [*un abus de ce droit ou un manquement au principe de la bonne foi*] could endow an act of alienation with the character of a breach of the Treaty; such misuse cannot be presumed, and it rests with the party who states that there has been such misuse to prove his statement.[52]

The important thing to note is that the doctrine of abuse of rights as applied to the Versailles Treaty concerned dispositions carried out before the treaty took effect on 10 January 1920. The doctrine was not used in interpreting the content of Article 256; it was used in determining its possible effects prior to the treaty entering into force, that is, arguably, before the conception of the state as an international law subject ought to have been substituted for the conception of the state as a national sovereign.[53]

---

[48] *Case of the Mavrommatis Palestine Concessions* (Jurisdiction), Series A No. 2 (1924) at 26.
[49] *Case concerning Certain German Interests in Polish Upper Silesia* (Merits), Series A No. 7 (1926) at 25–31. Cf. the observations appended by Judge Finlay, *ibid.*, p. 84.
[50] *Ibid.*, pp. 37–9, 42 and also 29–31.
[51] As for the links to good faith: see *ibid.*, pp. 38–9 and 42.
[52] *Ibid.*, p. 30; and also Dionisio Anzilotti, *Cours de droit internaional* (Paris, 1929), p. 373.
[53] Cf. the Polish Goverment in Series C No. 9-I at 122, 41 and 51 and Series C No. 11 at 625–34, 953–6, 182–5 and 275. However, some commentators have given the 'doctrine' of abuse of rights as applied in the *Upper Silesia* case a much broader reading, thereby associating it with the national principle of self-containedness: see Bin Cheng,

On this basis, and also relying on a principle of state succession,[54] the liquidation had been contrary to the Geneva Convention as well as the strict conception of vested rights.[55] And so more proceedings followed about this factory in the course of which the notion of 'incidental' juris-diction became essential.[56]

In 1927, at the twelfth session, the Permanent Court admitted the German Government's claim to indemnity under Article 23(1) of the Geneva Convention, although the clause was limited to 'the construction and application of Articles 6 to 22'. Counsel for the German Government had previously referred to this question of jurisdiction as a 'problème délicat'.[57] However, Judge Anzilotti had agreed with President Huber on the principle of incidental jurisdiction,[58] and the proceedings were quickly disposed of, Judge Moore taking part in the work of the drafting committee.[59] According to the *motifs*, the Permanent Court's jurisdiction covered disputes 'bearing upon the applicability of these articles' in the Geneva Convention, thus also questions of reparation for '[i]t is a prin-ciple of international law that the breach of an engagement involves an obligation to make reparation in an adequate form'.[60] The opposite interpretation would leave the Permanent Court with 'a jurisdiction

General Principles of Law as Applied by International Courts and Tribunals (London, 1953), p. 128; cf. H. Lauterpacht, *The Function of Law in the International Community* (Oxford, 1933), pp. 288–9; H. Lauterpacht, *The Development of International Law by the Permanent Court of International Justice* (London, 1934), pp. 53–4; and Roberto Ago, YILC 1970-II, p. 193 and YILC 1971-II.1, p. 221. See also Lauterpacht, YILC 1953-II, pp. 109–10; Fitzmaurice, YILC 1956-II, pp. 112–13 and 121–2; Waldock, YILC 1962-II, p. 47 and YILC 1965-II, p. 44; and the International Law Commission, YILC 1962-II, p. 175 and YILC 1966-II, p. 202.

[54] Series A No. 7 (1926) at 41.

[55] Notably *ibid.*, pp. 21–2, 32–3 and 42; and also *Case concerning the Factory at Chorzów* (Claim for Indemnity) (Jurisdiction), Series A No. 9 (1927) at 27–8.

[56] However, it may be noted that also in its judgment on the merits in the *Upper Silesia* case the Permanent Court referred to a principle of incidental jurisdiction, the Permanent Court holding that it 'will not examine, save as an incidental and preliminary point, the possible existence of rights under German municipal law': Series A No. 7 (1926) at 42 and also 19.

[57] See Series C No. 9-I at 71, which in the following proceedings was emphasised by the Polish Government: see Series C No. 13-I at 26 and 57.

[58] See Huber, 'Tagebuch', 28 February 1925.

[59] See Moore to Chamberlain, 25 July 1927, Moore papers 58. Besides Judge *ad hoc* Ehrlich, only Judge de Bustamante and Deputy-Judge Yovanovitch voted against the *dispositif*; cf. *Case concerning the Factory at Chorzów* (Claim for Indemnity) (Jurisdiction), Series A No. 9 (1927) at 32; but see Huber to de Bustamante, 21 July 1927, Huber papers 24.1; and de Bustamante to Moore, 22 July 1927, Moore papers 57.

[60] Series A No. 9 (1927) at 20–1; and also *Case concerning the Factory at Chorzów* (Claim for Indemnity) (Merits), Series A No. 17 (1928) at 27–8, 29 and 47.

[that] . . . instead of settling a dispute once and for all, would leave open the possibility of further disputes'.[61] Lauterpacht was justified in relating this decision to a principle of effectiveness.[62] But it must be emphasised that this effectiveness was based on the Geneva Convention and its purpose,[63] and to some degree on 'the fundamental conceptions by which the movement in favour of general arbitration has been characterized'.[64] It did not involve an analogical interpretation reflecting a notion of a court of justice in some national legal systems.

The objection of the Polish Government to the Permanent Court's jurisdiction was characterised as a restrictive interpretation of the compromissory clause.[65] It made the Permanent Court emphasise the hierarchical superiority of the dynamic structure of international legal argument based on the conception of the state as an international sovereign:

It has been argued repeatedly in the course of the present proceedings that in case of doubt the Court should decline jurisdiction. It is true that the Court's jurisdiction is always a limited one, existing only in so far as States have accepted it; consequently, the Court will, in the event of an objection – or when it has automatically to consider the question – only affirm its jurisdiction provided that the force of the arguments militating in favour of it is preponderant. The fact that weighty arguments can be advanced to support the contention that it has no jurisdiction cannot of itself create a doubt calculated to upset its jurisdiction. When considering whether it has jurisdiction or not, the Court's aim is always to ascertain whether an intention on the part of the Parties exists to confer jurisdiction upon it. The question as to the existence of a doubt nullifying its jurisdiction need not be considered when, as in the present case, this intention can be demonstrated in a manner convincing to the Court [qui satisfait la conviction de la Cour].[66]

---

[61] Ibid., p. 25; and also Case concerning Certain German Interests in Polish Upper Silesia (Merits), Series A No. 7 (1926) at 46.

[62] Lauterpacht, Development by the Permanent Court, p. 72; and see also more generally the joint dissenting opinion of Judges Lauterpacht, Wellington Koo and Spender in Case concerning the Aerial Incident of July 27th, 1955 (Preliminary Objections), ICJ Reports [1959] 127 at 192. However, other courts could possibly have entertained this dispute had the Permanent Court declined jurisdiction: cf. Series A No. 9 (1927) at 25–32.

[63] Series A No. 9 (1927) at 24–5.

[64] Ibid., pp. 21–2; and also ibid., p. 23 on the different categories of legal disputes listed in Article 13(2) of the Covenant.

[65] See ibid., pp. 21, 22 and 24.

[66] Ibid., p. 32. Cf. Border and Transborder Armed Actions (Jurisdiction and Admissibility), ICJ Reports [1988] 69 at para. 16. Referring to the just-quoted passage from the judgment of the Permanent Court, an arbitral tribunal set up under the ICSID Convention inferred: 'Thus, jurisdictional instruments are to be interpreted neither restrictively nor expansively, but rather objectively and in good faith, and jurisdiction will be

In the judgment on the merits, delivered at the fourteenth session in 1928, the Permanent Court ruled that it had no jurisdiction over the submission of the German Government concerning Polish claims to a set-off against the German claims relating to the factory. The Permanent Court admitted that questions regarding payment arose 'quite naturally out of its jurisdiction to award monetary compensation', but it added that:

> this principle would be quite unjustifiably extended if it were taken as meaning that the Court might have cognizance of any question whatever of international law even quite foreign to the convention under consideration, for the sole reason that the manner in which such question is decided may have an influence on the effectiveness of the reparation asked for. Such an argument seems hardly reconcilable with the fundamental principles of the Court's jurisdiction [la base de la compétence de la Cour], which is limited to cases specially provided for in treaties and conventions in force.[67]

The Permanent Court had entertained the claim for indemnity in order to settle the case concerning the factory at Chorzów, and not in order to decide other matters which were neither incidental nor preliminary and so could only be undertaken if the international sovereigns had given their consent.[68] This was opposite to the analogical interpretation advocated by Judge Nyholm, according to whom '[i]n international law no principle can be raised which would establish on this subject a difference between national and international law'.[69]

Prior to the judgment on the merits, while still at the twelfth session, the Permanent Court had had in a new judgment to give an interpretation of its previous judgment on the merits in the *Upper Silesia* case. The application for an interpretation was filed by the German Government due to a rather exotic interpretation of previous judgments advanced by the Polish Government. What is of interest here is not that the

---

found to exist if – but only if – the force of the arguments militating in favor of it is preponderant': *Southern Pacific Properties (Middle East) Limited* v. *Egypt* (Jurisdiction No. 2), 3 ICSID Reports 131 (1988) at 144.

[67] *Case concerning the Factory at Chorzów* (Claim for Indemnity) (Merits), Series A No. 17 (1928) at 61–2; cf. *ibid.*, pp. 38–9; and *Case concerning the Factory at Chorzów* (Claim for Indemnity) (Jurisdiction), Series A No. 9 (1927) at 32–3. See also Series D No. 2, Add.3 (1936) at 106–15; and Dionisio Anzilotti, 'La Demande reconventionnelle en procédure internationale' (1930) 57 *Journal du droit international* 857.

[68] Cf. Ibrahim F. I. Shihata, *The Power of the International Court to Determine Its Own Jurisdiction* (The Hague, 1965), p. 196.

[69] Series A No. 17 (1928) at 98. An interpretation based on a contrast with national law was suggested by Judge *ad hoc* Rabel: see *ibid.*, p. 69.

Permanent Court rejected this interpretation,[70] but that for the first time it had to apply Article 60 of the Statute, which provided: 'The judgment is final and without appeal. In the event of dispute as to the meaning or scope of the judgment, the Court shall construe it upon the request of any party.' This provision had already caused some discussion in 1925 when the Chamber for Summary Procedure had been preparing the second judgment in the *Neuilly Treaty* case. According to President Huber, Article 60 had then 'given rise to a somewhat extensive correspondence between members of the Chamber for Summary Procedure'.[71] In the end, the Chamber, consisting of Judges Huber, Loder and Weiss, had overcome the problem by instead relying on a Special Agreement.[72]

One reason for Article 60 being controversial was indicated by previous advisory opinions. Thus, in the *Jaworzina* opinion, it had been stated that '[i]n the absence of an express agreement between the parties, the arbitrator is not competent to interpret, still less modify, his award by revising it'.[73] As was made clear in 1926 when revising the Rules of Court, the judges disagreed as to whether Article 60 vested the Permanent Court with compulsory jurisdiction. While Judges Anzilotti, de Bustamante and Finlay answered this in the affirmative,[74] Judge Moore 'could not agree that Article 60 of the Statute gave the Permanent Court compulsory jurisdiction'.[75] President Huber thought that 'it was possible to construe Article 60 as establishing for cases of interpretation a jurisdiction which was compulsory', 'the fundamental question' being whether 'jurisdiction for purposes of interpretation was, so to speak, incidental'.[76] In 1926, as in the second judgment in the *Neuilly Treaty* case, a definitive interpretation of Article 60 had not been reached and so the question reappeared at the end of the twelfth session as the German Government asked the Permanent Court to interpret its previous judgments, the Polish Government objecting.[77]

Unsurprisingly, in his dissenting opinion Judge Anzilotti stated that Article 60 established 'the compulsory jurisdiction of the Court for a

---

[70] See *Interpretation of Judgments Nos. 7 and 8 (the Chorzów Factory)*, Series A No. 13 (1927) at 19.

[71] Series D No. 2, Add.1 (1926) at 174.

[72] Cf. *Interpretation of Judgment No. 3 (Interpretation of Paragraph 4 of the Annex following Article 179 of the Treaty of Neuilly)*, Series A No. 4 (1925) at 5–6.

[73] *Question of Jaworzina (Polish–Czechoslovakian Frontier)*, Series B No. 8 (1923) at 38; and likewise *Polish Postal Service in Danzig*, Series B No. 11 (1925) at 37.

[74] See Series D No. 2, Add.1 (1926) at 175 and 176 (Judge Anzilotti), 177 (Judge de Bustamante) and 177 (Judge Finlay).

[75] *Ibid.*, p. 178.   [76] *Ibid.*, pp. 175 and 178.

[77] Cf. Series C No. 13-V at 47 and 28–9. The German Government had suggested that the objections should be joined to the merits: see *ibid.*, pp. 64 and 10.

certain category of disputes'.[78] The judgment was not quite as clear, one explanation being that it was supported by Judge Moore, who, however, left The Hague before the judgment was delivered.[79] That being said, the *motifs* were surely consonant with the view expressed by Judge Anzilotti.[80] Judge Anzilotti dissented because of his rather narrow conception of the Permanent Court's – compulsory – jurisdiction under Article 60. 'It appears to me to be clear', Judge Anzilotti stated, 'that a binding interpretation of a judgment can only have reference to the binding portion of the judgment construed', this being the *dispositif*, as opposed to the *motifs*.[81] The majority took a broader view, as it gave Article 60 an effective interpretation supported by the notion of incidental jurisdiction.[82] In its view:

it is clear . . . that, although it is not contested that the terms of the operative part of the judgment do not contain the reservation in question, the fact that the grounds for the judgment contain a passage which one of the Parties construes as a reservation . . . or as affirming a right inconsistent with the situation at law which the other Party considers as established with binding force, allows of the Court's being validly requested to give an interpretation fixing the true meaning and scope of the judgment in question.[83]

It may be noted that Judge Anzilotti expressly stated that his view reflected 'principles obtaining in civil procedure',[84] an analogy which he justified by reference to Article 59 of the Statute and the principle of *res judicata*. In Judge Anzilotti's view, 'if there be a case in which it is legitimate to have recourse, in the absence of conventions and customs, to "the general principles of law recognized by civilized nations", mentioned in No. 3 of Article 38 of the Statute, that case is assuredly the present one'.[85] Although Judge Anzilotti did not convince the majority, this was a plausible example of an international lawyer's use of analogies from national law, a domestic analogy based on the openness of

[78] Series A No. 13 (1927) at 23.   [79] *Ibid.*, p. 22.   [80] See *ibid.*, pp. 10 and also 21.

[81] *Ibid.*, pp. 23–4; and see the Polish Government, Series C No. 13-V at 47–50 and 29–32; and *Amco Asia Corporation and Others v. Indonesia* (Resubmitted Case) (Jurisdiction), 1 ICSID Reports 543 (1998) at 551.

[82] *Ibid.*, pp. 14 and 19–21.

[83] *Ibid.*, p. 14; and see Åke Hammarskjöld, 'The Permanent Court of International Justice and the Development of International Law' (1935) 14 *International Affairs* 797 at 799; and also Series D No. 2, Add.3 (1936) at 335. See also Antonio Sanchez de Bustamante y Sirvén, *The World Court* (New York, 1925), p. 293.

[84] Series A No. 13 (1927) at 27.

[85] Judge Anzilotti relied on the work of the Advisory Committee of Jurists: see Advisory Committee of Jurists, *Procès-Verbaux of the Proceedings of the Committee (16 June–24 July 1920, with Annexes)* (The Hague, 1920), pp. 315 (Ricci-Busatti), 316 and 335 (Phillimore) and also 593 (Descamps).

the treaty provisions in question, as opposed to a national lawyer's analogical interpretation the vehicle of which is national law and not the
treaty.

The Mavrommatis case again

Also at the twelfth session when the Permanent Court was deciding
on the preliminary objections in the *Chorzów Factory* case, the *Mavrommatis* case returned to the Permanent Court. In accordance with the
judgment on the merits in 1925, Mavrommatis had been granted new
concessions. Now he claimed that these concessions had been breached
and loss suffered, and so the Greek Government once again approached
the Permanent Court, relying on Article 26 of the Mandate. As in 1924,
the British Government denied that the compromissory clause was
applicable.

'The Court', the *motifs* stated, 'sees no reason to depart from a construction which clearly flows from the previous judgments the reasoning of
which it still regards as sound, more especially seeing that the two Parties have shown a disposition to accept the point of view accepted by the
Court.'[86] This statement may not excite writers on precedent in the International Court and its predecessor,[87] yet it expressed a not-so-unusual
reservation as to the precedential value of former rulings, at least in the
field of jurisdiction.[88] Given that the drafting committee had been composed of Judge Moore as well as President Huber and Judge Anzilotti,[89]
there was no guarantee of strict adherence to what in 1924 had survived
from the first drafting committee. The British Government was actually
successful in its objection to the Permanent Court's jurisdiction. Later,
Moore wrote to Professor Manley O. Hudson:

---

[86] *Case of the Readaptation of the Mavrommatis Jerusalem Concessions* (Jurisdiction), Series A
No. 11 (1927) at 18. The pleading governments had taken the former judgments for
granted, but they had disagreed over their interpretation: see, respectively, Series C
No. 13-III at 48–51 (Greek Government) and 20–1, 39–40 and 90 (British Government).

[87] See Mohamed Shahabuddeen, *Precedent in the World Court* (Cambridge, 1996), p. 17. Cf.
Series E No. 4 (1927–8) at 293.

[88] See Michel de la Grotte, 'Les Afffaires traitées par la Cour permanente de Justice
internationale pendant la periode 1926–1928' (1929) 10 *RDILC* 387 at 397; and, for
similar statements, *Case concerning Certain German Interests in Polish Upper Silesia* (Merits),
Series A No. 7 (1926) at 31; *Case concerning the Factory at Chorzów* (Claim for Indemnity)
(Jurisdiction), Series A No. 9 (1927) at 26–7; and *Case of Free Zones of Upper Savoy and the
District of Gex* (Third Phase), Series A/B No. 46 (1932) at 161.

[89] Huber, 'Tagebuch', 24 September 1927. See also Moore to Borchard, 2 October 1927,
Borchard papers 6.92: 'I keep very busy, especially as I am so often put on the court's
drafting committees. During the past ten days I have been working on the committee
to prepare the next judgment that is to be delivered.'

As you know, dissenting and separate opinions (the latter not being always dissenting or wholly so) sometimes turn out to be more important than the principal opinion. I think that the dissenting opinions in the first Mavrommatis case were far more instructive than the principal opinion, or opinion of the court; and the court in the end tacitly acknowledged this fact when on the third hearing it held that it had no jurisdiction.[90]

Judges Altamira and Nyholm and Judge *ad hoc* Caloyanni appended dissenting opinions, while the fourth dissenter who made no declaration might have been Judge Loder.[91] The majority's basis for distinguishing the new case was the view that the mere granting of concessions did not provide for 'public ownership or control' and so did not in itself fall within Articles 11 and 26 of the Mandate.[92] Support for this view could be found in the judgment from 1924, in which the granting of the Rutenberg concessions had been seen as a special case.[93] Nevertheless, if the majority had been as impressed by analogical interpretation as some judges in 1924, perhaps Article 26, or Article 11, could have been put into use, at least *prima facie*.[94] Some of the dissenters followed this course: Judge Altamira referred to a conception of 'juridical common sense [*bon sense juridique*]',[95] while Judge Nyholm held that 'the jurisdiction of the Court as regards the Mandate should be general'.[96] Others might have been discouraged from such analogical interpretation by the meagre outcome of the previous proceeding in the judgment on the merits in 1925.[97]

But there was a caveat. As for the readapted concessions, which the Permanent Court had dealt with in its judgment on the merits in 1925 due to a supplementary Special Agreement, it could be said, to quote the *Chorzów Factory* case, that 'a jurisdiction of this kind, instead of settling a dispute once and for all, would leave open the possibility of further disputes'.[98] Perhaps the majority was reluctant to give a *Special* Agreement

---

[90] Moore to Hudson, 14 January 1934, Moore papers 178 and Hudson papers 134A.1.

[91] See also de la Grotte, '1926-1928', p. 399.

[92] Series A No. 11 (1927) at 17; cf. the Greek Government in Series C No. 13-III at 470, 49-50 and 54.

[93] See *Case of the Mavrommatis Palestine Concessions* (Jurisdiction), Series A No. 2 (1924) at 18-23, which should be compared to *The Mavrommatis Jerusalem Concessions* (Merits), Series A No. 5 (1925) at 17.

[94] Cf. Series A No. 11 (1927) at 22; and see the dissenting opinion of Judge Altamira, *ibid.*, pp. 37 and 45.

[95] *Ibid.*, p. 44.   [96] *Ibid.*, p. 31.

[97] However, see the dissenting opinions of Judges Nyholm and Altamira, *ibid.*, pp. 29-30 and 45, respectively.

[98] *Case concerning the Factory at Chorzów* (Claim for Indemnity) (Jurisdiction), Series A No. 9 (1927) at 25; cf. Series A No. 11 (1927) at 14; and see Series C No. 13-III at 472-4

with quite a limited scope an effective interpretation.[99] Besides, the Greek Government had not relied on this in argument before the Permanent Court, and so 'the Court does not find it necessary to consider the question whether, in certain cases, it might have jurisdiction to decide disputes concerning the non-compliance with the terms of one of its judgments'.[100]

Special agreements

Difficulties in determining the scope of a state's consent to a specific proceeding had already been hinted at in 1925 in the second judgment in the *Neuilly Treaty* case. This case, which concerned Bulgaria's payment of reparations, was the first case submitted to the Permanent Court under a Special Agreement. It had been decided by the Chamber of Summary Procedure in 1924, the *motifs* being so summary that any analysis of them would be speculative.[101] When the Greek Government requested an interpretation of the judgment under Article 60 of the Statute, the Bulgarian Government submitted observations without disputing the Permanent Court's jurisdiction. This led the Chamber to refer to an 'agreement between the Parties'.[102] However, this implied 'agreement' was only invoked so as to dispense with the conditions for the Permanent Court's jurisdiction under Article 60. The 'agreement' was not given the wider effect of a Special Agreement under Article 36(1) of the Statute and so it did not vest the Permanent Court with jurisdiction to reply to a request that was outside the scope of its previous judgment.[103]

Instead, a crucial question as to implied Special Agreements fell to be decided at the thirteenth session in 1928.[104] In 1925, the Chamber

---

(Greek Government). This point was emphasised in the individual note submitted by Judge Pessôa: see Epitácio Pessôa, *Côrte permanente de justiça international (1923–1930)* (Rio de Janeiro, 1960), pp. 147–50. When it became clear that he was in the minority, Judge Pessôa left The Hague: see Twelfth session, *Procès-Verbal* 54 (1 October 1927), reproduced in *ibid.*, pp. 114–15. See also Series A No. 11 (1927) at 24.

[99] Cf. *Case concerning the Factory at Chorzów* (Claim for Indemnity) (Jurisdiction), Series A No. 9 (1927) at 13.

[100] Series A No. 11 (1927) at 14. Cf. *ibid.*, pp. 31 (Judge Nyholm) and 46 (Judge Altamira).

[101] The judgment had been drafted single-handedly by Judge Huber, who had been very much in doubt as to the result: see Huber, *Denkwürdigkeiten*, p. 283.

[102] *Interpretation of Judgment No. 3 (Interpretation of Paragraph 4 of the Annex following Article 179 of the Treaty of Neuilly)*, Series A No. 4 (1925) at 6.

[103] See *ibid.*, pp. 6–7; cf. Series C No. 6 at 17–18.

[104] See also Series D No. 2 (1922) at 149 and 201; and Series D No. 2, Add.1 (1926) at 82, 85, 88, 90 and 96.

of Summary Procedure had consisted of Judges Huber, Loder and Weiss, but it was the full Court that in 1928 decided the *Minority Schools* case brought by the German Government. The compromissory clause in Article 23(1) of the Geneva Convention, also relied upon in the *Upper Silesia* case, clearly did not vest the Permanent Court with jurisdiction. The Permanent Court noted, however, that the Polish Government objected to the Permanent Court's jurisdiction only in its *duplique*,[105] while its *contre-mémoire* had been confined to the merits of the case.[106] According to the majority, this order of events was sufficient to confer jurisdiction on the Permanent Court.[107] The *motifs* explained that '[t]he acceptance by a State of the Court's jurisdiction in a particular case is not, under the Statute, subordinated to the observance of certain forms', thus a Special Agreement could be implied.[108] In addition, the Permanent Court referred to the judgment on the merits in the *Mavrommatis* case, according to which 'the Court has accepted as sufficient for the purpose of establishing its jurisdiction a mere declaration made by the Respondent in the course of the proceedings'.[109] In the *Minority Schools* case, however, *forum prorogatum* was the sole source of jurisdiction, not as in the *Mavrommatis* case merely a source of supplementary jurisdiction.

Three of the dissenters, including Judge Huber, who had been the architect of the second judgment in the *Neuilly Treaty* case,[110] insisted that this was equivalent to establishing a third mode of jurisdiction in addition to Special Agreements and compromissory clauses.[111] According to Judge Huber, the position of the majority 'appears difficult to reconcile with the conceptions which, at the time of the preparation of

---

[105] Series C No. 14-II at 312. At the oral pleadings the Polish Government again dealt with the merits before developing its preliminary objection: *ibid.*, p. 58.

[106] Although see *ibid.*, pp. 219–20 and 224–5; and also the dissenting opinions of Judges Huber and Negulesco in *Rights of Minorities in Upper Silesia (Minority Schools)*, Series A No. 15 (1928) at 49 and 67, respectively; cf. *ibid.*, p. 20.

[107] Cf. Series D No. 2, Add.1 (1926) at 82 (Judge Loder), 85 (Judge Nyholm) and 90 (Judge Anzilotti); see, however, *ibid.*, p. 88 (Judge Moore).

[108] Series A No. 15 (1928) at 23–4.   [109] *Ibid.*, p. 23.

[110] See Huber to Loder, 5 December 1924, Huber papers 24.1; and Huber, 'Tagebuch', 12 March 1925.

[111] Series A No. 15 (1928) at 52 (Judge Huber), 57 (Judge Nyholm) and 69 (Deputy-Judge Negulesco). Judge Nyholm and Deputy-Judge Negulesco also relied on a principle of restrictive interpretation: *ibid.*, pp. 57 and 69, respectively. Deputy-Judge Negulesco and also Judge Rostworowski repeated this view, again being in a minority, in Series D No. 2, Add.3 (1936) at 69–72, 92–3 and 154–60. Similarly, Walther Schücking, *Vertrauliche Bemerkungen zur Frage der Revision des Statuts des Weltgerichtshofs*, undated, Schücking papers (Koblenz) 32, p. 13; cf. Series D No. 2, Add.3 (1936) at 69.

the Statute, were current in Government circles in regard to compulsory arbitration'.[112] 'Michel de la Grotte', although he considered the decision of the majority equitable, was unwilling to take 'un pas aussi gigantesque' towards compulsory jurisdiction.[113] The question was not so much whether consent could be implied, or 'presumed',[114] as whether consent had to be given before proceedings were instituted. After all, as Judge Huber emphasised, Article 36(1) of the Statute, and also Article 14 of the Covenant, referred to 'cases which the parties refer to it'.[115]

Subsequently, and in accordance with judgments in the *Chorzów Factory* case,[116] Judge Anzilotti based the result in the *Minority Schools* case on the view that 'according to the Statute and the Covenant, the Court always had jurisdiction if the parties were agreed'.[117] In his view, referring to the *Mavrommatis* case, '[c]'est là, si l'on veut, une interprétation assez large du Statut; mais l'on peut se demander si une interprétation différente, d'un formalisme rigide, ne serait pas en contraste avec la nature même et le but de la fonction attribuée à la Cour'.[118] It may also have been of some importance that the German Government had invoked the same compromissory clause as in the *Upper Silesia* case and the subsequent *Chorzów Factory* case, proceedings in which the Polish Government had not been slow to raise preliminary objections.

Conclusions

In this period the Permanent Court's contentious jurisdiction gave rise to the same general questions as other issues affected by treaty law, namely

---

[112] Series A No. 15 (1928) at 52.   [113] De la Grotte, '1926–1928', p. 423.

[114] See for the use of this word Hammerskjöld, 'Observations on the Memorandum Prepared by Dr Manley O. Hudson on the Adhesion of the United States of America to the Protocol of the Permanent Court of International Justice', p. 6, which was enclosed with Hammarskjöld to Hudson, 1 February 1929, Hudson papers 82.4. As for the majority view, one commentator has referred to 'the PCIJ's reliance on the rationale of that which is not prohibited is permitted': see Sienho Yee, '*Forum Proragatum* in the International Court' (1999) 42 *GYIL* 147 at 163.

[115] Series A No. 15 (1928) at 51–2; and also Deputy-Judge Negulesco, *ibid.*, pp. 69–70; and Phillimore in Advisory Committee, *Procès-verbaux*, p. 235. Cf. Judge Anzilotti's dissenting opinion in *Interpretation of the Statute of the Memel Territory* (Merits), Series A/B No. 49 (1932) at 351; and see also The '*Société Commerciale de Belgique*', Series A/B No. 78 (1939) at 178; and *Corfu Channel Case* (Preliminary Objections), ICJ Reports [1947–8] 15 at 28.

[116] See *Case concerning the Factory at Chorzów* (Claim for Indemnity) (Jurisdiction), Series A No. 9 (1927) at 25; and *Case concerning the Factory at Chorzów* (Claim for Indemnity) (Merits), Series A No. 17 (1928) at 37.

[117] Series D No. 2, Add.3 (1936) at 67.

[118] Anzilotti, 'Demande reconventionnelle', p. 863.

whether a treaty has been concluded and how to interpret it. To a large degree, in answering these questions, majorities relied on, respectively, the conception of the state as an international sovereign and the conception of the state as an international law subject. Accordingly, whether the Permanent Court had been vested with jurisdiction was determined by a consensual test that overshadowed a textual interpretation of the Statute, for example the use in Article 36(1) of the term 'parties', as distinct from 'party'. In the majority decisions there was hardly any trail of reasoning based on analogical interpretation. The notion of a court of justice could hardly have been imposed on Special Agreements so long as they were liable to a strict textual interpretation, or even a subjective interpretation.[119] More generally, compromissory clauses were subjected to an objective interpretation in accordance with a principle of effectiveness, as opposed to an extraneous notion of a court of justice; it vested the Permanent Court with incidental jurisdiction, the prime example being the judgment in the *Chorzów Factory* case concerning the claim for indemnity.

From the beginning, the principle of incidental jurisdiction had had the support of President Huber and Judge Anzilotti. While Judge Anzilotti maintained his insistence on the consensual test for jurisdiction, at least in the *Upper Silesia* case, that insistence did not influence his interpretation of compromissory clauses once concluded; thus, he was not an exponent of subjective interpretation. President Huber, for his part, took a strict view on when a Special Agreement had to have been concluded, notably in the *Minority Schools* case. But once it was concluded, he too favoured an 'effective' interpretation. It seemed as if he no longer saw the Permanent Court's contentious jurisdiction against a background coloured by the international law of coexistence. These were indications of leading members of the bench not abiding by their original, professorial views conceived in harmony with the *Buchrecht*.

When revising the Rules of Court in 1926, Judge Anzilotti proposed that 'the Court should only deal with the question of jurisdiction when it had before it the merits of the case', that is, 'a plea to jurisdiction, if any, shall be filed after the filing of the Case by the applicant'.[120] In support of this proposal, Judge Anzilotti referred to 'the experience gained in the Mavrommatis and Upper Silesian cases'. While the Registrar was

---

[119] Cf. Arbitrator Huber in *Affaire des biens britanniques au Maroc espagnol*, 2 RIAA 615 (1924) at 626.

[120] Series D No. 2, Add.1 (1926) at 79 and 267; see also Deputy-Judge Beichmann and Judge Moore in Series D No. 2 (1922) at 201 and 214, respectively.

against, Judge Anzilotti's colleagues agreed to the proposal.[121] There was some discussion as to whether preliminary objections could be joined to the decision on the merits. President Huber was against and Judge Anzilotti remained somewhat undecided;[122] no decision was taken on this point.

The *Mosul* opinion and treaty interpretation

Preliminary questions

The *Mosul* case arose out of a dispute over the delimitation of the frontier between Turkey and Iraq, then a mandate of the United Kingdom. Part of the dispute was a delicate question as to the interpretation of Article 3(2) of the Lausanne Treaty, which vested the Council of the League with powers as regards this delimitation. The *Mosul* opinion has been selected for a careful study because it contains a number of often-quoted statements concerning treaty interpretation. It also added to the understanding of the nature of the Council. Like the decisions on contentious jurisdiction, the *Mosul* opinion provides an important example of the Permanent Court determining the competence of an international organ.

However, the first question to be decided had nothing to do with the Lausanne Treaty. Because Turkey was not at the time a member of the League of Nations, and because the Turkish Government did not seem to have consented to the Council requesting an advisory opinion regarding the powers conferred on it by Article 3(2),[123] the Permanent Court had to consider the precedential value of the second line of reasoning in the *Eastern Carelia* opinion. This was the line of reasoning that had turned on the competence of the Permanent Court, as opposed to the Council. In 1925, when the Permanent Court was differently composed, it distinguished the *Eastern Carelia* opinion in an open-ended statement (not an order). One reason was that the advisory opinion requested in

---

[121] *Ibid.*, p. 93. As for Hammarskjöld's views, see *ibid.*, pp. 84 and also 309–10; they were later vindicated: see Series D No. 2, Add.3 (1936), at 819–20 and also 84–94, 148–9, 644–6 and 733.

[122] See Series D No. 2, Add.1 (1926) at 89, and at 83 and 90, respectively. Cf. *ibid.*, pp. 82 (Judge Loder) and 86 (Judge Weiss).

[123] Cf. *Official Journal* 1925, pp. 1381–2; and *Official Journal* 1926, p. 122; see also Amery's memorandum, 30 September 1925, FO 371 E6156/32/65; and Sir Cecil Hurst in 'Minutes of the Conference of State Signatories of the Protocol of Signature of the Statute of the Permanent Court of International Justice, Held at Geneva from September 1st to 23rd, 1926' (League of Nations Document V.Legal.1926.V.26, 1926), p. 24.

the *Mosul* case would not be equivalent to deciding the dispute before the Council because the request 'referred not to the merits of the affair but to the competence of the Council'.[124] There was no need for specific consent to the Permanent Court exercising advisory jurisdiction where in doing so it did not fill in for, but merely assisted, the Council, which was 'duly seized'.[125] 'Michel de la Grotte' took the view that this was not an overruling of the second line of reasoning in the *Eastern Carelia* opinion.[126] So did Hammarskjöld in a quasi-official publication,[127] and in the Permanent Court's annual report an effort was made to demonstrate that 'the Court has in practice been careful not to reverse precedents established by itself in previous judgments and opinions, and to explain apparent departures from such precedents'.[128]

Although no vote was given, there was no evidence that it had been controversial to distinguish the *Mosul* case from the *Eastern Carelia* case. What had initially troubled members of the Permanent Court was the silence of the Statute and the Rules on the matter of judges *ad hoc* in advisory proceedings. The presence of only a British judge on the bench generated a problem of inequality that had been nagging several judges, including President Huber.[129] Judge Moore, who was absent, later wrote, referring to the *Eastern Carelia* opinion, that:

the force of this precedent was afterwards impaired, first, by the Council's resolution of censure or dissent; and, secondly, by the action of the Court in the Mosul case, the full history of which has never been written. Some accurate inferences may be found in Brigg's article in the *Revue de droit international*. What happened

---

[124] Series E No. 2 (1925–6) at 164; and also *Article 3, Paragraph 2, of the Treaty of Lausanne (Frontier between Turkey and Iraq)*, Series B No. 12 (1925) at 18; as to the relevance of Article 5 of the Covenant in this context, see Fromageot in 'Conference of Signatories 1926', pp. 21 and 26.

[125] Series E No. 2 (1925–6) at 164. See similarly *Interpretation of Peace Treaties*, ICJ Reports [1950] 65 at 72; cf. the dissenting opinions of Judges Winiarski, Zoricic and Krylov, *ibid.*, pp. 89–92, 102–4 and 108–11, respectively. It was followed in *Legal Consequences for States of the Continued Presence of South Africa in Namibia (South West Africa) notwithstanding Security Council Resolution 276 (1970)*, ICJ Reports [1971] 12 at paras. 31–3.

[126] Michel de la Grotte, 'La Cour permanente de Justice internationale en 1925' (1926) 7 *RDILC* 321 at 335–6.

[127] Åke Hammarskjöld, 'La Cour permanente de Justice internationale à la neuvième session de l'Assemblée de la Société des Nations' (1928) 9 *RDILC* 665 at 717 and 723–5; and see Hammarskjöld to de Visscher, 14 November 1928, Hammarskjöld papers 488.

[128] Series E No. 3 (1926–7) at 218, referring to *ibid.*, p. 226 concerning the *Mosul* opinion.

[129] Huber, 'Tagebuch', 13 October 1925; and 17 October 1925; and Huber to Moore, 23 November 1925, Huber papers 24.1 and Moore papers 177. See also Series D No. 2, Add.1 (1926) at 192, 253 and 267 and, on equality, *ibid.*, pp. 25, 29, 32, 186, 189, 193 and 253; likewise, Démètre Negulesco, 'L'évolution de la procédure des avis consultatifs de la Cour permanente de Justice internationale' (1936) 57 *Recueil des Cours* 5 at 24–5.

in the Mosul case eventually led to the adoption of the rule allowing national judges to the parties in advisory proceedings. Anzilotti, Loder and I constituted the committee by which the rule was drafted. Anzilotti strongly favored it. Loder, who had previously opposed such a rule, declared, after I read my draft of the report, that he was 'convinced'. This took place one evening in my office at the Wittebrug. I shall never forget the scene, and Loder's straightforward and hearty declaration – the declaration of an honest mind.[130]

Principles of treaty interpretation

As for the actual opinion, President Huber had exercised more influence on the *motifs* than the advice. According to his *Tagebuch*, when the Permanent Court adopted the *Mosul* opinion:

[j]e déclare que, quoique je me fus placé dans ma première note à un point de vue différent de celui qui a été adopté par la Cour, par rapport à la première question, et bien que je continue à considérer mes arguments comme forts, je me suis convaincu, surtout lors de la rédaction du projet d'avis, que la thèse de la majorité peut être soutenue par des arguments très sérieux et que je finis par me rallier à l'opinion de la grande majorité de la Cour, estimant que d'une manière générale, et avant tout dans un cas de l'importance de la présente affaire, on devrait se rallier à la majorité afin d'obtenir l'unanimité, aussi longtemps qu'une pareille attitude est compatible avec la conscience juridique.[131]

According to Judge Nyholm, the session at which the Permanent Court decided the *Mosul* case had 'some (but not many) dramatic scenes'.[132] An inside view on the deliberations between the ten members of the Permanent Court participating in the case confirms the influence exercised by the President on the *motifs*.[133] At the meeting at which the Permanent

---

[130] Moore to Borchard, 11 September 1931, Moore papers 63; see also Moore to Borchard, 8 July and 8 August 1928, both Borchard papers 6.93. As for the amendment to the Rules, see Series E No. 4 (1927–8) at 72–8, which may be compared to Advisory Committee, *Procès-verbaux*, p. 731. Briggs' article on the *Mosul* opinion did not deal with the *Eastern Carelia* opinion: it had the form of a critical analysis of the reasoning on the merits, which, in his view, 'n'ajoutent aucun lustre à la réputation d'une grande Cour internationale': Herbert Whittaker Briggs, 'L'avis consultatif no. 12 de la Cour permanente de Justice internationale dans l'affaire de Mossoul' (1927) 8 *RDILC* 626 at 655. Later, Moore wrote that 'I have . . . always thought that the Mosul case was unfortunate in having apparently weakened the force of the admirable and independent position taken by the Court, by a majority of seven to four, in the Eastern Carelia case': Moore to de Wolf, 23 December 1930, Moore papers 172 and NARA 500 C114/Advisory opinions/90; see also Moore to Walsh, 19 January 1926, Moore papers 172.

[131] Huber, 'Tagebuch', 18 November 1925.

[132] Nyholm to Moore, 23 November 1925, Moore papers 177.

[133] See Ninth session, *Procès-Verbal* 12 (18 November 1925), Moore papers 172.

Court adopted the opinion, there was a vote between two texts, text A and text B. Text B was adopted against the votes of Judges Altamira, Nyholm and Weiss and Deputy-Judge Negulesco. In addition, although agreeing to the advice, Deputy-Judge Beichmann made a statement in which he gave reasons different from the *motifs*. Judge Anzilotti cast a vote against the draft opinion, while he remained undecided whether to support the alternative reasoning proposed by Deputy-Judge Beichmann. Judge Loder, for his part, 'stated that for purely practical considerations he would not separate himself from the majority, although a part of the draft did not satisfy his conception of logic'. This left only three judges who did not at this point express misgivings about the *motifs*, namely President Huber, Judge Finlay and Deputy-Judge Yovanovitch.

The final, in Huber's words 'très serieux', *motifs* of the *Mosul* opinion were rich in statements as to a hierarchy between various principles of treaty interpretation, respectively emphasising text, preparatory work, subsequent practice and the conception of the state as a national sovereign. Compared to previous decisions these statements were couched in more significant, general language, and for the first time the Permanent Court laid down the potentially far-reaching principle later codified in Article 32 of the Vienna Convention on the Law of Treaties that preparatory work holds only a secondary and limited position in treaty interpretation.[134] Most of the ideas contained in the *motifs* reflected Max Huber's understanding of treaty interpretation. When the issue was later debated by the Institut de Droit International, Huber explained the rationale behind some of the principles articulated during his presidency, including the passages regarding the importance of preparatory work, which, as emphasised repeatedly by the Institut's first rapporteur, seemed inconsistent.[135]

As for the specific case, Article 3(2) of the Lausanne Treaty provided that if the Turkish and British Governments had not reached agreement

---

[134] For earlier pronouncements as to the importance of preparatory work: see *International Labour Organization and the Conditions of Agricultural Labour*, Series B No. 2 (1922) at 41; *Question of Jaworzina (Polish–Czechoslovakian Frontier)*, Series B No. 8 (1923) at 41; *Case of the Mavrommatis Palestine Concessions* (Jurisdiction), Series A No. 2 (1924) at 24–8; *Exchange of Greek and Turkish Populations*, Series B No. 10 (1925) at 16 and 22; and *The Mavrommatis Jerusalem Concessions* (Merits), Series A No. 5 (1925) at 47. The reluctance expressed in the first opinion was emphasised in Åke Hammarskjöld, 'The Early Work of the Permanent Court of International Justice' (1922–3) 36 *HLR* 704 at 719; see also Démètre Négulesco, 'La Jurisprudence de la Cour permanente de Justice internationale' (1926) 33 *RGDIP* 194 at 202; and Arbitrator Beichmann in *Affaire des réparations allemandes selon l'article 260 du Traité de Versailles*, 1 RIAA 429 (1924) at 435–6.
[135] (1950) 43-I *Annuaire*, pp. 380 and 391.

on the frontier between Turkey and Iraq within nine months, 'the dispute shall be referred to the Council of the League of Nations'. The British Government resorted to this provision and both governments took part in the deliberations of the Council. Eventually, however, the Turkish Government objected to the Council making a binding decision without its consent. The Council requested the Permanent Court's opinion on this point, that is, whether the decision to be taken was 'an arbitral award, a recommendation or a simple mediation'; it also asked how the decision should be taken and whether the interested parties should take part in the vote.

In the tense atmosphere of the case, the Permanent Court opened its *motifs* by distinguishing the application of law from political decision-making. Thus, interpreting Article 3(2) of the Lausanne Treaty, the Permanent Court 'must . . . in the first place, endeavour to ascertain from the wording of this clause what the intention of the contracting Parties was; subsequently, it may be considered whether – and if so, to what extent – factors other than the wording of the Treaty must be taken into account for this purpose'.[136] This general formula introduced what appeared to be, at least partly, a subjective approach to treaty interpretation based on the conception of the state as an international sovereign. The 'purpose' of interpretation was to 'ascertain' the common intention of the international sovereigns. As Max Huber later explained, 'l'essentiel d'un contrat, d'une convention, d'un traité est la volonté concordante des parties'. 'Sans cette concordance', he added, 'il n'y a pas de contrat et en conséquence ni droits et ni obligations qui pourraient en résulter.'[137] This train of thought suited the *Mosul* opinion well, as it helped the Permanent Court to underline its non-political mission, being the simple 'mouthpiece' of the international sovereigns. It may be doubted, however, if the general formula was more than casual embellishment. In his note to the Institut, Huber immediately abandoned the subjective approach because 'la certitude de la règle juridique est l'intérêt qui prime'. In his view, '[i]l faut donc chercher la volonté des parties dans le texte conventionnel, d'abord dans les clauses relatives à la contestation, ensuite dans l'ensemble de la convention, ensuite dans le droit international général, et enfin dans les principes généraux de droit reconnus par les nations civilisées'.[138]

---

[136] *Article 3, Paragraph 2, of the Treaty of Lausanne (Frontier between Turkey and Iraq)*, Series B No. 12 (1925) at 19.

[137] (1952) 44-I *Annuaire*, p. 199.

[138] *Ibid.*, pp. 200–1. Cf. Négulesco, 'La Jurisprudence de la Cour', pp. 203–4.

In the *Mosul* opinion, the substantive argument was based on the conception of the state as a national sovereign and the need to separate it from other national sovereigns. While the 'terms, taken by themselves', were not clear, that is, they did 'not expressly indicate the nature of the action to be undertaken by the Council',[139] the *motifs* bore evidence of the unhappiness about territorial disputes that flowed from the international law of coexistence, just as in the previous *Jaworzina* opinion.[140] The Council had the power to draw the definitive frontier because it was 'natural that any article designed to fix a frontier should, if possible, be so interpreted that the result of the application of its provisions in their entirety should be the establishment of a precise, complete and definitive frontier'.[141] The interpretation of Article 3(2) having been shaped by the international law of coexistence, the result was said also to follow from the meaning of the text of Article 3(3) concerning the situation 'pending the decision to be reached'. This text was then 'clear'.[142]

In the same breath, the *motifs* switched to an objective interpretation, which emphasised not the intention of the international sovereigns, nor the needs of the national sovereigns, but the obligations of the international law subjects under the 'clear' text. This significant paragraph resulted:

Since the Court is of opinion that Article 3 is in itself sufficiently clear . . . the question does not arise whether consideration of the work done in preparation of the Treaty of Lausanne (*les travaux préparatoires*) would also lead to the conclusions set out above. Nevertheless, it may be well also to consider Article 3 and the construction which the Court has placed on it, in the light of the negotiations at Lausanne, for the Turkish Government has cited certain facts connected with those negotiations in support of its adverse opinion.[143]

The first sentence echoed the *Jaworzina* opinion in which the Permanent Court had ruled out the preparatory work of a treaty provision relating to questions of territorial sovereignty.[144] In the former decision, however, drafted by Judges Anzilotti, Huber and Weiss,[145] the subordination of the preparatory work to the text had been restricted to the specific context of territorial disputes. As regards such disputes, the conception of the state as an international sovereign easily yielded to the conception of the state as a national sovereign and the international law of coexistence.

[139] See Series B No. 12 (1925) at 20 and also 23–4.
[140] See also the British Government, Series C No. 10 at 202–3.
[141] Series B No. 12 (1925) at 20.   [142] *Ibid.*, pp. 21–2.   [143] *Ibid.*, p. 22.
[144] *Question of Jaworzina (Polish–Czechoslovakian Frontier)*, Series B No. 8 (1923) at 41.
[145] Huber, *Denkwürdigkeiten*, p. 281.

Also in the *Mosul* opinion the majority relied heavily on the international law of coexistence, yet the subordinate status of the preparatory work was not expressly confined to territorial disputes.

In his note to the Institut, which was in fact addressed to Lauterpacht as the Institut's rapporteur on the matter, Huber wrote that '[l]e texte signé est, sauf de rares exceptions, la seule et la plus récente expression de la volonté commune des parties'.[146] In other words, Huber took the view that there could hardly be any contradiction of importance between the text and the preparatory work. The text was seen as the final expression of the common intention of the parties. To the extent that the text was 'clear', so was the intention. In the event that the preparatory work contradicted the 'clear' text, one had to infer that the parties had changed their intentions before adopting the final text.[147]

The British Government had argued that this ought to be a generally applicable principle.[148] Assuming that this was also the Permanent Court's position, Lauterpacht very much regretted the subordinate status of preparatory work.[149] He persistently advanced the argument that in paragraphs like the above-quoted, although one sentence subordinated preparatory work to a 'clear' text, the next sentence resorted to such preparatory work, thereby contradicting the superiority of the 'clear' text. In the *Mosul* opinion, however, having dealt with the contentions of the Turkish Government based on the preparatory work, the Permanent Court simply concluded by restating the hierarchy; the supreme considerations were 'a grammatical and logical point of view as well as . . . the rôle assigned to . . . [the] article in the Peace Treaty'.[150]

The relevant, and open-ended, Article 3 of the Lausanne Treaty had been envisaged because the two governments had been unable to negotiate a solution to the frontier dispute. It was an agreement to disagree. An examination of the preparatory work could well have proved nothing but the absence of a common intention. Besides, it would seem that the Permanent Court examined the preparatory work already characterised as obsolete in order to deal with all the parties' arguments,[151] especially a party not appearing before the Permanent Court (nor having appointed

---

[146] (1952) 44-I *Annuaire*, p. 199.

[147] See also *Case concerning the Factory at Chorzów* (Claim for Indemnity) (Interim Measure of Protection), Series A No. 12 (1925) at 24.

[148] See Series C No. 10 at 200 and 20–3; and also Series C No. 2 at 197; and Series C No. 13-IV at 27 and 1867–8.

[149] H. Lauterpacht, 'Les Travaux préparatoires et l'interprétation des traités' (1934) 48 *Recueil des Cours* 713 at 768–9 and 790.

[150] Series B No. 12 (1925) at 23.

[151] See similarly the British Government: Series C No. 10 at 207–19 and 33–42.

a judge *ad hoc*). In Hammarskjöld's words, the Permanent Court's practice at that time was that 'elle ne s'est jamais crue obligée de combattre des arguments qui auraient pu être avancés contre la solution finalement adoptée par elle', but only 'si ces arguments n'ont pas été effectivement formulés par les intéressés'.[152]

Related to the inferior status of preparatory work, and the underpinning rationale as explained in Huber's note, was in the *Mosul* opinion the treatment of subsequent practice. 'The facts subsequent to the conclusion of the Treaty of Lausanne can', the *motifs* read, 'only concern the Court in so far as they are calculated to throw light on the intention of the Parties at the time of the conclusion of that Treaty.'[153] Thus, what was important was not the intention of the parties before concluding the treaty, nor after concluding it, but when concluding it, for the intention could have changed in the intervals. According to Huber:

[l]a liberté dans laquelle les parties fixent les clauses d'un traité ou s'engagent par leur signature ou ratification, rend acceptable la règle suivant laquelle ces clauses lient les parties indépendamment de l'interprétation qu'elles lui donnent plus tard ou des intentions qui les auraient déterminées lors des négociations.[154]

In other words, in treaty interpretation the conception of the state as an international law subject prevailed. Of course, an interpreter who was committed to subjective treaty interpretation would not have been convinced by such arguments. For it was equally possible that the intention had not been changed in the intervals and that, for example, the preparatory work was immensely valuable for determining the intentions of the parties. But then in the *Mosul* opinion, the Permanent Court's treatment of arguments as to the subsequent practice of the parties illustrated just how far away it was in this context from deviating from the conception of the state as an international law subject and conceiving of the state as an international sovereign.

---

[152] (1927) 33-I *Annuaire*, p. 586; and see Charles de Visscher, *Problèmes d'interprétation judiciaire en droit international public* (Paris, 1963), p. 117. Alternatively, the explanation might have been the Permanent Court's desire to please all the competing schools: see J. P. Fockema Andreae, *An Important Chapter from the History of Legal Interpretation: The Jurisdiction of the First Permanent Court of International Justice, 1922–1940* (Leiden, 1948), p. 135; by the same token, the latter writer noted that '[f]ortunately . . . there were never any accidents, for the history of origin always confirmed the result to which the treaty text had led and thus the Court has so far not had to account for the consequences of its doctrine'.

[153] Series B No. 12 (1925) at 24.

[154] (1952) 44-I *Annuaire*, p. 199; see also *Free City of Danzig and International Labour Organization*, Series B No. 18 (1930) at 29.

On the one hand, the Permanent Court mentioned that at one point all members of the Council, including the British and the Turkish representatives, had voted in favour of the future proposal being binding. This vote was seen as a consequence of Article 3(2): 'For', the Permanent Court said, 'it cannot be assumed that the representatives of the Parties would have declared that they accepted the solutions to be given by the Council as definitive, if, in their view, this constituted a new undertaking going beyond the scope of the obligations entered into under Article 3 of the Treaty.'[155] This argument could only convince those who had already abandoned the conception of the state as an international sovereign.

On the other hand, there was the argument of the Turkish Government that the Council had felt constrained to ask for an advisory opinion. This argument was also based on subsequent practice; yet it was treated quite differently. The Permanent Court held that:

[t]his argument appears to rest on the following principle: if the wording of a treaty provision is not clear, in choosing between several admissible interpretations, the one which involves the minimum of obligations for the Parties should be adopted. This principle may be admitted to be sound. In the present case, however, the argument is valueless, because, in the Court's opinion, the wording of Article 3 is clear. Moreover, the attitude of the Council in the matter is sufficiently explained by a natural desire not to set aside the views of one of the Parties as to the rôle of the Council, without previously obtaining the Court's opinion upon this legal question.[156]

It should not be forgotten, however, that the text had 'cleared' only after the Permanent Court had identified a need for international law providing a frontier, thus relying on the conception of the state as a national sovereign, as opposed to the conception of the state as an international sovereign.

The Permanent Court happily applied a hierarchy between general principles of treaty interpretation, but this hierarchy would merely seem to have ornamented a conclusion dictated by the international law of coexistence.[157] Whether an argument was related to a superior or an inferior principle of treaty interpretation to a certain extent depended on whether the argument led to the same conclusion as the international law of coexistence. For example, the argument that the two governments

---

[155] Series B No. 12 (1925) at 25.
[156] *Ibid.* This step was regretted in Briggs, 'Mossoul', pp. 640 and 655.
[157] Likewise, *Territorial Dispute (Libya v. Chad)*, ICJ Reports [1994] 6 at para. 47; cf. Judge Shahabuddeen's separate opinion, *ibid.*, pp. 46–9.

had accepted the binding character of the Council's future proposal was related to a superior principle of treaty interpretation. In contrast, although similarly based on subsequent deliberations in the Council, the arguments advanced by the Turkish Government against the Permanent Court's interpretation were related to inferior principles of treaty interpretation, namely those concerning the preparatory work and restrictive interpretation. In this way, the *Mosul* opinion illustrated the Permanent Court's use of international legal argument at the time. Basically, in treaty interpretation, the Permanent Court preferred the conception of the state as an international law subject and objective interpretation to the conception of the state as an international sovereign and subjective interpretation. This was so, even though references to the latter conception could help drafting a decision in a delicate political atmosphere. Furthermore, the dynamic structure of international legal argument easily yielded to a part of the basic structure, namely the international law of coexistence, at least if substantively clear, while it trumped the national principle of self-containedness. Accordingly, the *Mosul* opinion contributed to an understanding of the hierarchy between the two structures and so the double structure of international legal argument.

The *motifs* should be compared to the statement of Deputy-Judge Beichmann at the meeting where the advisory opinion was adopted. Deputy-Judge Beichmann rejected an interpretation of Article 3(2) of the Lausanne Treaty in accordance with the international law of coexistence. In his view, Article 3(2) did not vest the Council with competence to make a binding decision and so, in looking for an alternative basis, arguably going outside the competence of the Permanent Court as determined by the questions referred to it concerning Article 3(2), he substituted the conception of the state as an international sovereign for the conception of the state as a national sovereign. He could 'only concur in the reply given in the opinion to the first question of the Council, in view of the declarations and votes of the parties at the Council meeting of September 30th, 1924; in my opinion, these declarations and votes constitute an undertaking from which neither party can withdraw without the consent of the other'.[158] Judge Anzilotti was inclined to take the same

---

[158] See Ninth session, *Procès-Verbal* 12 (18 November 1925), Moore papers 172. The majority confirmed the view that the Council was 'composed of representatives of Members, that is to say, of persons delegated by their respective Governments, from whom they receive instructions and whose responsibility they engage': see Series B No. 12 (1925) at 29; and also Henry G. Schermers and Niels M. Blokker, *International Institutional Law* (3rd edn, The Hague, 1995), p. 246.

view: 'As I cannot deny the possible existence, apart from Article 3 of the Treaty of Lausanne, of declarations made by the parties undertaking in advance to accept the Council's recommendation as binding; and as I am convinced that it is most desirable in the present case that the Court's conclusions should have the appearance of unanimity, I will not avail myself of the right to append to the Opinion a statement of my personal views.'

The nature of the Council

The second question put before the Permanent Court in the *Mosul* case concerned the procedure for it to follow when acting under Article 3(2) of the Lausanne Treaty. Unlike the British Government, the Permanent Court did not treat this question in complete isolation from the Covenant,[159] although the institutional characteristics of the Council had been neglected in the *motifs* when determining its powers under Article 3(2). It could have been argued that because the Council, when acting under Article 15 of the Covenant, only issued recommendations, and because it normally acted only by unanimity, it had not been given the power to make a binding decision. That, however, would have been neglecting the international law of coexistence and so the Permanent Court took the view that Article 15 'only sets out the minimum obligations which are imposed upon States'; it concluded that the Council had been conferred with 'powers wider than those resulting from the strict terms of Article 15'.[160] This view was redolent of Huber, an early analysis of whose had concluded that the Covenant was an open-ended 'Kodifikation der praktischen Politik', which future statesmen could give a wider or a narrower field of application.[161] However, as Turkey had not been a member of the League when agreeing to the Lausanne Treaty, there was room for doubt as to whether this opportunity had been seized upon. Such doubt was indeed articulated by 'Michel de la Grotte',[162] who

---

[159] Cf. Series C No. 10 at 220–5 and 43–51.

[160] Series B No. 12 (1925) at 26–8 and 31. Cf. *South-West Africa – Voting Procedure*, ICJ Reports [1955] 67 at 75.

[161] Cf. Max Huber, 'Die konstruktiven Grundlagen des Völkerbundsvertrages' (1922–3) 12 *Zeitschrift für Völkerrecht* 1 at 2, 6 and 17–18; and see also Max Huber, 'Die Fortbildung des Völkerrechts auf dem Gebiete des Prozess- und Landkriegsrechts durch die II. internationale Friedenskonferenz im Haag 1907' (1908) 2 *Jahrbuch des öffentlichen Rechts der Gegenwart* 470 at 477.

[162] De la Grotte, '1925', p. 338. Cf. Louis Le Fur, 'L'affaire de Mossoul' (1926) 33 *RGDIP* 60 at 88–91.

also knew the views of Deputy-Judge Beichmann and Judge Anzilotti, and it might well have been what caused President Huber's initial dissent.

Adapting the Council's decision-making to its wider powers, the majority envisaged two general principles. On the one hand, this being an institutional question under the international law of cooperation, as distinct from the substantive question and the need for a frontier under the international law of coexistence, the conception of the state as an international sovereign re-emerged. Thus, the 'observance of the rule of unanimity is naturally and even necessarily indicated'.[163] In explaining why this principle was mandatory, the *motifs* repeated Huber's early analysis and also the joint dissenting opinion in *The Wimbledon*:

Only if the decisions of the Council have the support of the unanimous consent of the Powers composing it, will they possess the degree of authority which they must have: the very prestige of the League might be imperilled if it were admitted, in the absence of an express provision to that effect, that decisions on important questions could be taken by a majority. Moreover, it is hardly conceivable that resolutions on questions affecting the peace of the world could be adopted against the will of those amongst the Members of the Council who, although in a minority, would, by reason of their political position, have to bear the larger share of the responsibilities and consequences ensuing therefrom.[164]

On the other hand, there was the 'well-known rule that no one can be judge in his own suit'.[165] Echoing Article 15(6) and (7) of the Covenant, which referred to reports 'unanimously agreed to by the members . . . other than the Representatives of one or more of the parties to the dispute', the Permanent Court struck a balance between the principles so that all members of the Council, including the parties to the dispute, took part in the vote, while the votes of the parties did not count when deciding whether 'unanimous agreement' had been achieved. 'There is', the *motifs* ended, 'nothing to justify a further derogation from the essential principles of unanimity and of the equal rights of Members.'[166]

There was probably no sharp distinction between the substantive and institutional questions in this case. The influence of the international

[163] Series B No. 12 (1925) at 29 and 30.
[164] *Ibid.*, p. 29. Cf. Huber, 'Konstruktiven Grundlagen', pp. 10–12; and Anzilotti to Hammarskjöld, 29 December 1925, Hammarskjöld papers 478. See also Paul Guggenheim, 'Max Huber, 1874–1960' (1961) 43 *Revue Internationale de la Croix-Rouge* 313 at 331.
[165] Series B No. 12 (1925) at 32; and see Series C No. 10 at 51.   [166] *Ibid.*, p. 32.

law of coexistence did not stop with the conclusion that the Council's decision was binding: it also produced a strong argument for none of the parties being able to veto the Council's decision, this being a principle of effectiveness.[167] It should be noted that Deputy-Judge Beichmann and Judge Anzilotti both supported the Permanent Court's answer to the second question.[168] Judge Anzilotti said that he was 'in full agreement with the Court as regards question No. 2', while Deputy-Judge Beichmann stated that 'it is, in my opinion, the reference to the rules laid down in Article 15 which constitutes the main argument against taking into account the votes of the representatives of the parties for the purposes of the required unanimity'.

Judge Huber's presidency and the understanding of sovereignty

No decision of the Permanent Court has been closer associated with the name of Max Huber than the judgment in *The Lotus*, decided in 1927 by the casting vote of President Huber in accordance with Article 55 of the Statute. Although essential parts of *The Lotus* were an unmistakable product of President Huber's drafting, this association was a dubious honour since the judgment has regularly been criticised for being 'extremely' positivist. Before coming to the commentators, and also to *The Lotus*, mention should first be made of the relaxed approach to state sovereignty displayed in decisions prior to *The Lotus*, including the *Mosul* opinion. Two tantalising decisions added to the conception of the state as an international sovereign and the dynamic structure of international legal argument as hierarchically privileged, namely the *Exchange of Populations* opinion and the second *Competence of the International Labour Organization* opinion.

The *Exchange of Populations* opinion had launched Judge Huber's presidency at the sixth session in 1925. According to a convention between Greece and Turkey on the exchange of populations in the aftermath of the war, exchange was not compulsory for persons 'established' in Constantinople. The meaning of this term being disputed, the Council

---

[167] Cf. Lauterpacht, *Development by the Permanent Court*, pp. 84 and 46–50. According to Lauterpacht, 'it would be difficult to find a decision of the Court which is more important from the point of view either of theory or of its practical consequences': *ibid.*, p. 49; this view was later confirmed in Judge Lauterpacht's separate opinion in *South-West Africa – Voting Procedure*, ICJ Reports [1955] 67 at 99–102, 105 and 109–12. See also L. Oppenheim, *International Law* (5th edn by H. Lauterpacht, London, 1935–7), vol. 1, p. 83, note 1 and p. 86, note 2.

[168] Ninth session, *Procès-Verbal* 12 (18 November 1925), Moore papers 172.

requested an advisory opinion upon its interpretation. The Permanent Court opened its reasoning by emphasising the dynamic structure of international legal argument, holding that:

the Court is satisfied that the difference of opinion which has arisen regarding the meaning and scope of the word 'established', is a dispute regarding the interpretation of a treaty and as such involves a question of international law. It is not a question of domestic concern [un rapport de droit interne] between the administration and the inhabitants; the difference affects [intéresse] two States which have concluded a Convention with a view to exchanging certain portions of their populations, and the criterion afforded by the word 'established' used in Article 2 of this Convention is precisely intended to enable the contracting States to distinguish the part of their respective populations liable to exchange from the part exempt from it.[169]

The textual arguments in which the motifs were so rich did not hint at the chaotic drafting.[170] Serious criticism had been levelled against a first draft produced by a committee chaired by Judge Weiss, and the motifs were only agreed on after the drafting committee had been enlarged with three of the most influential members of the bench, namely President Huber, Judge Anzilotti and Deputy-Judge Beichmann.[171] This fact casts some light on the Permanent Court's response to the key contention of the Turkish Government, according to which the term 'established' had to be seen as a reference to the Turkish law on domicile. The Permanent Court's response had a bearing on the majority decision in The Wimbledon, which none of the new members of the drafting committee had supported. This part of the Exchange of Populations opinion was not a textual exercise; the Permanent Court held:

The principal reason why the Turkish Delegation has maintained the theory of an implicit reference to local legislation appears to be that, in their opinion, a contrary solution would involve consequences affecting Turkey's sovereign rights [la souveraineté nationale]. But, as the Court has already had occasion to point out in its judgment in the case of The Wimbledon, 'the right of entering into international engagements is an attribute of State sovereignty'.[172]

---

[169] Exchange of Greek and Turkish Populations, Series B No. 10 (1925) at 17–18. The Permanent Court also referred to 'a principle which is self-evident, according to which a State which has contracted valid international obligations is bound to make in its legislation such modifications as may be necessary to ensure the fulfilment of the obligations undertaken': ibid., p. 20.

[170] Cf. ibid., pp. 18–20.

[171] Huber, 'Tagebuch', 5 February 1925, 6 February 1925, 16 February 1925 and 17 February 1925.

[172] Series B No. 10 (1925) at 21.

This was a virtual reconstruction of the *Wimbledon* statement.[173] In *The Wimbledon*, the Permanent Court had substituted the conception of the state as an international sovereign for the conception of the state as a national sovereign, holding that all kinds of treaty obligations could be undertaken by a state. Nevertheless, the Permanent Court had made room for the conception of the state as a national sovereign, being sympathetic to, at least verbally, the national principle of self-containedness by giving a restrictive interpretation to treaty rules.[174] Now the *Exchange of Populations* opinion employed the *Wimbledon* statement as an argument against such a principle of restrictive interpretation.[175] In their joint dissenting opinion in *The Wimbledon*, Judges Anzilotti and Huber had expressed serious doubts as to the conception of Germany as an international sovereign in respect of '*Das Diktat von Versailles*'.[176] In contrast, as was underlined in the *Exchange of Populations* opinion, the scheme for exchange was (interpreted to be) 'absolutely equal and reciprocal'.[177] To put it differently, it was a conceivable outcome of two international sovereigns striking a bargain. 'It is', the Permanent Court held, 'impossible to admit that a convention which creates obligations of this kind, construed according to its natural meaning, infringes the sovereign rights [*la souveraineté*] of the High Contracting Parties.'[178] So long as the conception of the state as an international sovereign had some reality (the treaty negotiations not being completely at variance with notions of sovereign equality, or independence),[179] the *Exchange of Populations* opinion indicated that there was hardly any room for the national principle of self-containedness.

The hierarchical superiority of the dynamic structure over the basic structure when the issue in question was categorised with the national principle of self-containedness was emphasised once again in the second *Competence of the International Labour Organization* opinion delivered

---

[173] Likewise, in the *Exchange of Populations* opinion the term 'self-contained' was not employed in the same sense as in *The Wimbledon*: see Series B No. 10 (1925) at 20 and Series A No. 1 (1923) at 23–4. Cf. Tsune-Chi Yü, *The Interpretation of Treaties* (New York, 1927), pp. 46–7, 106, 108, 142, 152 and 193; and also Jan Klabbers, 'Clinching the Concept of Sovereignty: Wimbledon Redux' (1998) 3 *Austrian Review of International & European Law* 345 at 363.

[174] See *Case of the SS Wimbledon*, Series A No. 1 (1923) at 24.

[175] Cf. the Turkish Government, Series C No. 7-I at 223–4 and 45.

[176] Series A No. 1 (1923) at 37. See also Max Huber in (1952) 44-I *Annuaire*, p. 201.

[177] Series B No. 10 (1925) at 20.   [178] *Ibid.*, p. 21.

[179] See expressly Judge Anzilotti's separate opinion in *Customs Regime between Germany and Austria (Protocol of March 19th, 1931)*, Series A/B No. 41 (1931) at 66–7.

at the eleventh session in 1926. In this, the fourth advisory opinion concerning the Constitution of the International Labour Organization, the Permanent Court was asked to consider whether the organisation had the power to draw up and propose legislation which, in order to protect employees, also regulated incidentally the same work when performed by employers. The Permanent Court held that this question of treaty interpretation was 'manifestly a question of law',[180] and it advocated a general principle of objective interpretation, focusing on the 'practical effect rather than . . . the predominant motive'.[181] 'Il est à remarquer', as one commentator observed in this context, 'que la Cour se trouvait alors présidée par M. Max Huber, dont on connaît par ses publications, l'importance qu'il attache au rôle social dans le domaine juridique.'[182] The opinion became known for applying a principle of effective treaty interpretation to the 'constitutional' document of an international organisation.[183]

While this elevated exercise in objective interpretation had found its final form through President Huber's collaboration with Judge Anzilotti, other parts of the *motifs* bore witness to the significant style of Judge Moore, who had prepared the first draft.[184] Thus, 'national sovereignty,

---

[180] *Competence of the International Labour Organization to Regulate, Incidentally, the Personal Work of the Employer*, Series B No. 13 (1926) at 14.

[181] *Ibid.*, p. 19.

[182] Marcelle Jokl, *De l'interprétation des traités normatifs d'après la doctrine et la jurisprudence internationales* (Paris, 1935), p. 176; cf. Jan Klabbers, 'The Life and Times of the Law of International Organizations' (2001) 70 *NJIL* 287 at 296–7.

[183] Series B No. 13 (1926) at 18–19; the Permanent Court relied on earlier opinions: see in particular *ibid.*, pp. 20–1, referring to *International Labour Organization and the Methods of Agricultural Production*, Series B No. 3 (1922) at 59. The principle of effective treaty interpretation was adopted by the International Court: see *Corfu Channel Case* (Merits), ICJ Reports [1949] 4 at 24; and *Reparation for Injuries suffered in the Service of the United Nations*, ICJ Reports [1949] 174 at 182–3; and also *Legality of the Use by a State of Nuclear Weapons in Armed Conflict*, ICJ Reports [1996] 66 at para. 25. See also Huber in (1952) 44-I *Annuaire*, p. 201.

[184] Huber, 'Tagebuch', 13 July 1926. The opinion was adopted in the presence of dissenting votes by Judges Loder and Pessôa. Originally, Judge Pessôa had declared that he would submit a dissenting opinion. However, 'M. Pessoa, après une conversation avec M. le Président Loder, déclare que, pour ne pas affaiblir l'autorité de la Cour, il se contentera de joindre le contenu de son avis dissident au procès-verbal de la séance ou sera approuvé le texte définitif de l'avis': see Eleventh session, *Procès-Verbal* 19
(19 July 1926), reproduced in Pessôa, *Côrte permanente*, pp. 110–11. As for his individual note and dissenting opinion, see *ibid.*, pp. 129–32 and 132–7, respectively. According to Judge Pessôa, Judge Loder agreed that the opinion of the majority contradicted the third advisory opinion delivered in 1922: see *ibid.*, p. 137; cf. Series B No. 13 (1926) at 20–1.

individual liberty, and various controversial theories of society and government' were classified as 'political principles'.[185] In a telling paragraph, the *motifs* recalled the Permanent Court's second advisory opinion, also concerning the powers of the International Labour Organization. In 1922, the Permanent Court had responded to an argument for restrictive interpretation based on the national principle of self-containedness by stating that '[t]here may be some force in this argument, but the question in every case must resolve itself into what the terms of the Treaty actually mean'.[186] Four years later, having quoted that passage, the Permanent Court was less polite:

So, in the present instance . . . the province of the Court is to ascertain what it was the Contracting Parties agreed to. The Court . . . is called upon to perform a judicial function, and, taking the question actually before it in connection with the terms of the Treaty, there appears to be no room for the discussion and application of political principles or social theories, of which, it may be observed, no mention is made in the Treaty.[187]

The linking of state sovereignty to the political process of treaty-making, as opposed to the application of treaty law, was clear enough. It suggested a preference for the dynamic structure of international legal argument and the conceptions of the state as an international sovereign and as an international law subject. Once the international sovereigns had concluded a treaty (then binding on the international law subjects), this preference militated against the use in treaty interpretation of arguments based on the conception of the state as a sovereign, whether national or international. It should be noted, however, that the Permanent Court's statements on sovereignty were kept at a general level, and indeed on this occasion the Permanent Court declined to be more specific.[188] It was perhaps not clear whether the statements, in addition

---

[185] Series B No. 13 (1926) at 21–2. In the *Eastern Carelia* opinion, Judge Moore had favoured an analogical interpretation and there was also evidence of the use of such interpretation in the second *Competence of the International Labour Organization* opinion: cf. *ibid.*, p. 20.

[186] *International Labour Organization and the Conditions of Agricultural Labour*, Series B No. 2 (1922) at 23. It may be noted that the Permanent Court had considered the view that the organisation's powers 'should not be extended by interpretation', while the actual argument 'much urged' by the French Government was that the provisions 'must be construed strictly and in the narrowest sense': Series C No. 1 at 174.

[187] Series B No. 13 (1926) at 23. A series of sovereignty-based principles of restrictive interpretation had been put before the Permanent Court: see Series C No. 12 at 195–7, 204–7, 212, 214–15 and 220.

[188] Series B No. 13 (1926) at 24; and similarly *Exchange of Greek and Turkish Populations*, Series B No. 10 (1925) at 17 and 23–5.

to the national principle of self-containedness, were also aimed at the international law of coexistence.

The Lotus

The Permanent Court meets the Buchrecht

A year later, at the twelfth session, the Permanent Court decided *The Lotus*. Its judgment attracted more attention among international lawyers than any other decision of the 1920s, at the time and ever since. It has been referred to as 'a mine of valuable material upon the subject of Jurisdiction'.[189] Technically, the Permanent Court was asked to interpret Article 15 of a Lausanne Convention concerning residence, business and jurisdiction. However, on the Permanent Court's reading, Article 15 referred to 'international law as it is applied between all nations belonging to the community of States'.[190] The Permanent Court made inquiries into the nature and the making of international law, issues which were at the heart of the *Buchrecht* and on which any sweeping statement, almost whatever its content, would have been controversial. The attention attracted by the judgment did not come as a surprise to the bench. The judges themselves had found the case exciting.[191] On the initiative of President Huber and Judge Moore, and independently of the parties, the Registrar had collected relevant legal material and distributed it to the judges.[192]

At the opening of the twelfth session, President Huber welcomed the new tendency among international lawyers to subject the Permanent Court's decisions to intense analysis.[193] In addition to 'les analyses pénétrantes' by 'Paul de Vineuil', President Huber pointed to Professor Gabriele Salvioli's and Professor J. H. W. Verzijl's theoretical and rather

---

[189] Oppenheim/Lauterpacht, *International Law*, vol. 1, p. 270, note 2.

[190] *The Case of the SS Lotus*, Series A No. 10 (1927) at 16; 'the community of States' was a translation of '*la communauté internationale*', a notion repeatedly employed by Dionisio Anzilotti in the context of so-called customary law: see Anzilotti, *Cours*, pp. 43, 63, 74 and 90.

[191] See John Bassett Moore, 'Permanent Court of International Justice: Session of 1927 – The "Lotus" Case', Moore papers 178.

[192] See Moore to Huber, 14 December 1926, Huber to Moore, 3 January 1927 and Huber to Weiss, 20 June 1927, all Huber papers 24.1 and Moore papers 177. Cf. Carsten Smith, *The Relation between Proceedings and Premises: A Study in International Law* (Oslo, 1962), p. 44.

[193] Präsidentreden, 15 June 1927, Huber papers 25.2.

critical evaluations of the Permanent Court's first years.[194] The new tendency demanded, he said, that the judges engaged in a constructive dialogue on their respective notes and drafts and that they showed the highest degree of carefulness when framing the *motifs*. Using a metaphor that had a clear bearing on *The Lotus*, President Huber compared 'our decisions to ships which are intended to be launched on the high seas of international criticism'.[195]

The facts of the case were simple. In 1926, a Turkish steamship suffered a collision on the high seas causing loss of life. The ship had collided with the *SS Lotus*, a mail steamer flying the French flag, which then sailed into a Turkish port to set ashore the survivors and obtain repairs. Here the French officer on watch at the time of the collision was arrested and was subsequently prosecuted and sentenced before the Turkish courts. The French Government protested the action taken against the officer and as a result the French and Turkish Governments signed a Special Agreement submitting to the Permanent Court the question whether Turkey had been justified in exercising criminal jurisdiction.[196]

One particular passage from the opening of the Permanent Court's reasoning on the merits was a red rag to the *Buchrecht*. According to the majority:

International law governs relations between independent States. The rules of law binding upon States therefore emanate from their own free will [*la volonté de ceux-ci*] as expressed in conventions or by usages generally accepted as expressing principles of law and established in order to regulate the relations between these co-existing independent communities [*la co-existence de ces communautés indépendantes*] or with a view to the achievement of common aims. Restrictions upon the independence of States cannot therefore be presumed.[197]

Among the first commentators, Professor J. L. Brierly wrote that this 'reasoning was based on the highly contentious metaphysical proposition of the extreme positivist school that the law emanates from the free will of sovereign independent States, and from this premiss

---

[194] J. H. W. Verzijl, 'Die Rechtsprechung des Ständigen Internationalen Gerichtshofes von 1922 bis Mai 1926' (1924–6) 13 *Zeitschrift für Völkerrecht* 489; and Gabriele Salvioli, 'La Jurisprudence de la Cour permanente de Justice internationale' (1926) 12 *Recueil des Cours* 3.

[195] Präsidentreden, 15 June 1927, Huber papers 25.2.

[196] It was this question, and not the case as such, which was submitted to the Permanent Court: see Series A No. 10 (1927) at 12–15; and de la Grotte, '1926–1928', pp. 389–90 and 393.

[197] Series A No. 10 (1927) at 18.

they argued that restrictions on the independence of States cannot be presumed'.[198] Brierly went on to say: 'Neither, it may be said, can the absence of restrictions; for we are not entitled to deduce the law applicable to a specific state of facts from the mere fact of sovereignty or independence.' At the same time, Professor Charles de Visscher observed that 'le raisonnement de la Cour nous fait toucher du doigt la conséquence la plus fâcheuse des doctrines positivistes en droit international'. One of the consequences so laid bare was that 'leurs conclusions sont peu progressives: elles représentent le droit à l'état *statique*; elles ne contribuent guère à assurer son développement'.[199] Professors Verzijl and Salvioli were both provoked by *The Lotus* to contribute their first analyses devoted to a single decision.[200]

These and other commentators linked the judgment to a term, 'positivism', from which most theorists spent the twentieth century trying to distance themselves.[201] *The Lotus* encouraged contemporary lawyers to adopt the notion of *obiter dictum* as a way to deny the various statements any precedential value.[202] However, there was more to *The Lotus* than 'positivism'. Manley O. Hudson, one of the few supporters of the judgment, later said that he suspected that writers 'had merely been repeating what Mr Brierly and Mr Charles de Visscher had written'.[203] 'Michel de la Grotte' went so far as to say that, 'étant donné le nombre d'études subjectives qui existent, il est peut-être opportun de présenter un bref exposé objectif'.[204]

---

[198] J. L. Brierly, 'The "*Lotus*" Case' (1928) 44 *LQR* 154 at 155. See also YILC 1950-I, p. 196.

[199] Charles de Visscher, 'Justice et médiation internationales' (1928) 9 *RDILC* 33 at 77–8.

[200] Gabriele Salvioli, 'Il caso del "Lotus"' (1927) 19 *Rivista* 521; and J. H. W. Verzijl, 'L'affaire du "Lotus" devant la Cour permanente de Justice internationale' (1928) 9 *RDILC* 1.

[201] See expressly Verzijl, 'L'affaire du "Lotus"', pp. 31–2.

[202] See John Fischer Williams, 'L'affaire du "Lotus"' (1928) 35 *RGDIP* 361 at 364–5; W. E. Beckett, 'Les Questions d'intérêt général au point de vue juridique dans la jurisprudence de la Cour permanente de Justice internationale' (1932) 39 *Recueil des Cours* 135 at 144; and Lauterpacht, *Development by the Permanent Court*, pp. 23–4 and 104. Cf. Judge Anzilotti in *Interpretation of Judgments Nos. 7 and 8 (the Chorzów Factory)*, Series A No. 13 (1927) at 24 and also the judgment, *ibid.*, pp. 19–21 and 14, which was interpreted in Hammarskjöld, 'Development of International Law', p. 799 and also in Series D No. 2, Add.3 (1936) at 335. See also de Bustamante, *World Court*, p. 293.

[203] YILC 1951-I, p. 336; cf. Hammarskjöld, 'Development of International Law', p. 804; and Anthony A. D'Amato, *The Concept of Custom in International Law* (Ithaca, 1971), pp. 178–9. Hudson had also said that '[t]he Hague Court had shown excessive discretion in the case of the *Lotus*' to the effect that '[a] further study of the problem could therefore usefully be made': YILC 1949, p. 42.

[204] De la Grotte, '1926–1928', p. 387.

In 1926, the Committee of Experts for the Progressive Codification of International Law had considered the criminal competence of states in respect of offences committed outside their territory. Brierly and de Visscher, who had prepared a report on the matter to the Committee, had partly disagreed, and the Committee concluded that 'international regulation of these questions by way of a general convention, although desirable, would encounter grave political and other obstacles'.[205] When the following year it fell to the Permanent Court to resolve the dispute as to Turkey's exercise of criminal jurisdiction over a French officer on a French ship, it was hardly surprising that the Permanent Court contemplated a residual principle, considering 'the very nature and existing conditions of international law' according to which '[i]nternational law governs relations between independent States'.[206]

The 'majority' reached the conclusion that the debate in the Committee of Experts had arguably conveyed, namely that there were no settled rules of international law applicable to the matter. Many commentators have been tempted to follow Professor Viktor Bruns and to relate *The Lotus* to the notion of a *non liquet*.[207] Although leading members of the Permanent Court had approved of that notion in theory,[208] the view on the bench was that, in respect of *The Lotus*, Bruns' analysis was 'tout à fait hors de route'.[209] More than any other decision of the Permanent Court, a proper analysis of the issues raised by *The Lotus* demands that due regard is paid to the conception of the state as a national sovereign. The premise already mentioned that '[i]nternational law governs relations between independent States' implied that prior to international law there were at least the independent states.[210] But the conception of the state as a national sovereign not only did away with the notion of a *non liquet* in the context of this judgment; it also pointed towards the preliminary question that divided the Permanent Court, namely whether there really was no applicable international law.

---

[205] *Codification Committee of Experts*, vol. 2, p. 9; see also Series C No. 13-II at 371–2 and 414.
[206] Series A No. 10 (1927) at 18.
[207] Viktor Bruns, 'Völkerrecht als Rechtsordnung I' (1929) 1 ZaöRV 1 at 53; cf. *ibid.*, pp. 1, 6, 22, 32 and 55; and Bruns to Hudson, 31 December 1927, Hudson papers 76.8.
[208] See in particular the dissenting opinion of Judge Huber in *Rights of Minorities in Upper Silesia (Minority Schools)*, Series A No. 15 (1928) at 54–5; and Huber, 'Konstruktiven Grundlagen', pp. 14 and 15–16. Indications of a similar view can be found in Anzilotti, *Cours*, pp. 81 and 117; but see Dionisio Anzilotti, *Corso di Diritto Internazionale* (4th edn, Padua, 1955), p. 105, note 4.
[209] Anzilotti to Huber, 5 March 1930, Huber papers 23.
[210] See Max Huber, *Die Staatensuccession: Völkerrechtliche und Staatsrechtliche Praxis in XIX. Jahrhundert* (Leipzig, 1898), pp. 4–8 and 24.

The division of the bench

Confronting the question whether there was any applicable international law relevant to the case involved a basic choice between the conceptions of the state as a national sovereign and as an international sovereign, each reflecting one of the two structures that make up the double structure of international legal argument. The pleadings of both governments had a bearing on the former conception. During the oral pleadings the Turkish Government, represented by Mr Mahmout Essat Bey, Minister of Justice, submitted:

Le principe fondamental qui domine la matière est le droit, pour tout Etat souverain, de légiférer librement, d'organiser ses autorités judiciaires et d'en fixer les compétences. Une restriction de cet attribut essentiel de la souveraineté ne peut être présumée; elle doit être prouvée par celui qui l'allègue. Une telle restriction ne peut résulter que d'une disposition claire et précise, d'un traité général ou spécial ou d'une règle certaine du droit des gens consacrée par une coutume générale bien établie et librement acceptée. En cas de doute, soit sur le sens d'un traité, soit sur l'existence d'une règle coutumière du droit des gens, c'est le principe de liberté qui doit prévaloir: *in dubio pro libertate*.[211]

In other words, having embraced the conception of the state as a national sovereign, the Turkish Government contended that no international law of coexistence was available, leaving the matter with the national principle of self-containedness and a presumption against international law (of cooperation).

Also, the French Government conceived of the state as a national sovereign, but unlike the Turkish Government it identified a need for international law to solve this case, thus leading it to the international law of coexistence. The French Government treated the state's criminal jurisdiction as *prima facie* limited to its own territory. Thus, Professor Basdevant, the French agent, said that '[à] l'intérieur de son cercle de compétence, dans son domaine, l'Etat peut invoquer sa souveraineté; mais, pour élargir sa compétence, il lui faut un titre reconnu par le droit international, il lui faut s'appuyer sur une règle du droit international'.[212]

---

[211] Series C No. 13-II at 134–5. The substance of this argument was in accordance with Professor Diena's opinion, *ibid.*, pp. 322 and 354; but the last phrase as such had been taken from Professor Mercier's opinion, *ibid.*, pp. 403 and 419. As for the origin of this phrase, Mercier had added 'Voir Rivier', but Alphonse Rivier employed the phrase '*in dubio pro libertate*' only in relation to servitudes, and certainly not in relation to jurisdiction in general: see Alphonse Rivier, *Principes du droit des gens* (Paris, 1896), vol. 1, p. 296; cf. *ibid.*, p. 284 and vol. 2, p. 123.

[212] Series C No. 13-II at 150–1.

The position of the French Government was adopted by the dissenters. Judge Weiss stated that the purpose of the international law of coexistence was 'to harmonize and reconcile the different sovereignties over which it exercises its sway', while Judge Loder referred to the territorial setting as 'a logical principle of law . . . a postulate upon which the mutual independence of States rests'.[213] A state 'cannot', Judge Loder added, extend its criminal law 'to offences committed by a foreigner in a foreign territory, without infringing the sovereign rights [la souveraineté] of the foreign State concerned, since in that State the State enacting the law has no jurisdiction'. 'To take the contrary view', Judge Altamira contended, 'would . . . be to neglect one of the fundamental conditions of the international community and would result in opening the door to continual conflicts which might involve most undesirable consequences.'[214] According to the dissenting opinion of Judge Nyholm:

In endeavouring to trace the general lines along which public international law is formed, two principles will be found to exist: the principle of sovereignty and the territorial principle, according to which each nation has dominion over its territory [est maître sur son territoire] and – on the other hand – has no authority to interfere in any way in matters taking place on the territories of other nations.[215]

The presumption of exclusive territorial jurisdiction was strong, as had previously, in 1910, been stated by the Permanent Court of Arbitration in the *North Atlantic Coast Fisheries* case.[216] Yet in *The Lotus* the six judges who formed the 'majority' held that '[r]estrictions upon the independence of States cannot . . . be presumed'.[217]

If these words, which will be referred to as 'the *Lotus* statement', are seen in the light of the conception of the state that the French and Turkish Governments shared, they imply that there was no need for the international law of coexistence. What comes into view then is the national principle of self-containedness. The conclusion drawn by the Turkish Government had been '*in dubio pro libertate*' and many commentators have indeed seen the *Lotus* statement as carrying the same

---

[213] See Series A No. 10 (1927) at 44 and 35 respectively; later Judge Weiss referred to 'the principle of sovereignty' and Judge Loder to 'the basic principle of the sovereignty and independence of States': *ibid.*, pp. 49 and 38. See also André Weiss, *Manuel de droit international privé* (9th edn, Paris, 1925), p. xxxvi.

[214] *Ibid.*, p. 103.

[215] *Ibid.*, p. 59. See also *ibid.*, pp. 68 (Judge Moore) and 95 (Judge Altamira). Judge Finlay restricted his reasoning 'to crimes committed at sea': *ibid.*, p. 51.

[216] *North Atlantic Coast Fisheries Case*, 11 RIAA 167 (1910) at 180.

[217] Series A No. 10 (1927) at 18.

meaning. 'The *Lotus* presumption' became the meaning of the *Lotus* state-ment.[218] However, there were several aspects of the Permanent Court's judgment in *The Lotus* that militated against this understanding of the *Lotus* statement.[219] First of all, although the Turkish Government had said '*in dubio pro libertate*', the Permanent Court creatively summarised the Turkish view as follows: 'the Turkish Government takes the view that Article 15 allows Turkey jurisdiction whenever such jurisdiction does not come into conflict with a principle of international law.'[220] The Turkish view which the Permanent Court discussed had been purged of any hint of a presumption, leaving a mere residual principle. On this interpretation, the Turkish Government's argument provided no ready-made solution if the situation under international law was unclear. What is more, in the *motifs* the *Lotus* statement was followed by this

---

[218] E.g., Brierly, '"*Lotus*" Case', p. 156, note 2; De Visscher, 'Justice et médiation internationales', p. 74; Walter Rebbe, *Der Lotusfall vor dem Weltgerichtshof* (Leipzig, 1932), p. 27; H. Lauterpacht, 'Restrictive Interpretation and the Principle of Effectiveness in the Interpretation of Treaties' (1949) 26 *BYIL* 48 at 58–9; Scelle, YILC 1950-II, pp. 133–4; Cheng, *General Principles of Law*, p. 306; Julius Stone, 'Fictional Elements in Treaty Interpretation: A Study in the International Judicial Process' (1953–4) 1 *Sydney Law Review* 344 at 354, note 55a; and Jacques-Michel Grossen, *Les Présomptions en droit international public* (Neuchatel, 1954), pp. 118–19. See more recently Martti Koskenniemi, *From Apology to Utopia: The Structure of International Legal Argument* (Helsinki, 1989), pp. 221–2; Jan Klabbers, *The Concept of Treaty in International Law* (The Hague, 1996), p. 68; Mojtaba Kazazi, *Burden of Proof and Related Issues: A Study on Evidence before International Tribunals* (The Hague, 1996), pp. 77–9 and 246; V. D. Degan, *Sources of International Law* (The Hague, 1997), pp. 100–1; Philippe Sands, 'Turtles and Torturers: The Transformation of International Law' (2001) 33 *NYUJILP* 527 at 529–30 and 548; Ian Brownlie, *Principles of Public International Law* (6th edn, Oxford, 2003), pp. 8, 12 and 288–9; Luc Reydams, *Universal Jurisdiction: International and Municipal Legal Perspectives* (Oxford, 2003), pp. 20–1; C. F. Amerasinghe, *Jurisdiction of International Tribunals* (The Hague, 2003), pp. 105 and 116; see also Alfred Verdross and Bruno Simma, *Universelles Völkerrecht: Theorie und Praxis* (3rd edn, Berlin, 1984), pp. 223 and 388. Cf. James Crawford, *The Creation of States in International Law* (Oxford, 1979), pp. 32–3 and 355. Support for 'the *Lotus* presumption' is also found in Judge Moreno Quintana's dissenting opinion in *Case concerning Right of Passage over Indian Territory* (Merits), ICJ Reports [1960] 6 at 91; Judge Ammoun's separate opinion in *North Sea Continental Shelf*, ICJ Reports [1969] 3 at 101; Judge Dillard's separate opinion in *Fisheries Jurisdiction (United Kingdom v. Iceland)*, ICJ Reports [1974] 3 at 59; and Judge Guillaume's separate opinion in *Legality of the Threat or Use of Nuclear Weapons*, ICJ Reports [1996] 226 at 291–2; and also President Bedjaoui's declaration, *ibid.*, p. 271; and Judge Shahabuddeen's dissenting opinion, *ibid.*, p. 426. In the *Legality of the Threat or Use of Nuclear Weapons* opinion, the International Court refrained from expressing an opinion on 'the questions of burden of proof' because the relevant states had either accepted or not disputed that 'their independence [*liberté*] [*sic*] was indeed restricted by the principles and rules of international law': *ibid.*, para. 22.
[219] And see the dissenting opinion of Judge Weiss, Series A No. 10 (1927) at 43.
[220] *Ibid.*, pp. 18 and also 20.

sentence: 'Now the first and foremost restriction imposed by international law upon a State is that – failing the existence of a permissive rule to the contrary – it may not exercise its power in any form in the territory of another State.'[221] If the *Lotus* statement had been a presumption against international law, or against restrictions imposed by international law, as the traditional reading has had it, not even the most careless, or deeply split, group of drafters would have started the next sentence, relating to 'the first and foremost restriction imposed by international law upon a State', with the connective 'now [or]'. Furthermore, a presumption or a burden of proof as to the content of international law fits badly with the fact that the Permanent Court itself had collected legal material and thus 'not confined itself to a consideration of the arguments put forward'.[222]

There was no reliance at all upon general presumptions in the *motifs*. Literally, the *Lotus* statement did not give expression to a presumption of freedom: it rejected a presumption against freedom. The general principle, which was clearly expressed elsewhere in the judgment, was the residual principle of state freedom ('*liberté*'),[223] not a presumption. In this context, a residual principle differed from a presumption in that it rested on a legal analysis which had determined that there were no rules, while a presumption, though rebuttable by legal analysis, provided a method of determining that there were no rules.[224] Commentators have focused on the *Lotus* statement and given it the form of a presumption, because they saw the judgment solely in the light of the basic structure of international legal argument and the conception of the state as a national sovereign. This was a misconception. True, Anzilotti referred to 'la règle *in dubio pro libertate*' in his textbook, but that *dubio* was not about the scope of international law; it was about what to do when no international law was applicable.[225] Thus, in Anzilotti's view, and in accordance with how the Permanent Court summarised the Turkish

---

[221] *Ibid.*, p. 18.

[222] *Ibid.*, pp. 31 and also 22. See similarly *Case relating to the Territorial Jurisdiction of the International Commission of the River Oder*, Series A No. 23 (1929) at 19.

[223] See *ibid.*, pp. 19, 21 and 30–2; similarly, in the context of treaty interpretation, Max Huber in (1952) 44-I *Annuaire*, p. 201. See, for a comparable example, *Société Ouest Africaine des Bétons Industriels v. Senegal* (Merits), 2 ICSID Reports 190 (1988) at 205–6 and 214.

[224] See further Ole Spiermann, '*Lotus* and the Double Structure of International Legal Argument' in Laurence Boisson de Chazournes and Philippe Sands (eds.), *International Law, the International Court of Justice and Nuclear Weapons* (Cambridge, 1999), p. 131 at pp. 132–6.

[225] Anzilotti, *Cours*, pp. 114–19; cf. as to unilateral declarations *ibid.*, pp. 350–1.

view in *The Lotus*, the principle *in dubio pro libertate* proper was identical with the residual principle of state freedom belonging to the dynamic structure, as distinct from a presumption.

Die soziologischen Grundlagen des Völkerrechts, which Max Huber republished the following year, was also instructive. Discussing the distinction between customary law (*Völkerrecht*) and non-binding customs (*Völkersitte*), Huber joined customary law and the international law of coexistence together and took the view that the essence of it was the territorial separation of states. Thus, as said in *The Lotus*, 'the first and foremost restriction imposed by international law upon a State is that . . . it may not exercise its power in any form in the territory of another State'.[226] Regarding the possibility of other parts of the international law of coexistence derogating from this principle, Huber wrote that 'es kann somit die Existenz solcher Normen nicht vermutet werden'.[227] Indeed, Huber made it his general position that 'hier muß die Vermutung für die Nichtexistenz einer die Autonomie beschränkenden Norm durch partikuläre oder allenfalls kollektive Satzung widerlegt werden'.[228] While the international law of coexistence offered territorial sovereignty, other international law came within the international law of cooperation where consent was required, but in respect of which no presumption was applied.[229]

What the Permanent Court dealt with in that critical passage of the judgment which led to the *Lotus* statement was the making of the international law of cooperation in such cases where the international law of coexistence did not apply. Clearly the Permanent Court assumed that only states could be international lawmakers, or sovereigns, and because states were 'independent', no state could legislate with binding effect on another state. 'The rules of law binding upon States therefore emanate from their own free will.'[230] This was the only way to make international law. Or, at least, '[r]estrictions upon the independence of States cannot therefore be presumed'.[231] It could not be presumed, by the French

---

[226] Series A No. 10 (1927) at 18; see also Arbitrator Huber in *Island of Palmas Case*, 2 RIAA 829 (1928) at 838; and Huber in (1931) 36-I *Annuaire*, pp. 78–9.

[227] Huber, *Soziologischen Grundlagen des Völkerrechts*, p. 47 (translation: 'the existence of such norms can therefore not be presumed').

[228] *Ibid.*, p. 48 (translation: 'here must the presumption of the non-existence of a norm which restricts the autonomy be refuted by a particular or perhaps a general rule').

[229] See for a similar proposition as regards state responsibility, Arbitrator Huber in *Affaire des biens britanniques au Maroc espagnol*, 2 RIAA 615 (1924) at 699.

[230] Series A No. 10 (1927) at 18.

[231] See also Bedjaoui, YILC 1974-II, p. 103; Schwebel, YILC 1978-I, p. 170; and Quentin-Baxter, YILC 1980-II.1, p. 257.

Government, that states could legislate with binding effect on other states; they were all sovereign. Accordingly, the *Lotus* statement pointed back to one of the other great statements on independence (as distinct from sovereignty), namely in the *Eastern Carelia* opinion, according to which 'the principle of independence of States' is 'a fundamental principle of international law [*la base même du droit international*]'.[232] In the *Eastern Carelia* opinion, as in *The Lotus*, the majority had relied on a residual principle of freedom without giving any support to a presumption against international law.

To put it differently, in his own copy of his textbook, Anzilotti made the observation that the opening of *The Lotus* was in accordance with the principle that 'toute activité de l'Etat . . . est protégée par le droit international dans ce sens qu'il interdit aux autres Etats de limiter, sans un titre juridique particulier, le libre développement de ladite activité'.[233] In 1931, in observations submitted to the Institut de Droit International, Max Huber also referred to the independence of states. He stated that 'le droit international commun', in my terminology the international law of coexistence, 'est basé . . . sur les Etats comme unités territoriales indépendantes'.[234] In Huber's view, '[d]ans ses propres frontières territoriales . . . [i]l n'y a que très peu de règles de droit commun applicables en l'espèce'.[235] He added the following remarks:

Je continue de penser que le principe proclamé par la Cour permanente de Justice internationale dans l'affaire du 'Lotus' est exact; mais il a été quelquefois mal interprété par les critiques du dit arrêt. L'absence d'une règle qui départagerait les droits des Etats et la liberté qui en résulte pour chaque Etat de faire ce qui n'est pas défendu ne signifie pas un état d'anarchie où chacun aurait le droit de passer outre à la situation créée par un autre Etat. Là où les libertés font une collision *réelle*, le droit *doit* fournir la solution, car le droit international, comme tout droit, repose sur l'idée de la *coexistence* de volontés de la même valeur.[236]

In *The Lotus*, the 'majority' and the dissenters did not divide on the notion of an international law of coexistence that separated the national sovereigns. Each and every judge would seem to have accepted this notion. The question was whether overlaps and conflicts between the criminal laws of different states disturbed coexistence to such a degree that the jurisdiction of each state to prescribe criminal law had to be limited to its territory. On the facts of the case, the majority answered this

---

[232] *Status of Eastern Carelia*, Series B No. 5 (1923) at 27.
[233] Anzilotti, *Cours*, p. 58. For the association of this principle with *The Lotus*, see Anzilotti, *Corso*, p. 58.
[234] (1931) 36-I *Annuaire*, p. 78.   [235] *Ibid.*, p. 79.   [236] *Ibid.*, and also pp. 84–5.

question of categorisation in the negative because, unlike the enforce-ment of national law, they did not see *The Lotus* as a case in which 'les libertés font une collision réelle'. Yet, having discussed jurisdiction to prescribe national law in general, the Permanent Court admitted that criminal law was a borderline case:

> Nevertheless, it has to be seen whether the foregoing considerations really apply as regards criminal jurisdiction, or whether this jurisdiction is governed by a different principle: this might be the outcome of the close connection which for a long time existed between the conception of supreme criminal jurisdiction and that of a State [*entre la suprême juridiction pénale et la notion d'Etat*], and also by the especial importance of criminal jurisdiction from the point of view of the individual [*la personnalité humaine*].[237]

This was a window, as it were, to the inherent vagueness of the inter-national law of coexistence. However, the window was immediately closed.[238] The majority seemed willing in this respect to adopt a mod-est approach, taking what could otherwise have been an inherently vague situation under the international law of coexistence, 'the existing lacunæ',[239] to be a situation not governed by international law. And so the dynamic structure of international legal argument and the resid-ual principle moved to the fore of the Permanent Court's reasoning. In the actual case, the validity of the French view depended on 'whether there is a custom having the force of law establishing it',[240] this 'custom' belonging to the international law of cooperation, as explained below. As already implied in the *Nationality Decrees* opinion, the international law of cooperation was not a challenge to the independence of states.

The majority's legal analysis

In 1926, Åke Hammarskjöld had written to the Institut de Droit Inter-national that 'la Cour s'est ralliée au point de vue suivant lequel, du moment que sa juridiction est limitée et dérive exclusivement de la volonté des parties, elle ne peut soulever *ex officio* des questions de droit

---

[237] Series A No. 10 (1927) at 20 and also 21 regarding 'precedents offering a close analogy to the case under consideration'. See also Antonio Sanchez de Bustamante y Sirvén, *The Territorial Sea* (New York, 1930), p. 125; and Antonio Sanchez de Bustamante y Sirvén, *Droit international public* (Paris, 1936), vol. 3, pp. 151–2.

[238] Cf. President Guillaume's separate opinion, paras. 4 and 14 in *Case concerning the Arrest Warrant of 11 April 2000*, ICJ Reports [2002] 3.

[239] Cf. Series A No. 10 (1927) at 19; and also, in a different context, Riphagen, YILC 1979-I, p. 212.

[240] Series A No. 10 (1927) at 21. In addition to 'custom', the words 'rule' and 'principle' were also used.

que les parties ne lui ont pas soumises'.[241] That view could hardly stand after *The Lotus*.[242] Although the Turkish and French Governments had both argued the case within the basic structure of international legal argument based on the conception of the state as a national sovereign, the Permanent Court focused on the categorisation of the issue of criminal jurisdiction within the dynamic structure that reflected the conception of the state as an international sovereign. Clearly the dynamic structure was taken to be hierarchically superior. That being said, the Permanent Court appeared to uphold the view that it ought to deal with the arguments 'effectivement formulés par les intéressés'.[243] The remaining part of the majority's reasoning subjected the three arguments of the French Government – regarding the content of the international law of coexistence – to careful scrutiny, in the course of which the Permanent Court did not challenge the presumption against extraterritorial jurisdiction that underlay the arguments. However, employing an effects doctrine, the majority justified Turkey's exercise of jurisdiction also on the premises of this presumption, namely by 'the so-called territorial principle'.[244]

Of course, the Permanent Court's readiness might also have been a reflection that not all members of the majority were fully convinced that the international law of coexistence did not apply to the case. Judge Moore had actually been part of the majority until the very point when the final judgment was to be adopted,[245] and he reached the same conclusion as the majority, but only by starting from within the international law of coexistence.[246] Judge Moore told Professor Borchard that '[w]hile I was obliged to dissent on one point, my opinion was more of a concurrence than of a dissent'.[247] The reason why Judge Moore

---

[241] (1927) 33-I *Annuaire*, p. 586; cf. Anzilotti, *Cours*, p. 120; and J. H. W. Verzijl, *The Jurisprudence of the World Court* (Leiden, 1965), vol. 1, p. 399. See also *Case concerning the Payment in Gold of Brazilian Federal Loans Contracted in France*, Series A No. 21 (1929) at 124; *Case relating to the Territorial Jurisdiction of the International Commission of the River Oder*, Series A No. 23 (1929) at 19; and *Case of Free Zones of Upper Savoy and the District of Gex* (Third Phase), Series A/B No. 46 (1932) at 138.

[242] Cf. Iain Scobbie, '*Res Judicata*, Precedent and the International Court: A Preliminary Sketch' (1999) 20 *AYIL* 299 at 305.

[243] (1927) 33-I *Annuaire*, p. 586.

[244] Series A No. 10 (1927) at 23 and 24; cf. *ibid.*, p. 30. The dissenters' criticism of the effects doctrine was brief and haphazard: see *ibid.*, pp. 37 (Judge Loder), 48 (Judge Weiss) and 61 (Judge Nyholm).

[245] See Huber, 'Epilog zu Denkwürdigkeiten', p. 7.   [246] Series A No. 10 (1927) at 68–70.

[247] Moore to Borchard, 18 September 1927, Moore papers 57 and Borchard papers 6.92. Indeed, Judge Moore added: 'My opinion was longer than I desired, but I felt that this

eventually appended a dissenting opinion, though he concurred in the *dispositif* (which he had voted against),[248] was what he had termed his 'conceptions of judicial proceedings'.[249] They had induced him to review on a more general basis 'the international validity' of the Turkish Criminal Code based on the passive personality principle, which applied generally to acts of foreigners committed abroad if the victim was 'a Turkish subject'.[250] Accordingly, the majority, which 'straddled the question of extraterritorial jurisdiction' and so 'tried hard to persuade me to join them', did not succeed.[251]

Judge Moore's approach clashed with the dualist views of, in particular, Judge Anzilotti. And this was important because, according to President Huber's *Tagebuch*, the drafting committee had decided 'que M. Anzilotti sera chargé de la rédaction entière, mais que les deux autres membres lui soumettront des esquisses ou fractions d'arrêt qui leur apparaîtront particulièrement opportuns'.[252] While the contribution of President Huber was clearly felt in relation to the opening of the majority's substantive argument, it was a view associated more with Judge Anzilotti than anybody else (leaving aside Triepel), namely that before an international court the validity of an act in national law was immaterial.[253] While Judge Moore considered the decisions of national courts as a national lawyer and in accordance with the traditions of the common

could not be helped when the position was taken in one of the dissents [namely, the dissenting opinion of Judge Finlay] that a ship was, for jurisdictional purposes, only a chattel and not a "place", and that *The Queen* v. *Keyn* was an international authority; and when the position was constantly taken by some in the discussions that, where the jurisdiction of a country even within its own territory was challenged on grounds of international law, the "burden of proof" rested upon such country to show that international law "permitted" it to do the act that was challenged.'

[248] Series A No. 10 (1927) at 65.

[249] On his conceptions, at least as regards this case: see Moore to Huber, 14 December 1926, Huber papers 24.1 and Moore papers 177.

[250] Series A No. 10 (1927) at 90 and also 65. As to his strong views on the passive personality principle: see John Bassett Moore, *Report on Extraterritorial Crime*, which was used in the *Cutting* case between the United States and Mexico; it has been reproduced in John Bassett Moore, *A Digest of International Law* (Washington DC, 1906), vol. 2, pp. 243–68. Judge Moore thought that '[i]n the "Lotus" case before the World Court I possessed a certain advantage over my colleagues by reason of the fact that the only publication cited to us was my report in the Cutting case': see Moore to Wigmore, 26 February 1940, Moore papers 178.

[251] Moore to Borchard, 29 August 1931, Borchard papers 7.98. In his usual style, Moore added that 'I may, without vanity, say that my opinion in the *Lotus* case is the only one that has a strictly legal character or is based on definite legal principles'.

[252] Huber, 'Tagebuch', 18 August 1927.

[253] Series A No. 10 (1927) at 23–4 and also 13 and 15.

law, the *motifs* treated those decisions as facts, or expressions of the attitude of the state to which the court belonged.[254]

Towards the end of the *motifs*, there was another unmistakable product of Judge Anzilotti's drafting, as the majority came back to the dynamic structure of international legal argument, which it treated as hierarchically superior. This was the rejection of the third French argument as to the existence of a principle of exclusive jurisdiction in case of ship collisions:

> Even if the rarity of the judicial decisions to be found among the reported cases were sufficient to prove in point of fact the circumstance alleged by the Agent for the French Government, it would merely show that States had often, in practice [en fait], abstained from instituting criminal proceedings, and not that they recognized themselves as being obliged to do so; for only if such abstention were based on their being conscious of having a duty to abstain [si l'abstention était motivée par la conscience d'un devoir de s'abstenir] would it be possible to speak of an international custom.[255]

This is a famous passage, which in 1969 the International Court related to the conception of *opinio juris sive necessitatis*.[256] The phrase 'their being conscious of having a duty' unmistakably corroborated the view of Judge Anzilotti that a customary rule was an '*accord tacite*',[257] the conclusion of which was a question of fact which the Permanent Court had to answer through interpretation.[258] One should be careful, however, not to take the just-quoted passage out of its context. In his textbook, Anzilotti drew a clear distinction between an international and a national context: while the existence of so-called customary international law was a matter of course in the international context, it appeared to be beyond the bounds of possibility in the national context.[259] Accordingly, Anzilotti

---

[254] Compare the dissenting opinion of Judge Moore, *ibid.*, pp. 71–83 and 85–9, with the *motifs*, *ibid.*, pp. 23, 27 and 28–30; see also John Bassett Moore, 'The Organization of the Permanent Court of International Justice' (1922) 22 *Columbia Law Review* 497 at 510. Cf. the dissenting opinion of Judge Altamira, Series A No. 10 (1927) at 96–7.

[255] Series A No. 10 (1927) at 28.

[256] See *North Sea Continental Shelf*, ICJ Reports [1969] 3 at paras. 77–8. It may be noted that in *The Lotus* the dissenting judges were quite insistent, as a matter of principle, about the need for consent: see Series A No. 10 (1927) at 34 (Judge Loder), 43–4 and 45 (Judge Weiss), 56 (Judge Finlay), 60 (Judge Nyholm) and 103 (Judge Altamira).

[257] See Anzilotti, *Cours*, pp. 67–8 and 73–7.

[258] See Series A No. 10 (1927) at 28; and likewise *Status of Eastern Carelia*, Series B No. 5 (1923) at 26 and 28.

[259] See Anzilotti, *Cours*, pp. 75, 76, 90, 91–2, 107–8, 117–18, 166–7, 174–5, 236–8, 242, 255 and 341–2, which must be compared with Anzilotti, *Corso*, p. 72, note 10. See also Anzilotti in (1932) 37 *Annuaire*, pp. 104–10; and *Nationality Decrees in Tunis and Morocco*,

defined custom as 'actes des Etats dans le domaine des relations interna-tionales, desquels résulte leur volonté de se comporter réciproquement et obligatoirement d'une certaine manière'.[260] The underlying distinc-tion between an international and a national context is akin to the distinction between the international law of coexistence, applying to 'une collision réelle', which Huber had alluded to when defending *The Lotus*,[261] and the national principle of self-containedness. It was not state consent, or *opinio juris*, that made Anzilotti refer to custom, but the inter-national law of coexistence, or so-called custom, that made him refer to state consent. Indeed, consent would not seem to be relevant to the international law of coexistence. Because outside the international con-text the above-quoted passage rather related to the conception of the state as an international sovereign and arguably expressed, what was required in the making of international law when outside the scope of the international law of coexistence, that is, in the making of the inter-national law of cooperation.[262] It certainly had no implications for the basic structure of international legal argument based on the conception of the state as a national sovereign.

State consent was not in evidence when at the end of the *motifs* the Permanent Court sought to justify – and, by the same token, restrict the implications and scope of – the holding that the specific case did not come within the international law of coexistence. The closing argument was that '[n]either the exclusive jurisdiction of either State, nor the limi-tations of the jurisdiction of each to the occurrences which took place on the respective ships would appear calculated to satisfy the requirements of justice and effectively to protect the interests of the two States'.[263]

Conclusions

Whether *The Lotus*, concerning 'international law as it is applied between all nations belonging to the community of States [*la communauté internationale*]',[264] was a manifest to extreme positivism depended, of course, on the meaning given to two terms, 'positivism' and 'extreme'. In what Verzijl later referred to as 'a curious instance of opposition by

Series B No. 4 (1923) at 27. Likewise, e.g., the dissenting opinions of Judge Finlay and Judge Nyholm, Series A No. 10 (1927) at 54 and 59, respectively. Cf. de Bustamante, *Droit international*, vol. 1, p. 51.

[260] Anzilotti, *Cours*, p. 74.   [261] (1931) 36-I *Annuaire*, p. 79.

[262] Cf. *Jurisdiction of the European Commission of the Danube between Galatz and Braila*, Series B No. 14 (1927) at 36–7.

[263] Series A No. 10 (1927) at 30.   [264] *Ibid.*, p. 16.

the community of States against a pronouncement of the International Court',[265] treaties were subsequently adopted that changed the principle of concurrent jurisdiction laid down by the Permanent Court.[266] This development is in full agreement with the double structure of international legal argument, as also demonstrated by *The Lotus*.[267]

In manifesting an international lawyer's approach to international legal argument, *The Lotus* represented a twofold challenge to the *Buchrecht* as it confirmed the hierarchy between the two structures of international legal argument also apparent in, for example, the *Mosul* opinion.[268] On the one hand, the judgment and the dissenting opinions taken as a whole demonstrated that the presence of a so-called custom depended not on consent, but on the basic structure of international legal argument and whether there was a collision of state interests considered to be sufficiently serious. On the other hand, in cases where no such serious collision was recognised, the existence of international law depended on consent and the dynamic structure of international legal argument prevailed. This may explain why *opinio juris* is seldom referred to where admitting the presence of and applying the international law of coexistence, or so-called customary law. Its main field of application is in cases where neither the international law of coexistence, nor the international law of cooperation, whether dressed up as 'custom' or not, apply.

Unlike a national lawyer's approach to international legal argument, the national principle of self-containedness was of no importance in either respect; accordingly, the Permanent Court did not embrace a presumption against international law, whether of cooperation or coexistence. On the contrary, the Permanent Court rejected a presumption in respect of the international law of cooperation. State consent could not simply be presumed. As stated in the *Eastern Carelia* opinion, whether an international sovereign had given its consent and thus was bound by a treaty was a question of fact, which was subject to demonstration.[269]

---

[265] J. H. W. Verzjil, *International Law in Historical Perspective* (Leiden, 1971), vol. 4, p. 53.

[266] See Article 1 of the International Convention for the Unification of Certain Rules relating to Penal Jurisdiction in Matters of Collision or other Incidents of Navigation from 1952; and also Article 11 of the Geneva Convention on the High Seas; and Article 97 of the United Nations Convention on the Law of the Sea.

[267] Still, the role of the International Law Commission in 'overruling' *The Lotus* is noteworthy: YILC 1950-II, p. 383, YILC 1955-II, p. 24 and YILC 1956-II, p. 281; and also the Special Rapporteur, J. P. A. François, YILC 1951-II, pp. 77–80, YILC 1952-I, p. 143, YILC 1954-II, pp. 13–14 and YILC 1956-II, p. 17. See also Brownlie, *Principles*, pp. 8–9, 20, 238–9 and 300–1.

[268] As for a possible third challenge, see Series A No. 10 (1927) at 26.

[269] Cf. *Status of Eastern Carelia*, Series B No. 5 (1923) at 26 and 28.

The most important link between *The Lotus* and the *North Sea Continental Shelf* cases is not the references to *opinio juris* as a way to cloak the international law of coexistence. It is the application in the latter judgment of a principle similar to the *Lotus* statement, namely that 'ratification' of a treaty by conduct, as opposed to the carrying out of certain prescribed formalities, 'is not lightly to be presumed'.[270]

President Anzilotti and fluvial law

The aftermath of The Lotus

The Lotus would not seem to have had a particularly helpful effect on judicial relations within the Permanent Court. The case had divided the judges at the end of Judge Huber's presidency, just as the *Mavrommatis* case had at the end of Judge Loder's presidency. Once again the Permanent Court faced a series of harshly worded dissenting opinions. Shortly afterwards, on President Huber's proposal, and as an indication of the crisis felt, it was agreed among the judges 'that dissenting opinions might be prepared quite independently of the judgment of the Court, that their object was to show the reasons for which a judge could not agree with the majority and that they were not intended to be a reasoned criticism of the judgment or opinion'.[271] Later it was also agreed that the dissenting opinions should be presented to the Permanent Court at the time of the second reading of the *motifs*.[272]

At the end of 1927, Judge Anzilotti was unanimously elected president.[273] It was reported at the time that 'Judge Anzilotti personally desired to withdraw his candidacy in view of the great inconvenience which he anticipated from enforced residence for three years in this city', that is, at The Hague, but 'it appears that he was given to understand that Mussolini desired him to accept the office if offered'.[274] That being said, '[h]e and Judge Moore are', according to a confidential biographic data circulated in the Department of State, 'unquestionably the dominating spirits in the Court'.[275] When subsequently looking back on

---

[270] See *North Sea Continental Shelf*, ICJ Reports [1969] 3 at paras. 28 and also 33 and 71.
[271] Series E No. 4 (1927–8) at 291.   [272] *Ibid.*
[273] Marcilly's dispatch, 12 December 1927, Quai d'Orsay 2400B; see originally Anzilotti to Huber, 16 February 1927, Huber papers 24.1; and Huber, 'Tagebuch', 25 June 1927, 11 July 1927, 20 July 1927, 23 July 1927, 27 July 1927, 15 August 1927 and 17 August 1927.
[274] Tobin to Secretary of State, 7 December 1927, NARA 500 C114/648.
[275] See the enclosures in Norweb to Secretary of State, 14 January 1927, NARA 500 C114/601.

the work of the Permanent Court, Manley O. Hudson took the view that Anzilotti was 'the best judge the Court has ever had' and 'in no sense "political" . . . for 18 years he has shown himself entirely independent'.[276]

In the speech President Anzilotti made at the opening of the thirteenth session, the first at which he presided, he appealed that 'each of us makes the others understand the whole of his ideas, and himself is able to appreciate the ideas of all the others'.[277] Judge Anzilotti's only dissenting opinion during his presidency opened as follows:

Very much to my regret I do not concur in the opinion of the Court and it is my duty to say so. Since, in my view, a dissenting opinion should not be a criticism of that which the Court has seen fit to say, but rather an exposition of the views of the writer, I shall confine myself to indicating as briefly as possible what my point of view is and the grounds on which it is based.[278]

The Danube opinion

In the *Danube* opinion, also delivered at the Permanent Court's twelfth session and thus before Judge Anzilotti took up the presidency, only Deputy-Judge Negulesco dissented. The case concerned the jurisdiction of the European Commission governed by the Convention establishing the Definitive Statute of the Danube between two points, Galatz and Braila. The agreement among the judges would seem to have been achieved by broadening the *motifs*, which included several parallel arguments for the advice, while at the same time avoiding some of the specific issues.[279] It had brought Judge Moore to the point of despair. As for the background, Judge Moore had told Justice Stone as follows:

The Court still sits. I do not know whether you ever saw the play called the 'Private Secretary'. The hero, when asked how he began the day, replies that he went to the club; and, when asked what he did at the club, replied: 'I sit'. So with the Court. We are now considering our deliverance in the Danube case, in which we had seven whole days of oral argument. Unfortunately, I was again elected a member of the drafting committee, a laborious post requited with anonymity and frequently inability to say what you want to say in your own way.[280]

---

[276] See Hudson to Stimson, 20 December 1938, Hudson papers 97.3; and Hudson to Green, 19 July 1939, Hudson papers 164.2.

[277] Series E No. 4 (1927–8) at 23.

[278] *Free City of Danzig and International Labour Organization*, Series B No. 18 (1930) at 18.

[279] Cf. *Jurisdiction of the European Commission of the Danube between Galatz and Braila*, Series B No. 14 (1927) at 68.

[280] Moore to Stone, 19 November 1927, Moore papers 59. Later, Moore wrote to Professor Borchard: 'My personal experience leads me to think that a thorough reading knowledge of French and a fair capacity to understand it when spoken are of prime

Eventually, Judge Moore appended his own observations to the Permanent Court's opinion. They opened as follows:

While concurring in the conclusions and generally in the reasoning of the Court's Opinion, which stands as a monument to the laborious care with which all views and suggestions have been considered, I desire to say that, in my opinion, the first and main question, whether 'under the law at present in force' the European Commission has the same powers from Galatz to Braila as it has below Galatz, shrinks on legal analysis into a small compass and is essentially simple.[281]

Some years later, however, Judge Moore called the *Danube* opinion '[o]ne of the most interesting advisory opinions ever given by the court'.[282] A few significant aspects may be pointed to. The advisory opinion contained a statement that nicely summarised the need for fluvial law as part of the international law of coexistence and the vagueness which at one point had characterised it:

Prior to 1815, the right to navigate rivers which separated or traversed two or more States was not regulated by any general principle or general act, and formed a subject of constant dispute. For the most part, each State sought to monopolize the navigation of streams flowing through its own territory, and even the right of an upper riparian State to access to the sea was denied. As the existence of such conditions not only hampered the development of commerce but also tended to prevent the growth of international relations appropriate to a state of peace, the Parties to the great international conflict which covered the concluding years of the XVIIIth century and the earlier part of the XIXth, introduced into the arrangements by which this long period of warfare was ended, provisions for the freedom of navigation of international streams.[283]

However, as the *Danube* opinion was concerned with the Definitive Statute, this was another great case on the hierarchies of principles of treaty interpretation, in particular that 'preparatory work should not be used for the purpose of changing the plain meaning of a text'.[284]

---

importance. In the Danube case in 1927, for instance, the record consisted of nearly fifteen hundred printed pages of French, of which no translation into English was made, and of which, morally speaking, none could have been made': Moore to Borchard, 17 September 1930, Moore papers 62.

[281] Series B No. 14 (1927) at 80; and likewise de la Grotte, '1926–1928', p. 399.

[282] John Bassett Moore, 'Notes on Some Cases Dealt with by the Permanent Court of International Justice' (1929), Moore papers 178, p. 6.

[283] Series B No. 14 (1927) at 38.

[284] *Ibid.*, pp. 31 and also 28 and 34–5. The preparatory work of the Versailles Treaty was confidential and not made available to the Permanent Court: see *ibid.*, p. 32 and Series C No. 13-IV at 2078–9 and 2087–8; and again in *Case relating to the Territorial*

The Permanent Court also restated the *Wimbledon* statement taking the form of a prelude to the dynamic structure of international legal argument, according to which 'restrictions on the exercise of sovereign rights accepted by treaty by the State concerned cannot be considered as an infringement of sovereignty'.[285] As in the *Mosul* opinion, and also in *The Lotus* regarding a Lausanne convention,[286] it was not so much an objective textual interpretation that such principles stimulated as a quick departure from the international law of cooperation.

In the *Danube* opinion, the old treaty regime to which the Definitive Statute referred was said to have created 'an uncertain and precarious situation';[287] and just as in the *Mosul* opinion, the open-ended provisions interpreted by the Permanent Court could be characterised as agreements to disagree, there being no common intention to unveil. Instead, the Permanent Court obtained what help it found necessary from the international law of coexistence, or an analogy of it, since this part of the decision concerned international river commissions as opposed to territorial states.[288] Thus, the European Commission was said to be fully competent in the Galatz–Braila sector, because 'the Definitive Statute obviously assures the internationalization, by means of two Commissions, of the entire course of the river, uninterruptedly from Ulm to the Black Sea',[289] and because the competence of the other commission, the International Commission, first began at Braila.[290] Moreover, 'it seems quite natural that the European Commission should also act along the same lines in the Galatz–Braila sector' as below Galatz.[291]

Another noteworthy aspect of the *Danube* opinion was that, while a stable and complementary division of competences was encouraged, the

Jurisdiction of the International Commission of the River Oder, Series A No. 23 (1929) at 8–9 and 42. In the latter decision, the Permanent Court also relied on the absence of Germany and two neutral states from the Paris Conference; see also the submissions of parties, Series C No. 17-II at 430–3 and 25–35. Cf. Yi-ting Chang, *The Interpretation of Treaties by Judicial Tribunals* (New York, 1933), pp. 107–8; but see also Series D No. 2, Add.1 (1926) at 124–32; and Series E No. 4 (1927–8) at 288–9; as well as Judge van Eysinga in *The Oscar Chinn Case*, Series A/B No. 63 (1934) at 136. The decisions may be compared to *Question of Jaworzina (Polish–Czechoslovakian Frontier)*, Series B No. 8 (1923) at 26.
[285] Series B No. 14 (1927) at 36.
[286] See *The Case of the SS Lotus*, Series A No. 10 (1927) at 16–17.
[287] Series B No. 14 (1927) at 27; and see the treatment of the Interpretative Protocol, *ibid.*, pp. 34–5.
[288] Cf. the observations submitted by Judge Moore, *ibid.*, p. 83.
[289] *Ibid.*, pp. 25 and also 27, 30, 45, 58–9 and 62.
[290] See *ibid.*, p. 25; cf. the observations submitted by Judge Nyholm, *ibid.*, pp. 73 and 76–7.
[291] *Ibid.*, p. 54.

national sovereign was not given preference over a treaty-based river commission. In distinguishing the powers of the two through an objective interpretation,[292] the Permanent Court pronounced:

When in one and the same area there are two independent authorities, the only way in which it is possible to differentiate between their respective jurisdictions is by defining the functions allotted to them. As the European Commission is not a State, but an international institution with a special purpose, it only has the functions bestowed upon it by the Definitive Statute with a view to the fulfilment of that purpose, but it has power to exercise these functions to their full extent, in so far as the Statute does not impose restrictions upon it.[293]

Unlike the dissenting opinion of Deputy-Judge Negulesco, the majority did not employ the national principle of self-containedness as a vehicle for restrictive treaty interpretation.[294] The attempt of Nicolas Politis, appearing on behalf of the Romanian Government, to invoke the *Lotus* presumption was unsuccessful.[295] On the contrary, the above-quoted passage hinted at the possibility of international institutions being vested with personality in international law.

The *Danube* opinion confirmed the hierarchy exemplified by *The Lotus* between the two structures of international legal argument. While there was no room for the national principle of self-containedness, which was trumped by the international law of cooperation in the context of an international river, the international law of cooperation was in turn presumed to be in accordance with the international law of coexistence. No doubt, this presumption was rebuttable, yet if the content of the international law of coexistence was reasonably clear it had a strong impact on treaty interpretation. This hierarchical relationship between the two makes up the thrust of an international lawyer's double structure of international legal argument.

The River Oder *case*

The *River Oder* case was a further illustration of the international law of coexistence being the driving force behind formulating a hierarchy of principles of treaty interpretation, it being understood at the time that the *motifs* had been produced by President Anzilotti.[296] The case was submitted to the Permanent Court under a Special Agreement concluded

---

[292] *Ibid.*, pp. 62–3 and 65–8.
[293] *Ibid.*, p. 64; and see González, YILC 1985-II.1, p. 111.   [294] Cf. *ibid.*, p. 109.
[295] Series C No. 13-IV, pp. 201 and see also 219; cf. Professor de Visscher, *ibid.*, p. 173.
[296] Scavenius to Munch, 11 September 1929, Rigsarkivet H-12-41.

between on the one hand Poland and on the other hand the United Kingdom, the Czechoslovak Republic, Denmark, France, Germany and Sweden, these being the seven states represented on the International Commission of the Oder. The main question was whether the competence of the International Commission under the Versailles Treaty extended to two tributaries situated in Polish territory. The judgment gave an affirmative answer and so was in favour of the six governments, Judges de Bustamante and Pessôa and Judge *ad hoc* Rostworoski each declaring a dissent.[297]

At the centre of the dispute, one found Article 331 setting out the scope of the internationalisation of, among others, the Oder, which, on the Permanent Court's interpretation, was equivalent to the territorial competence of the International Commission.[298] The essential phrase was 'all navigable parts of these river systems which naturally provide more than one State with access to the sea'. The upper reaches of both tributaries were situated in Polish territory, and the Polish Government contended, *inter alia*, that these were outside the treaty regime.[299] The six governments submitted that by 'parts' the provision alluded to entire tributaries, or sub-tributaries.[300]

'[T]he text being doubtful',[301] the *motifs* continued by rejecting the appeal made by Charles de Visscher on behalf of the Polish Government to a principle of restrictive interpretation based on the national principle of self-containedness.[302] In the Permanent Court's words:

[t]his argument, though sound in itself, must be employed only with the greatest caution. To rely upon it, it is not sufficient that the purely grammatical analysis of a text should not lead to definite results; there are many other methods of interpretation, in particular, reference is properly had to the principles underlying the matter to which the text refers; it will be only when, in spite of all pertinent considerations, the intention of the Parties still remains doubtful, that that interpretation should be adopted which is most favourable to the freedom of States.[303]

In other words, a sovereignty-based principle of restrictive interpretation was watered down, more or less brought to approximate the residual principle of freedom; it certainly could not apply to issues coming within the international law of coexistence, as opposed to the national

---

[297] *Case relating to the Territorial Jurisdiction of the International Commission of the River Oder,* Series A No. 23 (1929) at 32.
[298] *Ibid.*, pp. 23–4.   [299] Series C No. 17-II at 414–7, 464–6, 470–1, 146–7 and 171.
[300] See *ibid.*, pp. 285–91, 305, 79–84 and 205.   [301] Series A No. 23 (1929) at 26.
[302] See Series C No. 17-II at 167–8 and 181–2.   [303] Series A No. 23 (1929) at 26.

principle of self-containedness. Accordingly, the Permanent Court went 'back to the principles governing international fluvial law', which in turn led it to 'the idea . . . of a community of interest of riparian States':

> This community of interest [*communauté d'intérêts*] in a navigable river becomes the basis of a common legal right [*une communauté de droit*], the essential features of which are the perfect equality of all riparian States in the use of the whole cause of the river and the exclusion of any preferential privilege of any one riparian State in relation to the others.[304]

Article 331 of the Versailles Treaty was interpreted in accordance with this '*Grundsätze des Miteigentums*' previously analysed by Huber.[305]

The clear language in which the Permanent Court was able to present the international law of coexistence, and let it determine its treaty interpretation, may have been part of the background why the Permanent Court did not apply the Barcelona Convention, which under Article 338 of the Versailles Treaty should have superseded parts of the regime that it had laid down (though not expressly Article 331).[306] Much to Judge Huber's regret the majority took the view that the relevant parts of the Barcelona Convention were not binding upon Poland due to Article 338 of the Versailles Treaty; Poland had to ratify not only the Versailles Treaty but also the Barcelona Convention.[307] It may be noted that ratification was a requirement, not solely according to Article 4 of the Barcelona Convention but also due to general principle; for, according to the majority, 'unless the contrary be clearly shown by the terms of that

---

[304] *Ibid.*, p. 27; and see the six governments in Series C No. 17-II at 290–1, 294–5, 87, 107–9, 112–13 and 220 and the Polish Government, *ibid.*, pp. 451–2 and 163.

[305] *Ibid.*, pp. 28–9; and Max Huber, 'Ein Beitrag zur Lehre von der Gebietshoheit an Grenzflüssen' (1907) 1 *Zeitschrift für Völkerrecht und Bundesstaatsrecht* 159 at 161–2. As to the general applicability of the idea of a community of interests, see Schwebel, YILC 1980-II.1, p. 189 and also YILC 1980-II.2, p. 127; McCaffrey, YILC 1986-II.1, p. 114; Gutiérrez in YILC 1990-I, p. 112; and also Jerome Lipper, 'Equitable Utilization' in A. H. Garretson *et al.* (eds.), *The Law of International Drainage Basins* (New York, 1967), p. 15 at p. 29; Eduardo Jimènez de Aréchaga, 'International Law in the Past Third of a Century' (1978) 159 *Recueil des Cours* 1 at 193; J. G. Lammers, *Pollution of International Watercourses: A Search for Substantive Rules and Principles of Law* (The Hague, 1984), pp. 506–7; and Steven C. McCaffrey, *The Law of International Watercourses – Non-Navigation Uses* (Oxford, 2001), p. 151. See also *Land, Island and Maritime Frontier Dispute* (El Salvador v. Honduras), ICJ Reports [1992] 351 at para. 406; and *Gabcíkovo-Nagymaros Project*, ICJ Reports [1997] at para. 85; cf. *ibid.*, para. 147.

[306] The six governments' arguments in relation to the Barcelona Convention led to the same result as reached by the Permanent Court: see Series C No. 17-II at 248, 281–3, 301, 49–51 and 67–8.

[307] Cf. Series A No. 23 (1929) at 20–2 and, for Judge Huber's observations, *ibid.*, p. 33. See also the Polish Government, Series C No. 17-II at 152–3.

article, it must be considered that reference was made to a Convention made effective in accordance with the ordinary rules of international law amongst which is the rule that conventions, save in certain exceptional cases, are binding only by virtue of their ratification'.[308]

Direct effect of treaty rules

At the thirteenth session, at which President Anzilotti took office and made his appeal to the judges to further the cause of collaboration, the Permanent Court delivered the unanimous *Jurisdiction of Courts* opinion concerning Danzig. Under Articles 100 and 102 of the Versailles Treaty, Danzig had been separated from Germany and made 'a Free City' in order to give Poland access to the sea. In 1928, the question was whether an agreement between Poland and the Free City, the so-called *Beamtenabkommen*, was directly effective on – or, in the Permanent Court's words,[309] 'directly applicable' to – individual railway officials as part of their '"contract of service", that is, "the series of provisions which constitute the legal relationship between the Railways Administration and its employees"'.[310] Only thereby would the agreement provide a basis for individual actions before the Danzig courts.

The question as to the direct effect of treaty rules presented an immense challenge to the Benthamite conception of international law, which only reflects the international law of coexistence. There would not be much room for direct effect, unless the Permanent Court treated the international law of cooperation as a different branch of international law that belonged to a distinct, hierarchically superior structure of international legal argument. The essential question was whether the judges would go along with the conception of the state as an international sovereign, one which could put in a treaty any rule it liked, including rules that had a direct effect on individuals, creating individual rights and obligations on which, according to international law, claims could be based before national authorities and courts.

The Polish Government contended that an international agreement (between two states or state-like entities) could not create rights and

---

[308] Series A No. 23 (1929) at 20; and also Brierly, YILC 1952-II, p. 53; cf. Lauterpacht, YILC 1953-II, p. 117; Fitzmaurice, YILC 1956-II, p. 123; Waldock, YILC 1962-II, pp. 50–1; and Articles 12–14 of the Vienna Convention on the Law of Treaties.

[309] *Jurisdiction of the Courts of Danzig (Pecuniary Claims of Danzig Railway Officials who have passed into the Polish Service, against the Polish Railways Administration)*, Series B No. 15 (1928) at 18.

[310] *Ibid.*, p. 23.

obligations for individuals.[311] The Permanent Court's response was memorable:

It may be readily admitted that, according to a well established principle of international law, the *Beamtenabkommen*, being an international agreement, cannot, as such, create direct rights and obligations for private individuals. But it cannot be disputed that the very object of an international agreement, according to the intention of the contracting Parties, may be the adoption by the Parties of some definite rules creating individual rights and obligations and enforceable by the national courts.[312]

In a sense this passage echoed the Benthamite conception. It also recalled Triepel's basic premise that international and national law were circles with no overlap. According to Anzilotti, who had been a member of the drafting committee, the Permanent Court's opinion 'ne dit pas qu'un traité, comme tel, peut créer des droits et des obligations pour des individus, sans besoin que les règles y afférentes soient incorporées dans le droit interne: il dit seulement que l'intention des Parties contractantes peut être celle d'adopter des règles déterminées créant des droits et des obligations pour des individus et susceptibles d'être appliquées par les tribunaux nationaux'.[313]

That being said, Anzilotti pointed to an argument that had been put at the end of the *motifs*, namely that if:

Poland would contend that the Danzig Courts could not apply the provisions of the *Beamtenabkommen* because they were not duly inserted in the Polish national law, the Court would have to observe that, at any rate, Poland could not avail herself of an objection which, according to the construction placed upon the *Beamtenabkommen* by the Court, would amount to relying upon the non-fulfilment of an obligation imposed upon her by an international engagement.[314]

Accordingly, the direct effect of the *Beamtenabkommen* could be based on the conception of the state as an international law subject *vis-à-vis*

---

[311] See Series C No. 14-I at 241, 358, 361, 53 and 70.   [312] Series B No. 15 (1928) at 17–18.
[313] Anzilotti, *Cours*, pp. 407–8 and also 133–4. See also de Bustamante, *World Court*, pp. 179–94; and Bruns, 'Völkerrecht als Rechtsordnung I', pp. 2 and 6–7. Cf. Huber, 'Fortbildung des Völkerrechts', pp. 504–5; and 540–5; and James Brown Scott (ed.), *The Proceedings of the Hague Peace Conferences: The Conference of 1907* (London, 1921), vol. 2, pp. 788–90.
[314] Series B No. 15 (1928) at 26–7; see similarly Judge Finlay in *Questions concerning the Acquisition of Polish Nationality*, Series B No. 7 (1923) at 26. Cf. *Case concerning the Factory at Chorzów* (Claim for Indemnity) (Jurisdiction), Series A No. 9 (1927) at 31; and Cheng, *General Principles of Law*, p. 149.

other states, as opposed to the conception of the state as an international sovereign adopting such rules as it chose. Perhaps not all members on the bench agreed with this categorisation, which may also have been the reason why parts of the *motifs* were couched in the language of subjective, as opposed to objective, interpretation.[315] In any case, it did not make much difference. The state had become an international law subject under the *Beamtenabkommen*, precisely because the state was a party to it, that is, because the state had acted as an international sovereign.[316]

On the facts of the specific case the Permanent Court concluded that the 'wording and general tenor of the *Beamtenabkommen* show that its provisions are directly applicable as between the officials and the Administration'.[317] The Permanent Court was not even close to applying a presumption according to which a treaty is not directly effective. Arguably, the Permanent Court had the opportunity to dismiss the direct effect of the *Beamtenabkommen* altogether, but it did not. The argument could have been based on Article 9, stipulating that under the *Beamtenabkommen* all matters 'shall be dealt with by the Polish State Railways Administration'. It could possibly have been argued that the Polish administration would only apply Polish law, so that the *Beamtenabkommen* foresaw implementation through Polish law. Yet the Permanent Court held that Article 9 'should not be construed in a manner which would make the applicability of the provisions of the *Beamtenabkommen* depend on their incorporation into a Polish Regulation'.[318]

Judge *ad hoc* Bruns, who had served in the case, wrote to Professor Hudson: 'The impressions I received of the Permanent Court were excellent, and I returned with a very high opinion of the standard of judicial capacity shown there and of the personalities of the leading judges.'[319] The *Jurisdiction of Courts* opinion confirmed that the national principle of

---

[315] Cf. Arbitrator Huber in *Affaire des biens britanniques au Maroc espagnol*, 2 RIAA 615 (1924) at 633–4.

[316] But see as to the direct effect of directives as between individuals in the context of European Community law, Case 148/78, *Pubblico Ministero v. Ratti* [1979] ECR 1629 at paras. 21–2; Case 152/84, *Marshall v. Southampton and South-West Hampshire Area Health Authority* [1986] ECR 723 at para. 48; Case C-91/92, *Faccini Dori v. Recreb* [1994] ECR I-3325 at paras. 29–30; Case C-192/94, *El Corte Inglés SA v. Blázquez Rivero* [1996] ECR I-1281 at paras. 15–17; and Case C-343/98, *Collino and Chiappero v. Telecom Italia Spa* [2000] ECR I-6659 at para. 20.

[317] Series B No. 15 (1928) at 18.   [318] *Ibid.*, p. 19. Cf. Grossen, *Les présomptions*, pp. 123–5.

[319] Bruns to Hudson, 10 March 1928, Hudson papers 76.8.

self-containedness did not breed powerful principles of treaty inter-pretation, but yielded to principles associated with the hierarchically superior, dynamic structure of international legal argument. The open-minded, though not eccentric, approach to the involvement of the individual in international law was not due to the 'special legal status' of the Free City.[320] The possibility of such involvement had been envis-aged by the Permanent Court when facing the treaty regimes of Polish Upper Silesia, notably in the *Minorities* opinions.[321]

At the thirteenth session, the Permanent Court dealt with a similar aspect of the Polish Minorities Treaty in the *Minorities Schools* case.[322] Nevertheless, commentators have tended to treat the *Jurisdiction of Courts* opinion as an exceptional decision which is liable to a narrow interpretation.[323]

National law and politics: new jurisdictional questions

Introduction

During Judge Anzilotti's presidency the Permanent Court delivered a number of decisions that deserve attention, besides the *River Oder* case and the *Jurisdiction of Courts* opinion. Thus, there were the *Minorities*

---

[320] Cf. *Free City of Danzig and International Labour Organization*, Series B No. 18 (1930) at 9 and 11.

[321] See *Questions relating to Settlers of German Origin in Poland*, Series B No. 6 (1923) at 25; and *Questions concerning the Acquisition of Polish Nationality*, Series B No. 7 (1923) at 16.

[322] See *Rights of Minorities in Upper Silesia (Minority Schools)*, Series A No. 15 (1928) at 32. See also the decision of the Arbitral Tribunal of Upper Silesia in *Steiner and Gross v. Poland*, 4 Annual Digest 291 (1928); and Georges Kaeckenbeeck, *The International Experiment of Upper Silesia* (London, 1942), pp. 49–54. One could also refer to *North American Dredging Company*, 4 RIAA 26 (1926), para. 6.

[323] Cf. Lauterpacht, *Development by the Permanent Court*, pp. 52–3, Brierly, YILC 1950-II, p. 229, note 24; Arnold D. McNair, *The Law of Treaties: British Practice and Opinions* (2nd edn, Oxford, 1961), p. 337; Ian Brownlie, 'The Place of the Individual in International Law' (1964) 50 *Virginia Law Review* 435 at 440; Wolfgang Friedmann, *The Changing Structure of International Law* (London, 1964), p. 239, note 17; and Christine Chinkin, *Third Parties in International Law* (Oxford, 1993), p. 13, note 63. See also Waldock, YILC 1964-II, p. 46 and the ensuing debate, YILC 1964-I, pp. 114–19. For a broad reading, see Oppenheim/Lauterpacht, *International Law*, vol. 1, p. 506; Paul W. Gormley, *The Procedural Status of the Individual before International and Supranational Tribunals* (The Hague, 1966), p. 40; and James Crawford, *International Law as an Open System: Selected Essays* (London, 2002), p. 27. See also in respect of the *LaGrand Case*, ICJ Reports [2001] 466 at para. 77: R. Y. Jennings, 'The *LaGrand* Case' (2002) 1 *LPICT* 13 at 45–9; and Ole Spiermann, 'The *LaGrand* Case and the Individual as a Subject of International Law' (2003) 58 *Zeitschrift für öffentliches Recht* 197 at 206–11.

Schools case and the *Communities* opinion on the conception of a minority and other minorities issues,[324] both interpreting and justifying the relevant parts of the minorities scheme. In addition, there was the *Greco-Turkish Agreement* opinion, termed by one commentator 'a most "spirited" advice',[325] in which the Permanent Court, very much relying on teleological interpretation, and a doctrine of implied powers, advised as to who had the competence to decide whether cases pending before a mixed commission should be referred to 'arbitration'.[326]

However, the most controversial decisions, providing some new examples of the use of international legal argument, were not these decisions on the merits of disputes, but a number of judgments concerning the Permanent Court's contentious jurisdiction, namely the *Loans* cases and the second and third phases of the *Free Zones* case. These proceedings also introduced some of the new judges who had been elected to fill the vacancies created by the resignation of Judge Moore and the deaths of Judges Finlay and Weiss.

Judge Hughes, the Loans *cases and Judge Fromageot*

Following the exceedingly long ordinary session in 1927, Judge Moore resigned. This was, according to a letter from President Anzilotti, 'a very hard blow to this Body', and, according to Judge Huber, 'the heaviest loss which the Court may suffer'.[327] The 'main reason' for Judge Moore's resignation was his desire to put out a collection of arbitral awards which he had been preparing for several years.[328] He found that this task was not consistent with remaining on the bench; for '[m]y share in the work of the Court was so heavy that I had always found it impossible, when at The Hague, to do anything else'.[329] Indeed, as for the ordinary session of 1927, he had stayed until the end 'bearing, with Huber and

---

[324] *Rights of Minorities in Upper Silesia (Minority Schools)*, Series A No. 15 (1928) at 32–4; and *Interpretation of the Convention between Greece and Bulgaria Respecting Reciprocal Emigration, Signed at Neuilly-sur-Seine on November 27th, 1919 (Question of the 'Communities')*, Series B No. 17 (1930) at 21.

[325] Andreae, *An Important Chapter*, p. 110.

[326] *Interpretation of the Greco-Turkish Agreement of December 1st, 1926 (Final Protocol, Article IV)*, Series B No. 16 (1928) at 18–19, 22, 24–5 and 26.

[327] See Anzilotti to Moore, 23 April 1928, Moore papers 176 and Huber to Moore, 23 April 1928, Moore papers 176, respectively.

[328] Moore to Drummond, 11 April 1928, Moore to Anzilotti, 12 April 1928 and Moore to Huber, 12 April and 7 May 1928, all Moore papers 176. See also Series E No. 4 (1927–8) at 20–1; and Max Huber, 'Schiedsrichterliche und richterliche Streiterledigung: Ein Überblick' (1961/6) 56 *Die Friedens-Warte* 105 at 109.

[329] Moore to Cardozo, 24 May 1928, Moore papers 176.

Anzilotti, a burden of work that precluded attention to anything else'.[330]
In September 1928, President Anzilotti wrote to Moore:

I . . . think the present a fitting moment to write and tell you how much my colleagues and I have felt your absence at the 13th and 14th sessions, and to repeat how much we appreciate that devotion to duty with which you, though far from your home, attended, during six years, the Sessions of the Court, and how we valued your contribution to its deliberations and your help in framing its judgments and opinions.

The sound advice which your past experience enabled you to afford us on all occasions was of the greatest assistance in enabling us to uphold the prestige of the Court during the earliest and perhaps most critical period.[331]

For his part, Moore objected to 'the popular impression of some restful sea voyages and refreshing care-free summers on the North Sea, marred only by occasional presence at the reading of a judgment or opinion that came out of the air'.[332] Quite to the contrary, Moore found that '[t]he discussions in the Chambre de Conseil, which, in a body made up as the Court is, necessarily occupy nine-tenths of the judges' time, are also far more onerous and wearing than a person who had not taken part in them could appreciate'.[333] His work on *International Adjudications Ancient and Modern* began to come out in 1929. As regards the introduction on adjudication of international disputes in the first volume, Moore wrote the following to Professor Borchard:

What I have prepared is, in its full development, a treatise on the subject, includ-ing the question of the adequacy of international law as it now stands for the purposes of an international judicial tribunal. This question is discussed ana-lytically, and the discussion constitutes in each phase a comparative study of international law and municipal law, with constant stress upon the fact that the rules of the former are derived from the latter.[334]

In previous years these analogies had often been felt in text wholly, or partly, drafted by Moore, the Permanent Court's advisory jurisdiction being an obvious example, and Judge Moore's dissenting opinion in *The Lotus* another.

Moore's successor, Charles Evans Hughes, a former Supreme Court Jus-tice and Secretary of State and a keen supporter of the Permanent Court,

---

[330] Moore to Stone, 30 March 1928, Moore papers 176.
[331] Anzilotti to Moore, 15 September 1928, Moore papers 176.
[332] Moore to Cardozo, 24 May 1928, Moore papers 176.
[333] Moore to Root, 24 May 1928, Moore papers 176 and Root papers 143.
[334] Moore to Borchard, 12 January 1929, Borchard papers 7.94.

was elected in September 1928 and was present at the two sessions in 1929, the sixteenth and the seventeenth, but he resigned the following year, having been appointed Chief Justice of the United States Supreme Court.[335] During his short career at the Permanent Court, Judge Hughes exercised a strong influence on his colleagues and, according to his biographer, he 'was a member of every drafting committee selected during his summer at The Hague'.[336] In Deputy-Judge Negulesco's words, Judge Hughes 'apportait à nos délibérations un intérêt et un agrément toutes spéciaux'.[337] Upon Judge Hughes' resignation, Judge Huber wrote the following lines:

I feel obliged to thank you with some lines for the admirable work you have done in the Court during the last session. I had often been very much discouraged, especially since Mr Moore and Lord Finlay had left the Court. When you came in with your immense legal and judicial experience, your broad conceptions of a real statesman and your personality which inspires unlimited confidence, the conditions of work in the Court were entirely changed. The whole atmosphere was changed to such a degree that my decision, otherwise beyond discussion for me, to withdraw from the Court at the end of the period, was considerably shaken.[338]

In the *Serbian Loans* case (as well as in the *Brazilian Loans* case), the first phase of the *Free Zones* case and the *River Oder* case, President Anzilotti and Judge Hughes were members of the drafting committees, together with a third member of the bench. Whereas President Anzilotti was a prominent international lawyer, and according to Huber 'der feinste und schärfste juristische Geist, der mir im Leben begegnet ist',[339] it has

---

[335] As for Judge Hughes' election, see *Records of Assembly: Plenary* 1928, pp. 72–3.

[336] See Merlo J. Pusey, *Charles Evans Hughes* (New York, 1963), pp. 643–4; and also Tobin to Secretary of State, 28 August 1929, NARA 500 C114/849. As to the general feeling, see Tobin to Secretary of State, 24 May 1929, NARA 500 C114/801. Hughes would seem to have continued to exercise influence: see Edward McWhinney, 'The Role and Mission of the International Court in an Era of Historical Transition' in Nandasiri Jasentuliyana (ed.), *Perspectives on International Law: Essays in Honour of Judge Manfred Lachs* (The Hague, 1995), p. 217 at p. 229.

[337] Negulesco to Hughes, 27 March 1930, Hughes papers 5.

[338] Huber to Hughes, 15 March 1930, Hughes papers 5. For his part, Judge Loder referred to Judge Hughes as 'that first-class man and first-class jurist': Loder to Moore, undated [1931], Moore papers 64. Upon his resignation, Judge Hughes had been told by Judge Loder that '[y]ou had brought such a good, fresh, wholesome breeze in it; it is a blow we shall not easily overcome': Loder to Hughes, February 1930, Hughes papers 5.

[339] Huber, 'Epilog zu Denkwürdigkeiten', p. 7 (translation: 'the finest and sharpest legal mind whom I have ever met'); see also Series E No. 4 (1927–8) at 28; and (1952) 44-II *Annuaire*, pp. 445–6.

been said about Judge Hughes that '[i]n part because he believed that international law and domestic law had a common base, and in part because of simple provincialism, Hughes perceived a substantial degree of continuity between the two'.[340] Moore recorded the following about his successor:

Mr Hughes was then promptly elected, but he resigned early in February, 1930, on his appointment by President Hoover as Chief Justice of the United States. In this position full play could be given to his exceptional gifts. On the Permanent Court of International Justice, he no doubt found himself handicapped by his want of knowledge of foreign languages and particularly of French. On talking with him afterwards concerning his experiences on the Permanent Court of International Justice, I found that he had a limited appreciation of the capacities of his colleagues, and notably of Anzilotti, the Italian Judge, a man of exceptional learning, exceeding industry and rare impartiality.[341]

Judge Hughes being more of a national lawyer, his influence seemed to have been most felt in the two *Loans* cases.[342] Both the *Serbian Loans* case between France and the Serb-Croat-Slovene State and the *Brazilian Loans* case between France and Brazil brought under special agreements, which were decided on the same day, turned on national law regulating various bonds held by French nationals. These two cases represented quite a challenge to some members, though probably not to Judge Hughes.

Previously, in the *Upper Silesia* case, the Permanent Court had agreed to give an 'abstract' or 'declaratory' judgment on whether a particular Polish law was in accordance with the Geneva Convention. On that occasion the Permanent Court had argued that '[f]rom the standpoint of International Law and of the Court which is its organ, municipal laws are merely facts which express the will and constitute the activities of States, in the same manner as do legal decisions or

---

[340] Richard D. Friedman, 'Charles Evans Hughes as International Lawyer' (1996) 90 *American Society Proceedings* 143 at 147; cf. Charles Evans Hughes, *The Supreme Court of the United States: Its Foundation, Methods and Achievements: An Interpretation* (New York, 1928), pp. 115–17 and 137–40. On the so-called 'Hughes doctrine' in the history of American constitutional law: see Hughes in (1929) 23 *American Society Proceedings*, pp. 194–6; and Louis Henkin, *Foreign Affairs and the United States Constitution* (2nd edn, Oxford, 1996), p. 197.

[341] John Bassett Moore, 'Resignation as a Judge of the Permanent Court of International Justice', undated, Moore papers 296-23.

[342] Cf. W. E. Beckett, 'Decisions of the Permanent Court of International Justice on Points of Law and Procedure of General Application' (1930) 11 *BYIL* 1 at 19–20.

administrative measures'.[343] To put it differently, in this context the Permanent Court conceived of the state as an international law subject, as opposed to a national sovereign.[344] And so, although the Permanent Court had no jurisdiction to give a – non-binding – advisory opinion at the request of states,[345] it could examine the conformity of a law to a treaty, just like other 'activities of States'.[346] The Permanent Court made no secret, however, that it would not go into a legal analysis of German or Polish national law 'save as an incidental or preliminary point',[347] and it upheld a clear-cut distinction between itself and national courts.[348]

In its final judgment on the merits in the *Chorzów Factory* case, the Permanent Court had articulated two principles relating to its contentious jurisdiction. On the one hand, it had referred to 'the general character of an international tribunal [*juridiction internationale*] which, in principle, has cognizance only of interstate relations'.[349] On the other hand, the Permanent Court had held that it 'is always competent once . . . [the parties] have accepted its jurisdiction'.[350] There was a tension between these two statements, for what if states under a Special Agreement submitted a dispute to the Permanent Court not limited to or even

---

[343] *Case concerning Certain German Interests in Polish Upper Silesia* (Merits), Series A No. 7 (1926) at 19; and see also *Interpretation of Judgments Nos. 7 and 8 (the Chorzów Factory)*, Series A No. 13 (1927) at 20–1.

[344] Cf. Krystyna Marek, 'Les Rapports entre le droit international et le droit interne à la lumière de la jurisprudence de la Cour permanente de Justice internationale' (1962) 66 *RGDIP* 260 at 268–94.

[345] See *Case concerning Certain German Interests in Polish Upper Silesia* (Jurisdiction), Series A No. 6 (1925) at 21; and *Case concerning Certain German Interests in Polish Upper Silesia* (Merits), Series A No. 7 (1926) at 34–5; likewise *Interpretation of the Greco-Bulgarian Agreement of December 9th, 1927 (Caphandaris–Molloff Agreement)*, Series A/B No. 45 (1932) at 87; but see Judge Anzilotti's dissenting opinion in *Interpretation of the Statute of the Memel Territory* (Merits), Series A/B No. 49 (1932) at 349–50.

[346] Cf. Anzilotti, *Cours*, p. 57.

[347] *Case concerning Certain German Interests in Polish Upper Silesia* (Merits), Series A No. 7 (1926) at 42 and also 19. See also *The Mavrommatis Jerusalem Concessions* (Merits), Series A No. 5 (1925) at 28–9; *Case concerning Certain German Interests in Polish Upper Silesia* (Jurisdiction), Series A No. 6 (1925) at 25; and Judge Anzilotti in *Interpretation of Judgments Nos. 7 and 8 (the Chorzów Factory)*, Series A No. 13 (1927) at 26.

[348] *Case concerning Certain German Interests in Polish Upper Silesia* (Jurisdiction), Series A No. 6 (1925) at 20; and similarly *Case concerning Certain German Interests in Polish Upper Silesia* (Merits), Series A No. 7 (1926) at 33–4 and 46; see also *Case concerning the Factory at Chorzów* (Claim for Indemnity) (Jurisdiction), Series A No. 9 (1927) at 25.

[349] *Case concerning the Factory at Chorzów* (Claim for Indemnity) (Merits), Series A No. 17 (1928) at 27 and also 28; cf. *Interpretation of the Greco-Turkish Agreement of December 1st, 1926 (Final Protocol, Article IV)*, Series B No. 16 (1928) at 23.

[350] *Ibid.*, p. 37, referring to *Rights of Minorities in Upper Silesia (Minority Schools)*, Series A No. 15 (1928) at 22–3.

concerned with 'interstate relations'? This was the question raised by the *Loans* cases.

In the *Serbian Loans* case, the Permanent Court examined its jurisdiction *ex officio* because, as made clear in the dissenting opinions of Judge Pessôa and Judge *ad hoc* Novacovitch,[351] the case 'seems at first sight to constitute a departure from the principles which the Court, in previous judgments, has laid down with regard to the conditions under which a State may bring before it cases relating to the private rights of its nationals'.[352] Although the dispute had been submitted to the Permanent Court under a Special Agreement, therefore being 'admissible as far as considerations of form are concerned',[353] Article 14 of the Covenant limited the Permanent Court's competence to 'international disputes'. As in the *Mavrommatis* case, the Permanent Court relied on the principle of diplomatic protection, yet it also had to argue that it could decide a case on the basis of national law. 'From a general point of view', the *motifs* read, 'it must be admitted that the true function [*fonction propre*] of the Court is to decide disputes between States or Members of the League of Nations on the basis of international law: Article 38 of the Statute contains a clear indication to this effect.'[354] That being said, the Permanent Court noted that according to Article 36(2) of the Statute states could agree to the Permanent Court having compulsory jurisdiction with regard to disputes concerning 'the existence of any fact which, if established, would constitute a breach of an international obligation'.[355] The Permanent Court inferred that 'it would be scarcely accurate to say that only questions of international law may form the subject of a decision of the Court'.

It was not clear, however, that the Permanent Court's jurisdiction covered questions of fact that did not have a bearing on 'an international obligation'. Although holding that the facts 'may be of any kind', the *motifs* did not quote the *Upper Silesia* case for the principle that international law treated national laws as mere facts, a principle on which President Anzilotti and Judge Hughes might have had different

---

[351] *Case concerning the Payment of Various Serbian Loans issued in France*, Series A No. 20 (1929) at 62–5 and 76–80 respectively; Judge Pessôa took a very strict view on the Permanent Court's jurisdiction: see his individual note reproduced in Pessôa, *Côrte permanente*, pp. 236–7; and also Laurita Pessôa Raja Gabaglia, *Epitacio Pessôa (1865–1942)* (Sao Paolo, 1951), pp. 775–6. On the other hand, the Permanent Court's jurisdiction was not questioned in the dissenting opinion of Judge de Bustamante, but see de Bustamante, *World Court*, p. 180.

[352] Series A No. 20 (1929) at 16.   [353] *Ibid.*, p. 17.   [354] *Ibid.*, p. 19.   [355] *Ibid.*

views.[356] Instead, the Permanent Court relied on a presumption of jurisdiction flowing from the existence of the Special Agreement.[357] In the end, internationalism and 'the general character of an international tribunal' yielded to consent as the Permanent Court's supreme guide, although, as emphasised in the *Brazilian Loans* case, 'the Court, which is a tribunal of international law, and which, in this capacity, is deemed itself to know what this law is, is not obliged also to know the municipal law of the various countries'.[358]

The judgment in the *Serbian Loans* case summarised developments that had occurred in private international law since the second half of the nineteenth century, a period characterised by extensive and divergent codifications in different systems of national law and an accelerating number of decisions rendered by national courts. Lawyers continued to share the ideal that, to use the words of Friedrich Carl von Savigny taken from his nominal contribution published in 1849, 'in cases of conflict of laws, the same legal relations . . . have to expect the same decision whether the judgment be pronounced in this state or in that'.[359] But at the beginning of the twentieth century, private international law had in practice come to be categorised with national law (and the national principle of self-containedness); these could no longer be issues concerning the interests of a plurality of states that, at least *prima facie*, came within international law, albeit for some decades this development had no great impact on the *Buchrecht*. While Hegel and John Austin did not impress lawyers in need of international law with their critique of the (international) legal character of public international law,[360] the parallel attack led by Carl Georg von Wächter and others, including Anzilotti, against the international (legal) character of private international law eventually prevailed,[361] or so it seemed. To subsequent generations, private

[356] Cf. Paul De Vineuil, 'La Cour permanente de Justice internationale en 1929' (1930) 11 *RDILC* 749 at 775.
[357] Series A No. 20 (1929) at 19; and see Åke Hammarskjöld, 'The Permanent Court of International Justice and its Place in International Relations' (1930) 9 *International Affairs* 467 at 485; cf. K. Lipstein, 'The Place of the Calvo Clause in International Law' (1945) 22 *BYIL* 130 at 142-3.
[358] *Case concerning the Payment in Gold of Brazilian Federal Loans contracted in France*, Series A No. 21 (1929) at 124.
[359] Friedrich Carl von Savigny, *A Treatise on the Conflict of Laws* (2nd edn, Edinburgh, 1880), pp. 69-70 (originally published 1849).
[360] Cf. G. W. F. Hegel, *Grundlinien der Philosophie des Rechts* (Cambridge, 1991), pp. 366-71 (originally published 1821); and John Austin, *The Province of Jurisprudence Determined* (Cambridge, 1995), pp. 20, 112 and 124 (originally published 1832).
[361] Cf. Carl Georg von Wächter, 'Über die Collision der Privatrechtsgesetze verschiedener Staaten' (1841) 24 *Archiv für die Civilistische Praxis* 230 at 237-40, 254, 261-5 and 311;

international law no longer found its justification in notions of comity between nations or the like but perhaps rather in theories of vested or acquired rights or simple common sense.[362] According to the *Serbian Loans* case:

Any contract which is not a contract between states in their capacity as subjects of international law is based on the municipal law of some country. The question as to which this law is forms the subject of that branch of law which is at the present day usually described as private international law or the doctrine of the conflict of laws. The rules thereof may be common to several states and may even be established by international conventions or customs, and in the latter case may possess the character of true international law governing the relations between states. But apart from this, it has to be considered that these rules form part of municipal law.[363]

Significantly, these observations were followed by paragraphs that conveyed the impression of the Permanent Court being guided by principles external to particular systems of national law when choosing the applicable law. Thus, having laid out its general approach to choice of law in a few sweeping statements, the Permanent Court noted that 'this would seem to be in accord with the practice of municipal courts in the absence of rules of municipal law concerning the settlement of conflicts of law'.[364] In other words, the *Serbian Loans* case alluded to doctrinal approaches to private international law by many considered overcome, such as Joseph Story's 'extra-municipal principles',[365] or von Savigny's 'international common law of nations having intercourse with one another',[366] which in turn indicated some need for complementing national law in cases such as the one before the Permanent Court. But, no doubt, it might also just have been that the Permanent Court was unwilling to adopt a particular *lex fori*, certainly an exotic notion in the

and see Dionisio Anzilotti, *Corsi di diritto internazionale privato e processuale* (Padua, 1996), pp. 91–115 and 387–92 (reproducing publications from 1918 and 1925); cf. Dionisio Anzilotti, *Studi critici di diritto internazionale private* (Rocca S. Casciano, 1898), pp. 117–30; and Dionisio Anzilotti, *Il diritto internazionale nei giudizi interni* (Bologna, 1905), pp. 122–58; see also Antonio Sanchez de Bustamante y Sirvén, *Derecho internacional privado* (3rd edn, Havana, 1943), vol. 1, pp. 22–7, 40–2 and 49–51.

[362] E.g., Arthur Nussbaum, 'Rise and Fall of the Law-of-Nations Doctrine in the Conflict of Laws' (1942) 42 *Columbia Law Review* 189. As for the doctrine of vested rights, see, notably, A. V. Dicey, *A Digest of the Law of England with Reference to the Conflict of Laws* (London, 1896), pp. 5, 9–10, 15 and 22–32; and Joseph H. Beale, *A Treatise on the Conflict of Laws* (New York, 1935), vol. 1, p. 64, and vol. 3, pp. 1967–75; and also John Westlake, *A Treatise on Private International Law* (7th edn by Norman Bentwich, London, 1925), p. 22.

[363] Series A No. 20 (1929) at 41.   [364] *Ibid.*

[365] Joseph Story, *Commentaries on the Conflict of Laws* (8th edn by Melville M. Bigelow, Boston, 1883), p. 10.

[366] Von Savigny, *Treatise on Conflict of Laws*, p. 70.

context of an international court, and approach private international law in the same way as a national court.

Be that as it may, what ultimately proved attractive to the Permanent Court was the principle of party autonomy seen against a background coloured by the principle that 'a sovereign State . . . cannot be presumed to have made the substance of its debt and the validity of the obligations accepted by it in respect thereof, subject to any law other than its own'.[367] Accordingly, despite the contention of the Serb-Croat-Slovene Government, the Permanent Court found Serbian law to be applicable. But then another caveat was entered as French law indeed applied to certain aspects of the case due to 'a generally accepted principle that a State is entitled to regulate its own currency'.[368] And so, having invoked two different principles that were both closely associated with the national principle of self-containedness, the Permanent Court ended up with French law. However, the argument of the Serb-Croat-Slovene Government that French law rendered a clause for payment in gold or at gold value null and void was met with scepticism on the bench. Moreover, the Permanent Court conveniently declined to undertake its own construction of French law; it 'would not be in conformity with the task for which the Court has been established and would not be compatible with the principles governing the selection of its members'.[369]

In a sense the *Loans* cases were to the Permanent Court's jurisdiction what the *Jurisdiction of Courts* opinion had been to the subjects of treaty rights and obligations: a manifestation of potential differences between the international law of coexistence and the international law of cooperation, and thus between the conception of the state as a national sovereign and the conception of the state as an international sovereign. In both instances the Permanent Court had given preference to the latter conception, thereby upholding the hierarchically superior position of the dynamic structure of international legal argument. The somewhat erratic categorisations in the *Serbian Loans* case of private international law issues within the static structure of international legal argument does not detract from this conclusion. Rather, it suggests that the uncertainty in respect of categorisation that had split the Permanent Court evenly in *The Lotus*, regarding the related issue of jurisdiction to legislate, persisted.

The *Loans* cases not only introduced Judge Hughes and a possibly less principled view as to the division between national and international law. Judge Weiss having died, the French Government had selected Henri

---

[367] Series A No. 20 (1929) at 42.   [368] *Ibid.*, p. 44.   [369] *Ibid.*, p. 46.

Fromageot, the *jurisconsulte* to the Ministry of Foreign Affairs, as a judge *ad hoc*.[370] Fromageot was responsible for the French Government's campaign, launched at the Ninth Assembly in September 1928, to revise the Statute.[371] According to Professor Hudson, the resolution of the Ninth Assembly on this issue had been the work of Fromageot and 'due in part to a dissatisfaction with the Court's judgment in the case of "The Lotus"'.[372] In March 1929, various amendments were worked out by Fromageot and eleven other members of a Committee of Jurists, including Elihu Root; they were appended to the Revision Protocol, which was adopted later the same year, subject to ratification. President Anzilotti and Judge Huber had taken part in the meetings of the Committee, but they had made it known that they did not see the need for a revision.[373] Indeed, they regarded the campaign as a scarcely veiled attack on the Permanent Court, and their and possibly also other judges' opposition to Fromageot was quite strong.[374] Judge Huber, who had regarded the oral arguments in the *Loans* cases as 'really interesting', wrote to Moore:

---

[370] Cf. H. Lauterpacht, 'Dissenting Opinions of National Judges and the Revision of the Statute of the Court' (1930) 11 *BYIL* 182 at 183–4;

[371] See *Records of Assembly: Committees* 1928, pp. 33–4 and 40; Hammarskjöld to Hudson, 22 November 1928, Hudson papers 82.4; Hurst to Campbell, 31 January 1929, FO 371 W1009/21/98; and also Committee of Jurists on the Statute of the Permanent Court of International Justice, 'Minutes of the Session Held at Geneva, March 11th–19th, 1929' (League of Nations Document C.166.M.66.1929.V, 1929), p. 94.

[372] Hudson to Root, 19 January 1929, Hudson papers 88.9; cf. Manley O. Hudson, *The Permanent Court of International Justice, 1920–1942* (2nd edn, New York, 1943), p. 132.

[373] Committee of Jurists, 'Minutes', pp. 8 and 94; cf. Hammarskjöld, 'Neuvième session', pp. 667–77. See also Oda to Hammarskjöld, 1 April 1931, Hammarskjöld papers 477; and Åke Hammarskjöld, 'Quelques aspects de la fonction consultative de la Cour permanente de Justice internationale' in *Festgabe für Max Huber zum sechzigsten Gerburtstag 28. Dezember 1934* (Zurich, 1934), p. 146 at pp. 162–3. It would seem to have been the hope of some judges that the revision had been undertaken not by the League of Nations but by a general diplomatic conference: see Norweb to Secretary of State, 12 December 1928, NARA 500 C114/735; and also Tobin to Secretary of State, 23 April 1926, NARA 500 C114/507, referring a conversation with President Huber.

[374] Cf. Hammarskjöld to [Hjalmar] Hammarskjöld, 23 March 1929 and 10 June 1929, both Hammarskjöld papers 30. This was also made clear in a publication in Hammarskjöld's own name in which the idea of 'la suprématie de Genève' was rejected and a general 'réexamen' of the Statute said to resemble 'le jeu d'enfant qui consiste à démonter les jouets pour voir ce qu'il y a dedans': see Hammarskjöld, 'Neuvième session', pp. 676–7. One purpose of this publication, which had been approved by President Anzilotti and Judge Huber (see Hammarskjöld to de Visscher, 14 November 1928, Hammarskjöld papers 488), had been to discourage individual members of the Permanent Court other than President Anzilotti and Judge Huber, the latter occupying the position of vice-president, from assisting the Committee of Jurists; cf. *ibid.*, pp. 685–6; and see Scavenius to Munch, 4 April 1929, Rigsarkivet H-12-1.

Since your departure the Court has undergone considerable changes. Your absence has been felt very strongly and we are glad that your seat is now taken by so eminent a lawyer from the US. The succession to the seats of Mr Weiss and Lord Finlay seems now less certain as it had appeared some months ago. Very much depends for the Court's future from these elections which, no doubt, prejudge those of the next years.[375]

Fromageot's career took an important turn two months after the *Loans* cases when, as had been expected, he was elected the new French member of the Permanent Court.[376] His appearance in the *Loans* cases had not impressed the Registrar. In a letter to his father, Hammarskjöld wrote that 'Fromageot är f.ö. en missräkning i domstolen. Liksom Weiss gör han ingenting annat ifråga om positiva insatsa än att peka på kommatering och ända "et" till "ainsi que"'.[377] But, of course, there was a difference between being a judge *ad hoc* and a fully-fledged judge.

The Free Zones *case, Judge Kellogg and Sir Cecil Hurst*

The *Free Zones* case was submitted to the Permanent Court under a Special Agreement between France and Switzerland. The case was dealt with in three 'phases', consisting of two orders in 1929 and 1930 and the final judgment in 1932, due to the controversial character of the Special Agreement. Whereas in the *Loans* cases the Permanent Court had been willing to decide disputes on the basis of national law, in the *Free Zones* case the majority of the Permanent Court distanced themselves from settling a dispute on the basis of extra-legal considerations, referred to in Article 38(2) of the Statute as a decision *ex aequo et bono*. There clearly was a difference between national law and a decision *ex aequo et bono*.

As for the facts, in 1603 and again in 1815–16 various acts had defined the 'free zones'. These were areas close to the Swiss frontier to which goods from Switzerland could be exported without customs duties being levied upon them. On the initiative of France, to which the areas now belonged, Article 435(2) of the Versailles Treaty stipulated that the free zones were 'no longer consistent with present conditions, and that it is for France and Switzerland to come to an agreement together with a view to settling between themselves the status of these territories'.

---

[375] Huber to Moore, 20 May 1929, Moore papers 61.

[376] See *Records of Assembly: Plenary* 1929, pp. 126 and 153.

[377] Hammarskjöld to [Hjalmar] Hammarskjöld, 7 July 1929, Hammarskjöld papers 30 (translation: 'Besides Fromageot is a mistake in the Court. Like Weiss, he does nothing in respect of positive changes than to point to punctuation and change "et" to "ainsi que"').

Having been unable to reach an agreement, France and Switzerland concluded the Special Agreement submitting the matter to the Permanent Court. In an order of 1929 the Permanent Court, acting under Article 1(1) of the Special Agreement, took the view that Article 435 of the Versailles Treaty did not itself abrogate the free zones, one reason being that Switzerland had accepted the Versailles Treaty subject to a reservation as to the zones.[378] Although Judge Nyholm, Deputy-Judge Negulesco and Judge *ad hoc* Dreyfus dissented,[379] the question was straightforward, the order reportedly being drafted by the Registrar.[380] Article 435 was seen as 'an authorization resulting from the disinterested attitude assumed by the Powers which had signed the old treaties'.[381]

Article 1(2) of the Special Agreement then provided that the Permanent Court, 'before pronouncing any judgment, shall accord to the two Parties a reasonable time to settle between themselves the new régime'. In its order, recalling the views previously expressed by Huber and a pronouncement in the *Jaworzina* opinion,[382] the Permanent Court held that:

> the judicial settlement of international disputes, with a view to which the Court has been established, is simply an alternative to the direct and friendly settlement of such disputes between the Parties; and consequently it is for the Court to facilitate, so far as is compatible with its Statute, such direct and friendly settlement.[383]

Yet the Permanent Court was not happy to give an interim decision as to which 'the constitutional provisions' of the Statute was silent, but which was akin to an advisory opinion, characterising it as 'strictly

---

[378] *Case of the Free Zones of Upper Savoy and the District of Gex* (First Phase), Series A No. 22 (1929) at 17–18.

[379] In his dissenting opinion, Judge Nyholm first applied a conception of a common 'legislator' ('how can it be imagined that a legislator should intend to maintain in force rules which he himself declares to be out of date?'), just to effectively abandon the conception of the state as an international law subject towards the end: see *ibid.*, pp. 23–4 and 26–7. Deputy-Judge Negulesco relied mainly on 'the clause rebus sic stantibus': *ibid.*, pp. 29–30, 36 and 39.

[380] See Hammarskjöld to [Hjalmar] Hammarskjöld, 17 August 1929, Hammarskjöld papers 30.

[381] See *Case of Free Zones of Upper Savoy and the District of Gex* (Third Phase), Series A/B No. 46 (1932) at 143 and also 137 and 140–1; similarly, Series A No. 22 (1929) at 16; and *Case of the Free Zones of Upper Savoy and the District of Gex* (Second Phase), Series A No. 24 (1930) at 27. Cf. Huber, *Denkwürdigkeiten*, pp. 131–7 and 145–52.

[382] *Question of Jaworzina (Polish–Czechoslovakian Frontier)*, Series B No. 8 (1923) at 56.

[383] Series A No. 22 (1929) at 13.

exceptional'.[384] True, President Anzilotti had introduced a wide inter-pretation of Article 48 of the Statute, which authorised 'orders for the conduct of the case', but for reasons of formality.[385]

The parties remained unable to reach a compromise as to the future of the zones. In late 1930, the Permanent Court had to confront Article 2 of the Special Agreement, which provided that 'the Court shall, by means of a single judgment rendered in accordance with Article 58 of the Court's Statute . . . settle for a period to be fixed by it and having regard to present conditions, all the questions involved in the execution of paragraph 2 of Article 435 of the Treaty of Versailles'. The two govern-ments had agreed to this text without agreeing on its meaning.[386] They had never abandoned their initial viewpoints articulated at the opening of the negotiations of the Special Agreement. Relying on the formula *ex aequo et bono*, the French Government wanted to vest the Permanent Court with the freedom enjoyed by the two governments if negotiat-ing a solution, the abandonment of the free zones being an option.[387] On the other hand, insisting that in law the free zones had not been abrogated, the Swiss Government merely wanted the Permanent Court to 'readapt' the zones to the new conditions.[388] The Swiss Government associated the Permanent Court's powers with considerations *de lege fer-enda* and, indeed, actual law-making,[389] but only in a narrow sense for it contended that the Permanent Court, a 'tribunal de caractère essen-tiellement juridique et judiciaire', could not disregard existing rights.[390]

By the time of the second phase of the *Free Zones* case, Judge Hughes had resigned and Frank B. Kellogg, another former Secretary of State, had filled the vacancy at the age of seventy-four.[391] In an individual opinion framed before the end of the oral pleadings,[392] Judge Kellogg

---

[384] See also Series A No. 24 (1930) at 14; and Series A/B No. 46 (1932) at 161. Judge Pessôa took exception to this, comparing the interim decision to an advisory opinion: see Series A No. 22 (1929) at 48–9 and also Seventeenth session, *Procès-Verbal* 20 (9 August 1929), reproduced in Pessôa, *Côrte permanente*, pp. 119–20, and his individual note, reproduced *ibid.*, pp. 250–1.

[385] Cf. Series E No. 11 (1934–5) at 95–7; and Series D No. 2, Add.3 (1936) at 830; see also Hudson, *Permanent Court*, pp. 557 and 585.

[386] Cf. Series A/B No. 46 (1932) at 163.

[387] Series C No. 17-I at 32; Series C No. 19-I at 468–77, 1564, 1671, 32–63, 101 and 293–323; and Series C No. 58 at 62–77 and 377–96.

[388] Series C No. 17-I at 142; Series C No. 19-I at 1242–3, 1712–36, 139–74 and 355–84; and Series C No. 58 at 449–53.

[389] Series C No. 19-I at 1227 and 171; and Series C No. 58 at 440–1.

[390] Series C No. 19-I at 373 and 382–3; and Series C No. 58 at 441.

[391] See *Records of Assembly: Plenary* 1930, p. 128.

[392] See Kellogg to Olds, 7 November 1930 and Kellogg to Root, 11 November 1930, both Kellogg papers 41; and also Kellogg to Hudson, 2 February 1931, Kellogg papers 86.4.

adopted an even stricter view than the Swiss Government. He did so by relying on past quotations of fellow Americans combined with the national lawyer's key virtue, the national principle of self-containedness. Matters that according to Judge Kellogg fell 'exclusively within the competence of a sovereign State',[393] and which he dubbed 'political', could not be decided by the Permanent Court even if submitted under a Special Agreement.[394] Indeed, Judge Kellogg took the view that 'it would be fatal to the Court to extend its jurisdiction to the political questions and involve the Court in political controversies which have no place in a Court of Justice'.[395] These were concerns different from those previously expressed by Judge Moore, who regarded Judge Kellogg's mind as presenting a 'muddle' and his individual opinion ('screed') to be 'absurd'.[396]

Judge Kellogg was convinced that the majority of the Permanent Court was in favour of the Permanent Court having jurisdiction,[397] and therefore he regarded his separate opinion as a dissenting opinion. However, side-stepping the general question of jurisdiction, five other members of the bench applied a very strong presumption that the parties did not want the Permanent Court to take into account 'considerations of pure expediency' and so they reached the same conclusion as Judge Kellogg.[398] This group of judges rendered the Permanent Court's order upon the casting vote of President Anzilotti.

This left six judges dissenting because they could 'see no sound reason why the liberty enjoyed by the Court in settling every question involved in the execution of Article 435, paragraph 2, is more restricted than that which the Parties themselves would have enjoyed'.[399] The dissenters were Judges Nyholm and Altamira, Deputy-Judges Yovanovitch and Negulesco, Judge *ad hoc* Dreyfus and also Sir Cecil Hurst, formerly the Legal Adviser

---

[393] Series A No. 24 (1930) at 41. Judge Kellogg was not familiar with the *Nationality Decrees* opinion: see Kellogg to Roseborough, 14 November 1931, Kellogg papers 44.

[394] Series A No. 24 (1930) at 34–8 and 43.

[395] Kellogg to Hudson, 2 February 1931, Kellogg papers 86.4.

[396] Moore to Borchard, 31 December 1931, Borchard papers 7.97. In Moore's view, a precise line between political and non-political questions, however defined, could not be drawn. Moore added that '[i]f parties agree on the formulation of certain issues, and ask a court to decide upon them, especially *ex aequo et bono*, it certainly would require a very extreme case to justify or enable a court to refuse to pass up on them because they were "political"'. In Moore's view, the election of Kellogg was not 'ideal': Moore to Borchard, 15 September 1930, Borchard papers 7.97. See also Lauterpacht, *Function of Law*, pp. 318–20.

[397] Kellogg to Ottis, 20 November 1930 and Kellogg to Hughes, 6 December 1930, both Kellogg papers 41; and Kellogg to Taylor, 28 October 1931, Kellogg papers 44. Similarly, Roseborough to Kellogg, 19 May 1932, Kellogg papers 45.

[398] Series A No. 24 (1930) at 10–11; and also Huber in (1934) 38 *Annuaire*, p. 235.

[399] Series A No. 24 (1930) at 27.

to the British Foreign Office for more than ten years, who in 1929 had filled the vacancy created by the death of Judge Finlay.[400] While Judge Hurst disagreed with Judge Kellogg as to the Permanent Court's right to decline jurisdiction under the Statute, he subscribed, as a matter of principle, to the strict view on the Permanent Court's non-political mission.[401] Like Judge Kellogg, Judge Hurst thought that hardly any international lawyer was international; he would have liked a Permanent Court composed largely of judges who had served in national courts and he himself approached international law as a national lawyer.[402] Judge Hurst was an advocate of the view that 'in many matters there were two different systems of international law, the continental systems and the Anglo-Saxon system'.[403]

It may be added that in his observations, referring to the characteristics distinguishing 'a Court of Justice', Judge Kellogg had said that '[i]t was most certainly a Court of this nature, and not a branch of a foreign office nor a chancellery, of which the Jurists Committee drafted the Statute when they met at The Hague'.[404] This observation was given a twist by some diplomats, for example in a despatch submitted by a United States diplomat at The Hague to the Secretary of State:

This observation is particularly interesting in view of the presence of Monsieur Fromag[e]ot and Sir Cecil Hurst on the Court . . . and in view of the intimation which has been confidentially made to me that Sir Cecil Hurst suddenly changed his point of view with regard to certain aspects of this case, as though in accordance with newly received instructions from his foreign office.

It has always seemed to this Legation a mistake that foreign office politicians such as Fromag[e]ot and Hurst should find a place on this international bench and that so many other members of the Court are professors and theoretical men rather than great lawyers and judges.[405]

---

[400] See *Records of Assembly: Plenary* 1929, pp. 126 and 153.

[401] See Series D No. 2, Add.3 (1936) at 372; Cecil Hurst, 'World Court' in Philip Gibbs (ed.), *Bridging the Atlantic* (London, 1943), p. 180 at p. 201; and John Eppstein, *Ten Years' Life of the League of Nations: A History of the Origins of the League and of its Development from AD 1919 to 1929* (London, 1929), p. 41. See also Johnson to Secretary of State, 16 February 1931, NARA 500 C114/1250.

[402] Cf. Hurst, 'World Court', pp. 190, 193 and 194; Cecil Hurst, 'The Permanent Court of International Justice' (1943) 59 *LQR* 312 at 325; and Cecil Hurst, 'A Plea for the Codification of International Law on New Lines' (1946) 32 *Grotius Transactions* 135 at 138; cf. *ibid.*, p. 150.

[403] Hurst in *Records of Assembly: Committees* 1920, p. 373; and see also Hurst's memorandum, September 1921, FO 371 W9576/22/98 and Hurst's minute, 30 November 1928, FO 371 W11377/309/98.

[404] Series A No. 24 (1930) at 37.

[405] Johnson to Secretary of State, 17 December 1930, NARA 500 C114/1218.

For his part, Judge Hurst had ended a conversation with the same diplomat 'by remarking that while to the mind of an Anglo-Saxon lawyer Judge Kellogg's observations were sound and irrefutable they can not be grasped by the professors and theoreticians of other nationalities on the Court, and by insinuating that perhaps the observations were made with a view to forwarding membership of the United States in the Court'.[406] A Danish diplomat at The Hague shared the above-quoted views of his American colleague and ventured that the narrowing of the majority in 1930, as compared to the first order of 1929, was an indication of a politicisation of the bench.[407]

The Permanent Court's decision of 1930 was a further order on the ground that 'although the Court, being a Court of justice, cannot disregard rights recognized by it, and base its decision on considerations of pure expediency, nevertheless there is nothing to prevent it, having regard to the advantages which a solution of this kind might present, to offer the Parties, who alone can bring it about, a further opportunity for achieving this end'.[408] This was clearly a convenient result, since, in Kellogg's words, '[t]he Court is in a most terrible muddle with twelve judges and apparently no two judges holding the same opinion'.[409] When subsequently addressing Moore, Judge Kellogg put his observations in a new light:

While the Court did not decide that it has a jurisdiction of purely political and economic questions for which there is no treaty right or principle of law, yet I did not wish France and Switzerland to send this case back to the Court with an amended special agreement which would authorize the Court to pass on any such question.[410]

As it turned out, the Special Agreement remained unchanged and the *Free Zones* case was decided on the merits in 1932. The decision was given by the bench that had sat on the second phase of the case in 1930,[411] the majority of which had indicated the general lines along

---

[406] Johnson to Secretary of State, 16 February 1931, NARA 500 C114/1250.

[407] Scavenius to Munch, 15 December 1930, Rigsarkivet H-12-12.

[408] Series A No. 24 (1930) at 15; and see Anzilotti to Huber, 2 August 1930, Huber papers 23. Behind the scenes, President Anzilotti strongly advocated that the governments reached an agreement: see *Documents diplomatiques suisses, 1848–1945* (Bern, 1979–92), vol. 10, p. 144; and also Series A/B No. 46 (1932) at 161.

[409] Kellogg to Ottis, 20 November 1930, Kellogg papers 41.

[410] Kellogg to Moore, 2 January 1931, Moore papers 172.

[411] Cf. Geneviève Guyomar, *Commentaire du Règlement de la Cour internationale de Justice: interprétation et pratique* (Paris, 1973), pp. 15 and 138–9.

which the case would finally be settled. A majority agreed in restricting the *dispositif* to upholding the old customs line, and a drafting committee was composed of Acting President Anzilotti, Judge Hurst and Deputy-Judge Beichmann.[412] At the same time, Judge Negulesco took a hint dropped by the French Government and held that the Permanent Court did not have jurisdiction,[413] while Judge Altamira engaged in another dissenting opinion, being based on 'governmental psychology',[414] which eventually won the support of Judge Hurst.[415]

As a result, the judgment was supported by the same six judges as the order of 1930, namely Judges Anzilotti, Huber, Kellogg, Loder and Oda and Deputy-Judge Beichmann. The Permanent Court did 'not dispute the rule invoked by the French Government that every Special Agreement, like every clause conferring jurisdiction upon the Court, must be interpreted strictly [*strictement*]',[416] not restrictively (*restrictement*), and it restated the presumption against it being empowered to dispose of rights; this would be 'contrary to the proper function of the Court',[417] which is 'to declare the law'.[418] The Permanent Court's freedom was of a different kind. It was not bound by the submissions of the parties; for 'it must be presumed that the Court enjoys the freedom which normally appertains to it, and that it is able, if such is its opinion, not only to accept one or other of the two propositions, but also to reject them both'.[419] The Permanent Court laid down a residual principle, according to which the territorial sovereignty of France was 'complete in so far as it had not been limited by the provisions of the treaties'.[420] However,

---

[412] See Series A/B No. 46 (1932) at 161–2 and 164–71; cf. *ibid.*, p. 169. See also Kellogg to Roseborough, 18 May 1932, Kellogg papers 45; Kellogg to Root, 8 June 1932, Root papers 148; and Swenson to Secretary of State, 20 June 1932, NARA 500 C114/1441.

[413] See Series A/B No. 46 (1932) at 187–99; and also Judge *ad hoc* Dreyfus, *ibid.*, p. 208, which should be compared to the position taken by the majority, *ibid.*, pp. 163–4. However, see Series C No. 58 at 75 *et seq.* referring twice to the *Eastern Carelia* opinion and also Judge Anzilotti's individual opinion in *Customs Regime between Germany and Austria (Protocol of March 19th, 1931)*, Series A/B No. 41 (1931) at 68–9. See also Roseborough to Kellogg, 12 May 1932, Kellogg papers 45; and Kammerer's despatch, 19 August 1932, Quai d'Orsay 2400C.

[414] Series A/B No. 46 (1932) at 182–3.

[415] Kellogg to Roseborough, 2 June 1932 and 3 June 1932, both Kellogg papers 45. Judge Altamira's preliminary note is kept by the Peace Palace Library, file Z 397-23. Hammarskjöld did not regard this as a dissent proper: see Hammarskjöld to [Hjalmar] Hammarskjöld, 26 June 1932, Hammarskjöld papers 30.

[416] Series A/B No. 46 (1932) at 138–9; see also Judge Huber in Series D No. 2, Add.1 (1926) at 88. Cf. as to admissibility, Series A/B No. 46 (1932) at 155–6.

[417] Series A/B No. 46 (1932) at 153 and also 161–2.

[418] *Ibid.*, p. 138.   [419] *Ibid.*   [420] *Ibid.*, pp. 164 and 166.

in response to the contention of the Swiss Government that the French authorities could not collect certain duties and taxes at the political frontier, it went further, holding that 'no such limitation necessarily ensues from the old provisions relating to the free zones' and added that 'in case of doubt a limitation of sovereignty must be construed restrictively'.[421] This statement did not relate to 'French fiscal legislation'; for even if that legislation had been in accordance with international law, the question was whether it could be enforced at the frontier. Yet the national principle of self-containedness had caused a presumption, even if only in respect of the territorial state's exercise of power on its own territory. This represented a wide departure from the *Danube* opinion and *The Lotus*, although the narrow majority in the *Free Zones* case also encompassed Judges Huber and Anzilotti.[422] It also gave a new function to a doctrine of abuse of rights, compared to the earlier pronouncement in the *Upper Silesia* case.[423] According to the Permanent Court:

[a] reservation must be made as regards the case of abuses of a right, since it is certain that France must not evade the obligation to maintain the zones by erecting a customs barrier under the guise of a control cordon. But an abuse cannot be presumed by the Court.[424]

If this consideration had had any impact on the Permanent Court's analysis it would seem to have been to the effect of a further restrictive interpretation. While the above-mentioned principle of restrictive interpretation led the Permanent Court to hold that a control cordon was not prohibited under the free zones regime, the doctrine of abuse of rights would seem in turn to have the potential on the basis of this freedom to evade other obligations, though admitted, such as 'the obligation to maintain the zones'. Both steps were in conflict with the international lawyer's approach to international legal argument that had taken form during the 1920s. They may have been caused by members of the narrow majority to whom a national lawyer's approach felt more natural, a change in the hierarchy between the structures of international legal argument which followed logically from the conception of the state as a

[421] *Ibid.*, p. 167; and similarly Series A No. 24 (1930) at 12.
[422] *The Case of the SS Lotus*, Series A No. 10 (1927) at 18–19; and *Jurisdiction of the European Commission of the Danube between Galatz and Braila*, Series B No. 14 (1927) at 63–4; but see, of course, *Case of the SS Wimbledon*, Series A No. 1 (1923) at 37.
[423] See *Case concerning Certain German Interests in Polish Upper Silesia* (Merits), Series A No. 7 (1926) at 30. Cf. Lauterpacht, *Development by the Permanent Court*, pp. 54–5; and García Amador, YILC 1960-II, p. 59.
[424] Series A/B No. 46 (1932) at 167.

national sovereign suggested by Judge Kellogg, possibly among others.[425] Alternatively, they may just be seen as another expression of the Permanent Court making the least of its jurisdiction and wanting to close an exceptional proceeding.[426] If so, it contradicted a principle of interpretation articulated in the first order in 1929, according to which 'in case of doubt, the clauses of a special agreement by which a dispute is referred to the Court must, if it does not involve doing violence to their terms, be construed in a manner enabling the clauses themselves to have appropriate effects'.[427]

Certainly Huber, for one, wanted the case to find a final solution. As for his experiences in 1932, he wrote the following to Moore:

I have now come back to the Court after an absence of one year and a half; that offers me an opportunity of seeing the Court with fresh eyes and with some detachment. But the impression is the same as I had during the last years of my term and I do not regret that I do no longer belong to the Court. The collaboration in a Court is satisfactory only when the large majority of the members have a large common ground of legal conceptions in international law and . . . the same sense and conception of judicial responsibility. I do not know what the new Court is, but I think, though it may be better than the old one, I should not find there the homogeneity and comprehension which seem to me indispensable for a really happy collaboration. How gratefully I remember yours![428]

Conclusions

The Permanent Court had a thought-provoking record in the 1920s. The United Kingdom was generally successful before the Permanent Court, so was Germany, with the exception of *The Wimbledon*, an early case brought by the Principal Allied and Associated Powers in the immediate aftermath of the Versailles Treaty. On the other hand, France, Turkey and

---

[425] As for the doctrine of abuse of rights, Judge Anzilotti later called it 'an extremely delicate one', making it seem less likely that he was among those who had promoted the doctrine in the context of the *Free Zones* case; cf. *The Electricity Company of Sofia and Bulgaria* (Preliminary Objection), Series A/B No. 77 (1939) at 98.

[426] Cf. Series A/B No. 46 (1932) at 168. And see *ibid.*, pp. 169–70; and the following award, *Affaire des Zones franches*, 3 RIAA 1455 (1933).

[427] Series A No. 22 (1929) at 13. The principle has been referred to by the Inter-American Court of Human Rights: see notably *Rodríguez Case* (Preliminary Objections), 95 ILR 237 (1987) at para. 30.

[428] Huber to Moore, 21 May 1932, Moore papers 64. As for the 'new' Court, Huber later wrote to Moore that he did 'not regret to belong no more to the Court in its present composition': Huber to Moore, 8 August 1934, Moore papers 67.

Poland were unsuccessful in most proceedings in which they declared an interest. Perhaps the cases that Poland lost to Germany were difficult to defend in legal terms. The same may also apply to many of Turkey's cases (leaving aside *The Lotus*), yet it has been said that the *Mosul* opinion, 'more than any other of the Court's Advisory Opinions, involved legal choices based on inarticulate major premises'.[429] When preparing the amendment to the Rules allowing for judges *ad hoc* in advisory proceedings, Judges Loder, Moore and Anzilotti submitted a report according to which 'of all the influences to which men are subject, none is more powerful, more pervasive, or more subtle, than the tie of allegiance that binds them to the land of their homes'.[430]

Representatives of the French Government had no illusions about any separation of international law from politics in the Permanent Court. While Judge Weiss was seen as being exceedingly loyal to his government,[431] other judges were accused of being 'germanophile'.[432] On the other hand, a French diplomat reported that 'les professeurs, dont M. Anzilotti et M. Huber sont les personnifications les plus représentatives, montrent parfois une indifférence excessive aux réalités politiques sur lesquelles ils opèrent et semblemt raffiner sur la beauté abstraite du droit'.[433] Of course, these were personal opinions, which might be more or less justified. Moore recalled a meeting with Loder at which

[w]hile congratulating himself on his exceptional judicial poise and impartiality, he strongly deprecated the general lack of this quality as a menace to the maintenance of an international judicature. From this general deprecation, however, he specially excepted Mr Weiss, whom he associated with himself as an example of freedom from bias or partiality, and of readiness to disregard the interests and sentiments of his own government and people.[434]

---

[429] George Schwarzenberger, *International Law as Applied by International Courts and Tribunals* (London, 1986), vol. 4, p. 245, who seemed to agree with the excessive critique advanced by Verzijl, 'Die Rechtsprechung des Ständigen Internationalen Gerichtshofes', p. 539; cf. Salvioli, 'Jurisprudence', p. 59, note 2; and Carl Schmitt, *Die Kernfrage des Völkerbundes* (Berlin, 1926), pp. 7, 10 and 82.

[430] Series E No. 4 (1927-8) at 75.

[431] See Clausel to Berthelot, 7 November 1927, 23 November 1927 and 29 November 1927, all Quai d'Orsay 2400B; and also Hammarskjöld's memorandum, 7 June 1920, League of Nations Archives 21-4762-88; and Hammarskjöld's note, 12 June 1920, Hammarskjöld papers 477. Cf. *The Case of the SS Lotus*, Series A No. 10 (1927) at 49.

[432] Cf. Benoist's despatch, 19 November 1923, Quai d'Orsay 2400C; Marcilly's despatch, 24 October 1927, Quai d'Orsay 2400B; and Kammerer's despatches, 10 June 1930, Quai d'Orsay 2400B and 26 January 1931, Quai d'Orsay 2400C.

[433] Marcilly's despatch, 24 October 1927, Quai d'Orsay 2400B.

[434] Moore to Finlay, 16 September 1926, Moore papers 177.

Moore's biographer noted about Moore's position that 'he was greatly annoyed by the intrigue for position – the good jobs were those of registrar and president judge – intrigue conducted on both personal and national scales. Thus, Judge Loder, a Dutchman, was elected president judge largely because the French managed to sidetrack Lord Finlay, the leading candidate.'[435]

Political bias would open up a gulf between the Permanent Court's decisions and international legal argument. It would be a serious objection to the analysis in this chapter, but it is also an objection almost impossible to sustain. One may see a link between the personal wealth of some of the original judges, a Western legal culture and the strict principle of vested rights articulated in the Permanent Court's decisions prior to the second general election. But such personal bias, or the general picture of inter-war politics, cannot explain the Permanent Court's decision-making. The leading members of the bench, Judges Huber, Anzilotti and Moore and Deputy-Judge Beichmann, were all respected as independent lawyers, as was Judge Finlay.[436] In his academic writings, Huber made mention of 'sociological' considerations and later he appreciated the emergence of international relations as a separate discipline.[437] This might have made Huber particularly vigilant against intervention that could disturb coexistence, and be contrary to the international law of coexistence, as suggested by the *Nationality Decrees* opinion and the *Mosul* opinion as well as one of his decisions in the *Moroccan Claims*. But Huber was conscious that 'sociology' and international law seldom overlapped. Just after his election, Huber had written to Judge Moore that '[t]he moral responsibility of the Court in deciding the first cases and in giving their argumentation is immense. The world is disgusted with politics of interest and influence and longs for an institution of real impartiality. We must not only be impartial but even try to avoid the appearance of partiality.'[438]

In 1931, Moore wrote to Loder about the Permanent Court that, 'looking back over its record, while we both were members of it, I feel content, especially as regards the vital matter of maintaining a judicial

---

[435] Edwin M. Borchard, *Moore's Memoirs*, undated, Moore papers 217, p. 693.
[436] Cf. Marcilly's despatch, 16 May 1925, Quai d'Orsay 2416; and Fleuriau to Briand, 19 November 1927, Quai d'Orsay 2400B.
[437] Huber, *Koexistenz und Gemeinschaft*, p. 5.
[438] Huber to Moore, 21 October 1921, Moore papers 176.

attitude in its decisions and opinions'.[439] According to Alexander Fachiri, an English barrister who had made the Permanent Court his special interest, '[t]he first Court set a high standard by its judicial impartiality and legal attainments; the Court is now firmly established as a normal and necessary part of our international life, and the task of the future is to build upon the sound foundation already laid'.[440] In particular under the presidencies of Judges Huber and Anzilotti, the Permanent Court had made an attempt to build up a jurisprudence. Professor Schücking had gained some useful experience and rather firm views as to the composition of the bench from his service as a judge *ad hoc* in two proceedings, including *The Wimbledon*. In his view, the ideal was to have on the bench persons 'die sowohl eine ausgedehnte wissenschaftliche Kenntnis des Völkerrechts wie eine praktische Erfahrung in bezug auf aussenpolitische Dinge haben'. Looking back on the 'first' Court, it was Schücking's impression 'dass die richterlichen Ziviljuristen für den Gerichtshof viel gefährlicher sind als die Professoren, weil sie weder aus praktischer politischer Tätigkeit noch aus fachwissenschaftlich völkerrechtlicher Vergangenheit eine Ahnung von den Problemen haben, über die sie zu Gericht sitzen'.[441] In his view, judges with judicial experience were indispensable, yet it would be disastrous to repress the professors (*der Berufsgelehrten*). He added that:

[d]er sicherste Beweis liegt in den Erfahrungen, die man mit der Präsidentschaft gemacht hat. Der erste Präsident Loder ist an sich ein glänzender Jurist gewesen, der als solcher deshalb auch aus dem Advokatenstande in das höchste Tribunal in Holland übernommen worden war. Aber die Führung seiner Präsidentschaft ist nicht nur aus Gründen seiner allzu autoritativen Formen sondern auch deshalb im Gerichtshof auf erbitterten Widerstand gestossen, weil nicht alle Richter ihm die nötige Sachkunde zubilligen konnten. Gegenwärtig wird der Gerichtshof im stärksten Maße von 2 Persönlichkeiten dirigiert, die beide Berufsgelehrte gewesen sind, nämlich Anzilotti und Huber. Bei der gegenwärtigen

---

[439] Moore to Loder, 27 August 1931, Moore papers 63.
[440] Alexander P. Fachiri, *The Permanent Court of International Justice: Its Constitution, Procedure and Work* (2nd edn, London, 1932), p. 31.
[441] See Walther Schücking, *Vertrauliche Bemerkungen zur Frage der Revision des Statuts des Weltgerichtshofs*, undated, Schücking papers (Koblenz) 32, pp. 1–2 (translation: 'who have both extensive scientific knowledge of international law and practical experience of international affairs'; 'that judges from civil law are much more dangerous for the Court than the professors, as they have neither past practical political occupation, nor been engaged in scientific work in international law which could give them an idea of the problems on which they sit in judgment').

Zusammensetzung des Gerichtshofs könnte ich mir überhaupt nicht denken, wie dieses Tribunal nur einigermaßen funktionieren sollte, wenn diese beiden Persönlichkeiten nicht vorhanden wären, obgleich ich auch Anzilotti ein wenig kritisch gegenüberstehe, weil er bei reichem wissen und glanzendem Scharfsinn fraglos sehr zu Spitzfindigkeit neigt.[442]

Most of the cases decided by the Permanent Court in the 1920s had to do with treaty interpretation. At one point, referring to the *International Labour Organization* opinions, Judge Huber had been talking about 'the "agricultural" question' as being 'a very interesting one, as it involves most delicate problems of interpretation of treaties', which 'is a chapter of International Law which is usually very poor even in big treatises on the Law of Nations'.[443] However, in 1928, when he had just delivered his award in the *Island of Palmas* case, Judge Huber wrote to Moore that:

it was a most interesting case from a legal point of view, a case of pure law of nations, not, as most of the cases decided by the Court, a question of interpretation of some badly drafted clauses of a convention, or a civil case, as Chorzow, international only by some connection with a treaty.[444]

Although mainly concerned with treaty interpretation, Moore explained that '[t]he Court itself has made it a point to cite its own decisions as precedents with a view to establish, by repetition and reaffirmation, the principles laid down'.[445] This tendency found expression in the lists of examples of such references given in the annual reports. On the first occasion just after the *Mosul* opinion, it was noted that '[i]t may be concluded from the above instances that the Court has in practice been careful not to reverse precedents established by itself in previous

---

[442] *Ibid.* (translation: 'The best proof lies in the experience that one has had with the presidency. The first president, Loder, was actually a brilliant jurist; therefore, he was also admitted from the Bar to the highest court in the Netherlands. However, his presidency met with fierce opposition on the bench not only on account of his all too authoritarian style but also because not all judges believed that he had the expertise needed. At present, the Court is forcefully presided over by two personalities, who have both been professors, namely Anzilotti and Huber. In its current composition, I could not at all imagine how this tribunal should function, even just reasonably well, in the absence of these two personalities, although I am also a little critical about Anzilotti. While he has profound knowledge and a brilliant mind, it is beyond question that he is inclining towards being too subtle.').

[443] Huber to Moore, 26 June 1922, Moore papers 177.

[444] Huber to Moore, 23 April 1928, Moore papers 176; and also Huber to Hudson, 23 April 1928, Hudson papers 78.7. See also Chang, *Interpretation of Treaties*, p. 185: 'The Permanent Court of International Justice has made few, if any, new rules in treaty interpretation.' Cf. Huber, 'Fortbildung des Völkerrechts', p. 473.

[445] Moore to Borchard, 16 January 1930, Borchard papers 7.97.

judgments and opinions, and to explain apparent departures from such precedents'.[446]

As in the foundational period, the decisions delivered between 1925 and 1930 confirmed that Article 38 of the Statute did not provide a framework within which the Permanent Court's decisions could be analysed. Again state consent was not everything in terms of international legal argument. Notably, the *Mosul* opinion underlined the potential of the international law of coexistence to influence treaty interpretation, while in other cases the Permanent Court's strict conception of vested rights guided the interpretation. Indeed, preparatory work was given a subordinate position in treaty interpretation in four decisions, the *Mosul* opinion, *The Lotus*, the *Danube* case and the *River Oder* case, all of which put a strong focus on the territorial setting under the international law of coexistence. It was relatively easy to construe treaty texts so that they were in accordance with the international law of coexistence; it would have been more of a challenge to do the same with the voluminous work done in preparation of those texts.

This second period in the Permanent Court's life emphasised that the room available for the national lawyer was limited. It has been said that '[t]he Court appears almost activist'.[447] The Permanent Court developed a preference for the dynamic structure of international legal argument based on the conception of the state as an international sovereign, most significantly in *The Lotus*, but also in the *Jurisdiction of Courts* opinion and the *Loans* cases. It only resorted to other concepts if the matter also came within the international law of coexistence. The national principle of self-containedness was reduced to a mere cipher, except in the *Free Zones* case. As exemplified by the *Mosul* opinion, the starting-point of

---

[446] See Series E No. 3 (1926–7) at 217–18 (referring to *ibid.*, p. 226, at which the *Mosul* opinion was distinguished from the *Eastern Carelia* opinion), Series E No. 4 (1927–8) at 292–3 and Series E No. 6 (1929–30) at 300. The examples were given under the heading of Article 59 of the Statute; already in the *Upper Silesia* case the Permanent Court held that 'the object of this article is simply to prevent legal principles accepted by the Court in a particular case from being binding upon other States or in other disputes': *Case concerning Certain German Interests in Polish Upper Silesia* (Merits), Series A No. 7 (1926) at 19. See also L. Oppenheim, *International Law* (4th edn by Arnold D. McNair, London, 1926), vol. 2, pp. 56–7; and W. E. Beckett, 'Decisions of the Permanent Court of International Justice on Points of Law and Procedure of General Application' (1930) 11 *BYIL* 1 at 1.

[447] Thomas J. Bodie, *Politics and the Emergence of an Activist International Court of Justice* (Westport, CT, 1995), p. 53. Cf. N. Politis, 'Méthodes d'interprétation du droit international conventionnel' in *Recueil d'etudes sur les sources du droit en l'honneur de François Gény* (1934), vol. 3, p. 375 at pp. 377 and 380.

the Permanent Court's treaty interpretation was generally found within the international law of cooperation, the conception of the state as an international law subject pointing in the direction of an objective interpretation. In matters of jurisdiction, there appeared to be a distinction between the Permanent Court's strictly textual interpretation of Special Agreements and its more teleological interpretation of compromissory clauses. On the other hand, the Permanent Court had given up analogical interpretation, with the possible exception of the interpretation of the Special Agreement in the *Free Zones* case. In general, with Judge Huber on the bench, the Permanent Court seldom interpreted treaties subjectively, that is, against a background coloured by the conception of the state as an international sovereign.

The period contributed another essential lesson. While the Permanent Court moulded an international lawyer's approach to international legal argument, international legal theory stuck to what was at least partly a national lawyer's approach, changing the hierarchy between the basic and dynamic structures of international legal argument in favour of the former. On their reading, the *Lotus* statement became the *Lotus* presumption, a dramatic expression of the national principle of self-containedness. Not that many commentators endorsed the *Lotus* presumption, although some did. But their reading of *The Lotus* exemplified the 'all-or-nothing' approach that the *Buchrecht* adopted, and adopts, in relation to the conception of the state as a sovereign. Either that conception was all-embracing, i.e. the *Lotus* presumption, or it was, as suggested by most theorists, completely abandoned. As explained in Chapter 3, neither of these alternatives has ever been attractive. The basic conceptual conflict in international legal argument is not the one between sovereignty and bindingness, but that between one national sovereign and more national sovereigns.

In developing an international lawyer's approach to international legal argument, Judge Huber and the other members of the bench had been greatly assisted by the Registrar. Well in advance of the second election to be held in 1930, Judge Huber had written to Moore about candidates:

I shall propose President Anzilotti and Mr Hammarskjöld, because these two guarantee more than anybody else the continuity of jurisprudence between the old and the new Court. The re-election of Anzilotti seems to be certain, if he – as, I think, he does – accepts a candidature. On the other hand, the candidature of Hammarskjöld, because he does not belong to a Great Power, needs special support if he has to have a serious chance of being elected.

Because you are fully acquainted with the very, very great services rendered by Hammarskjöld to the Court, I take the liberty of suggesting to you whether you might take into consideration a possible proposition of Hammarskjöld by the American group. If the candidature of Hammarskjöld would be supported by some of those groups to which actual or former members of the PCIJ belong, it would become evident for the Assembly and Council that these nominations are based on special experience and are worthy of special consideration. Few members of the electoral bodies are familiar with the interior working of the Court and no few may be inclined to underrate the work of a 'registrar'. For this reason it seems to be highly desirable that the immense work done by the Registrar in the background would be made at least indirectly recognizable to the electors.

I feel sure that you will not consider my letter as an inadmissible intervention in the business of other people; my suggestion is made only in the interest of the Court which will be considerably changed and which could therefore be in need of a young element which combines with an exceptional capacity of work a unique experience of the past of the Court.[448]

In his reply, Moore wrote: 'Personally I think it of the utmost importance that Anzilotti should continue to be a member of the Court and, besides feeling in the same way concerning yourself, I also think it of the highest importance that there should continue to be a judge from Switzerland.'[449]

---

[448] Huber to Moore, 7 May 1930, Moore papers 62.
[449] Moore to Huber, 31 May 1930, Moore papers 62.

7   A national lawyer's approach, 1931–1940

The Permanent Court as composed after the second general election

President Adatci and other new judges

The second general election of judges took place on 25 September 1930.[1] Those re-elected were Judges Altamira (sixty-four years old), Anzilotti (sixty-one years old) and de Bustamante (sixty-five years old), who had been ordinary members of the Permanent Court since 1922; Judges Negulesco (fifty-five years old) and Wang (forty-nine years old), who had also been members of the Permanent Court since 1922, though in the first nine years as deputy-judges; and Judges Hurst (sixty years old), Fromageot (sixty-six years old) and Kellogg (seventy-four years old) (ages stated as at the end of 1930).

Only Judges Negulesco and Wang were younger than Judge Huber; Judge Huber, however, had eventually declined to stand for re-election. Huber's influence had diminished during Judge Anzilotti's presidency, partly because he had taken up the presidency of the International Committee of the Red Cross. Yet his departure was a serious blow to an international lawyer's approach to international legal argument, one which combined the international law of coexistence with the dynamic structure of international legal argument, having the conception of the state as an international sovereign as its starting-point. The main exponent of this approach remaining on the bench was Judge Anzilotti, since Deputy-Judge Beichmann did not secure re-election. Indeed, no Scandinavian candidate succeeded. Åke Hammarskjöld lost the last seat on the bench by a whisker to a South American, Francisco José Urrutia (Colombia).

---

[1] See *Records of Assembly: Plenary* 1930, pp. 134–40 and 188.

The other new judges were Minéitcirô Adatci (Japan), Jonkheer W. J. M. van Eysinga (the Netherlands), J. Gustavo Guerrero (El Salvador), Baron Rolin-Jaequemyns (Belgium), Count Rostworowski (Poland) and Walther Schücking (Germany).[2] All new judges were members of the Permanent Court of Arbitration, and except for the German judge they were all fully acquainted with the League organs.

Three of the new judges, Adatci (sixty years old), Guerrero (fifty-four years old) and Urrutia (sixty years old), had long careers in diplomacy behind them. Adatci had been a delegate to the Paris Peace Conference and a member of the Advisory Committee of Jurists. In 1920, he had called the Advisory Committee's making of a draft-scheme 'a social miracle', but in the same breath he had advised his colleagues to 'be modest and practical', quoting the proverb that '[w]ho attempts too much does nothing well'.[3] His prior opposition to the compulsory jurisdiction of the Permanent Court foreshadowed the amendments inserted in the draft Statute by the Council. Subsequently, Adatci obtained a reputation in the Council for being 'a born settler';[4] in Moore's view, Adatci 'had been very conversant with international affairs and had always shown good judgment and good temper'.[5] In early 1931, having received more votes than any other candidate in the Assembly, a narrow majority elected him president of the Permanent Court.[6] Guerrero, for ten years a leading figure in the Assembly, was elected vice-president. Both Adatci and Guerrero had previously been assigned to diplomatic posts at Paris, and

[2] See in general Series E No. 7 (1930–31) at 21–41.

[3] Advisory Committee of Jurists, *Procès-Verbaux of the Proceedings of the Committee (16 June–24 July 1920, with Annexes)* (The Hague, 1920), pp. 542–3; and see Ole Spiermann, '"Who Attempts Too Much Does Nothing Well": The 1920 Advisory Committee of Jurists and the Statute of the Permanent Court of International Justice' (2002) 73 *BYIL* 187 at 187, 232–5 and 238–9.

[4] Malkin's note, 20 July 1931, FO 371 C5576/673/3. Cf. Masatoshi Matsushita, *Japan in the League of Nations* (New York, 1929), pp. 104–9 and 161–2.

[5] John Bassett Moore, 'Nomination of Candidates for the Permanent Court of International Justice', 18 June 1930, Moore papers 178, p. 2. One may also quote Hudson. Speaking of Judge Adatci's successor, elected in 1935, Hudson wrote: 'Indeed all of his activities seem to have been either in the diplomatic service or in the Foreign Office. The same might have been said of Judge Adatci, but on several occasions when I hinted at this point in my articles on the Court I received prompt reminders from Mr Adatci's friends that he was a jurist and not a diplomat; he had been judge of a Prize Court during the Russo-Japanese War': Hudson to Moore, 6 March 1935, Moore papers 178. An example of such a 'reminder' was Adatci to Hudson, 28 October 1930 and Hudson to Adatci, 14 November 1930, both Hudson papers 83.7. Cf. Dorothy V. Jones, *Toward a Just World: The Critical Years in the Search for International Justice* (Chicago, 2002), pp. 20–1 and 96–7.

[6] See Kammerer's despatch, 26 January 1931, Quai d'Orsay 2400C.

Adatci had obviously allied himself with Fromageot.[7] At the time of the election of the new president, a rather disillusioned Judge Anzilotti had written to Huber that part of Judge Adatci's campaign for the presidency had been Judge Fromageot declaring his candidacy 'agréable au Quai d'Orsay'.[8] In the view of Hurst, President Adatci 'was a diplomat and somewhat lacking in forcefulness'.[9] Of the three diplomats Urrutia probably had the best reputation as a lawyer. Like Guerrero he was a proud exponent of the pan-American approach to international law.[10]

Rolin-Jaequemyns (sixty-seven years old) was the son of one of the founders of the *Revue de droit international et de législation comparée* and of the Institut de Droit International. He had followed in his father's footsteps while practising as a national lawyer before the Belgian courts. Having attended the Paris Peace Conference in 1919, he spent most of the 1920s as a member of the Belgian Government, regularly attending the Assembly of the League.

Three of the new judges, none of whom would seem to have been particularly forceful personalities, had for a long time held chairs in international law, namely van Eysinga (fifty-two years old), Rostworowski (sixty-six years old) and Schücking (fifty-five years old). Van Eysinga, an expert in international fluvial law, had begun his career in the Netherlands Ministry of Foreign Affairs. He had represented his country at numerous sessions of the Assembly and Loder regarded him as indeed the

---

[7] This had been evident in the preparations of the session of the Advisory Committee of Jurists in 1920: see Adatci to Hammarskjöld, 3 June 1920 and Hammarskjöld's memorandum, 7 June 1920, both League of Nations Archives 21-4762-88; and also Spiermann, 'Advisory Committee', pp. 193 and 258. In 1928, Fromageot suggested that Adatci should be appointed a member and president of the Committee of Jurists preparing the revision of the Statute of the Permanent Court. This proposal was communicated to the League of Nations: see letter to Giraut, 3 December 1928, Quai d'Orsay 2399B.

[8] Anzilotti to Huber, 24 January 1931, Huber papers 23. Drawing a comparison with the 'first' Court, a French diplomat wrote that '[l]'état d'esprit de M. Adatci, rompu aux négociations politiques, mêlé à la vie internationale depuis trente ans, est tout différent et sa loyauté est bien connue': Kammerer's despatch, 26 January 1931, Quai d'Orsay 2400C.

[9] Hurst to Malkin, 31 March 1935, FO 371 W2976/55/98. See also Anzilotti to Huber, 4 March 1931, Huber papers 23; and A.-G. Frangulis, 'Adatci (Minèitcirô)' in A.-G. Frangulis (ed.), *Dictionnaire Diplomatique* (Paris, 1957), vol. 5, p. 13 at p. 14. President Adatci did not make full use of his presidential powers: see Series E No. 9 (1932–3) at 174; and Series D No. 2, Add.3 (1936) at 809.

[10] E.g., Francisco José Urrutia, 'La Codification du droit international en Amérique' (1928) 22 *Recueil des Cours* 85; and see also Haroldo Valladao, 'Francisco José Urrutia' (1950) 43-II *Annuaire*, p. 519 at p. 520.

'right man for Geneva'.[11] Rostworowski had often been present at the Assembly as a delegate of Poland. It has been said that as a professor he 'qui n'avait pas des dons d'orateur, enseignait sans éclat'.[12] In previous years, Rostworowski had sat as judge *ad hoc* on three cases, all decided against Poland. In 1923, on his first appearance before the Permanent Court, in the *Minorities* cases, he had invoked his authority as 'an old professor' and advised the new Court to interpret treaties restrictively, having regard to the national principle of self-containedness.[13]

Schücking had also served as a judge *ad hoc*. When first he sat on *The Wimbledon* his then inadequate English and French language skills had prevented him from participating in the oral deliberations.[14] Schücking was well known among German-speaking international lawyers as an ardent supporter of the notion of international organisation.[15] It seemed to be generally agreed that he approached international law as a national lawyer.[16] An advocate of analogical interpretation,[17] he had given to the Hague Peace Conferences the name of a '*Weltstaatenbund*'.[18] The

[11] Loder to Moore, undated [1931], Moore papers 64; cf. Max Huber, *Denkwürdigkeiten, 1907-1924* (Zurich, 1974), p. 50. Loder had reportedly supported another Dutch candidate: see despatch of 19 July 1930, Quai d'Orsay 2400B. It has been said that in 1932 Sir Eric Drummond, who had been Secretary-General of the League of Nations since 1919, preferred van Eysinga as his successor. However, van Eysinga declined to stand 'on the grounds that he preferred to retain his seat as an associate justice in the Permanent Court of International Justice at The Hague, especially since there appeared to be a likelihood that he might be chosen president of the court': see James Barros, *Betrayal from Within: Joseph Avenol, Secretary-General of the League of Nations, 1933-1940* (New Haven, 1969), pp. 2 and 7.

[12] B. Winiarski, 'Comte Michel Rostworowski' (1950) 43-II *Annuaire*, p. 505 at p. 507.

[13] See Series C No. 3-I at 493.

[14] See Series E No. 1 (1922-5) at 171; and Huber, *Denkwürdigkeiten*, p. 279; and also W. J. M. van Eysinga, 'Walther Schücking als internationaler Richter' (1935) 35 *Die Friedens-Warte* 213 at 214; and Åke Hammarskjöld, 'Persönliche Eindrücke aus Walther Schückings Richtertätigkeit' (1935) 35 *Die Friedens-Warte* 214 at 216. See also Hammarskjöld to [Hjalmar] Hammarskjöld, 7 December 1935, Hammarskjöld papers 30.

[15] See Walther Schücking, 'Die Organisation der Welt' in *Staatsrechtliche Abhandlungen: Festgabe für Laband* (Tübingen, 1908), p. 533; and also Pitman B. Potter, 'Origin of the Term "International Organization"' (1945) 39 *AJIL* 803 at 805.

[16] See notably Hammarskjöld, 'Persönliche Eindrücke', pp. 215-16; and also Max Huber, 'Walther Schücking und die Völkerrechtswissenschaft' (1935) 35 *Die Friedens-Warte* 197 at 198; and van Eysinga, 'Schücking als internationaler Richter', p. 213. See also, e.g., Walther Schücking, *Der Staatenverband der Haager Konferenzen* (Munich, 1912), pp. 8-9.

[17] See Schücking, *Staatenverband der Haager Konferenzen*, pp. 46-9, 74-6, 124-35, 149 and 289-312.

[18] See Schücking, 'Organisation der Welt', p. 610; and also Schücking, *Staatenverband der Haager Konferenzen*. Cf. (1913) 15 *Die Friedens-Warte* 294-5; and Walther Schücking and Hans Wehberg, *Die Satzung des Völkerbundes* (2nd edn, Berlin, 1924), pp. 86 and 560.

immediate substantive implications were negligible, certainly not constituting a threat to the key conception of the state as a national sovereign
cherished by national lawyers and also, in *The Wimbledon*, by Judge *ad hoc*
Schücking.[19] Schücking had attended the Paris Peace Conference without being able to impress the diplomats with his lofty ideals.[20] His seat
in the *Reichstag* had not resulted in him gaining experiences with the
League organs. Instead, his enthusiasm about the League found schol-
arly expression in the commentary on the Covenant which he published
with Professor Hans Wehberg.[21] According to Schücking, '[l]'époque de
désorganisation de la communauté des Etats européens . . . touche à sa
fin',[22] the Statute of the Permanent Court representing, among other
texts, 'un développement du droit constitutionnel'.[23]

In total the new bench was composed of eight 'old' and seven 'new'
judges. In 1931, Judges Anzilotti, de Bustamante and Hurst were members of the Institut de Droit International, as were President Adatci and
Judges Rolin-Jaequemyns, Rostworowski, Schücking and Urrutia, while
Judges Altamira and Negulesco remained *associés* until, respectively, 1934
and 1936.[24] The increase in the number of ordinary judges had been
decided by the Assembly pursuant to Article 3 of the Statute. It was in
accordance with an amendment to the Statute contained in the Revision Protocol signed in 1929, which, however, did not take effect until
1936, partly due to the opposition of Cuba (and Judge de Bustamante).[25]
In the Revision Protocol, the increase in the number of ordinary judges

[19] Cf. Schücking, *Staatenverband der Haager Konferenzen*, pp. 81, 95, 113–19, 139–41, 237–40,
244, 289–90 and 324; and see Walther Schücking, 'Le Développement du Pacte de la
Société des Nations' (1927) 20 *Recueil des Cours* 353 at 429.

[20] Cf. Walther Schücking, 'Der Völkerbundsentwurf des Deutschen Regierung' in
P. Munch (ed.), *Les Origines et l'oeuvre de la Société des Nations* (Copenhagen, 1923), vol. 1,
p. 138; for the text of the German draft, see David Hunter Miller, *The Drafting of the
Covenant* (New York, 1928), vol. 2, pp. 744–61.

[21] Schücking and Wehberg, *Satzung des Völkerbundes*. It should be noted, however, that,
like most Germans, Schücking recommended a revision of the Covenant: see, e.g.,
Walther Schücking, *Die Revision der Völkerbundssatzung im Hinblick auf den Kelloggpakt*
(Berlin, 1931), p. 40.

[22] Schücking, 'Développement du Pacte', pp. 354 and also 368–9, 379–80 and 397–8. Cf.
ibid., pp. 433 and 450.

[23] *Ibid.*, p. 360; and see *ibid.*, pp. 362–3.

[24] See (1931) 36-II *Annuaire*, pp. xii–xxiv; (1934) 38 *Annuaire*, p. 518; and (1936) 39-II
Annuaire, p. 11.

[25] See Moore to Borchard, 17 September 1930, Moore papers 62 and Borchard papers 7.97;
Kammerer's memorandum, 1 September 1930, Quai d'Orsay 2399C; memorandum,
21 November 1930, NARA 500 C114/1183; Malkin's memorandum, 2 February 1931, FO
371 W976/142/98; and also Manley O. Hudson, 'The Cuban Reservations and the
Revision of the Statute of the Permanent Court of International Justice' (1932)

was paired with the abolition of the posts of deputy-judges; this eventually took place in 1936, the four persons elected to the posts in 1930 never having been called upon.[26]

Modification of the Rules

The Revision Protocol contained other amendments that aimed at enhancing the Permanent Court's permanency and its status as 'a real judicial body'.[27] In 1930, having realised that the Revision Protocol was not about to take effect, the Assembly recommended that the Permanent Court modify the Rules of Court in the light of the Revision Protocol.[28] Judges van Eysinga, Fromageot, Hurst and Urrutia had taken part in the drafting of the amendments, and at the twentieth ordinary session opening on 15 January 1931 the new bench happily undertook this task,[29] arguably stretching the provisions of the original Statute in order to provide, in particular, for a quasi-permanent session opening on 1 February.[30]

Other 'urgent' proposals were also introduced when modifying the Rules. A majority furthered the notion of assimilating judgments and advisory opinions, in form as well as in respect of procedure, by combining the publication of the Permanent Court's decisions in a single publication series.[31] The notion of assimilation developed by the Permanent

26 AJIL 590; L. Oppenheim, *International Law* (5th edn by H. Lauterpacht, London, 1935–7), vol. 2, p. 48, note 1; and George Schwarzenberger, *International Law as Applied by International Courts and Tribunals* (London, 1986), vol. 4, p. 233, note 52. Indeed, revised Article 16 of the Statute concerning incompatibilities would seem to have been aimed at, in particular, Judge de Bustamante, the senior partner of a Havana law firm: see Hurst's minute, 30 November 1928, FO 371 W11377/309/98; and the Lord Chancellor's minute, 13 December 1928, FO 371 W11812/309/78; cf. Hudson, YILC 1951-I, p. 129. It should be added that Cuba ratified the Revision Protocol without reservations on 14 March 1932. In the end, the entry into force was achieved by adopting a negative clause for approval: see *Records of Assembly: Plenary* 1935, pp. 94 and 124–5.

[26] Cf. as to the interpretation of Article 25 of the Statute: Series D No. 2, Add.1 (1926) at 22–4 and 304; and Series E No. 7 (1930-1) at 289.

[27] See Committee of Jurists on the Statute of the Permanent Court of International Justice, 'Minutes of the Session Held at Geneva, March 11th–19th, 1929' (League of Nations Document C.166.M.66.1929.V, 1929), pp. 110 and 118; cf. *Records of Assembly: Plenary* 1928, p. 55.

[28] *Records of Assembly: Plenary* 1930, p. 132.

[29] See Rules of Court amended on 21 February 1931, Series D No. 1 (2nd edn, 1931) at 23–49.

[30] On this 'quasi-permanency', see Hammarskjöld in Series D No. 2, Add.2 (1931) at 173.

[31] See Series E No. 7 (1930-1) at 339–43 and also Series D No. 2, Add.2 (1931) at 64 and 126.

Court had been approved in what became Article 68 of the Statute when eventually the Revision Protocol took effect. It provided that '[i]n the exercise of its advisory functions, the Court shall further be guided by the provisions of the Statute which apply in contentious cases to the extent to which it recognizes them to be applicable'. According to Hammarskjöld, who may have had a role in framing it, this provision 'finally consecrates the Court's conception of Advisory Opinions as a special kind of arbitral award differing from ordinary awards in the method of submission and the force of *res judicata*'.[32]

The Permanent Court in its new composition also considered the scheme of deliberations. Criticism, also from within the Permanent Court, had prevented Judge Fromageot from putting the scheme on the agenda for the Committee of Jurists which met in 1929,[33] but now he addressed the matter. He was supported by Judge Hurst, who disliked commencing the deliberations with written notes. That implied, in Judge Hurst's view, 'a great risk that a judge having once committed himself to an opinion on paper will not change it'.[34] Judge Fromageot suggested a number of other changes, including an exchange of views on procedural and substantive aspects of the case between the written and the oral pleadings.[35] These two suggestions were adopted on an experimental and provisional basis in a resolution of 20 February 1931.[36] As a consequence, no individual notes were supposed to be written until two meetings had been held in the course of which 'chaque juge a fait connaître son sentiment'. Judge Guerrero considered this to be more in accordance with diplomatic practice.[37] On his part, Judge Anzilotti pointed to the fact that the system with individual, written notes had its

---

[32] Hammarskjöld to Lape, 24 August 1929, Root papers 144; and see as to the background Norweb to Secretary of State, 25 February 1929, NARA 500 C114/763. See also Fromageot in 'Minutes of the Conference Regarding the Revision of the Statute of the Permanent Court of International Justice and the Accession of the United States of America to the Protocol of Signature of That Statute, Held at Geneva from September 4th to 12th, 1929' (League of Nations Document C.514.M.173.1929.V, 1929), p. 48. Hudson told Root that '[l]ast fall I was surprised to find that M. Fromageot was of the opinion that the Court had gone too far in assimilating its procedure with reference to advisory opinions to its procedure in contested cases': Hudson to Root, 19 January 1929, Hudson papers 88.9.

[33] See Hurst's note, 3 October 1928, FO 371 W8655/309/98; and also Åke Hammarskjöld, 'La Cour permanente de Justice internationale à la neuvième session de l'Assemblée de la Société des Nations' (1928) 9 *RDILC* 665 at 672–3 and 687.

[34] Series D No. 2, Add.2 (1931) at 292, 122 and 218.

[35] *Ibid.*, pp. 13, 216 and 225.   [36] *Ibid.*, pp. 267 and 300–1.

[37] *Ibid.*, p. 220; and similarly in Thirty-second session, *Procès-Verbal* 1 (15 May 1934), van Eysinga papers 127, p. 7.

advantages, but he added that these were 'advantages which, however, also depended to some extent on the composition of the Court'.[38]

In practice the revised deliberations scheme was not felt to be a complete success. When adopted by the Permanent Court, it had been agreed, on the proposal of Judge Guerrero, 'that the text of this resolution, which introduced a new practice, by way of experiment should only be published if and when a decision to that effect were taken by the Court at the conclusion of its next session'.[39] At the following session, it was agreed, on the proposal of Judge Hurst, supported by Judge Fromageot, not to insert the resolution in the Annual Report,[40] and indeed the resolution continued to be deliberately omitted from the Annual Reports.[41] Hammarskjöld wrote to Huber that 'the resolution of February 20th is by no means strictly applied: the clear tendency is to revert to the practice of the Court in its old composition'.[42] However, the deliberations had acquired an oral and collective beginning. A majority view would have emerged prior to the written notes, which could no longer be seen as a test of the individual judge's study of the case and apprehension of its points.[43]

On 21 February 1931, at the last meeting of the twentieth session, President Adatci,

before closing the session, desired specially to thank all his colleagues who had attended it for the willing, cordial and friendly collaboration which they had extended to him. That collaboration was of happy augury for the future of the Court's activities, and convinced him that he had done right in overcoming his original hesitation in accepting the heavy responsibilities resting upon the President of the Court. His thanks were addressed first and foremost to M. Anzilotti, his predecessor, who had always been ready with clear and full explanations regarding the practice previously followed by the Court. He also thanked M. van Eysinga for having been kind enough to undertake the task, sometimes a laborious one, of reading the Court's minutes. He desired to pay special tribute

---

[38] Series D No. 2, Add.2 (1931) at 219; and previously Series D No. 2, Add.1 (1926) at 58.
[39] Series D No. 2, Add.2 (1931) at 267.
[40] Twenty-fourth session, Distr. 2351 (1 February 1932), Annex 1, Schücking papers (Koblenz) 35, p. 17.
[41] See Series E No. 7 (1930–1) at 297–8; and Series E No. 10 (1933–4) at 162–3; cf. Series E No. 12 (1935–6) at 196–7.
[42] Hammarskjöld to Hudson, 25 November 1931, Hudson papers 130.11; cf. Series D No. 2, Add.3 (1936) at 398.
[43] Cf. Charles Evans Hughes, 'The World Court as a Going Concern' (1930) 16 *American Bar Association Journal* 151 at 155. As to the use of the written notes, see Series E No. 8 (1931–2) at 268; and Series E No. 10 (1933–4) at 162–3; cf. Manley O. Hudson, 'The Twenty-Third Year of the Permanent Court of International Justice' (1945) 39 *AJIL* 1 at 6.

to the energy of the Registrar, who though barely convalescent, had spared no pains to serve the interests of the work of the session. He hoped that the Registrar would continue to devote his efforts to the service of the great cause of international justice. Lastly he thanked the Deputy-Registrar and the staff of the Registry which, throughout the whole session, had worked extremely hard and shown unremitting zeal.

The judges were about to separate and the President would remain alone responsible for the functioning of the Court. He hoped that his colleagues would continue from afar to lend him their assistance and that they would not hesitate to come to his help, should circumstances require it. In any case he asked them, at the next session, frankly to state their opinion in regard to any decisions which the President might have had to take in the meantime.[44]

President Adatci soon asked Hammarskjöld as to 'l'appréciation de la Cour sur la valeur juridique des considérants qui ont motivé le dispositif des arrêts et des avis'; he added that '[d]ans le monde scientifique de mon pays, il y a une divergence de vues assez marquée à ce sujet'.[45] Back in 1930, Hammarskjöld had noted that 'it is . . . true that a court with an unchanging composition is not likely – though always free to do so – to reverse its previous decisions except on very good grounds, which it will be careful to explain'.[46] Hammarskjöld had not then stated explicitly what applied to a bench, the composition of which had changed.

Discontinuity

In 1928, when the negotiations on the revision of the Statute of the Permanent Court were upcoming, Sir Cecil Hurst made the following observations, echoing his views on the result produced by the first general election of judges in 1921:

I have been surprised at the frequency with which during the last few years I have heard criticisms made upon the Court on the ground that it contains too many professors. The criticisms are well-founded. Professors make bad judges. What is required is people who have had practical experience and not professorial experience. At the same time, it would be undesirable to make any change in the wording of the Statute on this point; but the adoption of a delicately worded

---

[44] Twentieth session, Procès-Verbal 51 (21 February 1931), Schücking papers (Koblenz) 33, pp. 4–5.

[45] Adatci to Hammarskjöld, 24 March 1931, Hammarskjöld papers 477. Cf., as regards the decision-making of the Assembly of the League of Nations: Adatci in Records of Assembly: Plenary 1921, p. 241: 'We must not lose sight of the fact that we are creating a precedent.'

[46] Åke Hammarskjöld, 'International Justice' in League of Nations, Ten Years of World Co-operation (London, 1930), p. 125 at p. 139.

recommendation advocating the choice as candidates of persons who have had practical or judicial experience of the application of international law would be free from objection.[47]

Sir Cecil and kindred spirits like Henri Fromageot were successful.[48] Despite criticism echoing the misgivings dating back to 1920 about such a recommendation throwing the Permanent Court open to diplomats,[49] first the Committee of Jurists, then the Conference of Signatories and finally the Tenth Assembly of the League of Nations adopted resolutions to the effect that 'in accordance with the spirit of Articles 2 and 39 of the Statute of the Court, the candidates nominated by the national groups should possess recognised practical experience in international law'.[50] Professor Jessup noted that 'the two new judges elected in September, 1929, – M. Fromageot and Sir Cecil Hurst, – are eminently qualified in this respect'.[51]

There was some discussion at the time whether the second general election had or had not resulted in a weaker composition of the Permanent Court. No doubt, the French Government was pleased with the outcome of the election and also the election as president and vice-president of two former diplomats both considered 'pro-françaises'.[52] The British Foreign Office had the impression that Judge Hurst found the

---

[47] Hurst's minute, 30 November 1928, FO 371 W11377/309/98.

[48] See Committee of Jurists, 'Minutes', pp. 129 and also 24–5.

[49] 'Conference of Signatories 1929', pp. 25–8 and 52–3. For example, according to Root, '[i]f the governments were entrusted with the preparation of the lists of candidates and also carried out the elections upon these lists, the Court would differ but little in character from the Council of the League of Nations': Advisory Committee, *Procès-verbaux*, p. 421. It would become, he had added, 'a body representing the various governments, instead of a body composed of picked and specially qualified men entrusted with the administration of justice regardless of any national considerations'.

[50] *Records of Assembly: Plenary* 1929, pp. 119–21 and also 'Conference of Signatories 1929', p. 82; the sentence continued: '. . . and that they should be at least able to read both the official languages of the Court and to speak one of them; it also considers it desirable that to the nominations there should be attached a statement of the careers of the candidates justifying their candidature.'

[51] Philip C. Jessup, 'The Permanent Court of International Justice: American Accession and Amendments to the Statute' (1929) 254 *International Conciliation* 7 at 25, note 44. Cf. B. Schenk von Stauffenberg, 'Die Revision des Statuts des Städigen Internationalen Gerichtshofs' (1936) 6 ZaöRV 89 at 94–5. According to Hudson, '[t]he recommendation about "practical experience in international law" was stoutly opposed by the Scandinavians, who saw it as a basis for the selection of foreign office advisers, such as Hurst and Fromageot, as judges': Hudson to Root, 20 September 1929, Root papers 144.

[52] Cf. Kammerer's despatches, 27 September 1930, Quai d'Orsay 2400B and 26 January 1931, Quai d'Orsay 2400C.

bench elected in 1930 'a considerable improvement on its predecessor'.[53] This was so even though the newcomers had no practical judicial experience. Judge Hurst wrote to Professor Hudson that '[i]t is very interesting work and I think the League has elected a pretty good lot to serve for the next nine years. But I rather wish that there had been rather fewer of us.'[54] For his part, Hudson wrote to the *New York Times* as well as his compatriots and some judges saying how 'delighted' he was with the new bench.[55] The article in the *New York Times* ended as follows:

With these new members, the court remains truly representative of 'the main forms of civilization and the principal legal systems of the world'. The judges come from North America, South America, Europe and Asia. Their experience covers every type of governmental activity, and their familiarity with the problems of current international life qualifies the court to deal intelligently with the cases that may come before it. So much of the business of the court grows out of the activities of the League of Nations that it is very important for the judges to have had experience in its work. In this respect it would be difficult to improve on the new roster. Fortunately, also, many of the new judges are thoroughly au courant with the development of international law, both in its theory and in its application.

On the whole, the election of the new judges should produce very general satisfaction throughout the world, and there is every prospect that they will continue the excellent record made by the court during the past nine years.[56]

As for less positive commentaries, Hudson was 'afraid of this thing and its effect in this country'.[57] However that may be, following the close of the Eleventh Assembly, a United States officer with the Secretariat,

---

[53] Malkin's note, 20 July 1931, FO 371 C5576/673/3.

[54] Hurst to Hudson, 14 October 1930, Hudson papers 85.12.

[55] Hudson to Kellogg, 27 September 1930, Kellogg papers 41. See also, e.g., Hudson to Adatci, 1 October and 16 October 1930 and Hudson to Anzilotti, 11 October 1930, all Hudson papers 83.7; Hudson wrote that '[t]he election has been very well received in this country, and I believe that the result is so satisfactory that it will facilitate the adhesion of the United States', Anzilotti replied that 'I am extremely glad that the election of the new judges has been well received in your country and that it will facilitate the adhesion of the United States': Anzilotti to Hudson, 11 October 1930, Hudson papers 83.7. Adatci replied: 'Je suis très heureux de pouvoir travailler avec M. Kellog[g]. Sa présence à la Cour rehausse singulièrement le prestige de celle-ci. Il manque malheureusement un ciment utile pour la composition de la Cour. Nous n'avons aucune personnalité représentant le système juridique du Nord de l'Europe; mais il faudrait peut-être ne pas chercher des tâches au soleil': Adatci to Hudson, 4 October 1930, Hudson papers 83.7.

[56] Hudson in *New York Times*, 12 October 1930, a copy of which is kept as Hudson papers 47.10.

[57] Hudson to Sweetser, 20 October 1930, Hudson papers 114.13.

Mr Arthur Sweetser, wrote to Hudson that '[t]he elections . . . have been unsatisfactory to a good many people, leaving the Court without a single judge with Bench experience and bringing in perhaps too much an element of men who have had political affiliations'.[58] The view articulated by Hudson that the bench 'would be difficult to improve on' was soon questioned by Hammarskjöld in his private correspondence with Hudson.[59]

There was a personal side to Hammarskjöld's doubts. He had been defeated in the election and afterwards he had been too blunt at Geneva.[60] What is more, many newcomers objected to his attitude of 'la Cour c'est moi'.[61] Hammarskjöld was convinced that his 'influence' would diminish, at least for some time, and he reminded Hudson that 'the new Court contains, if I remember correctly, three ex-members of the Council and five ex-legal advisers to members of the Council'.[62] To Anzilotti, Hammarskjöld wrote that '[m]y opinion is that the spirit of the Court will be entirely changed, as yourself, M. Rolin-Jaequemyns and M. Wang will be unable in the long run to offer sufficient resistance'.[63] In a letter to his father, Hammarskjöld was even more frank as he wrote that '[d]en verkligen sorgen' (the true regret) was that the Permanent Court in its new composition would be subordinated to 'Fromageot–Hurst, mot hvilken de relativt självständiga elementer – Adatci, Anzilotti, Rolin-Jaequemyns och Wang – icke kunna göra sig gällande'.[64]

This concern, even if exaggerated, echoed the worries shared by Judges Anzilotti and Huber when in 1929 Judges Fromageot and Hurst were first elected to the Permanent Court. Their legal qualifications were not as

---

[58] Sweetser to Hudson, 10 October 1930, Hudson papers 114.13.

[59] Hammarskjöld to Hudson, 29 October 1930 and Recano to Hudson, 15 November 1930, both Hudson papers 113.10. See also an anonymous writer's contribution, 'The Work of the Eleventh Assembly Relating to the Permanent Court of International Justice' (1931) 12 *BYIL* 107 at 108 and 123–4.

[60] See Hammarskjöld's note, 27 September 1930, Hammarskjöld papers 486; but see Hammarskjöld's note, 13 September 1934, Hammarskjöld papers 502.

[61] See van Eysinga to Huber, 4 March 1931, Huber papers 23; cf. Series D No. 2, Add.2 (1931) at 139 *et seq.*, 153 *et seq.* and 208–9; and also Manley O. Hudson, *The Permanent Court of International Justice, 1920–1942* (2nd edn, New York, 1943), p. 305.

[62] Hammarskjöld to Hudson, 29 November 1930, Hudson papers 113.10; cf. Paul de Vineuil, 'La Cour permanente de Justice internationale en 1929' (1930) 11 *RDILC* 600 at 604.

[63] Hammarskjöld to Anzilotti, 29 September 1930, Hammarskjöld papers 478.

[64] Hammarskjöld to [Hjalmar] Hammarskjöld, 30 September 1930, Hammarskjöld papers 30 (translation: 'Fromageot–Hurst against which the relatively independent members, Adatci, Anzilotti and Wang, will not be able to assert themselves'). As to Judge Wang's view, see 14 UNCIO, pp. 94 and 828.

such disputed, indeed, according to Elihu Root, 'both the gentlemen named are of the highest character and quality',[65] but it was objected that 'leur entrée simultanée dans la Cour peut-elle créer l'impression d'un certain parallelisme entre le Conseil de la Société des Nations et la Cour'.[66] Actually, the British and French groups of the Permanent Court of Arbitration had avoided nominating nationals of the other country. The explanation was simple: 'on ne voudrait pas donner prise aux critiques déjà formulées à Genève sur l'entente des "jurisconsultes de la couronne" français et anglais.'[67] Having been each other's equivalents at the Foreign Office and the Quai d'Orsay, they had developed a mutual understanding that had been of some political importance in the aftermath of the First World War.[68] Perhaps they did not agree on more points of substantive law than lawyers in general, but their overarching conceptions of the Permanent Court's proper functioning were similar. They regarded the *motifs* of many of the past decisions as being too long and too theoretical.[69]

An early illustration of Judges Hurst and Fromageot's combined impact was an advisory opinion delivered in 1930 at the eighteenth session, according to which the Free City of Danzig could not become a member of the International Labour Organization. Six members of the bench, including Judges Fromageot and Hurst, supported the advice and produced some very short *motifs*, a substantial part of which were the reasons for giving a narrow interpretation to the request for an opinion.[70] Both President Anzilotti and Judge Huber appended dissenting opinions that were longer than the *motifs*. In particular, Judge Huber invoked the Permanent Court's 'traditional conception of advisory opinions' and

---

[65] Root to Moore, 1 May 1929, Moore papers 178; and likewise Root to Hughes, 27 June 1929, Root papers 144.

[66] Huber to Soldati, 9 June 1929, Huber papers 26; and, e.g., Anzilotti to Huber, 10 April 1929, Huber papers 23; and Tobin to Secretary of State, 28 August 1929, NARA 500 C114/849, referring Judge Loder's similar view.

[67] Massigli to Berthelot, 15 May 1930, Quai d'Orsay 2400A.

[68] Arnold D. McNair, 'Sir Cecil James Barrington Hurst, GCMG, KCB, QC, LLD' (1962) 38 *BYIL* 400 at 401.

[69] Committee of Jurists, 'Minutes', pp. 24 and 65–6; and also Briand to Marcilly, 29 December 1928, Quai d'Orsay 2399B. Max Sørensen, *Les Sources du droit international: Etude sur la jurisprudence de la Cour permanente de Justice internationale* (Copenhagen, 1946), p. 183 referred to 'le déclin persistant de la doctrine comme source de droit international'. Cf. R. Y. Jennings, 'The Role of the International Court of Justice' (1997) 58 *BYIL* 1 at 24.

[70] *Free City of Danzig and International Labour Organization*, Series B No. 18 (1930) at 9–10 and 15.

remonstrated with the majority about not giving 'an answer of such usefulness as those concerned may well have expected'.[71]

As representatives of their respective governments, Hurst and Fromageot disagreed on whether dissenting opinions were desirable.[72] Personally, however, Hurst leaned towards the French view that in an international court such opinions were undesirable:

Dissenting opinions are a good system for any system of law which is approaching finality, but for one which is in the formative stage it is more questionable whether a single opinion is not more conducive to a clear understanding of the principles applicable. In a case like the 'Lotus', where the Court was divided six to six and the case decided by the casting vote of the President, or other cases where the Court has given a decision by a narrow majority of one (e.g. the Mavrommatis Jurisdiction point) it is not easy for the practitioner or the student to derive all the help from the decision which he would be able to do if there were but a single opinion to consider.[73]

As indications of the general feeling at The Hague, some diplomats put a neologism, 'Cour de politique internationale',[74] into use, which echoed Hans Wehberg's frank note in *Die Friedens-Warte* on the upcoming election of Judge Weiss' successor published in the beginning of 1929. Having categorised Fromageot as an unwelcome, conservative element, Wehberg had added:

Denn sollte Fromageot in den Gerichtshof gewählt werden, so wird die natürliche Folge die sein, daß auch die Auswärtigen Aemter der anderen Mächte Wert darauf legen, ihre Rechtsbeistände in den Gerichtshof hineinwählen zu lassen. Der Gerichtshof wird dann eines Tages in seiner Mehrheit aus früheren Kronjuristen und außerdem, wenn man die Wahl von Hughes als symptomatisch

---

[71] *Ibid.*, pp. 29 and 36. Judge Anzilotti, as President of the Permanent Court, was reticent about his view on the majority's approach: see *ibid.*, p. 18; cf. Judge Huber's dissenting opinion, *ibid.*, p. 31. See also Huber to Louter, 22 October 1931, Huber papers 23.

[72] Committee of Jurists, 'Minutes', p. 50; and Hurst to Chamberlain, 4 April 1929, FO 371 W3108/21/98.

[73] Hurst's memorandum, 30 November 1928, FO 371 W11377/309/98. While Hurst did not find support at home (see the Lord Chancellor's minute, 13 December 1928, FO 371 W11812/309/78), his German and French counterparts, Gaus and Fromageot, were reported to be 'strongly in favour' of his view: 'What they say is that a judge ought to decide according to his conscience and that the present system renders it quite impossible for a judge who is a national of a small country and has to sit as judge in a case affecting that country to do otherwise than decide in favour of his own country': Hurst's minute, 12 December 1928, FO 371 W11901/309/98. Cf. Gilbert Guillaume, 'Some Thoughts on the Independence of International Judges vis-à-vis States' (2003) 2 *LPICT* 163 at 166.

[74] Scavenius to Munch, 15 December 1930, Rigsarkivet H-12-12.

betrachtet, aus früheren Ministern bestehen, während in Wahrheit berühmte Völkerrechtsgelehrte von internationaler Gesinnung den idealen Richtertypus darstellen, aus dem der Haager Gerichtshof in seiner Mehrheit zusammengesetzt sein muß.[75]

Just before the second general election Judge Loder had written to Moore: 'Politics play an important "rôle" in Geneva, and we have already Government candidates! The same fault the Great Powers have made in 1907. And it is quietly said, they are like the Bourbons: they forget nothing, and they learn nothing.'[76] Later, probably in the late summer of 1931, Loder said that 'I fear with you that it is actually sliding down to a political club'.[77] And then in November 1931 he came down to a conclusion: 'I do not regret to be no more a member of what has become a political club. The German–Austrian case has done much harm to the Court, with its merely ridiculous argumentation.'[78]

Moore very much agreed in this analysis of both the election and the *Customs Regime* opinion delivered at the twenty-second session.[79] Before

---

[75] Hans Wehberg, 'Zur Wahl des französischen Mitgliedes des Weltgerichtshofs' (1929) 29 *Die Friedens-Warte* 17 at 17 (translation: 'Should Fromageot be elected to the Court, the natural consequence of his election will be that the foreign offices of the other Great Powers will also take labour to have their legal advisers elected to the Court. Consequently, the Court shall one day have a majority of former crown jurists and in addition, if the election of Hughes is seen as symptomatic, former ministers, while in truth the ideal judge – and the majority of the Hague Court should be comprised of such judges – is a renowned expert on international law with an international outlook.'). Schücking had commented on the concerns aired by Wehberg, saying that they could not be rejected out of hand. Yet he was convinced that in addition to former judges and professors in international law, former diplomats were needed on the bench; 'Ihnen wird niemand das höchste Maß von Kenntnissen und Erfahrungen auf dem Gebiet des internationalen Rechts und seiner Anwendung bestreiten können': see Walther Schücking, 'Vertrauliche Bemerkungen zur Frage der Revision des Statuts des Weltgerichtshofs', undated, Schücking papers (Koblenz) 32, pp. 2–3 (translation: 'Nobody can argue that they do not have the highest degree of knowledge and experience as regards the field of international law and its practical application'). Cf. Thomas M. Franck, 'Some Psychological Factors in International Third-Party Decision-Making' (1966–7) 19 *Stanford Law Review* 1217 at 1234, note 73.

[76] Loder to Moore, 19 September 1930, Moore papers 62; and likewise Loder to Hughes, February 1930, Hughes papers 5.

[77] Loder to Moore, undated [1931], Moore papers 64; and also Johnson to Secretary of State, 18 February 1931, NARA 500 C114/1265, referring to a conversation with Loder.

[78] Loder to Moore, 19 November 1931, Moore papers 64.

[79] On the election, see Moore to Borchard, 28 September 1930, Borchard papers 7.97. Moore was particularly concerned with the election of the three South Americans. In his view, '[t]he concession of the presidency of the Assembly, so often made to Latin America, is now in principle carried into the Court'. Noting the re-election of 'Altamira – Senator and historian', Moore added: 'May he not be honoured with the presidency of the court next year, and thus, as representing the mother, becomingly shelter the three stray chicks?'

the advisory opinion had been delivered, Moore had told Professor Borchard that he had 'never been able to see any legal ground on which the Austro-German customs agreement could be held to violate the treaties'; in his view, '[t]he opinion in this case will definitely show whether the present court is a political board or a judicial body'.[80] And so it did, Moore opining a month later that:

[t]he Court has dealt itself a blow from which it cannot be expected to recover unless it is brought to its senses by an effective public rebuke. The cause for which Huber and I, particularly, consistently and strenuously fought, not always with entire success, is, with the change in the personnel of the Court, for the time being lost.[81]

Professor Verzijl, who at this point had begun producing regular case-notes, observed that '[t]he statements of reasons for the decisions had already greatly deteriorated of late (even before the renovation of the Court – under the influence of new Judges?), but this latest Advisory Opinion bears away the palm in this respect'.[82]

In Hammarskjöld's view, the *Customs Regime* opinion bore out his concerns about the Permanent Court in its new composition.[83] Under the pseudonym of 'André Becker', Hammarskjöld later reviewed all the Permanent Court's decisions delivered in 1930 and 1931, emphasising 'cette . . . brièveté dans l'exposé des motifs qu'on a pu observer, d'une manière générale, dans les avis à partir de 1930'.[84] This review also noted the 'profonds changements' in the Permanent Court's composition that had taken effect in 1930, Judges Fromageot and Hurst coming on to the bench.[85] At the time, in a letter to Hudson, Hammarskjöld explained why he had been so critical of Hudson's speaking of a bench that was hard or difficult to improve on:

Of course I quite saw your reasons for striking that note; but my fear was – as I think I said at once – that if achievements of the Court thus ideally composed were subsequently severely criticized, the very statement that the composition could not be improved upon would inevitably be read as a somewhat sweeping condemnation of the whole institution, thus defeating its own object.

[80] Moore to Borchard, 17 August 1931, Borchard papers 7.98.
[81] Moore to Borchard, 11 September 1931, Moore papers 63. Indeed, Moore called the *Customs Regime* opinion 'an unfortunate aftermath' of the period 1922 to 1927 in which he served on the bench: see John Bassett Moore, 'Permanent Court of International Justice at The Hague', 27 December 1943, Moore papers 180, pp. 40–6.
[82] J. H. W. Verzijl, *The Jurisprudence of the World Court* (Leiden, 1965), vol. 1, p. 262.
[83] Hammarskjöld to [Hjalmar] Hammarskjöld, 7 October 1931, Hammarskjöld papers 30.
[84] André Becker, 'La Cour permanente de Justice internationale en 1930–1931' (1932) 13 *RDILC* 524 at 563 and also 541–2, 542, 547, 555 and 559.
[85] *Ibid.*, p. 524.

And I am afraid that this is exactly what has happened, no matter whether the criticism is sound or not.[86]

Self-restraint in treaty interpretation

The Customs Regime *opinion*

The *Customs Regime* opinion was a watershed in the history of the Permanent Court because it significantly damaged the Permanent Court's reputation. This was partly due to the obscurity of the *motifs*, although perhaps it was partly a consequence of a decline in enthusiasm among commentators and politicians, many of whom had been 'optimists', for this project of international justice. The *Customs Regime* opinion conveniently provided the cynics with capital. Obscurity makes it a less useful illustration of international legal argument; yet, and in addition to the past careers of the judges, the *Customs Regime* opinion offered some reasons for the decline in the standard of the Permanent Court's legal reasoning, as underlined by Verzijl and Hammarskjöld. In particular, there was a new flavour of national lawyers being drawn towards the basic structure of international legal argument based on the conception of the state as a national sovereign.

The *Customs Regime* opinion was the most politically sensitive dispute to be referred to the Permanent Court. By 1931, the Great Depression had reached its peak. European statesmen remained incapable of quick action, while Germany and Austria planned to assimilate their tariff policies and enter into a politically sensitive customs union. The plan created considerable anxiety, especially within the French Government, as movements in both Germany and Austria worked towards full political union. On the initiative of the British Government, the Council requested an advisory opinion as to whether the planned customs union was compatible with the obligations undertaken by Austria in Article 88 of the Saint-Germain Treaty and in a Geneva Protocol of 1922 not to 'compromise' or 'threaten' its 'independence' without the consent of the Council. It was regarded as a case of urgency by all the governments involved, and also by the Permanent Court.[87]

Before the Permanent Court, the pleading governments advanced some highly principled arguments as to Austria's independence. Representing the German Government, Professor Viktor Bruns drew a clear

---

[86] Hammarskjöld to Hudson, 18 January 1932, Hudson papers 113.10; and see also von Stauffenberg, 'Revision des Statuts', p. 92.

[87] See Adatci to Schücking, 27 May 1931, Schücking Papers (Koblenz) 33.

distinction between independence and sovereignty, where independence 'signifie que, dans le cadre de sa compétence, l'Etat agit par lui-même, par ses propres organes'.[88] Bruns rightly criticised the French, Italian and Czechoslovak Governments for overlooking that distinction in their written submissions.[89] On the other hand, acting on behalf of the French Government, Professor Basdevant took the view that the term 'independence' as employed in the two treaty texts had a wider meaning than according to the international law of coexistence.[90]

On the bench, which consisted of all fifteen ordinary judges,[91] the conceptual issue apparently raised some difficulty. It is true that the three opinions to which the proceeding gave rise would seem to have followed Bruns, defining 'independence' in opposition to a state's being subject to another state (not to its being subject to international law).[92] However, at least at the opening of the deliberations, this had been a minority view. On 20 August 1931, only Judge van Eysinga had voted against the following proposition:

Dans l'article 88 du traité de Saint-Germain, l'indépendance de l'Autriche doit-elle s'entendre du maintien de son existence dans ses frontières actuelles comme Etat séparé restant seul maître de ses décisions?[93]

---

[88] Series C No. 53 at 227.

[89] *Ibid.*, pp. 219–37, referring to the various memoirs: *ibid.*, pp. 119–22 and 128 (French Government), 156–7 (Italian Government) and 166–7 (Czechoslovak Government); cf. *ibid.*, p. 53 (German Government).

[90] *Ibid.*, pp. 394–5 and 399–406; see also *ibid.*, pp. 451 and 468.

[91] In an order, the Permanent Court had decided that there was no need for the appointment of judges *ad hoc* by Austria and Czechoslovakia, since 'all governments which, in the proceedings before the Court, come to the same conclusion, must be held to be in the same interest for the purposes of the present case': *Customs Regime between Germany and Austria (Protocol of March 19th, 1931)*, Series A/B No. 41 (1931) at 89–90. As regards Austria, President Adatci and Judges Altamira, Anzilotti, Rostworowski and Wang dissented, holding that 'Austria is a Party to the dispute with reference to which the Court's opinion is asked, whereas Germany is not': *ibid.*, p. 91.

[92] *Ibid.*, pp. 45–6, 57 and 77; and see Scelle in YILC 1949, pp. 88–9 and 189 (but contrast El-Erian in YILC 1978-I, p. 47); cf. the rhetorical argument of the dissenters, Series A/B No. 41 (1931) at 86. See also Antonio Sanchez de Bustamante y Sirvén, *Droit international public* (Paris, 1934), vol. 1, pp. 219–20. In his individual note, Schücking wrote: 'il est vrai que le mot "souveraineté", de nos jours, est assez discrédité, mais c'est seulement parce qu'on a combiné aux temps de l'absolutisme et de l'étatisme exagéré par la philosophie de Hegel une conception qui pose l'Etat au-dessus du droit. Evidemment, une telle conception est impossible dans notre époque d'interdépendance des Etats. Mais, au lieu d'abolir la notion de la souveraineté, il faudrait lui donner un contenu raisonnable': Schucking papers (Koblenz) 32.

[93] Distr. 2133, Schücking papers (Münster) XII.1. Having regard to the specific obligations imposed on Austria, Judge van Eysinga took the view that '[i]l est clair que cette indépendance que le Traité de Saint-Germain et le Protocole No. I de 1922

But only eight members of the Permanent Court gave their approval of this proposition with the following qualification:

... sous réserve des obligations assumées par elle dans les traités en vigueur ou résultant pour elle du droit international?

Those opposed to the qualification were President Adatci and Judges Anzilotti, de Bustamante, van Eysinga, Hurst, Kellogg and Schücking.[94]

The crucial issue was not, however, the meaning of 'independence' but whether this independence would be 'compromised' or 'threatened' by the planned customs union. On this point, the pleadings had been haphazard, almost as if the governments had been shy of the issue. The bench divided into three groups. Seven judges signing the joint dissenting opinion, namely President Adatci and Judges van Eysinga, Hurst, Kellogg, Rolin-Jaequemyns, Schücking and Wang, essentially declined to calculate the dangers to Austria's independence. This was considered a 'political' question.[95] The authoritative version of the dissenting opinion was English and indeed it was Judge Hurst who on 1 September 1931 had submitted a 'Draft of Dissenting Opinion – Sir Cecil Hurst's Revised Text'.[96] The dissenting opinion bore some resemblance to Judge Kellogg's observations in the *Free Zones* case, to which Judge Hurst had paid considerable regard at the first session in 1931 (but on which no agreement had been reached among the judges).[97] President Adatci was also a strong supporter of the view.[98] Judge Schücking, for his part, gave the word 'independence' a very technical interpretation, which interestingly involved the principle that 'il faut interpréter les textes de manière à ne pas étendre les restrictions à la liberté d'action du débiteur au-delà

---

reconnaissent à l'Austriche est autre chose que p.e. celle de la France ou de la Suède': see van Eysinga's note, van Eysinga papers 137.

[94] They found support for their view in, e.g., Sakutaro Tachi, *La Souveraineté et l'indépendance de l'état et les questions intérieures en droit international* (Paris, 1930), pp. 36–54, 68, 112–13 and 119. See also Judge Anzilotti's separate opinion in Series A/B No. 41 (1931) at 66–7; but cf. the joined dissenting opinion, *ibid.*, pp. 77–8 and 86.

[95] Series A/B No. 41 (1931) at 82 and also 75; and Adatci to van Eysinga, undated [1931], van Eysinga papers 137; cf. Louis Le Fur, 'Règles générales du droit de la paix' (1935) 54 *Recueil des Cours* 5 at 267–8.

[96] See Draft of Dissenting Opinion, 1 September 1931, van Eysinga papers 137.

[97] See also McNair, 'Cecil Hurst', p. 402. Judge Hurst had proposed that the Permanent Court ought to make up its mind as to the view advocated by Judge Kellogg and inform the Council accordingly: see Hurst's note, 28 January 1931, Distr. 1838, Adatci papers 38; and also Johnson to Secretary of State, 16 February 1931, NARA 500 C114/1250.

[98] See Adatci's draft note, 14 August 1931, Hammarskjöld papers 477.

du minimum encore compatible avec le texte'.[99] It has been said that, on this occasion, Judge Schücking co-operated with Judge Kellogg.[100]

In contrast, the question of the dangers to Austria's independence was explicitly addressed in the separate opinion that Judge Anzilotti appended to the Permanent Court's decision, relying on considerations of 'a political and economic kind'.[101] Seven other judges reached the same conclusion as Judge Anzilotti, namely that the planned customs union would endanger Austria's independence, including Judge Fromageot, who thereby came to the same conclusion as the French Government. However, the *motifs* were marred by disagreements among the seven judges. While they opened by describing the position of Austria as 'a sensitive point in the European system' and 'an essential feature of the existing political settlement',[102] the dangers to which Austria's independence was exposed were not elaborated on in public.[103] Indeed, Judge de Bustamante did not agree that Austria's independence would be threatened by taking part in the planned customs union. However, the Geneva Protocol provided that Austria 'shall not violate her economic independence by granting to any State a special régime or exclusive advantages calculated to threaten this independence', and Judge de Bustamante took the extraordinary view, shared by none of his colleagues, that a 'special régime' was a violation of the Geneva Protocol even if implying no threat to Austria's independence.[104] In contrast, Judges Altamira, Fromageot, Guerrero, Negulesco, Rostworowski and Urrutia saw a threat to Austria's independence and so a violation of the Saint-Germain Treaty as

---

[99] See Schücking's note, 17 August 1931, Schücking papers (Koblenz) 32; and also G. van Hecke, 'Relecture de l'avis consultatif sur le projet d'union douanière austro-allemande' in Marianne Dony (ed.), *Mélanges en hommage à Michel Waelbroeck* (Bruxelles, 1999), p. 255 at pp. 259–60. For a similar view, see the memorial submitted by the Austrian Government, Series C No. 53 at 86–7. Wehberg quoted Schücking as having suggested that 'alle politischen Streitfragen' should be submitted to arbitration and settled on the basis of 'Billigkeit': see Hans Wehberg, 'Das Gutachten des Weltgerichtshofs in der Zollunionsfrage' (1931) 31 *Die Friedens-Warte* 301 at 302.

[100] See Christoph-Bernhard Schücking, 'Walther Schücking: Ein Lebensbild' in *Fünfzig Jahre Institut für Internationales Recht an der Universität Kiel* (Kiel, 1965), p. 174 at p. 191.

[101] Series A/B No. 41 (1931) at 68; and also, as regards the nature of the Council, *ibid.*, pp. 57, 61–2 and 69–70.

[102] *Ibid.*, pp. 42 and also 45.

[103] Cf. Judge Anzilotti's separate opinion, *ibid.*, pp. 56, 68 and 70–3.

[104] See Distr. 2133, Schücking papers (Münster) XII.1; and also Series A/B No. 41 (1931) at 52. It may be noted that only Judges van Eysinga, Hurst, Kellogg and Rolin-Jaequemyns took the view that the Vienna Protocol did not constitute a 'special régime'.

well as the Geneva Protocol.[105] The advice as such did not pronounce on the conformity of the proposed customs union with the Saint-Germain Treaty.[106]

When discussing the draft opinion at the meeting at which it was adopted, Judge van Eysinga suggested the deletion of two pages.[107] Judges Fromageot and Rostworowski, who had been members of the drafting committee, countered this suggestion, which eventually was defeated by the seven members of the Permanent Court who supported the *motifs*. Judge van Eysinga won the support of only President Adatci and Judge Wang, while Judges Altamira, Anzilotti, Hurst, Jaequemyns and Kellogg abstained. In the end, Judge Anzilotti cast a vote against the *motifs*, while the seven dissenters abstained.

The *Customs Regime* opinion has generally been regarded as a misfortune for the Permanent Court.[108] Professor Hans Morgenthau was almost alone in seeing the opinion as an attempt to find a legal solution for a political dispute.[109] Most commentators considered that it imposed a political solution on a legal dispute. This view had already gained some

---

[105] *Ibid.*, p. 53 and see also *ibid.*, pp. 47–8; cf. *ibid.*, p. 49.

[106] See J. L. Brierly, 'The Advisory Opinion of the Permanent Court on the Customs Régime between Germany and Austria' (1933) 3 *ZaöRV* 68 at 71; and H. Lauterpacht, *The Development of International Law by the International Court* (London, 1958), p. 48.

[107] See Twenty-second session, *Procès-Verbal* 39 (1 September 1931), Schücking papers (Koblenz) 33. Judge van Eysinga also suggested that the dissenting opinion was considerably shortened, concentrating on Series A/B No. 41 (1931) at 78–82: see van Eysinga to Hurst, undated, van Eysinga papers 137.

[108] E.g., Edwin M. Borchard, 'The Customs Union Advisory Opinion' (1931) 25 *AJIL* 711 at 715–16; Manley O. Hudson, 'The World Court and the Austro-German Customs Régime' (1931) 17 *American Bar Association Journal* 791 at 793; Ferenc A. Váli, 'The Austro-German Customs Regime before the Permanent Court, Considered with Reference to the Proposed Federation of Danubian States' (1932) 18 *Grotius Transactions* 79 at 88–92; Brierly, 'Customs Régime', p. 74; and A. de Lapradelle, 'Les Vies et les oeuvres: in memoriam Edouard Rolin-Jaequemyns, Albéric Rolin, Elihu Root' (1937) 19 *Revue de Droit International* 3 at 6.

[109] See Hans Morgenthau, *Politics among Nations* (5th edn, New York, 1973), p. 408; and also Carl Bilfinger, 'Der Streit um die deutsch-österreichische Zollunion' (1931) 3 *ZaöRV* 163 at 163; Julius Stone, *Legal Control of International Conflict: A Treatise on the Dynamics of Disputes – and War-Law* (London, 1954), p. 150; Wolfgang Friedmann, *The Changing Structure of International Law* (London, 1964), p. 155, note 6; Rosenne, YILC 1966-I.1, p. 32; and Martti Koskenniemi, *From Apology to Utopia: The Structure of International Legal Argument* (Helsinki, 1989), p. 210. Cf. Hans Morgenthau, *Die internationale Retchspflege, ihr Wesen und ihre Grenzen* (Leipzig, 1929), pp. 112–19; and Hans Morgenthau, 'Positivism, Functionalism, and International Law' (1940) 34 *AJIL* 260 at 280 and 282.

ground before the advisory opinion was delivered,[110] and it was fuelled by the combination of Judge Anzilotti's boldness, the obscurity of the *motifs* and the dissenters' scarcely veiled accusations.[111] Moore was unwavering in his support of the joint dissenting opinion, as was Professor Borchard.[112] Judge Schücking took the view that:

die Sache nach meinen Dafürhalten [ist] für uns noch verhältnismässig günstig ausgegangen. Die formelle Niederlage hat unserer Regierung den Rückzug erleichtert, der aus politischen Gründen auch bei einem Obsiegen notwendig gewesen wäre. Auf der anderen Seite war das Gutachten des Weltgerichtshofs mit 7 gegen 8 Stimmen für uns ein moralischer Sieg. Das Ansehen des Gerichtshofs selbst hat freilich durch das völlige Auseinanderfallen und die Herausstellung eines französischen Blocks in der Welt sehr gelitten.[113]

That being said, Manley O. Hudson, one of the few adherents to the majority opinion, was right in arguing that 'the question before the Court could hardly have been answered without some appreciation of the political situation which led to the treaties themselves'.[114] There are

---

[110] See Edwin M. Borchard, 'The Theory and Sources of International Law' in *Recueil d'etudes sur les sources du droit en l'honneur de François Gény* (Paris, 1934), vol. 3, p. 328 at p. 353; and also Borchard to Moore, 27 August 1931, Moore papers 63 and Borchard papers 7.98. In an earlier letter, also reporting from The Hague, Professor Borchard wrote that '[t]here seems to be considerable agreement here that the present Court is immeasurably weaker (in juridical calibre) than the original Court': see Borchard to Moore, 17 August 1931, Moore papers 63.

[111] Series A/B No. 41 (1931) at 75.

[112] See Borchard, 'Customs Union Advisory Opinion', pp. 715–16; and Moore to Huber, 19 August 1931, Huber papers 7; and Moore to Borchard, 15 September 1932, Moore papers 64. Borchard had been corresponding with Moore regarding his case note on the *Customs Regime* opinion: see Moore to Borchard, 11 September 1931 and 2 October 1931, Moore papers 63 and Borchard papers 7.98; and also Jessup to Borchard, 8 December 1931 and 12 December 1931, Jessup papers A205.

[113] Schücking to Colm, 3 November 1931, Schücking papers (Münster) XII.1 (translation: 'in my opinion the case had a relatively favourable outcome for us. The formal defeat has made the retreat of our government easier, a retreat which would also have been necessary for political reasons in case of victory. On the other hand, the opinion of the World Court with seven votes against eight was a moral victory for us. The standing of the Court itself has certainly suffered from the complete disintegration and the manifestation of a French block.'). Cf. Detlev Acker, *Walther Schücking (1875–1935)* (Münster, 1970), p. 204.

[114] Hudson, 'Austro-German Customs Régime', p. 793; and similarly Philip C. Jessup, 'The Customs Union Advisory Opinion' (1932) 26 *AJIL* 105 at 108 and 110; Charles de Visscher, 'La Cour permanente de Justice internationale et sa contribution au développement du droit international' (1936) 22 *Bulletin de la Classe des Lettres et des Sciences Morales et Politiques* 151 at 156–7; and Huber to Louter, 22 October 1931, Huber papers 23.

similarities between the joint dissenting opinion in the *Customs Regime* case and the widely criticised judgment in the so-called second phase of the *South West Africa* case.[115] Remarkably, in a book devoted to the argument that all international disputes are justiciable, Hersch Lauterpacht took the view that as for the *Customs Regime* case '[i]t is conceivable that the Court could have arrived at an opinion to the effect that the treaty provisions were so vague as to be meaningless, and that therefore no question of their violation arose'.[116]

An entire dimension of the proceeding was neglected by most commentators. Thus, Hammarskjöld wrote to Hudson that '[n]one of the explanations I have seen so far – whether simply straightforward and brutal or ingenious and complicated – is the correct one; but I suppose something has got to be said'.[117] Although emphasising that 'le délibéré "est et demeure secret"',[118] 'André Becker' analysed the *Customs Regime* opinion in detail. In Hammarskjöld's view, 'André Becker' wrote 'something which strikes me as fundamentally accurate'.[119] More than anything else, he put the advisory proceeding in the context of the Council's more comprehensive decision-making process. The consequence of all three opinions would have been, had the planned customs union not been abandoned by the Austrian and German Governments just before the advisory opinion was delivered, that the dispute would have been back on the Council's table. In particular, the dissenting opinion, on the face of it an unsophisticated exercise in treaty interpretation, held that the Council was better equipped to apply the treaty provisions in question.[120]

---

[115] *South West Africa* (Second Phase), ICJ Reports [1966] 6; and see G. G. Fitzmaurice, 'Sir Cecil Hurst (1870–1963)' (1963) 50-II *Annuaire*, p. 462 at p. 473; cf. Edward McWhinney, *Judicial Settlement of International Disputes: Jurisdiction, Justiciability and Judicial Law-Making on the Contemporary International Court* (Dordrecht, 1991), p. 45.

[116] H. Lauterpacht, *The Function of Law in the International Community* (Oxford, 1933), p. 156, note 1. But see also Dietrich Schindler, 'Les Progrès de l'arbitrage obligatoire depuis la création de la Société des Nations' (1933) 46 *Recueil des Cours* 233 at 255.

[117] Hammarskjöld to Hudson, 25 November 1931, Hudson papers 130.11.

[118] Becker, '1930–1931', p. 549.

[119] Hammarskjöld to Moore, 29 January 1934, Moore papers 178.

[120] Becker, '1930–1931', pp. 554–5. And see the draft of President Adatci's written note that had indeed been prepared by Hammarskjöld, 14 August 1931, Hammarskjöld papers 477. In the *motifs*, it was noted that Article 88 of the Saint-Germain Treaty and the Geneva Protocol, 'without imposing any absolute veto upon Austria, simply [*simplement*] require her to abstain or, in certain circumstances, to obtain the consent of the Council of the League of Nations', Series A/B No. 41 (1931) at 44; see also Judge Anzilotti's separate opinion, *ibid.*, pp. 57 and 69–70.

Another indication of the 'new' Court's special understanding of the domain and workings of the Council was the following passage taken from its first decision, the rather uncontroversial *Minorities School* opinion, concerning a *modus vivendi* adopted by the Council while the *Minorities School* case had been pending before the 'first' Court:

> Though, in accordance with the rules of law, the interpretation given by the Court to the terms of the Convention has retrospective effect – in the sense that the terms of the Convention must be held to have always borne the meaning placed upon them by this interpretation – it does not follow that the results of the purely practical measures to which the Council legitimately had recourse in order temporarily to obviate the difficulties resulting from the uncertainty prevailing as to the meaning of the rules to be applied, are necessarily null and void.[121]

To sum up, the *Customs Regime* opinion was a monument to judicial self-restraint. This was particularly due to the joint dissenting opinion, but even Judge Anzilotti had considered whether the Permanent Court should refrain from giving an opinion.[122] It was the first illustration of Judge Anzilotti feeling 'totalement isolé et dans l'impossibilité de faire quelque chose de bon'.[123] Years later, in 1939, a British diplomat noted about Judge Anzilotti's position: 'The present Italian Judge, Professor Anzilotti, is (though he never agrees with anybody else) a very useful member of the Court, and I understand that his colleagues are anxious that he should stand again.'[124] Still, Judge Anzilotti became 'the great dissenter' while it was the joint dissenting opinion, not the

---

[121] *Access to German Minority Schools in Polish Upper Silesia*, Series A/B No. 40 (1931) at 19. The remark that 'the interpretation given by the Court to the terms of the Convention has retrospective effect' was hardly of general application, thus it should not be seen as a rejection of a principle of 'dynamic' treaty interpretation; cf. J. P. Fockema Andreae, *An Important Chapter from the History of Legal Interpretation: The Jurisdiction of the First Permanent Court of International Justice, 1922–1940* (Leiden, 1948), pp. 25–6 and 105–6. As to the nature of the Council, see also *Interpretation of the Statute of the Memel Territory* (Jurisdiction), Series A/B No. 47 (1932) at 248.

[122] Series A/B No. 41 (1931) at 68–9; and likewise Moore to Hammarskjöld, 19 January 1934, Hammarskjöld papers 483. Contrary to many other commentators, Moore was also highly critical of Judge Anzilotti's separate opinion, which he associated with a conception of the Permanent Court's advisory jurisdiction as different from his own: see Moore to Brierly, 15 February 1932, Moore papers 178.

[123] Anzilotti to Huber, 5 October 1931, Huber papers 23.

[124] Cadogan's minute, 23 February 1939, and Malkin's note, 7 March 1939, both FO 371 W3446/107/98. In Hudson's view, Judge Anzilotti 'is the best judge the Court has ever had': Hudson to Stimson, 20 December 1938, Hudson papers 97-3. Cf. Charles de Visscher, 'Dionisio Anzilotti' (1951) 6 *La Comunità Internazionale* 247 at 251–2; Edvard Hambro, 'Dissenting and Individual Opinions in the International Court of Justice'

confused *motifs*, that foreshadowed many of the dominating themes around which majorities would gather in the following years, the first example arguably being the unanimous *Railway Traffic* opinion also delivered at the twenty-second session.[125] Moore wrote that he had 'an impression that the court began to decline after the decision in the case of the German–Austrian commercial treaty'.[126]

The Employment of Women *opinion*

Following the *Customs Regime* opinion, the *Employment of Women* opinion delivered at the twenty-sixth session in 1932 was the best example during Judge Adatci's presidency of the interpretation of a treaty the subject matter of which was not already covered by the international law of coexistence. The *motifs* were supported by six judges, none of whom had been on the bench for long, namely President Adatci and Judges van Eysinga, Guerrero, Hurst, Negulesco and Urrutia. The result was a rather short opinion marred by its self-restraint and strictly focusing on textual interpretation.

The question was whether Article 3 of the Convention concerning Employment of Women During the Night, adopted in 1919 by the International Labour Conference, applied to women who held positions of supervision or management and were not ordinarily engaged in manual work. The majority answered the question in the affirmative, relying on the text of Article 3:

Women without distinction of age shall not be employed during the night in any public or private industrial undertaking, or in any branch thereof, other than an undertaking in which only members of the same family are employed.

According to the International Labour Organization, the nub of the matter was whether to adopt a textual ('la thèse littérale') or an historical interpretation ('la thèse historique'): the former led to an affirmative answer to the question referred, while the latter supported an answer in

---

(1956) 17 ZaöRV 229 at 229, note 3; and Ernst Rabel, *The Conflict of Laws: A Comparative Study* (2nd edn by Ulrich Drobnig, Ann Arbor, 1958), vol. 1, p. 17.

[125] Cf. Judge Anzilotti's observations in *Railway Traffic between Lithuania and Poland (Railway Sector Landwarów–Kaisiadorys)*, Series A/B No. 42 (1931) at 123 and also *ibid.*, pp. 112, 119 and 120. In preparing the *Railway Traffic* opinion, President Adatci had been exceedingly interested in the preparatory work of the Council's resolutions and other previous undertakings in the dispute: see Adatci to van Eysinga, 17 June 1931, van Eysinga papers 135.

[126] John Bassett Moore, '1926: Permanent Court of International Justice', undated, Moore papers 180.

the negative.[127] Although refraining from expressing a definite conclusion, the Organization let there be no doubt that it favoured the textual approach.[128] So did, and very explicitly so, the British Government, also appearing before the Permanent Court.[129] The sole dissenting voice was raised by the German Government, which based its opposition upon 'la thèse de la raison', arguing that owners and also women in high positions must be exempted and that a principle of equality between the sexes ought to be observed.[130]

The Permanent Court heard two English lawyers, Mr Phelan, appearing as representative of the International Labour Organization, and Mr Fachiri, counsel for the British Government. Phelan emphasised that the method of interpretation adopted in this case would influence the whole of 'international labour legislation',[131] while Fachiri warned that 'if this Convention is not to apply to women in positions of supervision and management, the door will be opened to further derogation', insecurity ensuing.[132] Fachiri found it opportune, towards the end of his speech, to make the following comments:

The suggestion is sometimes made that we in England take a narrow, legalistic view founded upon our peculiar system of law, which is in contrast with the more liberal principles of, say, Roman law. I submit with respect that this opinion is quite mistaken. As I shall endeavour to show, the construction which my Government advocates is not the result of any exclusively English rules, but the result of what, if I may be permitted to do so, I would call common sense, upon which sound principles of law everywhere are based.[133]

A third English lawyer, Judge Hurst, was a member of the drafting committee together with President Adatci and Judge Negulesco.[134] According to the *motifs*, which closely resembled the oral submissions of the British Government, '[t]he wording of Article 3, considered by itself, gives rise to no difficulty; it is general in its terms and free from ambiguity or obscurity'.[135] 'If, therefore', the majority added, 'Article 3 . . . is to be

---

[127] Series C No. 60 at 173 and 180.
[128] See *ibid.*, pp. 180 and 173–80 and also 208–9. See also the other organisations appearing before the Permanent Court: *ibid.*, pp. 196 and 198.
[129] *Ibid.*, pp. 183, 218 and 221.   [130] *Ibid.*, pp. 238 and also 188.
[131] *Ibid.*, pp. 207, 211 and 213–14; see also *ibid.*, p. 240.
[132] *Ibid.*, pp. 216 and 236–7 and also 186–7; see also *ibid.*, pp. 247–8.
[133] *Ibid.*, pp. 232 and also 234–5.
[134] Twenty-sixth session, *Procès-Verbal* 7 (25 October 1932), van Eysinga papers 127, p. 5.
[135] *Interpretation of the Convention of 1919 concerning Employment of Women during the Night*, Series A/B No. 50 (1932) at 373.

interpreted in such a way as not to apply to women holding posts of supervision and management and not ordinarily engaged in manual work, it is necessary to find some valid ground for interpreting the provisions otherwise than in accordance with the natural sense of the words.'

In the remaining part of the *motifs*, the Permanent Court considered and rejected various such grounds. First, it considered whether there was a general presumption to the effect that conventions adopted by the International Labour Conference only applied to manual workers unless otherwise provided.[136] It also considered the possible implications of the agenda of the Conference in 1919, which had included the revision of conventions adopted at Berne in 1906, one of which concerned the employment of women during the night and was expressly confined to manual workers.[137] Furthermore, the Permanent Court examined the preparatory work, which convinced the majority that the original aim of not deviating from the stipulations of the Berne Convention had been replaced by a policy of all draft conventions presented to the International Labour Conference being drawn up in uniform language.[138]

There were two more grounds which the Permanent Court considered in the *motifs* and which might have been of greater significance. First, it noted that the Convention Limiting the Hours of Work in Industrial Undertakings to Eight in the Day and Forty-Eight in the Week, also adopted in 1919 at the International Labour Conference, explicitly exempted persons who held positions of supervision or management.[139] This Convention applied to men as well as women. Secondly, the Permanent Court held:

It has been stated that in 1919, when the Convention was adopted at Washington, very few women actually held positions of supervision or management in industrial undertakings, and that the application of the Convention to women holding such posts was never considered. Even if this were so, however, it does not by itself afford sufficient reason for ignoring the terms of the Convention. The mere fact that, at the time when the Convention . . . was concluded, certain facts or situations, which the terms of the Convention in their ordinary meaning are wide enough to cover, were not thought of, does not justify interpreting those of its provisions which are general in scope otherwise than in accordance with their terms.[140]

---

[136] *Ibid.*, pp. 374–6.   [137] *Ibid.*, pp. 376–7.
[138] *Ibid.*, pp. 378–80.   [139] *Ibid.*, p. 381.   [140] *Ibid.*, p. 377.

The majority was successful in keeping a distance from the conception of the state as an international sovereign as well as the conception of the state as a national sovereign and the national principle of self-containedness. However, the alternative that it offered was not particularly encouraging. The majority turned objective treaty interpretation based on the conception of the state as an international law subject into a textual exercise indebted to formalism. Its insistence on considering the arguments against its textual interpretation separately was indicative.

While four of the dissenters voted against the advice on the ground of a subjective interpretation,[141] thus relying on the preparatory work and the conception of the state as an international sovereign, what struck Judge Anzilotti, and probably strikes a present-day reader, was the complete absence of a teleological interpretation, not to mention a dynamic interpretation. The Permanent Court had been presented with the argument that an interpretation without foundation in the known intentions of the parties would amount to an act of legislation.[142] The introductory paragraph of Judge Anzilotti's dissenting opinion seems worthwhile quoting:

I do not see how it is possible to say that an article of a convention is clear until the subject and aim of the convention have been ascertained, for the article only assumes its true import in this convention and in relation thereto. Only when it is known what the Contracting Parties intended to do and the aim they had in view is it possible to say either that the natural meaning of terms used in a particular article corresponds with the real intention of the Parties, or that the natural meaning of the terms used falls short of or goes further than such intention. In the first alternative it may rightly be said that the text is clear and that it is impossible, on the pretext of interpretation, to endow it with an import other than that which is consistent with the natural meaning of the words. In the other alternative, since the words have no value save as an expression of the intention of the Parties, it will be found either that the words have been used in a wider sense than normally attaches to them (broad interpretation) or that they have been used in a narrower sense than normally attaches to them (narrow interpretation).[143]

---

[141] See the declaration of Judges Fromageot, Rolin-Jaequemyns, Rostworowski and Schücking, *ibid.*, p. 382.

[142] See the International Labour Organization and the British Government in Series C No. 60 at 179–80, 181, 185 and 233, respectively, and also Georges Fischer, *Les Rapports entre l'Organisation internationale du Travail et la Cour permanente de Justice internationale* (Berne, 1946), p. 343.

[143] Series A/B No. 50 (1932) at 383.

Although Judge Anzilotti referred to the conception of the state as an international sovereign, he was not led to a subjective interpretation based on the intentions of the law-makers. Rather it brought him back to the context in which the Convention had been adopted. Thus, having stated that '[t]he first question which arises . . . is what is the subject and aim of the convention in which occurs the article to be interpreted',[144] he put the Convention in the context of Part XIII of the Versailles Treaty and held that the focus of the International Labour Organization was on manual workers and that the Convention should be interpreted accordingly.[145] In commenting on the textual interpretation in the *motifs*, Judge Anzilotti stated that:

this argument, which in itself is sufficiently weak, for it has no regard to the nature of the Convention in which the expression is used, loses all its force when we observe that this expression is used in documents relating to labour legislation to designate women industrial workers.[146]

Commentators who appreciated the first part of the *motifs* in *The Wimbledon* were bound also to be impressed by the *Employment of Women* opinion.[147] Professor Bin Cheng has said that, generally speaking, 'the Permanent Court of International Justice has developed the teleological approach of interpreting the intention of the parties so that it is the real and practical aim pursued by the contracting parties that is enforced'.[148] However, referring to Judge Anzilotti's dissenting opinions in *The Wimbledon* and the *Employment of Women* opinion, among others, he added that '[i]n many cases, Anzilotti would have preferred to go much further than the Court, a fact which explains many of his dissenting opinions'.[149] Noting Judge Anzilotti's 'contribution', and emphasising that only six of the fifteen members of the Permanent Court had supported the *motifs*, Professor Charles Cheney Hyde wrote that 'it may not be too late to endeavor to convince the court that the real significance of words as symbols of common design depends upon what the evidence reveals; that that evidence may contradict what the bare form of a text

---

[144] *Ibid.*   [145] *Ibid.*, pp. 384–7.   [146] *Ibid.*, p. 388.

[147] See Marcelle Jokl, *De l'interprétation des traités normatifs d'après la doctrine et la jurisprudence internationales* (Paris, 1935), pp. 44–5.

[148] Bin Cheng, *General Principles of Law as Applied by International Courts and Tribunals* (London, 1953), p. 116.

[149] *Ibid.*, p. 116, note 54.

purports to establish, and that in case of a conflict, the evidence should be accepted as the key to a correct interpretation'.[150]

The obvious problem with turning objective interpretation into formalism was the abandonment of a teleological or dynamic interpretation also suggested by the conception of the state as an international law subject. Accordingly, objective interpretation appeared altogether less attractive; for, as stated by Judge Anzilotti, purely textual arguments are seldom convincing. This might have been a reason why other principles of treaty interpretation gained more ground in these years, compared to the Permanent Court in its old composition: besides restrictive interpretation in accordance with the national principle of self-containedness, subjective interpretation and preparatory work would also seem to have earned a more important role. For example, the *Lighthouses* case, which was decided in 1934, gave prominence to the national principle of self-containedness and used preparatory work in the interpretation of a text that was not 'clear'.[151] In other decisions, preparatory work was simply used when interpreting treaties.[152]

As a matter of treaty interpretation, the international law of coexistence makes a universally convincing argument while the national principle of self-containedness does not. Therefore, it was relatively easy for the 'first' Court to discard arguments based on preparatory work, and some other principles of treaty interpretation, because it did so in relation to treaties already considered in the light of, and clarified by, the international law of coexistence. In contrast, a court that restricted the international law of cooperation by reference to the national principle

---

[150] Charles Cheney Hyde, 'Judge Anzilotti on the Interpretation of Treaties' (1933) 27 *AJIL* 502 at 506; and see also Julius Stone, 'Fictional Elements in Treaty Interpretation: A Study in the International Judicial Process' (1953–4) 1 *Sydney Law Review* 344 at 357.

[151] *Lighthouses Case between France and Greece*, Series A/B No. 62 (1934) at 13 and 33 (Judge Anzilotti).

[152] E.g., *Minority Schools in Albania*, Series A/B No. 64 (1935) at 21, 30 and 32; and *The Borchgrave Case* (Preliminary Objections), Series A/B No. 72 (1937) at 164–7; and also the joint dissenting opinion in *Interpretation of the Statute of the Memel Territory* (Merits), Series A/B No. 49 (1932) at 342–6; and see *The Oscar Chinn Case*, Series A/B No. 63 (1934) at 136 (Judge van Eysinga); as well as *The Pajzs, Csáky, Esterházy Case* (Merits), Series A/B No. 68 (1936) at 76 (Judge Hudson); and *The Electricity Company of Sofia and Bulgaria* (Preliminary Objection), Series A/B No. 77 (1939) at 126 (Judge Hudson). Later Hudson said that he had drafted the judgment in the *Borchgrave* case: see Hudson to Wigmore, 21 May 1942, Hudson papers 100.8; and Series E No. 14 (1937–8) at 138. See also H. Lauterpacht, 'Les Travaux préparatoires et l'interprétation des traités' (1934) 48 *Recueil des Cours* 713 at 771–6.

of self-containedness might well have found it useful to boost its reasoning arguing that the states as international sovereigns had indeed not intended to interfere with self-containedness. That some of the newcomers would have first-hand knowledge of preparatory work could also be part of the explanation.[153]

Conclusions

One may ask whether self-restraint prevented the Permanent Court from fully using the double structure of international legal argument. What is politically sensitive is determined according to political, as opposed to legal, notions. Judicial self-restraint may reduce the use of international legal argument in specific cases, but although objective, teleological interpretation is the usual main target, as in the *Employment of Women* opinion, it is not necessarily the same aspects of international legal argument which are neglected in all cases of self-restraint.

Self-restraint was at least partly a consequence of a change in the hierarchical relationship between the structures of international legal argument. The *Customs Regime* opinion taught lawyers the lesson that the interpretation of treaties, the subject matter of which fell well outside the international law of coexistence, could easily give rise to accusations of political bias. The definition of the political could hardly be seen in isolation from what was regarded as essential to a national sovereign. Like Judges Hurst and Kellogg, many of the new judges, including President Adatci and Judges van Eysinga, Rolin-Jaequemyns and Schücking, seemed to approach international law as national lawyers, who espoused the conception of the state as a national sovereign also in relation to the international law of cooperation.[154] Anzilotti had already written to Huber that:

la Cour est composée d'hommes médiocres, qui toutefois font de leur mieux pour se comprendre et y arrivent presque toujours. Je ne vois pas d'hommes superieurs, au sens véritable de mot, dans cette Cour; person ne, par exemple, qui puisse être, même de loin, comparé à vous ou à Beichmann. En revanche tout le monde prend part à la discussion et les résultats sont presque toujours le produit d'une convergence d'opinions originairement diverses ou opposées; ce qui n'arrivait pas souvent dans l'ancienne Cour. Le temps seul pourra nous dire jusqu'à quel point cette condition est preférable à l'oligarchie de la première

---

[153] Cf. Judge Fromageot's observations in *Access to, or Anchorage in, the Port of Danzig of Polish War Vessels*, Series A/B No. 43 (1931) at 149.

[154] As for Judge Kellogg, see also David Bryn-Jones, *Frank B. Kellogg: A Biography* (New York, 1937), pp. 278–9.

Cour dans la dernière période de sa vie; plus encore, jusqu'à quel point la politique reste etrangère aux discussions.[155]

In its annual report, the Permanent Court soon stopped recording the cases in which it had referred to previous decisions.[156] There were some early indications of the Permanent Court in its new composition regarding itself as being free to deviate from the decisions of the 'first' Court. The *Greco-Bulgarian Agreement* opinion delivered at the twenty-fourth session provides an illustration. It concerned the claims of the Greek Government to set off the Bulgarian reparations debt against its debt under a Greco-Bulgarian Agreement from 1927, or to have the payment of the latter debt suspended due to the moratorium on certain war debts. In accordance with the *Chorzów Factory* case, the Permanent Court held that the compromissory clause contained in the Greco-Bulgarian Agreement did not extend to these claims; its jurisdiction in respect of 'a question incidental or preliminary to another question' did not imply jurisdiction in relation to these claims.[157] However, the opinion was given by a narrow majority against the votes of President Adatci and Judges Altamira, van Eysinga, Rostworowski, Schücking and Judge *ad hoc* Papazoff; none of the dissenters appended a dissenting opinion.[158]

In the early 1930s, much of the explicit reasoning in the Permanent Court's decisions, however brief, was centred on the international law of coexistence, notions about territorial sovereignty and the national principle of self-containedness.[159] The hierarchical relationship between the dynamic and basic structures of international legal argument was changing so that under the international law of cooperation more room was given not merely to the international law of coexistence, but also to the national principle of self-containedness. This change was best

---

[155] Anzilotti to Huber, 4 March 1931, Huber papers 23; and similarly Anzilotti to Hammarskjöld, 27 September 1930, Hammarskjöld papers 478; cf. more subtly Series D No. 2, Add.3 (1936) at 161, note 1. One may compare Anzilotti's account just quoted to Judge Fromageot's suggestion of making the representation on drafting committees of opposing views compulsory: see Series D No.2, Add.2 (1931) at 221.

[156] Cf. Series E No. 8 (1931–2) at 272.

[157] See *Interpretation of the Greco-Bulgarian Agreement of December 9th, 1927 (Caphandaris-Molloff Agreement)*, Series A/B No. 45 (1932) at 85–6; and *Case concerning the Factory at Chorzów* (Claim for Indemnity) (Merits), Series A No. 17 (1928) at 61–2.

[158] Neither Judge Schücking nor Judge van Eysinga considered the *Chorzów Factory* case in their written notes: see van Eysinga's note, 20 February 1932, van Eysinga papers 140. Cf. Series D No. 2, Add.3 (1936) at 105–17.

[159] As to the latter, see e.g. *Railway Traffic between Lithuania and Poland (Railway Sector Landwarów-Kaisiadorys)*, Series A/B No. 42 (1931) at 121, which must be compared with Judge Anzilotti's dissenting opinion, *ibid.*, p. 123.

illustrated by two decisions from 1932: the opinion in the *Treatment of Polish Nationals* case and the judgment in the *Memel Territory* case.

Statehood, territory and sovereignty

The Free City of Danzig

'André Becker' considered the *Treatment of Polish Nationals* opinion a step 'dans la direction d'un retour à la pratique d'avant 1930',[160] at least in respect of the quantity of the *motifs*. Both Judge Fromageot and Judge Hurst appended separate opinions to the opinion, which was actually criticised by Judge Hurst for being too long and too theoretical.[161] But besides an unprecedented number of references to former decisions of the Permanent Court, an exercise in which Hammarskjöld had probably been helpful, there was a host of links to the work of the Council,[162] confirming, if nothing else, that the Permanent Court's composition had changed.

The Versailles Treaty had separated Danzig from Germany and made it 'a Free City' in order to give Poland access to the sea, while providing local self-government. In exercising its autonomy the Free City had agreed not to discriminate against Polish nationals, and in 1932, at its twenty-third session, the Permanent Court responded to a request for an opinion on the proper interpretation of the principle of non-discrimination.

In elaborating upon this principle, the Polish Government pleaded that various treaties and also the Danzig Constitution were relevant.[163] According to Article 103 of the Versailles Treaty, the Constitution was placed under the guarantee of the League of Nations. But, in respect of Poland, the Permanent Court held that the Danzig Constitution 'is and remains the Constitution of a foreign State', thus being a matter 'of domestic concern' to Danzig. Accordingly, and referring to 'the ordinary rules governing relations between States', '[t]he general principles of international law apply to Danzig subject, however, to the treaty provisions binding upon the Free City'.[164] This line of reasoning was, of

---

[160] Becker, '1930–1931', p. 563.
[161] *Treatment of Polish Nationals and other Persons of Polish Origin or Speech in the Danzig Territory*, Series A/B No. 44 (1932) at 53 and 57.
[162] As regards the Council's work, see *ibid.*, pp. 21, 25, 32, 37 and 39.
[163] See Series C No. 56 at 106–10 and 245.
[164] See Series A/B No. 44 (1932) at 23–5 and also 31. Similarly, *Consistency of Certain Danzig Legislative Decrees with the Constitution of the Free City*, Series A/B No. 65 (1935) at 50; and

course, another expression of the dualist view, just like the *Upper Silesia* case.[165] However, the opinion of the Permanent Court was rather more about shaping the Free City of Danzig in the image of a sovereign state.[166] Dualism only came to the Permanent Court's mind because the Free City was seen as a fully-fledged sovereign entity, a state.

Since 1922 the Free City had been on the list prepared by the Permanent Court of states entitled to appear before it, yet the legal consequences were not clear.[167] The Permanent Court in its old composition had not taken a clear stand in any of its three decisions concerning the Free City, the first being the *Postal Service* opinion delivered in 1925 at the seventh session. Then, because the Polish Government and the Free City had both assumed that states could rely on a general principle of restrictive interpretation, a passionate discussion had taken place as to whether the Free City was a state.[168] Due to internal disagreement, however, the majority of the Permanent Court had side-stepped the issue, holding that 'the rules as to a strict or liberal construction of treaty stipulations can be applied only in cases where ordinary methods of interpretation have failed'.[169] Judge Anzilotti had always been willing to consider the Free City a state, but then he was willing to treat most subjects of international law in that way.[170] The Permanent Court in its new composition also saw the Free City as a state, but here in the sense of a national sovereign. In this way, the international law of coexistence was

also, previously, *Free City of Danzig and International Labour Organization*, Series B No. 18 (1930) at 15; cf. *ibid.*, p. 11. It ought to be added that in the *Treatment of Polish Nationals* opinion this was said in the context of 'the compulsory arbitration [*juridiction arbitrale obligatoire*] of those organs', that is, the organs of the League: see Series A/B No. 44 (1932) at 22.

[165] See *Case concerning Certain German Interests in Polish Upper Silesia* (Merits), Series A No. 7 (1926) at 19, which was indeed referred to in Series A/B No. 44 (1932) at 25; again Judge Anzilotti was a member of the majority.

[166] Eager support for this view was found in the pleadings of the Free City: see Series C No. 56 at 80–4, 174 and 326–30; cf. the Polish Government: *ibid.*, pp. 115–16, 245 and 359–61; but see *ibid.*, pp. 108–9 and 234.

[167] Series E No. 1 (1922–5) at 260; and see Hudson, *Permanent Court*, pp. 393–4.

[168] See Series C No. 8 at 371, 397 and 408–9 (Polish Government); *ibid.*, pp. 428, 435–7 and 486 (Free City); and *ibid.*, pp. 413, 420 and 454–5 (Polish Government).

[169] *Polish Postal Service in Danzig*, Series B No. 11 (1925) at 39; and see Finlay to Huber, 9 May 1925, Huber papers 24.1. Likewise, the dissenting opinion of Judge Huber in *Free City of Danzig and International Labour Organization*, Series B No. 18 (1930) at 29–30 and 31, referring to 'the character of a State necessary for being a Member of the Organization [*les caractères étatiques requis pour être Membre de l'Organisation*]'.

[170] See Dionisio Anzilotti, *Cours de droit internaional* (Paris, 1929), pp. 125 and 231–2; and also *Free City of Danzig and International Labour Organization*, Series B No. 18 (1930) at 19–21.

made directly applicable to an entity in respect of which there was an indisputable need for coexistence: already in the *Polish War Vessels* opinion, delivered in late 1931, also at the twenty-third session, the majority had applied to the Free City a strong presumption flowing from the international law of coexistence against a state exercising 'special rights and privileges' on the territory of another state.[171] A key question raised by the *Treatment of Polish Nationals* opinion was whether the Free City could also rely on the national principle of self-containedness, whatever the implications, if any.

While in relation to the League, the Free City was treated as a *sui generis* entity, in relation to Poland it was a state, a national sovereign. In the two proceedings that resulted in advisory opinions at the twenty-third session, this double-sided conception of the Free City was not directly challenged by the dissenters, who were, besides Judge Rostworowski,[172] Judges Urrutia and Fromageot and, in the *Treatment of Polish Nationals* opinion, also Judge Guerrero and, arguably, Judges Hurst and Rolin-Jaequemyns. However, they gave more weight to the Versailles Treaty under which the Free City was established,[173] and so they appeared to agree with the Polish Government in conceiving of the Free City as being *sui generis* also in relation to Poland. The dissenters certainly did not subject the rights of the latter to a restrictive interpretation such as the conception of Danzig as a national sovereign might have invited them to.[174] Among the dissenters Judge Fromageot would seem to have been the vanguard.[175] An illustration of his way of reasoning was found in the *Polish War Vessels* opinion. In the *motifs*, the majority was 'prepared to take notice' of the promise to Poland at the time of the peace settlement of free and secure access to the sea, but it considered it 'a matter of history' and it was 'not prepared to adopt the view that the text of the Treaty of Versailles can be enlarged by reading into it stipulations which are said to result from the proclaimed intentions of the authors

---

[171] See *Access to, or Anchorage in, the Port of Danzig of Polish War Vessels*, Series A/B No. 43 (1931) at 142. The effect of this presumption was helped by the Permanent Court adopting a textual approach to treaty interpretation: see *ibid.*, pp. 142, 143–4, 145 and 147; cf. Judge Rostworowski's dissenting opinion, *ibid.*, pp. 156–8 and 160.

[172] However, see his dissenting opinion appended to the *Polish War Vessels* opinion in which the Free City was referred to as a 'country': *ibid.*, p. 160.

[173] See *Access to, or Anchorage in, the Port of Danzig of Polish War Vessels*, Series A/B No. 43 (1931) at 149–50 and Series A/B No. 44 (1932) at 45–6 and 53–4.

[174] Series A/B No. 44 (1932) at 47–8 and 50–2.

[175] Cf. Swenson to Secretary of State, 30 December 1931, NARA 500 C114/1380, who accused Judge Fromageot of political bias.

of the Treaty, but for which no provision is made in the text itself'.[176] Judge Fromageot, for his part, took the view that 'the recognition, made in the written negotiations preceding the Treaty of Peace, of a right on the part of Poland to "free and secure access to the sea", a right inherent in the creation of the State of Poland and of the Free City of Danzig, cannot be regarded as a mere historical fact without significance and renders it impossible equitably to exclude from such free access, for the purposes of their nautical requirements, Polish war vessels or any other Polish ships other than merchant ships'.[177]

As for the majority's use of international legal argument, the status of the Free City had grown in importance because the Permanent Court in its new composition allowed more room for the conception of the state as a national sovereign and the basic structure of international legal argument. It was not only that the international law of coexistence influenced treaty interpretation, as in the *Polish War Vessels* opinion,[178] but also that regard was paid to the national principle of self-containedness.[179] It would seem to have been this principle, not the residual principle of state freedom, that was echoed when in the *Treatment of Polish Nationals* opinion the Permanent Court explained that '[t]he State is at liberty, either by means of domestic legislation or under a convention, to grant to minorities rights over and above those assured by the Minorities Treaty'.[180]

That line accompanied the Permanent Court's interpretation of the ban on discrimination due to nationality contained in Article 33 of the Paris Convention, which Poland and the Free City had entered into in accordance with Article 104 of the Versailles Treaty, paragraph five of which laid down that the future treaty should 'provide against any discrimination within the Free City of Danzig to the detriment of citizens of Poland and other persons of Polish origin or speech'. Article 33 consisted of two parts. The first part provided for reciprocity so that the 'provisions' of the Minorities Treaty binding upon Poland were made applicable to the Free City in respect of its minorities. According to the

---

[176] *Access to, or Anchorage in, the Port of Danzig of Polish War Vessels*, Series A/B No. 43 (1931) at 144.

[177] *Ibid.*, p. 149. Cf. Judge Hurst's separate opinion in Series A/B No. 44 (1932) at 58.

[178] See *Access to, or Anchorage in, the Port of Danzig of Polish War Vessels*, Series A/B No. 43 (1931) at 144–5; and Series A/B No. 44 (1932) at 21–4 and 31–2.

[179] See also on behalf of the Free City, Series C No. 56 at 395 and 174; cf., however, the brilliant argument advanced by Professor de Visscher on behalf of the Polish Government: *ibid.*, p. 265.

[180] Series A/B No. 44 (1932) at 40.

second part, the Free City should 'provide, in particular, against any discrimination, in legislation or in the conduct of the administration, to the detriment of nationals of Poland and other persons of Polish origin or speech, in accordance with Article 104, paragraph 5, of the Treaty of Versailles'.

As for the first part of Article 33, the Permanent Court noted that it referred to 'not national treatment, but the régime of minority protection'.[181] The second part of Article 33 was characterised by the Permanent Court as 'a further guarantee' of the obligations undertaken in the first part, nothing more. According to the Permanent Court, the Free City was only prevented from discriminating between Polish nationals and other foreigners, not between Polish nationals and Danzig citizens.[182] It was at this point that the Permanent Court referred to the sovereignty of the Free City, and to it being 'at liberty, either by means of domestic legislation or under a convention' to grant a better position to foreigners. If neglecting such references to the conception of the state as a national sovereign, and the restrictive interpretations that it might justify from a national lawyer's point of view, the *motifs* would be jejune, leaving one with the assurance that the interpretation given to Article 33 'cannot be said to be unreasonable or unjust'.[183] In particular, the argument that the Polish Government made 'a very important addition [to Article 33], namely, a standard of comparison', would seem to have been shorthand for the Polish Government not having adopted the standard of comparison that gave Article 33 the narrowest scope possible.[184] It may be noted that Judge van Eysinga, for one, in his written note had advocated a principle of restrictive interpretation by reference to the national principle of self-containedness; he had begun his note as follows:

Dans un certain sens, la question du traitement des nationaux polonais et des autres personnes d'origine ou de langue polonaise dans le territoire de la Ville libre de Dantzig doit être résolue, par qui de droit, sur la base de la Constitution dantzikoise, et même de toute autre disposition de la législation dantzikoise applicable au cas d'espèce dont il s'agit.[185]

It is true that at an early point, referring to the *German Settlers* opinion, the Permanent Court held that 'the prohibition against discrimination,

---

[181] *Ibid.*, pp. 34–5 and also 38–9.
[182] *Ibid.*, pp. 29–30 and also 34–5, 36–7 and 41.   [183] *Ibid.*, pp. 40 and also 28.
[184] Cf. *ibid.*, p. 29. Thus, there was a 'natural' standard of comparison ingrained in the discrimination ban, fitting it into a scheme of minority protection as opposed to a 'special régime' of national treatment: *ibid.*, pp. 29 and 37.
[185] Van Eysinga's note, van Eysinga papers 139.

in order to be effective, must ensure the absence of discrimination in fact as well as in law'.[186] That, however, was not indicative of the reasoning in 1932, which did not take the rationale behind minority protection very far.[187] It had been suggested by the Polish Government that if the Permanent Court opted for the narrow standard of comparison, namely other foreigners as opposed to Danzig citizens, it would be possible for the Free City to exclude all Polish nationals from its territory.[188] The Permanent Court admitted that this would be 'irreconcilable' with the rationale for having a Free City. But it held that the 'admission of foreigners to the territory of a State is a question which is not necessarily connected with the legal status of persons within its territory'.[189]

Here the Permanent Court's *motifs* came to an end. They were supported by a majority of seven, consisting of President Adatci and Judges Altamira, Anzilotti, van Eysinga and Wang as well as two Germans, namely Judge Schücking and Judge *ad hoc* Bruns (who had been nominated by the Free City).[190] Before the Permanent Court had set to draft the *motifs*, Schücking had written to a German diplomat that:

Über diesem letzten Prozess waltet kein glücklicher Stern, namentlich ist die Danziger Sache weder in den Schriftsätzen, noch in der mündlichen Verhandlung so gründlich und umfassend vertreten worden, wie das die Wichtigkeit und die besondere Schwierigkeit der Angelegenheit erfordert hätte. Wenn ich auch mit dem Danziger Richter, Herrn Professor Bruns in der besten Harmonie und in weitgehendster wissenschaftlicher Übereinstimmung in der Auffassung der Probleme zusammenarbeite, so ist der Erfolg leider sehr zweifelhaft. Wir werden in den Weihnachtsferien daheim die ausführlichen schriftlichen Gutachten ausarbeiten, die schon am 8. Januar in Haag einlaufen müssen. Erfreulicherweise steht mir dazu auch hier ein vortrefflicher Apparat zur Verfügung.[191]

---

[186] Series A/B No. 44 (1932) at 28.   [187] *Ibid.*

[188] On such teleological interpretation, see Series C No. 56 at 123–4, 129–31, 255–60 and 272–3.

[189] Series A/B No. 44 (1932) at 41.

[190] Cf. Series D No. 2, Add.3 (1936) at 17–23 and 26–31.

[191] Schücking to Zech-Burkersroda, 19 December 1931, Schücking papers (Koblenz) 33 (translation: 'The latest proceeding did not take place under a lucky star, that is, the Danzig case, which neither in the written pleadings nor in the oral pleadings was given the thorough and extensive treatment that the importance and particular complexity of the matter demanded. Even though I work together with the Danzig judge, Professor Bruns, in the best spirit of harmony and on the basis of a shared scientific view on the problems, it is unfortunately unlikely that our efforts shall meet with success. During the Christmas vacation we shall draft the detailed written opinion, working at home. The opinion must be handed in at The Hague already on 8 January. Fortunately, I have also here an excellent apparatus at my disposal.').

Two principled steps were taken in the *motifs*. The first step was to conceive of the Free City as a state as opposed to a treaty-based entity, thereby moving towards inter-nationalism and making the full basic structure of international legal argument based on the conception of the state as a national sovereign available.[192] Secondly, treaty obligations of the Free City not to discriminate were interpreted restrictively, the *motifs* suggesting a preference for the conception of the state as a national sovereign and the national principle of self-containedness over the conception of the state as a subject under the international law of cooperation. In the *Minorities* opinions from 1923 there had been a hint of the national principle of self-containedness, but now this was considerably strengthened. No wonder that in 1932 Judge Schücking wrote the following to a colleague:

Nach meinen persönlichen Erfahrungen beim Weltgerichtshof aus dem grossen Prozess zwischen Polen und Danzig, bei dem es sich um die Rechtsstellung der polnischen Staatsbürger in Danzig handelt, würde es besonders nützlich sein, wenn der Begriff der égalité du traitément oder des traitément national, wie andere Verträge sagen, das vielfach Ausländern zugesichert ist, einmal historisch, dogmatisch und rechtspolitisch untersucht würde. Man ist in den neuesten Verträgen vielfach von dieser Formel wieder abgekommen, weil sie zahlreiche Zweifel in sich birgt, denn in der Regel wird der Staat nicht darauf verzichten und es liegt schliesslich in der Bedeutung der Staatsbürger als eines wesentlichen Elementes, des Staatsbegriffs, dass der Staat doch immer wieder einen grundsätzlichen Underschied macht zwischen seine eigenen Bürgern, und den Staatsfremden, die er zugelassen hat.[193]

Given that the national principle of self-containedness would seem to have been at the centre of the majority's reasoning, it is significant that the *motifs* accommodated a statement to the effect that because the text of Article 33 was not 'absolutely clear, it may be useful to recall here

---

[192] Cf. James Crawford, *The Creation of States in International Law* (Oxford, 1979), pp. 165–6.

[193] Schücking to Radbruch, 16 April 1932, Schücking papers (Koblenz) 25 (translation: 'According to my personal experience at the World Court in the big proceeding between Poland and Danzig concerning the law regulating the treatment of Polish citizens in Danzig, it would be particularly useful to submit the concept of *égalité du traitément* or national treatment, as other treaties would have it, a right guaranteed to a great number of foreigners, to a combined historical, dogmatical and political analysis. This concept has fallen out of use in many of the newest treaties because it gives rise to much doubt as the state generally does not renounce its rights. Finally, it seems to go to the very heart of the meaning of citizenship as one of the essential elements of the concept of state that the state time and again draws a fundamental distinction between its own citizens and the foreigners that it has admitted to its territory.').

somewhat in detail' the preparatory work of the Conference of Ambassadors back in 1920.[194] This preparatory work did not, however, help the Permanent Court; for it merely reproduced the question of which 'standard of comparison' to apply.[195] In the 1930s, the only example of subordinating preparatory work to a 'clear' text (but here, unlike decisions of the Permanent Court in its old composition, unrelated to the international law of coexistence) was the short judgment on the preliminary objection taken by the Lithuanian Government in the *Memel Territory* case.[196] The objection only related to two of the six questions raised by the applicants and it was easily disposed of, Judges Rolin-Jaequemyns and Rostworowski and Judge *ad hoc* Römer'is dissenting.[197]

The Memel Territory

In the judgment on the merits in the *Memel Territory* case later in 1932, at the twenty-fifth session, the members of the bench were given the opportunity to reconsider some of the basic assumptions underlying the *Treatment of Polish Nationals* opinion. The new case concerned the Memel Territory, a former part of Germany that had been acquired by the Principal Allied and Associated Powers under Article 99 of the Versailles Treaty. The territory was subsequently invaded by Lithuania (which, like Poland in respect of Danzig, sought an outlet to the sea), and in the Paris Convention the Principal Allied and Associated Powers formally transferred, 'subject to the conditions contained in this Convention, all the rights and titles ceded to them by Germany' to Lithuania. Article 2 of the Convention stipulated that the Memel Territory 'shall constitute, under the sovereignty of Lithuania, a unit enjoying legislative, judicial, administrative and financial autonomy within the limits prescribed by the Statute set out in Annex I'.

The dispute between the Principal Allied and Associated Powers and Lithuania arose when the representative of the Lithuanian Government

---

[194] Series A/B No. 44 (1932) at 33 and also 29–30 and 37. Cf. Judge Hurst's separate opinion, *ibid.*, pp. 56 and 57.

[195] *Ibid.*, p. 37.

[196] *Interpretation of the Statute of the Memel Territory* (Jurisdiction), Series A/B No. 47 (1932) at 249; see also the dissenting opinions in Series A/B No. 44 (1932) at 56 and 57; and *Interpretation of the Statute of the Memel Territory* (Merits), Series A/B No. 49 (1932) at 342–6.

[197] Judge Rolin-Jaequemyns was alone in appending a dissenting opinion in which he relied on a report of a Committee of Jurists appointed by the Council of the League of Nations: *ibid.*, pp. 256–7. Although this Committee had been appointed two years after the relevant treaty had been concluded, the majority did not reject as a matter of principle its relevance in terms of treaty interpretation: see *ibid.*, p. 252.

in the Memel Territory, the Governor, dismissed the President of the Directorate, who was the chief executive in the autonomous entity. This was the reaction to the President of the Directorate having undertaken direct negotiations with the German Government without the knowledge of the Lithuanian Government. The dispute was brought before the Council by the German Government, but under Article 17 of the Paris Convention only the Principal Allied and Associated Powers could refer the dispute to the Permanent Court.

It was not disputed before the Permanent Court that the Memel Territory was part of the Lithuanian state, and that this state was sovereign. However, while the Lithuanian Government inferred that the Statute of the Memel Territory should be interpreted restrictively,[198] the Principal Allied and Associated Powers saw the Statute and the autonomy of the Memel Territory as a condition for Lithuania's sovereignty over the territory,[199] assimilating the arrangement to a 'federal' state.[200]

The opening of the *motifs* held that the Statute of the Memel Territory, which was annexed to the Paris Convention, would be treated as a treaty and not as a part of Lithuanian law, as claimed by the Lithuanian Government.[201] It was also stated that the autonomy conferred on the Memel Territory 'was to be real and effective'.[202] Nevertheless, the Statute was soon placed against a background coloured by the conception of the state as a national sovereign. The majority of the Permanent Court paid much regard to what was called the 'full sovereignty [*propre souveraineté*]' that Lithuania enjoyed 'over the ceded territory, subject to the limitations imposed on its exercise'.[203] This was contrasted with 'the autonomy of Memel', which 'was only to operate within the limits so fixed and expressly specified [*dans les limites ainsi fixées et spécifiées*]'. The *leitmotif* was that the 'wide measure of . . . decentralization . . . should not disturb the unity of the Lithuanian State and should operate within the framework of Lithuanian sovereignty'.[204] In other words, Lithuania was to be treated as the national sovereign, also in respect of the Memel Territory.

---

[198] Series C No. 59 at 45, 61, 202, 212, 302, 307, 314 and 348–9.
[199] *Ibid.*, pp. 177 and 275–6.
[200] See for this characterisation: *ibid.*, pp. 28 and 274; it was opposed by the Lithuanian Government: *ibid.*, pp. 46–52, 210–26 and 311.
[201] Cf. *ibid.*, pp. 44–5; and see *Interpretation of the Statute of the Memel Territory* (Merits), Series A/B No. 49 (1932) at 300.
[202] Series A/B No. 49 (1932) at 300.   [203] *Ibid.*, p. 313.   [204] *Ibid.*

The *motifs* contained a residual principle, also laid down in Article 7 of the Statute of the Memel Territory,[205] according to which, 'in the absence of provisions to the contrary in the Convention or its annexes, the rights ensuing from the sovereignty of Lithuania must apply'.[206] However, the question was whether this principle was not preceded by a presumption against powers coming within the autonomy of the Memel Territory, just as in the pleadings of the Lithuanian Government. The Permanent Court held that the Governor could dismiss the President of the Directorate, although the Statute only gave such powers to the Chamber of Representatives in the Memel Territory. According to the Permanent Court, the right to dismiss the President of the Directorate, 'though it results from the Statute . . . is not regulated by it',[207] the underpinning notion being the conception of Lithuania as a national sovereign dressed in the language of necessity:

The dismissal of the President of the Directorate by the Governor would constitute a legitimate and appropriate measure of protection of the interests of the State only in cases in which the acts complained of were serious acts calculated to prejudice the sovereign rights of Lithuania and violating the provisions of the Memel Statute, and when no other means are available.[208]

The Permanent Court had taken the view that '[b]oth the autonomy as defined and the sovereignty were intended to be effective'.[209] The President of the Directorate, allegedly not travelling in that capacity, had made an attempt to secure better terms for Memel agricultural products than those enjoyed by Lithuania generally. In holding that this was 'an act against which Lithuania was entitled to protect herself',[210] the majority arguably promoted the 'sovereignty' of Lithuania at the expense of the 'autonomy' of the Memel Territory.[211] According to Judge *ad hoc* Römer'is, '[d]ans les remarquables motifs de cet arrêt, la Cour repousse résolument la suggestion d'une soi-disant division de la souveraineté entre la République de Lithuanie et le Territoire de Memel. La souveraineté étatique est une, et c'est la souveraineté de la Lithuanie.'[212]

---

[205] *Ibid.*, pp. 316 and 341.   [206] *Ibid.*, pp. 313–14.   [207] *Ibid.*, p. 321.
[208] *Ibid.*, pp. 319 and also 323.   [209] *Ibid.*, p. 317.
[210] *Ibid.*, p. 326.   [211] Cf., *ibid.*, pp. 317, 319 and 323.
[212] Michel Römer'is, 'La Juridiction dite "Statutaire" en Lithuanie en ce qui concerne le Territoire autonome de Memel' (1936) 2 *Revue internationale française du droit des gens* 361 at 364.

It should be added that with respect to some subordinated points also submitted for decision, the Permanent Court was able on the facts of the case to produce a compromise. Applying a set of domestic analogies to the Memel Territory, the Permanent Court held that the Governor and the new President of the Directorate acted in contravention of the Memel Statute when dissolving the Chamber of Representatives because the new President had never received its confidence.[213] But there was a caveat:

The Court thinks it well to add that its function in the present case is limited to that of interpreting the Memel Statute in its treaty aspect. It has arrived at the conclusion that on the proper construction of the Statute the Governor ought not to have taken certain action which he did take. It does not thereby intend to say that the action of the Governor in dissolving the Chamber, even though it was contrary to the treaty, was of no effect in the sphere of municipal law. This is tantamount to saying that the dissolution is not to be regarded as void in the sense that the old Chamber is still in existence, and that the new Chamber since elected has no legal existence.[214]

Accordingly, the suggestion seemed to be that in the last analysis the Chamber of Representatives was governed by national law, as opposed to international law, or by the Statute in its national law aspect, as distinct from its 'treaty aspect'. It is a rather curious conclusion for an international court to draw from the dualist distinction between international and national law on which the majority relied in the opening of the motifs,[215] and it is difficult to dissociate it from the national principle of self-containedness (a different question being whether the consequence under international law of the breach of the Statute would have been the invalidity of the new election to the Chamber). The references in the motifs to the Statute in its 'treaty aspect' raised the question whether the majority was really more concerned with its national law aspect. Indeed, the Permanent Court relied on a tradition of constitutional law,[216] and the thrust of its reasoning would seem to be rooted in constitutional law, inseparably bound up with the conception of the state as a national sovereign. This would also explain the proposition, unattainable in international law, that Lithuania was not responsible for acts of the autonomous entity.[217]

---

[213] Series A/B No. 49 (1932) at 300 and 333–7, arguably reflecting an analogical interpretation; but cf. ibid., p. 336.

[214] Ibid., p. 336; thereby, the Permanent Court's judgment came close to taking the form of an advisory opinion: cf. ibid., pp. 336–7 and 350 (Judge Anzilotti).

[215] Ibid., p. 300.   [216] Ibid., pp. 320 and 334.   [217] Ibid., p. 329.

Judge Urrutia distanced himself from the Permanent Court's deductions from sovereignty, as did Judges Altamira, de Bustamante, van Eysinga and Schücking in their joint dissenting opinion, and apparently also Judge Anzilotti.[218] They employed the residual principle of state freedom that is linked to the international law of cooperation, as distinct from the presumption related to the national principle of self-containedness. For example, in his written note Judge van Eysinga submitted:

C'est à juste titre qu'on a relevé que l'autonomie n'est pas une notion fixe qu'on n'aurait qu'à appliquer au Territoire de Memel, mais que l'autonomie memeloise n'est autre chose que le régime stipulé dans la Convention de Paris. De la même facon, la souveraineté n'est non plus une notion fixe; la souveraineté absolue l'est; mais les Etats de ce temps ne la possèdent pas. La souveraineté de tel Etat est l'ensemble de ce que le droit international, tant général que particulier, a laissé à sa compétence exclusive. . . . La souveraineté de la Lithuanie sur le Territoire de Memel n'est pas quelque chose en fonction de laquelle l'autonomie memeloise doit être comprise; cette souveraineté n'est autre chose que ce que la Convention de Paris a laissé à la compétence exclusive de la Lithuanie, et à quoi n'appartient pas le droit de révoquer le président du Directoire.[219]

As in the *Treatment of Polish Nationals* opinion, the Permanent Court's judgment in the *Memel Territory* case exemplified the majority's focus on the world as an aggregate of absolute and undivided sovereigns. The Permanent Court approached the 'constitutions' of both the Free City of Danzig and the Memel Territory, searching for *the* entity that could be presented as the holder of sovereignty. The Permanent Court did not accept a pragmatic, unclear setting with divided powers which, as said in the latter ruling, would 'disturb the unity of the Lithuanian State'.[220] So if a new entity arose it was either fully sovereign and passed the test of statehood (the Free City of Danzig) or it was fully not-sovereign and failed the test (the Memel Territory). In respect of the Free City, it could be said that if it were not treated as a state the international law of cooperation would have produced an entity that could disturb the international law of coexistence (although that was not strictly relevant to the specific issue dealt with in the *Treatment of Polish Nationals* opinion); the most likely alternative would have been to apply the international law of coexistence indirectly through interpreting the treaties

---

[218] *Ibid.*, pp. 339, 346–7 and 354, respectively; Judge Anzilotti primarily dissented on jurisdictional grounds: *ibid.*, pp. 349–54.

[219] Van Eysinga's note, van Eysinga papers 141.   [220] Series A/B No. 49 (1932) at 313.

governing the Free City.[221] The Memel Territory, on the other hand, did not replace Lithuania in relation to the international law of coexistence. That entity could have been conceived independently of the conception of the state as a national sovereign, had it not been for the majority's use of presumptions that were considered attributes of statehood.

This was the kind of argument that had been avoided during Judge Huber's presidency, for example in *The Lotus* and the *Danube* opinion. Now it was reintroduced. It was not that the judges were blind to the weaknesses of the national principle of self-containedness. Indeed, besides President Adatci and Judge Wang, and also Judge Urrutia, who dissented in both cases, the judges who advanced this line of argument in one of the decisions criticised it in general terms in the other decision. Yet in both cases the reasoning was expressed, in more or less direct terms, through the national principle of self-containedness and the accompanying principle of restrictive interpretation, signifying a change in the hierarchy between the two structures of international legal argument.

The Eastern Greenland *case*

A related decision, also dealing with the basic structure of international legal argument, although the international law of coexistence instead of the national principle of self-containedness, was the subsequent judgment rendered in 1933 at the twenty-sixth session in the *Eastern Greenland* case. It concerned the competing claims of Denmark and Norway to eastern parts of Greenland. This was the only time the Permanent Court was called upon to decide a territorial dispute (as distinct from a frontier dispute). At the outset, following the pleading governments, the Permanent Court adopted what seemed a traditional doctrine, according to which:

a claim to sovereignty based not upon some particular act or title such as a treaty of cession but merely upon continued display of authority, involved two elements each of which had to be proved: the intention and will to act as sovereign, and some actual exercise or display [*manifestation ou exercice effectif*] of such authority.[222]

In addition, the Permanent Court laid down two substantive principles, which it said were derived from international jurisprudence. First, competing claims to 'territorial sovereignty' were resolved by deciding 'which

---

[221] Cf. Méir Ydit, *Internationalised Territories: From the 'Free City of Cracow' to the 'Free City of Berlin'* (Leiden, 1961), pp. 224–7; and Crawford, *Creation of States*, pp. 165–6.
[222] *Legal Status of Eastern Greenland*, Series A/B No. 53 (1933) at 45–6.

of the two is the stronger'.[223] Thus, as suggested by the *Treatment of Polish Nationals* opinion and also the *Memel Territory* case, the basic assumption was that there could be no more than one sovereign in respect of given territory. In separating competing state powers, 'the actual exercise of sovereign rights' would be the yardstick to measure the strength of the respective claims to 'territorial sovereignty'. Secondly, provided that there was no 'superior claim', tribunals had 'been satisfied with very little in the way of the actual exercise of sovereign rights', or so the Permanent Court said.[224] This principle indicated that in defining state powers the crux of the matter was not 'the actual exercise of sovereign rights' but rather 'the intention and will to act as sovereign'.

What mattered here was the separation of state powers, whatever their origin and definition, and the prime means of separation was territorial borders. Certainly, national law, whether Norwegian law or Danish law, was of no use in this respect. The *Eastern Greenland* case is a classic demonstration of how the international law of coexistence works. There was a need for international law separating state powers, which was translated into a need for drawing territorial borders. The need did not, however, imply that an operational legal principle was available. In settling the actual dispute, the Permanent Court carried out a hugely complicated act of balancing the competing claims, which indicated that no rule met the imperative need for a solution.[225]

No wonder the Permanent Court was inclined to suspend the balancing test in favour of some special solution under the international law of cooperation. There were three lines of argument employed by the majority in ruling that Denmark had title to the whole of Greenland. Two lines of argument belonged to the international law of cooperation,

---

[223] *Ibid.*, p. 46.

[224] *Ibid.*; and see *ibid.*, pp. 45–64, applying this principle in the interest of 'finality, stability and effectiveness', H. Lauterpacht, *The Development of International Law by the Permanent Court of International Justice* (London, 1934), p. 81. In particular, one may point to the interpretation of the word 'Greenland', in Danish legislative and administrative acts as well as treaties: Series A/B No. 53 (1933) at 49–51, 52, 63 and 68. Cf. *Western Sahara*, ICJ Reports [1975] 12 at paras. 91–2 and 116; and *Case concerning Maritime Delimitation and Territorial Questions between Qatar and Bahrain* (Merits), ICJ Reports [2001] 40 at para. 198.

[225] See also Charles Cheney Hyde, 'The Case Concerning the Legal Status of Eastern Greenland' (1933) 27 AJIL 732 at 738. As for the formula of *animus possidendi*, cf. Alf Ross, *A Textbook in International Law* (London, 1947), p. 147; quoted in J. L. Brierly, *The Law of Nations* (6th edn by Sir Humphrey Waldock, Oxford, 1963), p. 163, note 2; and Ian Brownlie, *Principles of Public International Law* (6th edn, Oxford, 2003), p. 134. Cf. Koskenniemi, *Apology to Utopia*, pp. 249–55.

one holding that various treaties between Denmark and Norway had attributed Greenland to Denmark,[226] the other arguing that Norway was bound by the Norwegian Foreign Minister's acceptance of the Danish claim (the Ihlen declaration).[227] It was probably these two lines of argument which made it possible for Hammarskjöld to write to the absent Judge Kellogg that the 'deliberation is progressing with exceptional celerity'.[228]

The third line of argument, though hardly decisive in the actual proceeding, was particularly interesting because it was confined to the inner logic of the international law of coexistence. This brought the Permanent Court back to questions concerning the scope of the international law of coexistence and the need for separating state powers. In other words, the Permanent Court in its new composition, as it were, revisited *The Lotus*, the task being, if not strictly speaking to define what powers to separate by way of territorial borders, then to define what exercises of power could be used in determining territorial borders. It was on this issue that the members of the bench fundamentally divided in 1933, as they had done in 1927. In the *Eastern Greenland* case, the *motifs*, which on this point were supported by a majority of ten, stated that '[l]egislation is one of the most obvious forms of the exercise of sovereign power'.[229] In this way, the majority in the *Eastern Greenland* case got close to the dissenters in *The Lotus*, who had given the international law of coexistence a wide scope, all state powers, legislation as well as enforcement, being *prima facie* restricted to the state's territory. In the *Eastern Greenland* case, Danish legislation for the whole of Greenland was seen as a strong indication of Danish sovereignty over the entire island.

---

[226] Series A/B No. 53 (1933) at 66–9; and see Wang to Hammarskjöld, 27 February 1933, Hammarskjöld papers 485.

[227] *Ibid.*, pp. 71–3; cf. *The Mavrommatis Jerusalem Concessions* (Merits), Series A No. 5 (1924) at 37; *Case of Free Zones of Upper Savoy and the District of Gex* (Third Phase), Series A/B No. 46 (1932) at 170; and *Case concerning the Legal Status of the South-Eastern Territory of Greenland*, Series A/B No. 48 (1932) at 285–7 and 288.

[228] Hammarskjöld to Kellogg, 21 February 1933, Kellogg papers 47. On 28 March 1933, the judges voted on which version should be authentic. Judges Anzilotti, van Eysinga, Hurst, Rolin-Jaequemyns, Schücking and Wang voted in favour of the English version, while Judges Fromageot, Guerrero, Negulesco, Rostworowski and Urrutia and Judge *ad hoc* Zahle preferred the French text: see Twenty-sixth session, *Procès-Verbal* 97 (28 March 1933), Schücking papers (Münster) XII.2, p. 3. As President Adatci and Judge *ad hoc* Vogt abstained, the English text would seem eventually to have been chosen as the authentic text by the casting vote of President Adatci.

[229] Series A/B No. 53 (1933) at 48 and also 46, 47, 53 and 62.

Only four members of the bench, namely Judges Anzilotti, Schücking and Wang as well as Judge *ad hoc* Vogt, took the view that the territorial limitation of state powers only applied to enforcement.[230] Judge Anzilotti, who was the only member of the 'majority' in *The Lotus* to sit on this case, characterised it as 'a profound difference', which was 'as exceptional as it is significant', that 'there were perhaps laws in force [in eastern parts of Greenland] but no authority to enforce them'.[231] Judge Anzilotti distanced himself from the majority by advancing as a historical fact, like Arbitrator Huber in the *Island of Palmas* case decided in 1928,[232] that '[i]nternational law established an ever closer connection between the existence of sovereignty and the effective exercise thereof, and States successfully disputed any claim not accompanied by such exercise'.[233] When it came to legislation as opposed to enforcement, Judge Anzilotti saw no need for the international law of coexistence to separate state powers. Accordingly, a state was free to legislate with effect for territory to which it had no title and Denmark's legislation for the whole of Greenland did not support its claim to sovereignty over the entire island.[234] Judge Anzilotti preferred to base the *dispositif* on the Ihlen declaration and thus the international law of cooperation as part of the dynamic structure of international legal argument, quite like *The Lotus*.[235]

---

[230] The Norwegian Government based a similar conclusion on the principle of effectiveness: Series C No. 62 at 437–45 and 457–66; Series C No. 63 at 1251 and 1299–1301; Series C No. 66 at 3229–45; and Series C No. 67 at 3602–29.

[231] Series A/B No. 53 (1933) at 83.

[232] *Island of Palmas Case*, 2 RIAA 829 (1928) at 839.

[233] Series A/B No. 53 (1933) at 84 and also *ibid*., pp. 96 (Judges Schücking and Wang) and 106 and 111 (Judge *ad hoc* Vogt).

[234] For a similar principle, see *Island of Palmas Case*, 2 RIAA 829 (1928) at 851, 855, 857 and 870; cf. *ibid.*, pp. 863–4 regarding 'the international law of the period'. See also Max Huber, *Die Staatensuccession: Völkerrechtliche und Staatsrechtliche Praxis in XIX. Jahrhundert* (Leipzig, 1898), pp. 42, 55, 131 and 132.

[235] Series A/B No. 53 (1933) at 76–7 and 86–94; cf. Anzilotti, *Cours*, pp. 262–3, 347–8, 363–4 and 374; and Edvard Hambro, 'The Ihlen Declaration Revisited' in *Grundprobleme des Internationalen Rechts: Festschrift für Jean Spiropoulos* (Bonn, 1957), p. 227 at pp. 235–6. Judge Kellogg, who did not sit in the *Eastern Greenland* case, was of the opinion that 'there is no principle of international law that would authorize the Secretary of State of Foreign Affairs to enter into a treaty or make a binding commitment of his country in the face of constitutional limitations to the contrary': Kellogg to Hudson, 30 April 1934, Hudson papers 93.2. Originally, and supported by Brierly and, to a certain degree, also by Lauterpacht, this view prevailed in the International Law Commission: see YILC 1950-I, pp. 88–9; YILC 1951-I, pp. 47–50 and 142; Brierly, YILC

Conclusions

In the early 1930s, the Permanent Court in its new composition contributed to the understanding of, in particular, the international law of
coexistence and its implications for the international law of cooperation.
There were significant signs of an interconnection between the international law of cooperation and the international law of coexistence.
Where the need for the international law of coexistence was inevitable,
but the 'rules' proved inherently vague, the international law of coexistence prompted a rigorous scrutiny of the international law of cooperation in order to satisfy the need; the prime example being the pursuit
of territorial borders in the *Eastern Greenland* case. On the other hand,
where there was a 'rule' as well as a need under the international law
of coexistence, this significantly influenced the interpretation of the
international law of cooperation. Thus, in the *Treatment of Polish Nationals* opinion, the international law of coexistence favoured a conception
of the Free City as a state-like entity in order not to disturb the general system of coexistence built on the basis of a plurality of national
sovereigns.

While the international law of coexistence had exercised comparable influence on treaty interpretation in decisions of the Permanent
Court in its old composition, the early 1930s witnessed a change in the
hierarchical relationship between the dynamic and basic structures of
international legal argument through the Permanent Court's wider use
of the national principle of self-containedness over the international
law of cooperation. Often the Permanent Court in its new composition
appeared to give way to this principle, for example in the *Treatment of Polish Nationals* opinion and the *Memel Territory* case. This was contrary to the
international lawyer's approach to international legal argument founded
in previous years, while buttressed by a national lawyer's approach.

National law

The focus of the Permanent Court in its new composition on the conception of the state as a national sovereign, and the basic structure of

1952-II, p. 52; Lauterpacht, YILC 1953-II, pp. 144 and 146–7; and also J. Mervyn Jones,
'Constitutional Limitations on the Treaty-Making Power' (1941) 35 *AJIL* 462 at 473; and
J. Mervyn Jones, *Full Powers and Ratifications: A Study in the Development of Treaty-Making
Procedure* (Cambridge, 1947), pp. 147–8. But see Fitzmaurice, YILC 1958-II, pp. 33–5;
Waldock, YILC 1963-II, pp. 44–5; Article 7(2)(a) of the Vienna Convention on the Law
of Treaties; YILC 1963-II, p. 192; and YILC 1966-II, p. 193.

international legal argument based thereon, was indicative of a national lawyer's approach. Indeed, the approach adopted by the Permanent Court in the mid-1930s to questions of national law strongly suggested that the second general election had produced a bench where more members basically thought as national lawyers. Leaving aside the subtle references to national law conceptions in various decisions, including a tradition of constitutional law that hinted at the thrust of the reasoning in the *Memel Territory* opinion,[236] three decisions centred on national law.

The first was the *Peter Pázmány University* case, an appeal by Czechoslovakia from a judgment of the Hungaro-Czechoslovak Mixed Arbitral Tribunal. The case concerned the rights of the Peter Pázmány University to some immovable property in the territory of the new state of Czechoslovakia. The Permanent Court upheld the judgment, recognising the property rights of the University. Having regard to Article 34(1) of the Statute, according to which only states or members of the League of Nations could be parties in cases before the Permanent Court, there had been some discussion among the judges as to whether the Permanent Court could decide on the appeal. Judge Anzilotti had submitted that:

[t]he chief difficulty, as he saw it, arose, not because the Court was being applied to as a court of appeal, but because the parties before the Court could not be the same as they were before the Mixed Arbitral Tribunal. If the Hungarian State was appearing before the Court to represent private individuals, it might seem difficult to declare that the Court was competent. If, on the other hand, the Hungarian State was appearing on its own behalf, the case was not an appeal, but a new application. The question of the Court's jurisdiction would bear an entirely different aspect if this had been an appeal against an arbitral award delivered in a dispute between two States.[237]

The case turned on the interpretation of certain technical provisions of the Trianon Treaty and various principles of Hungarian law, including the definition of a legal person. No doubt was expressed in the *motifs* as

---

[236] *Interpretation of the Statute of the Memel Territory* (Merits), Series A/B No. 49 (1932) at 320 and 334.

[237] Twenty-sixth session, *Procès-Verbal* 8 (26 October 1932), Schücking papers (Münster) XII.1 and van Eysinga papers 127, p. 8; and see Twenty-fifth session, *Procès-Verbal* 54 (18 July 1932) and *Procès-Verbal* 59 (25 July 1932), van Eysinga papers 127; Twenty-eighth session, *Procès-Verbal* 3 (12 May 1933) and *Procès-Verbal* 4 (15 May 1933), van Eysinga papers 127; *Appeal from a Judgment of the Hungaro-Czechoslovak Mixed Arbitral Tribunal (the Peter Pázmány University v. the State of Czechoslovakia)*, Series A/B No. 61 (1933) at 221 and 248–9; Series D No. 2, Add.3 (1936) at 336–59, 444–6, 651–2, 734 and 878–9; Series E No. 9 (1932–3) at 163–4; and Schücking, 'Développement du Pacte', pp. 418–19.

to the Permanent Court being competent to apply Hungarian national law,[238] as allowed for in the relevant treaty provisions,[239] yet it was applied on an uneven basis. At some points, Hungarian law was treated as facts in relation to which the Permanent Court employed a burden of proof, while in other respects it was simply applied, the real facts being subsumed under its rules.[240] Unlike the *Loans* cases, the Permanent Court flatly ignored *dicta* of national courts on the ground that they were *obiter*, a notion the impact of which was certainly not universally agreed upon as between the several national legal systems.[241]

Treating national law as law, rather than fact, differed from decisions of the Permanent Court in its old composition. Yet this approach was followed in the *Lighthouses* case, concerning the validity of a concession under Ottoman law, and in the *Legislative Decrees* opinion, concerning the constitutionality of certain decrees adopted by the National-Socialist Party in the Free City.

The latter case was submitted in the form of a request for an advisory opinion and not under a Special Agreement. The opinion was rendered in 1935 at the thirty-fifth session. Judge Anzilotti appended a strongly argued dissent against entertaining such questions of national law where it was not 'necessary for the settlement of international disputes, or in order to answer questions of international law'.[242] Perhaps for this reason, the majority acknowledged that 'the interpretation of the Danzig Constitution is primarily an internal question of the Free City'.[243] However, 'the international element in the problem' flowed from the Danzig Constitution being under the guarantee of the League. 'This element', the Permanent Court added, 'is not excluded by the fact that . . . the Court will have to examine municipal legislation of the Free City, including the Danzig Constitution.'[244] Three years before, in

---

[238] See Series A/B No. 61 (1933) at 221; cf. the preliminary exchange of views in Series C No. 73 at 783–819.

[239] See Series A/B No. 61 (1933) at 232 and 236–8; and also A. Hammarskjöld, 'Le Cour permanente de Justice internationale et le droit international privé' (1934) 29 *Revue critique de droit international* 315 at 342.

[240] As for the treatment of Hungarian law as facts, see Series A/B No. 61 (1933) at 230, 231–2, 233–4 and 239. Hungarian law was simply applied in other respects, including legal personality: see *ibid.*, pp. 230–1 and 234–6 and also Bedjaoui, YILC 1970-II, p. 140.

[241] Cf. Series A/B No. 61 (1933) at 235–6.

[242] *Consistency of certain Danzig Legislative Decrees with the Constitution of the Free City*, Series A/B No. 65 (1935) at 61–2 and also 62–3; cf. Series C No. 77 at 175–7.

[243] *Ibid.*, p. 50.   [244] *Ibid.*

the *Treatment of Polish Nationals* opinion, the Permanent Court had indicated that, in relation to the League, as opposed to Poland, the Free City was an odd, treaty-based entity belonging to the international law of cooperation. In the *Legislative Decrees* opinion, no trace of this conception remained. The Free City was conceived of as a national sovereign also in relation to the League, the only abnormality being that the latter could pronounce on the constitutionality of its acts.[245] One consequence was that according to the Permanent Court there was no 'existing dispute between two or more States or Members of the League of Nations' and so under Article 71(2) of the Rules of Court no access for the Free City to a judge *ad hoc*.[246]

The most significant illustration of the Permanent Court's familiarity with national law was the reasoning on the merits in the *Lighthouses* case. Indeed, according to C. Wilfred Jenks, '[t]here could hardly be clearer authority for the proposition that the Court will, when necessary, interpret and apply rules of municipal law'.[247] The case, which was decided at the thirty-first session in 1934, had been submitted to the Permanent Court under a Special Agreement between France and Greece. The overall question was whether the Greek Government, as a successor to the Ottoman Empire, was obliged to respect a concessionary contract concluded in 1913 between the Ottoman Government and a French firm renewing a previous concession. The Permanent Court interpreted the Special Agreement so as to cover not only questions of national law but also matters relating to state succession. This aspect of the international law of coexistence was not, however, of much importance to the

---

[245] Cf. *ibid.*, pp. 49 and also 62 (Judge Anzilotti); cf. *ibid.*, pp. 70–1 regarding the right to a judge *ad hoc*.

[246] *Ibid.*, pp. 70–1 and 6; and previously *Minority Schools in Albania*, Series A/B No. 64 (1935) at 6. The Permanent Court would not seem to have been prevented from interpreting Article 31 of the Statute to which Article 71(2) of the Rules referred so that the Free City had been granted a judge *ad hoc*. Cf. *Legal Consequences for States of the Continued Presence of South Africa in Namibia (South West Africa) notwithstanding Security Council Resolution 276* (1970), ICJ Reports [1971] 12 at paras. 35–9; Eduardo Jimènez de Aréchaga, 'Judges ad hoc in Advisory Proceedings' (1971) 31 *ZaöRV* 697 at 709–11; and, critically, Shabtai Rosenne, 'The Composition of the Court' in Leo Gross (ed.), *The Future of the International Court of Justice* (Dobbs Ferry, 1976), p. 377 at p. 413.

[247] C. Wilfred Jenks, 'The Interpretation and Application of Municipal Law by the Permanent Court of International Justice' (1938) 19 *BYIL* 67 at 73. All decisions mentioned by Jenks as examples of the Permanent Court finding national law to be inapplicable or irrelevant were rendered by the Permanent Court in its old composition: see *ibid.*, pp. 84–6.

decision.[248] The *motifs* turned on the condition, laid down in Article 9 of Protocol XII to the Lausanne Treaty, that concessions must have been 'duly entered into'.

The Permanent Court had dealt with this phrase in its judgment on the merits in the *Mavrommatis* case. In 1925, the Permanent Court had held that such a question of Ottoman law was 'not . . . a point of law falling by its intrinsic nature properly within its jurisdiction as an International Court'.[249] Accordingly, it had been treated as a question of fact in respect of which the respondent, the British Government, had the burden of proof. Now, in 1934, that same question was seen as a question of law.[250] In its review of the Ottoman Government's application of Ottoman law, the Permanent Court showed reluctance only when considering certain open-ended requirements laid down in the Ottoman Constitution. And this reluctance was not due to Ottoman law not being 'law' but because, the Permanent Court held, '[i]t is a question of appreciating political considerations and conditions of fact, a task which the Government, as the body possessing the requisite knowledge of the political situation, is alone qualified to undertake'.[251] Leaving aside this early articulation of a doctrine of the margin of appreciation, made famous later in the century by the European Court of Human Rights, the nub of the matter was whether the Ottoman Government had been authorised under Ottoman law to conclude the concessionary contract. The authorisation was found in a Decree, the legality of which was held to be unaffected by the military occupation of parts of the Ottoman Empire. For '[i]n constitutional law', the Permanent Court said, 'nothing short of definite cession can produce legal effects prejudicing the rights of the lawful sovereign. The question, which arises in international law, whether the Succession State can be bound by a contract or a law made during military occupation lies entirely outside this subject.'[252]

This was dualism, although with Judge Anzilotti dissenting. But it was more than that, since the majority had made a reservation about a

---

[248] *Lighthouses Case between France and Greece*, Series A/B No. 62 (1934) at 13–17 and 25–6, thereby rejecting the French Government's view, Series C No. 74 at 39, 167 and 335. Cf. Bedjaoui, YILC 1969-II, p. 87; and also YILC 1969-I, p. 55.

[249] *The Mavrommatis Jerusalem Concessions* (Merits), Series A No. 5 (1925) at 29.

[250] Series A/B No. 62 (1934) at 20–4; cf. Judge Anzilotti's dissenting opinion: *ibid.*, pp. 37 and 38.

[251] Series A/B No. 62 (1934) at 22; and see Series C No. 74 at 161–2 and 239 (French Government); cf. *ibid.*, p. 322 (Greek Government).

[252] Series A/B No. 62 (1934) at 24; and also *Lighthouses in Crete and Samos*, Series A/B No. 71 (1937) at 103.

'definite cession' of territory. This is an illustration of how the treatment of national law as law went hand in hand with the international law of coexistence under the basic structure of international legal argument, national lawyers being champions of both. In principle, of course, the Ottoman legislator could have sanctioned any violation of international law in its national law. So what the Permanent Court must have envisaged here was not the end of the national sovereign, but the end of the national principle of self-containedness, the beginning of the international law of coexistence. If the Ottoman legislator had promulgated concessions in respect of territory formally belonging to another state, a conflict between state interests over jurisdiction to legislate would have arisen, for which, following the *Eastern Greenland* case, the international law of coexistence should and would provide a solution.

Up to the point of a 'definite cession', however, the territorial state's activities on its territory were treated as not giving rise to sufficiently serious disputes with other states; thus they belonged to the national principle of self-containedness. This was consistent with the view laid down in the *Treatment of Polish Nationals* opinion and the *Memel Territory* case that there could be no more than one sovereign in respect of given territory. It was not denied by the majority that this approach seemed too mechanical or too generalised,[253] and that in specific cases the international law of coexistence could have a broader bearing, as evidenced by the *Upper Silesia* case.[254] But, as the Permanent Court held in 1934, '[e]ven if there had been a generally accepted rule of international law forbidding a sovereign State from taking measures in respect of occupied territory, the Parties to the contract of 1913 might have had in view the possibility that special provisions in the future peace treaties would subsequently accord recognition to the concessions'.[255]

President Hurst and his time

The *Peter Pázmány University* case was the last case disposed of during Judge Adatci's presidency. The decision was virtually unanimous, with

---

[253] But see the French Government: Series C No. 74 at 168.
[254] See *Case concerning Certain German Interests in Polish Upper Silesia* (Merits), Series A No. 7 (1926) at 30.
[255] Series A/B No. 62 (1934) at 19.

only Judge *ad hoc* Hermann-Otavský dissenting.[256] Judge Kellogg, who had left The Hague in the course of the deliberations, received this elated letter from President Adatci:

la Cour est entrée en délibérations très minutieuses de tous les points que j'ai relevés dans mon schéma. Elle a nommé son Comité de rédaction. Cette fois-ci, nous avons partagé la tâche entre nous quatre: MM. Anzilotti, Wang, Hammarskjöld et moi-même. Nous avons rédigé chacun une partie de l'arrêt. Le projet d'arrêt a été accueilli favorablement par la Cour. Peu d'amendements ont été proposés, et, comme vous avez déjà dû le constater, le texte de l'arrêt se présente bien; il est cohérent et répond à tous les points qui ont été soulevés par les Parties devant la Cour. J'ai l'impression que cet arrêt est un des meilleurs que la Cour ait prononcés depuis sa création. Déjà la monde scientifique se montre très favorable à l'endroit de cet arrêt.[257]

It was obviously true that the *motifs* in the *Peter Pázmány University* case were far more detailed than what had by then become the standard for decisions of the Permanent Court. President Adatci's letter confirmed what Judge Anzilotti had written to Huber in 1931, namely that the Permanent Court in its new composition was more dependent on consensus.[258] In the 1930s the relationship between the judges *qua* lawyers had become less hierarchical.[259] It was collegiate closer to the ideal of an international court representing, as Article 9 of the Statute admonished, 'the main forms of civilization and the principal legal systems of the world'. But often it also generated much more controversy among the judges over the *motifs*, which resulted in ellipses and inconsistencies.

Characteristically, Hammarskjöld had changed the aim of his articles reviewing the Permanent Court's work. The articles on the years 1930 and 1931 were signed 'André Becker', and the articles on the two following years 'A. Engelsdoerfer'. While originally intended to correct misconceptions among commentators, the new articles, written in a more

---

[256] According to Judge Kellogg, this was a 'dissenting opinion in which no one is interested but the party writing it': Kellogg to Hudson, 31 January 1934, Hudson papers 93.2.

[257] Adatci to Kellogg, 20 December 1933, Kellogg papers 48.

[258] See also Hammarskjöld to Huber, 19 January 1933, Hammarskjöld papers 453; cf. Hammarskjöld to [Hjalmar] Hammarskjöld, 8 June 1932 and 10 June 1936, both Hammarskjöld papers 30.

[259] This development would seem to have continued in the International Court: see G. G. Fitzmaurice, 'The Future of Public International Law and of the International Legal System in the Circumstances of Today' in Institut de Droit International, *Livre du centenaire, 1873–1973: Evolution et perspectives du droit international* (Basel, 1973), p. 196 at p. 288; and Jennings, 'Role of the International Court', p. 33.

secretive style, took the approach of correcting the Permanent Court.[260] The overall question was whether the practices of the Permanent Court in its old composition had been upheld, it being known that '[q]ui dit période de transition, dit d'habitude période de crise'.[261] The conclusion of 'André Becker' was that continuity had been broken,[262] while 'A. Engelsdoerfer' concluded that 'd'une manière générale, la continuité existe' but 'on a plutôt l'impression qu'il s'agit d'une coïncidence'.[263]

In late 1933, Judge Hurst was elected as the new president of the Permanent Court. A United States diplomat reported as follows on the election:

I have it from reliable sources that when the question of the election of President for the ensuing three year period came up the name of Sir Cecil was the most prominent in the list of those discussed. Privately there was some objection raised. However, when the time came for voting Sir Cecil was elected unanimously, one blank vote having been cast, by Sir Cecil himself.[264]

It had been assumed that Judge Adatci would not stand for re-election, yet 'det är nog', Hammarskjöld wrote, 'en äfven inom domstolen ganska spridd uppfattning att om man lägger utslagsrösten i Hursts (d.v.s. Fromageots) händer, så är detta början till slutet för hele institutionen'.[265] President Hurst was quoted as having said that '[a]ll things in this world have more than one side and thus it is with the truth; personal conviction is an important factor'.[266] During his presidency between 1934 and 1936, Judge Hurst appended more dissenting opinions to the Permanent Court's decisions than any other president of the Permanent Court.[267] In

---

[260] See Huber to Hammarskjöld, 15 November 1932, Hammarskjöld papers 453; and Hammarskjöld to de Visscher, 7 January 1933, Hammarskjöld papers 486.

[261] Becker, '1930-1931', p. 538; see also A. Engelsdoerfer, 'La Cour de la Haye en 1932-1933' (1934) 15 RDILC 249 at 268-9.

[262] Becker, '1930-1931', p. 563; see also Hammarskjöld to van Eysinga, 26 September 1930, Hammarskjöld papers 481; and Hammarskjöld to Ruegger, 29 September 1930, Hammarskjöld papers 484.

[263] Engelsdoerfer, 'La Cour de la Haye en 1932-1933' (1935) 16 RDILC 443 at 472-3. Cf. Minéitcirô Adatci, 'Foreword' in Permanent Court of International Justice, Ten Years of International Jurisprudence, 1922-1932 (Leiden, 1932), p. 5 at p. 5.

[264] Swenson to Secretary of State, 5 December 1933, NARA 500 C114/1529; and also Scavenius to Udenrigsministeriet, 11 December 1933, Rigsarkivet H-12-16.

[265] Hammarskjöld to [Hjalmar] Hammarskjöld, 26 November 1933, Hammarskjöld papers 30 (translation: 'there appears to be a widespread view, even within the Court, that if Hurst (and thus Fromageot) is entrusted with the casting vote, this will be the beginning of the end of the entire institution'). Cf. Series E No. 10 (1933-4) at 153.

[266] As quoted in Andreae, An Important Chapter, p. 8.

[267] So his contribution to the Permanent Court's work clearly did not find its place only in the Permanent Court's decisions: cf. W. E. Beckett, 'Sir Cecil Hurst's Services to

September 1935, Hammarskjöld referred to it as 'a fact that during the last two years the element of judicial experience had been completely lacking within the Court'.[268]

Judge Hurst's presidency saw the conclusion in 1936 of a thorough revision of the Rules of Court, which had been started in 1931.[269] It took five years to complete the revision mainly because the Revision Protocol only took effect on 1 February 1936. Another reason was that the Permanent Court's advisory jurisdiction was controversial, at least in the United States. Thus, it would seem to have been no coincidence that the revision only came to an end after the Permanent Court had been 'defeated' in the United States Senate in January 1935.[270] On 17 March 1936, the Permanent Court adopted a slightly revised resolution on its deliberation practice, which was printed in its annual report.[271]

The Permanent Court was influenced by the decaying political climate of the 1930s in various ways. In an attempt to meet budgetary restraints, Judge Fromageot proposed suspending the publication of acts and documents relating to the decisions of the Permanent Court in Series C.[272] He was not able, however, to win the support of his colleagues, who were satisfied with Hammarskjöld's explanation why Series C was essential, namely due to 'a) le risque de voir publier des recueils non autorisés et incorrects; b) l'intérêt scientifique des publications dont il s'agit; c) l'autorité plus grande résultant pour les décisions de la Cour de la possibilité de les comparer avec les arguments présentés par les Parties'.

The Permanent Court's workload was very much influenced by the decay.[273] 'A. Engelsdoerfer' quoted 'M. A. Hammarskjöld, Greffier de la

International Law' (1949) 24 *BYIL* 1 at 3; and McNair, 'Cecil Hurst', p. 402; see also Charles de Visscher, 'Sir Cecil Hurst' (1964) 13 *ICLQ* 1 at 3; and Fitzmaurice, 'Cecil Hurst', pp. 473–4.

[268] Hammarskjöld's report, 25 September 1935, Hammarskjöld papers 502.

[269] See Rules of Court adopted on 11 March 1936, Series D No. 1 (3rd edn, 1936) at 28–57. Judges Anzilotti and van Eysinga cast votes against the revised Rules: see Series D No. 2, Add.3 (1936) at 744–6.

[270] E.g., Hammarskjöld to Kellogg, 7 December 1934, Hurst to Kellogg, 11 December 1934 and 10 January 1935, and Hammarskjöld to Kellogg, 1 March 1935, all Kellogg papers 49; and also Hammarskjöld to [Hjalmar] Hammarskjöld, 27 January 1935, Hammarskjöld papers 30.

[271] See Series E No. 12 (1935–6) at 196–7.

[272] Twenty-seventh session, *Procès-Verbal* 2 (29 March 1933), van Eysinga papers 127, p. 3.

[273] See Manley O. Hudson, 'The Twelfth Year of the Permanent Court of International Justice' (1934) 28 *AJIL* 1 at 18; Manley O. Hudson, 'The Thirteenth Year of the Permanent Court of International Justice' (1935) 29 *AJIL* 1 at 1; and Manley O. Hudson, 'The Eighteenth Year of the Permanent Court of International Justice' (1940) 34 *AJIL* 1 at 1, 16 *et seq.* and 21–2.

Cour', for the view that 'l'année 1933 a été pour la Cour une année de désistements'.[274] Three cases had been withdrawn earlier in 1933,[275] and later, after the election of Judge Hurst as president, Germany's new government withdrew two more cases.[276] This would seem to be why President Hurst wrote to Professor Hudson that his new 'position is not so much burdensome as worrying'.[277] Just after the *Lighthouses* case had been decided at the beginning of 1934, the year in which the greatest number of states were bound by the Optional Clause after it had blossomed in 1929–30,[278] the new president wrote to Judge Kellogg: 'We are all a little worried at the lack of any new cases for the Court to deal with. In these days where all international organs are being attacked it would be better if the Court were full of work. However, we must wait.'[279]

In 1935, the Permanent Court delivered the *Albanian Minority Schools* opinion and the *Legislative Decrees* opinion.[280] Professor Louis Le Fur related both opinions to an embryonic human rights movement;[281] in his view, having referred to the *Customs Regime* opinion, 'les deux cas précédents constitueront la meilleure réhabilitation, si elle en avait besoin, de cette procédure si utile'.[282] However, the two advisory opinions delivered in 1935 were the last of the Permanent Court. In his usual uncompromising style, Hammarskjöld saw Judge Hurst's election as president as an immediate reason for states being less willing to submit

[274] Engelsdoerfer, '1932–1933', p. 469.

[275] See *Case concerning the Delimitation of the Territorial Waters between the Island of Castellorizo and the Coasts of Anatolia*, Series A/B No. 51 (1933); *Legal Status of the South-Eastern Territory of Greenland*, Series A/B No. 55 (1933); and *Appeals from Certain Judgments of the Hungaro-Czechoslovak Mixed Arbitral Tribunal*, Series A/B No. 56 (1933).

[276] *Case concerning the Administration of the Prince von Pless*, Series A/B No. 59 (1933); and *Case concerning the Polish Agrarian Reform and the German Minority*, Series A/B No. 60 (1933).

[277] Hurst to Hudson, 19 February 1934, Hudson papers 92.16.

[278] Series E No. 11 (1934–5) at 50 and 258–68.

[279] Hurst to Kellogg, 23/24 March 1934 and similarly Hurst to Kellogg, 7 April 1934, both Kellogg papers 48; see also Kellogg to Hudson, 9 May 1934, Hudson papers 93.2; and Hurst to Kellogg, 4 September 1934, Kellogg papers 49. President Hurst's view was probably shared by those who, like Judge Anzilotti, saw the Permanent Court as 'now almost the only hope of the friends of international peace': Anzilotti to Hudson, 20 October 1933, Hudson papers 91.9.

[280] *Minority Schools in Albania*, Series A/B No. 64 (1935) and *Consistency of Certain Danzig Legislative Decrees with the Constitution of the Free City*, Series A/B No. 65 (1935), respectively.

[281] Louis Le Fur, 'L'activité de la Cour permanente de Justice internationale en 1934–1936' (1937) 44 *Revue politique et parlementaire* 48 at 60.

[282] *Ibid.*, p. 61.

disputes to the Permanent Court.[283] It could be asked whether in this context the Permanent Court took a broader view on its contentious jurisdiction. A possible example was the *Lighthouses* case. Notwithstanding that 'there was no agreement between them [that is, the parties to the case] as to what the words meant in the Special Agreement', the Permanent Court held that it had jurisdiction in accordance with the wider interpretation of the agreement.[284]

There emerged a general trend of joining preliminary objections not concerning the Permanent Court's jurisdiction to the decision on the merits of the case, beginning with the *Prince von Pless* case between Germany and Poland, which was first dealt with at the twenty-sixth session in 1933.[285] In response to the Polish Government's preliminary objection that local remedies had not been exhausted, the Permanent Court held that 'it will certainly be an advantage' to know the decision of the Supreme Polish Administrative Tribunal.[286] In practice, if the principle of exhaustion of local remedies applied in the first place, that amounted to upholding the preliminary objection, the Permanent Court exceptionally maintaining the case in its docket with a view to the possibility of the Polish court not upholding the appeal.[287] The case saw two more preliminary objections being joined to the merits. As to the objection that there was not yet a dispute between the German and Polish Governments, the Permanent Court stated that that could 'only be decided on the basis of a full knowledge of these facts, such as can only be obtained from the proceedings on the merits'.[288] In addition, the Permanent Court

---

[283] See Hammarskjöld to [Hjalmar] Hammarskjöld, 6 December 1933, 4 March 1934, 17 March 1935 and 31 May 1935, all Hammarskjöld papers 30.

[284] *Lighthouses Case between France and Greece*, Series A/B No. 62 (1934) at 17; cf. Judge Anzilotti's dissenting opinion, *ibid.*, p. 30. Another example may have been an arbitral award rendered by Arbitrators Guerrero, Mayer and Politis, in which the principle of incidental jurisdiction articulated in the *Upper Silesia* case was associated with analogical interpretation: *Affaire des chemins de fer Zeltweg–Wolfsberg et Unterdrauburg-Woellan*, 3 RIAA 1795 (1934) at 1803.

[285] The decision having the form of an order, the vote was not given: see also Series E No. 9 (1932–3) at 171; and Series E No. 10 (1933–4) at 161.

[286] *Case concerning the Administration of the Prince von Pless* (Jurisdiction), Series A/B No. 52 (1933) at 16.

[287] See Judge Anzilotti in *The Electricity Company of Sofia and Bulgaria* (Preliminary Objection), Series A/B No. 77 (1939) at 98; and also *Brown v. United Kingdom*, 6 RIAA 120 (1923) at 129, decided by an arbitral tribunal of which Henri Fromageot was the president. On whether the principle of exhaustion of local remedies applies in the first place, see C. F. Amerasinghe, *Local Remedies in International Law* (2nd edn, Cambridge, 2004), pp. 39–40.

[288] *Case concerning the Administration of the Prince von Pless* (Jurisdiction), Series A/B No. 52 (1933) at 14.

raised the question *ex officio* whether Germany as a member of the Council of the League could demand an indemnity in respect of the Prince, a Polish national. The Permanent Court held that 'as the latter question – which the Court feels called upon to raise *proprio motu* – concerns the merits, the Court cannot pass upon the question of jurisdiction until the case has been argued upon the merits'.[289] This was hardly an overruling of the previous judgment on *forum prorogatum* in 1928; it was rather the Permanent Court cultivating the Polish Government's objection – while affording the German Government a fair opportunity to reply.[290]

In 1936, an explicit provision on the possibility of joining a preliminary objection to the merits was adopted in Article 62(5) of the Rules of Court. In principle, this was uncontroversial,[291] and in four cases after the revision preliminary objections were joined to the merits, some of which concerned the Permanent Court's jurisdiction, as opposed to admissibility.[292] There was, however, a contrast to the previous decisions in the *Mavrommatis* case and the *Upper Silesia* case in which the Permanent Court had preferred to make provisional incursions into the merits in order to decide on its jurisdiction in a separate judgment.[293] So long as the Permanent Court ruled on the objections before deciding on the merits, the trend of joining them to the merits, which became the norm in an abnormal period,[294] was not of much importance – apart from showing the true nature of the so-called 'preliminary' objections in those cases. One should not jump to the conclusion that the joining of preliminary objections to the merits as a general trend was witness to an extended conception of the Permanent Court's jurisdiction.

Indeed, Hammarskjöld rather saw it as a result of 'impotence', although with respect to the *Losinger* case between Switzerland and

---

[289] *Ibid.*, p. 15.

[290] As for indications of the argument: see the pleadings of the Polish Government, Series C No. 70 at 250; cf. *ibid.*, pp. 135, 238–9 and 284; see also Verzijl, *Jurisprudence of the World Court*, vol. 1, pp. 319–20.

[291] See Series D No. 2, Add.1 (1926) at 79–93 and Series D No. 2, Add.3 (1936) at 768, 870, 95, 149–50, 646–9 and 705–8.

[292] *The Pajzs, Csáky, Esterházy Case* (Preliminary Objections), Series A/B No. 66 (1936) at 9; *The Losinger & Co. Case* (Preliminary Objection), Series A/B No. 67 (1936) at 23–4; *The Panevezys–Saldutiskis Railway Case* (Preliminary Objections), Series A/B No. 75 (1938) at 56; and *The Electricity Company of Sofia and Bulgaria* (Preliminary Objection), Series A/B No. 77 (1939) at 78 and 82–3. Cf. *The Borchgrave Case* (Preliminary Objections), Series A/B No. 72 (1937).

[293] Cf. *Case of the Mavrommatis Palestine Concessions* (Jurisdiction), Series A No. 2 (1924) at 23; and *Case concerning Certain German Interests in Polish Upper Silesia* (Jurisdiction), Series A No. 6 (1925) at 15.

[294] Cf. Etienne Grisel, *Les Exceptions d'incompétence et d'irrecevabilité dans la procédure de la Cour internationale de Justice* (Berne, 1968), pp. 181–2.

Yugoslavia, as for which the order on joining preliminary objections to the merits was delivered in 1936, it was also explained by Judge Rolin-Jaequemyns being seriously ill.[295] For his part, Judge *ad hoc* Huber was struck by what he considered the low standard of the deliberations.[296] According to the Yugoslav Government, the Permanent Court did not have jurisdiction under the Optional Clause contained in Article 36(2) of the Statute 'when the fact of which the foreigner complains does not constitute the violation of an international obligation'.[297] However, while Article 36(2)(c) gave the Permanent Court jurisdiction in disputes concerning 'the existence of any fact which, if established, would constitute a breach of an international obligation', Article 36(2)(b) concerned 'any question of international law'. Still the Permanent Court did not reject the plea to its jurisdiction. On the contrary, the Permanent Court held that it 'may be regarded . . . as a part of the defence on the merits, or at any rate as being founded on arguments which might be employed for the purposes of that defence' and that, 'in those circumstances, the Court might be in danger, were it to adjudicate now upon the plea to the jurisdiction, of passing upon questions which might be employed to the merits of the case, or of prejudicing their solution'.[298]

A likely example of the decaying political atmosphere influencing the Permanent Court's work during Judge Hurst's presidency was the *Legislative Decrees* opinion about changes in criminal law that threatened the *Rechtsstaat*. It must have been difficult not to hear a voice in that decision seeking to teach the (uninstructable) National-Socialists a lesson.[299]

At the time there emerged a more positive attitude among theorists towards a concept of *jus cogens*, that is, the view that there are rules from

---

[295] Hammarskjöld to [Hjalmar] Hammarskjöld, 22 June 1936 and 27 June 1936, both Hammarskjöld papers 30. See also Manley O. Hudson, *International Tribunals: Past and Future* (Washington DC, 1944), p. 70.

[296] Hammarskjöld to [Hjalmar] Hammarskjöld, 10 June 1936, Hammarskjöld papers 30.

[297] Series C No. 78 at 127.

[298] *The Losinger & Co. Case* (Preliminary Objection), Series A/B No. 67 (1936) at 23.

[299] Cf. Le Fur, '1934–1936', p. 60; and J. Gustave Guerrero, *L'ordre international: hier – aujourd'hui – demain* (Neuchâtel, 1945), p. 41. On the occasion of the death of Judge Schücking, who was of Jewish descent: see also President Hurst, Series C No. 77 at 164–5; as well as Hammarskjöld to [Hjalmar] Hammarskjöld, 6 August 1935, Hammarskjöld papers 30; A. de Lapradelle, *Maitres et doctrines du droit des gens* (2nd edn, Paris, 1950), p. 339; Schücking, 'Walther Schücking', pp. 181 and 192–5; Acker, *Schücking*, pp. 204–5; Peter Hoffmann, *Stauffenberg: A Family History, 1905–1944* (Cambridge, 1995), p. 105; and Frank Bodendiek, *Walther Schückings Konzeption der internationalen Ordnung: Dogmatische Strukturen und ideengeschichtliche Bedeutung* (Berlin, 2001), pp. 77–81.

which no treaty may derogate.[300] This trend was encouraged by some judges on the bench. Protocol XII to the Lausanne Treaty dealt with in the *Lighthouses* case stipulated that the Balkan States, as successors to territories detached from the Ottoman Empire, had a wider obligation to recognise concessions granted by the Ottoman Empire than had the Principal Allied and Associated Powers. 'This discrimination', the Permanent Court held, 'was, however, intentionally made and it does not suffice, in itself, to support objections to the Article.'[301] Later the same year in the *Oscar Chinn* case, and as possibly hinted at by that line of argument, two members of the bench took the view that in some cases the opposite conclusion would be correct. The Belgian Congo had since 1885 been regulated by the General Act of the Conference at Berlin, but

---

[300] Cf. H. Lauterpacht, *Private Law Sources and Analogies of International Law* (London, 1927), pp. 168–9; Ch. Rousseau, 'De la compatibilité des normes juridiques contradictoires dans l'ordre international' (1932) 39 *RGDIP* 133; Friedrich August von der Heydte, 'Glossen zu einer Theorie der allgemeinen Rechtsgrundsätze' (1933) 33 *Die Friedens-Warte* 289 at 297–8; Charles de Visscher, 'Contribution à l'étude des sources du droit international' in *Recueil d'etudes sur les sources du droit en l'honneur de François Gény* (Paris, 1934), vol. 3, p. 389 at p. 394; Jean Ray, 'Des conflits entre principes abstraits et stipulations conventionelles' (1934) 48 *Recueil des Cours* 635 at 702; Alfred Verdross, 'Les Principes généraux du droit dans la jurisprudence internationale' (1935) 52 *Recueil des Cours* 195 at 205–6; and Louis Le Fur, *Précis de droit international public* (3rd edn, Paris, 1937), pp. 186–7; and also *Case of the SS Wimbledon*, Series A No. 1 (1923) at 25; and *Case concerning Certain German Interests in Polish Upper Silesia* (Merits), Series A No. 7 (1926) at 29–30. The positive attitude was partly related to criticism of the Versailles Treaty: see Alfred Verdross, 'Anfechtbare und nichtige Staatsverträge' (1935) 15 *Zeitschrift für öffentliches Recht* 289 at 291–2; and E. H. Carr, *The Twenty Years' Crisis, 1919–1939: An Introduction to the Limits of Legal Imagination in International Affairs* (London, 1946), p. 188, note 1; and also *Case of the SS Wimbledon*, Series A No. 1 (1923) at 47. On the conception as such, see Alfred Verdross, 'Forbidden Treaties in International Law' (1937) 31 *AJIL* 571 at 571, note 3; and also Lauterpacht, *Function of Law*, p. 318; and Arnold D. McNair, *The Law of Treaties: British Practice and Opinions* (Oxford, 1938), pp. 112–13. Cf. H. Lauterpacht, 'The Chinn Case' (1935) 16 *BYIL* 164 at 165–6.

[301] *Lighthouses Case between France and Greece*, Series A/B No. 62 (1934) at 27. Discrimination made Judge Anzilotti found his dissenting opinion 'rather upon equity than upon law': *ibid.*, p. 38. Judge Anzilotti had previously mentioned the possibility of arguments based on a concept of *jus cogens*: see *Customs Regime between Germany and Austria (Protocol of March 19th, 1931)*, Series A/B No. 41 (1931) at 64; and also Anzilotti, *Cours*, p. 257. See also *Case of the Free Zones of Upper Savoy and the District of Gex* (Second Phase), Series A No. 24 (1930) at 27; and Huber in *Free City of Danzig and International Labour Organization*, Series B No. 18 (1930) at 29; and *Aaland Islands Case*, Official Journal 1920, Special Supplement No. 3 (1920) at 17–18. Cf. *Jurisdiction of the European Commission of the Danube between Galatz and Braila*, Series B No. 14 (1927) at 23. In Sørensen's view, the case law of the Permanent Court did not lend support to a 'droit public européen': see Sørensen, *Sources du droit international*, pp. 78 and 95 and also 247.

in 1919, a number of states, but not all parties to the older Act, had derogated from it by adopting the Saint-Germain Convention revising the General Act of Berlin. Judge van Eysinga saw the Berlin Act as an example of 'a highly institutionalized statute, or rather a constitution established by treaty, by means of which the interests of peace, those of "all nations" as well as those of the natives, appeared to be most satisfactorily guaranteed'.[302] According to Judge van Eysinga, 'a régime, a statute, a constitution' was opposite to a *jus dispositivum*, that is, 'a number of contractual relations between a number of States, relations which may be replaced as regards some of these States by other contractual relations'.[303] On the same occasion, Judge Schücking said that '[t]he Court would never, for instance, apply a convention the terms of which were contrary to public morality'.[304] To his friend, Professor Wehberg, Judge Schücking wrote:

M. E. kann an diesem Urteil nicht Kritik genug geübt werden aus folgendem Grunde. Es ist in meinem Augen sehr traurig, dass das Gericht nicht gewagt hat in eine Untersuchung darüber einzutreten, ob die Konvention v. S. Germain, auf welche die Parteien sich gestützt, überhaupt gültiges Recht ist order nicht. M. E. war es evident, dass die Kongo Akte nicht durch einen Teil der Vertragsstaaten aufgehoben oder abgeändert werden konnte, weil ihre Wortlaut nur gemeinsame Revision vorsieht und weil es sich bei ihrem Inhalt (Neutralität!) aus Normen handelt, bei denen eine Aufhebung in kleineren Kreise für die Beziehungen gewisser Staaten inter se überhaupt undenkbar ist. Wenn zum die Sieger-staaten in demselben Jahr, in dem sie im Pact versprechen, die internat. Verpflichtungen scrupulös einzuhalten, ganz munteranbar sich die Kongoakte in S. Germain revidieren, um sich von lästigen Fesseln für die einzel-staatliche Souveränität zu befreien, so war das einfach ein Scandal, der als solcher vom Gerichtshof gebrandmarkt werden musste. Der Gerichtshof musste sich weigern, diese faule

---

[302] *The Oscar Chinn Case*, Series A/B No. 63 (1934) at 133.   [303] *Ibid.*, pp. 133–4.

[304] *Ibid.*, p. 150; and see Verdross, 'Principes généraux dans la jurisprudence', pp. 243–4; Lauterpacht, YILC 1953-II, pp. 155 and 156; Fitzmaurice, YILC 1958-II, p. 45; and De Luna, YILC 1966-I.1, p. 39; but cf. Dionisio Anzilotti, *Corso di Diritto Internazionale* (4th edn, Padua, 1955), p. 97, note 7 and p. 288, note 4. As remarked upon by one commentator, the views of Judges Schücking and van Eysinga 'ont trouvé un écho considérable en doctrine': Herbert A. F. Eisele, *L'affaire Oscar Chinn devant la Cour permanente de Justice internationale* (Ambilly, 1970), p. 23, note 26. To hold that the Statute of the International Court, and to some extent also its Rules, have the character of *jus cogens* because two states cannot derogate from them at will is certainly to give a new and much broader meaning to the term: see Georges Abi-Saab, 'Cours générale de droit international public' (1987) 207 *Recueil des Cours* 9 at 259; Georges Abi-Saab, 'De l'evolution de la Cour internationale: reflexions sur quelques tendances recentes' (1992) 99 *RGDIP* 273 at 282; and Robert Kolb, *Théorie du ius cogens international: Essai de relecture du concept* (Paris, 2001), pp. 211–48 and *passim*.

Konvention anzuwenden. Ich spreche hier wirklich nicht aus Rechthaberei, aber warum geht der Gerichtshof einer Untersuchung dieser Frage aus dem Wege? Die Sondervoten von Eysinga und mir beweisen doch, dass alle diese Fragen im Gerichtshof aufgetaucht sind. Viellicht hätte man uns widerlegen können und aus der Kongoakte ableiten, dass doch partielle Modificationen im engeren Kreise möglich seien, vielleicht hätte man beweisen können, dass trotz eines Verbotes partieller Abänderungen im engeren Kreise, die betr. Verträge unter den Zuwiderhandelnden gültig und nur durch die dritten Staaten anfechtbar seien, aber wenn man diese Probleme totschweigt, so muss jeder Unbefangene den Eindruck haben, dass man nicht den Mut gehabt hat an die Dinge heranzugehen, weil man dann die Ungültigkeit der Konvention von S. Germain hätte schlussfolgern müssen, an der etliche Grossmächte beleidigt. Ich mache mir schwere Sorge, dass die moralische Autorität des Gerichtshofes abermals einem schweren Stoss erlitten hat. Was soll überhaupt aus dem Völkerrecht werden, wenn es niemals ein jus cogens geben kann, dessen Überschreitung durch Individualverträge einfach nichtig ist, selbst wenn die Parteien selbst sich auf Unabänderlichkeit verpflichtet hatten. Die ganze Frage ist von ungeheurer Bedeutung für die Zukunft des Völkerrechts.[305]

---

[305] Schücking to Wehberg, 18 December 1934, Wehberg papers 199/80 (translation: 'In my opinion, this judgment cannot be criticised too much for the following reasons. It is in my eyes very sad that the Court did not dare to engage in an analysis of whether the Saint-Germain Convention on which the parties relied was valid law at all or not. In my opinion, it was evident that the Congo Act could not be repealed or changed by some of the parties because its wording only foresaw a collective revision and because according to its content (neutrality), it had to do with norms which it was completely unthinkable that a smaller group could have repealed in their relationships *inter partes*. When the victorious states, in the same year as they promised in the Covenant unscrupulously to keep the international obligations in the S. Germain, completely revised the Congo Act, freeing themselves from the tiresome restrictions put upon the sovereignty of the single state, it was simply a scandal, which the Court should have branded as such. The Court should have refused to apply this faulty convention. I am not herein really speaking about *Rechthaberei*, but why did the Court avoid an analysis of this question? The dissenting opinions of van Eysinga and I show that these questions all surfaced in the Court. Perhaps one could come to a different conclusion, deducing from the Congo Act that partial modifications in smaller groups were permissible, [or] perhaps one could prove that despite a ban on partial changes in smaller groups the treaty in question was valid as between those contravening it and so could only be challenged by third states, but since this question was passed over in silence, any impartial person must get the impression that one did not have the courage to tackle the question because one would then have had to conclude that the Convention was invalid, in opposition to quite a few Great Powers. I worry that once again the moral authority of the Court has sufferred a serious blow. What is to become of international law in the first place if there is no *jus cogens*, the transgression of which simply entails the invalidity of specific treaties, even where the parties have bound themselves not to change it. This whole question is of supreme importance for the future of international law.').

It is true that the main focus of Judge Schücking's concept of *jus cogens* differed from what has been laid down in Article 53 of the Vienna Convention on the Law of Treaties, in that the Berlin Act could be changed if all parties to it agreed.[306] However that may be, the question of *jus cogens* had not been raised by any of the parties to the *Oscar Chinn* case,[307] and there was no general support for the analogical interpretation advanced by Judge Schücking, according to which '[i]t is an essential principle of any court, whether national or international, that the judges may only recognize legal rules which they hold to be valid'.[308] As defined by the parties, the case had to do with the interpretation of the Saint-Germain Convention, as opposed to its validity. And so the conception of the state as a national sovereign once again became the dominating theme of the *motifs*.

Discrimination and sovereignty

The Oscar Chinn case

In the *Treatment of Polish Nationals* opinion, the Permanent Court had interpreted principles of non-discrimination so that the treatment of Polish nationals was compared to the treatment of other foreigners, as opposed to Danzig nationals. The interpretative potential of a strong focus on state sovereignty was illustrated more thoroughly now. In the *Oscar Chinn* case, decided at the thirty-third session in 1934, a narrow majority upheld the line of argument adopted in the *Treatment of Polish Nationals* opinion, while in the *Albanian Minority Schools* opinion, which was decided at the following session, a larger majority refused to see discrimination bans against a background coloured by the national principle of self-containedness.

The *Oscar Chinn* case concerned river transportation in the Belgian Congo during the Great Depression. The Belgian Government had subsidised a single company (under partial government control) so that this company could lower its fares. Intervening on behalf of the company's competitor, Mr Chinn, a British subject, the British Government contended that the subsidies to the Belgian company were incompatible with various treaty obligations undertaken by Belgium. This was not an

---

[306] *The Oscar Chinn Case*, Series A/B No. 63 (1934) at 148–9; and also Eisele, *Oscar Chinn*, p. 58.
[307] *The Oscar Chinn Case*, Series A/B No. 63 (1934) at 80 and also 122–3 (President Hurst).
[308] *Ibid.*, p. 149; but see Waldock, YILC 1963-II, p. 57 and YILC 1964-II, p. 41.

easy case for the Permanent Court. The judgment was adopted with six votes to five, Judges Altamira, Anzilotti, van Eysinga and Schücking as well as President Hurst dissenting. Judge van Eysinga wrote to Professor Hudson that:

[t]his Chinn-case was one of those cases which, when it was introduced before the Court, gave to some people the impression to be a petty case; to the contrary very important questions of law were at stake. And although I refrain as much as possible from giving dissenting opinions, I thought it my duty to give a rather long one this time.[309]

The president, who thought that 'these equal divisions are not good for the Court', wrote to the absent Judge Kellogg that '[t]he Drafting Committee had a good deal of difficulty with the preparation of the Judgment; the first text which they put forward encountered a great deal of opposition and was ultimately withdrawn, and replaced by a new draft'.[310] Apparently one or two further drafts were quashed, making Hammarskjöld talk more about impotence.[311]

In the end, the Permanent Court's judgment was written by members of the bench who gave credit to the national principle of self-containedness. On the Great Depression, they noted that '[t]he Belgian Government was the sole judge of this critical situation and of the remedies that it called for – subject of course to its duty of respecting its international obligations'.[312] This formula was put into use as the Permanent Court argued that the subsidies did not violate the principle of freedom of trade in the Saint-Germain Convention. Comparing it with the older Berlin Act, the Permanent Court said that it 'cannot be supposed that the contracting Parties adopted new provisions with the idea that they might lend themselves to a broad interpretation going beyond what was expressly laid down'.[313]

The Permanent Court's conclusion that the subsidies did not violate the freedom of trade was supported by 'their temporary character and the fact that they applied to companies entrusted by the State with the conduct of public services' as well as by 'the exceptional

---

[309] Van Eysinga to Hudson, 12 February 1935, Hudson papers 95.3 and van Eysinga papers 126.

[310] Hurst to Kellogg, 11 December 1934, Kellogg papers 49; cf. Hurst to Kellogg, 16 November 1934, Kellogg papers 49. As for concern about the many divisions, see also Hudson to Root, 15 February 1933, Hudson papers 88-9.

[311] Hammarskjöld to [Hjalmar] Hammarskjöld, 30 November 1934, Hammarskjöld papers 30.

[312] *The Oscar Chinn Case*, Series A/B No. 63 (1934) at 79.   [313] *Ibid.*, p. 84.

circumstances'.[314] One might have thought that entrusting a single company with 'the conduct of public services' in itself would *prima facie* have been contrary to freedom of trade, but the Permanent Court held that even if the subsidised company took advantage of the situation – and endeavoured to concentrate 'in its hands the business of its competitors' – it had not been proved 'that this was the motive and the aim of the action of the Belgian Government'. Thus, intent was a condition for violating this aspect of international law, as if the national sovereign and its actions were unrelated to the international sovereign which had consented to the treaty obligations, let alone the international law subject bound by them.[315] Leaving aside the very first advisory opinion delivered in 1922, and perhaps the judgments on the merits in the *Mavrommatis* case and in the *Free Zones* case, this was the first and only time that the Permanent Court relied on a conception of good faith.[316] Responding to a further contention of the Belgian Government, the majority ended this part of the *motifs* stating: 'However legitimate and unfettered governmental action in connection with the management and subsidizing of national shipping may be, it is clear that this does not authorize a State to evade on this account [*à ce propos*] its international obligations.'[317]

The Permanent Court also had to decide to what extent the sovereignty of Belgium, and other parties to the Saint-Germain Convention, was restricted by treaty provisions which obliged them 'to maintain between their respective nationals and those of States, Members of the League of Nations, which may adhere to the present Convention a complete commercial equality'.[318] The majority of the Permanent Court held that Belgium would observe its obligations so long as it did not discriminate between its own nationals and nationals of the other parties to the Convention due to their nationality. It could discriminate, however, on the basis of the public or private nature of the national businesses.[319]

---

[314] *Ibid.*, p. 86.
[315] Cf. President Hurst's dissenting opinion, *ibid.*, pp. 115–18; on the point of freedom of trade, President Hurst agreed with the majority, see *ibid.*, pp. 124–6.
[316] Cf. *Nomination of the Workers' Delegate to the International Labour Conference*, Series B No. 1 (1922) at 20; *The Mavrommatis Jerusalem Concessions* (Merits), Series A No. 5 (1925) at 43; and *Case of Free Zones of Upper Savoy and the District of Gex* (Third Phase), Series A/B No. 46 (1932) at 167; and see also Andreae, *An Important Chapter*, pp. 59–60 and 101–2. It was possibly due to an analogy drawn from French administrative law: see Eisele, *Oscar Chinn*, p. 91.
[317] Series A/B No. 63 (1934) at 86.
[318] Cf. as for the Belgian Government's view, Series C No. 75 at 296–8.
[319] Series A/B No. 63 (1934) at 86–7.

This was not a broad interpretation, to put it mildly. While the majority saw the reference to 'nationals' as defining, and limiting, the substance of the ban on discrimination, it could have been treated as simply determining who could rely on a general ban on discrimination. As emphasised by the dissenters, this was supported by a teleological interpretation.[320] However, the national principle of self-containedness had assisted the majority in reaching the more restrictive interpretation. In his dissenting opinion, Judge Altamira recalled the *Wimbledon* statement, thereby emphasising the conception of the state as an international sovereign, as distinct from a national sovereign.[321]

The Albanian Minority Schools *opinion*

The next decision of the Permanent Court, the *Albanian Minority Schools* opinion delivered at the thirty-fourth session in 1935, clarified the rationale behind many of the contemporary treaties and declarations concerning the protection of minorities and so was also about interpreting discrimination bans. There were eight judges in the majority, including Judges Altamira, Anzilotti, van Eysinga and Schücking, who had all dissented in the *Oscar Chinn* case. They sidestepped arguments based on the national principle of self-containedness and gave a wide reading to minority protection.[322] It is no surprise that this decision has been seen as '[p]erhaps the most interesting example' of the Permanent Court exercising its jurisdiction as a guardian of group rights.[323] Minority protection was not merely about placing the minorities 'on a footing of perfect equality'. It was also about 'the preservation of their racial pecularities, their traditions and their national characteristics'.[324] So, in addition to the negative obligation not to discriminate, which had been

---

[320] See *ibid.*, pp. 101–2 (Judge Altamira), 111–12 (Judge Anzilotti), 136 (Judge van Eysinga) and 148 (Judge Schücking); cf. President Hurst's dissenting opinion, reaching the same conclusion as the British Government, *ibid.*, p. 128.

[321] *Ibid.*, p. 93; see also *ibid.*, p. 102; and Günther Jaenicke, 'International Trade Conflicts before the Permanent Court of International Justice and the International Court of Justice' in Ernst-Ulrich Petersmann and Günther Jaenicke (eds.), *Adjudication of International Trade Disputes in International and National Economic Law* (Fribourg, 1992), p. 43 at p. 53.

[322] See *Minority Schools in Albania*, Series A/B No. 64 (1935) at 22.

[323] See Thomas M. Franck, 'Individuals and Groups of Individuals as Subjects of International Law' in Rainer Hofmann (ed.), *Non-State Actors as New Subjects of International Law* (Berlin, 1999), p. 97 at p. 102; cf. Patrick Thornberry, *International Law and the Rights of Minorities* (Oxford, 1991), p. 43.

[324] Series A/B No. 64 (1935) at 17.

the key issue in the pleadings before the Permanent Court,[325] there was a positive obligation to generate a reality within which the minorities could be equal.[326]

Four members of the majority, Judges Fromageot, Guerrero, Rolin-Jaequemyns and Urrutia, had also supported the sovereignty-based reasoning in the *Oscar Chinn* case. They might have thought that the scheme for the protection of minorities should be given a wider interpretation than such special regimes as dealt with in the *Oscar Chinn* case and also in the *Treatment of Polish Nationals* opinion; or perhaps they wanted to treat the states involved in the three proceedings differently for some other reason.[327]

Judges Negulesco and Rostworowski, who had also been in the majority in the *Oscar Chinn* case, joined President Hurst in a dissenting opinion which was drafted in the language of the president.[328] Again, what was advanced was an interpretation based on the national principle of self-containedness, and so also this treaty obligation was turned into a narrow principle of non-discrimination.[329]

New judges and President Guerrero

Changes on the bench

In 1935, the vacancy created the year before by the death of Judge Adatci was filled with the election of another Japanese, Harukazu Nagaoka, a fifty-eight year old, experienced diplomat who had frequently been involved in the work of the League.[330] Hudson was not alone in thinking of Nagaoka 'as a diplomat and not as a jurist'.[331] Three elections were held in 1936 to fill the vacancies created in 1935 and 1936 by the death of Judge Schücking and the resignations of Judges Kellogg and Wang.[332] The successful candidates were Åke Hammarskjöld (Sweden),

---

[325] See the Greek Government in Series C No. 76 at 94 and 149–50.

[326] See Series A/B No. 64 (1935) at 19–20, referring also to the *German Settlers* opinion and the *Acquisition of Nationality* opinion.

[327] *Ibid.*, pp. 7–10 and 16.   [328] See McNair, 'Cecil Hurst', p. 404.

[329] Series A/B No. 64 (1935) at 27, 29 and 32; cf. the Albanian Government, Series C No. 76 at 86 and 126; cf. *ibid.*, pp. 123–4.

[330] See *Records of Assembly: Plenary* 1935, pp. 69–70.

[331] See Hudson to Moore, 6 March 1935, Moore papers 178; see also Sweetser to Hudson, 11 March 1935, Moore papers 178. According to Cadogan's minute, 23 February 1939, FO 371 W3446/107/98, '[t]he present Japanese judge, Mr Nagaoka, though an old friend of mine, is, I understand, quite useless as a member of the Court'.

[332] See *Records of Assembly: Plenary* 1936, pp. 110–11.

Manley O. Hudson (United States) and Cheng Tien-Hsi (China). When being told of Judge Wang's resignation, Hammarskjöld's reaction had been that '[d]å Anzilotti numera ä otillräknelig, var han den sista använbara domaren';[333] in Moore's view, '[t]he loss to the Court probably is irreparable'.[334] Judge Wang himself had been of the opinion that none of the possible Chinese candidates were competent, even his friend Cheng Tien-Hsi (fifty-two years old).[335] However, in 1939, Hudson noted that Cheng Tien-Hsi had been 'a judge of the . . . [Permanent Court] since 1936 who has made an excellent name there as a first-rate judge'.[336]

As for Hudson (fifty years old), it was almost symbolic that this ardent supporter of the League and the Permanent Court left for The Hague shortly after 'the World Court' had been defeated in the United States Senate. In Hammarskjöld's view, '[l]a saut de la trinité Moore-Hughes-Kellogg à Hudson est érronée à un moment où la Cour a certainement besoin de vois s'enforcer son autorité'.[337] Hudson being concerned about possible aversion provoked by the intense campaign in favour of his candidacy, Hammarskjöld reassured him in the following words:

The question before the States at Geneva will be whether or not it is expedient to elect an American to succeed Mr Kellogg. That question will be settled on purely political grounds in conversations between delegates before the election. If it is answered in the affirmative, the nominee of the American group will be elected, since there is only one, no matter whether he has fifty other nominations or none, no matter what individuals and Governments may feel about the methods employed to secure this result, and even without regard to the personal qualifications of the candidate concerned.[338]

Hammarskjöld (forty-three years old) had stepped down from his position as Registrar of the Permanent Court, a position in which he had exercised more influence on the Permanent Court's work than most of its members. Like Hudson, he was a passionate personality. President Hurst had for a long time sought his election because:

[a]s Registrar he has become too powerful, and it would be good for the Court and for him that after thirteen and a half years of service as Registrar he should

---

[333] Hammarskjöld to [Hjalmar] Hammarskjöld, 18 January 1936, Hammarskjöld papers 30 (translation: '[a]s Anzilotti can no longer be counted on, he was the last useful judge').
[334] Moore to Hudson, 31 January 1936, Hudson papers 95.10.
[335] Hammarskjöld to [Hjalmar] Hammarskjöld, 6 July 1936, Hammarskjöld papers 30; and see Tien-Hsi Cheng, East & West: Episodes in Sixty Years' Journey (London, 1951), p. 171.
[336] Hudson to Green, 19 July 1939, Hudson papers 164.2.
[337] Hammarskjöld to Huber, 8 November 1935, Huber papers 25.3.
[338] Hammarskjöld to Hudson, 4 January 1936, Hudson papers 167.12.

be elected to a judgeship. I cannot say that he is a popular person: he is formal and rigid, and possesses no sense of humour; but of his qualifications for the post I entertain no doubt.[339]

At the time of his election, some government representatives had apparently asked Hammarskjöld to bring back the 'old' Court.[340] The Permanent Court subsequently elected Julio López Oliván, a former Deputy-Registrar, as the new Registrar.[341]

The new judges made interesting debuts in the *Pajzs, Csáky, Esterházy* case. The case involved the technical details of a series of agreements on agrarian reforms and nationalisation in the Balkan states, which had been concluded in order to end a deadlock in proceedings before various Mixed Arbitral Tribunals. It was decided by a majority of eight to six, with Judges Anzilotti, van Eysinga, Hammarskjöld, Hudson and Nagaoka as well as Judge *ad hoc* Tomcsányi dissenting. Although the other dissenters generally supported the dissenting opinion of Judge Hudson,[342] only Judge van Eysinga did not append his own dissenting opinion to the judgment. Judge Hudson would seem to have come on the bench with weighty arguments but little authority. In particular, though expressly referring to parts of Judge Hudson's opinion, Judges Anzilotti and Hammarskjöld also had their reservations. They disagreed as to why the Permanent Court had jurisdiction to entertain the cases on appeal.[343] In addition, Judge Hammarskjöld wanted to cover many more aspects in his criticism of the *motifs* than the other dissenters.[344]

In private, Judge Hammarskjöld admitted that only the third general election scheduled for 1939 could save the Permanent Court.[345] An officer with the Registry, Berthold von Stauffenberg, expressed similar concerns in a short article concerning the entering into force of the Revision Protocol. Noting that the Permanent Court no longer had the confidence of the organs of the League, he said: 'Nicht eine Änderung des Statuts allein kann des Prestige des Gerichtshofs wieder erhöhen. Sie kann nur

---

[339] Hurst to Malkin, 31 March 1935, FO 371 W2976/55/98.
[340] Hammarskjöld to [Hjalmar] Hammarskjöld, 9 October 1936, Hammarskjöld papers 30.
[341] Series E No. 13 (1936–7) at 46.
[342] *The Pajzs, Csáky, Esterházy Case* (Merits), Series A/B No. 68 (1936) at 66 (van Eysinga), 67 and 71 (Judge Anzilotti), 72 (Judge Nagaoka), 86 (Judge Hammarskjöld) and 90 (Judge *ad hoc* Tomcsányi).
[343] See *ibid.*, pp. 79, 68–9 and 86, respectively.   [344] *Ibid.*, pp. 87–9.
[345] Hammarskjöld to [Hjalmar] Hammarskjöld, 11 December 1936, Hammarskjöld papers 30.

dann von glücklicher Wirkung sein, wenn ihr in der Zukunft die Wahl unabhängiger und überlegener Richterpersönlichkeiten folgt.'[346]

Although in 1936 two new, independent voices had come onto the bench, none of them was given much of a hearing. At a time when Judge Anzilotti was losing faith even in his dissenting project,[347] Judge Hudson became a new 'great' dissenter (at least in quantitative terms), submitting five dissenting opinions and one separate opinion in what were essentially eight proceedings. That number was only rivalled by Judge van Eysinga; it was twice the number of individual opinions by Judge Anzilotti in the same period. It would seem that Judge Hudson was a member of the drafting committee only when deciding on the preliminary objections in the *Borchgrave* case.[348] Judge Hudson's individual opinions were 'd'une manière générale très minutieusement motivées, contiennent surtout une abondance de références aux précédents de la Cour'.[349] As regards Judge Hammarskjöld, the Permanent Court sustained, in Hudson's words, 'a grievous loss' when he died in July 1937.[350] To Moore, Judge Hudson wrote that '[t]he youngest member of the Court – he was not yet 45 when he died – he was also the best informed with regard to its precedents and its history, and it will be difficult indeed to replace him'.[351]

In 1938, a broadly experienced Finnish lawyer, Rafael W. Erich (then fifty-nine years old), was elected to fill the vacancy.[352] Already the year before, due to the death of Judge Rolin-Jaequemyns, another Belgian, Charles de Visscher (then fifty-two years old), had been elected.[353] He was a distinguished professor in international law, the Secretary-General

---

[346] Von Stauffenberg, 'Revision des Statuts', p. 95 (translation: 'A revision of the Statute cannot alone enhance the prestige of the Court. Such a revision can only produce felicitous effects if, in the future, it is followed by the election of independent and superior personalities as judges.').

[347] Cf. Anzilotti to Huber, 9 October 1935 and 17 October 1935, both Huber papers 23.

[348] Cf. Wigmore to Hudson, 18 May 1942 and Hudson to Wigmore, 21 May 1942, both Hudson papers 100.8. See also Judge Hudson's dissenting opinion in *The Panevezys–Saldutiskis Railway Case*, Series A/B No. 76 (1939) at 43.

[349] Sørensen, *Sources du droit international*, p. 174.

[350] Manley O. Hudson, 'The Sixteenth Year of the Permanent Court of International Justice' (1938) 32 *AJIL* 1 at 1.

[351] Hudson to Moore, 23 July 1937, Moore papers 73. See also President Guerrero in Series C No. 82 at 207; and Max Huber, 'In Memoriam Åke Hammarskjöld (1893–1937)' in Åke Hammarskjöld, *Juridiction internationale* (Leiden, 1938), p. 7 at pp. 9 and 16–25.

[352] See *Records of Assembly: Plenary* 1938, pp. 92–3.

[353] See *Official Journal* 1937 Special Supplement No. 166, p. 35.

of the Institut de Droit International, and also the editor who had published Åke Hammarskjöld's pseudonymous comments on the Permanent Court's work.

In late 1936, Judge Guerrero, vice-president since 1931, was elected as the new president. However, not much changed during his presidency, at least not in the first three years. The tendency to focus on the conception of the state as a national sovereign was upheld in the Permanent Court's last judgments on the merits, which were delivered in 1937 in the *Meuse* case and the second *Lighthouses* case.[354]

The second Lighthouses *case*

The second *Lighthouses* case was a sequel to the case decided by the Permanent Court in 1934, again using what had then been called a 'definite cession' as the dividing line between the national principle of self-containedness and the international law of coexistence. As in 1934, the basic structure of international legal argument was the background against which the Permanent Court interpreted Article 9 of Protocol XII to the Lausanne Treaty. It provided that concessionary contracts concerning 'territories detached from Turkey after the Balkan wars' were binding on the successor state if entered into by the Ottoman authorites 'before the coming into force of the treaty providing for the transfer of the territory'. According to the majority, '[t]his provision leaves no room for a break in continuity of the sovereignty over the territories' and so the word 'detached' 'connotes the entire disappearance of any political link'.[355] This was in accordance with the contention of the French Government that had centred on independence,[356] while the Greek Government had focused on autonomy, or (effective) sovereignty.[357]

The argument that due to autonomy Crete and Samos did come within Article 9,[358] or that the Ottoman Government had not been competent under Ottoman law to enter into a contract applying to these islands,[359]

---

[354] Technically the Permanent Court's judgment in the *Société Commerciale de Belgique* case was not only about preliminary objections, but there was really nothing for the Permanent Court to say about the merits: cf. *The 'Société Commerciale de Belgique'*, Series A/B No. 78 (1939) at 175–8.

[355] *Lighthouses in Crete and Samos*, Series A/B No. 71 (1937) at 101 and 103.

[356] Series C No. 82 at 15–16, 148–50, 212–15, 219–20 and 257–9.

[357] *Ibid.*, pp. 77–8, 171–5, 238, 242–3, 249–50 and 271.

[358] *Ibid.*, pp. 232–3, 243, 270 and 273.

[359] *Ibid.*, pp. 62, 250, 267–8 and 274. Cf. Judge Hurst's dissenting opinion: Series A/B No. 71 (1937) at 107 and 109.

it being not 'duly entered into', did not gain a hearing.[360] This might partly have been due to the Permanent Court's restrictive interpretation of the Special Agreement, somewhat in contrast with the first *Lighthouses* case.[361] It was remarkable, as emphasised by Verzijl, that the Permanent Court's interpretation of the Special Agreement in this case, as in the *Oscar Chinn* case, appeared to imply the abandonment of the principle *curia jus novit*.[362]

The Meuse *case*

The *Meuse* case concerned an international river mainly used as a reservoir for other waterways. At the beginning of its judgment, the Permanent Court held that it would not consider 'the general rules of international law', but limit its argument to interpreting the treaty of 1863 concerning the diversion of water from the river Meuse.[363] Although not primarily concerning navigation, this approach was quite different from the readiness shown by the Permanent Court in the *River Oder* case to have its treaty interpretation reflect the international law of coexistence. The Permanent Court might have felt its narrow approach justified by the circumstances in which the treaty had been concluded in 1863.[364]

That being said, behind the treaty the majority saw the conception of the state as a national sovereign and so the basic structure of international legal argument as the hierarchically superior. It held that canals exclusively situated within the territory of one state raised no questions under the treaty, an interpretation that was in accordance with

---

[360] However, see the dissenters' argument that in any case Ottoman law did not apply to Crete, being autonomous, and that the concessionary contract had not been duly entered into: Series A/B No. 71 (1937) at 109 (Judge Hurst), 126 and 128–9 (Judge Hudson) and 139–40 (Judge *ad hoc* Séfériadès). Cf. Judge van Eysinga's separate opinion: *ibid.*, pp. 112–15.

[361] Cf. *ibid.*, pp. 100–1 and 103 about what 'is decisive in this case'; cf. Judge Hudson's dissenting opinion, *ibid.*, pp. 117–22 and 124–5. Accordingly, the results reached in the judgment should not be generalised: cf. Crawford, *Creation of States*, pp. 233–7.

[362] *Ibid.*, pp. 100–1; and *The Oscar Chinn Case*, Series A/B No. 63 (1934) at 80; and see Verzijl, *Jurisprudence of the World Court*, vol. 1, pp. 398–9, 403 and 491; and also *Affaire relative à la concession des phares de l'Empire ottoman*, 12 RIAA 155 (1956) at 193; cf. Verdross, 'Anfechtbare und nichtige Staatsverträge', p. 298. The apparent rejection of the principle *curia jus novit* was approved of in Sørensen, *Sources du droit international*, pp. 46–7.

[363] *The Diversion of Water from the Meuse*, Series A/B No. 70 (1937) at 16; cf. *ibid.*, pp. 9 and 12.

[364] *Ibid.*, pp. 12–13.

the national principle of self-containedness.[365] And with respect to one state's interpretation of the treaty to the effect that the state could supervise the activities on the other state's territory, the majority held that such a right would presumably have been granted on a reciprocal basis.[366] Seemingly, the rationale behind that presumption, which was different from the *Exchange of Populations* opinion, was that a derogation from the national principle of self-containedness should be justified in terms of the international law of coexistence. The treaty was, according to the *motifs*, 'an agreement freely concluded between two States seeking to reconcile their practical interests with a view to improving an existing situation rather than to settle a legal dispute concerning mutually contested rights'.[367]

This being the purpose of the treaty, according to the majority, arguments akin to a teleological interpretation were used so as to narrow the obligations under the treaty. Article 1 of the treaty determined that all canals below Maastricht should be fed from one new intake ('the treaty feeder'). Article 4 was quite explicit as to the quantity of water to be taken through the treaty feeder. The question was how to treat the passage of water through new locks (as opposed to new intakes which would have been contrary to Article 1). Despite the rather specific indications in Article 4, the Permanent Court stated that it

would be prepared to consider that the use of the Neerhaeren Lock is contrary to the Treaty, notwithstanding the existence and functioning of lock 19 [provided for in the Treaty], if it were shown that the use of the Neerhaeren Lock contravened the object of the Treaty, that is to say if it were shown that the use of the Neerhaeren Lock produced an excessive current in the Zuid-Willemsvaart or a deficiency of water in the Meuse.[368]

It could be said to be a rather high threshold for a breach of treaty that the activity had to undermine the whole purpose underlying the treaty.[369] Indeed, in his dissenting opinion, relying on Article 4, Judge

---

[365] *Ibid.*, p. 26 and similarly pp. 27, 29–30 and 32; see also *ibid.*, p. 18. For a more communitarian argument, see Judge van Eysinga, *ibid.*, p. 72; and also *Case relating to the Territorial Jurisdiction of the International Commission of the River Oder*, Series A No. 23 (1929) at 27.

[366] *Ibid.*, p. 20.

[367] *Ibid.* Cf. Judge Altamira's dissenting opinion, *ibid.*, p. 39; and see also Judge van Eysinga's separate opinion, *ibid.*, pp. 63–4.

[368] *Ibid.*, p. 23.

[369] As for internal canals, the Permanent Court had held that they were not in breach of the Treaty 'provided that the diversion of water at the treaty feeder and the volume

Anzilotti said that the object of Article 1 was 'to exclude any feeding of the canals in question with water withdrawn from the Meuse elsewhere than at the treaty feeder';[370] he added that the fact that there had been no excessive current in the Zuid-Willemsvaart 'could not have the effect of legalizing a withdrawal of water from the Meuse which is, in itself, contrary to the Treaty'.[371]

However, the majority had an additional argument in support of its conclusion. Emphasising that both parties to the case had built new locks that allegedly were significantly bigger than lock 19 mentioned in the treaty, it held:

The Court cannot refrain from comparing the case of the Belgian lock with that of the Netherlands lock at Bosscheveld. Neither of these locks constitutes a feeder, yet both of them discharge their lock-water into the canal, and thus take part in feeding it with water otherwise than through the treaty feeder, though without producing an excessive current in the Zuid-Willemsvaart. In these circumstances, the Court finds it difficult to admit that the Netherlands are now warranted in complaining of the construction and operation of a lock of which they themselves set an example in the past.[372]

Judge Hudson associated this principle with a notion of equity known to Anglo-American lawyers,[373] while Judge Anzilotti held that 'this submission . . . is so just, so equitable, so universally recognized, that it must be applied in international relations also. In any case, it is one of these "general principles of law recognized by civilized nations" which the Court applies in virtue of Article 38 of its Statute.'[374]

---

of water to be discharged therefrom to maintain the normal level and flow in the Zuid-Willemsvaart is not affected': *ibid.*, p. 26 and also p. 27.

[370] *Ibid.*, p. 46; and also Judge van Eysinga's separate opinion, *ibid.*, pp. 59–60 and 67.

[371] *Ibid.*, p. 47.   [372] *Ibid.*, p. 25.

[373] *Ibid.*, pp. 77–80. Cf. the separate opinions of Judges Jessup and Ammoun in *North Sea Continental Shelf*, ICJ Reports [1969] 3 at 84 and 138, respectively; Judge Dillard's separate opinion in *Fisheries Jurisdiction (United Kingdom v. Iceland)*, ICJ Reports [1974] 3 at 63; Judge Schwebel's dissenting opinion in *Case concerning Military and Paramilitary Activities in and against Nicaragua* (Provisional Measures), ICJ Reports [1984] 169 at 198; Judge Evensen's dissenting opinion in *Continental Shelf (Tunisia v. Libya)*, ICJ Reports [1982] 18 at 290–1; Judge Weeramantry's separate opinion in *Maritime Delimitation in the Area between Greenland and Jan Mayen*, ICJ Reports [1993] 38 at 234 and 236; Judge Koroma's separate opinion and Judge *ad hoc* Skubiszewski's dissenting opinion in *Gabčíkovo-Nagymaros Project*, ICJ Reports [1997] 7 at 151–2 and 238–9, respectively; and also McCaffrey, YILC 1986-II.1, p. 132, note 330.

[374] Series A/B No. 70 (1937) at 50. Cf. Waldock, YILC 1963-II, p. 74; and Al-Khasawneh, YILC 1992-I, p. 158.

The Optional Clause

The Phosphates in Morocco *case*

In 1938 and 1939, the Permanent Court's work centred on preliminary objections taken in three different cases submitted under the Optional Clause. The main hurdle faced by the Permanent Court was how to interpret reservations formulated by states when accepting the Optional Clause. In the *Phosphates in Morocco* case between France and Italy, the Permanent Court held that:

[t]he declaration, of which the ratification was deposited by the French Government on April 25th, 1931, is a unilateral act by which that Government accepted the Court's compulsory jurisdiction. This jurisdiction only exists within the limits within which it has been accepted. In this case, the terms on which the objection *ratione temporis* submitted by the French Government is founded, are perfectly clear . . . In these circumstances, there is no occasion to resort to a restrictive interpretation that, in case of doubt, might be advisable in regard to a clause which must on no account be interpreted in such a way as to exceed the intention of the States that subscribed to it.[375]

What the Permanent Court alluded to was a restrictive interpretation of the scope of the unilateral, sovereign act by which consent to be bound by the Optional Clause had been expressed.[376] Although another empty gesture, the reference to a principle of restrictive interpretation was significant: it had not been pleaded before the Permanent Court. Taking objection to the Permanent Court's jurisdiction under the Optional Clause, the French Government had only once dealt with principles of interpretation in general, and then, at the opening of its oral pleadings, it had not argued a restrictive interpretation but an 'interprétation stricte'.[377] The Permanent Court indicated that this view could be given a twist, something which would reflect neither the conception of the state as an international law subject nor as an international sovereign. While the conception of the state as an international sovereign prompts a subjective interpretation of the law-making act, focusing on the intention underpinning the act, it does not promote a restrictive interpretation. The suggestion seemed to be that behind the conception of the state as

---

[375] *Phosphates in Morocco Case* (Preliminary Objections), Series A/B No. 74 (1938) at 23–4.

[376] It was the acceptance that was to be interpreted restrictively, not the restrictions put on that acceptance: see H. Lauterpacht, 'Restrictive Interpretation and the Principle of Effectiveness in the Interpreation of Treaties' (1949) 26 *BYIL* 48 at 65; but cf. Lauterpacht, *Development by the International Court*, pp. 340 and 96.

[377] Series C No. 85 at 1026; and see also *ibid.*, pp. 1027 and 1044.

an international sovereign, which is particularly apt in the context of reservations, the Permanent Court sensed the conception of the state as a national sovereign (and the national principle of self-containedness).

The reservation in question restricted the French acceptance of the Optional Clause to 'disputes which may arise after the ratification of the present declaration with regard to situations or facts subsequent to such ratification'. Before the Permanent Court the phrase 'situations or facts' had been the subject of brilliant arguments by Professors Roberto Ago and Jules Basdevant. Representing the French Government, Basdevant had related the reservation to 'le fait ou la situation d'où est né le différend'.[378] On the facts of the case that meant 'the dahirs of 1920' and an administrative decision of 1925. It was in this context that Professor Basdevant recommended an 'interprétation stricte'. In contrast, the Italian Government held that the relevant 'situations or facts' were those that incurred state responsibility under international law.[379] The written pleadings had centred on theories of continuous breach;[380] orally, however, Ago primarily relied on a general notion of state responsibility, according to which responsibility had only been incurred when in the specific case a definitive decision had been taken by the state in question.[381] Neither the 'dahirs' nor the administrative decision were definitive because there were local remedies available; thus Ago, arguing for the Italian Government, fixed the violation to a much later point in time.

The Permanent Court reached the same conclusion as the French Government, largely by adopting a similar interpretation of the phrase 'situations and facts'.[382] Ago, unsurprisingly, considered this a 'very restrictive' interpretation.[383] The Permanent Court did not look upon the French reservation with suspicion; it had been inserted, the Permanent Court explained, 'in order both to avoid, in general, a revival of old disputes, and to preclude . . . [disputes] dating from a period when the State whose action was impugned was not in a position to foresee the legal proceedings'.[384] In consequence, the phrase 'situations or facts subsequent to such ratification' comprised the factors out of which

---

[378] Ibid., pp. 1024 and also p. 1295; and Series C No. 84 at 23–4 and 716–22.

[379] For clear statements: see Series C No. 85, pp. 1231 and 1331.

[380] Series C No. 84 at 488–99 and 851–9, partly relying on Case of the Mavrommatis Palestine Concessions (Jurisdiction), Series A No. 2 (1924) at 35. See also Ago, YILC 1978-II.1, pp. 40–5 and 49–50; the report of the International Law Commission, YILC 1978-II.2, pp. 95–6; and Arangio-Ruiz, YILC 1988-II.1, pp. 14–15.

[381] Series C No. 85 at 1224–33 and 1330–4.   [382] Series A/B No. 74 (1938) at 24–9.

[383] YILC 1978-II.1, p. 44.   [384] Series A/B No. 74 (1938) at 24.

the dispute originally arose and not 'subsequent factors which either presume the existence or are merely the confirmation or development of earlier situations or facts constituting the real causes of the dispute'. This line of reasoning expressed how the situation looked from the point of view of national law. If prior to its acceptance of the Optional Clause a state under its national law had established a situation contrary to its international obligations, this situation would be covered by the reservation; it appeared irrelevant whether in international law the situation was qualified as a continuing breach of the state's international obligations.[385]

The Permanent Court was so sure of this 'national' approach that it misrepresented Ago's 'international' approach.[386] According to the Permanent Court, the Italian Government had not argued that there was no violation of international law before a 'definitive' decision had been taken, but that 'this violation only became definitive as a result of certain acts subsequent to' 1925.[387] Having said that, the Permanent Court added that the administrative decision taken in 1925 was 'a definitive act which would, by itself, directly involve international responsibility'.[388] Unlike Ago, the Permanent Court did not use the term 'definitive' to signify the exhaustion of local remedies. It followed the French Government in viewing such exhaustion as a procedural condition for exercising diplomatic protection, as opposed to a substantive condition for incurring state responsibility.[389]

As the administrative decision had been taken before 'the crucial date', which was sometime in 1931, the dispute fell within the French reservation and the Permanent Court had no jurisdiction under the Optional Clause. On this occasion, it was not decided whether in certain cases the exhaustion of local remedies was a further – procedural – condition for the Permanent Court's jurisdiction under the Optional Clause. This

---

[385] Cf. ibid., pp. 25–7.   [386] Cf. YILC 1978-II.1, pp. 41–2.
[387] Series A/B No. 74 (1938) at 27.   [388] Ibid., p. 28.
[389] See Series C No. 85 at 1048 and 1294. Cf. the Italian Government: ibid., pp. 1210–12 and 1332–3; and also Ago, YILC 1977-II.1, p. 29; and the report of the International Law Commission, YILC 1977-II.2, pp. 35–6 and 39–40; but contrast James Crawford, 'Second Report on State Responsibility' (United Nations Document A/CN.4/498, 1999), para. 146; and John Dugard, 'Second Report on Diplomatic Protection' (United Nations Document A/CN.4/514, 2001), paras. 33, 46 and 63–6; and see James Crawford, *The International Law Commission's Articles on State Responsibility: Introduction, Text and Commentaries* (Cambridge, 2002), p. 23. For a rather pragmatic view, see C. H. M. Waldock, 'The Plea of Domestic Jurisdiction before International Legal Tribunals' (1954) 31 *BYIL* 96 at 101.

question had been the subject of extended debate in the *Phosphates in Morocco* case,[390] whereas, in the subsequent *Panevezys–Saldutiskis Railway* case, the Lithuanian and Estonian Governments agreed on the principle being applicable to a case concerning the nationalisation of a railway.[391]

In its judgment in the *Panevezys–Saldutiskis Railway* case, the Permanent Court noted this agreement.[392] As if recalling a principle of domestic jurisdiction akin to that dealt with in the *Nationality Decrees* opinion, the Permanent Court held that '[i]n principle, the property rights and the contractual rights of individuals depend in every State on municipal law and fall therefore more particularly within the jurisdiction of municipal tribunals'.[393] Although the question was preliminary and incidental to the Permanent Court's jurisdiction, it was not willing to decide whether there were local remedies to exhaust:

> The question whether or not the Lithuanian courts have jurisdiction to entertain a particular suit depends on Lithuanian law and is one on which the Lithuanian courts alone can produce a final decision. It is not for this Court to consider the arguments which have been addressed to it for the purpose either of establishing the jurisdiction of the Lithuanian tribunals by adducing particular provisions of the laws in force in Lithuania, or of denying the jurisdiction of those tribunals by attributing a particular character (seizure *jure imperii*) to the act of the Lithuanian Government. Until it has been clearly shown that the Lithuanian courts have no jurisdiction to entertain a suit by the *Esimene* Company as to its title to the Panevezys–Saldutiskis railway, the Court cannot accept the contention of the Estonian Agent that the rule as to exhaustion of local remedies does not apply in this case because Lithuanian law affords no means of redress.[394]

Perhaps using a less 'national' approach, the Permanent Court could have entertained one, if not both, of the cases now dismissed. It is tempting to associate the 'national' approach to the conception of the state as a national sovereign aired in the *Phosphates in Morocco* case when referring to a principle of restrictive interpretation. In the same breath, one may consider whether the hard and fast pronouncements in the

---

[390] See Series C No. 85 at 1091 and 1201.

[391] See Series C No. 86 at 42–8 and 194–205.

[392] *The Panevezys–Saldutiskis Railway Case*, Series A/B No. 76 (1939) at 18; among the dissenters only Judge van Eysinga explicitly disagreed on this point: *ibid.*, pp. 36–7. Cf. Amerasinghe, *Local Remedies*, p. 252.

[393] *Ibid.*, p. 18.

[394] *Ibid.*, p. 19; and also Judge Urrutia in *The Electricity Company of Sofia and Bulgaria* (Preliminary Objection), Series A/B No. 77 (1939) at 107; cf. Guerrero in Shabtai Rosenne (ed.), *Committee of Experts for the Progressive Codification of International Law* (New York, 1972), vol. 1, pp. 91 and 94.

just-quoted passage from the *Panevezys–Saldutiskis Railway* case, including the rigid burden of proof, was a reflection of again conceiving national law as facts, or rather a tribute to a peculiar notion of domestic jurisdiction and thus the national principle of self-containedness.[395] However, in particular in the *Phosphates in Morocco* case, the view taken might well have been that the 'national' approach was in accordance with 'the will of the State',[396] and thus acceptable under a subjective interpretation advocated by the conception of the state as an international sovereign.

The Electricity Company *case*

The Permanent Court's judgment in the *Electricity Company* case had a bearing on both of the preceding judgments, but, unlike them, this dispute was actually entertained. The case had been submitted by the Belgian Government against Bulgaria under the Treaty of Conciliation, Arbitration and Judicial Settlement of 1931 concluded between Belgium and Bulgaria, as well as under the Optional Clause. As for the relationship between Belgium and Bulgaria, strong arguments could be produced for the treaty having been substituted for the Optional Clause so that the Permanent Court's jurisdiction was conditional upon diplomatic negotiations and the exhaustion of local remedies pursuant to Articles 1 and 3 of the treaty. At one point, Henri Rolin, counsel for the Belgian Government, had taken this view, but he had subsequently abandoned it.[397] Significantly, the Bulgarian Government, which objected to the Permanent Court's jurisdiction, vigorously opposed Rolin's original view.[398]

Four members of the bench, Judges Anzilotti, van Eysinga, Hudson and Urrutia, found that the Optional Clause had been suspended and that the admissibility of the dispute depended on the treaty.[399] Local remedies had clearly not been exhausted since the case was pending before the Bulgarian Cour de Cassation at the time of the Belgian Government's application, and this 'irregularity . . . was not removed by the

---

[395] Cf. Judge Anzilotti's dissenting opinion in *The Electricity Company of Sofia and Bulgaria* (Preliminary Objection), Series A/B No. 77 (1939) at 99; and also Judge Hudson's separate opinion in *The 'Société Commerciale de Belgique'*, Series A/B No. 78 (1939) at 184.

[396] Series A/B No. 74 (1938) at 24.

[397] Series C No. 88 at 406–7 and 415.

[398] *Ibid.*, pp. 436–7; and see also Judge *ad hoc* Papazoff, *The Electricity Company of Sofia and Bulgaria* (Preliminary Objection), Series A/B No. 77 (1939) at 146–9.

[399] See Series A/B No. 77 (1939) at 88 and 91–2 (Judge Anzilotti), 103–4 (Judge Urrutia), 110–11 (Judge van Eysinga) and 126–31 (Judge Hudson).

judgment rendered on March 16th, 1938, by the Bulgarian Court of Cassation, for in the meantime . . . the Treaty of 1931 had expired'.[400] Three of the judges, but not Judge van Eysinga, consequently ruled in favour of the Bulgarian Government's preliminary objection.[401] In contrast, the majority of nine took the view that the Optional Clause remained an independent source of jurisdiction, which applied to this case.[402]

There were two essential steps in bringing the dispute within the Optional Clause. First, the Permanent Court faced a reservation similar to that in the *Phosphates in Morocco* case. It presented no trouble here, however, since the administrative decision starting the dispute had been taken eight years after the critical date in 1926:

It is true that a dispute may presuppose the existence of some prior situation or fact, but it does not follow that the dispute arises in regard to that situation or fact. A situation or fact in regard to which a dispute is said to have arisen must be the real cause of the dispute.[403]

Secondly, there was the question of applying the principle of exhaustion of local remedies to the Optional Clause. This question was not dealt with in the *motifs*, nor had it been raised by the Bulgarian Government. Yet the *Electricity Company* case was not necessarily in conflict with the *Panevezys–Saldutiskis Railway* case.[404] The Bulgarian Cour de Cassation had given its decision shortly after the proceeding had been instituted by the Belgian Government, and at the end of his speech Rolin had indeed relied on the *Prince von Pless* case.[405]

In particular, the Permanent Court's judgment should not be seen as implicitly approving the presumption of jurisdiction advocated by the Belgian Government.[406] The treaty had expired only days after the Belgian Government had filed its application and, as emphasised by Judge van Eysinga, had the Permanent Court declined jurisdiction the Belgian Government could immediately have filed a new application under the

---

[400] See the *motifs*, *ibid.*, pp. 79–80.

[401] As for Judge van Eysinga's position: see *ibid.*, pp. 114–15.

[402] *Ibid.*, pp. 76 and 80–3; and also Judge de Visscher's separate opinion, *ibid.*, pp. 137–8.

[403] See *ibid.*, pp. 81–2. See also *Case concerning Right of Passage over Indian Territory* (Merits), ICJ Reports [1960] 6 at 35–6; cf. the dissenting opinions of Judges Winiarski and Badawi and Judge Chagla, *ibid.*, pp. 71–4 and 116–18, respectively.

[404] Cf. *ibid.*, pp. 90 (Judge Anzilotti), 104 (Judge Urrutia) and 137–8 (Judge de Visscher); another view was again taken by Judge van Eysinga, *ibid.*, p. 113.

[405] Series C No. 88 at 432; cf. the Bulgarian Government, *ibid.*, p. 384.

[406] Cf. *ibid.*, p. 435; and see Charles de Visscher, *Problèmes d'interprétation judiciaire en droit international public* (Paris, 1963), p. 215.

Optional Clause.[407] As it had done previously in the 1930s,[408] the Permanent Court upheld an objection to its jurisdiction in respect of one of the submissions on the ground that there had been no prior dispute between the governments.[409] This step certainly reflected a good deal of self-restraint.[410]

Judicial caution

On Hersch Lauterpacht's reading, the late decisions on preliminary objections justified an entire new chapter on 'judicial caution'.[411] Possibly they also contributed something else, namely a national lawyer's approach to the Permanent Court's jurisdiction.

In the *Electricity Company* case, the majority upheld the view that acceptances under the Optional Clause did not constitute a multilateral treaty but a collection of unilateral declarations. True, the Permanent Court adopted the term 'agreements' when referring to the treaty and the Optional Clause together,[412] but, unlike the treaty, acceptances under the Optional Clause were never referred to in the singular. The Permanent Court saw that Optional Clause as a repository for declarations, which in a specific case could establish 'the juridical bond between the two States'.[413] It was left for the dissenters to see the Optional Clause as the framework of 'an agreement [that] came into existence between the two States accepting the compulsory jurisdiction of the Court'.[414] Construing reservations to a state's adherence to the Optional Clause has to do with the law-making act of the international sovereign, as distinct from a treaty text the content of which is binding on the participating states conceived of as international law subjects. It would not

---

[407] Series A/B No. 77 (1939) at 114; and similarly Judge Erich, *ibid.*, pp. 144–5.

[408] See *Interpretation of the Statute of the Memel Territory* (Merits), Series A/B No. 49 (1932) at 323; cf. *Case concerning the Administration of the Prince von Pless* (Jurisdiction), Series A/B No. 52 (1933) at 14.

[409] Series A/B No. 77 (1939) at 83.

[410] Cf. *Case of the Mavrommatis Palestine Concessions* (Jurisdiction), Series A No. 2 (1924) at 15; and *Case concerning Certain German Interests in Polish Upper Silesia* (Jurisdiction), Series A No. 6 (1925) at 14; and also Judge van Eysinga's dissenting opinion, Series A/B No. 77 (1939) at 116.

[411] Lauterpacht, *Development by the International Court*, pp. 95–8, 100–2 and 113–14.

[412] *The Electricity Company of Sofia and Bulgaria* (Preliminary Objection), Series A/B No. 77 (1939) at 75–6.

[413] *Ibid.*, p. 81.

[414] *Ibid.*, pp. 87 (Judge Anzilotti) and 103 (Judge Urrutia); cf. *ibid.*, p. 121 (Judge Hudson). But see also *Case concerning the Legal Status of the South-Eastern Territory of Greenland*, Series A/B No. 48 (1932) at 269 and 270.

be surprising if this prompted a more subjective approach to interpretation, but only as regards the reservations: within the scope of the consents actually given by the respective states, with all their reservations, ordinary treaty obligations had been undertaken. Basically, there was nothing special about the acceptances of the Optional Clause compared to other treaties or treaty provisions.[415] Indeed, a principle of strict reciprocity was part of the Optional Clause.[416] Nevertheless, behind the Optional Clause the majority might have seen the conception of the state as a national sovereign, leading them to the national principle of self-containedness. The first two decisions in which the Permanent Court had declined jurisdiction under the Optional Clause had a ring of restrictive interpretation. As was arguably made explicit in the *Phosphates in Morocco* case, the continuing focus on the unilateral declarations was equivalent to a continuing focus on the state seen in isolation and possibly not only the state as an international sovereign but also, or instead, as a national sovereign.

On the other hand, there was the tendency towards joining preliminary objections not strictly concerned with the Permanent Court's jurisdiction to the merits and, all in all, to defer making a decision on them as long as possible. These objections did not have much of a bearing on the treaty aspect of the Permanent Court's jurisdiction, that being a possible reason why they escaped a general tendency of restrictive treaty interpretation. The tendency to join preliminary objections to the merits

---

[415] In theory, the Optional Clause had been conceived as a set of bilateral relations, just as multilateral treaties in general when later a broader view on reservations was accepted: see Max Huber, 'Die Fortbildung des Völkerrechts auf dem Gebiete des Prozess – und Landkriegsrechts durch die II. internationale Friedenskonferenz im Haag 1907' (1908) 2 *Jahrbuch des öffentlichen Rechts der Gegenwart* 470 at 526; Max Huber, 'Gemeinschafts – und Sonderrecht unter Staaten' in *Festschrift Otto Gierke zum Siebzigsten Geburtstag* (Weimar, 1911), p. 817 at p. 839; and Huber in (1927) 33-I *Annuaire*, pp. 766–7; and also Åke Hammarskjöld, 'The Permanent Court of International Justice and Its Place in International Relations' (1930) 9 *International Affairs* 467 at 476; de Vineuil, '1929', p. 750; Guiliano Enriques, 'L'acception, sans réciprocité, de la juridiction obligatoire de la Cour permanente de Justice internationale' (1932) 13 *RDILC* 834 at 846–9 and 857–8; Manley O. Hudson, 'Obligatory Jurisdiction under Article 36 of the Statute of the Permanent Court of International Justice' (1933–4) 19 *Iowa Law Review* 190 at 204 and 210; Viktor Bruns, *Der internationale Richter* (Uppsala, 1934), p. 6; and Hudson, *Permanent Court*, p. 473, note 12; cf. C. H. M. Waldock, 'Decline of the Optional Clause' (1955/6) 32 *BYIL* 244 at 250–4. See also de Visscher, *Problèmes d'interprétation judiciaire*, pp. 199–203.

[416] See *Phosphates in Morocco Case* (Preliminary Objections), Series A/B No. 74 (1938) at 22; and *The Electricity Company of Sofia and Bulgaria* (Preliminary Objection), Series A/B No. 77 (1939) at 81.

may also be associated with national lawyers favouring an analogical interpretation reflecting their notion of a court of justice. Notably, in the *Panevezys–Saldutiskis Railway* case, the Permanent Court declared that it was entitled to join objections to the merits 'whenever the interests of the good administration of justice require it'.[417] In the *Electricity Company* case, the objection that the case belonged to the defendant's domestic jurisdiction evaporated into thin air as it was joined to the merits.[418] Another kind of preliminary objection joined to the merits concerned the principle of exhaustion of local remedies. In the *Panevezys–Saldutiskis Railway* case, the Permanent Court gave national courts a broad margin in determining whether remedies were effective and if they had been exhausted.[419] And, as illustrated by the *Prince von Pless* case and the *Electricity Company* case, the Permanent Court was also willing to wait for the remedies to be exhausted, if that was only a matter of time, the alternative being to decline jurisdiction.[420]

Conclusions

The *Electricity Company* case gave rise to two more published orders,[421] then in 1940 the active life of the Permanent Court came to an abrupt

[417] *The Panevezys–Saldutiskis Railway Case* (Preliminary Objections), Series A/B No. 75 (1938) at 56; and see Judge Hudson's dissenting opinion in *The Panevezys–Saldutiskis Railway Case*, Series A/B No. 76 (1939) at 44–5, also referring to *Case of the Mavrommatis Palestine Concessions* (Jurisdiction), Series A No. 2 (1924) at 16. Cf. *Case concerning the Barcelona Traction, Light and Power Company, Limited* (Preliminary Objections), ICJ Reports [1963] 6 at 41–6; *Military and Paramilitary Activities in and against Nicaragua* (Jurisdiction and Admissibility), ICJ Reports [1984] 392 at para. 76; *Military and Paramilitary Activities in and against Nicaragua* (Merits), ICJ Reports [1986] 14 at paras. 38–41; and *Questions of Interpretation and Application of the 1971 Montreal Convention Arising from the Aerial Incident at Lockerbie* (Preliminary Objections) (*Libya* v. *United Kingdom*), ICJ Reports [1998] 9 at para. 49 and (*Libya* v. *United States*), ICJ Reports [1998] 115 at para. 48.

[418] *The Electricity Company of Sofia and Bulgaria* (Preliminary Objection), Series A/B No. 77 (1939) at 78 and 82–3; and also Judge van Eysinga's dissenting opinion, *ibid.*, p. 117. Moreover, as regards nationality of claims, see *The Panevezys–Saldutiskis Railway Case*, Series A/B No. 76 (1939) at 16–18; and also Judge Hudson's dissenting opinion, *ibid.*, pp. 45–8; cf. Judges de Visscher and Rostworowski's separate opinion, *ibid.*, pp. 24–5; Judge van Eysinga's dissenting opinion, *ibid.*, pp. 30–1; and Judge Erich's dissenting opinion, *ibid.*, pp. 49–51.

[419] *The Panevezys–Saldutiskis Railway Case*, Series A/B No. 76 (1939) at 19.

[420] *Case concerning the Administration of the Prince von Pless* (Jurisdiction), Series A/B No. 52 (1933) at 16; and *The Electricity Company of Sofia and Bulgaria* (Preliminary Objection), Series A/B No. 77 (1939).

[421] *The Electricity Company of Sofia and Bulgaria* (Interim Measures of Protection), Series A/B No. 79 (1939); and *The Electricity Company of Sofia and Bulgaria* (Attendance), Series A/B No. 80 (1940). It may be noted that the former order had been prepared by a

end. By then, the third general election of judges due for 1939 had been suspended.[422] However, before the suspension in December 1939, the scheduled election had provoked judges to evaluate the preceding period in the Permanent Court's life. According to Judge Hurst, Judge Fromageot had suggested, possibly with the concurrence of President Guerrero, that the British and French Governments should draw up 'a list of not less than ten judges' and press for them being elected.[423] Eventually, Judge Hurst himself did not support that suggestion.[424] He was less enthusiastic about the present bench than he had been nine years before. He wanted the field from which candidates 'in practice' were drawn to be widened so as to ensure that the Permanent Court's position and authority were 'maintained'.[425]

Over the previous years, Judges Fromageot and Hurst, neither of whom sought re-election in 1939, had been prominent members of the group of former diplomats on the bench. They had had a vital impact on the Permanent Court's work, which the Permanent Court in yet another composition could have found it difficult to erase, even if desirable.[426] The *motifs* of the Permanent Court's decisions had been much reduced in length, and in the *Phosphates in Morocco* case, the statement of facts had even been omitted.[427] There was no flow of grand statements on international law and certainly no *dicta* that attracted as much citation as the *Wimbledon* statement and the *Lotus* statement continued to do.[428] Self-restraint found yet another expression, as the Permanent Court in

rapporteur, a system which most members of the bench had otherwise been against: see Series E No. 16 (1939–45) at 189 and Series D No. 2 (1922) at 78; see also Guyomar, *Commentaire du règlement*, p. 146.

[422] See *Records of Assembly: Plenary 1939*, p. 6.

[423] Hurst to Malkin, 19 January 1939, FO 371 W1679/107/98.

[424] Hurst to Malkin, 2 November 1939, FO 371 W16213/107/98.

[425] Malkin's minute, 14 April 1938, FO 371 W4945/956/98; cf. *Report of the Informal Inter-Allied Committee on the Future of the Permanent Court of International Justice*, Cmd 6531 (1944), p. 7.

[426] Cf. Shabtai Rosenne, *The International Court of Justice: An Essay in Political and Legal Theory* (Leiden, 1957), pp. 430–2.

[427] See Judicial Year 1938, *Procès-Verbal* 20 (3 June 1938), van Eysinga papers 127, pp. 8–9; and also Judge van Eysinga in *Phosphates in Morocco Case* (Preliminary Objections), Series A/B No. 74 (1938) at 35. According to Judge Anzilotti, the reason for omitting the statement of facts was that the judgment quoted the application filed by the Italian Government, which contained a similar statement: Distr. 4073, van Eysinga papers 155.

[428] See Åke Hammarskjöld, 'The Permanent Court of International Justice and the Development of International Law' (1935) 14 *International Affairs* 797 at 799; Manley O. Hudson, 'The Twentieth Year of the Permanent Court of International Justice' (1942) 36 *AJIL* 1 at 5; and Hudson, *Permanent Court*, pp. 605–6. Characteristically, when in a

some decisions defined its task not as applying the law but as merely reviewing the application of the law by other institutions.[429]

One may ask whether the reduction in legal reasoning was also indicative of the judges being willing to take other, political considerations into account.[430] From a French perspective, the second general election had certainly been a turning-point. Judge Fromageot became a leading member of a Permanent Court, the president and vice-president of which were considered 'pro-françaises'.[431] France was successfully involved in three contentious proceedings started after 1930 and also in the *Customs Regime* case, the one decision that brought the question of political bias to the mind of all commentators.[432] Yet only guesswork can answer questions as to possible political bias. There appeared to be many reasons for the reduction in legal reasoning in the 1930s, which witnessed the decay of the League, of the Permanent Court, and of the internationalist project itself. Judges Fromageot and Hurst opposed what they regarded as an academic standard for constructing long *motifs*. Moreover, the 'oligarchy' of the 'first' Court had been a passing phase. In subsequent periods, the bench had more voices, making the construction of long *motifs* much more difficult. And, as was made clear in the joint dissenting opinion in the *Customs Regime* case, many of the new 'voices' considered teleological considerations 'political' and were unwilling to make them an integral part of treaty interpretation.

Relying on a work published by Professor Reut-Nicolussi in 1940, *Unparteilichkeit im Völkerrecht*, Wilhelm Grewe submitted the following judgment of the Permanent Court, which appears to go back to the first edition of his history of international law completed in 1944:

> dissenting opinion Judge Read referred to the use of a principle of effectiveness in the Permanent Court, all his examples were taken from the 1920s: see *Interpretation of Peace Treaties* (Second Phase), ICJ Reports [1950] 221 at 232–5. Bin Cheng opened his analysis on general principles with four quotations taken from opinions framed by Judge Anzilotti: see Cheng, *General Principles of Law*, p. 29; another widely used source in the book was the arbitral awards of Arbitrator Huber. See also Andreae, *An Important Chapter*, pp. 53 and 129; and Antonio Cassese, *International Law* (Oxford, 2001), p. 157.

[429] Cf. *Lighthouses Case between France and Greece*, Series A/B No. 62 (1934) at 22; *The Oscar Chinn Case*, Series A/B No. 63 (1934) at 79 and 86; and *The Panevezys–Saldutiskis Railway Case*, Series A/B No. 76 (1939) at 19. See also *Nomination of the Workers' Delegate to the International Labour Conference*, Series B No. 1 (1922) at 25–6.

[430] Cf. Martens in James Brown Scott (ed.), *The Proceedings of the Hague Peace Conferences: The Conference of 1899* (London, 1920), pp. 740, 748 and 615.

[431] Cf. Kammerer's despatches, 27 September 1930, Quai d'Orsay 2400B and 26 January 1931, Quai d'Orsay 2400C.

[432] Cf. *Report of the Informal Inter-Allied Committee*, pp. 17, 19–20 and 21–2. See also Schwarzenberger, *International Law as Applied*, p. 258.

The experience with . . . [ad hoc] judges was hardly encouraging. They generally voted in favour of the State that appointed them. In most cases (although there were some remarkable exceptions) this also applied to the regular judges when their countries were before the Court. At times this shifted the judgment of the Court in a political direction, as for example in the highly controversial Advisory Opinion of 1931 on the question of a customs union between Germany and Austria.[433]

However, much was soon taken away from Reut-Nicolussi's analysis of 'absence of impartiality on the part of the judges of the Permanent Court of International Justice'. Thus, it was not a question of 'corrupt judges'. 'The problem was', according to Grewe, 'much more intricate': 'With remarkable self-criticism, the English judge Lord Davey summarised the problem with the following remark: "All English judges are impartial, but not all of them have the strength to free themselves from their prejudices".[434] As for the 'distinct inclination to support and vote in favour of one's own country', Grewe added:

Of course this inclination was all the more evident when several of the States represented on the bench were guided by the same interests. This was the case in the 1931 Advisory Opinion on the German–Austrian customs union, which lacked the impartiality and objectivity required for a judicial finding and was instead more of a political decision.[435]

In other words, Grewe's judgment that the members of the Permanent Court were not impartial seems only to have been aimed at those judges who in specific proceedings had the nationality of one of the parties, or other states interested. This view goes back to Reut-Nicolussi, who in an English summary of his work noted that 'the majority of its decisions prove that States may successfully place before a bench of professional judges any controversies that they are willed to settle by the methods

---

[433] Wilhelm G. Grewe, *The Epochs of International Law* (3rd edn, Berlin, 2000), p. 614; and see Eduard Reut-Nicolussi, *Unparteilichkeit in Völkerrecht* (Innsbruck, 1940), pp. 202–12 and 241–6 (as regards judges *ad hoc*) and 212–28 and 3 (as regards the *Customs Union* opinion). As for Reut-Nicolussi's discussion as to his own impartiality, see *ibid.*, pp. 212–13; as for the reactions of Huber and others to his ideas, see *ibid.*, p. 6. Cf. Hudson, *Permanent Court*, pp. 355–60; William Samore, 'National Origins v. Impartial Decisions: A Study of World Court Holdings' (1956) 34 *Chicago-Kent Law Review* 198 at 201–2; Franck, 'Psychological Factors', pp. 1230 and 1247; Thomas R. Hensley, 'National Bias and the International Court of Justice' (1968) 12 *Midwest Journal of Political Science* 568 at 585; Il Ro Suh, 'Voting Behaviour of National Judges in International Courts' (1969) 63 *AJIL* 224 at 230; and Stephen M. Schwebel, 'National Judges and Judges Ad Hoc of the International Court of Justice' (1999) 48 *ICLQ* 889 at 893.

[434] Grewe, *Epochs of International Law*, p. 615; the quotation is taken from Reut-Nicolussi, *Unparteilichkeit in Völkerrecht*, p. 244.

[435] Grewe, *Epochs of International Law*, pp. 615–16.

of legal procedure'.[436] That explains why Grewe was able to conclude that 'despite its deficiencies, the Court during this period had acquired prestige and authority'.[437]

So far as can be judged from the *motifs*, the use of international legal argument changed in about 1931, although the differences cannot be explained in terms of Article 38 of the Statute. It may be recalled that in 1937 Hersch Lauterpacht maintained among four lessons of the history of the law of nations the following:

The third moral is that the progress of International Law depends to a great extent upon whether the legal school of international jurists prevails over the diplomatic school. The legal school desires International Law to develop more or less on the lines of Municipal Law, aiming at the codification of firm, decisive, and unequivocal rules of International Law, and working for the establishment of international courts for the purpose of the administration of international justice. The diplomatic school, on the other hand, considers International Law to be, and prefers it to remain, rather a body of elastic principles than of firm and precise rules. The diplomatic school opposes the establishment of international courts, because it considers diplomatic settlement of international disputes, and, failing this, arbitration, preferable to international administration of justice by international courts composed of permanently appointed judges. There is, however, no doubt that international courts are urgently needed, and that the rules of International Law require now an authoritative interpretation and administration such as only an international court can supply.[438]

The Permanent Court in its new composition sided with the dissenters in *The Lotus*; and in doing so, gave more room for the international law of coexistence and, notably, territorial sovereignty. Thus, the *Eastern Greenland* case and the two *Lighthouses* cases indicated that the Permanent Court saw legislative powers as *prima facie* limited to the state's own territory. The other side of this approach to international legal argument was the weakening of the international law of cooperation. It was not

---

[436] Eduard Reut-Nicolussi, 'The Permanent Court of International Justice Viewed as an Experiment' (1941) 7 *Research and Progress* 107 at 112; see also the conclusions, not without hope, in Reut-Nicolussi, *Unparteilichkeit in Völkerrecht*, pp. 244–9; and Eduard Reut-Nicolussi, 'The Reform of the Permanent Court of International Justice' (1939) 25 *Grotius Transactions* 135 at 147–9.

[437] Grewe, *Epochs of International Law*, p. 616. See also as for the International Court of Justice, G. Terry, 'Factional Behaviour on the International Court of Justice: An Analysis of the First and Second Courts (1945–1951) and the Sixth and Seventh Courts (1961–1967)' (1975) 10 *Melbourne University Law Review* 59 at 117; and Edith Brown Weiss, 'Judicial Independence and Impartiality: A Preliminary Inquiry' in Fisler Damrosch (ed.), *The International Court of Justice at a Crossroads* (Dobbs Ferry, 1987), p. 123 at pp. 130–2.

[438] Oppenheim/Lauterpacht, *International Law*, vol. 1, pp. 81–2.

only interpreted with a firm view to the international law of coexistence. The scope of the international law of cooperation was regularly restricted by the national principle of self-containedness. In addition there were some possible examples of analogical interpretation, as in the *Memel Territory* case and the *Panevezys–Saldutiskis Railway* case.

By comparing the *Treatment of Polish Nationals* opinion to the *Memel Territory* case, or the *Oscar Chinn* case to the *Albanian Minority Schools* opinion, one can see that the more remarkable expressions of a national lawyer's approach to international law attracted opposition. But when not taken to extremes, this approach drew widespread support from the bench. Hence, also, the relaxed attitude towards national law, which in numerous decisions was treated straightforwardly as law. The change in the hierarchical relationship between the dynamic and basic structures of international legal argument, the international law of cooperation giving some way for the national principle of self-containedness, was ubiquitous and not just a reflection of the subject matter of some of the cases decided in the 1930s.

It may seem a paradox that in this period, probably the greatest 'optimist' to be associated with the work of the Permanent Court occupied a permanent position on the bench, namely Professor Schücking. In his own words, '[w]o sind denn diese Zukunftsjuristen des Völkerrechts? Ich kenne an allen deutschen Universitäten nur einen, nämlich den Professor Walther Schücking in Marburg.'[439] According to Schücking, Professor Max Huber's work might have been a consequence of Schücking's *Die Organisation der Welt*. However, he saw Huber as being too sceptical.[440] Conversely, Huber saw himself as someone who had been and continued to be 'in vielen Fragen weit weniger optimistisch und draufgängerisch'.[441] In 1930, Schücking referred to his election to the Permanent Court in the following way:

---

[439] Schücking, *Staatenverband der Haager Konferenzen*, p. 8, note 1 ('[w]here are these international jurists who have their eyes fixed on the future? In all the German universities I know of but one, namely, Professor Walther Schücking of Marburg.').

[440] Schücking, *Staatenverband der Haagerkonferenzen*, p. 33; cf. *ibid.*, pp. 67–8. See also *ibid.*, pp. 4–5 – referring to Max Huber, *Die Soziologischen Grundlagen des Völkerrechts* (Berlin, 1928), pp. 84–95 – and *ibid.*, pp. 11, 32–3, 51–2 and 93–4.

[441] Huber to Wehberg, 14 September 1935, Wehberg papers 199/61 (translation: 'in many questions much less optimistic and energetic'); and see also Huber, 'Walther Schücking', p. 197. According to a letter from van Eysinga to Schücking, '[s]owie Max Huber mir neulich sagte, hat keiner der Richter es so verdient im Hofe aufgenommen zu werden als Sie': van Eysinga to Schücking, 18 November 1930, Schücking papers (Koblenz) 33 (translation: '[a]s Max Huber told me recently, no judge has deserved to come on the bench so much as you').

Dieser äussere Erfolg meiner Lebensarbeit kommt mir noch immer ganz märchenhaft vor, denn leider Gottes ist es in dieser Welt doch keineswegs die Regel, dass die Pioniere einer Idee in ihrem Leben auch schliesslich den äusseren Erfolg davon tragen und dass ihr Idealismus sozusagen mit harten Gulden baren Geldes bezahlt wird, von allen ideellen Werten des Erfolges abgesehen.[442]

Unlike Judge Huber, who had taken part in founding an international lawyer's approach to international legal argument, which in regard to treaty interpretation meant objective interpretation in the light of object and purpose, Judge Schücking turned out to be a defender of state sovereignty, invoking a principle of restrictive interpretation and the national principle of self-containedness on a regular basis.[443] His notion of international organisation was a projection of national law onto international law. However, rather than drawing any significant conclusions from the general projection, when it came to the use of international legal argument to specific cases, the national lawyer focused on defending the national sovereign and its unfettered powers within a national legal system. It may be doubted whether Judge Schücking's reference to a concept of *jus cogens* in the *Oscar Chinn* case was an exception.

---

[442] Schücking to Wehberg, 3 October 1930, Wehberg papers 199/80 (translation: 'This outward success of my life work still strikes me as something fabulous and unreal, as it is unfortunately not at all the way of this world that the pioneers of an idea reap its outward success in their own life time and that their idealism is repaid, as it were, in hard guilder, disregarding for the moment the non-material value of the success.'); cf. Schücking, *Staatenverband der Haagerkonferenzen*, pp. vii and 1–6, 26–7, 32–6, 69–70, 82–3, 178–81, 232 and 273–5.

[443] Cf. Acker, *Schücking*, pp. 203–4; and Bodendiek, *Walther Schückings Konzeption*, p. 294.

PART 4

General conclusions

8   The legacy of the Permanent Court

International law as a complementary legal system

As an institution, or a project of international justice, the Permanent Court was a success, being the framework within which the world first experienced the development of an international judiciary. What remains so attractive about the Permanent Court is simply that it was a pioneering institution. During the negotiations of the Charter of the United Nations, there was little doubt that an International Court should be part of the institutional arrangement, and that it would be closely modelled on the Permanent Court. Despite the significant political changes in the world since 1945, many of which have been given legal form, there has been no decline in the international judiciary, and no change in the basic framework laid down after 1921 for the Permanent Court. At the turn of the twenty-first century, there were several active international courts in existence in addition to the principal judicial organ of the United Nations.

Many of the decisions of the Permanent Court concerned the interpretation of treaties that are now obsolete; most of them had emerged out of the conclusion of the First World War and most did not survive yet another upheaval of the world. More than sixty years later, there are often more recent and less eccentric precedents to cite. While many fields of international law are informed with quotations from various decisions of the Permanent Court, the exotic names of which are commonplace, the use of such quotations often has no relation to the original context and may indeed only be lingering on as echoes from a distant past.

Yet it takes a simplistic conception of history – or an equally flawed 'optimist' interpretation of the evolution of international law – to conclude that international legal argument as used in the Permanent

393

Court is no longer relevant. The structures of international legal argument then used were not a result of the *interbellum*, its political or other circumstances; they are part of a conceptual deep structure ingrained in internationalism at all times. The model of international legal argument used in Chapters 5 to 7 to analyse decisions of the Permanent Court is the same model that in Chapters 2 and 3 was detailed by reference to numerous decisions rendered long after the Permanent Court had been abolished in 1946. Of course, the scope and content of the international law of cooperation has changed, so to a certain extent has the content of the international law of coexistence. But the essence of internationalism and so the double structure of international legal argument has remained.

The basis of the double structure of international legal argument is the notion of international law being a complementary – and residual – legal system. It is coordinated with, yet separate from, national law. Each lawyer has a national legal system as his or her native tongue, as it were. But each has also to use international law when approaching issues that are international, either in kind or in form, in the sense that they interest a plurality of national sovereigns, or states. Such issues are not suitable for regulation in the national legal system of one state. Instead, issues international in kind are referred from national law to the international law of coexistence, while issues international in form are allocated to the international law of cooperation, as opposed to national law. In this way, the international grows out of the national, bindingness grows out of sovereignty. The two resulting structures of international legal argument connect the national and the international, or the lawyer's native tongue and this foreign language to which international law may be compared: the basic structure advances from issues national in kind to issues international in kind, or from the national principle of self-containedness to the international law of coexistence; the dynamic structure advances from contracts international in form, or the international law of cooperation, to the residual principle of state freedom.

Each and every issue may be categorised within both the basic and the dynamic structure: if the issue gives rise to a conflict between the interests of different national sovereigns, it is international in kind and is categorised with the international law of coexistence, instead of the national principle of self-containedness; if the issue is covered by a contract entered into by sovereign states, it comes under the international law of cooperation and otherwise the residual principle of freedom. These categorisations are determined separately in each structure, yet international legal argument is not indeterminate; for it does not simply have two single structures, but one double structure. It is international law, and not some extraneous force, nor international lawyers themselves, which determines the hierarchical relationship between the two structures.

As a matter of international law, it does not make sense to inquire whether the double structure of international legal argument is good or bad; for it is part of the conceptual deep structure within which international law is conceived, analysed and used. There is no choice, nor an alternative. On the other hand, the double structure underlines which difficulties may confront lawyers turned international. In particular, in taking up the language of international law, there may be differences in dialect between lawyers from different national legal systems. Some may also have a strong accent, suggesting that it is not always that easy for lawyers undertaking issues international in kind or form to dissociate themselves from their native tongue. From the point of view of the national lawyer, the scope of the international law of coexistence is relatively uncontroversial. But as regards its content as well as the scope and content of the international law of cooperation, there is a continuing and real risk that an international lawyer resorts to his or her native tongue, thereby obscuring international legal reasoning.

Of course, a collegiate judicial body cannot be treated as a disembodied institutional voice. The Permanent Court accommodated the work of thirty judges, four deputy-judges, twenty-three judges *ad hoc* and two registrars over a period of nineteen years in sixty-five proceedings leading to thirty-two judgments and twenty-seven advisory opinions as well as 137 orders. It would be a surprise if a perusal of these activities bred clear-cut, consistent or inclusive conclusions as to the use of international legal argument.[1] Indeed, one may surmise that such conclusions can only be the products of commentator's not being fully conversant with the Permanent Court, or indifferent to its use of international legal argument, using what is displayed as the Permanent Court's 'case law' as a window for the commentator's own agenda.

Yet there are certain trends and principles in the use of international legal argument in the Permanent Court, which fit into the double

---

[1] Cf. *Admission of a State to the United Nations (Charter, Art. 4)*, ICJ Reports [1947–8] 57 at 63; and also the joint dissenting opinion by Judges Basdevant, Winiarski and Read and Sir Arnold McNair, *ibid.*, p. 84.

structure, a description of which enhances the understanding of international legal argument in practice and dissolves some classic problems of international legal theory. While international legal theory has
been obsessed with the dichotomy between sovereignty and bindingness, the cardinal dichotomy in practice is one national sovereign versus more national sovereigns, or the national versus the international,
the national lawyer versus the international lawyer. A practitioner may
object that to the extent that the trends and principles referred to in
Chapters 5 to 7 have a bearing on international legal argument in practice, the double structure developed in Chapter 3, and within which they
fit, merely repeats, albeit in a novel phraseology, what has always been
known. It is certainly a well-known dilemma of legal academia that the
more ingenious and surprising the results, the less likely that they are
results *de lege lata*, as opposed to *de lege ferenda*. But then structures of
international legal argument are not confined to the results to which
arguments may lead, but also involve the arguments and processes as
such. For his or her part, a theorist may object that the trends and principles referred to, fitting the model of international legal argument, are
just further examples of a hidden agenda being read into the decisions of
an international court. No doubt, the trends and principles do not strike
the untrained eye. But using a model of international legal argument
to expose structures is a far cry from reading them into the decisions.
The objections, both the practical and the theoretical, are really to be
joined to the merits, as it were. The answers to them lie in the analysis
undertaken in Chapters 5 to 7. Any such objection ought to be sustained
by careful studies of the pleadings before the Permanent Court as well
as the *motifs* and the separate opinions, coupled with, it would seem,
indispensable archival material.

Technically speaking, all the cases before the Permanent Court had to
do with treaty interpretation. But treaty interpretation in the Permanent
Court was marked by differences, partly due to disagreement about the
hierarchical relationship between the two structures of international
legal argument. In the conclusions to the three chapters devoted to the
decisions of the Permanent Court, a variety of examples of the practical use of international legal argument have been given; they cannot
be explained in terms of a unitary structure. For example, Article 38
of the Statute does not provide a language in which the Permanent
Court's work and the several differences between various decisions can
be expressed. On the other hand, patterns emerge when studying the

decisions in the light of the double structure of international legal argument and the hierarchical relationship between the two structures which compose it.

The double structure also sheds light on some of the overall differences between the decisions of the Permanent Court in its old and in its new composition, which have been explained as a modification in the hierarchical relationship between the basic and the dynamic structures of international legal argument. To use the analogy, there were marked accents on the bench in the 1930s. It can hardly be argued that a radical change in international law coincided with the second general election in 1930. Instead, one might take the differences in international legal argument as evidence of international law really representing the vanishing point not only of jurisprudence, but also of normativity. But then one is assuming that the use of international legal argument in the Permanent Court in its old and new composition was equally valid and so the question is begged. The differences between the 'first' and the 'new' Court regarding the hierarchical relationship between the basic and dynamic structures, and also the categorisation of issues within the double structure, were not necessarily indicative of the freedom enjoyed by lawyers when using international legal argument. Rather, different lawyers at different times used the double structure differently; these could be differences between right and wrong international legal argument, between successful and ill-starred international lawyers.

On the basis of the model developed in Chapter 3, three aspects of international legal argument of particular interest to the analysis were pointed out, the third aspect being its variety reflecting the categorisation of issues within the double structure of international legal argument, and the hierarchical relationship between the basic and dynamic structures. In the Permanent Court, this aspect was dependent on the two first-mentioned aspects: (1) the role in international legal argument of the national lawyer and of the conception of the state as a national sovereign; and (2) the role of the international lawyer, as distinct from any national lawyer, notably in treaty interpretation but also in determining the content of the international law of coexistence. The accents prevalent in the 1930s raised the question whether in some cases international lawyers should not distance themselves from national lawyers and the fundamental conceptions ingrained in national law, especially the conception of the state as a national sovereign.

The national lawyer

The double structure of international legal argument is underpinned by the notion that international law is inter-national law, the logical consequence of having several states and several national legal systems. No lawyer would have come round to international law had it not been for national law, or the insufficiency of national law. There may be many cultural and sociological reasons why human societies develop law in the first place, vesting some 'promises', 'commands' and 'ideas' with a binding quality. However, having once explained, or even just assumed, the existence of national law, the reasons why international law develops are plain. The definition of international law is not a painstaking conundrum comparable to the philosophical discussions about the concept of law. International law governs promises, and the resulting agreements, between states (then conceived as international sovereigns), and while international law knows no super-state, a single international sovereign, it also governs clashes of interests between the several states (then conceived as national sovereigns). Here, national lawyers identify the interests of more than one state and so they need a common legal system; for it would be odd if a dispute between two or more sovereign states was made subject to the national law of one. International law can only achieve this purpose if treated as a legal system in its own right, the validity of which does not depend on national legal systems. Nevertheless, international law relates to national law and refers back to the national lawyer sometimes being an international lawyer. This is evidently so with the international law of coexistence. But, similarly, the international law of cooperation is a branch of international law only because contracts are not allocated to national law. In other words, while the content of international law is determined in international law, its scope is due to the insufficiency of national law.

The decisions of the Permanent Court provided numerous references to the international law of coexistence. Having been part of lawyers' law for centuries, it contributed the most stable aspect of international legal argument in the Permanent Court. In the 1920s, of the two general principles of treaty interpretation that were not only articulated but also repeated, one principle laid down the subordinate status of preparatory work. This principle had been developed in the *Mosul* case, *The Lotus*, the *Danube* opinion and the *River Oder* case, where treaty interpretation had reflected the international law of coexistence. Whatever the interpretations given to the statements afterwards, in their original context they served treaty interpretation by swiftly excluding the possibility of treaty provisions deviating from the international law of coexistence. In all four decisions the relevant aspect of the international law of coexistence was the separation of territorial sovereigns. The leading role given to territorial sovereignty in treaty interpretation was also demonstrated by the *Jaworzina* opinion and the *Monastery of Saint-Naoum* opinion, both displaying a dislike for territorial disputes.

Where it came to other rule-like aspects of the international law of coexistence, the 'first' Court employed these rules, normally referred to as belonging to 'general' international law,[2] in the form of subsidiary arguments for treaty interpretations already arrived at. In particular, this was the case with the strict conception of vested rights (which to some would seem reminiscent of a Western tradition and so, in the enlarged world of today, possibly an example of analogical interpretation). On the other hand, in *The Lotus* the majority seemed willing to take what could otherwise have been an inherently vague situation under the international law of coexistence to be a situation not governed by international law; the definition in the *Serbian Loans* case of private international law as part of national law was to the same effect.

In the 1930s, the 'new' Court gave the international law of coexistence a broader scope, as hinted at in the *Eastern Greenland* case. It covered not only the exercise of state authority but state activities in general, including legislation and administrative decision-making. The two *Lighthouses* cases and the *Meuse* case interpreted treaty regimes so that they did not encroach upon the national principle of self-containedness, but merely regulated what would otherwise have come within the international law of coexistence. In the *Treatment of Polish Nationals* opinion and the *Memel Territory* case, treaty-based entities were construed so that they could not disturb the notion of the world being the sum of territorially separated, national sovereigns.

These decisions did not relate solely to the international law of coexistence. Indeed, the main difference between the 'first' Court and the 'new' Court was what to do when outside that arena, and in particular how to interpret and apply the international law of cooperation. It

---

[2] E.g., *Status of Eastern Carelia*, Series B No. 5 (1923) at 27; *Case of the SS Wimbledon*, Series A No. 1 (1923) at 28; *Questions relating to Settlers of German Origin in Poland*, Series B No. 6 (1923) at 36; *Case of the Mavrommatis Palestine Concessions* (Jurisdiction), Series A No. 2 (1924) at 16; *Case concerning Certain German Interests in Polish Upper Silesia* (Merits), Series A No. 7 (1926) at 42; *The Case of the SS Lotus*, Series A No. 10 (1927) at 27; *Interpretation of Judgments Nos. 7 and 8 (the Chorzów Factory)*, Series A No. 13 (1927) at 19; and *Case relating to the Territorial Jurisdiction of the International Commission of the River Oder*, Series A No. 23 (1929) at 26.

was in this context that the national principle of self-containedness was entertained. The question was whether the conception of the state as an international law subject and so the dynamic structure of international legal argument trumped the conceptions of the state as a sovereign, whether national or international, and the basic structure, or, to put it differently, whether international lawyers were ever anything but national lawyers.

The international lawyer

Issues come within the international law of coexistence because they have to do with serious conflicts between state interests; on the other hand, issues come within the international law of cooperation, because agreements have been concluded the parties to which are states. They are international in form, but not necessarily in kind. Accordingly, there is no coordination between the international law of cooperation and national law. This was what prompted the theory of dualism, and thus *Völkerrecht und Landesrecht*. When interpreting and applying treaties, lawyers may be able to distance themselves from their being national lawyers and to approach the rules as international lawyers. But there is always the possibility that the international lawyer turns into a national lawyer. International legal theory has known many examples of this, hence the 'pessimist' and 'optimist' evaluations of international law. Such accents may also influence treaty interpretation.

In the 1930s, if a treaty did not have a bearing on the international law of coexistence, the 'new' Court was often willing to interpret it restrictively, as in the *Treatment of Polish Nationals* opinion, the *Memel Territory* case, the *Oscar Chinn* case and the *Meuse* case and perhaps also the *Phosphates in Morocco* case. There were also some possible examples of analogical interpretation, as in the *Panevezys–Saldutiskis Railway* case. Restrictive and analogical interpretations are linked to the conception of the state which is an integral part of national law, i.e. the state as a national sovereign: restrictive interpretation is an attempt to give this conception as broad a scope as possible, by restricting obligations under the international law of cooperation; analogical interpretation is about recreating the conception by construing the international law of cooperation in its image. A further illustration not only of judicial self-restraint but also of what room to give the national lawyer is the *Customs Regime* opinion. When negotiating treaties in what is an inherently political process, politicians transfer political principles, ideas and considerations to the international law of cooperation. Yet in the *Customs Regime* opinion the dissenters seemed to regard some considerations as being notoriously political and outside the province of international law, just because they were alien to the international law of coexistence, or embedded in the conception of the state as a national sovereign. An example to the same effect was the separate opinion appended by Judge Kellogg to the second order in the *Free Zones* case.

The 'first' Court had adopted a different approach. It had only applied a presumption against restrictions on the territorial state's freedom to exercise power in the *Free Zones* case. In this exceptional proceeding, the presumption might have served the purpose of the Permanent Court making the least of its broad jurisdictional powers under the Special Agreement, or it might have been a testimony to the upcoming changes in the Permanent Court's use of international legal argument. Previously, a presumption had been completely avoided in the *Danube* opinion and the *River Oder* case. In general, the 'first' Court had no difficulties in drawing the full consequences of a treaty having been concluded and new issues being transferred to the international law of cooperation. Indeed, the second principle of treaty interpretation cultivated in the 1920s countered the tendency of governments pleading a general principle of restrictive treaty interpretation before the Permanent Court. Treaty provisions were normally given an objective, effective interpretation in the light of the conception of the state as an international law subject. A prime example of the approach adopted by the 'first' Court had to do with the involvement of individuals in international law. Article 34 of the Statute provided that only states could be parties in cases before the Permanent Court. This provision had been drafted with a view to the international law of coexistence, which always has states as its – often only – subjects. However, in the *Jurisdiction of Courts* opinion, the Permanent Court rejected a presumption against individuals being subjects under treaty rules. While the international law of coexistence mainly applies to states, politicians can put whatever rule they like in a treaty, including rules that have a direct effect on individuals.

The Permanent Court in its old composition consisted of some of the most distinguished jurists. In the 1920s, Judges Huber, Anzilotti and Moore, Deputy-Judge Beichmann and the Registrar, Åke Hammarskjöld, produced a series of remarkable decisions. The national lawyer was given some space, but not too much. Thus, the national principle of self-containedness was essentially avoided. The 'first' Court articulated an international lawyer's approach to international legal argument, which due to a fixed hierarchy between the two structures of international legal argument had three layers: first, the conception of the state as a national sovereign and the international law of coexistence; secondly, the conception of the state as an international law subject and the international law of cooperation, which generally required an objective interpretation of agreed texts (although if regulating the same issues as the international law of coexistence, the latter was likely to influence that interpretation); and, thirdly, the conception of the state as a national sovereign and the residual principle of state freedom.

It is the second layer that is questioned under a national lawyer's approach to international legal argument. Changing the hierarchical relationship between the two structures of international legal argument and the international law of cooperation will be subject to a restrictive interpretation, or perhaps an analogical one, in accordance with the conception of the state as a national sovereign. This approach was adopted in the 1930s, after the election of a number of forceful personalities, whose claims to judgeships were not, or not primarily, their expertise in international law. It also underlay various misreadings of the decisions of the 'first' Court, including *The Lotus* and the *Jurisdiction of Courts* opinion, which were assimilated into the *Buchrecht*. Some subsequent international courts have adopted a similar approach, employing a comparative law methodology in their own Tower of Babel. On the other hand, many more lawyers today portray themselves as being principally international lawyers. According to Manfred Lachs:

> There are . . . a number of international judges who have had the benefit of being educated in several different cultures. They have thus had not only early access to, but direct contact with, a plurality of the 'principal legal systems of the world'. This is increasingly the case, with the growth of international intellectual contacts and the gradual forging of universal law. Moreover, within the context of an international tribunal, members learn swiftly to understand each other better, to influence and be influenced by the previously unfamiliar. The time necessary for their mutual accommodation is reduced by the cross-cultural contacts they have already enjoyed in other legal fora.[3]

Mohammed Bedjaoui, writing in 2000 about the Hague bench, states that '[t]he national cultural experience blends into the background of everyday working life in common and the collective international

---

[3] Manfred Lachs, 'A Few Thoughts on the Independence of Judges of the International Court of Justice' (1986–7) 25 *Columbia Journal of Transnational Law* 593 at 595.

experience'.[4] Still, background has remained important in the eyes of most commentators.[5] For example, according to Gilbert Guillaume, 'it would appear . . . that while the nationality of regular judges has sometimes had some influence on their point of view, that is probably because

[4] Mohammed Bedjaoui, 'Expediency in the Decisions of the International Court of Justice' (2000) 71 *BYIL* 1 at 6–7; holding that '[i]n short, and in many respects, there is nothing here to distinguish international judges from domestic ones', Bedjaoui added that 'the "function of adjudication" . . . is largely the same for both: all that changes is the setting, which here is international'. See also Mohammed Bedjaoui, 'L'opportunité dans les décisions de la Cour internationale de Justice' in Laurence Boisson de Chazournes and Vera Gowlland-Debbas (eds.), *The International Legal System in Quest of Equity and Universality: Liber Amicorum Georges Abi-Saab* (The Hague, 2001), p. 563 at pp. 569–70; cf. as regards the International Law Commission, James Crawford, 'Universalism and Regionalism from the Perspective of the Work of the International Law Commission' in Alain Pellet (ed.), *International Law on the Eve of the Twenty-First Century: Views from the International Law Commission* (New York, 1997), p. 99 at p. 109.

[5] See Mohammed Bedjaoui, 'The "Manufacture" of Judgments at the International Court of Justice' (1991) 3 *Pace Yearbook of International Law* 29 at 48 and 57–8; and also Raoul Genet, *Précis de jurisprudence de la Cour permanente de Justice internationale* (2nd edn, Vienna, 1939), pp. 2–3; Edvard Hambro, 'Dissenting and Individual Opinions in the International Court of Justice' (1956) 17 *ZaöRV* 229 at 246–7; André Gros, 'A propos de cinquante années de justice internationale' (1972) 76 *RGDIP* 5 at 9–10; Taslim Olawale Elias, 'Does the International Court of Justice, as It Is Presently Shaped, Correspond to the Requirements Which Follow from Its Functions as the Central Judicial Body of the International Community? – Report' in H. Mosler and R. Bernhardt (eds.), *Judicial Settlement of International Disputes* (Berlin, 1974), p. 19 at pp. 23, 27 and 29; Shabtai Rosenne, 'The Composition of the Court' in Leo Gross (ed.), *The Future of the International Court of Justice* (Dobbs Ferry, 1976), p. 377 at pp. 382–5; Manfred Lachs, 'Le Droit international à l'aube du XXIe siècle' (1992) 99 *RGDIP* 529 at 539; Christopher Gregory Weeramantry, 'Expanding the Potential of the World Court' in Nandasiri Jasentuliyana (ed.), *Perspectives on International Law: Essays in Honour of Judge Manfred Lachs* (The Hague, 1995), p. 309 at pp. 327–8; Elihu Lauterpacht, 'The Juridical and the Meta-Juridical in International Law' in Jerzy Makarczyk (ed.), *Theory of International Law at the Threshold of the 21st Century: Essays in Honour of Krzysztof Skubiszewski* (The Hague, 1996), p. 215 at pp. 233–4; Mohamed Shahabuddeen, *Precedent in the World Court* (Cambridge, 1996), pp. 203–8; Georges Abi-Saab, 'Substantive Requirements or The Portrait of the Jurist as an International Judge' in Connie Peck and Roy S. Lee (eds.), *Increasing the Effectiveness of the International Court of Justice* (The Hague, 1997), p. 166 at pp. 169–72; and C. F. Amerasinghe, 'Judges of the International Court of Justice: Election and Qualifications' (2001) 14 *IJIL* 335 at 339 and 345; see also Edward McWhinney, *The World Court and the Contemporary International Law-Making Process* (Alphen aan den Rijn, 1979), p. 13 and *passim*; Edward McWhinney, 'The Legislative Rôle of the World Court in an Era of Transition' in Rudolf Bernhard *et al.* (eds.), *Völkerrecht als Rechtsordnung – Internationale Gerichtsbarkeit – Menschenrechte: Festschrift für Hermann Mosler* (1983), p. 567 at p. 567; Edward McWhinney, *The International Court of Justice and the Western Tradition of International Law* (Dordrecht, 1987), pp. 151–3 and *passim*; and Edward McWhinney, *Judicial Settlement of International Disputes: Jurisdiction, Justiciability and Judicial Law-Making on the Contemporary International Court* (Dordrecht, 1991), pp. xiv–xvi, 25–30, 40, 42, 44–5, 46, 49, 65–6, 71, 106–7, 124–5, 133 and 156–7.

of their attachment to the cultural values particular to their home country'.[6] National legal systems are the framework in which they have all been educated and also the situation in which many have earned their living, at least in some phases of their careers. Apart from that, in certain respects, they have to depend on the conception of the state as a national sovereign because international law does so.

This national lawyer's approach must be rejected as a matter of international law. Referring issues from national law to the international law of coexistence just in order to let the content of the international law of coexistence reflect some specific national legal system would be pointless. Similarly, contracts between sovereign states are allocated to the international law of cooperation because they are binding and shall be given full effect. In the Permanent Court, the more remarkable examples of restrictive interpretation were criticised by significant minorities. Yet a national lawyer's approach has been adopted so often because lawyers have not been aware of its implications (or being aware, have accepted the parochialism that naturally follows). As the international legal system has been dealt with in isolation, there has been no occasion for considering the role of the national lawyer, let alone evaluating those cases where it has been excessive. On the other hand, that the better approach is the international lawyer's approach as adopted by the Permanent Court in the 1920s is a lesson that cannot be learned once, a hindrance that international law could not simply overcome in the 1920s. It is a daily quest for international lawyers. International law being this complementary and residual legal system that owes its existence to national law, there is always the risk that the international lawyer fails to restraint the national lawyer lurking within him or her.

---

[6] Gilbert Guillaume, 'Some Thoughts on the Independence of International Judges vis-à-vis States' (2003) 2 *LPICT* 163 at 167–8; referring to Thomas R. Hensley, 'National Bias and the International Court of Justice' (1968) 12 *Midwest Journal of Political Science* 568 at 581–5; and Michele Sicart-Bozec, *Les Juges du tiers monde à la Cour internationale de Justice* (Paris, 1986), pp. 185 and 297.

Appendix
List of Advisory Opinions, Judgments and Orders of the Permanent Court of International Justice

Note: This appendix lists all decisions published in Series A and B between 1922 and 1930 and in Series A/B between 1931 and 1940, that is, all advisory opinions and judgments of the Permanent Court and also a small number of orders. It gives the official name of the decision; its number in the General List and the date of registration; the references to official publications regarding the decision (i.e., Series A, Series B or Series A/B, and the publication of related acts and documents in Series C); the decision's kind, its date, the final vote (if available in the official publications) and the authentic language of the decision; and the participating judges, deputy-judges and judges *ad hoc* (the names of judges and deputy-judges not sitting on the case are struck out; the names of dissenting judges are underlined; the names of judges appending a declaration or a separate opinion are put in italics). The folios of the General List in respect of all cases submitted to the Permanent Court are reproduced in Series E No. 16 (1939–45) at 92–147. Chronological indexes of orders of the Permanent Court are contained in Series E No. 11 (1934–5) at 95–100; Series E No. 12 (1935–6) at 149–50; Series E No. 13 (1936–7) at 108–9; Series E No. 14 (1937–8) at 99; Series E No. 15 (1938–9) at 83; and Series E No. 16 (1939–45) at 88.

First Ordinary Session (15 June–12 August 1922)

Series B No. 1	**Nomination of the Workers' Delegate to the**
Series C No. 1	**International Labour Conference**
	General List No. 2; 27 May 1922
	Advisory opinion, 31 July 1922; Final vote: not available; French
	Loder; Weiss; Finlay; ~~Barbosa~~; Nyholm; Moore; de Bustamante; Altamira; Oda; Anzilotti; ~~Huber~~ ~~Yovanovitch~~; Beichmann; Negulesco; ~~Wang~~
Series B No. 2	**International Labour Organization and the**
Series C No. 1	**Conditions of Agricultural Labour**
	General List No. 1; 27 May 1922

Advisory opinion, 12 August 1922; Final vote: not available; English

Loder; <u>Weiss</u>; Finlay; ~~Barbosa~~; Nyholm; Moore; de Bustamante; Altamira; Oda; Anzilotti; ~~Huber Yovanovitch; Beichmann~~; <u>Negulesco</u>; ~~Wang~~

Series B No. 3 **International Labour Organization and the Methods**
Series C No. 1 **of Agricultural Production**

General List No. 3; 20 July 1922

Advisory opinion, 12 August 1922; Final vote: not available; English

Loder; Weiss; Finlay; ~~Barbosa~~; Nyholm; Moore; de Bustamante; Altamira; Oda; Anzilotti; ~~Huber Yovanovitch; Beichmann~~; Negulesco; ~~Wang~~

Second Extraordinary Session (8 January–7 February 1923)

Series B No. 4 **Nationality Decrees in Tunis and Morocco**
Series C No. 2 General List No. 4; 10 November 1922

Advisory opinion, 7 February 1923; Final vote: not available; French

Loder; Weiss; Finlay; ~~Barbosa~~; Nyholm; Moore; ~~de Bustamante; Altamira; Oda~~; Anzilotti; Huber ~~Yovanovitch~~; Beichmann; Negulesco; ~~Wang~~

Third Ordinary Session (15 June–15 September 1923)

Series B No. 5 **Status of Eastern Carelia**
Series C No. 3-I and II General List No. 7; 30 April 1923

Advisory opinion, 23 July 1923; Final vote: not available; English

Loder; <u>Weiss</u>; Finlay; ~~Barbosa~~; <u>Nyholm</u>; Moore; de Bustamante; <u>Altamira</u>; Oda; Anzilotti; Huber ~~Yovanovitch; Beichmann; Negulesco~~; Wang

Series A No. 1 **Case of the SS Wimbledon**
Series C No. 3-I and II General List No. 5; 16 January 1923

1) Judgment, 28 June 1923 (intervention); Final vote: not available; French

Loder; Weiss; Finlay; ~~Barbosa~~; Nyholm; Moore; de Bustamante; Altamira; Oda; <u>Anzilotti</u>; <u>Huber</u> ~~Yovanovitch; Beichmann; Negulesco~~; Wang Schücking

2) Judgment, 17 August 1923 (merits); Final vote: not available; French

Loder; Weiss; Finlay; ~~Barbosa~~; Nyholm; Moore; de
Bustamante; Altamira; Oda; <u>Anzilott</u>; <u>Huber</u>
~~Yovanovitch~~; ~~Beichmann~~; ~~Negulesco~~; Wang
<u>Schücking</u>

Series B No. 6
Series C No. 3-I and III

**Questions relating to Settlers of German Origin in
Poland**
General List No. 6; 5 March 1923
Advisory opinion, 10 September 1923; Final vote: not
available; English
Loder; Weiss; Finlay; ~~Barbosa~~; Nyholm; Moore; de
Bustamante; Altamira; Oda; Anzilotti; Huber
~~Yovanovitch~~; ~~Beichmann~~; ~~Negulesco~~; Wang

Series B No. 7
Series C No. 3-I and III

**Questions concerning the Acquisition of Polish
Nationality**
General List No. 8; 16 July 1923
Advisory opinion, 15 September 1923; Final vote: not
available; French
Loder; Weiss; *Finlay*; ~~Barbosa~~; Nyholm; ~~Moore~~; de
Bustamante; Altamira; Oda; Anzilotti; Huber
~~Yovanovitch~~; ~~Beichmann~~; ~~Negulesco~~; Wang

Fourth Extraordinary Session (12 November–6 December 1923)

Series B No. 8
Series C No. 4

**Question of Jaworzina (Polish–Czechoslovakian
Frontier)**
General List No. 9; 2 October 1923
Advisory opinion, 6 December 1923; Final vote: not
available; French
Loder; Weiss; Finlay; Nyholm; ~~Moore~~; ~~de Bustamante~~;
~~Altamira~~; Oda; Anzilotti; Huber; Pessôa
Yovanovitch; Beichmann; ~~Negulesco~~; Wang

Fifth Ordinary Session (16 June–4 September 1924)

Series A No. 2
Series C No. 5-I

**Case of the Mavrommatis Palestine Concessions
(Jurisdiction)**
General List No. 12; 5 June 1924
Judgment, 30 August 1924; Final vote: not available;
French
Loder; Weiss; <u>Finlay</u>; Nyholm; <u>Moore</u>; <u>de Bustamante</u>;
Altamira; <u>Oda</u>; Anzilotti; Huber; <u>Pessôa</u>
~~Yovanovitch~~; ~~Beichmann~~; ~~Negulesco~~; ~~Wang~~
Caloyanni

Series B No. 9   Question of the Monastery of Saint-Naoum (Albanian
Series C No. 5-II   Frontier)
                        General List No. 13; 19 June 1924
                        Advisory opinion, 4 September 1924; Final vote: not
                        available; French
                        Loder; Weiss; Finlay; Nyholm; Moore; de Bustamante;
                        Altamira; Oda; Anzilotti; Huber; Pessôa
                        ~~Yovanovitch; Beichmann; Negulesco; Wang~~
Series A No. 3   Interpretation of Paragraph 4 of the Annex following
Series C No. 6   Article 179 of the Treaty of Neuilly
                        General List No. 11; 3 June 1924
                        Judgment, 12 September 1924; Final vote: not
                        available; French
                        Loder; Weiss; Huber

Sixth Extraordinary Session (12 January–26 March 1925)

Series B No. 10   Exchange of Greek and Turkish Populations
Series C No. 6 (Add.)   General List No. 15; 20 December 1924
                         Advisory opinion, 21 February 1925; Final vote: not
                         available; French
                         Huber; Loder; Weiss; Finlay; Nyholm; ~~Moore~~;
                         ~~de Bustamante~~; Altamira; Oda; Anzilotti; ~~Pessôa~~
                         Yovanovitch; Beichmann; Negulesco; ~~Wang~~
Series A No. 4   Interpretation of Judgment No. 3
Series C No. 6 (Add.)   (Interpretation of Paragraph 4 of the Annex following
                         Article 179 of the Treaty of Neuilly)
                         General List No. 14; 29 November 1924
                         Judgment, 26 March 1925; Final vote: not available;
                         French
                         Loder; Huber; Weiss
Series A No. 5   The Mavrommatis Jerusalem Concessions (Merits)
Series C No. 7-II   General List No. 10; 13 May 1924
                         Judgment, 26 March 1925; Final vote: not available;
                         French
                         Huber; Loder; Weiss; Finlay; Nyholm; ~~Moore~~;
                         ~~de Bustamante~~; <u>Altamira</u>; Oda; Anzilotti; ~~Pessôa~~
                         Yovanovitch; Beichmann; Negulesco; ~~Wang~~;
                         Caloyanni

Seventh Extraordinary Session (14 April–16 May 1925)

Series B No. 11   Polish Postal Service in Danzig
Series C No. 8   General List No. 16; 16 March 1925

Advisory opinion, 16 May 1925; Final vote: not
available; English
Huber; Loder; Weiss; Finlay; ~~Nyholm~~; ~~Moore~~; ~~de
Bustamante~~; Altamira; Oda; Anzilotti; ~~Pessôa~~
Yovanovitch; Beichmann; Negulesco; Wang

Eighth Ordinary Session (15 June–2 August 1925)

Series A No. 6
Series C No. 9-I

Case concerning Certain German Interests
in Polish Upper Silesia (Jurisdiction)
General List No. 19; 20 June 1925
Judgment, 25 August 1925; Final vote: not available;
French
Huber; Loder; Weiss; Finlay; Nyholm; ~~Moore~~; de
Bustamante; Altamira; Oda; *Anzilotti*; Pessôa
~~Yovanovitch~~; ~~Beichmann~~; ~~Negulesco~~; Wang
Rostworowski; Rabel

Ninth Extraordinary Session (22 October–21 November 1925)

Series B No. 12
Series C No. 10

Article 3, Paragraph 2, of the Treaty of
Lausanne (Frontier between Turkey and Iraq)
General List No. 20; 26 September 1925
Advisory opinion, 21 November 1925; Final vote: not
available; French
Huber; Loder; Weiss; Finlay; Nyholm; ~~Moore~~;
~~de Bustamante~~; Altamira; ~~Oda~~; Anzilotti; ~~Pessôa~~
Yovanovitch; Beichmann; Negulesco; ~~Wang~~

Tenth Extraordinary Session (2 February–25 May 1926)

Series A No. 7
Series C No. 11-I to III

Case concerning Certain German Interests
in Polish Upper Silesia (Merits)
General List Nos. 18 and 18 *bis*; 16 May 1925 and
25 August 1925
Judgment, 25 May 1926; Final vote: not available;
French
Huber; Loder; ~~Weiss~~; *Finlay*; Nyholm; ~~Moore~~;
~~de Bustamante~~; Altamira; ~~Oda~~; Anzilotti; ~~Pessôa~~
Yovanovitch; Beichmann; Negulesco; ~~Wang~~
Rostworowski; Rabel

Eleventh Ordinary Session (15 June–31 July 1926)

Series B No. 13
Series C No. 12

Competence of the International Labour
Organization to regulate, incidentally, the Personal
Work of the Employer
General List No. 21; 23 March 1926
Advisory opinion, 23 July 1926; Final vote: not
available; English
Huber; Loder; Weiss; Finlay; Nyholm; Moore; de
Bustamante; Altamira; Oda; Anzilotti; Pessôa
~~Yovanovitch~~; ~~Beichmann~~; ~~Negulesco~~; ~~Wang~~

Series A No. 8
Series C No. 16-I

Denunciation of the Treaty of November 2nd,
1865, between China and Belgium (Interim Measure
of Protection)
General List No. 22; 26 November 1926
1) Order, 8 January 1927
Huber
2) Order, 15 February 1927
Huber

Twelfth Ordinary Session (15 June–16 December 1927)

Series A No. 8 (*cont.*)
Series C No. 16-I

Denunciation of the Treaty of November 2nd,
1865, between China and Belgium (Interim Measure
of Protection)
General List No. 22; 26 November 1926
3) Order, 18 June 1927; Final vote: not available; French
Huber; Loder; ~~Weiss~~; Finlay; Nyholm; Moore; de
Bustamante; Altamira; Oda; Anzilotti; Pessôa
Yovanovitch; ~~Beichmann~~; ~~Negulesco~~; ~~Wang~~

Series A No. 9
Series C No. 13-I

Case concerning the Factory at Chorzów
(Claim for Indemnity) (Jurisdiction)
General List No. 26; 14 April 1927
Judgment, 26 July 1927; Final vote: 10–3; French
Huber; Loder; ~~Weiss~~; Finlay; Nyholm; Moore; de
Bustamante; Altamira; Oda; Anzilotti; Pessôa
Yovanovitch; ~~Beichmann~~; ~~Negulesco~~; ~~Wang~~
Rabel; <u>Ehrlich</u>

Series A No. 10
Series C No. 13-II

The Case of the SS Lotus
General List No. 24; 4 January 1927
Judgment, 7 September 1927; Final vote: 6–6; French
Huber; <u>Loder</u>; <u>Weiss</u>; <u>Finlay</u>; <u>Nyholm</u>; <u>Moore</u>; de
Bustamante; <u>Altamira</u>; Oda; Anzilotti; Pessôa
~~Yovanovitch~~; ~~Beichmann~~; ~~Negulesco~~; ~~Wang~~
Bey

Series A No. 11 Series C No. 13-III	**Case of the Readaptation of the Mavrommatis Jerusalem Concessions (Jurisdiction)** General List No. 27; 28 May 1927 Judgment, 10 October 1927; Final vote: 7–4; French Huber; Loder; ~~Weiss~~; Finlay; <u>Nyholm</u>; Moore; ~~de Bustamante~~; <u>Altamira</u>; Oda; Anzilotti; ~~Pessôa Yovanovitch~~; Beichmann; Negulesco; ~~Wang~~ <u>Caloyanni</u>
Series A No. 12	**Case concerning the Factory at Chorzów (Claim for Indemnity) (Interim Measure of Protection)** General List No. 26; 14 April 1927 Order, 21 November 1927; Final vote: not available; French Huber; Loder; ~~Weiss~~; Finlay; Nyholm; Moore; ~~de Bustamante~~; Altamira; Oda; Anzilotti; ~~Pessôa Yovanovitch~~; Beichmann; Negulesco; ~~Wang~~
Series B No. 14 Series C No. 13-IV	**Jurisdiction of the European Commission of the Danube between Galatz and Braila** General List No. 23; 20 December 1926 Advisory opinion, 8 December 1927; Final vote: 9–1; English Huber; Loder; ~~Weiss~~; Finlay; *Nyholm*; *Moore*; ~~de Bustamante~~; Altamira; Oda; Anzilotti; ~~Pessôa Yovanovitch~~; Beichmann; <u>Negulesco</u>; ~~Wang~~
Series A No. 13 Series C No. 13-V	**Interpretation of Judgments Nos. 7 and 8 (the Chorzów Factory)** General List No. 30; 18 October 1927 Judgment, 16 December 1927; Final vote: 8–3; French Huber; Loder; ~~Weiss~~; Finlay; Nyholm; ~~Moore~~; de Bustamante; Altamira; Oda; <u>Anzilotti</u>; ~~Pessôa Yovanovitch~~; Beichmann; Negulesco; ~~Wang~~ Rabel; Ehrlich

Thirteenth Extraordinary Session (6 February–26 April 1928)

Series A No. 14	**Denunciation of the Treaty of November 2nd, 1865, between China and Belgium** General List No. 22; 26 November 1926 Order, 21 February 1928; Final vote: not available; French Anzilotti; Huber; Weiss; ~~Finlay~~; Loder; Nyholm; ~~Moore~~; ~~de Bustamante~~; Altamira; Oda; ~~Pessôa~~ Yovanovitch; Beichmann; Negulesco; Wang

Series B No. 15	Jurisdiction of the Courts of Danzig
Series C No. 14-I	(Pecuniary Claims of Danzig Railway Officials who
	have passed into the Polish Service, against the Polish
	Railways Administration)
	General List No. 29; 26 September 1927
	Advisory opinion, 3 March 1928; Final vote: 13–0;
	English
	Anzilotti; Huber; Weiss; ~~Finlay~~; Loder; Nyholm; ~~Moore~~;
	~~de Bustamante~~; Altamira; Oda; ~~Pessôa~~
	Yovanovitch; Beichmann; Negulesco; Wang
	Ehrlich; Bruns
Series A No. 15	**Rights of Minorities in Upper Silesia**
Series C No. 14-II	**(Minority Schools)**
	General List No. 31; 2 January 1928
	Judgment, 26 April 1928; Final vote: 8–4; French
	Anzilotti; <u>Huber</u>; Weiss; ~~Finlay~~; Loder; <u>Nyholm</u>; ~~Moore~~;
	~~de Bustamante~~; Altamira; ~~Oda~~; ~~Pessôa~~
	Yovanovitch; Beichmann; <u>Negulesco</u>; Wang
	<u>Schücking</u>; Rostworowski

Fourteenth Ordinary Session (15 June–13 September 1928)

Series A No. 16	**Denunciation of the Treaty of November 2nd, 1865,**
	between China and Belgium
	General List No. 22; 26 November 1926
	Order, 13 August 1928; Final vote: not available; French
	Anzilotti; Huber; ~~Weiss~~; Finlay; Loder; Nyholm; ~~Moore~~;
	de Bustamante; Altamira; Oda; Pessôa
	~~Yovanovitch~~; Beichmann; ~~Negulesco~~; ~~Wang~~
Series B No. 16	**Interpretation of the Greco-Turkish Agreement of**
Series C No. 15-I	**December 1st, 1926 (Final Protocol, Article IV)**
	General List No. 35; 9 June 1928
	Advisory opinion, 28 August 1928; Final vote: 10–0;
	French
	Anzilotti; Huber; ~~Weiss~~; Finlay; Loder; Nyholm; ~~Moore~~;
	de Bustamante; Altamira; Oda; Pessôa
	~~Yovanovitch~~; Beichmann; ~~Negulesco~~; ~~Wang~~
Series A No. 17	**Case concerning the Factory at Chorzów**
Series C No. 15-II	**(Claim for Indemnity) (Merits)**
	General List No. 25; 8 February 1927
	Judgment, 13 September 1928; Final vote: 9–3; French
	Anzilotti; Huber; ~~Weiss~~; <u>Finlay</u>; Loder; <u>Nyholm</u>; *de*
	Bustamante; *Altamira*; Oda; Pessôa; ~~Hughes~~

~~Yovanovitch~~; Beichmann; ~~Negulesco~~; ~~Wang~~
Rabel; <u>Ehrlich</u>

Sixteenth Extraordinary Session (13 May–12 July 1929)

Series A No. 18	**Denunciation of the Treaty of November 2nd,**
Series C No. 16-I	**1865, between China and Belgium**

General List No. 22; 26 November 1926
Order, 25 May 1929; Final vote: not available; French
Anzilotti; Huber; ~~Weiss~~; ~~Finlay~~; Loder; Nyholm; de
Bustamante; Altamira; Oda; Pessôa; Hughes
~~Yovanovitch~~; Beichmann; Negulesco; ~~Wang~~

Series A No. 19	**Case concerning the Factory at Chorzów**
Series C No. 16-II	**(Claim for Indemnity) (Expert Enquiry)**

General List No. 25; 8 February 1927
Order, 25 May 1929; Final vote: not available; French
Anzilotti; Huber; ~~Weiss~~; ~~Finlay~~; Loder; Nyholm; de
Bustamante; Altamira; Oda; Pessôa; Hughes
~~Yovanovitch~~; Beichmann; Negulesco; ~~Wang~~

Series A No. 20	**Case concerning the Payment of Various**
Series C No. 16-III	**Serbian Loans issued in France**

General List No. 34; 25 May 1928
Judgment, 12 July 1929; Final vote: 9–3; French
Anzilotti; Huber; ~~Weiss~~; ~~Finlay~~; Loder; ~~Nyholm~~; <u>de
Bustamante</u>; Altamira; Oda; <u>Pessôa</u>; Hughes
~~Yovanovitch~~; Beichmann; Negulesco; ~~Wang~~
Fromageot; <u>Novacovitch</u>

Series A No. 21	**Case concerning the Payment in Gold of**
Series C No. 16-IV	**Brazilian Federal Loans contracted in France**

General List No. 33; 27 April 1928
Judgment, 12 July 1929; Final vote: 9-2; French
Anzilotti; Huber; ~~Weiss~~; ~~Finlay~~; Loder; ~~Nyholm~~; <u>de
Bustamante</u>; Altamira; Oda; <u>Pessôa</u>; Hughes
~~Yovanovitch~~; Beichmann; Negulesco; ~~Wang~~
Fromageot

Seventeenth Ordinary Session (17 June–10 September 1929)

Series A No. 22	**Case of the Free Zones of Upper Savoy and**
Series C No. 17-I	**the District of Gex (First Phase)**

General List No. 32; 29 March 1928
Order, 19 August 1929; Final vote: not available; French
Anzilotti; ~~Weiss~~; ~~Finlay~~; Loder; *Nyholm*; de Bustamante;
Altamira; Oda; Huber; *Pessôa*; Hughes

~~Yovanovitch~~; ~~Beichmann~~; *Negulesco*; Wang;
Dreyfus

Series A No. 23 | Case relating to the Territorial Jurisdiction
Series C No. 17-II | of the International Commission of the River Oder
General List No. 36; 29 November 1928
Judgment, 10 September 1929; Final vote: 9–3; English
Anzilotti; *Huber*; ~~Weiss~~; ~~Finlay~~; Loder; Nyholm; de
Bustamante; Altamira; Oda; Pessôa; Hughes
~~Yovanovitch~~; ~~Beichmann~~; Negulesco; Wang
Rostworowski

Eighteenth Ordinary Session (16 June–26 August 1930)

Series B No. 17 | Interpretation of the Convention between
Series C No. 18-I | Greece and Bulgaria respecting reciprocal
Emigration, signed at Neuilly-sur-Seine on November
27th, 1919 (Question of the 'Communities')
General List No. 37; 20 January 1930
Advisory opinion, 31 July 1930; Final vote: 13–0; French
Anzilotti; Huber; Loder; Nyholm; de Bustamante;
Altamira; Oda; Pessôa; ~~Hughes~~; Fromageot; Hurst
Yovanovitch; ~~Beichmann~~; ~~Negulesco~~; ~~Wang~~
Caloyanni; Papazoff

Series B No. 18 | Free City of Danzig and International
Series C No. 18-II | Labour Organization
General List No. 38; 17 May 1930
Advisory opinion, 26 August 1930; Final vote: 6–4;
English
Anzilotti; Huber; Loder; Nyholm; de Bustamante;
Altamira; Oda; ~~Pessôa~~; ~~Hughes~~; Fromageot; Hurst
Yovanovitch; ~~Beichmann~~; ~~Negulesco~~; ~~Wang~~

Nineteenth Extraordinary Session (23 October–6 December 1930)

Series A No. 24 | Case of the Free Zones of Upper Savoy and
Series C No. 19-I | the District of Gex (Second Phase)
General List No. 32; 29 March 1928
Order, 6 December 1930; Final vote: 6–6; French
Anzilotti; Loder; Nyholm; ~~de Bustamante~~; Altamira;
Oda; Huber; ~~Pessôa~~; ~~Fromageot~~; Hurst; Kellogg
Yovanovitch; Beichmann; Negulesco; ~~Wang~~
Dreyfus

Twenty-First Extraordinary Session (20 April–15 May 1931)

Series A/B No. 40   Access to German Minority Schools in
Series C No. 52   Polish Upper Silesia
                       General List No. 40; 2 February 1931
                       Advisory opinion, 15 May 1931; Final vote: 11–1; French
                       Adatci; Guerrero; Kellogg; Rolin-Jaequemyns;
                       Rostworowski; Fromageot; ~~de Bustamante~~; Altamira;
                       Anzilotti; ~~Urrutia~~; Hurst; Schücking; Negulesco; van
                       Eysinga; ~~Wang~~

Twenty-Second Extraordinary Session (16 July–15 October 1931)

Series A/B No. 41   Customs Régime between Germany and Austria
Series C No. 53   (Protocol of March 19th, 1931)
                       General List No. 41; 21 May 1931
                       Advisory opinion, 5 September 1931; Final vote: 8–7;
                       French
                       Adatci; *Guerrero*; Kellogg; Rolin-Jaequemyns;
                       Rostworowski; *Fromageot*; de Bustamante; *Altamira*;
                       Anzilotti; Urrutia; Hurst; Schücking; *Negulesco*; van
                       Eysinga; Wang
Series A/B No. 42   Railway Traffic between Lithuania and Poland
Series C No. 54   (Railway Sector Landwarów–Kaisiadorys)
                       General List No. 39; 31 January 1931
                       Advisory opinion, 15 October 1931; Final vote: 13–0;
                       French
                       Adatci; ~~Guerrero~~; ~~Kellogg~~; Rolin-Jaequemyns;
                       Rostworowski; Fromageot; de Bustamante; *Altamira*;
                       Anzilotti; Urrutia; Hurst; Schücking; Negulesco; ~~van
                       Eysinga~~; Wang
                       Stasinskas

Twenty-Third Extraordinary Session (5 November 1931–4 February 1932)

Series A/B No. 43   Access to, or Anchorage in, the Port of Danzig of
Series C No. 55   Polish War Vessels
                       General List No. 44; 28 September 1931
                       Advisory opinion, 11 December 1931; Final vote: 11–3;
                       English
                       Adatci; Guerrero; ~~Kellogg~~; Rolin-Jaequemyns;
                       Rostworowski; Fromageot; ~~de Bustamante~~; Altamira;

Anzilotti; <u>Urrutia</u>; Hurst; Schücking; Negulesco; ~~van Eysinga~~; Wang
Bruns

Series A/B No. 44
Series C No. 56
Treatment of Polish Nationals and other Persons of Polish Origin or Speech in the Danzig Territory
General List No. 42; 28 May 1931
Advisory opinion, 4 February 1932; Final vote: 9–4; French
Adatci; <u>Guerrero</u>; ~~Kellogg~~; *Rolin-Jaequemyns*; <u>Rostworowski</u>; <u>Fromageot</u>; ~~de Bustamante~~; Altamira; Anzilotti; <u>Urrutia</u>; *Hurst*; Schücking; ~~Negulesco~~; van Eysinga; Wang
Bruns

Twenty-Fourth Ordinary Session (1 February–8 March 1932)

Series A/B No. 45
Series C No. 57
Interpretation of the Greco-Bulgarian Agreement of December 9th, 1927 (Caphandaris–Molloff Agreement)
General List No. 45; 28 September 1931
Advisory opinion, 8 March 1932; Final vote: 8–6; English
<u>Adatci</u>; Guerrero; ~~Kellogg~~; Rolin-Jaequemyns; <u>Rostworowski</u>; Fromageot; ~~de Bustamante~~; <u>Altamira</u>; Anzilotti; Urrutia; Hurst; <u>Schücking</u>; ~~Negulesco~~; <u>van Eysinga</u>; Wang
Caloyanni; <u>Papazoff</u>

Twenty-Fifth Extraordinary Session (18 April–11 August 1932)

Series A/B No. 46
Series C No. 58
Case of Free Zones of Upper Savoy and the District of Gex (Third Phase)
General List No. 32; 29 March 1928
Judgment, 7 June 1932; Final vote: 6–5; French
Anzilotti; Loder; <u>Altamira</u>; Oda; Huber; <u>Hurst</u>; Kellogg; <u>Yovanovitch</u>; Beichmann; <u>Negulesco</u>; <u>Dreyfus</u>

Series A/B No. 47
Series C No. 68
Interpretation of the Statute of the Memel Territory (Jurisdiction)
General List No. 50; 31 May 1932
Judgment, 24 June 1932; Final vote: 13–3; French
Guerrero; Kellogg; <u>Rolin-Jaequemyns</u>; <u>Rostworowski</u>; Fromageot; de Bustamante; Altamira; Anzilotti;

Urrutia; Adatci; Hurst; Schücking; Negulesco; van
Eysinga; Wang
Römer'is

Series A/B No. 48   **Case concerning the Legal Status of the**
Series C Nos. 68–69   **South-Eastern Territory of Greenland**
General List Nos. 52 and 53; 18 July 1932
1) Order, 2 August 1932; Final vote: not available;
French
Adatci; Guerrero; Kellogg; Rolin-Jaequemyns;
Rostworowski; Fromageot; de Bustamante; Altamira;
Anzilotti; Urrutia; Hurst; Schücking; Negulesco; van
Eysinga; Wang
Vogt; Zahle
2) Order, 3 August 1932; Final vote: not available;
French
Adatci; Guerrero; Kellogg; Rolin-Jaequemyns;
Rostworowski; Fromageot; de Bustamante; Altamira;
Anzilotti; Urrutia; Hurst; Schücking; Negulesco; van
Eysinga; Wang
Vogt; Zahle

Series A/B No. 49   **Interpretation of the Statute of the Memel**
Series C No. 59   **territory (Merits)**
General List No. 47; 11 April 1932
Judgment, 11 August 1932; Final vote: 10-5; French
Guerrero; ~~Kellogg~~; Rolin-Jaequemyns; Rostworowski;
Fromageot; de Bustamante; Altamira; Anzilotti;
Urrutia; Adatci; Hurst; Schücking; Negulesco; van
Eysinga; Wang
Römer'is

Twenty-Sixth Extraordinary Session (14 October 1932–5 April 1933)

Series A/B No. 50   **Interpretation of the Convention of 1919**
Series C No. 60   **concerning Employment of Women during the Night**
General List No. 48; 12 May 1932
Advisory opinion, 15 November 1932; Final vote: 6–5;
French
Adatci; Guerrero; ~~Kellogg~~; Rolin-Jaequemyns;
Rostworowski; Fromageot; ~~de Bustamante~~; ~~Altamira~~;
Anzilotti; Urrutia; Hurst; Schücking; Negulesco; van
Eysinga; ~~Wang~~

Series A/B No. 51   **Case concerning the Delimitation of the**
Series C No. 61   **Territorial Waters between the Island of Castellorizo**
and the Coasts of Anatolia

General List No. 46; 18 November 1931
Order, 26 January 1933; Final vote: not available;
French
Adatci; Guerrero; ~~Kellogg~~; Rolin-Jaequemyns;
Rostworowski; ~~Fromageot~~; ~~de Bustamante~~; ~~Altamira~~;
Anzilotti; Urrutia; Hurst; Schücking; Negulesco; van
Eysinga; Wang

Series A/B No. 52   **Case concerning the Administration of the**
Series C No. 70   **Prince von Pless (Jurisdiction)**
General List Nos. 49 and 55; 18 May 1932 and
8 October 1932
Order, 4 February 1933; Final vote: not available;
French
Adatci; Guerrero; ~~Kellogg~~; Rolin-Jaequemyns;
Rostworowski; Fromageot; ~~de Bustamante~~; ~~Altamira~~;
Anzilotti; Urrutia; Hurst; Schücking; Negulesco; van
Eysinga; Wang

Series A/B No. 53   **Legal Status of Eastern Greenland**
Series C Nos. 62–67   General List No. 43; 12 July 1931
Judgment, 5 April 1933; Final vote: 12–2; English
Adatci; Guerrero; ~~Kellogg~~; Rolin-Jaequemyns;
Rostworowski; Fromageot; ~~de Bustamante~~; ~~Altamira~~;
<u>Anzilotti</u>; Urrutia; Hurst; *Schücking*; Negulesco; van
Eysinga; *Wang*
<u>Vogt</u>; Zahle

Twenty-Eighth Extraordinary Session (10 May–16 May 1933)

Series A/B No. 54   **Case concerning the Administration of the**
Series C No. 70   **Prince von Pless (Interim Measures of Protection)**
General List Nos. 49 and 55; 18 May 1932 and
8 October 1932
Order, 11 May 1933; Final vote: not available; French
Adatci; Guerrero; ~~Kellogg~~; Rolin-Jaequemyns;
Rostworowski; Fromageot; ~~de Bustamante~~; ~~Altamira~~;
Anzilotti; Urrutia; Hurst; Schücking; Negulesco; van
Eysinga; Wang

Series A/B No. 55   **Legal Status of the South-Eastern Territory**
Series C Nos. 68–69   **of Greenland**
General List Nos. 52 and 53; 18 July 1932
Order, 11 May 1933; Final vote: not available; French
Adatci; Guerrero; ~~Kellogg~~; Rolin-Jaequemyns;
Rostworowski; Fromageot; ~~de Bustamante~~; ~~Altamira~~;
Anzilotti; Urrutia; Hurst; Schücking; Negulesco; van
Eysinga; Wang

Series A/B No. 56	**Appeals from certain Judgments of the**
Series C No. 68	**Hungaro-Czechoslovak Mixed Arbitral Tribunal**
	General List Nos. 51, 54, 56, 57; 11 July 1932, 25 July
	1932, 24 October 1932, 24 October 1932
	Order, 12 May 1933; Final vote: not available; French
	Adatci; Guerrero; ~~Kellogg~~; Rolin-Jaequemyns;
	Rostworowski; Fromageot; ~~de Bustamante~~; ~~Altamira~~;
	Anzilotti; Urrutia; Hurst; Schücking; Negulesco; van
	Eysinga; Wang
Series A/B No. 57	**Case concerning the Administration of the**
Series C No. 70	**Prince von Pless (Prorogation)**
	General List Nos. 49 and 55; 18 May 1932 and 8
	October 1932
	Order, 4 July 1933; French
	Adatci

Twenty-Ninth Extraordinary Session (10 July–29 July 1933)

Series A/B No. 58	**Case concerning the Polish Agrarian Reform and the**
Series C No. 71	**German Minority (Interim Measures of Protection)**
	General List No. 60; 3 July 1933
	Order, 29 July 1933; Final vote: not available; French
	Adatci; Guerrero; ~~Kellogg~~; <u>Rolin-Jaequemyns</u>;
	Rostworowski; Fromageot; ~~de Bustamante~~; ~~Altamira~~;
	Anzilotti; Urrutia; Hurst; <u>Schücking</u>; Negulesco; <u>van</u>
	<u>Eysinga</u>; Wang

Thirtieth Extraordinary Session (20 October–15 December 1933)

Series A/B No. 59	**Case concerning the Administration of the Prince**
Series C No. 70	**von Pless**
	General List Nos. 49 and 55; 18 May 1932 and
	8 October 1932
	Order, 2 December 1933; Final vote: not available;
	French
	Adatci; Guerrero; Kellogg; Rolin-Jaequemyns;
	Rostworowski; Fromageot; de Bustamante; ~~Altamira~~;
	Anzilotti; ~~Urrutia~~; Hurst; Schücking; Negulesco; van
	Eysinga; Wang
Series A/B No. 60	**Case concerning the Polish Agrarian**
Series C No. 71	**Reform and the German Minority**
	General List No. 60; 3 July 1933
	Order, 2 December 1933; Final vote: not available;
	French

Adatci; Guerrero; Kellogg; Rolin-Jaequemyns;
Rostworowski; Fromageot; de Bustamante; ~~Altamira~~;
Anzilotti; ~~Urrutia~~; Hurst; Schücking; Negulesco; van
Eysinga; Wang

Series A/B No. 61   **Appeal from a Judgment of the**
Series C Nos. 72–73   **Hungaro-Czechoslovak Mixed Arbitral Tribunal (the**
Peter Pázmány University v. the State of
Czechoslovakia)
General List No. 58; 9 May 1933
Judgment, 15 December 1933; Final vote: 12–1; French
Adatci; Guerrero; ~~Kellogg~~; Rolin-Jaequemyns;
Rostworowski; Fromageot; ~~de Bustamante~~; ~~Altamira~~;
Anzilotti; ~~Urrutia~~; Hurst; Schücking; Negulesco; van
Eysinga; Wang
Hermann-Otavský; de Tomcsányi

Thirty-First Ordinary Session (1 February–22 March 1934)

Series A/B No. 62   **Lighthouses Case between France and**
Series C No. 74   **Greece**
General List No. 59; 23 May 1933
Judgment, 17 March 1934; Final vote: 10–2; French
Hurst; Guerrero; ~~Kellogg~~; Rolin-Jaequemyns;
Rostworowski; Fromageot; ~~de Bustamante~~; ~~Altamira~~;
Anzilotti; Adatci; ~~Urrutia~~; Schücking; Negulesco; *van
Eysinga*; Wang
Séfériadès

Thirty-Third Extraordinary Session (22 October–12 December 1934)

Series A/B No. 63   The Oscar Chinn Case
Series C No. 75   General List No. 61; 1 May 1934
Judgment, 12 December 1934; Final vote: 6–5; French
Guerrero; ~~Kellogg~~; Rolin-Jaequemyns; Rostworowski;
Fromageot; ~~de Bustamante~~; Altamira; Anzilotti; ~~Adatci~~;
Urrutia; Hurst; Schücking; Negulesco; van Eysinga;
~~Wang~~

Thirty-Fourth Ordinary Session (1 February–10 April 1935)

Series A/B No. 64   **Minority Schools in Albania**
Series C No. 76   General List No. 62; 23 January 1935
Advisory opinion, 6 April 1935; Final vote: 8–3; French

Hurst; Guerrero; ~~Kellogg~~; Rolin-Jaequemyns;
Rostworowski; Fromageot; ~~de Bustamante~~; Altamira;
Anzilotti; ~~Adatci~~; Urrutia; Schücking; Negulesco; van
Eysinga; ~~Wang~~

Thirty-Fifth Extraordinary Session (28 October–4 December 1935)

Series A/B No. 65
Series C No. 77

Consistency of certain Danzig Legislative
Decrees with the Constitution of the Free City
General List No. 63; 30 September 1935
Advisory opinion, 4 December 1935; Final vote: 9–3;
English
Hurst; Guerrero; ~~Kellogg~~; Rolin-Jaequemyns;
Rostworowski; Fromageot; de Bustamante; Altamira;
Anzilotti; Urrutia; ~~Schücking~~; ~~Negulesco~~; van Eysinga;
Wang; Nagaoka

Judicial Year 1936

Series A/B No. 66
Series C Nos. 79–80

The Pajzs, Csáky, Esterházy Case
(Preliminary Objections)
General List Nos. 65 and 66; 6 December 1935 and
4 March 1936
Order, 23 May 1936; Final vote: not available
Hurst; Guerrero; ~~Kellogg~~; Rolin-Jaequemyns;
Rostworowski; Fromageot; de Bustamante; Altamira;
Anzilotti; Urrutia; ~~Schücking~~; Negulesco; van Eysinga;
~~Wang~~; Nagaoka
de Tomcsányi; Zoricic

Series A/B No. 67
Series C No. 78

The Losinger & Co. Case (Preliminary Objection)
General List Nos. 64 and 67; 23 November 1935 and 27
March 1936
Order, 27 June 1936; Final vote: not available
Hurst; Guerrero; ~~Kellogg~~; ~~Rolin-Jaequemyns~~;
Rostworowski; Fromageot; de Bustamante; Altamira;
Anzilotti; Urrutia; ~~Schücking~~; Negulesco; van Eysinga;
~~Wang~~; Nagaoka
Huber; Zoricic

Series A/B No. 68
Series C Nos. 79–80

The Pajzs, Csáky, Esterházy Case (Merits)
General List Nos. 65 and 66; 6 December 1935 and
4 March 1936
Judgment, 16 December 1936; Final vote: 8–6; French
Hurst; Guerrero; ~~Rolin-Jaequemyns~~; Rostworowski;
Fromageot; de Bustamante; Altamira; Anzilotti;

~~Urrutia~~; Negulesco; <u>van Eysinga</u>; <u>Nagaoka</u>; ~~Cheng~~;
<u>Hudson</u>; <u>Hammarskjöld</u>
<u>de Tomcsányi</u>; Zoricic

Series A/B No. 69   **The Losinger & Co. Case**
General List Nos. 64 and 67; 23 November 1935 and
27 March 1936
Order, 14 December 1936; Final vote: not available
Hurst; Guerrero; ~~Rolin-Jaequemyns~~; Rostworowski;
Fromageot; de Bustamante; Altamira; Anzilotti;
~~Urrutia~~; Negulesco; van Eysinga; Nagaoka; ~~Cheng~~;
Hudson; Hammarskjöld
Huber; Zoricic

Judicial Year 1937

Series A/B No. 70   **The Diversion of Water from the Meuse**
Series C No. 81   General List No. 69; 1 August 1936
Judgment, 28 June 1937; Final vote: 10–3; French
Guerrero; *Hurst*; Rostworowski; Fromageot; de
Bustamante; <u>Altamira</u>; <u>Anzilotti</u>; ~~Urrutia~~; Negulesco;
<u>van Eysinga</u>; Nagaoka; Cheng; *Hudson*; ~~Hammarskjöld~~;
de Visscher

Series A/B No. 71   **Lighthouses in Crete and Samos**
Series C No. 82   General List No. 70; 27 October 1936
Judgment, 8 October 1937; Final vote: 10–3; French
Guerrero; <u>Hurst</u>; Rostworowski; Fromageot; de
Bustamante; Altamira; ~~Anzilotti~~; Urrutia; Negulesco;
van Eysinga; ~~Nagaoka~~; Cheng; <u>Hudson</u>; ~~Hammarskjöld~~;
de Visscher
Séfériadès

Series A/B No. 72   **The Borchgrave Case (Preliminary**
Series C No. 83   **Objections)**
General List No. No. 73; 29 June 1937
Judgment, 6 November 1937; Final vote: 12–0; English
Guerrero; Hurst; Rostworowski; Fromageot; de
Bustamante; Altamira; ~~Anzilotti~~; Urrutia; Negulesco;
van Eysinga; ~~Nagaoka~~; Cheng; Hudson; ~~Hammarskjöld~~;
de Visscher

Judicial Year 1938

Series A/B No. 73   **The Borchgrave Case (Discontinuance)**
Series C No. 83   General List No. 72; 5 March 1937
Order, 30 April 1938; Final vote: not available

Guerrero; Hurst; Rostworowski; Fromageot; de
Bustamante; Altamira; ~~Anzilotti~~; Urrutia; Negulesco;
van Eysinga; ~~Nagaoka~~; Cheng; Hudson; ~~Hammarskjöld~~;
de Visscher

Series A/B No. 74	**Phosphates in Morocco Case (Preliminary**
Series C Nos. 84–85	**Objections)**

General List No. 71; 16 December 1936
Judgment, 14 June 1938; Final vote: 11–1; French
Guerrero; Hurst; Rostworowski; Fromageot; de
Bustamante; Altamira; Anzilotti; Urrutia; Negulesco;
van Eysinga; ~~Nagaoka~~; *Cheng*; ~~Hudson~~; ~~Hammarskjöld~~;
de Visscher

Series A/B No. 75	**The Panevezys–Saldutiskis Railway Case**
Series C No. 86	**(Preliminary Objections)**

General List Nos. 74 and 76; 2 November 1937 and 15
March 1938
Order, 30 June 1938; Final vote: not available; French
Guerrero; Hurst; Rostworowski; Fromageot; de
Bustamante; Altamira; Anzilotti; Urrutia; Negulesco;
van Eysinga; Nagaoka; Cheng; ~~Hudson~~; ~~Hammarskjöld~~;
de Visscher
Strandman; Römer'is

Judicial Year 1939

Series A/B No. 76	**The Panevezys–Saldutiskis Railway Case**
Series C No. 86	General List Nos. 74 and 76; 2 November 1937 and 15

March 1938
Judgment, 28 February 1939; Final vote: 10–4; French
Guerrero; Hurst; *Rostworowski*; Fromageot; ~~de~~
~~Bustamante~~; Altamira; ~~Anzilotti~~; ~~Urrutia~~; Negulesco;
van Eysinga; Nagaoka; Cheng; Hudson; *de Visscher*; Erich
Strandman; *Römer'is*

Series A/B No. 77	**The Electricity Company of Sofia and Bulgaria**
Series C No. 88	**(Preliminary Objection)**

General List No. 78; 25 November 1938
Judgment, 4 April 1939; Final vote: 9–5; French
Guerrero; Hurst; Rostworowski; Fromageot; ~~de~~
~~Bustamante~~; Altamira; Anzilotti; Urrutia; ~~Negulesco~~;
van Eysinga; Nagaoka; Cheng; Hudson; *de Visscher*; Erich
Papazoff

Series A/B No. 78	**The 'Société Commerciale de Belgique'**
Series C No. 87	General List No. 77; 5 May 1938

Judgment, 15 June 1939; Final vote: 13–2; French

Guerrero; Hurst; Rostworowski; Fromageot; ~~de Bustamante~~; Altamira; Anzilotti; Urrutia; Negulesco; <u>van Eysinga</u>; Nagaoka; Cheng; <u>Hudson</u>; de Visscher; Erich

Ténékidès

Series A/B No. 79 Series C No. 88	**The Electricity Company of Sofia and Bulgaria** **(Interim Measures of Protection)** General List No. 75; 26 January 1938 Order, 5 December 1939; Final vote: not available; French Guerrero; Hurst; ~~Rostworowski~~; Fromageot; ~~de Bustamante~~; ~~Altamira~~; Anzilotti; ~~Urrutia~~; Negulesco; van Eysinga; ~~Nagaoka~~; Cheng; ~~Hudson~~; de Visscher; Erich

Judicial Year 1940

Series A/B No. 80 Series C No. 88	**The Electricity Company of Sofia and Bulgaria** General List No. 75; 26 January 1938 Order, 26 February 1940; Final vote: not available; French Guerrero; Hurst; ~~Rostworowski~~; Fromageot; ~~de Bustamante~~; Altamira; Anzilotti; ~~Urrutia~~; Negulesco; van Eysinga; ~~Nagaoka~~; Cheng; Hudson; de Visscher; Erich

Bibliography

Abi-Saab, Georges, *Les Exceptions préliminaires dans la procédure de la Cour internationale* (Paris, 1967)

'Cours générale de droit international public' (1987) 207 *Recueil des Cours* 9

'De l'évolution de la Cour internationale: reflexions sur quelques tendances recentes' (1992) 99 *Revue Générale de Droit International Public* 273

'The International Court as a World Court' in Vaughan Lowe and Malgosia Fitzmaurice (eds.), *Fifty Years of the International Court of Justice: Essays in Honour of Sir Robert Jennings* (Cambridge, 1996), p. 3

'Substantive Requirements or The Portrait of the Jurist as an International Judge' in Connie Peck and Roy S. Lee (eds.), *Increasing the Effectiveness of the International Court of Justice* (The Hague, 1997), p. 166

'Whither the International Community?' (1998) 9 *European Journal of International Law* 248

Acker, Detlev, *Walther Schücking (1875–1935)* (Münster, 1970)

Adatci, Minéitcirô, 'Foreword' in Permanent Court of International Justice, *Ten Years of International Jurisprudence, 1922–1932* (Leiden, 1932), p. 5

Advisory Committee of Jurists, *Procès-Verbaux of the Proceedings of the Committee (16 June–24 July 1920, with Annexes)* (The Hague, 1920)

Documents Presented to the Committee Relating to Existing Plans for the Establishment of a Permanent Court of International Justice (The Hague, 1920)

Ago, Roberto, 'Le Délit international' (1939) 68 *Recueil des Cours* 419

'Science juridique et droit international' (1956) 90 *Recueil des Cours* 849

'Droit positif et droit international' (1957) 3 *Annuaire français de droit international* 14

'Positive Law and International Law' (1957) 51 *American Journal of International Law* 691

'Pluralism and the Origins of the International Community' (1977) 3 *Italian Yearbook of International Law* 3

'The First International Communities in the Mediterranean World' (1982) 53 *British Yearbook of International Law* 213

'Rencontres avec Anzilotti' (1992) 3 *European Journal of International Law* 92

Akande, Dapo, 'Nuclear Weapons, Unclear Law? Deciphering the *Nuclear Weapons* Advisory Opinion of the International Court' (1997) 68 *British Yearbook of International Law* 165

Åkermark, Athanasia Spiliopoulou, *Justifications of Minority Protection in International Law* (London, 1997)

Allain, Jean, *A Century of International Adjudication: The Rule of Law and its Limits* (The Hague, 2000)

   'The Continued Evolution of International Adjudication' in *Looking Ahead: International Law in the 21st Century – Proceedings of the 29th Annual Conference of the Canadian Council on International Law* (The Hague, 2002), p. 50

Allott, Philip, 'Language, Method and the Nature of International Law' (1971) 45 *British Yearbook of International Law* 79

   Eunomia: New Order for a New World (Oxford, 1990)

   '*Mare Nostrum*: A New International Law of the Sea' (1992) 86 *American Journal of International Law* 764

   'The Concept of International Law' (1999) 10 *European Journal of International Law* 23

   The Health of Nations: Society and Law beyond the State (Cambridge, 2002)

Altamira y Crevea, Rafael, *El proceso ideológico del Proyecto de Tribunal de Justicia Internacional* (Madrid, 1921)

   'El Tribunal Permanente de Justicia Internacional' (1925–6) 6 *Anales de la Universidad de Valencia* 155

   La Sociedad de las Naciones y el Tribunal Permanente de Justicia Internacional (Madrid, 1931)

   A History of Spain from the Beginnings to the Present Day (New York, 1949)

Amerasinghe, C. F., 'Interpretation of Texts in Open International Organizations' (1994) 65 *British Yearbook of International Law* 175

   'International Law and the Concept of Law: Why International Law is Law' in Jerzy Makarczyk (ed.), *Theory of International Law at the Threshold of the 21st Century: Essays in Honour of Krzysztof Skubiszewski* (The Hague, 1996), p. 79

   Principles of the Institutional Law of International Organizations (Cambridge, 1996)

   'Theory with Practical Effects: Is International Law Neither Fish Nor Fowl? Reflections on the Characterization of International Law' (1999) 37 *Archiv des Völkerrechts* 1

   'Judges of the International Court of Justice: Election and Qualifications' (2001) 14 *Leiden Journal of International Law* 335

   'The Historical Development of International Law: Universal Aspects' (2001) 39 *Archiv des Völkerrechts* 367

   Jurisdiction of International Tribunals (The Hague, 2003)

   Local Remedies in International Law (2nd edn, Cambridge, 2004)

American Law Institute, *Restatement (Third) of the Law of the Foreign Relations of the United States, as Adopted and Promulgated May 14, 1986* (2 vols., St Paul, MN, 1987)

Amr, Mohamed Samed M., *The Role of the International Court of Justice as the Principal Judicial Organ of the United Nations* (The Hague, 2003)

Andreae, J. P. Fockema, *An Important Chapter from the History of Legal Interpretation: The Jurisdiction of the First Permanent Court of International Justice, 1922–1940* (Leiden, 1948)

Anghie, Antony, 'Finding the Peripheries: Sovereignty and Colonialism in Nineteenth Century International Law' (1999) 40 *Harvard International Law Journal* 1

'Colonialism and the Birth of International Institutions: Sovereignty, Economy, and the Mandate System of the League of Nations' (2002) 34 *New York University Journal of International Law and Politics* 513

Anzilotti, Dionisio, *La filosofia del diritto e la sociologia* (Florence, 1892)

Studi critici di diritto internazionale private (Rocca S. Casciano, 1898)

Teoria generale della responsabilità dello stato nel diritto internazionale (Florence, 1902)

Il diritto internazionale nei giudizi interni (Bologna, 1905)

'La Responsabilité internationale des états à raison des dommages soufferts par des étrangers' (1906) 13 *Revue Générale de Droit International Public* 5 and 285

Cours de droit international (Paris, 1929)

'Der Ständige Internationale Gerichtshof (Cour permanente de Justice internationale)' in Julius Magnus (ed.), *Die Höchsten Gerichte der Welt* (Leipzig, 1929), p. 623

'La riconvenzione nella procedura internazionale' (1929) 21 *Rivista di Diritto Internazionale* 309

'La Demande reconventionnelle en procedure internationale' (1930) 57 *Journal du Droit International* 857

Corso di Diritto Internazionale (4th edn, Padua, 1955)

Corsi di diritto internazionale privato e processuale (Padua, 1996)

Appleton, Lewis, *Historic Record of the Triumphs of International Arbitration from 1789 to 1899* (London, 1899)

Arai-Takahashi, Y., *The Margin of Appreciation Doctrine and the Principle of Proportionality in the Jurisprudence of the ECHR* (Oxford, 2002)

Arangio-Ruiz, Gaetano, 'The Plea of Domestic Jurisdiction before the International Court of Justice: Substance or Procedure?' in Vaughan Lowe and Malgosia Fitzmaurice (eds.), *Fifty Years of the International Court of Justice: Essays in Honour of Sir Robert Jennings* (Cambridge, 1996), p. 440

Aréchaga, Eduardo Jiménez de, 'Judges ad hoc in Advisory Proceedings' (1971) 31 *Zeitschrift für ausländisches öffentliches Recht und Völkerrecht* 697

'International Law in the Past Third of a Century' (1978) 159 *Recueil des Cours* 1

'The Work and the Jurisprudence of the International Court of Justice 1947–1986' (1987) 58 *British Yearbook of International Law* 1

Aubain, L., 'Un Nouveau protocole de Vienne?' (1934) 15 *Revue de Droit International et de Législation Comparée* 129

Aust, Anthony, *Modern Treaty Law and Practice* (Cambridge, 2000)

Austin, John, *The Province of Jurisprudence Determined* (Cambridge, 1995) (originally published 1832)

Baker, P. J., 'The Obligatory Jurisdiction of the Permanent Court of
    International Justice' (1925) 6 *British Yearbook of International Law* 68
Barros, James, *Betrayal from Within: Joseph Avenol, Secretary-General of the League of
    Nations, 1933–1940* (New Haven, 1969)
Basdevant, Jules, 'Affaire du Vapeur 'Wimbledon': Observations' (1924) 6 *Revue
    de Droit Maritime Comparé* 100
    'Règles générales du droit de la paix' (1936) 58 *Recueil des Cours* 473
    Peace Through International Adjudication? (Philadelphia, 1949)
    'La Place et le rôle de la justice internationale dans les relations entre états
    et à l'égard des organisations internationales' in Centre de sciences
    politiques de l'Institut d'études juridiques de Nice, *Les affaires étrangères*
    (Paris, 1959), p. 331
Baxter, Richard, *The Law of International Waterways – With Particular Regard to
    Interoceanic Canals* (Cambridge, 1964)
Beale, Joseph H., *A Treatise on the Conflict of Laws* (3 vols., New York, 1935)
Beaulac, Stéphane, *The Power of Language in the Making of International Law: The
    Word Sovereignty in Bodin and Vattel and the Myth of Westphalia* (Leiden, 2004)
Becker, André, 'La Cour permanente de Justice internationale en 1930–1931'
    (1932) 13 *Revue de Droit International et de Legislation Comparée* 524
Beckett, W. E., 'The Exercise of Criminal Jurisdiction over Foreigners' (1925) 6
    British Yearbook of International Law 44
    'Criminal Jurisdiction over Foreigners' (1927) 8 *British Yearbook of International
    Law* 108
    'The Case of the *Lotus*' (1928) 9 *British Yearbook of International Law* 131
    'Decisions of the Permanent Court of International Justice on Points of Law
    and Procedure of General Application' (1930) 11 *British Yearbook of
    International Law* 1
    'Les Questions d'intérêt général au point de vue juridique dans la
    jurisprudence de la Cour permanente de Justice internationale' (1932) 39
    Recueil des Cours 135
    'Les Questions d'intérêt général au point de vue juridique dans la
    jurisprudence de la Cour permanente de Justice internationale (juillet
    1932–juillet 1934)' (1934) 50 *Recueil des Cours* 193
    'Sir Cecil Hurst's Services to International Law' (1949) 24 *British Yearbook of
    International Law* 1
Bederman, David J., 'The 1871 London Declaration, Rebus Sic Stantibus and a
    Primitive View of the Law of Nations' (1988) 82 *American Journal of
    International Law* 1
    'Grotius and His Followers on Treaty Construction' (2001) 3 *Journal of the
    History of International Law* 18
    International Law in Antiquity (Cambridge, 2001)
Bedjaoui, Mohammed, 'Problèmes récents de succession d'états dans les états
    nouveaux' (1970) 130 *Recueil des Cours* 455
    'La "Fabrication" des arrets de la Cour internationale de Justice' in *Le droit
    international au service de la paix, de la justice et du developpement: Mélanges
    Michel Virally* (Paris, 1991), p. 87

'The "Manufacture" of Judgments at the International Court of Justice' (1991)
   3 *Pace Yearbook of International Law* 29
The New World Order and the Security Council (Dordrecht, 1994)
'Expediency in the Decisions of the International Court of Justice' (2000) 71
   British Yearbook of International Law 1
'L'opportunité dans les décisions de la Cour internationale de Justice' in
   Laurence Boisson de Chazournes and Vera Gowlland-Debbas (eds.), *The
   International Legal System in Quest of Equity and Universality: Liber Amicorum
   Georges Abi-Saab* (The Hague, 2001), p. 563
Bentham, Jeremy, *A Fragment on Government; or a Comment on the Commentaries*
   (2nd edn, London, 1823)
   An Introduction to the Principles of Morals and Legislation (2nd edn, London, 1823)
   'Principles of International Law' in John Bowring (ed.), *The Works of Jeremy
   Bentham* (Edinburgh, 1843), vol. 2, p. 535
   A Comment on the Commentaries and, A Fragment on Government (London, 1977)
Bergbohm, Karl Magnus, *Staatsverträge und Gesetze als Quellen des Völkerrechts*
   (Dorpat, 1877)
Berlia, G., 'Contribution à l'interprétation des traités' (1965) 114 *Recueil des Cours*
   287
Berman, Nathaniel, 'A Perilous Ambivalence: Nationalist Desire, Legal
   Autonomy, and the Limits of the Interwar Framework' (1992) 33 *Harvard
   International Law Journal* 353
   '"But the Alternative is Despair": European Nationalism and the Modernist
   Renewal of International Law' (1993) 106 *Harvard Law Review* 1792
   'Imperial Rivalry and the Genealogy of Human Rights: *The Nationality Decrees
   Case*' in American Society of International Law, *Proceedings of the 94th Annual
   Meeting* (Washington DC, 2000), p. 51
   'The *Nationality Decrees Case*, or, Of Intimacy and Consent' (2000) 13 *Leiden
   Journal of International Law* 265
Bernhardt, Rudolf, 'Thoughts on the Interpretation of Human-Rights Treaties'
   in Franz Matscher and Herbert Petzold (eds.), *Protecting Human Rights: The
   European Dimension, Studies in Honour of Gérard J. Wiarda* (Cologne, 1988),
   p. 65
Bilfinger, Carl, 'Der Streit um die deutsch-österreichische Zollunion' (1931) 3
   Zeitschrift für ausländisches öffentliches Recht und Völkerrecht 163
Binding, Karl, *Die Gründung des Norddeutschen Bundes: Ein Beitrag zur Lehre von der
   Staatenschöpfung* (Leipzig, 1889)
Bleckmann, Albert, *Allgemeine Staats- und Völkerrechtslehre: Vom Kompetenz- zum
   Kooperationsvölkerrecht* (Cologne, 1995)
Blondel, André, 'Les Principes généraux de droit devant la Cour permanente de
   Justice internationale et la Cour international de Justice' in *Recueil d'études
   de droit international: En hommage à Paul Guggenheim* (Geneva, 1968), p. 201
Bluntschli, Johann Caspar, *Das moderne Völkerrecht der civilisirten Staaten als
   Rechtsbuch dargestellt* (3rd edn, Nördlingen, 1878)
Bodansky, Daniel, '*Non Liquet* and the Incompleteness of International Law' in
   Laurence Boisson de Chazournes and Philippe Sands (eds.), *International*

Law, the International Court of Justice and Nuclear Weapons (Cambridge, 1999), p. 153

Bodendiek, Frank, 'Walther Schücking und Hans Wehberg: Pazifistische Völkerrechtslehre in der ersten Hälfte des 20. Jahrhunderts' (1999) 74 *Die Friedens-Warte* 79

Walther Schückings Konzeption der internationalen Ordnung: Dogmatische Strukturen und ideengeschichtliche Bedeutung (Berlin, 2001)

Bodie, Thomas J., *Politics and the Emergence of an Activist International Court of Justice* (Westport, CT, 1995)

Bodin, Jean, *The Six Books of a Commonweale* (Cambridge, MA, 1962) (originally published 1576)

On Sovereignty (Cambridge, 1992) (originally published 1576)

Borchard, Edwin M., 'The Mavrommatis Concessions Case' (1925) 19 *American Journal of International Law* 728

'The Customs Union Advisory Opinion' (1931) 25 *American Journal of International Law* 711

'The Theory and Sources of International Law' in *Recueil d'etudes sur les sources du droit en l'honneur de François Gény* (Paris, 1934), vol. 3, p. 328

'John Bassett Moore' (1946) 32 *American Bar Association Journal* 32

Bos, Maarten, *A Methodology of International Law* (Amsterdam, 1984)

Bourgeois, Léon, *Pour la Société des Nations* (Paris, 1910)

L'oeuvre de la Société des Nations (1920–1923) (Paris, 1923)

Bourquin, Maurice, 'Régles générales du droit international de la paix' (1931) 35 *Recueil des Cours* 5

Bravo, Luigi Ferrari, 'La Cour internationale de Justice aujourd'hui' in Kalliopi Kaufa (ed.), *International Law of the Turn of the Century* (Thesaurus Acroasion, vol. 27) (Thessaloniki, 1998), p. 17

Bredimas, Anna, *Methods of Interpretation and Community Law* (Amsterdam, 1978)

Brierly, J. L., 'Le Fondement du caratère obligatoire du droit international' (1928) 23 *Recueil des Cours* 467

'The "*Lotus*" Case' (1928) 44 *Law Quarterly Review* 154

'The Advisory Opinion of the Permanent Court on the Customs Régime between Germany and Austria' (1933) 3 *Zeitschrift für ausländisches öffentliches Recht und Völkerrecht* 68

'The Basis of Obligation in International Law' in Hersch Lauterpacht and Humphrey Waldock (eds.), *The Basis of Obligation in International Law and Other Papers by the Late James Leslie Brierly* (Oxford, 1958), p. 1

The Law of Nations (6th edn by Sir Humphrey Waldock, Oxford, 1963)

Briggs, Herbert Whittaker, 'L'avis consultatif no. 12 de la Cour permanente de Justice internationale dans l'affaire de Mossoul' (1927) 8 *Revue de Droit International et de Législation Comparée* 626

Brown, Chester, 'The Evolution and Application of Rules Concerning Independence of the "International Judiciary"' (2003) 2 *Law and Practice of International Courts and Tribunals* 63

Brownlie, Ian, 'The Individual before Tribunals Exercising International
    Jurisdiction' (1962) 2 *International and Comparative Law Quarterly* 701
    'The Relations of Nationality in Public International Law' (1963) 39 *British
    Yearbook of International Law* 284
    'The Place of the Individual in International Law' (1964) 50 *Virginia Law
    Review* 435
    'The Reality and Efficacy of International Law' (1981) 52 *British Yearbook of
    International Law* 1
    'International Law at the Fiftieth Anniversary of the United Nations: General
    Course on Public International Law' (1995) 255 *Recueil des Cours* 9
    *The Rule of Law in International Affairs: International Law at the Fiftieth Anniversary
    of the United Nations* (The Hague, 1998)
    Principles of Public International Law (6th edn, Oxford, 2003)
Bruns, Viktor, 'Völkerrecht als Rechtsordnung I' (1929) 1 *Zeitschrift für
    ausländisches öffentliches Recht und Völkerrecht* 1
    'Völkerrecht als Rechtsordnung II' (1933) 3 *Zeitschrift für ausländisches
    öffentliches Recht und Völkerrecht* 445
    Der internationale Richter (Uppsala, 1934)
    'Mineitciro Adatci: Ein Nachruf' (1935) 5 *Zeitschrift für ausländisches öffentliches
    Recht und Völkerrecht* 1
    'La Cour permanente de Justice internationale, son organisation et sa
    compétence' (1937) 62 *Recueil des Cours* 551
Brus, Marcel M. T. A., *Third Party Dispute Settlement in an Interdependent World:
    Developing a Theoretical Framework* (Dordrecht, 1995)
Bryn-Jones, David, *Frank B. Kellogg: A Biography* (New York, 1937)
Buffard, Isabelle and Karl Zemanek, 'The "Object and Purpose" of a Treaty: An
    Enigma?' (1998) 3 *Austrian Review of International and European Law* 311
Bunn-Livingstone, Sandra L., *Juricultural Pluralism vis-à-vis Treaty Law: State Practice
    and Attitudes* (The Hague, 2002)
de Bustamante y Sirvén, Antonio Sanchez, *La Cour permanente de Justice
    internationale* (The Hague, 1923)
    'La función consultiva del Tribunal Permanente de Justicia Internacional'
    (1924) 73 *Revista general de legislación y jurisprudencia* 519
    The World Court (New York, 1925)
    The World Court and the United States (Atlanta, GA, 1929)
    The Territorial Sea (New York, 1930)
    Droit international public (5 vols., Paris, 1934–9)
    'The First Court of International Justice and the Causes of its Dissolution' in
    Norman Bentwick, A. S. de Bustamante, Donald A. MacLean, Gustav
    Radbruch and H. A. Smith, *Justice and Equality in the International Sphere*
    (London 1936), p. 31
    Manual de derecho internacional privado (3rd edn, Havana, 1943)
    Derecho internacíonal privado (3 vols., 3rd edn, Havana, 1943)
    Manual de derecho internacional público (4th edn, Havana, 1947)

Byers, Michael, 'Conceptualising the Relationship between *Jus Cogens* and *Erga Omnes* Rules' (1997) 66 *Nordic Journal of International Law* 211
  Custom, Power and the Power of Rules (Cambridge, 1999)
  (ed.), *The Role of Law in International Politics: Essays in International Relations and International Law* (Oxford, 2000)
Bynkershoek, Cornelius van, *Quaestionum Juris Publici Libri Duo* (Oxford, 1930) (originally published 1737)
Caloyanni, A., 'L'organisation de la Cour permanente de Justice internationale et son avenir' (1931) 38 *Recueil des Cours* 655
Camara, José Sette, 'Behind the World Bench' in Manuel Rama-Montaldo (ed.), *El derecho internacional en un mundo en transformación: Liber amicorum en homenaje al Profesor Eduardo Jiménez de Aréchaga* (Montevideo, 1994), p. 1069
Capitant, Henri, *Notice sur la vie et les travaux de M. André Weiss* (Paris, 1931)
Carr, E. H., *The Twenty Years' Crisis, 1919–1939: An Introduction to the Study of International Relations* (2nd edn, London, 1946)
Carty, Anthony, *The Decay of International Law?: A Reappraisal of the Limits of Legal Imagination in International Affairs* (Manchester, 1986)
Carty, Anthony and Richard Smith, *Sir Gerald Fitzmaurice and the World Crisis: A Legal Adviser in the Foreign Office, 1932–1945* (The Hague, 2000)
Cassese, Antonio, *International Law* (Oxford, 2001)
Cavaglieri, Arrigo, 'Règles générales du droit de la paix' (1929) 26 *Recueil des Cours* 544
  Corso di diritto internazionale (3rd edn, Naples, 1934)
Cavaré, Louis, 'L'arrêt du "Lotus" et le positivisme juridique' (1930) 10 *Travaux Juridiques et Economiques de l'Université de Rennes* 144
Chang, Yi-ting, *The Interpretation of Treaties by Judicial Tribunals* (New York, 1933)
Cheng, Bin, *General Principles of Law as Applied by International Courts and Tribunals* (London, 1953)
  'United Nations Resolutions on Outer Space: "Instant" International Customary Law?' (1965) 5 *Indian Journal of International Law* 23
  'Some Remarks on the Constituent Element(s) of General (or So-Called Customary) International Law' in Antony Anghie and Garry Sturgess (eds.), *Legal Visions of the 21st Century: Essays in Honour of Judge Christopher Weeramantry* (The Hague, 1998), p. 377
  '*Opinio Juris*: A Key Concept in International Law That Is Much Misunderstood' in Sienho Yee and Wang Tieya (eds.), *International Law in the Post-Cold War World: Essays in Memory of Li Haopei* (London, 2001), p. 56
Cheng, C. H., *Essai critique sur l'interprétation des traités dans la doctrine et la jurisprudence de la Cour permanente de Justice internationale* (Paris, 1941)
Cheng, Tien-Hsi, *China Moulded by Confucius: The Chinese Way in Western Light* (London, 1946)
  East & West: Episodes in Sixty Years' Journey (London, 1951)
Chinkin, Christine, *Third Parties in International Law* (Oxford, 1993)

Collette, Jean, *Les Principes de droit des gens dans la jurisprudence de la Cour permanente de Justice internationale* (Paris, 1932)

Committee of Jurists on the Statute of the Permanent Court of International Justice, 'Minutes of the Session Held at Geneva, March 11th–19th, 1929' (League of Nations Document C.166.M.66.1929.V, 1929)

Corten, Olivier, *L'utilisation du 'raisonnable' par le juge international: Discours juridique, raison et contradictions* (Brussels, 1997)

Cosnard, Michel, 'Sovereign Equality: "The Wimbledon Sails on"' in Michael Byers and Georg Nolte (eds.), *United States Hegemony and the Foundations of International Law* (Cambridge, 2003), p. 117

Cotterrell, Roger, *The Sociology of Law: An Introduction* (2nd edn, London, 1992)

Couvreur, Philippe, 'Charles de Visscher and International Justice' (2000) 11 *European Journal of International Law* 905

Crawford, James, *The Creation of States in International Law* (Oxford, 1979)
'Negotiating Global Security Threats in a World of Nation-States: Issues and Problems of Sovereignty' (1995) 38 *American Behavioral Scientist* 867
'Universalism and Regionalism from the Perspective of the Work of the International Law Commission' in Alain Pellet (ed.), *International Law on the Eve of the Twenty-First Century: Views from the International Law Commission* (New York, 1997), p. 99
International Law as an Open System: Selected Essays (London, 2002)
The International Law Commission's Articles on State Responsibility: Introduction, Text and Commentaries (Cambridge, 2002)

Crawford, James and Anthony Sinclair, 'The UNIDROIT Principles and their Application to State Contracts' (2002) *ICC International Court of Arbitration Bulletin: Special Supplement* 57

Crawford, James and Thomas Viles, 'International Law on a Given Day' in Konrad Ginther, Gerhard Hafner, Winfried Lang, Hanspeter Neuhold and Lilly Sucharipa-Behrmann (eds.), *Völkerrecht zwischen normativem Anspruch und politischer Realität: Festschrift für Karl Zemanek zum 65. Geburtstag* (Berlin, 1994), p. 45

Cuban Society of International Law, *At the Service of Justice: Bustamante and the Permanent Court of International Justice, 1922–1930* (Havana, 1930)

D'Amato, Anthony A., *The Concept of Custom in International Law* (Ithaca, 1971)
'Customary International Law: A Reformulation' (1998) 4 *International Legal Theory* 1

Danelski, David J. and Joseph S. Tulchin (eds.), *The Autobiographical Notes of Charles Evans Hughes* (Cambridge, MA, 1973)

Darby, W. Evans, *International Tribunals: A Collection of the Various Schemes Which Have Been Propounded and of Instances Since 1815* (London, 1900)

Davis, John W., 'The World Court Settles the Question' (1932) *Atlantic Monthly* 119

Decencière-Ferrandière, André, 'Essai critique sur la justice internationale' (1934) 41 *Revue Générale de Droit International Public* 148

Degan, V. D., *L'interprétation des accords en droit international* (The Hague, 1963)
   Sources of International Law (The Hague, 1997)
Deibel, Terry L., *Le Secrétariat de la Société des Nations et l'internationalisme
   américain, 1919–1924* (Geneva, 1972)
Derevitzky, Pierre, *Les Principes du droit international tels qu'ils se dégagent de la
   jurisprudence de la Cour permanente de Justice internationale* (Paris, 1932)
Descamps, Le Chevalier, *Essai sur l'organisation de l'arbitrage international*
   (Brussels, 1898)
Detter De Lupis, Ingrid, *The Concept of International Law* (Uppsala, 1987)
Dexter, Byron, *The Years of Opportunity: The League of Nations, 1920–1926* (New York,
   1967)
Dicey, A. V., *A Digest of the Law of England with Reference to the Conflict of Laws*
   (London, 1896)
Diggelmann, Oliver, *Anfänge der Völkerrechtssoziologie: die Völkerrechtskonzeptionen
   von Max Huber und Georges Scelle im Vergleich* (Zurich, 2000)
Donner, A. M., 'The Constitutional Powers of the Court of Justice of the
   European Communities' (1974) 11 *Common Market Law Review* 127
Douma, J., *Bibliography of the International Court Including the Permanent Court,
   1918–1964* (Leiden, 1966)
Duguit, Léon, *Traité de droit constitutionnel* (5 vols., 3rd edn, Paris, 1927–30)
Dunne, Michael, *The United States and the World Court, 1920–1935* (London, 1988)
   'William Howard Taft, Charles Evans Hughes and the Permanent Court of
   International Justice' in William D. Pederson and Norman W. Provizer
   (eds.), *Great Justices of the US Supreme Court* (New York, 1993), p. 185
Dupuy, Pierre-Marie, 'The Danger of Fragmentation or Unification of the
   International Legal System and the International Court of Justice' (1999) 31
   New York University Journal of International Law and Politics 791
Dupuy, René-Jean, *La Communauté internationale entre le mythe et l'histoire* (Paris,
   1986)
Dworkin, Ronald, *Law's Empire* (London, 1986)
Ehrlich, Ludwik, 'L'interprétation des traités' (1928) 24 *Recueil des Cours* 5
Eisele, Herbert A. F., *L'affaire Oscar Chinn devant la Cour permanente de Justice
   internationale* (Ambilly, 1970)
Eissen, Marc-André, 'La Cour européenne des Droits de l'Homme' (1986)
   102 *Revue du Droit Public et de la Science Politique en France et à l'Etranger*
   1539
Elias, Taslim Olawale, 'Does the International Court of Justice, as It Is Presently
   Shaped, Correspond to the Requirements which Follow from Its Functions
   as the Central Judicial Body of the International Community? – Report' in
   H. Mosler and R. Bernhardt (eds.), *Judicial Settlement of International Disputes*
   (Berlin, 1974), p. 19
   'Methodological Problems Faced by the International Court of Justice in the
   Application of International Law' in Bin Cheng (ed.), *International Law:
   Teaching and Practice* (London, 1982), p. 135
   United Nations Charter and the World Court (The Hague, 1989)

Engelsdoerfer, A., 'La Cour de la Haye en 1932–1933' (1934) 15 *Revue de Droit International et de Législation Comparée* 249

'La Cour de la Haye en 1932–1933' (1935) 16 *Revue de Droit International et de Législation Comparée* 299 and 443

Enriques, Giuliano, 'L'acception, sans réciprocité, de la juridiction obligatoire de la Cour permanente de Justice internationale' (1932) 13 *Revue de Droit International et de Législation Comparée* 834

Eppstein, John, *Ten Years' Life of the League of Nations: A History of the Origins of the League and of its Development from AD 1919 to 1929* (London, 1929)

Erich, R., *Studier i internationell rättskipning* (Lund, 1943)

van Essen, J. L. F., 'A Reappraisal of Oscar Chinn' in *Symbolae Verzijl* (The Hague, 1958), p. 145

Eyffinger, Arthur, *The International Court of Justice, 1946–1996* (The Hague, 1996)

The 1899 Hague Peace Conference: 'The Parliament of Man, the Federation of the World' (The Hague, 1999)

Eyma, Jean, *La Cour de Justice Centre Américaine* (Paris, 1928)

van Eysinga, W. J. M., 'Walther Schücking als internationaler Richter' (1935) 35 *Die Friedens-Warte* 213

'Walther Schücking' (1937) 18 *British Yearbook of International Law* 155

Fachiri, Alexander P., 'Interpretation of Treaties' (1929) 23 *American Journal of International Law* 745

'The International Court: American Participation; Statute Revision' (1930) 11 *British Yearbook of International Law* 85

The Permanent Court of International Justice: Its Constitution, Procedure and Work (2nd edn, London, 1932)

Falk, Richard A., *The Role of Domestic Courts in the International Legal Order* (Syracuse, 1964)

The Status of Law in International Society (Princeton, 1970)

Fastenrath, Ulrich, *Lücken im Völkerrecht* (Berlin, 1991)

Feinberg, Nathan, 'La Juridiction et la jurisprudence de la Cour permanente de Justice internationale en matière de mandats et de minorités' (1937) 59 *Recueil des Cours* 591

Fernandes, Raoul, *La Société des Nations: sa genèse, ses buts, sa constitution, ses moyens d'action et ses résultats* (Geneva, 1925)

Fischer, Georges, *Les Rapports entre l'Organisation internationale du Travail et la Cour permanente de Justice internationale* (Berne, 1946)

Fitzmaurice, G. G., 'The Law and Procedure of the International Court of Justice: Treaty Interpretation and Certain Other Treaty Points' (1951) 28 *British Yearbook of International Law* 1

'The General Principles of International Law Considered from the Standpoint of the Rule of Law' (1957) 92 *Recueil des Cours* 1

'The Law and Procedure of the International Court of Justice, 1951–54: Treaty Interpretation and Other Treaty Points' (1957) 34 *British Yearbook of International Law* 203

'Some Problems Regarding the Formal Sources of International Law' in
  Symbolae Verzijl (The Hague, 1958), p. 153
'The Law and Procedure of the International Court of Justice 1954–9: General
  Principles and Sources of International Law' (1959) 36 *British Yearbook of
  International Law* 183
'Sir Cecil Hurst (1870–1963)' (1963) 50-II *Annuaire de l'Institut de Droit
  International* 462
'Vae Victis or Woe to the Negotiators' (1971) 65 *American Journal of
  International Law* 358
'The Future of Public International Law and of the International Legal
  System in the Circumstances of Today' in Institut de Droit International,
  Livre du centenaire, 1873–1973: Evolution et perspectives du droit international
  (Basel, 1973), p. 196
'The Problem of Non-Liquet: Prolegomena to a Restatement' in *Mélanges offerts
  à Charles Rousseau: La Communauté internationale* (Paris, 1974), p. 89
'Enlargement of the Contentious Jurisdiction of the Court' in Leo Gross (ed.),
  The Future of the International Court of Justice (Dobbs Ferry, 1976), p. 461
'Some Reflections on the European Convention on Human Rights – and on
  Human Rights' in Rudolf Bernhardt, Wilhelm Karl Geck, Günther Jaenicke
  and Helmut Steinberg (eds.), *Völkerrecht als Rechtsordnung, Internationale
  Gerichtsbarkeit, Menschenrechte: Festschrift für Hermann Mosler* (Berlin, 1983),
  p. 203
The Law and Procedure of the International Court of Justice (Cambridge, 1986)
Fitzmaurice, Malgosia, 'The Optional Clause System and the Law of Treaties:
  Issues of Interpretation in Recent Jurisprudence of the International Court
  of Justice' (1999) 20 *Australian Year Book of International Law* 127
Fleming, Denna Frank, *The United States and the World Court, 1920–1966* (2nd edn,
  New York, 1968)
Franck, Thomas M., 'Some Psychological Factors in International Third-Party
  Decision-Making' (1966–7) 19 *Stanford Law Review* 1217
  The Power of Legitimacy among Nations (New York, 1990)
  Fairness in International Law and Institutions (Oxford, 1995)
  'Individuals and Groups of Individuals as Subjects of International Law' in
  Rainer Hofmann (ed.), *Non-State Actors as New Subjects of International Law*
  (Berlin, 1999), p. 97
Frangulis, A.-G., 'Adatci (Minéitcirô)' in A.-G. Frangulis (ed.), *Dictionnaire
  diplomatique* (Paris, 1957), vol. 5, p. 13
Friedman, Richard D., 'Charles Evans Hughes as International Lawyer' in
  American Society of International Law, *Proceedings of the 90th Annual Meeting*
  (Washington DC, 1996), p. 143
Friedmann, Wolfgang, 'Some Impacts of Social Organization on International
  Law' (1956) 50 *American Journal of International Law* 475
  Law in a Changing Society (London, 1959)
  'Half a Century of International Law' (1964) 50 *Virginia Law Review* 1333

The Changing Structure of International Law (London, 1964)

Law in a Changing Society (2nd edn, London, 1972)

Frowein, Jochen Abr., 'Das Staatengemeinschaftsinteresse: Probleme bei Formulierung und Durchsetzung' in Kay Hailbronner, Georg Ress and Torsten Stein (eds.), *Staat und Völkerrechtsordnung: Festschrift für Karl Doehring* (Berlin, 1989), p. 219

'Unilateral Interpretation of Security Council Resolutions: A Threat to Collective Security?' in Christiane Philipp (ed.), *Liber amicorum Günther Jaenicke: Zum 85. Geburtstag* (Berlin, 1998), p. 97

Le Fur, Louis, 'L'affaire de Mossoul' (1926) 33 *Revue Générale de Droit International Public* 60 and 209

'La Coutume et les principes généraux du droit comme sources du droit international public' in *Recueil d'etudes sur les sources du droit en l'honneur de François Gény* (Paris, 1934), vol. 3, p. 362

'Règles générales du droit de la paix' (1935) 54 *Recueil des Cours* 5

'L'activité de la Cour permanente de Justice internationale en 1934–1936' (1937) 44 *Revue Politique et Parlementaire* 48

Précis de droit international public (3rd edn, Paris, 1937)

Gabaglia, Laurita Pessôa Raja, *Epitacio Pessôa (1865–1942)* (Sao Paolo, 1951)

Gaja, Giorgio, 'Positivism and Dualism in Dionisio Anzilotti' (1992) 3 *European Journal of International Law* 123

Gallus, 'L'acte générale d'arbitrage' (1930) 11 *Revue de Droit International et de Legislation Comparée* 190, 413 and 878

'L'acte générale a-t-il une réelle utilité?' (1931) 8 *Revue de Droit International* 377

Ganshof van der Meersch, Walter J., 'Le Caractère "autonome" des termes et la "marge d'appréciation" des gouvernements dans l'interprétation de la Convention européenne des Droits de l'Homme' in Franz Matscher and Herbert Petzold (eds.), *Protecting Human Rights: The European Dimension, Studies in Honour of Gérard J. Wiarda* (Cologne, 1988), p. 201

Garnier-Coignet, Jean, 'Procédure judiciaire et procédure arbitrale: Étude de droit international positif' (1930) 6 *Revue de Droit International* 123

Gassner, Ulrich M., *Heinrich Triepel: Leben und Werk* (Berlin, 1999)

Genet, Raoul, 'Un probleme de presences' (1933) 14 *Revue de Droit International et de Législation Comparée* 254

Précis de jurisprudence de la Cour permanente de Justice internationale (2nd edn, Vienna, 1939)

Gentili, Alberico, *De Legationibus Libri Tres* (New York, 1924) (originally published 1585)

De Iure Belli Libri Tres (Oxford, 1933) (originally published 1612)

Geny, François, *Méthode d'interprétation et sources en droit privé positif* (2 vols., 2nd edn, Paris, 1919)

Golden, Jeffrey B., 'The World Court: The Qualifications of the Judges' (1978) 14 *Columbia Journal of Law and Social Problems* 1

Golsong, Heribert, 'Role and Functioning of the International Court of Justice: Proposals Recently Made on the Subject' (1971) 31 *Zeitschrift für ausländisches öffentliches Recht und Völkerrecht* 673

Goodrich, Leland M., 'The Nature of the Advisory Opinions of the Permanent Court of International Justice' (1938) 32 *American Journal of International Law* 738

Gormley, W. Paul, *The Procedural Status of the Individual before International and Supranational Tribunals* (The Hague, 1966)

Gottlieb, Gidon, 'The Nature of International Law: Towards a Second Concept of Law' in Cyril E. Black and Richard A. Falk (eds.), *The Future of the International Legal Order* (Princeton, 1972), vol. 4, p. 331.

Gounelle, Max, *La Motivation des actes juridiques en droit international public* (Paris, 1979)

Gowlland-Debbas, Vera, 'Judicial Insights into Fundamental Values and Interests of the International Community' in A. S. Muller, D. Raic and J. M. Thuránszky (eds.), *The International Court of Justice: Its Future Role after Fifty Years* (The Hague, 1997), p. 327

Goy, Raymond, 'La Cour permanente de Justice internationale et les droits de l'homme' in *Liber amicorum Marc-André Eissen* (Brussels, 1995), p. 199

Gregory, Charles Noble, 'An Important Decision by the Permanent Court of International Justice' (1923) 17 *American Journal of International Law* 298

Greig, Don, '"International Community", "Interdependence" and All That . . . Rhetorical Correctness?' in Gerard Kreijen, Marcel Brus, Jorri Duursma, Elisabeth de Vos and John Dugard (eds.), *State, Sovereignty, and International Governance* (Oxford, 2002), p. 521

Grewe, Wilhelm G., *The Epochs of International Law* (3rd edn, Berlin, 2000)

Grisel, Etienne, *Les Exceptions d'incompétence et d'irrecevabilité dans la procédure de la Cour internationale de Justice* (Berne, 1968)

Gros, André, 'A propos de cinquante années de justice internationale' (1972) 76 *Revue Générale de Droit Internationale Public* 5
  'Concerning the Advisory Role of the International Court of Justice' in Wolfgang Friedmann, Louis Henkin and Oliver Lissitzyn (eds.), *Transnational Law in a Changing Society: Essays in Honor of Philip C. Jessup* (New York, 1972), p. 313
  'La Recherche du consensus dans les décisions de la Cour internationale de Justice' in Rudolf Bernhard, Wilhelm Karl Geck, Günther Jaenicke and Helmut Steinberg (eds.), *Völkerrecht als Rechtsordnung – Internationale Gerichtsbarkeit – Menschenrechte: Festschrift für Hermann Mosler* (Berlin, 1983), p. 351
  'La Cour internationale de Justice 1946–1986: Les Reflexions d'un juge' in Yoram Dinstein (ed.), *International Law at a Time of Perplexity: Essays in Honour of Shabtai Rosenne* (Dordrecht, 1989), p. 289

Grossen, Jacques-Michel, *Les Présomptions en droit international public* (Neuchâtel, 1954)

Grotius, Hugo, *De Iure Praedae Commentarius* (London, 1950) (original manuscript finished 1604)

De Jure Belli ac Pacis Libri Tres (Oxford, 1925) (originally published 1625)

de la Grotte, Michel, 'La Cour permanente de Justice internationale en 1925' (1926) 7 *Revue de Droit International et de Législation Comparée* 202 and 321

'Les Affaires traitées par la Cour permanente de Justice internationale pendant la periode 1926–1928' (1929) 10 *Revue de Droit International et de Législation Comparée* 225 and 387

Grzybowski, Kazimierz, 'Interpretation of Decisions of International Tribunals' (1941) 35 *American Journal of International Law* 482

Guerrero, J. Gustave, *La Codification du droit international* (Paris, 1930)

L'ordre international: Hier – aujourd'hui – demain (Neuchâtel, 1945)

Guggenheim, Paul, *Lehrbuch des Völkerrechts: Unter Berücksichtigung der internationalen und schweizerischen Praxis* (2 vols., Basel, 1948–51)

'Les Deux éléments de la coutume en droit international' in *La Technique et les principes du droit public: Etudes en l'honneur de Georges Scelle* (Paris, 1950), vol. 1, p. 275

'L'origine de la notion de l'"opinio juris sive necessitatis" comme deuxième élément de la coutume dans l'histoire du droit des gens' in *Hommage d'une génération de juristes au Président Basdevant* (Paris, 1960), p. 258

'Max Huber, 1874–1960' (1961) 41 *Revue Internationale de la Croix-Rouge* 313

Traité de droit international public: Avec mention de la pratique internationale et suisse (2nd edn, Geneva, 1967), vol. 1

Guillaume, Gilbert, *La Cour internationale de Justice à l'aube du XXIème siècle* (Paris, 2003)

'Some Thoughts on the Independence of International Judges vis-à-vis States' (2003) 2 *Law and Practice of International Courts and Tribunals* 163

Guyomar, Geneviève, *Commentaire du règlement de la Cour internationale de Justice: Interprétation et pratique* (Paris, 1973)

Commentaire du règlement de la Cour internationale de Justice adopté le 14 avril 1978: Interprétation et pratique (Paris, 1983)

Haemmerlé, Jean, *La Coutume en droit des gens d'après la jurisprudence de la CPJI* (Paris, 1936)

Haggenmacher, Peter, 'La Doctrine des deux éléments du droit coutumier dans la pratique de la Cour internationale' (1986) 90 *Revue Générale de Droit International Public* 5

Hambro, Edvard, 'The International Court of Justice' (1949) 3 *Yearbook of World Affairs* 188

'The Reasons behind the Decisions of the International Court of Justice' (1954) 7 *Current Legal Problems* 212

'Dissenting and Individual Opinions in the International Court of Justice' (1956) 17 *Zeitschrift für ausländisches öffentliches Recht und Völkerrecht* 229

'The Ihlen Declaration Revisited' in *Grundprobleme des Internationalen Rechts: Festschrift für Jean Spiropoulos* (Bonn, 1957), p. 227

'Les Opinions individuelles et dissidentes des membres de la Cour internationale de Justice' (1964) 34 *Nordisk Tidsskrift for International Ret* 181

Hammarskjöld, Åke, 'Le Règlement de la Cour permanente de Justice internationale' (1922) 3 *Revue de Droit International et de Legislation Comparée* 125

'The Early Work of the Permanent Court of International Justice' (1922–3) 36 *Harvard Law Review* 704

'Le Règlement revisé de la Cour permanente de Justice internationale' (1927) 8 *Revue de Droit International et de Legislation Comparée* 322

'Sidelights on the Permanent Court of International Justice' (1927) 25 *Michigan Law Review* 327

'La Cour permanente de Justice internationale à la neuvième session de l'Assemblée de la Société des Nations' (1928) 9 *Revue de Droit International et de Legislation Comparée* 665

'International Justice' in League of Nations, *Ten Years of World Co-operation* (London, 1930), p. 125

'The Permanent Court of International Justice and Its Place in International Relations' (1930) 9 *International Affairs* 467

'La Cour permanente de Justice internationale et le droit international privé' (1934) 29 *Revue Critique de Droit International* 315

'Quelques aspects de la fonction consultative de la Cour permanente de Justice internationale' in *Festgabe für Max Huber zum sechzigsten Geburtstag 28. Dezember 1934* (Zurich, 1934), p. 146

'L'Organisation internationale du Travail et la Cour de La Haye' in *Mélanges offerts à Ernest Mahaim* (Paris, 1935), p. 545

'Persönliche Eindrücke aus Walther Schückings Richtertätigkeit' (1935) 35 *Die Friedens-Warte* 214

'Quelques aspects de la question des mesures conservatoires en droit international positif' (1935) 5 *Zeitschrift für ausländisches öffentliches Recht und Völkerrecht* 5

'The Permanent Court of International Justice and the Development of International Law' (1935) 14 *International Affairs* 797

'Les Avis consultatifs à la seizième session de l'Assemblée' (1936) 17 *Revue de Droit International et de Legislation Comparée* 65

Juridiction internationale (Leiden, 1938)

Hannikainen, Lauri, *Peremptory Norms (Jus Cogens) in International Law* (Helsinki, 1988)

Haraszti, György, *Some Fundamental Problems of the Law of Treaties* (Budapest, 1973)

Hardy, Jean, 'The Interpretation of Plurilingual Treaties by International Courts and Tribunals' (1961) 37 *British Yearbook of International Law* 72

Härle, Elfried, *Die allgemeinen Entscheidungsgrundlagen des Ständigen Internationalen Gerichtshofes* (Berlin, 1933)

Hart, H. L. A., 'Definition and Theory in Jurisprudence' in H. L. A. Hart, *Essays in Jurisprudence and Philosophy* (Oxford, 1983), p. 21

The Concept of Law (2nd edn, Oxford, 1994)

van Hecke, G., 'Relecture de l'avis consultatif sur le projet d'union douanière austro-allemande' in Marianne Dony (ed.), *Mélanges en hommage à Michel Waelbroeck* (Brussels, 1999), p. 255

Hegel, G. W. F., *Grundlinien der Philosophie des Rechts* (Cambridge, 1991) (originally published 1821)

Heffter, August Wilhelm, *Das europäische Völkerrecht der Gegenwart auf den bisherigen Grundlagen* (8th edn by F. Heinr. Geffcken, Berlin, 1888)

Henkin, Louis, 'International Law: Politics, Values and Functions' (1989) 216 *Recueil des Cours* 9

International Law: Politics and Values (Dordrecht, 1995)

Foreign Affairs and the United States Constitution (2nd edn, Oxford, 1996)

Hensley, Thomas R., 'National Bias and the International Court of Justice' (1968) 12 *Midwest Journal of Political Science* 568

Herzog, Peter, 'The Need for a Comparative Perspective' in Thomas E. Carbonneau (ed.), *Resolving Transnational Disputes Through International Arbitration* (Charlottesville, 1984), p. 75

von der Heydte, Friedrich August, 'Glossen zu einer Theorie der allgemeinen Rechtsgrundsätze' (1933) 33 *Die Friedens-Warte* 289

Higgins, Rosalyn, 'The International Court of Justice and Human Rights' in Karel Wellens (ed.), *International Law: Theory and Practice – Essays in Honour of Eric Suy* (The Hague, 1998), p. 691

'The ICJ, the ECJ, and the Integrity of International Law' (2003) 52 *International and Comparative Law Quarterly* 1

Hoffmann, Peter, *Stauffenberg: A Family History, 1905–1944* (Cambridge, 1995)

Hogg, James F., 'The International Court: Rules of Treaty Interpretation' (1958–9) 43 *Minnesota Law Review* 369 and (1959–60) 44 *Minnesota Law Review* 5

Hoijer, Olaf, *La Solution pacifique des litiges internationaux avant et depuis la Société des Nations* (Paris, 1925)

Holland, Thomas Erskine, *The Elements of Jurisprudence* (13th edn, Oxford, 1924)

Holmbäck, Åke, *Der ständige internationale Gerichtshof in den Jahren 1922–1929: Einige Tatsachen* (Königsberg Pr., 1930)

van Hoof, G. J. H., *Rethinking the Sources of International Law* (Deventer, 1983)

Hoogensen, Gunhild, 'Bentham's International Manuscripts Versus the Published "Works"', (2001) 4 *Journal of Bentham Studies* 1

Houlard, Maurice, *La Nature juridique des traités internationaux et son application aux théories de la nullité, de la caducité et de la révision des traités* (Bordeaux, 1936)

Huber, Max, *Die Staatensuccession: Völkerrechtliche und Staatsrechtliche Praxis im XIX. Jahrhundert* (Leipzig, 1898)

'Ein Beitrag zur Lehre von der Gebietshoheit an Grenzflüssen' (1907) 1 *Zeitschrift für Völkerrecht und Bundesstaatsrecht* 29 and 159

'Die Fortbildung des Völkerrechts auf dem Gebiete des Prozess- und Landkriegsrechts durch die II. internationale Friedenskonferenz im Haag 1907' (1908) 2 *Jahrbuch des öffentlichen Rechts der Gegenwart* 470

'Die Gleichheit der Staaten' in F. Berolzheimer (ed.), *Recht wissenschaftliche Beiträge: Juristische Festgabe des Auslandes zu Josef Kohlers 60. Geburtstag* (Stuttgart, 1909), p. 88

'Gemeinschafts- und Sonderrecht unter Staaten' in *Festschrift Otto Gierke zum Siebzigsten Geburtstag* (Weimar, 1911), p. 817

'Die geschichtlichen Grundlagen des heutigen Völkerrechts' (1922–3) 16 *Wissen und Leben* 261

'Die konstruktiven Grundlagen des Völkerbundsvertrages' (1922–3) 12 *Zeitschrift für Völkerrecht* 1

'Die Schweizerische Neutralität und der Völkerbund' in P. Munch (ed.), *Les Origines et l'oeuvre de la Société des Nations* (Copenhagen, 1924), vol. 2, p. 68

Die soziologischen Grundlagen des Völkerrechts (Berlin, 1928)

'Walther Schücking und die Völkerrechtswissenschaft' (1935) 35 *Die Friedens-Warte* 197

'In Memoriam Åke Hammarskjöld (1893–1937)' in Å. Hammarskjöld, *Juridiction internationale* (Leiden, 1938), p. 7

Vermischte Schriften (3 vols., Zurich, 1948)

Das Völkerrecht und der Mensch (St Gallen, 1952)

'Prolegomena und Probleme eines internationalen Ethos' (1955–6) 53 *Die Friedens-Warte* 305

Koexistenz und Gemeinschaft: Völkerrechtliche Erinnerungen aus sechs Jahrzehnten (Zurich, 1956) (reprinted from *Züricher Student*)

Vermischte Schriften (vol. 4, Zurich, 1957)

'On the Place of the Law of Nations in the History of Mankind' in *Symbolae Verzijl* (The Hague, 1958), p. 190

'Schiedsrichterliche und richterliche Streiterledigung: Ein Überblick' (1961/6) 56 *Die Friedens-Warte* 105

Denkwürdigkeiten, 1907–1924 (Zurich, 1974)

Hudson, Manley O., 'Advisory Opinions of National and International Courts' (1923–4) 37 *Harvard Law Review* 970

'The Second Year of the Permanent Court of International Justice' (1924) 18 *American Journal of International Law* 1

'Les Avis consultatifs de la Cour permanente de Justice internationale' (1925) 8 *Recueil des Cours* 345

'The Fifth Year of the Permanent Court of International Justice' (1927) 21 *American Journal of International Law* 26

The Advisory Opinions of the World Court: An Address Delivered at the Annual Meeting of the National Council for Prevention of War (Washington DC, 1929)

'Advisory Opinions' in American Society of International Law, *Proceedings of the 24th Annual Meeting* (Washington DC, 1930), p. 63

'The World Court and the Austro-German Customs Régime' (1931) 17 *American Bar Association Journal* 791

'The Cuban Reservations and the Revision of the Statute of the Permanent Court of International Justice' (1932) 26 *American Journal of International Law* 590

'Obligatory Jurisdiction under Article 36 of the Statute of the Permanent Court of International Justice' (1933–4) 19 *Iowa Law Review* 190

'The Twelfth Year of the Permanent Court of International Justice' (1934) 28 *American Journal of International Law* 1

'International Engagements and Their Interpretation by the Permanent Court of International Justice' in Max Radin and A. M. Kidd (eds.), *Legal Essays in Tribute to Orrin Kip McMurray* (Berkeley, 1935), p. 187

'The Thirteenth Year of the Permanent Court of International Justice' (1935) 29 *American Journal of International Law* 1

'Åke Hammarskjöld' (1937) 31 *American Journal of International Law* 703

'The Sixteenth Year of the Permanent Court of International Justice' (1938) 32 *American Journal of International Law* 1

'The Eighteenth Year of the Permanent Court of International Justice' (1940) 34 *American Journal of International Law* 1

'The Twentieth Year of the Permanent Court of International Justice' (1942) 36 *American Journal of International Law* 1

The Permanent Court of International Justice, 1920–1942 (2nd edn, New York, 1943)

International Tribunals: Past and Future (Washington DC, 1944)

'The Twenty-Third Year of the Permanent Court of International Justice' (1945) 39 *American Journal of International Law* 1

'The Twenty-Fourth Year of the World Court' (1946) 40 *American Journal of International Law* 1

'The Succession of the International Court of Justice to the Permanent Court of International Justice' (1957) 51 *American Journal of International Law* 569

Hueck, Ingo J., 'The Discipline of the History of International Law: New Trends and Methods on the History of International Law' (2001) 3 *Journal of the History of International Law* 194

Hughes, Charles Evans, 'The Permanent Court of International Justice' in American Society of International Law, *Proceedings of the 17th Annual Meeting* (Washington DC, 1923), p. 75

'The Development of International Law' in American Society of International Law, *Proceedings of the 19th Annual Meeting* (Washington DC, 1925), p. 1

The Supreme Court of the United States: Its Foundation, Methods and Achievements – An Interpretation (New York, 1928)

'The World Court as a Going Concern' (1930) 16 *American Bar Association Journal* 151

Hurst, Cecil, *The Permanent Court of International Justice* (London, 1931) (reprinted from *The Solicitors' Journal*)

'The Permanent Court of International Justice' (1943) 59 *Law Quarterly Review* 312

'World Court' in Philip Gibbs (ed.), *Bridging the Atlantic* (London, 1943), p. 180

'A Plea for the Codification of International Law on New Lines' (1946) 32 *Transactions of the Grotius Society* 135

Hussain, Ijaz, *Dissenting and Separate Opinions at the World Court* (Dordrecht, 1984)

Hyde, Charles Cheney, 'The Interpretation of Treaties by the Permanent Court of International Justice' (1930) 24 *American Journal of International Law* 1

'Judge Anzilotti on the Interpretation of Treaties' (1933) 27 *American Journal of International Law* 502

'The Case Concerning the Legal Status of Eastern Greenland' (1933) 27 *American Journal of International Law* 732

International Law Chiefly as Interpreted and Applied in the United States (3 vols., 2nd edn, Boston, 1947)

Informal Inter-Allied Committee, *Report of the Informal Inter-Allied Committee on the Future of the Permanent Court of International Justice, 10th February 1944*, Cmd 6531 (London, 1944)

International Centre for Settlement of Investment Disputes, *History of the ICSID Convention: Documents Concerning the Origin and the Formulation of the Convention* (4 vols., Washington DC, 1968)

Jackson, William D., 'Thinking About International Community and Its Alternatives' in Kenneth W. Thompson (ed.), *Community, Diversity, and a New World Order: Essays in Honor of Inis L. Claude, Jr* (Lanham, 1994), p. 3

Jacobs, Francis G., 'Varieties of Approach to Treaty Interpretation: With Special Reference to the Draft Convention on the Law of Treaties before the Vienna Diplomatic Conference' (1969) 18 *International and Comparative Law Quarterly* 318

Jaenicke, Günther, 'International Trade Conflicts before the Permanent Court of International Justice and the International Court of Justice' in Ernst-Ulrich Petersmann and Günther Jaenicke (eds.), *Adjudication of International Trade Disputes in International and National Economic Law* (Fribourg, 1992), p. 43

Janis, Mark W., 'Jeremy Bentham and the Fashioning of "International Law"' (1984) 78 *American Journal of International Law* 405

Jarvin, Sigvard and Yves Derains (eds.), *Collection of ICC Arbitral Awards 1974–1985* (Paris, 1990)

Jellinek, Georg, *Die rechtliche Natur der Staatenverträge: Ein Beitrag zur juristischen Construction des Völkerrechts* (Vienna, 1880)

Die Lehre von den Staatenverbindungen (Vienna, 1882)

Jenks, C. Wilfred, 'The Interpretation and Application of Municipal Law by the Permanent Court of International Justice' (1938) 19 *British Yearbook of International Law* 67

'The Scope of International Law' (1954) 31 *British Yearbook of International Law* 1

The Prospects of International Adjudication (London, 1964)

Jennings, R. Y., 'The Progress of International Law' (1958) 34 *British Yearbook of International Law* 334

The Acquisition of Territory in International Law (Manchester, 1963)

'What is International Law and How Do We Tell It When We See It?' (1981) 37 *Schweizerisches Jahrbuch für internationales Recht* 59

'Gerald Gray Fitzmaurice' (1985) 55 *British Yearbook of International Law* 1

'The Judicial Function and the Rule of Law' in *International Law at the Time of its Codification: Essays in Honour of Roberto Ago* (Milan, 1987), vol. 3, p. 139

'The Internal Judicial Practice of the International Court of Justice' (1988) 59 *British Yearbook of International Law* 31

'The Collegiate Responsibility and Authority of the International Court of Justice' in Yoram Dinstein (ed.), *International Law at a Time of Perplexity: Essays in Honour of Shabtai Rosenne* (Dordrecht, 1989), p. 343

'An International Lawyer Takes Stock' (1990) 39 *International and Comparative Law Quarterly* 513

'The "World Court" is Necessarily a Regional Court' in Daniel Bardonnet (ed.), *The Peaceful Settlement of International Disputes in Europe: Future Prospects* (Dordrecht, 1991), p. 305

'The International Court of Justice after Fifty Years' (1995) 89 *American Journal of International Law* 493

'International Lawyers and the Progressive Development of International Law' in Jerzy Makarczyk (ed.), *Theory of International Law at the Threshold of the 21st Century: Essays in Honour of Krzysztof Skubiszewski* (The Hague, 1996), p. 413

'The Judiciary, International and National, and the Development of International Law' (1996) 45 *ICLQ* 1

'The Role of the International Court of Justice' (1997) 58 *British Yearbook of International Law* 1

Collected Writings of Sir Robert Jennings (2 vols., The Hague, 1998)

'The *LaGrand* Case' (2002) 1 *Law and Practice of International Courts and Tribunals* 13

Jessup, Philip C., 'The Permanent Court of International Justice: American Accession and Amendments to the Statute' (1929) 254 *International Conciliation* 7

The United States and the World Court (Boston, 1929)

'The Customs Union Advisory Opinion' (1932) 26 *American Journal of International Law* 105

Elihu Root (2 vols., New York, 1938)

A Modern Law of Nations: An Introduction (Hamden, 1947)

Transnational Law (New Haven, 1956)

Jokl, Marcelle, *De l'interprétation des traités normatifs d'après la doctrine et la jurisprudence internationales* (Paris, 1935)

Jones, Dorothy V., *Toward a Just World: The Critical Years in the Search for International Justice* (Chicago, 2002)

Jones, J. Mervyn, 'Constitutional Limitations on the Treaty-Making Power' (1941) 35 *American Journal of International Law* 462

Full Powers and Ratifications: A Study in the Development of Treaty-Making Procedure (Cambridge, 1947)

Kaeckenbeeck, Georges, 'The Protection of Vested Rights in International Law' (1936) 17 *British Yearbook of International Law* 1

The International Experiment of Upper Silesia (London, 1942)

Kaikobad, Kaiyan Homi, *The International Court of Justice and Judicial Review: A Study of the Court's Powers with Respect to Judgments of the ILO and UN Administrative Tribunals* (The Hague, 2000)

Karl, Wolfram, *Vertrag und spätere Praxis im Völkerrecht* (Berlin, 1983)

Kastanas, Elias, *Unité et diversité: Notions autonomes et marge d'appréciation des états dans la jurisprudence de la Cour européenne des Droits de l'Homme* (Brussels, 1996)

Kaufmann, Erich, *Das Wesen des Völkerrechts und die clausula rebus sic stantibus* (Tübingen, 1911)

Probleme der Internationalen Gerichtsbarkeit (Leipzig, 1932)

'Règles générales du droit de la paix' (1935) 54 *Recueil des Cours* 313

'La Concurrence de titres juridictionnels: Observations au sujet de l'arrêt de la Cour permanente de Justice internationale du 4 avril 1939' (1940) 21 *Revue de Droit International et de Legislation Comparée* 34 (also in *Gesammelte Schriften* (Göttingen, 1960), vol. 2, p. 269)

Gesammelte Schriften (3 vols., Göttingen, 1960)

'Max Huber: ein großer Rechtsgelehrter' in Erich Kaufmann, *Gesammelte Schriften* (Göttingen, 1960), vol. 3, p. 378

Kaufmann, Hans, *Die Gutachten des Ständigen Internationalen Gerichtshofes als Mittel zwischenstaatlicher Streitschlichtung* (Basel, 1939)

Kazazi, Mojtaba, *Burden of Proof and Related Issues: A Study on Evidence Before International Tribunals* (The Hague, 1996)

Kearney, Richard D., 'Sources of Law and the International Court of Justice' in Leo Gross (ed.), *The International Court of Justice: Consideration of Requirements for Enhancing Its Rôle in the International Legal Order* (New York, 1976), p. 610

Keith, Kenneth James, *The Extent of the Advisory Jurisdiction of the International Court of Justice* (Leiden, 1971)

Kellogg, Frank B., 'Limits of the Jurisdiction of the Permanent Court of International Justice: Observations by Mr Kellogg, Judge, on Order of the Court (December 6, 1930) in the Case of the Free Zones of Upper Savoy and the District of Gex' (1931) 25 *American Journal of International Law* 203

Kelsen, Hans, 'Les Rapports de système entre le droit interne et le droit international public' (1926) 14 *Recueil des Cours* 231

Das Problem der Souveränität und die Theorie des Völkerrechts (2nd edn, Tübingen, 1928)

'Théorie générale du droit international public' (1932) 42 *Recueil des Cours* 121

'Contribution à la théorie du traité international' (1936) 10 *Revue Internationale de la Théorie du Droit* 253

'Théorie du droit international coutumier' (1939) 1 *Revue Internationale de la Théorie du Droit* 253

Law and Peace in International Relations (Cambridge, MA, 1942)

General Theory of Law and State (Cambridge, MA, 1945)

Principles of International Law (New York, 1952)

Principles of International Law (2nd edn by Robert W. Tucker, New York, 1966)

Kennedy, David, 'Theses about International Law Discourse' (1980) 23 *German Yearbook of International Law* 353

'The Move to Institutions' (1986–7) 8 *Cardozo Law Review* 841

International Legal Structures (Baden-Baden, 1987)

'A New World Order: Yesterday, Today, and Tomorrow' (1994) 4 *Transnational Law and Contemporary Problems* 329

'International Law and the Nineteenth Century: History of an Illusion' (1996) 65 *Nordic Journal of International Law* 385

'Les Clichés revisités, le droit international et la politique' in Pierre-Marie Dupuy and Charles Leben (eds.), *Droit international 4* (2000), p. 7

'When Renewal Repeats: Thinking Against the Box' (2000) 32 *New York University Journal of International Law and Politics* 335

'My Talk at the ASIL: What is New Thinking in International Law?' in American Society of International Law, *Proceedings of the 94th Annual Meeting* (Washington DC, 2000), p. 104

Kirgis, Frederic L., 'Elihu Root, James Brown Scott and the Early Years of the ASIL' in American Society of International Law, *Proceedings of the 90th Annual Meeting* (Washington DC, 1996), p. 139

Klabbers, Jan, 'The Sociological Jurisprudence of Max Huber: An Introduction' (1992) 43 *Austrian Journal of Public and International Law* 197

The Concept of Treaty in International Law (The Hague, 1996)

'Clinching the Concept of Sovereignty: Wimbledon Redux' (1998) 3 *Austrian Review of International and European Law* 345

'The Life and Times of the Law of International Organizations' (2001) 70 *Nordic Journal of International Law* 287

An Introduction to International Institutional Law (Cambridge, 2002)

Kolb, Robert, *La Bonne foi en droit international public* (Geneva, 2000)

Théorie du ius cogens international: Essai de relecture du concept (Paris, 2001)

Kopelmanas, Lazare, 'Quelques réflexions au sujet de l'art. 38, 3, du Statut de la Cour permanente de Justice internationale' (1936) 43 *Revue Générale de Droit International Public* 285

'Custom as a Means of the Creation of International Law' (1937) 18 *British Yearbook of International Law* 127

Korhonen, Outi, 'Liberalism and International Law: A Centre Projecting a Periphery' (1996) 65 *Nordic Journal of International Law* 481

International Law Situated: An Analysis of the Lawyer's Stance Towards Culture, History and Community (The Hague, 2000)

Koroma, A. G., 'International Justice in Relation to the International Court of Justice' in Kalliopi Koufa (ed.), *International Justice* (Thesaurus Acroasium, vol. 26) (Thessaloniki, 1997), p. 421

Koskenniemi, Martti, *From Apology to Utopia: The Structure of International Legal Argument* (Helsinki, 1989)

'The Future of Statehood' (1991) 32 *Harvard International Law Journal* 397

'International Law in a Post-Realist Era' (1995) 16 *Australian Yearbook of International Law* 1

'Lauterpacht: The Victorian Tradition in International Law' (1997) 8 *European Journal of International Law* 215

'Between Commitment and Cynicism: Outline for a Theory of International Law as Practice' in *Collection of Essays by Legal Advisers of States, Legal Advisers of International Organizations and Practitioners in the Field of International Law* (New York, 1999), p. 495

'Carl Schmitt, Hans Morgenthau, and the Image of Law in International Relations' in Michael Byers (ed.), *The Role of Law in International Politics* (Oxford, 2000), p. 17

The Gentle Civilizer of Nations: The Rise and Fall of International Law, 1870–1960 (Cambridge, 2001)

Krabbe, Hugo, *Die moderne Staats-idee* (The Hague, 1919)

Kunz, Joseph L., 'La Primauté du droit des gens' (1925) 6 *Revue de Droit International et de Legislation Comparée* 556

'The Meaning and the Range of the Norm *Pacta Sunt Servanda*' (1945) 39 *American Journal of International Law* 180

Kutscher, Hans, 'Methods of Interpretation as Seen by a Judge at the Court of Justice' in *Judicial and Academic Conference 27–28 September 1976* (Luxembourg, 1976), vol. 1, p. 1

Lachs, Manfred, 'The Law of Treaties: Some General Reflections on the Report of the International Law Commission' in Pierre Lalive and Jacques Freymond (eds.), *Recueil d'études de droit international en hommage à Paul Guggenheim* (Geneva, 1968), p. 391

The Teacher in International Law: Teachings and Teaching (The Hague, 1982)

'A Few Thoughts on the Independence of Judges of the International Court of Justice' (1986–7) 25 *Columbia Journal of Transnational Law* 593

'Quelques réflexions sur la communauté internationale' in *Le Droit international au service de la paix, de la justice et du developpement: Mélanges Michel Virally* (Paris, 1991), p. 349

'Le Droit international à l'aube du XXIe siècle' (1992) 99 *Revue Générale de Droit International Public* 529

Lammers, J. G., *Pollution of International Watercourses: A Search for Substantive Rules and Principles of Law* (The Hague, 1984)

Lange, Chr. L., 'Préparation de la Société des Nations pendant la guerre' in P. Munch (ed.), *Les Origines et l'oeuvre de la Société des Nations* (Copenhagen, 1923), vol. 1, p. 1

de Lapradelle, A., *Influence de la Société des Nations sur le développement du droit des gens* (Paris, 1932–3)

'Les Vies et les oeuvres: In memoriam Edouard Rolin-Jaequemyns, Albéric Rolin, Elihu Root' (1937) 19 *Revue de Droit International* 3

Les Grands cas de la jurisprudence internationale (Paris, 1939)

Maitres et doctrines du droit des gens (2nd edn, Paris, 1950)

Laun, Rudolf, *Der Wandel der Ideen Staat und Volk als äussering des Weltgewissens* (Barcelona, 1933)

Laurain, André, *La Protection des intérêts privés devant la Cour permanente de Justice internationale* (Paris, 1939)

Laurent, F., *Droit civil international* (vol. 1, Brussels, 1880)

Lauterpacht, Elihu, *Aspects of the Administration of International Justice* (Cambridge, 1991)

'The Juridical and the Meta-Juridical in International Law' in Jerzy Makarczyk (ed.), *Theory of International Law at the Threshold of the 21st Century: Essays in Honour of Krzysztof Skubiszewski* (The Hague, 1996), p. 215

Lauterpacht, H., *Private Law Sources and Analogies of International Law* (London, 1927)

'Decisions of Municipal Courts as a Source of International Law' (1929) 10 *British Yearbook of International Law* 65

'Dissenting Opinions of National Judges and the Revision of the Statute of the Court' (1930) 11 *British Yearbook of International Law* 182

'The British Reservations to the Optional Clause' (1930) 10 *Economica* 137

'The So-Called Anglo-American and Continental Schools of Thought in International Law' (1931) 12 *British Yearbook of International Law* 31

The Function of Law in the International Community (Oxford, 1933)

'Les Travaux préparatoires et l'interprétation des traités' (1934) 48 *Recueil des Cours* 713

The Development of International Law by the Permanent Court of International Justice (London, 1934)

'The Chinn Case' (1935) 16 *British Yearbook of International Law* 164

'Règles générales du droit de la paix' (1937) 62 *Recueil des Cours* 99

'Restrictive Interpretation and the Principle of Effectiveness in the Interpretation of Treaties' (1949) 26 *British Yearbook of International Law* 48

'Foreword' in Oliver J. Lissitzyn, *The International Court of Justice: Its Roles in the Maintenance of International Peace and Security* (New York, 1951), p. v

'The Problem of the Revision of the Law of War' (1952) 29 *British Yearbook of International Law* 360

'Some Observations on the Prohibition of "Non Liquet" and the Completeness of the Law' in *Symbolae Verzijl* (The Hague, 1958), p. 196

The Development of International Law by the International Court (London, 1958)

International Law – Being the Collected Papers of Hersch Lauterpacht (5 vols., Cambridge, 1970–2004)

'The Revision of the Statute of the International Court of Justice' (2002) 1 *Law and Practice of International Courts and Tribunals* 55

Lavalle, Roberto, 'About the Alleged Customary Law Nature of the Rule Pacta Sunt Servanda' (1983) 33 *Österreichische Zeitschrift für öffentliches Recht und Völkerrecht* 9

League of Nations, *The Permanent Court of International Justice* (Geneva, 1921)

Lesaffer, Randall, 'The Grotian Tradition Revisited: Change and Continuity in the History of International Law' (2002) 73 *British Yearbook of International Law* 103

Lienau, Robert Albrecht, *Stellung und Befugnisse des Präsidenten des Ständigen Internationalen Gerichtshofes* (Kiel, 1938)

Lillich, Richard B. and G. Edward White, 'The Deliberative Process of the International Court of Justice: A Preliminary Critique and Some Possible Reforms' (1976) 70 *American Journal of International Law* 28

Lipper, Jerome, 'Equitable Utilization' in A. H. Garretson, R. D. Hayton and C. J. Olmstead (eds.), *The Law of International Drainage Basins* (New York, 1967), p. 15

Lipstein, K., 'Conflict of Laws before International Tribunals' (1941) 27 *Transactions of the Grotius Society* 142

  'The Place of the Calvo Clause in International Law' (1945) 22 *British Yearbook of International Law* 130

von Liszt, Franz, *Das Völkerrecht* (12th edn by Max Fleischmann, Berlin, 1925)

Lloyd, Lorna, *Peace Through Law: Britain and the International Court in the 1920s* (London, 1997)

Loder, B. C. J., *La Cour permanente de Justice internationale: Discours prononcé à la conférence de l'Association de droit international ('International Law Association'), à Portsmouth, le 28 mai 1920* (unknown, 1920)

  'The Permanent Court of International Justice and Compulsory Jurisdiction' (1921–2) 2 *British Yearbook of International Law* 6

  La Différence entre l'arbitrage international et la justice internationale (The Hague, 1923) (also in (1923) 9 *Bulletin de l'Institut Intermédiare International* 257)

  Speech delivered by Dr B. C. J. Loder at the Banquet Given by the Anglo-Batavian Society, in London on February 28th, 1923, in the Inner Temple Hall (The Hague, 1923)

Lorenzen, Ernest G., *Selected Articles on the Conflict of Laws* (New Haven, 1947)

Lowe, A. V., 'Public International Law and the Conflict of Laws: The European Response to the United States Export Administration Regulations' (1984) 33 *International and Comparative Law Quarterly* 515

  'The Politics of Law-Making: Are the Method and Character of Norm Creation Changing?' in Michael Byers (ed.), *The Role of Law in International Politics* (Oxford, 2000), p. 207

MacCormick, Neil, 'Beyond the Sovereign State' (1994) 54 *Modern Law Review* 1

Macdonald, R. St J., 'The Margin of Appreciation' in R. St J. Macdonald, F. Matscher and H. Petzold (eds.), *The European System for the Protection of Human Rights* (Dordrecht, 1993), p. 83

Mackenzie, Ruth and Philippe Sands, 'International Courts and Tribunals and the Independence of the International Judge' (2003) 44 *Harvard International Law Journal* 271

de Magyary, Geza, *Die internationale Schiedsgerichtsbarkeit im Völkerbunde* (Berlin, 1922)

  La Juridiction de la Cour permanente de Justice internationale (Paris, 1931)

Mahoney, Paul, 'Judicial Activism and Judicial Self-Restraint in the European Court of Human Rights: Two Sides of the Same Coin' (1990) 11 *Human Rights Law Journal* 57

Mancini, G. Federico, 'The Making of a Constitution for Europe' (1989) 26
    Common Market Law Review 595
Mandelstam, A. Nicolayévitch, 'La Conciliation internationale d'après le
    pacte et la jurisprudence du Conseil de la Société des Nations' (1926) 14
    Recueil des Cours 333
Marek, Krystyna, 'Les Rapports entre le droit international et le droit interne à
    la lumière de la jurisprudence de la Cour permanente de Justice
    internationale' (1962) 66 *Revue Générale de Droit International Public*
    260
    Identity and Continuity of States in Public International Law (2nd edn, Geneva,
    1968)
von Martens, Georg Friedrich, *Précis du droit des gens moderne de l'Europe fondé sur
    les traités et l'usage* (2 vols., Göttingen, 1789)
    Précis du droit des gens moderne de l'Europe (2nd edn by Charles Vergé, Paris,
    1864)
Massart, Eugenio, *La giurisdizione di costituzionalità nella Società delle Nazioni* (Pisa,
    1931)
    La Corte permanente di Giustizia internazionale e gli interessi privati (Pisa, 1932)
Matscher F., 'Methods of Interpretation of the Convention' in R. St J.
    Macdonald, F. Matscher and H. Petzold (eds.), *The European System for the
    Protection of Human Rights* (Dordrecht, 1993), p. 63
Matsushita, Masatoshi, *Japan in the League of Nations* (New York, 1929)
McCaffrey, Stephen C., *The Law of International Watercourses – Non-Navigation Uses*
    (Oxford, 2001)
McNair, Arnold D., 'The Council's Request for an Advisory Opinion' (1926) 7
    British Yearbook of International Law 1
    'La Termination et la dissolution des traités' (1928) 22 *Recueil des Cours* 463
    The Law of Treaties: British Practice and Opinions (Oxford, 1938)
    The Development of International Justice (New York, 1954)
    The Law of Treaties: British Practice and Opinions (2nd edn, Oxford, 1961)
    'Sir Cecil James Barrington Hurst, GCMG, KCB, QC, LLD' (1962) 38 *British
    Yearbook of International Law* 400
    The Expansion of International Law (Jerusalem, 1962)
McRae, Donald M., 'The Contribution of International Trade Law to the
    Development of International Law' (1996) 260 *Recueil des Cours* 99
    'The WTO in International Law: Tradition Continued or New Frontier?' (2000)
    3 *Journal of International Economic Law* 27
McWhinney, Edward, *The World Court and the Contemporary International
    Law-Making Process* (Alphen aan den Rijn, 1979)
    'The Legislative Rôle of the World Court in an Era of Transition' in Rudolf
    Bernhard, Wilhelm Karl Geck, Günther Jaenicke and Helmut Steinberg
    (eds.), *Völkerrecht als Rechtsordnung – Internationale Gerichtsbarkeit –
    Menschenrechte: Festschrift für Hermann Mosler* (Berlin, 1983), p. 567
    *Supreme Courts and Judicial Law-Making: Constitutional Tribunals and Constitutional
    Review* (Dordrecht, 1986)

The International Court of Justice and the Western Tradition of International Law (Dordrecht, 1987)

Judicial Settlement of International Disputes: Jurisdiction, Justiciability and Judicial Law-Making on the Contemporary International Court (Dordrecht, 1991)

'"Internationalizing" the International Court: The Quest for Ethno-Cultural and Legal-Systemic Representativeness' in Emmanuel G. Bello and Bola A. Ajibola (eds.), *Essays in Honour of Judge Taslim Olawale Elias* (Dordrecht, 1992), p. 277

'The Role and Mission of the International Court in an Era of Historical Transition' in Nandasiri Jasentuliyana (ed.), *Perspectives on International Law: Essays in Honour of Judge Manfred Lachs* (The Hague, 1995), p. 217

'The International Court and Judicial Law-Making: Nuclear Tests Re-visited' in Jerzy Makarczyk (ed.), *Theory of International Law at the Threshold of the 21st Century: Essays in Honour of Krzysztof Skubiszewski* (The Hague, 1996), p. 215

Memorial Hall of the M. Adachi Foundation, *Dr M. Adachi: Conscience of the World* (Tokyo, 1969)

Mendelson, Maurice, 'The Subjective Element in Customary International Law' (1995) 66 *British Yearbook of International Law* 177

Merrills, J. G., *Anatomy of International Law: A Study of the Role of International Law in the Contemporary World* (2nd edn, London, 1981)

The Development of International Law by the European Court of Human Rights (2nd edn, Manchester, 1993)

'The Optional Clause Revisited' (1993) 64 *British Yearbook of International Law* 244

International Dispute Settlement (3rd edn, Cambridge, 1998)

'The Contribution of the Permanent Court of Arbitration to International Law and to the Settlement of Disputes by Peaceful Means' in P. Hamilton, H. C. Requena, L. van Scheltinga and B. Shifman (eds.), *The Permanent Court of Arbitration: International Arbitration and Dispute Resolution* (The Hague, 1999), p. 3

Meyer, Howard N., *The World Court in Action: Judging among the Nations* (Lanham, 2002)

Miller, David Hunter, *The Drafting of the Covenant* (2 vols., New York, 1928)

Mirkine-Guetzévitch, B., 'Droit international et droit constitutionnel' (1931) 38 *Recueil des Cours* 311

de Montesquieu, Charles, *The Spirit of the Laws* (Cambridge, 1989) (originally published 1748)

Moore, John Bassett, *History and Digest of International Arbitrations to Which the United States Has Been a Party* (6 vols., Washington DC, 1898)

A Digest of International Law (8 vols., Washington DC, 1906)

'The Organization of the Permanent Court of International Justice' (1922) 22 *Columbia Law Review* 497

International Law and Some Current Illusions and Other Essays (New York, 1924)

'The Permanent Court of International Justice' (1924) 197 *International Conciliation* 91

'General Introduction' and 'Notes on the Historical and Legal Phases of the Adjudication of International Disputes' in John Bassett Moore (ed.), *International Adjudications Ancient and Modern: History and Documents, Modern Series* (New York, 1929), vol. 1, pp. vii and xv

'Fifty Years of International Law' (1936–7) 50 *Harvard Law Review* 395

The Collected Papers of John Bassett Moore (7 vols., New Haven, 1944)

Morellet, Jean, *L'organisation de la Cour permanente de Justice internationale* (Paris, 1921)

Morgenthau, Hans, *Die internationale Rechtspflege: Ihr Wesen und ihre Grenzen* (Leipzig, 1929)

'Positivism, Functionalism, and International Law' (1940) 34 *American Journal of International Law* 260

Politics among Nations: The Struggle for Power and Peace (5th edn, New York, 1973)

Moser, Johann Jakob, *Deutsches auswärtiges Staatsrecht* (Leipzig, 1772)

Mosler, Hermann, 'Völkerrecht als Rechtsordnung' (1976) 36 *Zeitschrift für ausländisches öffentliches Recht und Völkerrecht* 6

The International Society as a Legal Community (Alphen aan den Rijn, 1980)

Mosler, H. and R. Bernhardt (eds.), *Judicial Settlement of International Disputes* (Berlin, 1974)

Münch, Fritz, 'Das Wesen der Rechtsprechung als Leitbegriff für die Tätigkeit des Internationalen Gerichtshofs' (1971) 31 *Zeitschrift für ausländisches öffentliches Recht und Völkerrecht* 712

Nafziger, James A. R., 'Some Remarks on the Writing Style of the International Court of Justice' in T. Buergenthal (ed.), *Contemporary Issues in International Law: Essays in Honor of Louis B. Sohn* (Kehl, 1984), p. 325

Negulesco, Démètre, 'La Jurisprudence de la Cour permanente de Justice internationale' (1926) 33 *Revue Générale de Droit International Public* 194

Conférence sur la jurisprudence de la Cour permanente de Justice internationale (Paris, 1927)

'L'évolution de la procédure des avis consultatifs de la Cour permanente de Justice internationale' (1936) 57 *Recueil des Cours* 5

Nippold, Otfried, *The Development of International Law After the World War* (Oxford, 1923)

Nolte, Georg, 'From Dionisio Anzilotti to Roberto Ago: The Classical International Law of State Responsibility and the Traditional Primacy of a Bilateral Conception of Inter-State Relations' (2002) 13 *European Journal of International Law* 1083

Nussbaum, Arthur, 'Rise and Fall of the Law-of-Nations Doctrine in the Conflict of Laws' (1942) 42 *Columbia Law Review* 189

A Concise History of the Law of Nations (2nd edn, New York, 1958)

Nyholm, D. G., *Le Tribunal mondial* (Cairo, 1918)

'La Cour permanente de Justice internationale' in P. Munch (ed.), *Les Origines et l'oeuvre de la Société des Nations* (Copenhagen, 1924), vol. 2, p. 241

O'Connell, D. P., *International Law* (2 vols., 2nd edn, London, 1970)

Oda, Shigeru, 'The Compulsory Jurisdiction of the International Court of
    Justice: A Myth?' (2000) 49 *International and Comparative Law Quarterly* 251
Oppenheim, L., *International Law* (2 vols., London, 1905–6)
    Die Zukunft des Völkerrecht (Leipzig, 1911)
    The League of Nations and Its Problems (London, 1919)
    The Future of International Law (Oxford, 1921)
    International Law (2 vols., 4th edn by Arnold D. McNair, London, 1926–8)
    International Law (2 vols., 5th edn by H. Lauterpacht, London, 1935–7)
Ost, François, 'The Original Canons of Interpretation of the European Court of
    Human Rights' in Mireille Delmas-Marty (ed.), *The European Convention for
    the Protection of Human Rights: International Protection Versus National
    Restrictions* (Dordrecht, 1992), p. 283
Paasivirta, Esa, *Participation of States in International Contracts and Arbitral
    Settlements of Disputes* (Helsinki, 1990)
Parry, Clive, *The Sources and Evidences of International Law* (Manchester, 1965)
    'The Law of Treaties' in Max Sørensen (ed.), *Manual of Public International Law*
    (London, 1968), p. 175
Paulus, Andreas L., *Die internationale Gemeinschaft im Völkerrecht: Eine Untersuchung
    zur Entwicklung des Völkerrechts im Zeitalter der Globalisierung* (Munich, 2001)
    'The Influence of the United States on the Concept of the "International
    Community"' in Michael Byers and Georg Nolte (eds.), *United States
    Hegemony and the Foundations of International Law* (Cambridge, 2003), p. 57
Perassi, Tomaso, 'Dionisio Anzilotti' (1953) 36 *Rivista di Diritto internazionale* 5
Pereira da Silva, Fernando, *La Réforme de la Cour permanente de Justice
    internationale: Le Protocole de 1929 et le veto de Cuba* (Paris, 1931)
Permanent Court of International Justice, *Ten Years of International Jurisprudence,
    1922–1932* (Leiden, 1932)
    The Permanent Court of International Justice at The Hague (Leiden, 1939)
Pessôa, Epitácio, *Côrte permanente de justiça internacional (1923–1930)* (Obras
    completas de Epitácio Pessôa, vol. 23) (Rio de Janeiro, 1960)
Petrén, Sture, 'Forms of Expression of Judicial Activity' in Leo Gross (ed.), *The
    Future of the International Court of Justice* (New York, 1976), p. 445
Philipse, A. H., *Les Fonctions consultatives de la Cour permanente de Justice
    internationale* (Lausanne, 1928)
Phillimore, Lord, 'Schemes for Maintaining General Peace' in *Peace Handbooks
    Issued by the Historical Section of the Foreign Office* (London, 1920), vol. 25,
    No. 160
    'Scheme for the Permanent Court of International Justice' (1920) 6
    Transactions of the Grotius Society 89
    'The Third Committee: The Permanent Court of International Justice' in Lord
    Robert Cecil and Lord Phillimore (eds.), *The First Assembly: A Study of the
    Proceedings of the First Assembly of the League of Nations* (London, 1921),
    p. 147
Phillimore, Robert, *Commentaries upon International Law* (3 vols., 3rd edn,
    London, 1879–85)

Pictet, Jean, 'Centenary of the Birth of Max Huber' (1974) 14 *International Review of the Red Cross* 631

Politis, N., *La Justice internationale* (Paris, 1924)

'Le Problème des limitations de la souveraineté et la théorie de l'abus des droits dans les rapports internationaux' (1925) 6 *Recueil des Cours* 5

'How the World Court Has Functioned' (1925–6) 4 *Foreign Affairs* 443

'Méthodes d'interprétation du droit international conventionnel' in *Recueil d'études sur les sources du droit en l'honneur de François Gény* (Paris, 1934), vol. 3, p. 375

Pollard, Robert Thomas, *China's Foreign Relations, 1917–1931* (New York, 1933)

Pollock, Ernest, 'The International Court of the League of Nations' (1921–3) 1 *Cambridge Law Journal* 29

Pomerance, Michla, *The Advisory Function of the International Court* (Baltimore, 1973)

'The United States and the Advisory Function of the Permanent Court of International Justice' in Yoram Dinstein (ed.), *International Law at a Time of Perplexity: Essays in Honour of Shabtai Rosenne* (Dordrecht, 1989), p. 567

The United States and the World Court as a 'Supreme Court of the Nations': Dreams, Illusions, and Disillusion (The Hague, 1996)

Potter, Pitman B., 'Origin of the Term "International Organization"' (1945) 39 *American Journal of International Law* 803

Pratap, Dharma, *The Advisory Jurisdiction of the International Court* (Oxford, 1972)

Prott, Lyndell V., 'The Role of the Judge of the International Court of Justice' (1974) 10 *Revue Belge de Droit International* 473

The Latent Power of Culture and the International Judge (Abingdon, 1979)

Pusey, Merlo J., *Charles Evans Hughes* (New York, 1963)

Rabel, Ernst, *The Conflict of Laws: A Comparative Study* (3 vols., 2nd edn by Ulrich Drobnig, Ann Arbor, 1958–64)

Raftopoulos, Evangelos, *The Inadequacy of the Contractual Analogy in the Law of Treaties* (Athens, 1990)

Ragazzi, Maurizio, *The Concept of International Obligations Erga Omnes* (Oxford, 1997)

Ranshofen-Wertheimer, Egon F., *The International Secretariat: A Great Experiment in International Administration* (Washington DC, 1945)

Ray, Jean, *Commentaire du Pacte de la Société des Nations selon la politique et la jurisprudence des organes de la Société* (Paris, 1930)

'Des Conflits entre principes abstraits et stipulations conventionnelles' (1934) 48 *Recueil des Cours* 635

Raz, Joseph, *The Authority of Law: Essays on Law and Morality* (Oxford, 1979)

Rebbe, Walter, *Der Lotusfall vor dem Weltgerichtshof* (Leipzig, 1932)

Registry of the International Court of Justice, *The International Court of Justice* (4th edn, The Hague, 1996)

Reisman, W. Michael, *Nullity and Revision: The Review and Enforcement of International Judgments and Awards* (New Haven, 1971)

'Lassa Oppenheim's Nine Lives' (1994) 19 *Yale Journal of International Law* 255

Remlinger, E., *Les Avis consultatifs de la Cour permanente de Justice internationale* (Paris, 1938)

Renault, Louis, *Introduction à l'étude de droit international* (Paris, 1879)

L'oeuvre de la Haye en 1899 et en 1907 (Stockholm, 1908)

L'oeuvre internationale (Paris, 1932)

Research Project in International Law under the Auspices of the Faculty of the Harvard Law School, 'Part III: The Law of Treaties' (1935) *Supplement to the American Journal of International Law* 651

Reut-Nicolussi, Eduard, 'The Reform of the Permanent Court of International Justice' (1939) 25 *Transactions of the Grotius Society* 135

Unparteilichkeit in Völkerrecht (Innsbruck, 1940)

'The Permanent Court of International Justice Viewed as an Experiment' (1941) 7 *Research and Progress* 107

Reuter, Paul, *An Introduction to the Law of Treaties* (2nd edn, London, 1995)

Reydams, Luc, *Universal Jurisdiction: International and Municipal Legal Perspectives* (Oxford, 2003)

Riese, Otto, 'Über den Rechtsschutz innerhalb der Europäischen Gemeinschaften' (1966) 1 *Europarecht* 24

Rigaux, François, 'An Exemplary Lawyer's Life (1884–1973)' (2000) 11 *European Journal of International Law* 877

Rivier, Alphonse, *Principes du droit des gens* (2 vols., Paris, 1896)

Roberts, Anthea Elizabeth, 'Traditional and Modern Approaches to Customary International Law: A Reconciliation' (2001) 95 *American Journal of International Law* 757

Robinson, Jacob, Oscar Karbach, Max M. Laserson, Nehemiah Robinson and Marc Vichniak, *Were the Minorities Treaties a Failure?* (New York, 1943)

Romano, Cesare P. R., 'The Proliferation of International Judicial Bodies: The Pieces of the Puzzle' (1999) 31 *New York University Journal of International Law and Politics* 709

Root, Elihu, 'The Constitution of an International Court of Justice' (1921) 15 *American Journal of International Law* 1

'The Permanent Court of International Justice' in American Society of International Law, *Proceedings of the 17th Annual Meeting* (Washington DC, 1923), p. 1

Men and Policies: Addresses (Cambridge, 1925)

Rosenne, Shabtai, *The International Court of Justice: An Essay in Political and Legal Theory* (Leiden, 1957)

'Sir Hersch Lauterpacht's Concept of the Task of the International Judge' (1961) 55 *American Journal of International Law* 825

The World Court: What It Is and How It Works (Leiden, 1962)

'On the Non-Use of the Advisory Competence of the International Court of Justice' (1963) 39 *British Yearbook of International Law* 1

The Law and Practice of the International Court (Leiden, 1965)

'Interpretation of Treaties in the Restatement and the International Law Commission's Draft Articles: A Comparison' (1966) 5 *Columbia Journal of Transnational Law* 205

'Bilateralism and Community Interest in the Codified Law of Treaties' in
Wolfgang Friedmann, Louis Henkin and Oliver Lissitzyn (eds.), *Transnational
Law in a Changing Society: Essays in Honor of Philip C. Jessup* (New York, 1972),
p. 202

Committee of Experts for the Progressive Codification of International Law (2 vols.,
New York, 1972)

Conference for the Codification of International Law [1930] (4 vols., New York, 1975)

'The Composition of the Court' in Leo Gross (ed.), *The Future of the
International Court of Justice* (Dobbs Ferry, 1976), p. 377

Developments in the Law of Treaties, 1945–1986 (Cambridge, 1989)

An International Law Miscellany (Dordrecht, 1993)

The World Court: What It Is and How It Works (5th edn, Dordrecht, 1995)

'The Contribution of the International Court of Justice to the United Nations'
in M. S. Rajan (ed.), *United Nations at Fifty and Beyond* (New Delhi, 1996),
p. 123

'Presentation' in Connie Peck and Roy S. Lee (eds.), *Increasing the Effectiveness of
the International Court of Justice* (The Hague, 1997), p. 466

The Law and Practice of the International Court, 1920–1996 (4 vols., The Hague,
1997)

'Updates to Law and Practice of the International Court of Justice
(1920–1996)' (2002) 1 *Law and Practice of International Courts and Tribunals* 129

The World Court: What It Is and How It Works (6th edn by Terry D. Gill, Leiden,
2003)

Ross, Alf, *A Textbook in International Law* (London, 1947)

On Law and Justice (London, 1958)

Rousseau, Ch., 'De la compatibilité des normes juridiques contradictoires dans
l'ordre international' (1932) 39 *Revue Générale de Droit International Public* 133

Principes généraux du droit international public (Paris, 1944)

Röben, Volker, 'Le Précédent dans la jurisprudence de la Cour internationale'
(1989) 32 *German Yearbook of International Law* 382

Römer'is, Michel, 'La Juridiction dite "Statutaire" en Lithuanie en ce qui
concerne le territoire autonome de Memel' (1936) 2 *Revue Internationale
Française du Droit des Gens* 361

'Le Système juridique des garanties de la souveraineté de la Lithuanie sur le
territoire de Memel' (1936) 43 *Revue Générale de Droit International Public* 257

Ruda, José María, 'The Opinions of Judge Dionisio Anzilotti at the Permanent
Court of International Justice' (1992) 3 *European Journal of International Law*
100

Ruegger, Paul, 'Die auswärtige Verwaltung als Magistratur des
völkerrechtlichen Verkehrs' in *Festgabe für Max Huber zum sechzigsten
Geburtstag 28. Dezember 1934* (Zurich, 1934), p. 167

*Max Huber: Zum Erschienen seiner 'Denkwürdigkeiten, 1907–1924' anlasslich seines
100. Geburtstage* (Zurich, 1974) (reprinted from (1974–5) 54 *Schweizer
Monatshefte Sonderbeilage* zu Heft 9)

Rundstein, Simon, 'La Cour permanente de Justice internationale comme
instance de recours' (1935) 43 *Recueil des Cours* 5

Salvioli, Gabriele, *La Corte Permanente di Giustizia Internazionale* (Rome, 1924)
'La Jurisprudence de la Cour permanente de Justice internationale' (1926) 12 *Recueil des Cours* 3
'Il caso del "Lotus"' (1927) 19 *Rivista di Diritto Internazionale* 521
'Les Rapports entre le jugement sur la compétence et celui sur la fond dans la jurisprudence internationale' (1929) 36 *Revue Générale de Droit International Public* 108
Samore, William, 'National Origins v. Impartial Decisions: A Study of World Court Holdings' (1956) 34 *Chicago-Kent Law Review* 198
Sands, Philippe, 'Turtles and Torturers: The Transformation of International Law' (2001) 33 *New York University Journal of International Law and Politics* 527
Sands, Philippe and Pierre Klein, *Bowett's Law of International Institutions* (5th edn, London, 2001)
von Savigny, Friedrich Carl, *A Treatise on the Conflict of Laws* (2nd edn, Edinburgh, 1880) (originally published 1849)
Scelle, Georges, *Précis de droit de gens* (2 vols., Paris, 1932–4)
'Essai sur les sources formelles du droit international' in *Recueil d'études sur les sources du droit en l'honneur de François Gény* (Paris, 1934), vol. 3, p. 400
Scerni, Mario, 'La Procédure de la Cour permanente de Justice internationale' (1938) 65 *Recueil des Cours* 565
Schachter, Oscar, 'Creativity and Objectivity in International Tribunals' in Rudolf Bernhard, Wilhelm Karl Geck, Günther Jaenicke and Helmut Steinberg (eds.), *Völkerrecht als Rechtsordnung – Internationale Gerichtsbarkeit – Menschenrechte: Festschrift für Hermann Mosler* (Berlin, 1983), p. 813
International Law in Theory and Practice (Dordrecht, 1991)
Schermers, Henry G. and Niels M. Blokker, *International Institutional Law* (3rd edn, The Hague, 1995)
Schindler, Dietrich, 'Les Progrès de l'arbitrage obligatoire depuis la création de la Société des Nations' (1928) 25 *Recueil des Cours* 237
'Contribution à l'étude des facteurs sociologiques et psychologiques du droit international' (1933) 46 *Recueil des Cours* 233
Die Schiedsgerichtsbarkeit seit 1914: Entwicklung und heutiger Stand (Stuttgart, 1938)
Schlochauer, Hans-Jürgen, 'The Permanent Court of International Justice' in Rudolf Bernhardt (ed.), *Encyclopedia of Public International Law* (Amsterdam, 1997), vol. 3, p. 988
Schmitt, Carl, *Die Kernfrage des Völkerbundes* (Berlin, 1926)
Der Nomos der Erde im Völkerrecht des Jus Publicum Europaeum (Cologne, 1950)
Schreuer, Christoph H., *The ICSID Convention: A Commentary* (Cambridge, 2001)
Schuyt, C. J. M., *Rechtssociologie: een terreinverkenning* (Rotterdam, 1971)
Schücking, Christoph-Bernhard, 'Walther Schücking: Ein Lebensbild' in *Fünfzig Jahre Institut für Internationales Recht an der Universität Kiel* (Kiel, 1965), p. 174
Schücking, Walther, 'Die Organisation der Welt' in *Staatsrechtliche Abhandlungen: Festgabe für Laband* (Tübingen, 1908), p. 533
Der Staatenverband der Haager Konferenzen (Munich, 1912)

Der Bund der Völker: Studien und Vorträge zum organisatorischen Pazifismus (Leipzig, 1918)

The International Union of the Hague Conferences (Oxford, 1918)

Ein neues Zeitalter?: Kritik am Pariser Völkerbundentwurf (Berlin, 1919)

'Der Völkerbundsentwurf des Deutschen Regierung' in P. Munch (ed.), *Les Origines et l'oeuvre de la Société des Nations* (Copenhagen, 1923), vol. 1, p. 138

'Le Développement du Pacte de la Société des Nations' (1927) 20 *Recueil des Cours* 353

Die Revision der Völkerbundssatzung im Hinblick auf den Kelloggpakt (Berlin, 1931)

Schücking, Walther and Hans Wehberg, *Die Satzung des Völkerbundes* (2nd edn, Berlin, 1924)

Schwarzenberger, George, *The League of Nations and World Order: A Treatise on the Principle of Universality in the Theory and Practice of the League of Nations* (London, 1936)

'The Development of International Economic and Financial Law by the Permanent Court of International Justice' (1942) 54 *Juridical Review* 21 and 80

'The Fundamental Principles of International Law' (1955) 87 *Recueil des Cours* 195

International Law as Applied by International Courts and Tribunals (3rd edn, London, 1957), vol. 1

The Frontiers of International Law (London, 1962)

International Law and Order (London, 1971)

International Law as Applied by International Courts and Tribunals (London, 1986), vol. 4

Schwebel, Stephen M., 'Reflections on the Role of the International Court of Justice' (1986) 61 *Washington Law Review* 1061

'The Docket and Decisionmaking Process of the International Court of Justice' (1989) 13 *Suffolk Transnational Law Journal* 543

'Was the Capacity to Request an Advisory Opinion Wider in the Permanent Court of International Justice Than It Is in the International Court of Justice' (1991) 62 *British Yearbook of International Law* 77

'The Roles of the Security Council and the International Court of Justice in the Application of International Humanitarian Law' (1995) 27 *New York University Journal of International Law and Politics* 731

'May Preparatory Work Be Used to Correct Rather Than Confirm the "Clear" Meaning of a Treaty Provision?' in Jerzy Makarczyk (ed.), *Theory of International Law at the Threshold of the 21st Century: Essays in Honour of Krzysztof Skubiszewski* (The Hague, 1996), p. 541

'National Judges and Judges Ad Hoc of the International Court of Justice' (1999) 48 *International and Comparative Law Quarterly* 889

Scobbie, Iain, 'Towards the Elimination of International Law: Some Radical Scepticism about Sceptical Radicalism' (1990) 61 *British Yearbook of International Law* 339

'The Theorist as Judge: Hersch Lauterpacht's Concept of the International Judicial Function' (1997) 8 *European Journal of International Law* 264

'*Res Judicata*, Precedent and the International Court: A Preliminary Sketch' (1999) 20 *Australian Yearbook of International Law* 299

Scott, James Brown, *The Status of the International Court of Justice* (New York, 1916)

'A Permanent Court of International Justice' (1920) 14 *American Journal of International Law* 581

The Project of a Permanent Court of International Justice and Resolutions of the Advisory Committee of Jurists (Washington DC, 1920)

The Proceedings of the Hague Peace Conferences: The Conference of 1899 (London, 1920)

The Proceedings of the Hague Peace Conferences: The Conference of 1907 (2 vols., London, 1920–1)

'A Permanent Court of International Justice' (1921) 15 *American Journal of International Law* 52

'The Permanent Court of International Justice' (1921) 15 *American Journal of International Law* 260

Séfériadès, S., 'Aperçus sur la coutume juridique internationale et notamment sur son fondement' (1936) 43 *Revue Générale de Droit International Public* 129

Sekino, Shoichi, 'Dr Minéitcirô Adatci: The Centenary of His Birth' (1970) 14 *Japanese Annual of International Law* 59

Sereni, Angelo Piero, *The Italian Conception of International Law* (New York, 1943)

Shahabuddeen, Mohamed, *Precedent in the World Court* (Cambridge, 1996)

Shany, Yuval, *The Competing Jurisdictions of International Courts and Tribunals* (Oxford, 2003)

Shihata, Ibrahim F. I., *The Power of the International Court to Determine Its Own Jurisdiction* (The Hague, 1965)

Sicart-Bozec, Michele, *Les Juges du tiers monde à la Cour internationale de Justice* (Paris, 1986)

Simma, Bruno, 'Self-Contained Regimes' (1985) 16 *Netherlands Yearbook of International Law* 111

'Bilateralism and Community Interest in the Law of State Responsibility' in Yoram Dinstein (ed.), *International Law at a Time of Perplexity: Essays in Honour of Shabtai Rosenne* (Dordrecht, 1989), p. 821

'From Bilaterlism to Community Interest in International Law' (1994) 250 *Recueil des Cours* 217

(ed.), *The Charter of the United Nations: A Commentary* (2nd edn, Oxford, 2002)

Simma, Bruno and Philip Alston, 'The Sources of Human Rights Law: Custom, Jus Cogens and General Principles' (1992) 12 *Australian Yearbook of International Law* 82

Simma, Bruno and Andreas L. Paulus, 'The "International Community": Facing the Challenge of Globalization' (1998) 9 *European Journal of International Law* 266

'The Responsability of Individuals for Human Rights Abuses in Internal Conflicts: A Positivist View' (1999) 93 *American Journal of International Law* 302

Simon, Denys, *L'interprétation judiciaire des traités d'organisations internationales: Morphologie des conventions et fonction juridictionnelle* (Paris, 1981)

Simpson, A. W. Brian, 'Hersch Lauterpacht and the Genesis of the Age of Human Rights' (2004) 120 *Law Quarterly Review* 49

Simpson, J. L. and Hazel Fox, *International Arbitration: Law and Practice* (London, 1959)

Sinclair, Ian, *The Vienna Convention on the Law of Treaties* (2nd edn, Manchester, 1984)

Skubiszewski, Krzysztof, 'Elements of Custom and the Hague Court' (1971) 31 *Zeitschrift für ausländisches öffentliches Recht und Völkerrecht* 810

Smith, Carsten, *The Relation between Proceedings and Premises: A Study in International Law* (Oslo, 1962)

Società italiana per l'organizzazione internazionale, *Opere di Dionisio Anzilotti* (4 vols., Padua, 1955–63)

Sohn, Louis B., 'The Function of International Arbitration Today' (1963) 108 *Recueil des Cours* 9

Spencer, John H., *L'interprétation des traités par les travaux préparatoires* (Paris, 1934)

Spender, Percy, 'The Office of the President of the International Court of Justice' (1965) 1 *Australian Yearbook of International Law* 9

Spiermann, Ole, '*Lotus* and the Double Structure of International Legal Argument' in Laurence Boisson de Chazournes and Philippe Sands (eds.), *International Law, the International Court of Justice and Nuclear Weapons* (Cambridge, 1999), p. 131

'The Other Side of the Story: An Unpopular Essay on the Making of the European Community Legal Order' (1999) 10 *European Journal of International Law* 763

'Humanitarian Intervention as a Necessity and the Threat or Use of *Jus Cogens*' (2002) 71 *Nordic Journal of International Law* 523

'"Who Attempts Too Much Does Nothing Well": The 1920 Advisory Committee of Jurists and the Statute of the Permanent Court of International Justice' (2002) 73 *British Yearbook of International Law* 187

'A National Lawyer Takes Stock: Professor Ross' Textbook and Other Forays into International Law' (2003) 14 *European Journal of International Law* 675

'The *LaGrand* case and the Individual as a Subject of International Law' (2003) 58 *Zeitschrift für öffentliches Recht* 197

Spiropoulos, Jean, *Die allgemeinen Rechtsgrundsätze im Völkerrecht: Eine Auslegung von Art. 38(3) des Statuts des Ständigen Internationalen Gerichtshofs* (Kiel, 1928)

von Stauffenberg, B. Schenk, 'Die Zuständigkeit des Ständigen Internationalen Gerichtshofs für die sogenannten politischen Streitigkeiten' (1934) 39 *Deutsche Juristen-Zeitung* 1325

Statut et règlement de la Cour permanente de Justice internationale: Eléments d'interprétation (Berlin, 1934)

'Das Urteil des Ständigen Internationalen Gerichtshofs im Fall Oscar Chinn, vom 12. Dezember 1934' (1935) 5 *Zeitschrift für ausländisches öffentliches Recht und Völkerrecht* 195

'Die Revision des Statuts des Ständigen Internationalen Gerichtshofs' (1936) 6 *Zeitschrift für ausländisches öffentliches Recht und Völkerrecht* 89

'Gutachten des Ständigen Internationalen Gerichtshofs vom 4. Dezember 1935 über die Vereinbarkeit gewisser Danziger Verordnungen mit der Verfassung der Freien Stadt' (1936) 6 *Zeitschrift für ausländisches öffentliches Recht und Völkerrecht* 153

Steinberger, Helmut, 'The International Court of Justice' in H. Mosler and R. Bernhardt (eds.), *Judicial Settlement of International Disputes* (Berlin, 1974), p. 193

Steiner, Arthur, 'Fundamental Conceptions of International Law in the Jurisprudence of the Permanent Court of International Justice' (1936) 30 *American Journal of International Law* 414

Stern, Birgitte, 'La Coutume au coeur du droit international' in *Mélanges offerts à Paul Reuter* (Paris, 1981), p. 479

Stevenson, John R., 'The Relationship of Private International Law to Public International Law' (1952) 52 *Columbia Law Review* 561

Stillmunkes, Pierre, 'Le *Forum prorogatum* devant la Cour permanente de Justice international et la Cour internationale' (1964) 68 *Revue Générale de Droit International Public* 665

Stone, Julius, 'Fictional Elements in Treaty Interpretation: A Study in the International Judicial Process' (1953–4) 1 *Sydney Law Review* 344

Legal Control of International Conflict: A Treatise on the Dynamics of Disputes – and War-Law (London, 1954)

'*Non Liquet* and the Function of Law in the International Community' (1959) 35 *British Yearbook of International Law* 124

Story, Joseph, *Commentaries on the Conflict of Laws* (8th edn by Melville M. Bigelow, Boston, 1883)

Strebel, Helmut, 'Erzwungener, verkappter Monismus des Ständigen Internationalen Gerichtshofes?: Eine Entgegnung' (1971) 31 *Zeitschrift für ausländisches öffentliches Recht und Völkerrecht* 855

Strupp, Karl, 'Le Droit du juge international de statuer selon l'équité' (1930) 33 *Recueil des Cours* 357

'Les Règles générales du droit de la paix' (1934) 47 *Recueil des Cours* 263

Stuyt, A. M., *Survey of International Arbitrations, 1794–1989* (3rd edn, Dordrecht, 1990)

Suh, Il Ro, 'Voting Behaviour of National Judges in International Courts' (1969) 63 *American Journal of International Law* 224

Sukiennicki, Wiktor, *La Souveraineté des états en droit international moderne* (Paris, 1927)

Suy, Eric, *Les Actes juridiques unilatéraux en droit international public* (Paris, 1962)

Sztucki, Jerzy, *Interim Measures in the Hague Court: An Attempt at a Scrutiny* (Deventer, 1983)

Sørensen, Max, 'The Modification of Collective Treaties without the Consent of All the Contracting Parties' (1938) 9 *Acta scandinavica juris gentium* 150

Les Sources du droit international: Etude sur la jurisprudence de la Cour permanente de Justice internationale (Copenhagen, 1946)

Manual of Public International Law (London, 1968)

Tachi, Sakutaro, *La Souveraineté et l'indépendance de l'état et les questions intérieures en droit international* (Paris, 1930)

Temperley, H. W. (ed.), *A History of the Peace Conference of Paris* (6 vols., London, 1920–4)

Terry, G., 'Factional Behaviour on the International Court of Justice: An Analysis of the First and Second Courts (1945–1951) and the Sixth and Seventh Courts (1961–1967)' (1975) 10 *Melbourne University Law Review* 59

Téson, Fernando R., 'The Kantian Theory of International Law' (1992) 92 *Columbia Law Review* 53

Thévenaz, Henri, *Les Compromis d'arbitrage devant la Cour permanente de Justice internationale* (Neuchâtel, 1938)

Thirlway, H. W. A., *International Customary Law and Codification* (Leiden, 1972)

Non-Appearance before the International Court of Justice (Cambridge, 1985)

'The Law and Procedure of the International Court of Justice, 1960–1989: Part One' (1989) 60 *British Yearbook of International Law* 1

'The Law and Procedure of the International Court of Justice, 1960–1989: Part Two' (1990) 61 *British Yearbook of International Law* 1

'The Law and Procedure of the International Court of Justice, 1960–1989: Part Three' (1991) 62 *British Yearbook of International Law* 1

'Concepts, Principles, Rules and Analogies: International and Municipal Legal Reasoning' (2002) 294 *Recueil des Cours* 269

Thornberry, Patrick, *International Law and the Rights of Minorities* (Oxford, 1991)

Toffin, Jean-Louis, *La Dissidence à la Cour permanente de Justice internationale* (Paris, 1937)

Tomuschat, Christian, 'Obligations Arising for States without or against Their Will' (1993) 241 *Recueil des Cours* 195

'Die internationale Gemeinschaft' (1995) 33 *Archiv des Völkerrechts* 1

de la Torriente, Cosme, 'Cuba, Bustamante and the Permanent Court of International Justice' (1922) 178 *International Conciliation* 349

Triepel, H., *Völkerrecht und Landesrecht* (Leipzig, 1899)

Die Zukunft des Völkerrechts (Leipzig, 1916)

Droit international et droit interne (Paris, 1920)

'Ferdinand von Martitz: Ein Bild seines Lebens und seines Wirkens' (1922) 30 *Niemeyers Zeitschrift für Internationales Recht* 155

'Les Rapports entre le droit interne et le droit international' (1923) 1 *Recueil des Cours* 77

Trindade, A. A. Cançado, *The Application of the Rule of Exhaustion of Local Remedies in International Law* (Cambridge, 1983)

Unger, Roberto Mangabeira, *The Critical Legal Studies Movement* (Cambridge, MA, 1983)

United Nations Conference on the Law of Treaties, *Official Records* (3 vols., New York, 1969–71)

Urrutia, Francisco José, 'La Codification du droit international en Amérique' (1928) 22 *Recueil des Cours* 85

La Corte Permanente de Justicia Internacional (Bogota, 1934)

Vagts, Detlev F., 'International Law in the Third Reich' (1990) 84 *American Journal of International Law* 661

Váli, Ferenc A., *Die Deutsch-Österreichische Zollunion* (Vienna, 1932)

'The Austro-German Customs Regime before the Permanent Court, Considered with Reference to the Proposed Federation of Danubian States' (1932) 18 *Transactions of the Grotius Society* 79

Servitudes of International Law: A Study of Rights in Foreign Territory (London, 1958)

Valladao, Haroldo, 'Francisco José Urrutia' (1950) 43-II *Annuaire de l'Institut de Droit International* 519

de Vattel, Emmerich, *Le Droit des gens ou principes de la loi naturelle* (Washington DC, 1916) (originally published 1758)

Verdross, Alfred, *Die Einheit des rechtlichen Weltbildes auf Grundlage der Völkerrechtsverfassung* (Tübingen, 1923)

Die Verfassung der Völkerrechtsgemeinschaft (Vienna, 1926)

'La Fondement du droit international' (1927) 16 *Recueil des Cours* 251

'Les Principes généraux du droit comme source du droit des gens' in *Recueil d'études sur les sources du droit en l'honneur de François Gény* (Paris, 1934), vol. 3, p. 383

'Anfechtbare und nichtige Staatsverträge' (1935) 15 *Zeitschrift für öffentliches Recht* 289

'Les Principes généraux du droit dans la jurisprudence internationale' (1935) 52 *Recueil des Cours* 195

'Forbidden Treaties in International Law' (1937) 31 *American Journal of International Law* 571

'Jus Dispositivum and Jus Cogens in International Law' (1966) 60 *American Journal of International Law* 55

'Entstehungsweisen und Geltungsgrund des universellen völkerrechtlichen Gewohnheitsrechts' (1969) 29 *Zeitschrift für ausländisches öffentliches Recht und Völkerrecht* 635

Verdross, Alfred and Bruno Simma, *Universelles Völkerrecht: Theorie und Praxis* (3rd edn, Berlin, 1984)

Verzijl, J. H. W., 'Die Rechtsprechung des Ständigen Internationalen Gerichtshofes von 1922 bis Mai 1926' (1924–6) 13 *Zeitschrift für Völkerrecht* 489

'La Classification des différends internationaux et la nature du litige anglo-turc relatif au vilayet de Mossoul' (1925) 6 *Revue de Droit International et de Législation Comparée* 732

'L'affaire du "Lotus" devant la Cour permanente de Justice internationale' (1928) 9 *Revue de Droit International et de Législation Comparée* 1

The Jurisprudence of the World Court (2 vols., Leiden, 1965)

International Law in a Historical Perspective (11 vols., Leiden, 1968–92)

de Vineuil, Paul, 'Les Leçons du quatrième avis consultatif de la Cour permanente de Justice internationale' (1923) 4 *Revue de Droit International et de Legislation Comparée* 291

'Les Résultats de la troisième session de la Cour permanente de Justice internationale' (1923) 4 *Revue de Droit International et de Legislation Comparée* 573

'L'affaire de Javorina devant la Cour permanente de Justice internationale' (1924) 5 *Revue de Droit International et de Legislation Comparée* 130

'La Dernière phase de l'affaire de Javorina' (1924) 5 *Revue de Droit International et de Legislation Comparée* 282

'Les Decisions de la cinquième session ordinaire de la Cour permanente de Justice internationale' (1925) 6 *Revue de Droit International et de Legislation Comparée* 80

'The Permanent Court of International Justice and the Geneva "Peace Protocol"' (1925) 17 *Rivista di Diritto Internazionale* 144

'La Cour permanente de Justice internationale en 1929' (1930) 11 *Revue de Droit International et de Legislation Comparée* 600 and 749

Vinogradoff, Paul, 'Historical Types of International Law' (1923) 1 *Bibliotheca Visseriana* 1

de Visscher, Charles, 'Justice et médiation internationales' (1928) 9 *Revue de Droit International et de Législation Comparée* 33

'Les Avis consultatifs de la Cour permanente de Justice internationale' (1929) 26 *Recueil des Cours* 5

'Contribution à l'étude des sources du droit international' in *Recueil d'études sur les sources du droit en l'honneur de François Gény* (Paris, 1934), vol. 3, p. 389

'La Cour permanente de Justice internationale et sa contribution au développement du droit international' (1936) 22 *Bulletin de la Classe des Lettres et des Sciences Morales et Politiques* 151

'Dionisio Anzilotti' (1951) 6 *La Comunità Internazionale* 247

'Coutume et traité en droit international public' (1955) 59 *Revue Générale de Droit International Public* 353

Problèmes d'interprétation judiciaire en droit international public (Paris, 1963)

'Sir Cecil Hurst' (1964) 13 *International and Comparative Law Quarterly* 1

Aspects récents du droit procédural de la Cour internationale de Justice (Paris, 1966)

Théories et réalités en droit international public (4th edn, Paris, 1970)

de Vitoria, Francisco, *De Indis Relectio Prior* (Washington DC, 1917) (originally published 1532)

Vogelsanger, Peter, *Max Huber: Recht, Politik, Humanität aus Glauben* (Frauenfeld, 1967)

Vogiatzi, Maria, 'The Historical Evolution of the Optional Clause' (2002) 2 *Non-State Actors and International Law* 41

Voïcu, Ioan, *De l'interprétation authentique des traités internationaux* (Paris, 1968)

von Wächter, Carl Georg, 'Über die Collision der Privatrechtsgesetze verschiedener Staaten' (1841) 24 *Archiv für die Civilistische Praxis* 230

Waldock, C. H. M., 'Forum Prorogatum or Acceptance of a Unilateral Summons to Appear before the International Court' (1948) 2 International and Comparative Law Quarterly 377

'The Plea of Domestic Jurisdiction before International Legal Tribunals' (1954) 31 British Yearbook of International Law 96

'Decline of the Optional Clause' (1955–6) 32 British Yearbook of International Law 244

'General Course on Public International Law' (1962) 106 Recueil des Cours 1

Aspects of the Advisory Jurisdiction of the International Court of Justice (Geneva, 1976)

'The Effectiveness of the System Set up by the European Convention on Human Rights' (1980) 1 Human Rights Law Journal 1

Walters, F. P., A History of the League of Nations (Oxford, 1952)

Walther, Henri, L'affaire du 'Lotus' ou de l'abordage hauturier en droit pénal international (Paris, 1928)

Walz, G.-A., 'Les Rapports du droit international et du droit interne' (1937) 61 Recueil des Cours 379

Warganeus, 'Un problème de présénces?' (1933) 4 Acta scandinavica juris gentium 158

Wartenweiler, Fritz, Max Huber: Spannungen und Wandlungen in Werden und Wirken (Zurich, 1953)

Weeramantry, Christopher Gregory, 'Expanding the Potential of the World Court' in Nandasiri Jasentuliyana (ed.), Perspectives on International Law: Essays in Honour of Judge Manfred Lachs (1995), p. 309

Wehberg, Hans, Das Problem eines internationalen Staatengerichtshofes (Munich, 1912)

The Problem of an International Court of Justice (Oxford, 1918)

'Der Pariser Völkerbunds-Entwurf' in Deutsche Liga für Völkerbund, Wilsons Völkerbundplan: Die Akte der Pariser Konferenz vom 14. Februar 1919 (Berlin, 1919), p. 6

'Zur Wahl des französischen Mitgliedes des Weltgerichtshofs' (1929) 29 Die Friedens-Warte 17

'Walther Schücking Richter am Weltgerichtshof' (1930) 30 Die Friedens-Warte 341

'Das Gutachten des Weltgerichtshofs in der Zollunionsfrage' (1931) 31 Die Friedens-Warte 301

Der Internationale Gerichtshof (Offenbach A.M., 1948)

Wehberg, Hans and Hans-Waldemar Goldschmidt, Der Internationale Gerichtshof: Entstehungsgeschichte, Analyse, Dokumentation (Berlin, 1973)

Weil, Prosper, 'Towards Relative Normativity in International Law?' (1983) 77 American Journal of International Law 413

Weiler, J. H. H., 'The Transformation of Europe' (1991) 100 Yale Law Journal 2403

The Constitution of Europe: 'Do the New Clothes Have an Emperor?' and Other Essays on European Integration (Cambridge, 1999)

Weinberger, Sheila, 'The Wimbledon Paradox and the World Court:
    Confronting Inevitable Conflicts between Conventional and Customary
    International Law' (1996) 10 *Emory International Law Review* 397
Weis, P., *Nationality and Statelessness in International Law* (2nd edn, Alphen aan
    den Rijn, 1979)
Weiss, André, *Traité théorétique et pratique de droit international privé* (6 vols., 2nd
    edn, Paris, 1907–13)
    Le Droit international d'hier et de demain (Bologna, 1916) (reprinted from *Scientia*)
    'Compétence ou incompétence, des tribunaux à l'égard des états étrangers'
    (1923) 1 *Recueil des Cours* 525
    Manuel de droit international privé (9th edn, Paris, 1925)
    'Préface' in Olof Hoijer, *Le Pacte de la Société des Nations: Commentaire théorique
    et pratique* (Paris, 1926), p. vii
Weiss, Edith Brown, 'Judicial Independence and Impartiality: A Preliminary
    Inquiry' in Lori Fisler Damrosch (ed.), *The International Court of Justice at a
    Crossroads* (Dobbs Ferry, 1987), p. 123
Wellens, Karel, *Economic Conflict and Disputes before the World Court, 1922–1995* (The
    Hague, 1996)
Westlake, John, *International Law* (2 vols., 2nd edn, Cambridge, 1910–13)
    The Collected Papers of John Westlake on Public International Law (Cambridge, 1914)
    A Treatise on Private International Law (7th edn by Norman Bentwich, London,
    1925)
White, Gillian, 'The Principle of Good Faith' in Vaughan Lowe and Colin
    Warbrick (eds.), *The United Nations and the Principles of International Law:
    Essays in Memory of Michael Akehurst* (London, 1994), p. 230
Whitton, John B., 'La Règle "pacta sunt servanda"' (1934) 49 *Recueil des Cours* 151
Williams, John Fischer, 'L'affaire du "Lotus"' (1928) 35 *Revue Générale de Droit
    International Public* 361
    'The Optional Clause (the British Signature and Reservations)' (1930) 11
    British Yearbook of International Law 63
Winiarski, B., 'Comte Michel Rostworowski' (1950) 43-II *Annuaire de l'Institut de
    Droit International* 505
Wolff, Christian, *Jus Gentium Methodo Scientifica Pertractatum* (Oxford, 1934)
    (originally published 1749)
Wolgast, Ernst, *Der Wimbledonprozeß* (Berlin, 1926)
Wood, Michael C., 'The Interpretation of Security Council Resolutions' (1998) 2
    Max Planck Yearbook of United Nations Law 73
Yasseen, Mustafa Kamil, 'L'interprétation des traités d'après la Convention de
    Vienne sur le droit des traités' (1976) 151 *Recueil des Cours* 1
Ydit, Méir, *Internationalised Territories: From the 'Free City of Cracow' to the 'Free City
    of Berlin'* (Leiden, 1961)
Yee, Sienho, '*Forum Prorogatum* in the International Court' (1999) 42 *German
    Yearbook of International Law* 147
    '*Forum Prorogatum* and the Advisory Proceedings of the International Court'
    (2001) 95 *American Journal of International Law* 381

'Towards an International Law of Co-Progressiveness' in Sienho Yee and Wang Tieya (eds.), *International Law in the Post-Cold War World: Essays in Memory of Li Haopei* (London, 2001), p. 18

Yourow, Howard Charles, *The Margin of Appreciation Doctrine in the Dynamics of the European Human Rights Jurisprudence* (The Hague, 1996)

Yü, Tsune-Chi, *The Interpretation of Treaties* (New York, 1927)

Zegveld, Liesbeth, *Accountability of Armed Opposition Groups in International Law* (Cambridge, 2002)

Zimmern, Alfred, *The League of Nations and the Rule of Law, 1918–1935* (London, 1936)

Zoller, Elisabeth, *La Bonne foi en droit international public* (Paris, 1977)

Index

Special Agreements
  Chorzów Factory case 225
  contentious jurisdiction 11, 226–8
  court of justice 229, 287
  effective interpretation 229, 292
  Free Zones case 284, 285, 286, 287, 289, 290, 298
  implied agreement 226, 227
  interstate relations 278
  Lighthouses cases 351, 358, 373
  Loans cases 277, 279, 280
  The Lotus 248
  Mavrommatis case 225
  Neuilly Treaty case 222
  River Oder case 267
  strict interpretation 290, 298, 324–5
state powers
  absolute power 80, 81
  enforcement 347
  exercise of sovereign rights 345
  Great Powers 7, 26, 67
  law of the sea 84
  separation *see* separating state powers
  supervening state powers 85–8
  territory *see* territory
state responsibility 87, 377, 378
state succession
  concessionary contracts 351
  territory 83, 187, 218
states
  collision of interests 54, 57, 81, 262
  conceptions *see* conceptions of state
  disputes, jurisdiction 9, 192
  international law subject *see* international law subjects
  residual freedom *see* residual principle of freedom
  security 178
  sovereign *see* national sovereigns; sovereignty
  territory *see* territory
  Triepel's theories 38–43
statutes
  ICJ *see* ICJ Statute
  PCIJ *see* PCIJ Statute
strict interpretation
  Employment of Women opinion 324–5
  Free Zones case 290
  Phosphates in Morocco case 376, 377
  Special Agreements 290, 298, 324–5
subjective interpretation
  intention of parties 98, 234, 328
  international sovereigns 100, 234, 327, 328
  reservations 382

schools of interpretation 98, 99–100, 104, 109, 239, 272, 329
Security Council resolutions 104
substantive law 70
sui generis, unilateral acceptance 103
Sweetser, Arthur 311
Switzerland
  Free Zones case 284–92
  Treaty of Versailles (1919) 285

teleological interpretation
  clarity 101
  compromissory clauses 298
  domestic analogies 112
  intention of parties 328
  international sovereigns 100
  League of Nations Covenant 156
  objective interpretation 100, 101, 330
  obligations 374
  politics 386
  purpose 100
territory
  cession 185, 352, 353
  conclusions 348
  criminal law *see* jurisdiction, states
  Eastern Greenland case 344–7, 388
  frontier delimitation 189, 230, 233–4, 235
  frontier disputes 189–91, 230–42
  good neighbourliness 87
  international frontiers 190
  international law of coexistence 185, 189–90, 235, 297, 345, 388
  international servitudes 177, 179
  Jaworzina opinion 189–90, 235
  The Lotus 346
  Memel case 339–44
  objective character 184
  self-determination 190
  separating state powers 89, 345
  state powers 83, 85, 346
  state succession 83, 187, 218
  statehood 332
  stronger claim/balancing test 344–5
  superior claim absent 345
  territorial principle 258
  The Wimbledon 175–86, 208
textual interpretation
  Employment of Women opinion 324–5, 327
  objective interpretation 98–9, 101, 327, 329
travaux préparatoires see preparatory work
treaties
  acquiescence 94
  bindingness 71, 100
  case law 24, 295–6
  conclusion 94
  custom 94

CAMBRIDGE STUDIES IN INTERNATIONAL AND COMPARATIVE LAW

Lightning Source UK Ltd.
Milton Keynes UK
15 January 2011

165784UK00001B/29/P